CUSTOM AND ITS INTERPRETATION IN INTERNATIONAL INVESTMENT LAW

VOLUME 2

At first glance, one may think of international investment law as a response to custom (or lack thereof), instead of a field of its application. However, in fact, the opposite is the case. The interpretation and application of customary rules and principles are the bread and butter of international investment law and arbitration. With a diverse range of expert contributors, this collection traces how customary international law is practised in international investment law. It considers how custom should be interpreted and how its rules and principles should be understood and applied by investor-state arbitral tribunals. Raising and addressing vital questions surrounding custom and international law, this collection is a necessary contribution to the scholarship of the theory and history of customary international law and international investment law. This title is also available as Open Access on Cambridge Core.

PANOS MERKOURIS is Professor of International Law at the University of Groningen. He is Principal Investigator of The Rules of Interpretation of Customary International Law (TRICI-Law) project (European Research Council [ERC] grant agreement no 759728). Professor Merkouris is an acclaimed author and has written extensively on the law of treaties, sources and interpretation, most recently coauthoring *Treaties in Motion* (2020) with Professor Malgosia Fitzmaurice.

ANDREAS KULICK is Senior Research Fellow at University of Tübingen, Germany. He is visiting professor at the Albert Ludwigs University Freiburg in the winter semester of 2023–2024. He has been a visiting fellow at the Lauterpacht Centre for International Law, NYU School of Law, and the European University Institute. He has written extensively on all aspects of international law, with a particular focus on international adjudication. Also, he regularly advises and represents States in proceedings before international courts and tribunals, including investment arbitration.

JOSÉ MANUEL ÁLVAREZ-ZARATE is Professor at Externado University of Colombia and Director of the Law and Economics Department where he runs the International Economic Law (IEL) program. He has written extensively on trade and investment matters and practices advising and representing in proceedings before local and communitarian tribunals, including investment arbitration.

MACIEJ ŻENKIEWICZ is Assistant Professor at Nicolaus Copernicus University in Toruń. He also teaches as a visiting professor at various universities, including Antonio de Nebrija University, Spain; Pontificia Universidad Católica del Perú, Peru; and Xi'an Jiaotong University School of Law, China. He is the author of various articles and monographs.

THE RULES OF INTERPRETATION OF CUSTOMARY INTERNATIONAL LAW

Established in 2021, the TRICI-Law Book Series is a limited series that aims to publish monographs and edited volumes on topics that shed light on legal interpretation in international law, with a particular emphasis on the interpretation of customary international law. Titles appearing in the series examine the interpretation of customary international law from a theoretical and practical perspective, and compare the characteristics of legal interpretation in international law across courts, regimes and sources as they have evolved and continue to do so through time. The TRICI-Law Book Series is a joint initiative between Cambridge University Press, the European Research Council and the University of Groningen.

The titles in this series are available as Open Access thanks to the generous funding from the European Research Council (ERC) under the European Union's Horizon 2020 Research and Innovation Programme (Grant Agreement No 759728) and the University of Groningen.

General Editor
Panos Merkouris
University of Groningen

CUSTOM AND ITS INTERPRETATION IN INTERNATIONAL INVESTMENT LAW

Volume 2

Edited by

PANOS MERKOURIS
University of Groningen

ANDREAS KULICK
University of Tübingen

JOSÉ MANUEL ÁLVAREZ-ZARATE
Externado University of Colombia

MACIEJ ŻENKIEWICZ
Nicholas Copernicus University of Toruń

Assistant Editor

KONRAD TURNBULL
University of Groningen

Shaftesbury Road, Cambridge CB2 8EA, United Kingdom

One Liberty Plaza, 20th Floor, New York, NY 10006, USA

477 Williamstown Road, Port Melbourne, VIC 3207, Australia

314–321, 3rd Floor, Plot 3, Splendor Forum, Jasola District Centre,
New Delhi – 110025, India

103 Penang Road, #05–06/07, Visioncrest Commercial, Singapore 238467

Cambridge University Press is part of Cambridge University Press & Assessment,
a department of the University of Cambridge.

We share the University's mission to contribute to society through the pursuit of
education, learning and research at the highest international levels of excellence.

www.cambridge.org
Information on this title: www.cambridge.org/9781009255424
DOI: 10.1017/9781009255462

© Cambridge University Press & Assessment 2024

This work is in copyright. It is subject to statutory exceptions and to the provisions
of relevant licensing agreements; with the exception of the Creative Commons version
the link for which is provided below, no reproduction of any part of this work may
take place without the written permission of Cambridge University Press.

An online version of this work is published at doi.org/10.1017/9781009255462
under a Creative Commons Open Access license CC-BY-NC-ND 4.0 which permits
re-use, distribution and reproduction in any medium for non-commercial purposes
providing appropriate credit to the original work is given. You may not
distribute derivative works without permission. To view a copy of this license, visit
https://creativecommons.org/licenses/by-nc-nd/4.0

All versions of this work may contain content reproduced under license from third parties.

Permission to reproduce this third-party content must be obtained from these
third-parties directly.

When citing this work, please include a reference to the DOI 10.1017/9781009255462

First published 2024

A catalogue record for this publication is available from the British Library

A Cataloging-in-Publication data record for this book is available from the Library of Congress

ISBN 978-1-009-25542-4 Hardback

Cambridge University Press & Assessment has no responsibility for the persistence
or accuracy of URLs for external or third-party internet websites referred to in this
publication and does not guarantee that any content on such websites is, or will
remain, accurate or appropriate.

CONTENTS

List of Contributors   *page* viii
Foreword: Custom and International Investment Law
HORACIO A GRIGERA NAÓN   xiv
Table of Cases   xvi
Table of International Treaties, Documents, and National Legislation   xxxvi
List of Abbreviations   xlvii

PART I   **Identifying Custom in International Investment Law**

1   The 'Minimum Standard of Treatment' in International Investment Law: The Fascinating Story of the Emergence, Decline and Recent Resurrection of a Concept
   PATRICK DUMBERRY   3

2   Recourse to Legal Experts for the Establishment and Interpretation of Customary Norms in Investment Law
   SAÏDA EL BOUDOUHI   23

3   The Identification of Customary International Law and International Investment Law and Arbitration: State Practice in Connection with Investor-State Proceedings
   DIEGO MEJÍA-LEMOS   46

4   Assessing Damages in Customary International Law: The Chorzów's Tale
   JOSÉ MANUEL ÁLVAREZ-ZARATE   71

PART II The Interpretation of Secondary Rules
         in International Investment Law

5 Uses of the Work of International Law Commission on State
   Responsibility in International Investment Arbitration
   SOTIRIOS-IOANNIS LEKKAS   93

6 Revisiting the Availability of Countermeasures in Investment
   Arbitration
   ANNA VENTOURATOU   123

7 Investment Tribunals, the Duty of Compensation in Cases of
   Necessity: A Customary Law Void?
   FEDERICA I PADDEU   151

8 A Riddle Wrapped in a Mystery Inside an Enigma: Equitable
   Considerations in the Assessment of Damages by Investment
   Tribunals
   EMMANUEL GIAKOUMAKIS   179

9 Conflict of Treaty Norms and Subsequent Agreements in
   Relation to the Interpretation of Treaties in International
   Investment Law
   ŁUKASZ KUŁAGA   211

PART III Interpreting Customary International Rules:
          Current Challenges

10 Police Powers in a Pandemic: Investment Treaty Interpretation
    and the Customary Presumption of Reasonable Regulation
    OLIVER HAILES   233

11 Bilateral Investment Treaties, Investor Obligations and
    Customary International Environmental Law
    MADHAV MALLYA   261

12 The Role of Customary International Law in International
    Investment Law Remedies: The Curious Case of Natural Resources
    FILIP BALCERZAK   284

13 A TWAIL Engagement with Customary International
    Investment Law: Some Strategies for Interpretation
    NINA MILEVA   307

PART IV **Concluding Thoughts: Custom and Its Interpretation in International Investment Law**

14 Custom and Its Interpretation in International Investment Law: Final Musings
    PANOS MERKOURIS, ANDREAS KULICK, JOSÉ MANUEL ÁLVAREZ-ZARATE, AND MACIEJ ŻENKIEWICZ   335

Bibliography   346
Index   374

CONTRIBUTORS

JOSÉ MANUEL ÁLVAREZ-ZARATE is Professor at Externado University of Colombia and Director of the Law and Economics Department where he runs the IEL program. He holds a degree in Administrative Law and a Ph.D. He was a visiting scholar at American University Washington College of Law in 2016–2017; a visiting professor at Fundación Getulio Vargas, Río de Janeiro, Brazil, October–November in 2015; and a visiting research fellow at the British Institute of International and Comparative Law, London, England in May–June, 2009. He has been teaching and practicing in the fields of IEL, economic administrative regulation, and dispute settlement for more than twenty-eight years and has been widely published. His legal experience includes consultancy for private and public entities in trade negotiations and international business, as well as acting before administrative courts, arbitration panels, the Andean Tribunal, and international arbitration.

FILIP BALCERZAK, LL.M., PH.D., attorney at law is admitted to the bar in two jurisdictions: Poland (adwokat) and Spain (abogado). He specializes in commercial dispute resolution at both national and international levels. He has successfully led cases for a variety of clients from different jurisdictions, utilizing his fluency in English and Spanish.

His experience includes advising and representing parties in international arbitrations (e.g., in ad hoc arbitrations with their seat in New York and London). He is an arbitrator at the Court of Arbitration at the Polish Chamber of Commerce and the Lewiatan Court of Arbitration.

He effectively combines professional and academic activities. He completed his LL.M. studies at the University of Ottawa, specializing in International Trade and Foreign Investment Law. Subsequently, he was granted a Ph.D. in public international law by Adam Mickiewicz University in Poznań (Ph.D. dissertation title: "Investor state arbitration and human rights," written in English). Currently, he is an associate professor (research) at the Faculty of Law and Administration of the Adam Mickiewicz University in Poznan. He has authored numerous publications on international investment arbitration.

PATRICK DUMBERRY is a full professor at the University of Ottawa (Civil Law Section). He holds a Ph.D. from the Graduate Institute for International Studies (Geneva). He practised international investment arbitration with law firms in Geneva (Lalive), Montreal (Norton Rose), as well as with Canada's Ministry of Foreign Affairs (Trade Law Bureau). He is the author of more than ninety publications in the fields of international investment law and international law, including the following books: *The Fair and Equitable Treatment Standard: A Guide to NAFTA Case Law on Article 1105* (Wolters Kluwer, 2013); *The Formation and Identification of Rules of Customary International Law in International Investment Law* (Cambridge University Press 2016); *A Guide to State Succession in International Investment Law* (Elgar 2018); *Fair and Equitable Treatment: Its Interaction with the Minimum Standard and Its Customary Status* (Brill 2018); *A Guide to General Principles of Law in International Investment Law* (Oxford University Press 2020); *Rebellions and Civil Wars: State Responsibility for the Conduct of Insurgents* (Cambridge University Press 2021).

SAÏDA EL BOUDOUHI is Professor of Public Law at the University of Paris 8 Vincennes Saint-Denis, and her specialties range from public international law, international economic law (investment and WTO law), the application of international law in domestic systems, and the law of international organizations. She earned her Ph.D. from the University of Paris 1 Panthéon-Sorbonne in 2009, completed her postdoctoral studies at the European University Institute, University of Florence, Italy, and was an invited researcher at the University of Arizona College of Law from 2019 to 2020.

EMMANUEL GIAKOUMAKIS is an Associate Lawyer at Steptoe & Johnson LLP, where he focuses his practice on public international law, with an emphasis on international investment law and State-to-State adjudication. He is also a D.Phil. candidate at the University of Oxford, Faculty of Law. He was formerly an Associate Legal Officer at the International Court of Justice (ICJ), where he advised the President of the Court on his judicial and presidential duties while also working on a wide range of international law disputes. Prior to that, he worked in different law firms as a legal advisor to governments and private corporations on various questions of public international law, including the law of treaties and State responsibility, investment arbitration, and international human rights law. He has held seminars at the Hague Academy of International Law (2019) and the Institut International de Droits de l'Homme (International Institute of Human Rights) (2018).

HORACIO A GRIGERA NAÓN is Distinguished Practitioner-in-Residence and Director of the Center on International Commercial Arbitration at the Washington College of Law. He is a former secretary general of the International Court of Arbitration of the International Chamber of Commerce and a practitioner in the field for over thirty years.

OLIVER HAILES is Assistant Professor of Law at the London School of Economics and Political Science, where he lectures public international law, international arbitration, international investment law, and transnational environmental law. He is Assistant General Editor of the ICSID Reports. Before arriving at the LSE, Oliver clerked for an appellate judge, practised commercial litigation, and held several research, teaching, and editorial roles. Recently, he was co-Editor-in-Chief of the Cambridge International Law Journal and a Research Associate with the PluriCourts Centre of Excellence at the University of Oslo.

ŁUKASZ KUŁAGA is Associate Professor in the Division of International and European Law at the Faculty of Law and Administration of Cardinal Stefan Wyszynski University in Warsaw and a legal expert in the Legal-Treaty Department of the Ministry of Foreign Affairs of the Republic of Poland. Currently Dr. hab. Łukasz Kułaga works on the consequences of aggression against Ukraine for international law. His other fields of expertise are international investment law, the use of force, immunities, the law of treaties, and the law of State responsibility.

ANDREAS KULICK (*Privatdozent, venia legendi et docendi, Tübingen; doctor iuris, Tübingen*; LLM, NYU School of Law; First and Second State Exams, Berlin) is a senior research fellow at University of Tübingen, Germany. He is a visiting professor at the Albert Ludwigs University Freiburg in the winter semester of 2023–2024. He has been a visiting fellow at the Lauterpacht Centre for International Law, NYU School of Law, and the WZB Berlin. His research focuses on public international law – in particular, on international dispute settlement, and on German and comparative constitutional law and theory. He has experience in advising and representing States in various matters of public international law before international courts and tribunals, including the European Court of Human Rights (ECtHR), International Tribunal for the Law of the Sea (ITLOS), and in ICSID proceedings, as well as before domestic courts. He is a member of the International Law Association (ILA) Study Group on Content and Evolution of the Rules of Interpretation in International Law. He is the author, inter alia, of *Global Public Interest in International Investment Law* (Cambridge University Press, 2012) and the editor of *Reassertion of Control over the Investment Treaty Regime* (Cambridge University Press, 2017), and has numerous publications in the area of public international law and beyond.

SOTIRIOS-IOANNIS LEKKAS is a postdoctoral researcher for the of the TRICI-Law project (ERC grant agreement no 759728) at the Department of Transboundary Legal Studies of the University of Groningen. His research focuses on the content and evolution of rules of interpretation in international law. Prior to this position, Sotirios worked as a judicial fellow at the ICJ and as a tutor in public international law at the University of Oxford, Faculty of Law. He holds a D Phil in Law from the University of Oxford. He has studied law in Athens and London (University College London), where he was awarded the George Schwarzenberger Prize in International Law by the University of London. He is also a member of the Bar in Athens, Greece (non-practicing).

MADHAV MALLYA is Associate Professor at the Jindal Global Law School. He has also taught at National Law University, Delhi, India; Lloyd Law College and the School of Law, Uttar Pradesh, India; and Bennett University, Uttar Pradesh, India. He completed his BBA LLB from Symbiosis Law Schools, Pune, Maharashtra, India, in 2010 and LLM from McGill University, Montreal, Canada, in 2011. He was also a doctoral student at McGill University from 2014 to 2016 and an accomplished scholarship student at the Centre for International Governance Innovation, Waterloo, Canada, in 2016. His areas of research and teaching interest include international investment law and public international law.

DIEGO MEJÍA-LEMOS, LLM, PH.D., serves as a scholar and practitioner of international law and dispute resolution. He holds, among others, graduate degrees from New York University and the National University of Singapore (NUS). He has participated in the representation of States in proceedings before international courts, including while working as a juriste international at Freshfields Bruckhaus Deringer's Paris Office.

Furthermore, he has provided support to arbitral tribunals conducting proceedings under the Permanent Court of Arbitration's auspices. Recently, he has held a postdoctoral fellowship at NUS and has been appointed as a distinguished research associate professor within the Xi'an Jiaotong University's 'Young Talent' program.

PANOS MERKOURIS is Professor of International Law at the University of Groningen. His five-year project on *The Rules of Interpretation of Customary International Law* was awarded an ERC Starting Grant (ERC grant agreement no 759728). He specialises in Interpretation, Law of Treaties, Sources of International Law, and Dispute Settlement. Professor Merkouris is currently a member of the editorial boards of the *Netherlands Yearbook of International Law* (NYIL), the *Leiden Journal of International Law* (LJIL), and the *International Community Law Review* (ICLR). He was also the co-rapporteur of the ILA Study Group on the Content and Evolution of Rules of Interpretation in International Law. He is the author of the monograph *Treaties in Motion* (CUP 2020, coauthored with Professor Fitzmaurice), *Article 31(3)(c) of the VCLT, and the Principle of Systemic Integration: Normative Shadows in Plato's Cave* (Martinus Nijhoff 2015). The latter has been cited with approval by a Chamber of the International Criminal Court. He has numerous publications on interpretation, law of treaties, and customary international law.

NINA MILEVA is a PhD researcher of the TRICI-Law project (ERC grant agreement no 759728) and a lecturer at the Department of Transboundary Legal Studies of the University of Groningen. Her research focuses on the interpretation of customary international law, and in particular, the development of a theory of interpretation of customary international law. Her research interests relate to the role of international law in the practice of domestic courts, the relationship between international and domestic law, international legal theory, and critical approaches to international law.

FEDERICA I PADDEU is a Derek Bowett Fellow in Law, Queens' College, and Fellow at the Lauterpacht Centre for International both at the University of Cambridge. Her work has been published in leading international law journals, including the British Yearbook of International Law, the European Journal of International Law, and the American Journal of International Law. A monograph based on her PhD dissertation "Justification and Excuse in International Law: Concept and Theory of General Defences," was published by CUP in 2018. She is a member of

Blackstone Chambers Academic Research Panel and admitted to practice in Venezuela, as a member of the Caracas (Distrito Federal) Bar.

KONRAD TURNBULL is a PhD researcher within the Department of Transboundary Legal Studies and Faculty of Economics & Business at the University of Groningen. Whilst his core research focuses on international courts' approaches in adjudicating cases of structural discrimination and the public's perception of the efficacy of these institutions, his research interests also include international investment law and the international leasing of public powers. He holds an LLB & LLM in International Human Rights from the University of Groningen, an LLM in International Comparative Law from The George Washington University Law School, and a BS in Digital Filmmaking from Shepherd University.

ANNA VENTOURATOU is a DPhil candidate and tutor in Public International Law. Her thesis explores the availability of the defenses codified in Part I, Chapter V of the Articles on the Responsibility of States for Internationally Wrongful Acts in international adjudication. She focuses on disputes before the ICJ, the WTO Dispute Settlement System, and Investment Arbitration. Her doctoral studies are supervised by Professor Catherine Redgwell, Chichele Professor of Public International Law at All Souls College, and Professor Miles Jackson, Associate Professor of Law at Jesus College. Anna has studied law at the University of Athens (LLB; LLM in Public International Law (dist)) and the University of Oxford (MJur (dist); MPhil). Her studies in Oxford have been supported by the University of Athens "A Gazis" Trust, the Peter Carter Graduate Scholarship in Law (Oxford Faculty of Law and Wadham College), and the Academy of Athens.

MACIEJ ŻENKIEWICZ is Assistant Professor of Public International Law at Nicolaus Copernicus Univeristy (Toruń, Poland) and a visiting professor at Faculty of Social Sciences of the Antonio de Nebrija University. He is an author of various articles and monographs: his latest publication (with contribution as the editor and author) is the book *International Investment Law* published in Spanish. He is a member of various forums, eg, SIEL or ISDS Academic Forum.

FOREWORD: CUSTOM AND
INTERNATIONAL INVESTMENT LAW

In international investment law, as in other fields of international law, the interaction between treaty practice (including their interpretation and application) and customary rules of international law has become a fertile ground for doctrinal discussion. Two issues related to this discussion are particularly worth mentioning at the outset of this volume on *Custom and International Investment Law*.

The first question is whether and how a large number of bilateral investment treaties (BITs) may contribute to the formation or declaration of customary rules of law related to the content of these treaties. In other words, the question may be framed as to whether the substantive protections recognized in a fairly similar manner in large numbers of BITs is an expression of a customary rule with the same content. Several international judgments have so far confirmed that a multilateral treaty may declare the content of a rule of international customary law. For example, many international investment arbitration tribunals have upheld the declaratory nature of customary rules contained in the 1969 Vienna Convention on the Law of Treaties, such as Articles 31 to 33 about treaty interpretation. In contrast, no international tribunal (different from investment arbitration tribunals), United Nations General Assembly resolution, or any other equally authoritative body so far has conclusively affirmed that the substantive provisions of BITs declare the content of customary rules of international law. In sum, the uncertainty remains about the customary nature of the rules included in BITs and their arbitral interpretations.

A second question refers to the application by international investment arbitration tribunals of customary international law that is recognized independently from the BITs. The extensive discussions by arbitral tribunals, government officials, and scholars about the scope of the minimum standard of treatment and the fair and equitable treatment standard in regard to different states and treaties are an example of the complexities involved in articulating this relationship between treaty and customary rules of international law. Some may even say that a state that systematically invokes a certain historic jurisprudence to prove the content of a customary rule is a persistent objector against the formation of new and more advanced customary rules on that matter.

The discussion about the existence of customary rules of international investment law may also be approached from the perspective of the effectiveness of those rules. This effectiveness depends to a large extent on the availability of an enforceable, international judicial remedy. States, of course, have the upper hand by modifying the judicial means of dispute settlement through new treaties, in application of the well-established principle of *lex posterior derogat priori*. Depending on how states modify the dispute settlement system, they will influence the interpretation and application of the substantive rules on international investment protection, even regardless of whether these can be classified as strictly of treaty or customary nature.

In conclusion, customary and treaty rules of international investment law develop in a simultaneous and potentially interrelated manner. Together, these sources form a dynamic body of rules that develop in the shadow of the states' powers and preferences in changing times. I congratulate the authors and editors of this volume for pointing to specific examples, case studies, and related legal developments that frame the broader discussion on how States want to treat foreign investments.

Washington, D.C., January 27, 2022

Horacio A Grigera Naón
Independent International Arbitrator
Director of the Center on International Commercial Arbitration
American University Washington College of Law

TABLE OF CASES

International Court of Justice (ICJ)

Aegean Sea Continental Shelf (Greece v Turkey) (Jurisdiction) [1978] ICJ Rep 3, 105
- Separate Opinion of Judge de Castro, 114

Ahmadou Sadio Diallo (Republic of Guinea v Congo) (Compensation) [2012] ICJ Rep 324, 73
- Declaration of Judge Greenwood, 210

Ahmadou Sadio Diallo (Republic of Guinea v Congo) (Merits) [2010] ICJ Rep 639, 73

Ahmadou Sadio Diallo (Republic of Guinea v Congo) (Preliminary Objections) [2007] ICJ Rep 582, 37

Ambatielos (Greece v UK) (Preliminary Objection) [1952] ICJ Rep 28, 220

Appeal Relating to the Jurisdiction of the ICAO Council under Article II, Section 2, of the 1944 International Air Services Transit Agreement (Bahrain, Egypt and United Arab Emirates v Qatar) (Judgment) [2020] ICJ Rep 172, 145

Appeal Relating to the Jurisdiction of the ICAO Council under Article 84 of the Convention on International Civil Aviation (Bahrain, Egypt, Saudi Arabia and United Arab Emirates v Qatar) (Judgment) [2020] ICJ Rep 81, 145

Application of the Convention on the Prevention and Punishment of the Crime of Genocide (Bosnia and Herzegovina v Serbia and Montenegro) (Judgment) [2007] ICJ Rep 43, 108, 117, 179, 181, 220

Application of the International Convention on the Elimination of All Forms of Racial Discrimination (Georgia v Russian Federation) (Preliminary Objections) [2011] ICJ Rep 70, 112, 140

Arbitral Award of 31 July 1989 (Guinea-Bissau v Senegal) [1991] ICJ Rep 53, 105

Armed Activities on the Territory of the Congo (Congo v Uganda) (Counter-Claims, Order of 29 November 2001) [2001] ICJ Rep 678, 148

Armed Activities on the Territory of the Congo (Congo v Uganda) (Judgment) [2005] ICJ Rep 168, 73

Armed Activities on the Territory of the Congo (Congo v Uganda) (Order of 8 September 2020) [2020] ICJ Rep 264, 208
- Opinion of Judge Sebutinde, 208

Armed Activities on the Territory of the Congo (Congo v Uganda) (Reparations) [2022] ICJ Rep 1, 182

- Separate Opinion of Judge Iwasawa, 189
- Separate Opinion of Judge Yusuf, 199

Arrest Warrant of 11 April 2000 (Congo v Belgium) (Judgment) [2002] ICJ Rep 3, 148, 286, 313

Avena and Other Mexican Nationals (Mexico v USA) (Judgment) [2004] ICJ Rep 12, 73, 286

Barcelona Traction, Light and Power Co, Ltd (Belgium v Spain) (Judgment) [1970] ICJ Rep, 9
- Separate Opinion of Judge Ammoun, 187

Certain Activities Carried Out by Nicaragua in the Border Area (Costa Rica v Nicaragua) (Compensation) [2018] ICJ Rep 15, 73

Certain Activities Carried Out by Nicaragua in the Border Area (Costa Rica v Nicaragua) (Judgment) [2018] ICJ Rep 15, 179

Competence of the General Assembly for the Admission of a State to the United Nations (Advisory Opinion) [1950] ICJ Rep 4, 108

Continental Shelf (Libya/Malta) (Merits) [1985] ICJ Rep 13, 202

Continental Shelf (Tunisia/Libya) (Merits) [1982] ICJ Rep 18, 187

Corfu Channel (United Kingdom v Albania) (Merits) [1949] ICJ Rep 4, 140

Diplomatic and Consular Staff in Tehran (USA v Iran) (Judgment) [1980] ICJ Rep 3, 181

Dispute Regarding Navigational and Related Rights (Costa Rica v Nicaragua) (Judgment) [2009] ICJ Rep 213, 140, 220, 221, 240, 243

Elettronica Sicula SpA (ELSI) (USA v Italy) (Judgment) [1989] ICJ Rep 15, 9, 138, 254, 318, 319

Fisheries Jurisdiction (Spain v Canada) (Jurisdiction) (Judgment) [1998] ICJ Rep 432, 246

Frontier Dispute (Burkina Faso/Republic of Mali) [1986] ICJ Rep 554, 187

Interpretation of Peace Treaties with Bulgaria, Hungary and Romania (Second Phase) (Advisory Opinion) [1950] ICJ Rep 221, 200

Jadhav (India v Pakistan) (Judgment) [2019] ICJ Rep 418, 141

Judgments of the Administrative Tribunal of ILO Upon Complaint Made Against UNESCO (Advisory Opinion) [1956] ICJ Rep 77, 182

Jurisdictional Immunities of the State (Germany v Italy) (Counter-Claim, Order of 6 July 2010) [2010] ICJ Rep 310, 148

Jurisdictional Immunities of the State (Germany v Italy: Greece intervening) (Judgment) [2012] ICJ Rep 99, 52

Legal Consequences of the Construction of a Wall in the Occupied Palestinian Territories (Advisory Opinion) [2004] ICJ Rep 136, 179, 286

Legal Consequences of the Separation of the Chagos Archipelago from Mauritius in 1965 (Advisory Opinion) [2019] ICJ Rep 95, 118

Legality of the Threat or Use of Nuclear Weapons (Advisory Opinion) [1996] ICJ Rep 226, 249

Maritime Delimitation and Territorial Questions (Qatar v Bahrain) (Jurisdiction and Admissibility) [1994] ICJ Rep 112, 105
Maritime Delimitation in the Area Between Greenland and Jan Mayen (Judgment) [1993] ICJ Rep 38
- Separate Opinion of Judge Weeramantry, 186

Maritime Delimitation in the Caribbean Sea and the Pacific Ocean (Costa Rica v Nicaragua) (Order of 31 May 2016) [2016] ICJ Rep 235, 44
Military and Paramilitary Activities in and against Nicaragua (Nicaragua v USA) (Merits) [1986] ICJ Rep 16, 107, 181, 239, 249, 270
Monetary Gold Removed from Rome in 1943 (Preliminary Question) [1954] ICJ Rep 19, 125
North Sea Continental Shelf Cases (Federal Republic of Germany/Netherlands; Federal Republic of Germany/Denmark) (Judgment) [1969] ICJ Rep 3, 186, 192, 202, 211
- Dissenting Opinion of Judge Tanaka, 312
- Dissenting Opinion of Vice-President Koretsky, 186

Nuclear Tests Case (Australia v France) (Judgment) [1974] ICJ Rep 253, 146, 271
Oil Platforms (Iran v USA) (Counter-Claim, Order of 10 March 1998) [1998] ICJ Rep 203, 148
Oil Platforms (Iran v USA) (Merits) [2003] ICJ Rep 161
- Declaration of Judge Koroma, 149
- Dissenting Opinion of Judge Al-Khasawneh, 149
- Separate Opinion of Judge Higgins, 148

Pulp Mills on the River Uruguay (Argentina v Uruguay) (Judgment) [2010] ICJ Rep 14, 220, 272, 313
Request for an Examination of the Situation in Accordance with Paragraph 63 of the Court's Judgment of 20th December 1974 in the Nuclear Tests (New Zealand v France) [1995] ICJ Rep 288
- Dissenting opinion by Judge ad hoc Sir Geoffrey Palmer, 271
- Dissenting opinion by Judge Weeramantry, 271

Right of Passage over Indian Territory (Portugal v India) (Judgment) [1960] ICJ Rep 6, 34
Right of Passage over Indian Territory (Portugal v India) (Observations and submissions of the Government of the Portuguese Republic on the Preliminary Objections of the Government of India) [1957] VIII ICJ Rep 629, 28
Rights of Nationals of the United States of America in Morocco (France v USA) (Judgment) [1952] ICJ Rep 176, 33
South West Africa Cases (Ethiopia v South Africa; Liberia v South Africa) (Preliminary Objection) [1962] ICJ Rep 319, 108
South West Africa Cases (Second Phase) (Ethiopia v South Africa; Liberia v South Africa) (Judgment) [1966] ICJ Rep 6, 201
- Pleadings, South West Africa, Vol XI, 34

Territorial and Maritime Dispute (Nicaragua v Colombia) (Judgment) [2012] ICJ Rep 624, 239
Tulip v Turkey (Award of 10 March 2014) ICSID Case No ARB/11/28, 109

TABLE OF CASES　　　　　　　xix

Permanent Court of International Justice (PCIJ)

Case Concerning the Factory at Chorzów (Germany v Poland) (Jurisdiction) [1927] PCIJ Rep Series A No 9, 146, 203
Case Concerning the Factory at Chorzów (Germany v Poland) (Merits) [1928] PCIJ Series A No 17, 72, 179, 285
Factory at *Chorzów* (Germany v Poland) (Claim for Indemnity, The Merits) [1928] PCIJ Series A No 17, 87
Free Zones of Upper Savoy and the District of Gex (France/Switzerland) (Order) [1929] PCIJ Ser A No 22, 112
German Interests in Polish Upper Silesia (Germany v Poland) (Merits) [1926] PCIJ Series A No 7, 80
Oscar Chinn Case (Britain v Belgium) (Judgment) [1934] PCIJ Series A/B No 63, 239
SS 'Lotus' (France v Turkey) (Judgment) [1927] PCIJ Series A No 10, 35
SS 'Wimbledon' (UK & ors v Germany) (Judgment) [1923] PCIJ Series A No 1, 238

International Tribunal for the Law of the Sea (ITLOS)

Responsibilities and Obligations of States Sponsoring Persons and Entities with Respect to Activities in the Area (Advisory Opinion of 1 February 2011) 2011 ITLOS Rep 10, 220
Southern Bluefin Tuna Cases (New Zealand v Japan; Australia v Japan) (Provisional Measures, Order of 27 August 1999) 1999 ITLOS Rep 280
  • Separate Opinion of Judge Laing, 268, 271
  • Separate Opinion of Judge Treves, 271
The M/V 'Saiga' (No 2) (Saint Vincent and the Grenadines v Guinea) (Judgment) [1999] 120 ITLOS Rep 10, 286

Arbitration

9REN v Spain (Award of 31 May 2019) ICSID Case No ARB/15/15, 304
AAPL v Sri Lanka (Final Award of 27 June 1990) ICSID Case No ARB/87/3, 83, 206
Achmea (I) v Slovakia (Award of 7 December 2012) UNCITRAL, PCA Case No 2008-13, 106, 209
Achmea (I) v Slovakia (Award on Jurisdiction, Arbitrability and Suspension of 26 October 2010) PCA Case No 2008-13, 214
Adamakopoulos & ors v Cyprus (Statement of Dissent of Professor Marcelo Kohen of 3 February 2020) ICSID Case No ARB/15/49, 226
ADC Affiliate Limited v Hungary (Award of 2 October 2006) ICSID Case No ARB/03/16, 73, 80, 84-6, 88, 210, 286
Addiko Bank v Croatia (Decision on Croatia's Jurisdictional Objection Related to the Alleged Incompatibility of the BIT with the EU Acquis of 12 June 2020) ICSID Case No ARB/17/37, 223, 224

Adem Dogan v Turkmenistan (Decision on Annulment of 15 January 2016) ICSID Case No ARB/09/9, 188

ADF Group Inc v USA (Award of 9 January 2003) ICSID Case No ARB(AF)/00/, 101

ADF Group Inc v USA (Canada's Second Article 1128 Submission of 19 July 2002) ICSID Case No ARB(AF)/00/1, 318

ADF Group Inc v USA (Final Post-Hearing Submission of Respondent United States of America on Article 1105(1) and *Pope & Talbot* of 1 August 2002) Case No ARB(AF)/00/1, 56

ADF Group Inc v USA (Post-Hearing Submission of Respondent United States of America on Article 1105(1) and *Pope & Talbot* of 27 June 2002) Case No ARB(AF)/00/1, 59

ADF Group Inc v USA (Transcript of Hearing: Day 2 of 16 April 2002) ICSID Case No ARB(AF)/00/1, 318

ADM v Mexico (Award of 21 November 2007) ICSID Case No ARB(AF)/04/05, 102, 126

ADM v Mexico (Concurring Opinion of Arthur W Rovine of 20 September 2007) ICSID Case No ARB(AF)/04/05, 132

ADM v Mexico (Decision on Request for Correction, Supplementary Decision, and Interpretation of 10 July 2008) ICSID Case No ARB(AF) 04/05, 205

Adriano Gardella SpA v Côte d'Ivoire (Award of 29 August 1997) ICSID Case No ARB/74/1, 82

A11Y v Czech Republic (Decision on Jurisdiction 9 February 2017) ICSID Case No UNCT/15/1, 215

AES Summit Generation Limited and AES–Tisza Erömü Kft v Hungary (Award of 23 September 2010) ICSID Case No ARB/07/22, 243

AGIP SpA v Congo (Award of 30 November 1979) ICSID Case No ARB/77/1, 82

AIG Capital Partners, Inc and CJSC Tema Real Estate Company Ltd v Kazakhstan (Award of 7 October 2003) ICSID Case No ARB/01/6, 197

Al Tamimi v Oman (Award of 3 November 2015) ICSID Case No ARB/11/33, 96, 245

Alabama Claims of USA v UK (Ad hoc Award of 14 September 1872) published in JB Moore (ed), *History and Digest of the International Arbitrations to Which the United States Has Been a Party,* Vol 1 (US GPO 1898), 79

Al-Bahloul v Tajikistan (Final Award of 8 June 2010) SCC Case No V (064/2008), 101, 289, 302, 303

Alghanim v Jordan (Award of 14 December 2017) ICSID Case No ARB/13/38, 110

Almâs v Poland (Award of 27 June 2016) PCA Case No 2015–13, 108

Amco Asia Corporation & ors v Indonesia (Award of 20 November 1984) ICSID Case No ARB/81/1, 82

Amco Asia Corporation & ors v Indonesia (Decision on Annulment of 16 May 1986) ICSID Case No ARB/81/1, 183

Amco v Indonesia (Award of 31 May 1990) ICSID Case No ARB/81/8, 297

TABLE OF CASES xxi

American International Group, Inc v Iran (Award of 7 December 1983) IUSCT Case No 2, 4 IUSCTR 96, 185

American Manufacturing & Trading, Inc v Republic of Zaire (Award of 21 February 1997) ICSID Case No ARB/93/1, 82, 182

AMF Aircraftleasing Meier & Fischer GmbH & Co KG, Hamburg (Germany) v Czech Republic (Final Award of 11 May 2020) PCA Case No 2017–15, 241

Amoco International Finance Corp v Iran (Partial Award of 14 July 1987) IUSCT Case No 56, 83 ILR 500, 83, 185

Amoco v Iran (Partial Award (Award No 310-56-3) of 14 July 1987) IUSCT Case No 56, 15 IUSCT 189, 286

Anglia v Czech Republic (Final Award of 10 March 2017) SCC Case No 2014/181, 215

Antin v Spain (Award of 15 June 2018) ICSID Case No ARB/13/31, 290

Ares v Georgia (Award of 26 February 2008) ICSID Case No ARB/05/23, 103

Arif v Moldova (Award of 8 April 2013) ICSID Case No ARB/11/23, 16, 287

Armas v Venezuela (Final Award of 26 April 2019) PCA Case No 2013–3, 107

Asian Agricultural Products Ltd v Republic of Sri Lanka (Final Award of 27 June 1990) ICSID Case No ARB/87/3, 245

Atlantic Triton Company Limited v Guinea (Award of 21 April 1986) ICSID Case No ARB/84/1, 187

Attaque de la caravane du maharao de Cutch (1927) II RIAA 821, 190

Award in Arbitration Regarding the Iron Rhine Railway Between the Kingdom of Belgium and the Kingdom of the Netherlands (Decision of 24 May 2005) XXVII UNRIAA 35, 220

Awdi v Romania (Award of 2 March 2015) ICSID Case No ARB/10/13, 107

AWG Group v Argentina (Award of 9 April 2015) UNCITRAL, 85

AWG Group v Argentina (Decision on Liability of 30 July 2010) UNCITRAL, 112
- Separate Opinion of Arbitrator Pedro Nikken, 12

Azinian v Mexico (Award of 1 November 1999) ICSID Case No ARB(AF)/97/2, 320

Bahgat v Arab Republic of Egypt (Final Award of 23 December 2019) PCA Case No 2012–07, 244

Bayindir v Pakistan (Award of 27 August 2009) ICSID Case No ARB/03/29, 117

Bear Creek Mining Corporation v Peru (Award of 30 November 2017) ICSID Case No ARB/14/21, 275, 302

Bear Creek Mining Corporation v Peru (Partial Dissenting Opinion of Professor Philippe Sands of 30 November 2017) ICSID Case No ARB/14/21, 275

Bear Creek Mining Corporation v Peru (Submission of Canada pursuant to Article 832 of the Canada-Peru Free Trade Agreement of 9 June 2016) ICSID Case No ARB/14/21, 55

Bernardus Henricus Funnekotter v Zimbabwe (Award of 22 April 2009) ICSID Case No ARB/05/6, 152

BG Group v Argentina (Final Award of 24 December 2007) UNCITRAL, 153, 299

Biedermann v Kazakhstan (Award of 1 January 1999) SCC Case No 97/1996, 82
Biens britanniques au Maroc espagnol (Spain v GB) (1925) II RIAA 615, 191
Bilcon v Canada (Award on Jurisdiction and Liability of 17 March 2015) PCA Case No 2009-04, 274, 322
Bilcon v Canada (Decision on Damages of 10 January 2019) PCA Case No 2009-04, 101
Binder v Czech Republic (Award on Jurisdiction of 6 June 2007) UNCITRAL, 215
Bischoff Case (1903) 10 RIAA, 252
Biwater Gauff v Tanzania (Award of 24 July 2008) ICSID Case No ARB/05/22, 104, 286
Bosh v Ukraine (Award of 25 October 2012) ICSID Case No ARB/08/11, 107
Brewer, Moller & Co Case (Germany v Venezuela) (1903) 10 RIAA 423, 243
British Caribbean Bank v Belize (Award of 19 December 2014) PCA Case No 2010-18, 85
Burlington Resources Inc v Ecuador (Decision on Reconsideration and Award of 7 February 2017) ICSID Case No ARB/08/05, 85
Busta v Czech Republic (Final Award of 10 March 2017) SCC Case No 2015/01, 215
Campbell (1931) II RIAA 1145, 190
Camuzzi International SA v Argentina (Decision on Objections to Jurisdiction of 11 May 2005) ICSID Case No ARB/03/2, 57
Camuzzi International SA v Argentina (Opinion of Anne-Marie Slaughter and William Burke-White of 19 July 2005) ICSID Case No ARB/03/02, 39
Camuzzi International SA v Argentina (Opinion of José E Alvarez of 12 September 2005) ICSID Case No ARB/03/02, 39
Canadian Cattlemen v USA (Award on Jurisdiction of 28 January 2008) UNCITRAL, 222
Canfor Corporation v USA and Tembec et al v USA and Terminal Forest Products Ltd v USA (Order of the Consolidation Tribunal of 7 September 2005) UNCITRAL, 220
Caratube v Kazakhstan (Award of 27 September 2017) ICSID Case No ARB/13/13, 302
Cargill, Inc v Mexico (Award of 18 September 2009) ICSID Case No ARB(AF)/05/02, 5
Casinos Austria v Argentina (Decision on Jurisdiction of 29 June 2018) ICSID Case No ARB/14/32, 107
Cengiz v Libya (Final Award of 7 November 2018) ICC Case No 21537/ZF/AYZ, 107
Chemin de fer de Sopron-Köszeg contre Autriche et Hongrie (1929) II RIAA 961, 198
Chemtura Corporation (formerly Crompton Corporation) v Canada (Award of 2 August 2010) UNCITRAL, 241
Chevron Corporation and Texaco Petroleum Corporation v Ecuador (Award of 31 August 2011) UNCITRAL, PCA Case No 34877, 26
Chevron Corporation and Texaco Petroleum Corporation v Ecuador (II) (Opinion of Jan Paulsson of 12 March 2012) PCA Case No 2009-23, 43
Claimant v Slovakia (Award of 5 March 2011) ad hoc Arbitration, 106
CME Czech Republic BV v Czech Republic (Final Award of 14 March 2003) UNCITRAL, 42
CME Czech Republic BV v Czech Republic (Partial Award of 13 September 2001) UNCITRAL, 287

CME Czech Republic BV v Czech Republic (Separate Opinion on the Issues at the Quantum Phase by Ian Brownlie of 14 March 2003) UNCITRAL, 198
CMS v Argentina (Annulment of 25 September 2007) ICSID Case No ARB/01/8, 101, 157
CMS v Argentina (Application for Annulment and Request for Stay of Enforcement of Arbitral Award of 8 September 2005) ICSID Case No ARB/01/8, 55
CMS v Argentina (Award of 12 May 2005) ICSID Case ARB/01/8 [390], 156
Colt Industries Operating Corporation v Republic of Korea (Order Taking Note of the Discontinuance of 3 August 1990) ICSID Case No ARB/84/2, 82
Compagnie de la Baie d'Hudson (1869) published in in Politis, N & de Lapradelle, AG (eds), *Recueil Des Arbitrages Internationaux (1856–1872)* (Pedone 1923), 191
Compañía de Aguas del Aconquija SA and Vivendi Universal SA v Argentina (Final Award of 20 August 2007) ICSID Case No ARB/97/3, 16, 80
Compañia del Desarrollo de Santa Elena SA v Costa Rica (Award of 17 February 2000) ICSID Case No ARB/96/1, 185
Company General of the Orinoco (1905) 10 RIAA 184, 157
ConocoPhillips v Venezuela (Award of 8 March 2019) ICSID Case No ARB/07/30, 74, 180
ConocoPhillips v Venezuela (Decision on Jurisdiction and Merits of 3 September 2013) ICSID Case No ARB/07/30, 101, 295
Continental Casualty v Argentina (Award of 5 September 2008) ICSID Case No ARB/03/9, 257
Continental Casualty v Argentina (Decision on the Application for Partial Annulment, and the Application for Partial Annulment of 16 September 2011) ICSID Case No ARB/03/9, 104
Corn Products v Mexico (Decision on Responsibility of 15 January 2008) ICSID Case No ARB/(AF)/04/1, 126
Cotesworth & Powell (Great Britain) v Colombia (Award of November 1875) published in JB Moore (ed), *History and Digest of the International Arbitrations to Which the United States Has Been a Party*, Vol 2 (US GPO 1898), 79
Crystallex International Corporation v Venezuela (Award of 4 April 2016) ICSID Case No ARB(AF)/11/2, 16, 85, 180
Cube v Spain (Decision on Jurisdiction, Liability and Partial Decision on Quantum of 19 February 2019) ICSID Case No ARB/15/20, 290
David Aven v Costa Rica (Final Award of 18 September 2018) ICSID Case No UNCT/15/3, 262
Delagoa Bay Railway (1900) published in JB Moore (ed), *History and Digest of the International Arbitrations to Which the United States Has Been a Party*, vol 2 (US GPO 1898) 1865, 78
Desert Line v Yemen (Award of 6 February 2008) ICSID Case No ARB/05/17, 102
Deutsche Amerikanische Petroleum Gesellschaft Oil Tankers (1926) 2 RIAA 777, 240
Deutsche Bank AG v Sri Lanka (Award of 31 October 2012) ICSID Case No ARB/09/02, 244
Devas v India (Decision on Jurisdiction and Merits of 25 July 2016) PCA Case No 2013-09, 111

USA (Dickson Car Wheel Company) v Mexico (1931) 4 RIAA 669, 240

Eastern Sugar BV (Netherlands) v Czech Republic (Partial Award of 27 March 2007) SCC Case No 88/2004, 215

Eco Oro Minerals Corp v Colombia (Decision on Jurisdiction, Liability and Directions on Quantum of 9 September 2021) ICSID Case No ARB/16/41, 249, 322, 340

Ecuador v USA (Expert Opinion of Prof Alain Pellet of 23 May 2012) PCA Case No 2012–5, 44

EDF (Services) Ltd v Romania (Award of 8 October 2009) ICSID Case No ARB/05/13, 342

EDF v Argentina (Award of 11 June 2012) ICSID Case No ARB/03/23, 102, 159, 197

EDF v Argentina (Decision on Annulment of 5 February 2016) ICSID Case No ARB/03/23, 104, 159

Eiser v Spain (Final Award of 4 May 2017) ICSID Case No ARB/13/36, 290

El Paso Energy International Company v Argentina (Award of 31 October 2011) ICSID Case No ARB/03/15, 15, 102, 222, 246, 296

El Paso Energy International Company v Argentina (Decision on Annulment of 22 September 2014) ICSID Case No ARB/03/15, 109

Electrabel v Hungary (Decision on Jurisdiction and Liability of 30 November 2012) ICSID Case No ARB/07/19, 102, 213

Eli Lilly and Company v Canada (Observations on Issues Raised in 1128 Submissions of the United States and Mexico of 22 April 2016), 57

Eli Lilly and Company v Canada (Observations on Issues Raised in 1128 Submissions of the United States and Mexico of 22 April 2016) Case No UNCT/14/2, 55

EnCana v Ecuador (Award of 3 February 2006) UNCITRAL, LCIA Case No UN3481, 101

Enkev v Poland (First Partial Award of 29 April 2014) PCA Case No 2013-01, 293

Enron v Argentina (Award of 22 May 2007) ICSID Case No ARB/01/3, 157, 224

Enron v Argentina (Decision on Annulment of 30 July 2010) ICSID Case No ARB/01/3, 113

Enron v Argentina (Decision on Jurisdiction of 14 January 2004) ICSID Case No ARB/01/3, 157, 224, 289

Eskosol v Italy (Decision on Termination Request and Intra-EU Objection of 7 May 2019) ICSID Case No ARB/15/50, 222

Europe Cement v Turkey (Award of 13 August 2009) ICSID Case No ARB(AF)/07/2, 293

European American Investment Bank AG (Austria) v Slovakia (Award on Jurisdiction of 22 October 2012) UNCITRAL, PCA Case No 2010–17, 215

Fedax NV v Venezuela (Award of 9 March 1998) ICSID Case No ARB/96/3, 82

Feldman v Mexico (Award of 16 December 2002) ICSID Case No ARB(AF)/99/1, 241

Foresight v Spain (Final Award of 14 November 2018) SCC Case No 2015/150, 288

France (Affaire Chevreau) v UK (Award of 9 June 1931) 2 RIAA 1113, 317

France (Feuillebois) v Mexico (1929) V RIAA 542, 198

Furst Claim (1960) 42 ILR 153, 240

F-W v Trinidad and Tobago (Award of 3 March 2006) ICSID Case No ARB/01/14, 100

TABLE OF CASES xxv

Gabon v Société Serete SA (Order Taking Note of the Discontinuance Issued by the Tribunal of 27 Feb 1978) ICSID Case No ARB/76/1, 82
Gavrilović v Croatia (Award of 26 July 2018) ICSID Case No ARB/12/39, 108
Gemplus v Mexico (Award of 16 June 2010) ICSID Cases Nos ARB(AF)/04/3 & ARB(AF)/04/4, 102
Genin, Eastern Credit Limited, Inc and AS Baltoil v Estonia (Award of 25 June 2001) ICSID Case No ARB/99/2, 259
Georges Pinson case (France/United Mexican States) (Award of 13 April 1928) 5 UNRIAA 329, 138
Glamis Gold, Ltd v United States (Award of 8 June 2009) UNCITRAL, 5, 245
Glamis Gold, Ltd v United States (Decision on Application and Submission by Quechan Indian Nation of 16 September 2005) UNCITRAL, 330
Gold Reserve Inc v Venezuela (Award of 22 September 2014) ICSID Case No ARB(AF)/09/1, 16, 85, 182, 304
Gold Reserve Inc v Venezuela (Venezuela's Motion to Dismiss Petition and to Deny Recognition of Arbitral Award, or in the Alternative, to Stay Enforcement of 12 June 2015) ICSID Case No ARB(AF)/09/1, 184
GPF GP Sàrl v Poland (Award on Jurisdiction (Not Public) of 15 February 2017) SCC Case No V 2014/168, 215
GPF GP Sàrl v Poland (Final Award of 29 April 2020) SCC Case No 2014/168, 217
Green Power Partners & SCE Solar v Spain (Award of 16 June 2022) SCC Case No V 2016/13, 225
Greentech Energy Systems A/S, NovEnergia II Energy & Environment (SCA) SICAR, and NovEnergia II Italian Portfolio SA v Italy (Final Award of 23 December 2018) SCC Case No V 2015/095, 251
Guadalupe Gas Products Corporation v Nigeria (Award of 22 July 1980) ICSID Case No ARB/78/1, 82
Hamester v Ghana (Award of 18 June 2010) ICSID Case No ARB/07/24, 102
Harington et autres (1862) published in N Politis & AG de Lapradelle (eds), *Recueil Des Arbitrages Internationaux (1856–1872)* (Pedone 1923), 191
Heny (1903) IX RIAA 125, 191
Himpurna California Energy Ltd (Bermuda) v PT (Persero) Perusahaan Listruik Negara (Indonesia) (Final Award of 4 May 1999) XXV YBCA 14, 196
Holiday Inns SA & ors v Morocco (Order Taking Note of the Discontinuance 17 October 1978) ICSID Case No ARB/72/1, 82
Houben v Burundi (Award 12 January 2016) ICSID Case No ARB/13/7, 73
Hrvatska Elektropriveda v Slovenia (Award of 17 December 2017) ICSID Case No ARB/05/24, 112
Hulley Enterprises v Russia (Final Award of 18 July 2014) PCA Case No AA 226, 298
Impregilo v Argentina (Award of 21 June 2011) ICSID Case No ARB/07/17, 113, 208
Industria Nacional de Alimentos (Luccetti) v Perú (Decision on Annulment of 5 September 2007) ICSID Case No ARB/03/4, 115

Infinito Gold v Costa Rica (Decision on Jurisdiction of 4 December 2017) ICSID Case No ARB/14/5, 107
Infrared v Spain (Award of 2 August 2019) ICSID Case No ARB/14/12, 299
Inmaris v Ukraine (Award of 1 March 2012) ICSID Case No ARB/08/8, 114
Innogy v Spain (Decision on Jurisdiction, Liability and Certain Issues of Quantum of 30 December 2019) ICSID Case No ARB/14/34, 107
Invesmart, BV v Czech Republic (Award of 26 June 2009) UNCITRAL, 243
Islamic Republic of Iran v USA (Award of 2 July 2014) IUSCT Case Nos A15(IV) and A24, 182
Island of Palmas case (Netherlands v USA) (1928) 2 RIAA 829, 239
Jan de Nul v Egypt (Decision on Jurisdiction of 16 June 2006) ICSID Case No ARB/04/13, 26, 102, 103
John Gill (1931) V RIAA 157, 191
JSW Solar & Wirtgen v Czech Republic (Final Award of 11 October 2017) PCA Case No 2014–03, 215
Junghans (Germany v Romania) (Part Two) (1940) III RIAA 1883, 198
Juvel & Bithell v Poland (Partial Final Award 26 February 2019) ICC Case No 19459/MHM, 215
Kaiser Bauxite Company v Jamaica (Decision on Jurisdiction and Competence of 6 July 1975) ICSID Case No ARB/74/3, 82
Kardassopoulos v Georgia (Award of 3 March 2010) ICSID Case No ARB/05/18, 296
Kardassopoulos v Georgia (Decision on Jurisdiction of 6 July 2007) ICSID Case No ARB/05/18, 107
Karkey Karadeniz Elektrik Uretim AS v Islamic Republic of Pakistan (Award of 22 August 2017) ICSID Case No ARB/13/1, 244
Khan Resources v Mongolia (Award on the Merits of 2 March 2015) UNCITRAL, 294
Klöckner Industrie-Anlagen GmbH & ors v Cameroon & Société Camerounaise des Engrais (Ad hoc Committee Decision on Annulment of 3 May 1985) ICSID Case No ARB/81/2, 205
Klöckner Industrie-Anlagen GmbH & ors v Cameroon & Société Camerounaise des Engrais (Award of 21 October 1983) ICSID Case No ARB/81/2, 82
Kügele v Polish State (1932) 6 ILR 69, 240
Kuwait v American Independent Oil Company (Award of 24 March 1982) Ad Hoc Arbitration, 66 ILR 518, 183
Landesbank Baden-Württemberg & ors v Spain (Decision on the Intra-EU Jurisdictional Objection of 25 February 2019) ICSID Case No ARB/15/45, 125, 213
Larsen v Hawaiian Kingdom (Award of 5 February 2001) UNCITRAL, 119 ILR 566, 125
Lemire v Ukraine (Award of 28 March 2011) ICSID Case No ARB/06/18, 208, 298
Les Laboratoires Servier, SAS, Biofarma, SAS and Arts et Techniques du Progres SAS v Republic of Poland (Final Award of 14 February 2012) UNCITRAL, 244
LESI v Algeria (Award of 10 January 2005) ICSID Case No ARB/03/08, 106
LETCO v Liberia (Award of 31 March 1986) ICSID Case No ARB/83/2, 82
Levi v Peru (Award of 26 February 2014) ICSID Case No ARB/10/17, 107

TABLE OF CASES

LG&E v Argentina (Award of 25 July 2007) ICSID Case No ARB/02/1, 162, 286
LG&E v Argentina (Decision on Liability of 3 October 2006) ICSID Case No ARB/02/1, 111
Libyan American Oil Company v Libya (Award of 12 April 1977) Ad Hoc Tribunal, 62 ILR 140, 186
Loan Agreement Between Italy and Costa Rica (1998) XXV RIAA 21, 182
Loewen Group, Inc and Raymond L Loewen v USA (Award of 26 June 2003) ICSID Case No ARB(AF)/98/3, 26, 110, 320
Loewen Group, Inc and Raymond L Loewen v USA (Opinion of Richard B Bilder (on international law governing state responsibility for treatment of foreign investors) of 16 March 2001) ICSID Case No ARB(AF)/98/3, 35
Loewen Group, Inc and Raymond L Loewen v USA (Second Submission of the Government of Canada Pursuant to NAFTA Article 1128 of 27 June 2002) ICSID Case No ARB(AF)/98/3, 56
Loewen Group, Inc and Raymond L Loewen v USA (Second Submission of the United Mexican States of 9 November 2001) ICSID Case No ARB(AF)/98/3, 58
Lone Pine Resources Inc v Canada (Gouvernement du Canada Contre-Mémoire of 24 July 2015) ICSID Case No UNCT/15/2, 241
Lone Pine Resources Inc v Canada (Observations of the Government of Canada on the Issues Raised in the Memorials Submitted by the United States of America and Mexico by Virtue of NAFTA Article 1128 of 22 September 2017) Case No UNCT/15/2, 57
Maffezini v Spain (Award of 13 November 2000) ICSID Case No ARB/97/7, 82
Maffezini v Spain (Decision on Jurisdiction of 25 January 2000) ICSID Case No ARB/97/7, 117
Magyar Farming v Hungary (Award of 13 November 2019) ICSID Case No ARB/17/27, 215
Mamidoil Jetoil Greek Petroleum Products Societe Anonyme SA v Albania (Award of 30 March 2015) ICSID Case No ARB/11/24, 259
Marfin v Cyprus (Award of 26 July 2018) ICSID Case No ARB/13/27, 215, 241
Masdar Solar v Spain (Award of 16 May 2018) ICSID Case No ARB/14/1, 74, 103, 213, 251, 290
MCI Power Group LC and New Turbine, Inc v Ecuador (Award of 31 July 2007) ICSID Case No ARB/03/6, 16, 56
Mercer International Inc v Canada (Submission of the United States of America of 8 May 2015) ICSID Case No ARB(AF)/12/3, 56
Merrill & Ring v Canada (Award of 31 March 2010) ICSID Administered Case No UNCT/07/1, 101
Mesa Power Group LLC v Canada (Observations on the Award on Jurisdiction and Merits in *William Ralph Clayton, William Richard Clayton, Douglas Clayton, Daniel Clayton and Bilcon of Delaware, Inc v Canada* of 14 May 2015) PCA Case No 2012-17, 56
Mesa Power Group LLC v Canada (Response to 1128 Submissions of 26 June 2015) PCA Case No 2012-17, 55

Metalclad v Mexico (Award of 30 August 2000) ICSID Case No ARB(AF)/97/1, 15, 73, 288

Metal-Tech Ltd v Uzbekistan (Award of 4 October 2013) ICSID Case No ARB/10/3, 207

Methanex v USA (Final Award of the Tribunal on Jurisdiction and Merits of 3 August 2005) UNCITRAL, 222, 264

Michael Ballantine and Lisa Ballantine v Dominican Republic (Submission of the United States of America of 22 September 2017) PCA Case No 2016–17, 57

Micula (I) v Romania (Decision on Jurisdiction and Admissibility of 24 September 2008) ICSID Case No ARB/05/20, 289

Micula (I) v Romania (Final Award of 11 December 2013) ICSID Case No ARB/05/20, 289

Middle East Cement Shipping and Handling Co SA v Egypt (Award of 12 April 2002) ICSID Case No ARB/99/6, 197

Mobil Investments Canada Inc & Murphy Oil Corporation v Canada (Decision on Liability and Principles of Quantum of 22 May 2012) ICSID Case No ARB(AF)/07/4, 5

Mobil Oil Corporation & ors v New Zealand (Decision on Liability of 6 January 1988) ICSID Case No ARB/87/2, 83

Mondev International Ltd v USA (Award of 11 October 2002) ICSID Case No ARB(AF)/99/2, 39, 107, 313, 319

Montijo (USA) v Colombia (Award of 10 April 1875) published in JB Moore (ed), *History and Digest of the International Arbitrations to Which the United States Has Been a Party,* Vol 2 (US GPO 1898), 79

Mr Franck Charles Arif v Moldova (Award of 8 April 2013) ICSID Case No ARB/11/23, 16

MTD Equity Sdn Bhd v Chile (Decision on Annulment of 21 March 2007) ICSID Case No ARB/01/7, 183

Murphy v Ecuador (Award of 6 May 2016) PCA Case No AA434, 298

Muszynianka v Slovakia (Award 7 of October 2020) PCA Case No 2017–08, 215

National Grid plc v Argentina (Decision on Jurisdiction of 20 June 2006) UNCITRAL, 220

Neptune (1797) 4 Moore Arbitrations 3843, 168
- Opinion of Mr Gore, 169
- Opinion of Mr Pinkney, 169
- Opinion of Mr Trumbull, 169

NextEra v Spain (Award of 12 March 2019) ICSID Case No ARB/14/11, 305

Noble Ventures Inc v Romania (Award of 12 October 2005) ICSID Case No ARB/01/11, 100, 342

North Atlantic Coast Fisheries Case (GB v USA) (1910) 11 RIAA 167, 239

Norwegian Shipowners' Claims (Norway v USA) (Award of 13 October 1922) I RIAA 307, 81, 199

Novenergia II v Spain (Final Award of 15 February 2018) SCC Case No 2015/063, 74, 298

Nykomb v Latvia (Arbitral Award of 16 December 2003) SCC Case No 118/2001, 101, 286

OAO Tatneft v Ukraine (Award on the Merits of 29 July 2014) PCA Case No 2008-8, 85

Occidental v Ecuador (Award of 5 October 2012) ICSID Case No ARB/06/11, 300

Oko Pankki Oyj, VTB Bank (Deutschland) AG and Sampo Bank Plc v Estonia (Award of 19 November 2007) ICSID Case No ARB/04/6, 16
Olin v Libya (Final Award of 25 May 2018) ICC Case No 20355/MCP, 106
Oliva (Italy) v Venezuela (1903) published in MM Whiteman, *Damages in International Law*, Vol III (US GPO 1943), 79
Oostergetel v Slovakia (Decision on Jurisdiction 30 April 2010) UNCITRAL, 215
Oostergetel v Slovakia (Final Award of 23 April 2012) UNCITRAL, 107
OperaFund v Spain (Award of 6 September 2019) ICSID Case No ARB/15/36, 74, 180, 286
Opinion in the Lusitania Cases (1923) VII RIAA 32, 180
Orinoco Steamship Company Case (1910) XI RIAA 16, 190
Orr and Laubenheimer and the Post-Glover Electric Company (1900) 15 RIAA 33, 157
PA Allard v Barbados (Award of 27 June 2017) PCA Case No 2012-06, 16
Pac Rim v El Salvador (Award of 14 October 2016) ICSID Case No ARB/09/12, 106
Paushok v Mongolia (Decision on Jurisdiction of 28 April 2011) UNCITRAL, 101
Pezold v Zimbabwe (Award of 28 July 2015) ICSID Case No ARB/10/15, 26, 104, 152, 289
Pezold v Zimbabwe (Procedural Order No 2 of 26 June 2012) ICSID Case No ARB/10/15, 330
Philip Morris v Uruguay (Award of 8 July 2016) ICSID Case No ARB/10/7, 242
Philip Morris v Uruguay (Concurring and Dissenting Opinion of Gary Born of 8 July 2016) ICSID Case No ARB/10/7, 244
Phillips Petroleum v Iran (Award of 29 June 1989 (Award No 425-39-2)) IUSCT Case No 39, 21 IUSCT 79, 205
Poggioli Case (1903) 10 RIAA 669, 241
Pope & Talbot Inc v Canada (Award in Respect of Damages of 31 May 2002) UNCITRAL, 221, 319
Pope & Talbot Inc v Canada (Award on the Merits of Phase II of 10 April 2001) UNCITRAL, 4
PV Investors v Spain (Final Award of 28 February 2020) PCA Case No 2012-14, 290
Quiborax v Bolivia (Award of 16 September 2015) ICSID Case No ARB/06/2, 88, 112, 244, 295
- Partially Dissenting Opinion of Brigitte Stern of 7 September 2015, 89
Railroad Development Corporation (RDC) v Guatemala (Award of 29 June 2012) ICSID Case No ARB/07/23, 7
Règlement des prestations effectuées dans la Ruhr (1927) II RIAA 797, 191
Renco (I) v Peru (Partial Award on Jurisdiction of 15 July 2016) ICSID Case No UNCT/13/1, 220
RENERGY v Spain (Award of 6 May 2022) ICSID Case No ARB/14/18, 225
Reynolds Jamaica Mines Limited and Reynolds Metals Company v Jamaica (Order Taking Note of the Discontinuance of 12 October 1977) ICSID Case No ARB/74/4, 82
Rompetrol v Romania (Award of 6 May 2013) ICSID Case No ARB/06/3, 101

Ron Fuchs v Georgia (Award of 3 March 2010) ICSID Case No ARB/07/15, 180
RREEF v Spain (Decision on Responsibility and on the Principles of Quantum of 30 November 2018) ICSID Case No ARB/13/30, 251, 290
Rumeli Telekom AS & or v Kazakhstan (Decision of ad hoc Committee of 25 March 2010) ICSID Case No ARB/05/16, 204
Rusoro Mining v Venezuela (Award of 22 August 2016) ICSID Case No ARB(AF)/12/5, 294
RWE v Spain (Decision on Jurisdiction, Liability and Certain Issues of Quantum of 30 December 2019) ICSID Case No ARB/14/34, 290
Saar Papier Vertriebs GmbH v Poland (Final Award of 16 October 1995) UNCITRAL, 82
Saint-Gobain v Venezuela (Decision on Liability and Quantum of 30 December 2016) ICSID Case No ARB/12/13, 103
Saipem v Bangladesh (Decision on Jurisdiction and Provisional Measures of 21 March 2007) ICSID Case No ARB/05/07, 102
Salini v Argentina (Decision on Jurisdiction of 23 February 2018) ICSID Case No ARB/15/39, 110
Saluka Investments BV v Czech Republic (Partial Award of 17 March 2006) UNCITRAL, 220, 246
Sanum Investments (I) v Laos (Judgment of the Court of Appeal of Singapore of 29 September 2016) PCA Case No 2013–13, [2016] SGCA 57, 223
Sapphire International Petroleums Ltd v NIOC (Award of 15 March 1963) 35 ILR 136, 209
SARL Benvenuti & Bonfant v Congo (Award of 8 August 1980) ICSID Case No ARB/77/2, 82
SAS v Bolivia (Award of 22 November 2018) PCA Case No 2013–15, 152
Savage case (1865) published in JB Moore (ed), *History and Digest of the International Arbitrations to Which the United States Has Been a Party,* Vol 2 (US GPO 1898), 81
SD Myers Inc v Canada (Dissenting Opinion of Professor Bryan P Schwarts of 30 December 2002) UNCITRAL, 87
SD Myers Inc v Canada (Partial Award of 13 November 2000) UNCITRAL, 7, 73
SD Myers Inc v Canada (Second Partial Award of 21 October 2002) UNCITRAL, 82
SD Myers Inc v Canada (Statement of Defence of 18 June 1999) UNCITRAL, 241
Sedco, Inc v National Iranian Oil Company and Islamic Republic of Iran (Award of 17 September 1985) IUSCT Case Nos 128 and 129, 241
Sedelmayer v Russia (Arbitration Award of 7 July 1998) SCC, 82
SEDITEX Engineering v Madagascar (Settlement by the Parties of 20 June 1983) ICSID Case No CONC/82/1, 82
Sempra Energy v Argentina (Award of 28 September 2007) ICSID Case No ARB/02/16, 39, 101, 224
Sempra Energy v Argentina (Decision on Objections to Jurisdiction of 11 May 2005) ICSID Case No ARB/02/16, 57
Sempra Energy v Argentina (Opinion of Anne-Marie Slaughter and William Burke-White of 19 July 2005) ICSID Case No ARB/02/16, 39

Sempra Energy v Argentina (Opinion of José E Alvarez of 12 September 2005) ICSID Case No ARB/02/16, 39

Sevilla Beheer & ors v Spain (Decision on Jurisdiction, Liability and the Principles of Quantum of 11 Feb 2022) ICSID Case No ARB/16/27, 213

Siag v Egypt (Award of 1 June 2009) ICSID Case No ARB/05/15, 26, 293

Siemens AG v Argentina (Award of 6 February 2007) ICSID Case No ARB/02/8, 80, 85

Société Ouest Africaine des Bétons Industriels v Senegal (Award of 25 February 1988) ICSID Case No ARB/82/1, 82

SolEs v Spain (Award of 31 July 2019) ICSID Case No ARB/15/38, 304

South American Silver v Bolivia (Award of 22 November 2018) PCA Case No 2013–15, 152, 290

Southern Pacific Properties (Middle East) Limited v Egypt (Award of 20 May 1992) ICSID Case No ARB/84/3, 82, 206

Spadafora (Colombia, Italy) (1904) XI RIAA 1, 198

Spence International Investments, et al v Costa Rica (Non-Disputing Party Submission of The Republic of El Salvador of 17 April 2015) ICSID Secretariat File No UNCT/13/2, 55

Spillane (1931) RIAA 290, 191

ST-AD v Bulgaria (Decision on Jurisdiction of 18 July 2013) PCA Case No 2011–06, 113

Starrett Housing Corporation v Iran (Final Award of 14 August 1987) IUSCT Case No 24, 182

Stati & ors v Kazakhstan (Award of 19 December 2013) SCC Case No V116/2010, 73

Staur Eiendom v Latvia (Award of 28 February 2020) ICSID Case No ARB/16/38, 104

Strabag & ors v Poland (Partial Award on Jurisdiction 4 March 2020) ICSID Case No ADHOC/15/1, 215

Suez & Interagua v Argentina (Decision on Annulment of 14 December 2014) ICSID Case No ARB/03/17, 115

Suez & Interagua v Argentina (Decision on Liability of 30 July 2010) ICSID Case No ARB/03/17, 242

Swiss Aluminium Limited & Icelandic Aluminium Company Limited v Iceland (Order of the Secretary-General Taking Note of the Discontinuance of 6 March 1985) ICSID Case No ARB/83/1, 82

Swisslion DOO Skopje v FYROM (Award of 6 July 2012) ICSID Case No ARB/09/16, 206

Tatneft v Ukraine (Decision on Merits of 29 July 2014) UNCITRAL, 102

Técnicas Medioambientales Tecmed, SA v Mexico (Award of 29 May 2003) ICSID No ARB(AF)/00/2, 16, 311

Teinver v Argentina (Award of 21 July 2017) ICSID Case No ARB/09/1, 101, 259

Teinver v Argentina (Decision on Annulment of 29 May 2019) ICSID Case No ARB/09/1, 115

Telefónica SA v Argentina (Decision of the Tribunal on Objections to Jurisdiction of 25 May 2006) ICSID Case No ARB/03/20, 222

Tesoro Petroleum Corporation v Trinidad and Tobago (Report of the Conciliation Commission of 27 November 1985) ICSID Case No CONC/83/1, 82

Tethyan Copper v Pakistan (Award of 12 July 2019) ICSID Case No ARB/12/1, 73, 303
Tethyan Copper v Pakistan (Decision on Stay of Enforcement of the Award of 17 September 2020) ICSID Case No ARB/12/1, 260
Texaco Overseas Petroleum et al v Libya (Ad hoc Award of 19 January 1977) 53 ILR 422, 238
The Masonic (1885) published in H La Fontaine, *Pasicrisie internationale* (Stämpfli 1902), 190
Tidewater v Venezuela (Annulment of 27 December 2016) ICSID Case No ARB/10/5, 101
Tidewater v Venezuela (Award of 13 March 2015) ICSID Case No ARB/10/5, 88
Too v Greater Modesto Insurance Associates and United States of America (Award of 29 December 1989) IUSCT Case No 880, 241
Total SA v Argentina (Award of 27 November 2013) ICSID Case No ARB/04/1, 189
Total SA v Argentina (Decision on Liability of 27 December 2010) ICSID Case No ARB/04/1, 16
Trail Smelter (United States, Canada) (1941) III RIAA 1920, 206
Tulip v Turkey (Decision on Annulment of 30 December 2015) ICSID Case No ARB/11/28, 109
Tza Yap Shum v Peru (Award of 7 July 2011) ICSID Case No ARB/07/6, 286
UAB E energija (Lithuania) v Republic of Latvia (Award of 22 December 2017) ICSID Case No ARB/12/33, 241
Unglaube v Costa Rica (Award of 16 May 2012) ICSID Case No ARB/08/1 & ICSID Case No ARB/09/20, 101, 286
Unión Fenosa v Egypt (Award of 31 August 2018) ICSID Case No ARB/14/4, 74, 101, 152, 298
United Utilities (Tallinn) v Estonia (Award of 21 June 2019) ICSID Case No ARB/14/24, 215
Urbaser v Argentina (Award of 8 December 2016) ICSID Case ARB/07/26, 163, 260, 262
USA (Harry Roberts) v Mexico (Award of 2 November 1926) 4 RIAA 77, 317
USA (Hopkins) v Mexico (1926) 4 RIAA 41, 317
USA (LFH Neer) v Mexico (Award of 15 October 1926) 4 RIAA 60, 7, 317
Vattenfall AB & ors v Germany (Decision on the Achmea Issue of 31 August 2018) ICSID Case No ARB/12/12, 213
Venezuela Holdings v Venezuela (Award of 9 October 2014) ICSID Case No ARB/07/27, 295
Venezuela Holdings v Venezuela (Decision on Annulment of 9 March 2017) ICSID Case No ARB/07/27, 58, 295
Venezuela US v Venezuela (Interim Award on Jurisdiction of 26 July 2016) PCA Case No 2013-34, 220
Vestey v Venezuela (Award of 15 April 2016) ICSID Case No ARB/06/4, 103
Veteran Petroleum v Russia (Final Award 18 July 2014) PCA Case No AA 228, 298
Victor Pey Casado v Chile (Opinion of Alejandro Arraez and Associates of 3 September 2002) ICSID Case No ARB/98/2, 27, 104
Victor Pey Casado v Chile (Resubmission Award of 13 September 2016) ICSID Case No ARB/98/2, 104
Vivendi (I) v Argentina (Annulment of 3 July 2002) ICSID Case No ARB/97/3, 101

Vivendi (I) v Argentina (Award of 21 November 2000) ICSID Case No ARB/97/3, 82
Vivendi (I) v Argentina (Final Award of 20 August 2007) ICSID Case No ARB/97/3, 16, 80, 180, 298
Vivendi (II) v Argentina (Final Award of 20 August 2007) ICSID Case No ARB/03/19, 85
Vivendi (II) v Argentina (Final Award of 20 August 2007) ICSID Case No ARB/03/19, 104
Vivendi (II) v Argentina (Decision on Liability of 30 July 2010) ICSID No ARB/03/19, 13
- Separate Opinion of Arbitrator Pedro Nikken, 13

Waste Management, Inc v Mexico ("Number 2") (Award of 30 April 2004) ICSID Case No ARB(AF)/00/3, 320
Watkins Holdings v Spain (Award 21 January 2020) ICSID Case No ARB/15/44, 73
Wena Hotels v Egypt (Award of 8 December 2000) ICSID Case No ARB/98/4, 82
White Industries v India (Final Award of 30 November 2011) UNCITRAL, 108, 298
Windstream v Canada (Award of 27 September 2016) PCA Case No 2013–22, 96, 322
Wintershall v Argentina (Award of 8 December 2008) ICSID Case No ARB/04/14, 287
World Duty Free Company v Republic of Kenya (Award of 4 October 2006) ICSID Case No Arb/00/7, 207
Yukos Universal Ltd v Russia (Final Award of 18 July 2014) UNCITRAL, PCA Case No 2005–04/AA227, 88
Yukos Universal Ltd v Russia (Interim Award on Jurisdiction and Admissibility of 30 November 2009) UNCITRAL, PCA Case No 2005–04/AA227, 26, 27

International Criminal Tribunal for the Former Yugoslavia (ICTY)

Tadić (Judgment) IT-94-1-A, AC (15 July 1999), 117

Special Tribunal for Lebanon (STL)

Prosecutor v Ayyash et al (Interlocutory Decision on the Applicable Law: Terrorism, Conspiracy, Homicide, Perpetration, Cumulative Charging) STL-11-01/I/AC/R176bis (16 February 2011), 50

European Court of Human Rights (ECtHR)

Jahn and others v Germany ECHR 2005-/VI 55, 252
Papamichalopoulos and Others v Greece (Article 50) (1995) Series A No 330-B, 286
Sporrong and Lönnroth v Sweden IHRL 36 (ECHR 1982), 254
Varnava & ors v Turkey (2009) ECHR 1313, 182

Court of Justice of the European Union (CJEU)

Case C-292/04 *Wienand Meilicke, Heidi Christa Weyde, Marina Stöffler v Finanzamt Bonn-Innenstadt* [2007] ECLI:EU:C:2007:132, 227

Joined Cases C-430/93 & C-431/93 *Jeroen van Schijndel and Johannes Nicolaas Cornelis van Veen v Stichting Pensioenfonds voor Fysiotherapeuten* [1995] ECLI:EU:C:1995:185, 30
- Opinion of Mr Advocate General Jacobs, 30

Opinion 1/17 *Accord ECG UE-Canada* [2019] ECLI:EU:C:2019:341, 224
- Opinion of Advocate General Bot, 226

Inter-American Court of Human Rights (IACHR)

Aloeboetoe et al v Suriname, IACtHR (Reparations and Costs, Judgment of 10 September 1993) IACHR Series C no 15, 76

Chaparro Álvarez and Lapo Íñiguez v Ecuador (Preliminary Objections, Merits, Reparations, and Costs, Judgment of 21 November 2007) IACHR Series C No 170, 254

The Environment and Human Rights (Advisory Opinion OC-23/17 of 15 November 2017) IACHR Series A 23, 239

Velásquez-Rodríguez & ors v Honduras, IACtHR (Reparations and Costs, Judgment of 21 July 1989) IACHR Series C No 7, 179

World Trade Organization (WTO)

WTO, *China – Measures Related to the Exportation of Rare Earths, Tungsten, and Molybdenum, AB-2014-3, AB-2014-5, AB-2014-6 – Reports of the Appellate Body* (7 August 2014) WT/DS431/AB/R, WT/DS432/AB/R, WT/DS433/AB/R, 215

WTO, *European Communities – Imposition of Anti-Dumping Duties on Imports of Cotton Yarn from Brazil – Report of the Panel* (4 July 1995) ADP/137, 214

WTO, *European Communities – Measures Affecting Asbestos and Asbestos-Containing Products – Communication of the Appellate Body* (8 November 2000) WT/DS135/9, 29

WTO, *European Communities – Measures Affecting Asbestos and Asbestos-Containing Products – Report of the Appellate Body* (12 March 2001) WT/DS135/AB/R, 271

WTO, *European Communities – Measures Affecting the Approval and Marketing of Biotech Products – Report of the Panel* (21 November 2006) WT/DS291R, WT/DS292R & WT/DS293R, 220

WTO, *European Communities – Measures Concerning Meat and Meat Products (Hormones) – Report of the Appellate Body* (13 February 1998) WT/DS26/AB/R, WT/DS48/AB/R, 272

WTO, *India – Measures Concerning the Importation of Certain Agricultural Products – Report of the Appellate Body* (4 June 2015) WT/DS430/AB/R, 257

WTO, *Mexico – Anti-Dumping Investigation of High Fructose Corn Syrup from the United States – Report of the Panel* (28 January 2000) WT/DS132/R, 126

WTO, *Mexico – Tax Measures on Soft Drinks and Other Beverages – Report of the Appellate Body* (6 March 2006) WT/DS308/AB/R, 126

WTO, *Mexico – Tax Measures on Soft Drinks and Other Beverages – Report of the Panel* (7 October 2005) WT/DS308/R, 126

WTO, *United States – Measures Affecting the Cross-Border Supply of Gambling and Betting Services – Report of the Panel* (10 November 2004) WT/DS285/R, 95

WTO, *United States – Measures Affecting the Production and Sale of Clove Cigarettes – Report of the Appellate Body* (4 April 2012) WT/DS406/AB/R, 220

WTO, *United States – Measures Concerning the Importation, Marketing and Sale of Tuna and Tuna Products – Report of the Appellate Body* (16 May 2012) WT/DS381/AB/R, 29

Domestic Cases

Al-Kharafi & Sons Co v Libya and Others (Judgment of the Cairo Court of Appeal of 3 June 2020) Ad Hoc Arbitration, 184

Argentina v NMC Capital (22 November 2012) Court of Cassation of Belgium, C.11.0688.F/1, 65

Boily v HMTQ 2017 FC 1021, 44

Borrowdale v Director-General of Health [2020] NZHC 2090, 255

Democratic Republic of the Congo and ors v FG Hemisphere Associates LLC (8 June 2011) Court of Final Appeal of the Hong Kong Special Administrative Region, FACV Nos 5, 6 & 7 of 2010, 61

Flores v Southern Peru Copper Corp, 414 F.3d 233 (2d Cir 2003), 32

Hindcastle Ltd v Barbara Attenborough Associates Ltd [1996] UKHL 19, 227

JPA & consorts v Kingdom of the Netherlands & De Nederlandsche Bank (23 October 2015) Court of Cassation of Belgium, C.14.0322.F, 68

K v Argentina (8 May 2007) German Federal Constitutional Court, Order of the Second Senate, 2 BvM 1/03, 62

Natoniewski v Federal Republic of Germany (29 October 2010) Poland Supreme Court, Ref No CSK 465/09, reproduced in (2010) 30 Polish YB Intl Law 299, 50

NML Capital v Argentine Republic (11 December 2014) Court of Cassation of Belgium, C.13.0537, 67

Partenreederei MS "Neptun" GmbH & Co KG v Arquimedes Lazaro R (14 January 2005) Court of Cassation of Belgium, C.03.0607.N, 67

Swissbourgh Diamond Mines (Pty) Limited & ors v Kingdom of Lesotho (27 November 2018) Court of Appeal of the Supreme Court of Singapore, Civil Appeal No 149 of 2017 [2018] SGCA 81, 60

The Paquete Habana, 175 US 677 (1900), 35, 98

The Scotia, 81 US 170 (1871), 32

TABLE OF INTERNATIONAL TREATIES, DOCUMENTS, AND NATIONAL LEGISLATION

Multilateral Treaties

1892 International Sanitary Convention (adopted 30 January 1892, entered into force 1 November 1893), 255

1920 Statute of the Permanent Court of International Justice (adopted 16 December 1920, entered into force 8 October 1921) 6 LNTS 389, 85

1945 Statute of the International Court of Justice (adopted 26 June 1945, entered into force 24 October 1945) 33 UNTS 993, 86, 95, 164, 242

1946 Constitution of the World Health Organization (adopted 22 July 1946, entered into force 7 April 1948) 14 UNTS 185, 255

1957 Treaty Establishing the European Community (adopted 25 March 1957, entered into force 1 January 1958) [1997] OJ C340/173, 213

1965 Convention on the Settlement of Investment Disputes Between States and Nationals of Other States (adopted 18 March 1965, entered into force 14 October 1966) 575 UNTS 159, 99, 128, 288

1966 International Covenant on Economic, Social and Cultural Rights (adopted 16 December 1966, entered into force 3 January 1976) 993 UNTS 3, 257

1967 ICSID Rules of Procedure for Arbitration Proceedings (Arbitration Rules) (adopted 25 September 1967, entered into force 1 January 1968), 27, 206, 329

1969 Vienna Convention on the Law of Treaties (adopted 23 May 1969, entered into force 27 January 1980) 1155 UNTS 331, 96, 125, 213, 246, 288

1982 United Nations Convention on the Law of the Sea (adopted 10 December 1982, entered into force 16 November 1994) 1833 UNTS 397, 124, 190

1991 Convention on Environmental Impact Assessment in a Transboundary Context (adopted 25 February 1991, entered into force 10 September 1997) 1989 UNTS 309, 272

1992 North American Free Trade Agreement (NAFTA) (adopted 17 December 1992, entered into force 1 January 1994) 32 ILM 289, 14, 96, 124, 265, 288, 322

1994 Agreement on the Application of Sanitary and Phytosanitary Measures (adopted 15 April 1994, entered into force 1 January 1995) 1867 UNTS 493, 257

1994 The Energy Charter Treaty (adopted 17 December 1994, entered into force 16 April 1998) 2080 UNTS 95, 96, 143, 213, 288

1995 Convention to Ban the Importation into Forum Island Countries of Hazardous and Radioactive Wastes and to Control the Transboundary Movement and

Management of Hazardous Wastes within the South Pacific Region (adopted 16 September 1995, entered into force 21 October 2001) 2161 UNTS 91, 269

2000 Cartagena Protocol on Biosafety to the Convention on Biological Diversity (adopted 29 January 2000, entered into force 11 September 2003) 39 ILM 1027, 269

2004 Free Trade Agreement Between Central America, the Dominican Republic and the United States of America (CAFTA) (adopted 5 August 2004, entered into force 1 January 2009), 18, 276

2005 International Health Regulations (adopted 23 May 2005, entered into force 15 June 2007) 2509 UNTS 79, 253

2007 Investment Agreement for the COMESA Common Investment Area (adopted 23 May 2007, not yet in force), 18, 242

2007 Treaty on the Functioning of the European Union (adopted 13 December 2007, entered into force 1 December 2009) [2016] OJ C202/1, 213

2009 Agreement Establishing the ASEAN-Australia-New Zealand Free Trade Area (adopted 27 February 2009, entered into force 10 January 2010) 2672 UNTS 3, 17, 227

2009 ASEAN Comprehensive Investment Agreement (adopted 26 February 2009, entered into force 24 February 2012), 18

2014 United Nations Convention on Transparency in Treaty-based Investor-State Arbitration (Mauritius Convention on Transparency) (adopted 10 December 2014, entered into force 18 October 2017) No 54749, 293

2016 Canada-European Union Comprehensive Economic and Trade Agreement (CETA) (Canada & EU) (adopted 30 October 2016, provisionally entered into force 21 September 2017), 4

2018 Comprehensive and Progressive Agreement for Trans-Pacific Partnership (CPTPP) (adopted 8 March 2018, entered into force 30 December 2018), 18

2019 Agreement Between the United States of America, the United Mexican States, and Canada (CUSMA) (adopted 10 December 2019, entered into force 1 July 2020), 18, 96, 124, 288

Bilateral Treaties

1794 Treaty of Amity, Commerce and Navigation between his Britannic Majesty and the United States of America (Jay Treaty) (Great Britain & US) (adopted 19 November 1794, entered into force 29 February 1796) 52 CTS 249, 169

1900 Protocol of an Agreement Between the United States and Nicaragua for the Arbitration of the Amount of Damages to be Awarded *Orr and Laubenheimer and the Post-Glover Electric Company* (Nicaragua & US) (adopted 22 March 1900, entered into force 22 March 1900, terminated 16 June 1900) 15 RIAA 35, 172

1902 As established by the terms of the Protocol Relating to the Settlement of Indemnities Between France and Venezuela (France & Venezuela) (adopted 19 February 1902) published in Ralston J & Sherman Doyle WT (eds), *Report of French-Venezuelan Mixed Claims Commission of 1902* (US GPO 1906), 174

1922 German–Polish Convention regarding Upper Silesia (Germany & Poland) (adopted 15 May 1922), 80

1959 Treaty between the Federal Republic of Germany and Pakistan for the Promotion and Protection of Investments (Germany & Pakistan) (adopted 25 November 1959, entered into force 28 April 1962) 457 UNTS 24, 242

1987 Agreement between the Government of the United Kingdom of Great Britain and Northern Ireland and the Government of the Polish People's Republic for the Promotion and Reciprocal Protection of Investments (UK & Poland) (adopted 8 December 1987, entered into force 14 April 1988), 217

1988 Agreement between the Polish People's Republic and Republic of Austria on Promotion and Protection of Investments (Austria & Poland) (adopted 24 November 1988, entered into force 1 November 1989, terminated 16 October 2019), 217

1990 Agreement Between the Government of Canada and the Government of the Republic of Poland for the Promotion and Reciprocal Protection of Investments (Canada & Poland) (adopted 6 April 1990, entered into force 22 November 1990), 294

1990 Agreement between the Government of the United Kingdom of Great Britain and Northern Ireland and the Government of the Czech and Slovak Federal Republic for the Promotion and Protection of Investments (UK & Czech Republic) (adopted 10 July 1990, entered into force 26 October 1992), 217

1990 Agreement Between the Government of the United Kingdom of Great Britain and Northern Ireland and the Government of the Republic of Argentina for the Promotion and Protection of Investments (UK & Argentina) (adopted 11 December 1990, entered into force 19 February 1993), 124

1990 Agreement between the Republic of Austria and the Czech and Slovak Federal Republic on the Promotion and Protection of Investments (Austria & Czech Republic) (adopted 15 October 1990, entered into force 1 October 1991), 217

1990 Poland Business and Economic Relations Treaty (USA & Poland) (adopted 21 March 1990, entered into force 6 August 1994), 294

1990 Treaty between the Federal Republic of Germany and the Czech and Slovak Federal Republic Concerning the Promotion and Reciprocal Protection of Investments (Germany & Czech Republic) (adopted 2 October 1990, entered into force 2 August 1992), 217

1991 Agreement on Encouragement and Reciprocal Protection of Investments between the Kingdom of the Netherlands and the Czech and Slovak Federal Republic (Netherlands & Czech Republic) (adopted 29 April 1991, entered into force 1 October 1992), 217, 246

2000 Agreement Between New Zealand and Singapore on a Closer Economic Partnership (New Zealand & Singapore) (adopted 14 November 2000, entered into force 1 January 2001), 143

2002 Agreement Between the Government of the Republic of Korea and the Government of Japan for the Liberalisation, Promotion and Protection of Investment (Japan & Korea) (adopted 22 March 2002, entered into force 1 January 2003), 143

2003 Agreement Between Japan and the Socialist Republic of Viet Nam for the Liberalization, Promotion and Protection of Investment' (Japan & Vietnam) (adopted 14 November 2003, entered into force 19 December 2004), 143

2003 China-Australia Free Trade Agreement (ChAFTA) (China & Australia) (adopted 24 October 2003, entered into force 20 December 2015), 227

2005 Free Trade Agreement Between The Republic of Korea and Singapore (Korea & Singapore) (adopted 4 August 2005, entered into force 2 March 2006), 17

2005 The Agreement Between the Belgian-Luxembourg Economic Union and the Republic of Peru on Mutual Encouragement and Protection of Investments (BLEU & Peru) (adopted 12 October 2005, entered into force 12 September 2008), 18

2005 Treaty Between the United States of America and The Oriental Republic of Uruguay Concerning the Encouragement and Reciprocal Protection of Investment (US & Uruguay) (adopted 4 November 2005, entered into force 31 October 2006), 17

2006 Agreement Between Japan and the Republic of the Philippines for an Economic Partnership (Japan & Philippines) (adopted 9 September 2006, entered into force 11 December 2008), 17, 143

2007 Agreement Between Japan & Brunei Darussalam for an Economic Partnership (Japan & Brunei) (adopted 18 June 2007, entered into force 31 July 2008), 17

2007 Agreement Between Japan and the Republic of Chile for a Strategic Economic Partnership (Japan & Chile) (adopted 27 March 2007, entered into force 3 September 2007), 143

2008 Agreement Between Japan and The Lao People's Democratic Republic for the Liberalisation, Promotion and Protection of Investment (Japan & Laos) (adopted 16 January 2008, entered into force 3 August 2008), 17

2008 Agreement Between The Government of Romania and The Government of Canada for the Promotion and Reciprocal Protection of Investments (Canada & Romania) (adopted 8 May 2009, entered into force 23 November 2011), 18

2008 Australia-Chile Free Trade Agreement (Australia & Chile) (adopted 30 July 2008, entered into force 6 March 2009), 18

2008 Canada-Colombia Free Trade Agreement (Canada & Colombia) (adopted 21 November 2008, entered into force 15 August 2011), 18, 340

2008 Free Trade Agreement between Canada and the Republic of Peru (Canada & Peru) (adopted 29 May 2008, entered into force 1 August 2009) Can TS 2009 No 15, 248

2009 Free Trade Agreement Between The Government of the People's Republic of China & The Government of The Republic of Peru (China & Peru) (adopted 28 April 2009, entered into force 1 March 2010), 17

2009 Comprehensive Economic Partnership Agreement Between India and The Republic of Korea (India & Korea) (adopted 7 August 2009; entered into force 1 January 2010), 17

2009 New Zealand – Malaysia Free Trade Agreement (NZ & Malaysia) (adopted 26 October 2009, entered into force 1 August 2010), 17

2012 Treaty Between the United States of America and The Government of The Republic of Rwanda Concerning the Encouragement and Reciprocal Protection of Investment (US & Rwanda) (adopted 19 February 2012, entered into force 1 January 2012), 17

2015 Free Trade Agreement between the Government of the Republic of Korea and the Government of the Socialist Republic of Viet Nam (Korea & Vietnam) (adopted 5 May 2015, entered into force 20 December 2015), 227

2016 Reciprocal Investment Promotion and Protection Agreement Between The Government of the Kingdom of Morocco and The Government of the Federal Republic of Nigeria (Morocco & Nigeria) (adopted 3 December 2016, not yet in force), 261

2018 Investment Protection Agreement Between the European Union and its Member States, of the One Part, and The Republic of Singapore, of the Other Part (EU & Singapore) (adopted 18 October 2018, not yet in force), 21

2018 Treaty Between The Republic of Belarus and The Republic of India on Investments (Belarus & India) (adopted 24 September 2018, not yet in force), 21, 22

2019 Investment Protection Agreement Between the European Union and its Member States, of the One Part, and the Socialist Republic of Viet Nam of the Other Part (EU & Vietnam) (adopted 30 June 2019, not yet in force), 21

2020 Agreement Between The Government of Hungary and The Government of The Kyrgyz Republic for the Promotion and Reciprocal Protection Of Investments (Hungary & Kyrgyzstan) (adopted 29 September 2020, entered into force 10 April 2022), 89

2020 Agreement Between The Government of the State of Israel and The Government of the United Arab Emirates on Promotion and Protection of Investments (Israel & UAE) (adopted 20 October 2020, not yet in force), 89

2021 Agreement Between Japan and Georgia for the Liberalisation, Promotion and Protection of Investment (Japan & Georgia) (adopted 29 January 2021, not yet in force), 89

Model/Draft Investment Agreements

African Union Commission, 'Draft Pan African Investment Code' (*AUC*, December 2016) <https://au.int/sites/default/files/documents/32844-doc-draft_pan-african_investment_code_december_2016_en.pdf>, 266

Belgium-Luxembourg Economic Union Model BIT 2019 (Belgium & Luxembourg) (adopted 28 March 2019), 22

Canada, '2004 Model Agreement for the Promotion and Protection of Investments' (Canadian Government, 2004) <https://investmentpolicy.unctad.org/international-investment-agreements/treaty-files/2820/download>, 265

ECOWAS, 'ECOWAS Common Investment Code (ECOWIC)' (*ECOWAS*, July 2018) <https://wacomp.projects.ecowas.int/wp-content/uploads/2020/03/ECOWAS-COMMON-INVESTMENT-CODEENGLISH.pdf>, 267

European Commission, 'Commission Draft Text TTIP – Investment: Transatlantic Trade and Investment Partnership' (*European Commission*, 2015) <http://trade.ec.europa.eu/doclib/docs/2015/september/tradoc_153807.pdf>, 22

European Commission, 'New EU-Mexico Agreement: The Agreement in Principle' (*European Commission*, 23 April 2018) (text agreed upon 21 April 2018, not yet in force) <https://trade.ec.europa.eu/doclib/docs/2018/april/tradoc_156791.pdf>, 22

Germany, 'Germany Model Treaty -2008' (*German Government*, 2008) <https://investmentpolicy.unctad.org/international-investment-agreements/treaty-files/2865/download>, 71

India, 'Model Text for the Indian Bilateral Investment Treaty' (*Indian Ministry of Finance*, 14 January 2016) <www.dea.gov.in/sites/default/files/ModelBIT_Annex_0.pdf>, 22, 124

Netherlands, 'Netherlands Model Investment Agreement' (*Netherlands Ministry of Foreign Affairs*, 22 March 2019) <www.rijksoverheid.nl/binaries/rijksoverheid/documenten/publicaties/2019/03/22/nieuwe-modeltekst-investeringsakkoorden/nieuwe+modeltekst+investeringsakkoorden.pdf>, 22

SADC, 'SADC Model Bilateral Investment Treaty Template: With Commentary' (SADC, July 2012) Art 13.1 <www.iisd.org/itn/wp-content/uploads/2012/10/sadc-model-bit-template-final.pdf>, 267

USTR, '2004 Model Bilateral Investment Treaty' (*USTR*, 2004) <https://ustr.gov/sites/default/files/U.S.%20model%20BIT.pdf>, 16, 265

USTR, '2012 U.S. Model Bilateral Investment Treaty' (*USTR*, 2012) <https://ustr.gov/sites/default/files/BIT%20text%20for%20ACIEP%20Meeting.pdf>, 265

International Documents

League of Nations

League of Nations, 'Bases of Discussion Drawn up by the Preparatory Committee of the Hague Codification Conference' (1929) LoN Doc C.75.M.69.1929.V, 191

League of Nations, 'Report of the Commission of Enquiry on the Incidents on the Frontier between Bulgaria and Greece, Doc No C.727.M.270.1925.VII (Annex 815)' (1926) 7 LNOJ 196, 157, 175

United Nations General Assembly

UNGA 'Report of the United Nations Conference on Environment and Development' (16 March 1992) UN Doc A/RES/47/190, 268

UNGA Res 73/203 'Identification of Customary International Law' (11 January 2019) UN Doc A/RES/73/203, 154

UNGA Res 1803 (XVII) 'Permanent Sovereignty Over Natural Resources' (14 December 1962) UN Doc A/5217, 238

UNGA Res 2625 (XXV) 'Declaration on Principles of International Law Concerning Friendly Relations and Cooperation Among States in Accordance with the Charter of the United Nations' (24 October 1970) UN Doc A/RES/2625(XXV), 239

UNGA Res 3171 (XXVIII) 'Permanent Sovereignty Over Natural Resources' (17 December 1973) UN Doc A/RES/3171(XXVIII), 8

UNGA Res 3281 (XXIX) 'Charter of Economic Rights and Duties of States' (12 December 1974) UN Doc A/RES/3281(XXIX), 9, 166, 237, 310

UNGA 'Responsibility of States for Internationally Wrongful Acts: Compilation of Decisions of International Courts, Tribunals and Other Bodies, Report of the Secretary-General' (1 February 2007) UN Doc A/62/62, 94

UNGA 'Responsibility of States for Internationally Wrongful Acts: Compilation of Decisions of International Courts, Tribunals and Other Bodies, Report of the Secretary-General' (17 April 2007) UN Doc A/62/62/Add.1, 94

UNGA 'Responsibility of States for Internationally Wrongful Acts: Compilation of Decisions of International Courts, Tribunals and Other Bodies, Report of the Secretary-General' (30 April 2010) UN Doc, A/65/76, 94

UNGA 'Responsibility of States for Internationally Wrongful Acts: Compilation of Decisions of International Courts, Tribunals and Other Bodies, Report of the Secretary-General' (30 April 2013) UN Doc A/68/72, 94

UNGA 'Responsibility of States for Internationally Wrongful Acts: Compilation of Decisions of International Courts, Tribunals and Other Bodies, Report of the Secretary-General' (21 April 2016) UN Doc A/71/80, 94

UNGA 'Responsibility of States for Internationally Wrongful Acts: Compilation of Decisions of International Courts, Tribunals and Other Bodies, Report of the Secretary-General' (26 April 2017) UN Doc A/72/81, 94

UNGA 'Responsibility of States for Internationally Wrongful Acts: Compilation of Decisions of International Courts, Tribunals and Other Bodies, Report of the Secretary-General, Addendum' (20 June 2017) A/71/80/Add.1, 93

UNGA 'Responsibility of States for Internationally Wrongful Acts: Compilation of Decisions of International Courts, Tribunals and Other Bodies, Report of the Secretary-General' (23 April 2019) UN Doc A/74/83, 94

UNGA, 'Report of the International Law Commission on the Work of its 52nd Session (Continued)' (4 December 2000) UN Doc A/C.6/55/SR.18, 165

Other International Reports & Documents

Belgium, 'Observations de la Belgique sur le sujet "détermination du droit international coutumier"' (67th United Nations General Assembly, 6th Commission, 2015) <https://legal.un.org/ilc/sessions/67/pdfs/french/icil_belgium.pdf>, 67

Belgium, 'Observations de la Belgique sur le sujet "formation et détermination du droit international coutumier"' (66th United Nations General Assembly, 6th Commission, 2014) <https://legal.un.org/ilc/sessions/66/pdfs/french/icil_belgium.pdf>, 49

Israel, 'ILC Draft Conclusions on Identification of Customary International Law – Israel's Comments and Observations' (70th United Nations General Assembly, 6th Commission, 2018) <https://legal.un.org/ilc/sessions/70/pdfs/english/icil_israel .pdf>, 50, 336

New Zealand, 'Draft Conclusions on the Identification of Customary International Law adopted by the International Law Commission (A/71/10 at Chapter V): Comments by the Government of New Zealand' (70th United Nations General Assembly, 6th Commission, 2018) <https://legal.un.org/ilc/sessions/70/pdfs/english/icil_new_ zealand.pdf>, 51

OECD, 'Intergovernmental Agreements Relating to Investment in Developing Countries' (*OECD*, 27 May 1984) OECD Doc No 84/14, 11

Singapore, 'Response of the Republic of Singapore to the International Law Commission's Request for Comments and Observations on the Draft Conclusions on Identification of Customary International Law' (70th United Nations General Assembly, 6th Commission, 2018) <https://legal.un.org/ilc/sessions/70/pdfs/ english/icil_singapore.pdf>, 53

UN Sub-Commission on the Promotion and Protection of Human Rights, 'Economic, Social and Cultural Rights: Norms on the Responsibilities of Transnational Corporations and Other Business Enterprises With Regard to Human Rights' (26 August 2003) UN Doc E/CN.4/Sub.2/2003/12/Rev.2, 281

UNCITRAL, 'Arbitration Rules of the United Nations Commission on International Trade Law' (15 December 1976) UN Doc A/31/98, 28

UNCTAD, 'Bilateral Investment Treaties 1995–2006: Trends in Investment Rulemaking' (UNCTAD, 2007) UN Doc UNCTAD/ITE/IIA/2006/5, 8

UNCTAD, 'Expropriation: *UNCTAD series on Issues in International Investment Agreements II*' (UNCTAD, 2012) UN Doc UNCTAD/DIAE/IA/2011/7, 71

UNCTAD, 'Fair and Equitable Treatment' (*UNCTAD Series on Issues in International Investment Agreements II*, 2012) UN Doc UNCTAD/DIAE/IA/2011/5, 6

UNCTAD, 'Investment Dispute Settlement Navigator' (*UNCTAD Investment Policy Hub*, 31 December 2019) <https://investmentpolicy.unctad.org/investment-dispute-settlement/>, 94

UNCTAD, 'World Investment Report 2022' (9 June 2022) UN Doc UNCTAD/ WIR/2022, 211

UNHRC, 'Report of the Special Representative of the Secretary General on the Issue of Human Rights and Transnational Corporations and Other Business Enterprises, John Ruggie' (7 April 2008) UN Doc A/HRC/8/5, 282

UNHRC, 'Report of the Special Representative of the Secretary-General on the Issue of Human Rights and Transnational Corporations and Other Business Enterprises,

John Ruggie: Guiding Principles on Business and Human Rights: Implementing the United Nations "Protect, Respect and Remedy" Framework' (21 March 2011) UN Doc A/HRC/17/31, 281

UNHRC, 'Text of the Third Revised Draft Legally Binding Instrument with the Textual Proposals Submitted by States During the Seventh Session of the Open-Ended Intergovernmental Working Group on Transnational Corporations and Other Business Enterprises With Respect to Human Rights' (28 February 2022) UN Doc A/HRC/49/65/Add.1, 281

USA, 'Comments from the United States on the International Law Commission's Draft Conclusions on the Identification of Customary International Law as adopted by the Commission in 2016 on First Reading' (70th United Nations General Assembly, 6th Commission, 2018) <https://legal.un.org/ilc/sessions/70/pdfs/english/icil_usa.pdf>

World Bank, 'Legal Framework for the Treatment of Foreign Investment, Vol 2: Report to the Development Committee and Guidelines on the Treatment of Foreign Direct Investment' (*World Bank Report*, 25 September 1992) reproduced in (1992) 31 ILM 1363, 294

International Law Commission (ILC)

ILC, 'Analytical Guide to the Work of the International Law Commission' (*ILC*, 14 April 2020) <https://legal.un.org/ilc/guide/9_6.shtml#top>, 98

ILC, 'Comments and Observations Received from Governments' (19 March, 3 April, 1 May and 28 June 2001) UN Doc A/CN.4/515 and Add.1–3, 165

ILC, 'Draft Articles on Responsibility of States for Internationally Wrongful Acts with Commentaries' (23 April–1 June and 2 July–10 August 2001) UN Doc A/56/10, reproduced in [2001/II – Part Two] YBILC 31, 72, 93, 123, 151, 180, 287

ILC, 'Draft Articles on the Law of Treaties with Commentaries' (4 May–19 July 1966) UN Doc A/CN.4/191, reproduced in [1966/II] YBILC 187, 123, 214

ILC, 'Draft Conclusions on Identification of Customary International Law, with Commentaries' (30 April–1 June and 2 July–10 August 2018) UN Doc A/73/10, reproduced in [2018/II – Part Two] YBILC 122, 46, 97, 154, 211, 313

ILC, 'Draft Conclusions on Subsequent Agreements and Subsequent Practice in Relation to the Interpretation of Treaties, with Commentaries' (30 April–1 June and 2 July–10 August 2018) UN Doc A/73/10, 219

ILC, 'Final Report of the Study Group on the Most-Favoured-Nation Clause' (29 May 2015) UN Doc A/CN.4/L.852, 229

ILC, 'Formation and Evidence of Customary International Law: Elements in the Previous Work of the International Law Commission that Could be Particularly Relevant to the Topic' (Memorandum by the Secretariat, 14 March 2013) UN Doc A/CN.4/659, 52

ILC, 'Guide to Practice on Reservations to Treaties' (26 April–3 June and 4 July–12 August 2011) UN Doc A/66/10, reproduced in [2011/II] YBILC 26, 220

ILC, 'Identification of Customary International Law: Comments and Observations Received From Governments' (14 February 2018) UN Doc A/CN.4/716, 51

ILC, 'Identification of Customary International Law: Statement of the Chairman of the Drafting Committee, Mr Mathias Forteau (Statement of the Chairman, 29 July 2015) <https://legal.un.org/ilc/documentation/english/statements/2015_dc_chairman_statement_cil.pdf>, 48

ILC, 'International Responsibility: Sixth Report by FV Garcia Amador, Special Rapporteur' (26 January 1961) UN Doc A/CN.4/134 reproduced in [1961/II] YBILC 1, 191

ILC, 'Preliminary Report on the Content, Forms and Degrees of International Responsibility (Part 2 of the Draft articles on State Responsibility), by Mr William Riphagen, Special Rapporteur' (1 April 1980) UN Doc A/CN.4/330 reproduced in [1980/II] YBILC 107, 182

ILC, 'Report of the International Law Commission on the Work of its 27th Session' (5 May-25 July 1975) UN Doc A/10010/Rev.1 reproduced in [1975/II] YBILC 47, 191

ILC, 'Report of the International Law Commission on the Work of its 31st Session' (14 May-3 August 1979) UN Doc A/34/10, 165, 181

ILC, 'Report of the International Law Commission on the Work of its 51st Session (Continued)' (20 December 1999) UN Doc A/C.6/54/SR.22, 165

ILC, 'Report of the International Law Commission on the Work of its 51st Session (Continued)' (13 January 2000) UN Doc A/C.6/54/SR.21, 165

ILC, 'Report of the International Law Commission on the Work of its 68th Session' (2 May-10 June and 4 July-12 August 2016) UN Doc A/71/10, 168

ILC, 'Report on Fragmentation of International Law: Difficulties Arising from the Diversification and Expansion of International Law, finalised by Martti Koskenniemi' (13 April 2006) UN Doc A/CN.4/L.682, 129, 213

ILC, 'Report on International Responsibility by Mr FV Garcia-Amador, Special Rapporteur' (20 January 1956) UN Doc A/CN.4/96, 78, 191

ILC, 'Report on the Fourth Session of the Asian-African Legal Consultative Committee (Tokyo, February 1961), by FV Garcia Amador, Observer for the Commission' (30 May 1961) UN Doc A/CN.4/139, 8

ILC, 'Second Report on General Principles of Law by Marcelo Vázquez-Bermúdez, Special Rapporteur' (9 April 2020) UN Doc A/CN.4/741, 98

ILC, 'Second Report on State Responsibility, by Mr James Crawford, Special Rapporteur' (17 March, 1 and 30 April, 19 July 1999) UN Doc A/CN.4/498 and Add.1-4, 165

ILC, 'State Responsibility: Comments and Observations Received by Governments' (25 March, 30 April, 4 May, 20 July 1998) UN Doc A/CN.4/488 and Add.1-3, 165

ILC, 'State Responsibility: Comments and Observations Received from Governments' (25 March 1998) UN Doc A/CN.4/488, 165

ILC, 'Statement of the Chairman of the Drafting Committee, Mr. Gilberto Saboia' (Statement of Chairman, 7 August 2014) <https://legal.un.org/ilc/sessions/66/pdfs/english/dc_chairman_statement_identification_of_custom.pdf>, 50

ILC, 'Summary Records of the 8th Session' (23 April-4 July 1956) [1956/1] YBILC 1, 318

ILC, 'Summary Record of the 370th Meeting' (1956) UN Doc A/CN.4/SR.370, 191
ILC, 'Summary Record of the 1614th Meeting' (18 June 1980) UN Doc A/CN.4/SR.1614, 165
ILC, 'Summary Record of the 1616th Meeting' (20 June 1980) UN Doc A/CN.4/SR.1616, 165
ILC, 'Summary Record of the 1617th Meeting' (23 June 1980) UN Doc A/CN.4/SR.1617, 165
ILC, 'Summary Record of the 2587th Meeting' (15 June 1999) UN Doc A/CN.4/SR.2587, 123
ILC, 'Summary Records of the Meetings of the 31st Session' (14 May-3 August 1979) UN Doc A/CN.4/SER.A/1979, 181
ILC, 'Summary Records of the Meetings of the 32nd Session' (5–25 July 1980) UN Doc A/CN.4/SER.A/1980, 182
ILC, 'Survey of International Law in Relation to the Work of Codification of the International Law Commission' (10 February 1949) UN Doc A/CN.4/1/Rev.1, 255
ILC, 'Third Report on State Responsibility, by Mr James Crawford, Special Rapporteur' (15 March, 15 June, 10 and 18 July and 4 August 2000) UN Doc A/CN.4/507, 182, 194
Wood M, 'First Report on Formation and Evidence of Customary International Law' (17 May 2013) UN Doc A/CN.4/L.663, 50
Wood M, 'Fourth Report on Identification of Customary International Law' (8 March 2016) UN Doc A/CN.4/695, 48
Wood M, 'Second Report on Identification of Customary International Law' (22 May 2014) UN Doc A/CN.4/L.672, 52
Wood M, 'Third Report on Identification of Customary International Law' (27 March 2015) UN Doc A/CN.4/682, 48

International Law Association (ILA)

ILA Study Group on Use of Domestic Law Principles in the Development of International Law, 'Report' (Sydney Conference, 2018), 181

Domestic Legislation

Real Decreto 463/2020, de 14 de marzo, por el que se declara el estado de alarma para la gestión de la situación de crisis sanitaria ocasionada por el COVID-19, 235

ABBREVIATIONS

AIDI	*Annuaire de l'Institut de droit international*
AJIL	*American Journal of International Law*
ALI	American Law Institute
AmUIntl LRev	*American University International Law Review*
Arb Intl	*Arbitration International*
ARSIWA	Articles on the Responsibility of States for Internationally Wrongful Acts
ASA Bulletin	*Swiss Arbitration Association Bulletin*
ASEAN	Association of Southeast Asian Nations
ASIL Proc	*American Society of International Law Proceedings*
ASR	Articles on State Responsibility
AUBLR	*American University Business Law Review*
AUC	African Union Commission
Aust YBIL	*Australian Yearbook of International Law*
BCLRev	*Boston College Law Review*
BHRJ	*Business and Human Rights Journal*
BIICL	British Institute of International and Comparative Law
BIT	Bilateral Investment Treaty
BLEU	Belgian–Luxembourg Economic Union
Braz J Int Law	*Brazilian Journal of International Law*
Br J A Leg Studies	*British Journal of American Legal Studies*
BYBIL	*British Yearbook of International Law*
CAAJ	Contemporary Asia Arbitration Journal
CAFTA	Free Trade Agreement Between Central America, the Dominican Republic and the United States of America
CanBar Rev	*Canadian Bar Review*
CanYBIL	*Canadian Yearbook of International Law*
CEPEJ	European Commission for the Efficiency of Justice
CETA	Comprehensive Economic and Trade Agreement between the European Union and Canada
Ch	Chapter
ChAFTA	China–Australia Free Trade Agreement

Chin J Int Law	*Chinese Journal of International Law*
CIGI	Centre for International Governance Innovation
CIL	Customary International Law
CIMVAL	Canadian Institute of Mining, Metallurgy and Petroleum on Valuation of Mineral Properties
Cir	Circuit
CJEU	Court of Justice of the European Union
CJIL	*Chicago Journal of International Law*
CLJ	*The Cambridge Law Journal*
CLP	*Current Legal Problems*
ColumJ Transnat'l L	*Columbia Journal of Transnational Law*
ColumLRev	*Columbia Law Review*
COMESA	Common Market for Eastern and Southern Africa
Cornell LRev	*Cornell Law Review*
CPTPP	Comprehensive and Progressive Agreement for Trans-Pacific Partnership
CUP	Cambridge University Press
CUSMA	Agreement Between the United States of America, the United Mexican States, and Canada
DCF	Discounted Cash Flow
Doc	Document
DSU	Dispute Settlement Understanding
ECOWAS	Economic Community of West African States
ECOWIC	ECOWAS Common Investment Code
ECT	Energy Charter Treaty
ECtHR	European Court of Human Rights
Ed/s	Editor/s
Edn	Edition
EEEI	European Expertise & Expert Institute
EIA	Environmental Impact Assessment
EJIL	*European Journal of International Law*
EJLS	*European Journal of Legal Studies*
ESIL	European Society of International Law
Esp	Especially
EU	European Union
EURAM	European American Investment Bank
FET	Fair and Equitable Treatment
FILJ	*Foreign Investment Law Journal*
FIPA	Foreign Investment Promotion and Protection Agreement
FTA	Free Trade Agreement
FTC	Federal Trade Commission

FTC	Free Trade Commission
GAJInt'l& CompL	*Georgia Journal of International and Comparative Law*
GATT	General Agreement on Tariffs and Trade
GPO	Government Printing Office
HarvILJ	*Harvard International Law Journal*
HKIAC	Hong Kong International Arbitration Centre
HLR	*Harvard Law Review*
HowLJ	*Howard Law Journal*
HPT	*History of Political Thought*
HUP	Harvard University Press
IACtHR	Inter-American Court of Human Rights
ICAO	International Civil Aviation Organization
ICC	International Chamber of Commerce
ICJ	International Court of Justice
ICLQ	*International & Comparative Law Quarterly*
ICLR	*International Community Law Review*
ICSID	International Centre for Settlement of Investment Disputes
ICSID Rep	*International Centre for Settlement of Investment Disputes Reports*
ICSID Rev	*International Centre for Settlement of Investment Disputes Review*
ICTY	International Criminal Tribunal for the Former Yugoslavia
IDI	Institut de Droit International
IFC	International Finance Corporation
IHEI	Institut des Hautes Etudes Internationales
IHR	International Health Regulations
IIA	International Investment Agreement
IISD	International Institute for Sustainable Development
IJGLS	*Indiana Journal of Global Legal Studies*
IJIL	*Indian Journal of International Law*
ILA	International Law Association
ILC	International Law Commission
ILM	*International Legal Materials*
Inc	Incorporated
Int'l L	*International Lawyer*
Intl Law	*International Law*
Int'l Org	*International Organization*
IOLR	*International Organizations Law Review*
ISDS	Investor-State Dispute Settlement
ITLOS	International Tribunal for the Law of the Sea

LIST OF ABBREVIATIONS

IUSCT	Iran–US Claims Tribunal
IYIL	*Italian Yearbook of International Law*
JEL	*Journal of Environmental Law*
JERL	*Journal of Energy & Natural Resources Law*
JIDS	*Journal of International Dispute Settlement*
JIEL	*Journal of International Economic Law*
JWIT	*The Journal of World Investment & Trade*
JWT	*Journal of World Trade*
LawAmer	*Lawyer of the Americas*
Law & Bus Rev Am	*Law and Business Review of the Americas*
Law & PolIntBus	*Law and Policy in International Business*
Ld	Lord
LGDJ	Librairie générale de droit et de jurisprudence
LoN	League of Nations
LQR	*Law Quarterly Review*
Max Planck YrbkUNL	*Max Planck Yearbook of United Nations Law*
McGill LJ	*McGill Law Journal*
MFA	Multifibre Arrangement
MichJInt'l Law	*Michigan Journal of International Law*
MichLRev	*Michigan Law Review*
Minn JIntlL	*Minnesota Journal of International Law*
MJIEL	*Manchester Journal of International Economic Law*
MLR	*Model Law Review*
MST	Minimum Standard of Treatment
MUP	Manchester University Press
NAFTA	North American Free Trade Agreement
NCJInt'l L& ComReg	*North Carolina Journal of International Law and Commercial Regulation*
NIEO	New International Economic Order
NILR	*Netherlands International Law Review*
Nord J Intl L	*Nordic Journal of International Law*
NYIL	*Netherlands Yearbook of International Law*
NYU Envtl LJ	*New York University Environmental Law Journal*
NYU J Intl L & Pol	*New York University Journal of International Law & Policy*
OECD	Organization for Economic Cooperation and Development
OJ	Official Journal
Ors	Others
OUP	Oxford University Press
PAIC	Pan African Investment Code
PCIJ	Permanent Court of International Justice
PHEIC	Public Health Emergency of International Concern

LIST OF ABBREVIATIONS

Polish YBInt'l Law	*Polish Yearbook of International Law*
PSNR	Permanent Sovereignty over Natural Resources
PUF	University Press of France
RBDI	*Revue Belge de Droit International*
RdC	*Recueil des cours* (abbreviation for collected courses of the Hague Academy, in references and bibliography)
RDILC	*Revue de Droit International et de Législation Comparée*
RDUT	*University of Toronto Faculty of Law Review*
RECIEL	*Review of European, Comparative & Environmental Law*
REDI	*Revista Española de Derecho Internacional*
Rev	Review
RIAA	*Reports of International Arbitration Awards*
RTD civ	*Revue trimestrielle de droit civil*
SADC	South African Development Committee
SCC	Stockholm Chamber of Commerce
Sess	Session
SFDI	French Society for International Law
SGCA	Strategic Goods (Control) Act
STL	Special Tribunal for Lebanon
Supp	Supplement
TDM	*Transnational Dispute Management*
TEL	*Transnational Environmental Law*
TFEU	Treaty on the Functioning of the European Union
Tr	Translation
TTIP	Transatlantic Trade and Investment Partnership
TTP	Trans-Pacific Partnership
TWAIL	Third World Approaches to International Law
UAE	United Arab Emirates
UCDavis JInt'l L& Pol'y	*UC Davis Journal of International Law and Policy*
UC Press	University of California Press
UKanLRev	*University of Kansas Law Review*
UKHL	United Kingdom House of Lords
U Miami Inter-Am L Rev	*University of Miami Inter-American Law Review*
UN	United Nations
UNCITRAL	United Nations Commission on International Trade Law
UNCTAD	United Nations Conference on Trade and development
UNGA	United Nations General Assembly
UNHRC	United Nations Human Rights Council
UNRIAA	*United Nations Report of Arbitration Awards*
UPaJConstL	*University of Pennsylvania Journal of Constitutional Law*
USA	United States of America
USTR	United States Trade Representative

UVA	University Press of Virginia
VaJInt'l L	*Virginia Journal of International Law*
VaLRev	*Virginia Law Review*
VCLT	Vienna Convention on the Law of Treaties
Wake Forest LRev	*Wake Forest Law Review*
WAMR	*World Arbitration and Mediation Review*
WTO	World Trade Organization
YB Intl Invest L&Pol	*Yearbook on International Investment Law & Policy*
YBWA	*Yearbook of World Affairs*
YJIL	*Yale Journal of International Law*
YLJ	*Yale Law Journal*

PART I

Identifying Custom in International
Investment Law

1

The 'Minimum Standard of Treatment' in International Investment Law

The Fascinating Story of the Emergence, Decline and Recent Resurrection of a Concept

PATRICK DUMBERRY

1 Introduction

This chapter examines the story of how the concept of the 'Minimum Standard of Treatment' (MST) first emerged, its subsequent decline and also its recent 'resurrection'.

The concept of MST crystallised as a rule of custom in the mid-twentieth century,[1] but in the 1960s and 1970s, Newly Independent States (NIS) began to challenge its existence. While the Standard ultimately survived these events, this opposition had another more subtle consequence: both developing and developed States now perceived the MST as ineffective in providing basic legal protection to foreign investors.[2] It is in this historical context that these States began frenetically signing bilateral investment treaties (BITs) for the promotion and protection of investments, which provided clearer rules on investment protection. I will argue in this chapter that States started to use the expression 'fair and equitable treatment' (FET) in their BITs because of the ambiguities surrounding the concept of the MST and the fact that many States had contested its legitimacy in the past. By the end of the 1990s, only a very small minority of BITs actually referred to the MST. By then, the concept had clearly lost its once prevailing importance as a source of investment protection for foreign investors. The MST's glory days were long gone.

---

[1] This is indeed the position taken by writers in the 1950s: RR Wilson, *The International Law Standard in Treaties of the United States* (HUP 1953) 103-4; G Schwarzenberger, *International Law*, Vol 1 (3rd edn, Stevens and Sons 1957) 206-7. See also M Paparinskis, *The International Minimum Standard and Fair and Equitable Treatment* (OUP 2013) 64-7, 83 ff; JE Alvarez, 'Bit on Custom' (2009) 42 NYUJIntlL&Pol 39.

[2] JW Salacuse, *The Law of Investment Treaties* (OUP 2010) 45-6.

The dynamics suddenly changed, however, when arbitral tribunals started to give a broader interpretation to FET clauses, thereby providing foreign investors with treatment protections *above and beyond* the traditional MST.[3] It was only then that States started to explicitly mention in their new BITs that the treatment offered to investors under the FET clause was, in fact, the same that was extended to all foreign investors under the MST under custom. The concept of the MST, which had almost been forgotten by States in the 1990s, was now centre stage in their quest to limit investors' rights under investment treaties. States' objectives were now to prevent future tribunals from developing their own idiosyncratic interpretations of the FET standard. In this respect, the most interesting and innovative FET clause is certainly Article 8.10 of the Canada–European Union Comprehensive Economic and Trade Agreement (CETA), which contains a closed list of elements that are considered by the parties to embody the standard.[4] States have thus somewhat 'rediscovered' the usefulness of the MST. The concept has now regained the prevalence that it had lost in the past decades as an important source of investment protection.

---

[3] A good illustration is *Pope & Talbot Inc v Canada* (Award on the Merits of Phase II, 10 April 2001) UNCITRAL [105–18].

[4] The final text of the agreement was released, following legal review, on 29 February 2016: Canada–European Union Comprehensive Economic and Trade Agreement (CETA) (Canada & EU) (adopted 30 October 2016, provisionally entered into force 21 September 2017) Article 8.10. The provision (entitled 'Treatment of Investors and of Covered Investments') reads as follows:

1. Each Party shall accord in its territory to covered investments of the other Party and to investors with respect to their covered investments fair and equitable treatment and full protection and security in accordance with paragraphs 2 through 6.
2. A Party breaches the obligation of fair and equitable treatment referenced in paragraph 1 if a measure or series of measures constitutes:
   (a) denial of justice in criminal, civil or administrative proceedings;
   (b) fundamental breach of due process, including a fundamental breach of transparency, in judicial and administrative proceedings;
   (c) Manifest arbitrariness;
   (d) Targeted discrimination on manifestly wrongful grounds, such as gender, race or religious belief;
   (e) Abusive treatment of investors, such as coercion, duress and harassment; or
   (f) A breach of any further elements of the fair and equitable treatment obligation adopted by the Parties in accordance with paragraph 3 of this Article.
3. The Parties shall regularly, or upon request of a Party, review the content of the obligation to provide fair and equitable treatment. The Committee on Services and Investment, established under Article 26.2.1(b) (Specialized Committee), may develop recommendations in this regard and submit them to the CETA Joint Committee for decision.

2 The Emergence of MST as a Rule of Customary International Law

Section 2.1 will define the concept of MST and examine its historical foundation. Section 2.2 will analyse the subsequent challenges to the MST's customary status, which was led by developing States in the 1960s and 1970s and eventually resulted, in the 1990s, in the new phenomenon of 'treatification'.

2.1 The Historical Foundation of the Minimum Standard of Treatment

Despite some disagreement between States on the existence of the MST in the last few decades (a point further examined below), the concept is now well recognised by States, tribunals and scholars as a rule of customary international law.[5] What is more controversial is determining the actual *content* of the standard. The MST is an *umbrella concept* that in *itself* incorporates different elements.[6] Based on an analysis of case law and reports by the Organisation for Economic Co-operation and Development (OECD) and United Nations Conference on Trade and Development

---

4. When applying the above fair and equitable treatment obligation, a tribunal may take into account whether a Party made a specific representation to an investor to induce a covered investment, that created a legitimate expectation, and upon which the investor relied in deciding to make or maintain the covered investment, but that the Party subsequently frustrated.
5. For greater certainty, 'full protection and security' refers to the Party's obligations relating to physical security of investors and covered investments.
6. For greater certainty, a breach of another provision of this Agreement, or of a separate international agreement does not establish a breach of this Article.
7. For greater certainty, the fact that a measure breaches domestic law does not, in and of itself, establish a breach of this Article. In order to ascertain whether the measure breaches this Article, the Tribunal must consider whether a Party has acted inconsistently with the obligations in paragraph 1.

[5] See, numerous States' pleadings, awards and work of scholars mentioned in P Dumberry, 'Fair and Equitable Treatment: Its Interaction with the Minimum Standard and its Customary Status' (2017) 1(2) BRP Int ILA 1, 5–7.

[6] A number of NAFTA tribunals have also endorsed this description: *Glamis Gold, Ltd v United States* (Award of 8 June 2009) UNCITRAL, Ad Hoc Tribunal [618]; *Cargill, Inc v Mexico* (Award of 18 September 2009) ICSID Case No ARB(AF)/05/02 [268]; *Mobil Investments Canada Inc & Murphy Oil Corporation v Canada* (Decision on Liability and on Principles of Quantum of 22 May 2012) ICSID Case No ARB(AF)/07/4 [135]. See also, A Newcombe & L Paradell, *Law and Practice of Investment Treaties: Standards of Treatment* (Kluwer 2009) 236.

(UNCTAD),[7] it may be observed that the MST encompasses (at the very least) an obligation for host States to prevent denial of justice and arbitrary conduct and also to provide investors with due process and 'full protection and security'.[8]

The historical aspects surrounding the emergence of the MST have already been the subject of substantial scholarship.[9] Suffice it to note that its origin is grounded in the international law doctrine of State responsibility for injuries to aliens.[10] It is rooted in a due diligence obligation for States to respect the rights of foreigners within their country. Before the twentieth century, there was a prevailing view that individuals conducting business in another State should be subject to the law of that State.[11] Several States, especially in Latin America, adopted this position to counter the so-called gunboat diplomacy and other types of interferences by Western States in their internal affairs that were often made under the pretext of protecting the interests of their nationals abroad.[12] It is in this context that many States rejected the idea of the existence of any obligation under international law to accord a 'minimum' level of protection to foreigners.

Despite this opposition, the MST gradually emerged in the early twentieth century.[13] The development of this standard of treatment stemmed from capital-exporting States' concern that many host States receiving investments lacked the most basic measures of protection for aliens and

---

[7] OECD, *International Investment Law: A Changing Landscape: A Companion Volume to International Investment Perspectives* (OECD Publishing 2005) 82; UNCTAD, 'Fair and Equitable Treatment' (*UNCTAD Series on Issues in International Investment Agreements II*, 2012) UN Doc UNCTAD/DIAE/IA/2011/5, 44 (referring to OECD, 'Fair and Equitable Treatment Standard in International Investment Law' (2004) *OECD Working Papers on International Investment 2004/03*, <http://dx.doi.org/10.1787/675702255435> accessed 10 May 2021).

[8] P Dumberry, *The Fair and Equitable Treatment Standard: A Guide to NAFTA Case Law on Article 1105* (Kluwer 2013) 25–8.

[9] Paparinskis (n 1) 39–83; T Weiler, *The Interpretation of International Investment Law: Equality, Discrimination and Minimum Standards of Treatment in Historical Context* (Martinus Nijhoff 2013). See also, more recently, M Pinchis-Paulsen, 'The Life and Death (and Re-Birth) of "Fair and" "Equitable Treatment": A Historical Examination of Twentieth Century International Trade and Investment Law Treaty-Making and Political Decision-Making' (PhD Thesis, King's College London 2017).

[10] H Dickerson, 'Minimum Standards' [2013] MPEPIL 845 [2].

[11] This period is examined in detail in Weiler (n 9) 337 ff.

[12] Weiler (n 9) 345, providing a number of examples of such interventions and referring to 'no fewer than one hundred instances of "protection by force" between 1813 and 1927 by the United States alone, including two dozen in the Twentieth century'.

[13] Weiler (n 9) 351; Paparinskis (n 1) 64, noting that at the time it focused almost exclusively on the non-discriminatory aspects of the treatment and on preventing denial of justice.

their property.[14] They argued that all governments were bound under international law to treat foreigners with at least a minimum standard of protection,[15] because the existing standard in many countries was considered too low.[16] The reasons for establishing such a standard were explained by the US Secretary of State, Mr Elihu Root, in an article published in 1910[17] and were reiterated some ninety years later by the North American Free Trade Agreement (NAFTA) *SD Myers* Tribunal.[18] International jurisprudence slowly developed the concept of a minimum standard of protection. While a number of cases have had a significant impact on the emergence of this standard, the best known is certainly the *Neer* case of 1926.[19]

The question of whether or not any customary rule in the field of investment arbitration had firmly crystallised after the Second World War is controversial.[20] However, it is safe to say that the MST was an established rule of custom at the time.[21] Section 2.2 examines a number of dramatic developments that occurred in the decades following the Second World War.

---

[14] MA Orellana, 'International Law on Investment: The Minimum Standard of Treatment (MST)' (2004) 3 TDM 1.
[15] C Schreuer & R Dolzer, *Principles of International Investment Law* (OUP 2008) 12–13.
[16] Salacuse (n 2) 47; JC Thomas, 'Reflections on Article 1105 of NAFTA: History, State Practice and the Influence of Commentators' (2002) 17(1) ICSID Rev 26.
[17] E Root, 'The Basis of Protection to Citizens Residing Abroad' (1910) 4 AJIL 521.
[18] *SD Myers Inc v Canada* (Partial Award of 13 November 2000) UNCITRAL [259]: 'The inclusion of a "minimum standard" provision is necessary to avoid what might otherwise be a gap. A government might treat an investor in a harsh, injurious and unjust manner, but do so in a way that is no different than the treatment inflicted on its own nationals. The "minimum standard" is a floor below which treatment of foreign investors must not fall, even if a government were not acting in a discriminatory manner'.
[19] *USA (LFH Neer) v Mexico* (Award of 15 October 1926) 4 RIAA 60. The Commission held that the 'propriety of governmental acts should be put to the test of international standards' and that 'the treatment of an alien, in order to constitute an international delinquency, should amounts to an outrage, to bad faith, to wilful neglect of duty, or to an insufficiency of governmental action so far short of international standards that every reasonable and impartial man would readily recognize its insufficiency' (ibid 61–2). For a critical assessment of the influence of this case, see *Railroad Development Corporation (RDC) v Guatemala* (Award of 29 June 2012) ICSID Case No ARB/07/23 [216]; *Mondev International Ltd v United States* (Award of 11 October 2002) ICSID Case No ARB(AF)/99/2 [115]; SM Schwebel, 'Is Neer Far from Fair and Equitable?' (2011) 27(4) Arb Intl 555, 555–61; J Paulsson & G Petrochilos, 'Neer-ly Misled?' (2007) 22(2) ICSID Rev 242–57.
[20] P Juillard, 'L'évolution des sources du droit des investissements' (1994) 250 RdC 76.
[21] Paparinskis (n 1) 64–7, 83 ff. On the contrary, AC Blandford in 'The History of Fair and Equitable Treatment Before the Second World War' (2017) 32(2) ICSID Rev 294 ff argues that in the period before the Second World War the MST that emerged was originally based on the concept of 'general principles recognised by civilized nations' (which are found in the *domestic laws* of States), and therefore, *not* based on customary international law.

2.2 Newly Independent States Challenging the MST

In the 1960s and 1970s, NIS revived opposition towards the existence of any customary rules in the field of investment law. They openly contested the *legitimacy* of the existing CIL and demanded a revision of these 'outdated' rules that did not take into account the fundamental changes that had occurred in the international community since the end of the colonisation period.[22] According to Abi-Saab, these States '[did] not easily forget that the same body of international law that they [were] now asked to abide by, sanctioned their previous subjugation and exploitation and stood as a bar to their emancipation'.[23]

Specifically, these States rejected having the obligation to provide any minimum standard of protection to foreign investors under CIL.[24] They insisted that they were bound to provide foreign investors only with the level of treatment existing under their domestic law.[25] They also contested the existence of any international law norms requiring compensation for expropriated foreign properties and supported a less stringent compensation requirement than the Hull formula.[26] At the time, developing States took the debate to the United Nations General Assembly where they represented the majority of States.[27] They used their status within the international body to advance their interests by way of resolutions and declarations,[28] which included Resolution 3171 adopted in 1973[29] and the 1974 *Charter of Economic Rights and Duties*

---

[22] AT Guzman, 'Why LDCs Sign Treaties That Hurt Them: Explaining the Popularity of Bilateral Investment Treaties' (1998) 38(4) VaJIntlL 64; Juillard (n 20) 76.

[23] G Abi-Saab, 'The Newly Independent States and the Rules of International Law: An Outline' (1962) 8 HowLJ 100. See also SN Guha-Roy, 'Is the Law of Responsibility of States for Injuries to Aliens a Part of Universal International Law?' (1961) 55 AJIL 866.

[24] M Sornarajah, *The International Law on Foreign Investment* (2nd edn, CUP 2004). See, for instance, ILC, 'Report on the Fourth Session of the Asian-African Legal Consultative Committee (Tokyo, February 1961), by FV Garcia Amador, Observer for the Commission' (30 May 1961) UN Doc A/CN4/139, 78, 82–4.

[25] SM Schwebel, 'Investor-State Disputes and the Development of International Law: The Influence of Bilateral Investment Treaties on Customary International Law' (2004) 98 ASIL Proc 27.

[26] Guzman (n 22) 647; UNCTAD, 'Bilateral Investment Treaties 1995–2006: Trends in Investment Rulemaking' (*UNCTAD*, 2007) UN Doc UNCTAD/ITE/IIA/2006/5, 48.

[27] Juillard (n 20) 84ff.

[28] M Byers, *Custom, Power and the Power of Rules: International Relations and Customary International Law* (CUP 1999) 41.

[29] UNGA, 'Permanent Sovereignty Over Natural Resources' (17 December 1973) UN Doc A/RES/3171(XXVIII).

of States.³⁰ Given the division between the developed and the developing States, the *Charter of Economic Rights and Duties of States* could hardly be considered a reflection of existing international law at the time.³¹ Another question is whether or not the effect of the attack by new States was to *destroy* the few rules of custom that existed after the Second World War. A number of writers believe this was the case.³² Without specifically taking a position on the impact that the contestation may have had on custom, the International Court of Justice (ICJ) in the famous *Barcelona Traction* case of 1970 simply noted that *no rule* of customary international law existed in the field of international investment law.³³

The more established position is that some customary rules (including the MST) *already existed* at the time the developing States started opposing them.³⁴ In the 1990 *Elettronica Sicula S.p.A. (ELSI)* case, the ICJ indeed referred explicitly to the existence of a 'minimum international standard'.³⁵ In fact, while it seems that the MST survived the assault by the developing States, it did not do so without some casualties. Thus, as noted by one writer, the strong contestation of a large segment of States has 'served to undermine the solidity of the traditional international legal framework for foreign investment'.³⁶ Thus, while the developed States held the view that

---

[30] UNGA, 'Charter of Economic Rights and Duties of States' (12 December 1974) UN Doc A/RES/3281(XXIX).
[31] Schwebel (n 25) 28; C Brower & J Tepe, 'The Charter of Economic Rights and Duties of States: A Reflection or Rejection of International Law?' (1975) 9(2) IntlLaw 295; D Carreau & P Juillard, *Droit international économique* (LGDJ 1998) 464; Salacuse (n 2) 75.
[32] Carreau & Juillard (n 31) 464–5; Sornarajah (n 24) 19–20, 89–93, 213; A Akinsanya, 'International Protection of Direct Foreign Investments in the Third World' (1987) 36 ICLQ 58; A Al Faruque, 'Creating Customary International Law Through Bilateral Investment Treaties: A Critical Appraisal' (2004) 44 IJIL 312, 312–13; J d'Aspremont, 'International Customary Investment Law: Story of a Paradox' in T Gazzini & E de Brabandere (eds), *International Investment Law: The Sources of Rights and Obligations* (Martinus Nijhoff 2012) 14.
[33] *Barcelona Traction, Light and Power Co, Ltd (Belgium v Spain)* (Judgment) [1970] 3 ICJRep 46–7, noting that 'it may at first sight appear surprising that the evolution of the law [on foreign investments] has not gone further and that no generally accepted rules in the matter have crystallized on the international plane'.
[34] See, Paparinskis (n 1) 83 ff; Alvarez (n 1) 39; JE Alvarez, 'The Public International Law Regime Governing International Investment' (2009) 344 RdC 292.
[35] *Elettronica Sicula SpA (ELSI) (USA v Italy)* (Judgment) [1989] 15 ICJRep 111 ('The primary standard laid down by Article V is "the full protection and security required by international law", in short, the "protection and security" must conform to the minimum international standard').
[36] Salacuse (n 2) 45–6, 75; Al Faruque (n 32) 294–5.

customary rules existed, they also acknowledged that their effectiveness was limited as a result of the vehement opposition of a large number of States.[37] In fact, both the developed and the developing States perceived these rules as ineffective in providing basic legal protection to foreign investors.

It is in this historical context that, in the 1990s, States began signing numerous BITs providing clearer rules on investment protection (a new phenomenon referred to as 'treatification'). At the time, a new consensus emerged regarding the necessity to offer better legal protections to foreign investments in order to accelerate economic development. Yet, there was still great uncertainty surrounding the types of legal protections that existed for foreign investors under custom. As explained by two scholars, Dolzer and von Walter, it is due to the fact that 'customary law was deemed be too amorphous and not be able to provide sufficient guidance and protection' to foreign investors that capital-exporting and developing States started frenetically concluding *ad hoc* BITs.[38] According to both Schreuer and Dolzer, as a result of the new climate of international economic relations of the 1990s, 'the fight of previous decades against customary rules protecting foreign investment had abruptly become anachronistic and obsolete'.[39] Consequently, by the 1990s, 'the tide had turned', and developing States were no longer opposed to the application of a minimum standard of protection under custom. Instead, they granted 'more protection to foreign investment than traditional customary law did, now on the basis of treaties negotiated to attract additional foreign investment'.[40]

Section 3 examines how this new phenomenon of 'treatification' was marked by the emergence of the FET standard and the decline of the MST as a source of investment protection for foreign investors.

3   The Emergence of the FET Standard in Investment Treaties

From the 1990s and onwards, States have included the FET standard in an overwhelming majority of BITs. I have explained elsewhere that less than 5%

---

[37] The member States of the OECD certainly believed at the time that these customary rules existed. See OECD, 'Draft Convention on the Protection of Foreign Property' (1967) 7 ILM 117, Notes and Comments to Article 1 (further discussed in Section 3).

[38] R Dolzer & A von Walter, 'Fair and Equitable Treatment – Lines of Jurisprudence on Customary Law' in F Ortino, L Liberti, A Sheppard & ors (eds), *Investment Treaty Law: Current Issues II* (BIICL 2007) 99. The same conclusion is reached by many writers, see long list in Dumberry (n 5) 18.

[39] Schreuer & Dolzer (n 15) 16.

[40] ibid.

of the BITs which I have examined do not include any formal and binding FET obligation for the host State of investments.[41] One of the most controversial questions discussed in scholarship is why States first began including the term FET in their BITs throughout the 1960s and 1970s, and why they have continued to do so (almost) uniformly thereafter in the 1990s.[42]

According to one view, Western States incorporated the concept of FET in their BITs to simply reflect the MST that existed under international law.[43] This approach has been endorsed by a number of writers.[44] These writers typically refer to the 1967 OECD Draft Convention[45] as representative of the position of developed States at the time on matters of protection of foreign investments.[46] This is because the OECD's Commentary to the 1967 Draft Convention indicated that the concept of FET flowed from the 'well established general principle of international law that a State is bound to respect and protect the property of nationals of other States'.[47] The Drafting Committee also added that the phrase FET refers to 'the standard set by international law for the treatment due by each State with regard to the property of foreign nationals' and that 'the standard required conforms in effect to the minimum standard which forms part of customary international law'.[48] The same position was also taken by OECD member States in 1984[49] and is confirmed by the practice of some

---

[41] P Dumberry, 'Has the Fair and Equitable Treatment Standard become a Rule of Customary International Law?' (2016) 8(1) JIDS 155, 155–78, examining 1,964 BITs that were available on the UNCTAD website at the time (February 2014). Yet, it should be added that even when a BIT does not contain an FET clause, it may be that an investor will be able to invoke the MFN clause contained in that treaty to rely on provisions found in *another* treaty entered into by the host State that provide for a 'better' treatment. This is because a BIT containing an FET clause arguably provides (at least in theory) foreign investors with a 'better' treatment than a treaty without such a provision. See, P Dumberry, 'The Importation of the Fair and Equitable Treatment Standard Through MFN Clauses: An Empirical Study of BITs' (2016) 17 ICSID Rev 229, 229–59.

[42] See, discussion in Dumberry (n 8) 31–5.

[43] See, analysis in Newcombe & Paradell (n 6) 268; Thomas (n 16) 44, 47; Carreau & Julliard (n 31) 454.

[44] See, for instance, JR Picherack, 'The Expanding Scope of the Fair and Equitable Treatment Standard: Have Recent Tribunals Gone Too Far?' (2008) 9(4) JWIT 264; Paparinskis (n 1) 160–3; S Montt, *State Liability in Investment Treaty Arbitration* (Hart 2009) 69; Blandford (n 21) 302.

[45] OECD (n 37) Notes and Comments to art 1.

[46] S Vasciannie, 'The Fair and Equitable Treatment Standard in International Investment Law and Practice' (1999) 70(1) BYBIL 99, 112–13; UNCTAD (n 7) 8; OECD (n 7) 4.

[47] OECD (n 37) 119.

[48] ibid.

[49] Thomas (n 16) 48 referring to: OECD, 'Intergovernmental Agreements Relating to Investment in Developing Countries' (*OECD*, 27 May 1984) OECD Doc No 84/14, 12 [36] ('[a]ccording to all Member countries which have commented on this point, fair and

Western States.[50] This narrative has, however, been subject to dissent by many scholars.[51] While it is possible that the OECD commentary reflected what their member States (all developed States) *themselves* viewed to be the CIL at the time, they were certainly not representative of what the developing States believed were their legal obligations in the 1960s.[52] In any event, as explained by two scholars, Newcombe and Paradell, the use of a 'different and more politically neutral term [FET] might be explained by the historical political sensitivities regarding the minimum standard of treatment', which was 'historically viewed with suspicion because of the legacy of gun-boat diplomacy and imperialism'.[53] This is also the position endorsed by Judge Nikken in his separate opinion in the *AWG Group v Argentina* case.[54] In sum, for these writers the concept of the FET 'may simply have been viewed as a convenient, neutral and acceptable reference' to the MST.[55]

A more convincing approach has been adopted by a number of other writers who suggest that the growing use of the term FET by Western States in their BITs was intended to counter the assertion made by developing States about the inexistence of any MST under international law.[56] Thus, Western States started including references to the FET standard *because* of the ambiguities surrounding the concept of the MST.[57] They started using this term as a result of the challenge mounted by developing States against the MST. Weiler provides a detailed account explaining how the United States started using the expression FET after the War and concluded that US negotiators embraced the term in the 1960s because the MST 'controversy had otherwise poisoned the well for treaty drafters'.[58]

---

equitable treatment introduced a substantive legal standard referring to general principles of international law even if this is not explicitly stated').

[50] See, examples examined by Newcombe & Paradell (n 6).
[51] T Kill, 'Don't Cross the Streams: Past and Present Overstatement of Customary International Law in Connection with Conventional Fair and Equitable Treatment Obligations' (2008) 106 MichLRev 853, 876–7; M Klein Bronfman, 'Fair and Equitable Treatment: An Evolving Standard' (2006) 10 Max Planck YrbkUNL 615.
[52] Kill (n 51) 879.
[53] Newcombe & Paradell (n 6) 263–4.
[54] *AWG Group v Argentina* (Decision on Liability of 30 July 2010) UNCITRAL, Separate Opinion of Arbitrator Pedro Nikken [14–15].
[55] Newcombe & Paradell (n 6) 263–4. See also, Montt (n 44) 69–70.
[56] See analysis in Thomas (n 16) 48. *Contra*: Paparinskis (n 1) 163.
[57] Weiler (n 9) 199, 211–12, 216, 227, 239–40; Vasciannie (n 47) 157–8.
[58] Weiler (n 9) 199 ff, 215. See also: K Vandevelde, *United States International Investment Agreements* (Kluwer 2002) 263.

The actual drafting language used by States in their BITs supports this approach. As pointed out by two authors, 'if the parties to a treaty want to refer to customary international law, one would assume that they will refer to it as such rather than using a different expression'.[59] For the vast majority of BITs that contain an FET clause that does *not* make any reference to international law, the standard should *not* be considered as an implicit reference to the MST.[60] As pointed out by Schreuer and Dolzer, '[a]s a matter of textual interpretation, it seems implausible that a treaty would refer to a well-known concept like the "minimum standard of treatment in customary international law" by using the expression "fair and equitable treatment"'.[61] This is especially the case considering the (above-mentioned) contentious debates between the developed and the developing States as to the very existence of an MST.[62] The FET standard should therefore *generally* be considered as an *independent* treaty standard with an autonomous meaning from the MST. This is the position adopted by a majority of writers.[63] It should be noted, however, that a number of

---

[59] Schreuer & Dolzer (n 15) 124. See also, Bronfman (n 51) 621; JP Laviec, *Protection et promotion des investissements, étude de droit international économique* (PUF 1985) 94; Salacuse (n 2) 226; Vasciannie (n 46) 105; UNCTAD (n 7) 13.

[60] UNCTAD (n 7) 13.

[61] Schreuer & Dolzer (n 15) 124. See also, Bronfman (n 52) 621; Laviec (n 59) 94; Salacuse (n 2) 226; Vasciannie (n 46) 105; UNCTAD (n 7) 13. This position is adopted in *Vivendi (II) v Argentina* (Decision on Liability of 30 July 2010) ICSID No ARB/03/19 [184], but rejected in the Separate Opinion of Arbitrator Pedro Nikken [10 ff].

[62] A Diehl, *The Core Standard of International Investment Protection: Fair and Equitable Treatment* (Kluwer 2012) 151; Vasciannie (n 46) 131; UNCTAD (n 7) 13; Salacuse (n 2) 226-7.

[63] See, FA Mann, 'British Treaties for the Promotion and Protection of Investments' (1981) 52 BYBIL 241, 244; Newcombe & Paradell (n 6) 263; R Dolzer & M Stevens, *Bilateral Investment Treaties* (Martinus Nijhoff 1995) 60; Vasciannie (n 47) 144; P Muchlinski, *Multinational Enterprises and the Law* (2nd edn, OUP 2007) 635-47; C McLachlan, L Shore & M Weiniger, *International Investment Arbitration: Substantive Principles* (OUP 2007) 226-47; Dolzer & Schreuer (n 15) 124-8; I Tudor, *The Fair and Equitable Treatment Standard in International Foreign Investment Law* (OUP 2008) 53-104; Diehl (n 62) 151-2; C Schreuer, 'Fair and Equitable Standard (FET): Interaction with Other Standards' (2007) 4(5) TDM 68; R Dolzer, 'Fair and Equitable Treatment: A Key Standard in Investment Treaties' (2005) 39(1) Intl Law 87; H Haeri, 'A Tale of Two Standards: 'Fair and Equitable Treatment' and the Minimum Standard in International Law' (2011) 27 Arb Intl 34; M Kinnear, A Biorklund & JFG Hannaford, *Investment Disputes Under NAFTA: An Annotated Guide to NAFTA Chapter 11* (Kluwer Law 2006) 7; MC Ryan, 'Glamis Gold, Ltd v The United States and the Fair and Equitable Treatment Standard' (2011) 56(4) McGill LJ 919, 932-4; Salacuse (n 2) 226-7: R Preiswerk, 'New Developments in Bilateral Investment Protection – With Special Reference to Belgian Practice' (1967) 3 RBDI 173, 186; N Blackaby, C Partasides, A Redfern & Ors, *Redfern and Hunter on International Arbitration* (OUP 2009) 494.

scholars have rejected this interpretation.[64] Yet, as logical and sound as it may be, this interpretation is *not* convincing *in certain particular cases* where a treaty *explicitly* links the FET to the standard existing under 'international law'.[65] The same is true whenever the FET clause is entitled 'MST' (such as NAFTA Article 1105) or when the parties to a treaty have expressly stated that their intention was in fact for the FET standard to make reference to the MST under custom.[66]

4 The 'Return' of the MST

By the year 2000, the concept of the MST had clearly lost its once prevailing importance as a source of investment protection for foreign investors. One could have assumed at the time that the MST's role would become limited to the traditional function played by customary rules under international law in the context of the proliferation of treaty norms.[67] It seemed at the time that the MST's glory days were long gone. That impression did not last very long.

When arbitral tribunals actually started to interpret FET clauses that had systematically been included in BITs for decades, States were considerably surprised by the outcome. The controversy began in the year 2000 when three Tribunals rendered awards that defined different aspects of the scope of the FET clause (Article 1105) contained in the NAFTA.[68] These

---

[64] Picherack (n 44) 260–2, 265, 291; Thomas (n 16) 50; G Mayeda, 'Playing Fair: The Meaning of Fair and Equitable Treatment in Bilateral Investment Treaties' (2007) 41(2) JWT 273, 273–91; Orellana (n 14) 7; B Choudhury, 'Evolution or Devolution? Defining Fair and Equitable Treatment in International Investment Law' (2005) 6(2) JWIT 297, 317–20; Sornarajah (n 24) 170 ff; C Leben, 'L'évolution du droit international des investissements' in SFDI & IHEI (eds), *Un accord multilatéral sur l'investissement: d'un forum de négociation à l'autre?* (Pedone 1999) 7–28; M Romero Jiménez, 'Considerations of NAFTA Chapter 11' (2001) 2 CJIL 243, 244; Paparinskis (n 1) 163; Montt (n 44) 302–10.

[65] One example is North American Free Trade Agreement (NAFTA) (adopted 17 December 1992, entered into force 1 January 1994) 32 ILM 289, Art 1105; see the analysis in Dumberry (n 8).

[66] The most well-known example is the NAFTA Free Trade Commission, 'Notes of Interpretation of Certain Chapter 11 Provisions' (*NAFTA FTC*, 31 July 2001) <https://2009-2017.state.gov/documents/organization/38790.pdf> accessed 10 May 2021 (further discussed below). See the analysis in Dumberry (n 8) 65–86.

[67] The MST would, for instance, remain the applicable legal regime of protection in the absence of any BIT and could also play a gap-filling role whenever a treaty, a contract or domestic legislation is silent on a given issue. See P Dumberry, *The Formation and Identification of Rules of Customary International Law in International Investment Law* (CUP 2016) 364 ff.

[68] On this debate, see Dumberry (n 8) 65 ff.

three NAFTA Tribunals interpreted the FET clause as providing investors with treatment protections *above and beyond* the MST.[69] In other words, under this approach, the level of the standard of treatment imposed on the host State would be higher than that existing under custom; foreign investors would be given *more rights*. Most importantly, these three Tribunals adopted this approach notwithstanding the important fact that under Article 1105 (entitled 'MST') the FET is clearly linked to the standard existing under 'international law'.

This NAFTA debate highlights the importance of the actual drafting of the FET clause. Arbitral tribunals (outside the NAFTA context) have given different interpretations to the scope of FET clauses depending on their actual drafting.[70] A 2012 UNCTAD report indicated that the drafting variations in FET clauses have in fact been interpreted as meaning *different content* as well as *different thresholds*.[71] Many arbitral tribunals have thus interpreted an unqualified (or 'stand-alone') FET clause as 'delinked from customary international law' and have, therefore, 'focused on the plain-meaning of the terms "fair" and "equitable,"' which 'may result in a low liability threshold and brings with it a risk for State regulatory action to be found in breach of it'.[72] This phenomenon has been recognised by many scholars.[73] The vast majority of tribunals have, in fact, interpreted an unqualified FET clause as having an autonomous character, which therefore, provides a higher level of protection than the MST.[74] Only a limited number of tribunals have interpreted an unqualified FET standard as an implicit reference to international law.[75] This situation contrasts with the rather confusing approach adopted by tribunals faced with an FET clause containing an explicit reference to 'international law'.[76] Tribunals have overall been divided on the proper interpretation and use of these words. While some tribunals have held that the term 'international law' found in an FET clause was a reference

---

[69] *Metalclad v Mexico* (Award of 30 August 2000) ICSID Case No ARB(AF)/97/1 [70, 76]; *SD Myers* (n 18) [266]; *Pope & Talbot* (n 3).
[70] Newcombe & Paradell (n 6) 263–4; Paparinskis (n 1) 94; OECD (n 7) 40.
[71] UNCTAD (n 7) 8.
[72] ibid 22.
[73] See, several writers mentioned in Dumberry (n 5) 33.
[74] See Newcombe & Paradell (n 6) 263–4, referring to many cases.
[75] See, for instance, *Siemens AG v Argentina* (Award of 17 January 2007) ICSID Case No ARB/02/8 [291].
[76] UNCTAD (n 7) 22. See, *El Paso Energy International Company v Argentina* (Award of 31 October 2011) ICSID Case No ARB/03/15 [331–7], for an overview of the different positions adopted by tribunals.

to the minimum standard under custom,[77] others have interpreted such an express reference in much the same way as an unqualified FET standard.[78] Others have simply decided not to take position on the issue.[79]

The broad interpretations of FET clauses adopted by some tribunals led many States to take concrete measures to effectively reduce tribunals' margin of appreciation when assessing the conformity of States' conduct with the FET standard. The most virulent and comprehensive reaction came from NAFTA parties. Under the aegis of the Free Trade Commission ('FTC'), they responded by issuing a 'Note of Interpretation', which interpreted the FET standard *restrictively* by expressly limiting the level of protection to be accorded to foreign investors to that existing under the MST under custom.[80] The Note itself rapidly became the centre of an important controversy amongst parties to NAFTA arbitration proceedings, arbitrators and scholars.[81]

Around the same time, States also started *explicitly* mentioning in their BITs that the FET standard was not only linked to 'international law', but that it was in fact a reference to the MST under customary international law.[82] Again, two of the NAFTA Parties (United States and Canada) started this trend when they adopted their respective Model BITs in 2004. For instance, Article 5(1) of the US Model BIT provides that '[e]ach Party shall accord to covered investments treatment in accordance with *customary* international law, including FET and full protection and security'.[83] Clearly, Canada and the United States decided to adopt such

---

[77] See, in particular, *MCI Power Group LC and New Turbine, Inc v Ecuador* (Award of 31 July 2007) ICSID Case No ARB/03/6 [369]; *Gold Reserve Inc v Venezuela* (Award of 22 September 2014) ICSID Case No ARB(AF)/09/1 [567].

[78] *See*, for instance, *Vivendi (I) v Argentina* (Final Award of 20 August 2007) ICSID Case No ARB/97/3 [7.4.5 ff]; *Técnicas Medioambientales Tecmed, SA v Mexico* (Award of 29 May 2003) ICSID No ARB(AF)/00/2 [155]; *Crystallex International Corporation v Venezuela* (Award of 4 April 2016) ICSID Case No ARB(AF)/11/2 [530]; *Mr Franck Charles Arif v Moldova* (Award of 8 April 2013) ICSID Case No ARB/11/23 [529]; *Total SA v Argentina* (Decision on Liability of 27 December 2010) ICSID Case No ARB/04/1 [125]; *Oko Pankki Oyj, VTB Bank (Deutschland) AG and Sampo Bank Plc v Estonia* (Award of 19 November 2007) ICSID Case No ARB/04/6 [216 & 231–7].

[79] One recent example is *PA Allard v Barbados* (Award of 27 June 2017) PCA Case No 2012-06 [193].

[80] NAFTA FTC (n 66).

[81] The controversy is examined in Dumberry (n 8) 65–80.

[82] UNCTAD (n 7) 29.

[83] USTR, '2004 Model Bilateral Investment Treaty' (USTR, 2004) <https://ustr.gov/sites/default/files/U.S.%20model%20BIT.pdf> accessed 10 May 2021 (hereinafter 'US Model BIT'). US Model BIT, Art 5(2) further states that 'For greater certainty, paragraph 1 prescribes the *customary international law minimum standard of treatment of aliens as the minimum standard of treatment to be afforded to covered investments*. The concepts of

language to refute the expanding interpretation applied by some NAFTA tribunals and to incorporate the clarification made in the NAFTA FTC Note of 2001.[84] The two BITs that the United States entered into after 2004 with Uruguay and Rwanda also contain the same clause referring specifically to the MST under custom.[85] Recent investment treaties of the United States, Canada and Mexico also contain the same FET clause.[86] While such specific language is clearly the result of the NAFTA experience, the phenomenon is not limited to the North American context as many States elsewhere have recently adopted the same types of FET clauses referring to the MST.[87]

'fair and equitable treatment' and 'full protection and security' do not require treatment in addition to or beyond that which is required by that standard, and do not create additional substantive rights...' (emphasis added).

[84] C Lévesque, 'Influences on the Canadian Model FIPA and US Model BIT: NAFTA Chapter 11 and Beyond' (2006) 44 CanYBIL 255; K Vandevelde, 'A Comparison of the 2004 and 1994 US Model BITs' (2008–2009) 1 YB Intl Invest L&Pol 291; C Lévesque & A Newcombe, 'Commentary on the Canadian Model Foreign Promotion and Protection Agreement' in C Brown (ed), *Commentaries on Selected Model Investment Treaties* (OUP 2013) 78–80.

[85] Treaty Between the United States of America and The Oriental Republic of Uruguay Concerning the Encouragement and Reciprocal Protection of Investment (US & Uruguay) (adopted 4 November 2005, entered into force 31 October 2006) Art 5(1)(2); Treaty Between the United States of America and The Government of The Republic of Rwanda Concerning the Encouragement and Reciprocal Protection of Investment (US & Rwanda) (adopted 19 February 2012, entered into force 1 January 2012) Art 5(1)(2).

[86] See many examples mentioned in Dumberry (n 5) 39–40. See also, *Adel A Hamadi Al Tamimi v Oman* (Award of 27 October 2015) ICSID Case No ARB/11/33 [382, 384 & 386], where the Tribunal interpreted the US–Oman FTA, which contains the same restrictive language as the US Model BIT.

[87] UNCTAD (n 7) 25, referring to the Agreement Establishing the ASEAN–Australia–New Zealand Free Trade Area (adopted 27 February 2009, entered into force 10 January 2010) 2672 UNTS 3; the Agreement Between Japan and the Republic of the Philippines for an Economic Partnership (Japan & Philippines) (adopted 9 September 2006, entered into force 11 December 2008); Free Trade Agreement Between The Government of the People's Republic of China & The Government of The Republic of Peru (China & Peru) (adopted 28 April 2009, entered into force 1 March 2010); New Zealand–Malaysia Free Trade Agreement (NZ & Malaysia) (adopted 26 October 2009, entered into force 1 August 2010); Comprehensive Economic Partnership Agreement Between India and The Republic of Korea (India & Korea) (adopted 7 August 2009; entered into force 1 January 2010). See also, Free Trade Agreement Between The Republic of Korea and Singapore (Korea & Singapore) (adopted 4 August 2005, entered into force 2 March 2006) Art 10.5; Agreement Between Japan and The Lao People's Democratic Republic for the Liberalisation, Promotion and Protection of Investment (Japan & Laos) (adopted 16 January 2008, entered into force 3 August 2008) Art 5; Agreement Between Japan & Brunei Darussalam for an Economic Partnership (Japan & Brunei) (adopted 18 June 2007, entered into force 31 July 2008) Art 59 (see 'Note'). See also, The Agreement Between the Belgian–Luxembourg Economic Union and the Republic of Peru on Mutual Encouragement and Protection of Investments (BLEU

Another recent and closely related phenomenon is States becoming 'more precise about the content of the FET obligation and more predictable in its implementation and subsequent interpretation'.[88] One example is the 2004 US Model BIT that clarifies that the obligation to provide FET under Article 5(1) 'includes the obligation not to deny justice in criminal, civil, or administrative adjudicatory proceedings in accordance with the principle of due process embodied in the principal legal systems of the world'. This addition is also featured in the United States' most recent BITs and FTAs as well as some of Canada's investment treaties.[89] The same approach was adopted in the recently signed Canada–United States–Mexico Agreement (CUSMA, which has replaced NAFTA)[90] as well as by other States in the context of ASEAN,[91] COMESA,[92] CAFTA-DR[93] and the new Transpacific Partnership agreement (without the United States).[94]

The efforts by many States to clarify the content of the FET standard in the last two decades have also had an impact on the solidification of the meaning of the MST. The next section further examines this phenomenon.

& Peru) (adopted 12 October 2005, entered into force 12 September 2008) Art 3; Australia–Chile Free Trade Agreement (Australia & Chile) (adopted 30 July 2008, entered into force 6 March 2009) Art 10.5.

[88] UNCTAD (n 7) 13, 29, 30.

[89] DA Gantz, 'The Evolution of FTA Investment Provisions: From NAFTA to the United States – Chile Free Trade Agreement' (2003) 19(4) AmUIntl LRev 679, 724 ff. See, for instance, Canada–Colombia Free Trade Agreement (Canada & Colombia) (adopted 21 November 2008, entered into force 15 August 2011) Art 805; Agreement Between The Government of Romania and The Government of Canada for the Promotion and Reciprocal Protection of Investments (Canada & Romania) (adopted 8 May 2009, entered into force 23 November 2011) Art II(2).

[90] Agreement Between the United States of America, the United Mexican States and Canada (CUSMA) (adopted 10 December 2019, entered into force 1 July 2020), see, Art 14.6(1). The provision only finds application in disputes involving a US or a Mexican investor against either Mexico or the United States. The chapter on investor-State dispute settlement does not apply to Canada and Canadian investors. The provision can only be invoked in disputes relating to 'covered government contracts' (mentioned at Annex 14-E), which includes oil and gas production, power generation, transportation, telecoms and certain other infrastructure investments.

[91] ASEAN Comprehensive Investment Agreement (adopted 26 February 2009, entered into force 24 February 2012) Art 11.

[92] Investment Agreement for the COMESA Common Investment Area (adopted 23 May 2007, not yet in force) Art 14.

[93] Free Trade Agreement Between Central America, the Dominican Republic and the United States of America (CAFTA) (adopted 5 August 2004, entered into force 1 January 2009) Art 10.5. On this clause, see, P Dumberry, '"Cross Treaty Interpretation" en Bloc or How CAFTA Tribunals Are Systematically Interpreting the FET Standard Based NAFTA Case Law' The Law and Practice of International Courts and Tribunals (forthcoming 2023).

[94] Comprehensive and Progressive Agreement for Trans-Pacific Partnership (CPTPP) (adopted 8 March 2018, entered into force 30 December 2018) Art 9.6.

5 CETA: The Ultimate Detailed FET Clause

The most interesting and innovative recent FET clause is Article 8.10 of the CETA entered into by Canada and the member States of the European Union.[95] That provision is the first FET clause contained in an IIA that specifically enumerates a *closed list* of the different situations resulting in a breach of the obligation.[96] The content of Article 8.10 is to a very large extent based on how NAFTA tribunals have interpreted Article 1105 over the last 25 years. Thus, NAFTA tribunals have recognised that the FET standard contains only a *limited number* of specific elements of protection and that it requires proof of a high threshold of severity and gravity in order to conclude that the host State has committed a breach.[97] Article 8.10 CETA seems to be the natural and logical outcome of States' willingness to ever increase the degree of specificity of the content of the FET clause in order to narrow its scope and to circumscribe its interpretation by tribunals.[98]

One of the most notable features of Article 8.10 CETA is the fact that it does *not* refer to 'international law', the MST or to custom. The parties certainly believed that there was no need to expressly link the FET to the standard existing under the MST precisely because the clause contains a comprehensive enumeration of the elements they considered to be comprised in the FET 'box'. In any event, the elements listed at Article 8.10 CETA are those which are generally considered to be existing under the concept of the MST. As such, the omission of a reference to the MST should not be interpreted as a possible setback to the contemporary

---

[95] CETA (n 4) Art 8.10. This clause is examined in P Dumberry, 'Fair and Equitable Treatment' in M Bungenberg & A Reinisch (eds), *Canada-European Union Comprehensive Economic and Trade Agreement (CETA): Article-by-Article Commentary* (Nomos/Hart 2021); P Dumberry, 'Fair and Equitable Treatment' in S Schacherer & MM Mbengue (eds), *Foreign Investment Under the Comprehensive Economic and Trade Agreement (CETA)* (Springer 2018) 95–126.
[96] The elements listed are mentioned above, see footnote 4. It should be added that under para 4 the concept of legitimate expectation is mentioned as a 'factor', which can be taken into account by a tribunal.
[97] My analysis of NAFTA case law, Dumberry (n 8) 125–275, suggests that only the prohibition of manifest arbitrary conduct, denial of justice and the obligation of due process are unambiguously stand-alone elements of the FET obligation under Article 1105.
[98] F Jadeau & F Gélinas, 'CETA's Definition of the Fair and Equitable Treatment Standard: Toward a Guided and Constrained Interpretation' (2016) 13(1) TDM 1, 2 ff; G Ünüvar, 'The Vague Meaning of Fair and Equitable Treatment Principle in Investment Arbitration and New Generation Clarifications' in AL Kjær & J Lam (eds), *Language and Legal Interpretation in International Law* (OUP 2022) 288–9, article available: (2016) 55(2) *iCourts Working Paper Series*, 22.

importance of that standard. One writer has recently correctly referred to Article 8.10 CETA as an MST clause with another name.[99]

6 Conclusion

This chapter has argued that States have started to use the expression FET in their investment treaties because of the ambiguities surrounding the concept of the MST and because of the fact that many States had heavily contested it in the past. By the end of the 1990s, the importance of the MST as a source of investment protection for foreign investors seems to be in sharp decline. Yet, soon after, States began to refer explicitly to the MST in FET clauses contained in their investment treaties. Their clear aim was to limit the scope of investors' rights under said clauses. The clearest illustration of this willingness is the CETA FET clause.

In my view, the degree of specificity of the CETA FET clause is a welcome development. The reference to the MST in IIAs has not been entirely successful at harmonising the interpretation of the standard and limiting its scope.[100] Thus, faced with the binding FTC Note that links the FET to the MST, several NAFTA tribunals (*Pope & Talbot, Mondev, ADF, Merrill & Ring* and *Bilcon*) have simply 'moved the goal post'.[101] They have thus interpreted CIL broadly by emphasising its evolutionary character. Under the CETA FET clause, a tribunal would no longer have the freedom to do that. In the CETA, the 'evolution' has effectively been *stopped* with the specific enumeration of elements contained in the FET clause.[102] In theory, one could argue that it is still possible for a tribunal to give a wide interpretation to any of the specific elements contained in the enumeration set out in Article 8.10 CETA. As such, even a closed list of what constitutes a FET breach would not prevent a Tribunal like *Merrill & Ring* to interpret the concept of arbitrariness or due process in a very broad manner.[103] The likelihood of such a possibility is somewhat diminished by the use of qualifiers in Article 8.10 CETA ('manifest' arbitrariness, 'fundamental'

---

[99] B Barrera, 'The Case for Removing the Fair and Equitable Treatment Standard from NAFTA' (2017) 128 CIGI Papers 10.
[100] Jadeau & Gélinas (n 98) 11 ff.
[101] P Dumberry, 'Moving the Goal Post! How Some NAFTA Tribunals Have Challenged the FTC Note of Interpretation on the Fair and Equitable Treatment Standard Under NAFTA Article 1105' (2014) 8(2) WAMR 251.
[102] There remains, of course, the possibility under CETA, Art 8.10(3) for the parties to review and update the content of the standard.
[103] See, C Henckels, 'Protecting Regulatory Autonomy through Greater Precision in Investment Treaties: The TPP, CETA and TTIP' (2016) 19(1) JIEL 27.

breach of due process') and, most importantly, the establishment of a permanent tribunal of first instance and an appellate tribunal.[104] This will ensure that the same adjudicators decide on every case, thereby allowing for a more consistent and coherent jurisprudence with regards to the FET standard.[105] This is ultimately the best safeguard against any future attempts by arbitral tribunals to adopt a broad interpretation of the FET standard.[106]

Ultimately, the CETA FET clause is emblematic of the fact that in this new century the pendulum is clearly swinging in the direction of States increasingly trying to regain control of investor-State arbitration.[107] For Stephan Schill, changes that have occurred in the last decade are 'aimed at shifting power back from arbitral tribunals to the contracting parties in order to regain control over the interpretation of the obligations' under investment treaties.[108] José Alvarez calls this recent phenomenon the 'Return of the State'.[109] The approach adopted by Canada and the EU in CETA is arguably the most vivid demonstration of States narrowly defining the FET clause in their treaties and leaving arbitrators with a limited margin of appreciation. The same closed list approach has been adopted by the EU in agreements subsequently concluded with three other States[110] and has also been followed by Belgium–Luxembourg and the Netherlands

---

[104] CETA, Arts 8.27–8. See, S Schacherer, 'TPP, CETA and TTIP Between Innovation and Consolidation – Resolving Investor–State Disputes Under Mega-Regionals' (2016) 7(3) JIDS 631; G Van Harten, 'ISDS in the Revised CETA: Positive Steps, But Is It a "Gold Standard"?' (*CIGI Investor-State Arbitration Commentary Series*, 20 May 2016) <www.cigionline.org/publications/isds-revised-ceta-positive-steps-it-gold-standard> accessed 10 May 2021; JA VanDuzer, 'Investor-State Dispute Settlement in CETA: Is It the Gold Standard?' (*CD Howe Institute Commentary No 459*, 4 October 2016) <www.cdhowe.org/sites/default/files/attachments/research_papers/mixed/Commentary%20459.pdf> accessed 10 May 2021.

[105] See Schacherer (n 104) 631.

[106] See also, CETA, Art 8.31(3) providing the possibility for the CETA Joint Committee to adopt a binding interpretation 'where serious concerns arise as regards matters of interpretation that may affect investment'.

[107] See, G Aguilar Alvarez & WW Park, 'The New Face of Investment Arbitration: NAFTA Chapter 11' (2003) 28 YJIL 365.

[108] S Schill, *The Multilateralization of International Investment Law* (CUP 2009) 271.

[109] JE Alvarez, 'The Return of the State' (2011) 20(2) Minn JIntlL 223, 223.

[110] See, Investment Protection Agreement Between the European Union and its Member States, of the One Part, and The Republic of Singapore, of the Other Part (EU & Singapore) (adopted 18 October 2018, not yet in force); Investment Protection Agreement Between the European Union and its Member States, of the One Part, and the Socialist Republic of Viet Nam of the Other Part (EU & Vietnam) (adopted 30 June 2019, not yet in force); European Commission, 'New EU-Mexico Agreement: The Agreement in Principle' (*European Commission*, 23 April 2018) (text agreed upon 21 April 2018, not yet in force)

in their respective Model BITs.¹¹¹ The latest Indian Model BIT (which, notably, does not use the terms FET or MST, but instead refers to the expression 'violation of customary international law') also contains a similar explicit list of FET elements.¹¹² There are good reasons to believe that the CETA FET clause will increasingly be used by other States in the future. The most interesting feature of such clauses is that they reflect the content of the MST as defined by tribunals in the last 25 years. The concept of the MST, which had almost been forgotten by States in the 1990s, is now centre stage in their quest to limit investors' rights under investment treaties. Its 'resurrection' is one of the most interesting developments of the last two decades.

<https://trade.ec.europa.eu/doclib/docs/2018/april/tradoc_156791.pdf> accessed 10 May 2021. It should be added that the proposed text of the (now doomed) Transatlantic Trade and Investment Partnership (TTIP) between the EU and the United States also contained an FET clause with similar language to that provided by Article 8.10. European Commission, 'Commission Draft Text TTIP – Investment: Transatlantic Trade and Investment Partnership' (*European Commission*, 2015) Art 3 <http://trade.ec.europa.eu/doclib/docs/2015/september/tradoc_153807.pdf> accessed 10 May 2021.

[111] Belgium–Luxembourg Economic Union Model BIT 2019 (Belgium & Luxembourg) (adopted 28 March 2019) Art 4; Netherlands, 'Netherlands Model Investment Agreement' (*Netherlands Ministry of Foreign Affairs*, 22 March 2019) Art 9 <www.rijksoverheid.nl/binaries/rijksoverheid/documenten/publicaties/2019/03/22/nieuwe-modeltekst-investeringsakkoorden/nieuwe+modeltekst+investeringsakkoorden.pdf> accessed 10 May 2021.

[112] India, 'Model Text for the Indian Bilateral Investment Treaty' (*Indian Ministry of Finance*, 14 January 2016) Art 3.1 <www.dea.gov.in/sites/default/files/ModelBIT_Annex_0.pdf> accessed 10 May 2021: 'No Party shall subject investments made by investors of the other Party to measures which constitute a violation of customary international law through: (i) Denial of justice in any judicial or administrative proceedings; or (ii) fundamental breach of due process; or (iii) targeted discrimination on manifestly unjustified grounds, such as gender, race or religious belief; or (iv) manifestly abusive treatment, such as coercion, duress and harassment (…)'. This type of clause is found in the Treaty Between The Republic of Belarus and The Republic of India on Investments (Belarus & India) (adopted 24 September 2018, not yet in force).

2

Recourse to Legal Experts for the Establishment and Interpretation of Customary Norms in Investment Law

SAÏDA EL BOUDOUHI

1 Introduction

This chapter will scrutinise the recourse to legal witnesses on points of international law through the lens of specific texture of customary international law. A general question raised is that of the legal basis and legitimacy of the recourse to international law expert witnesses in investment arbitration, but answering it requires distinguishing between different sources of international law and paying a specific attention to customary rules. Indeed, the formal justification and legitimacy of the practice of expert witnesses on issues of international law may well depend on the type of norms involved. The recourse to legal expertise may be more justified – and thus more legitimate – for the establishment or interpretation of customary norms than for the interpretation of treaty norms. This entails a secondary question to which little attention has been paid other than in passing in international law: whether customary international law is a matter of fact that must be pleaded before investment tribunals or a matter of law that must be raised in argument by the parties in their submissions is a central question. To answer the question, a close look will be paid to the way international customary law is proved before investment tribunals. The question relates more generally to the issue of custom determination or custom interpretation.

The lack of scholarly attention on the dichotomy may be due to the absence of procedural consequences attached to the distinction between points of law and points of fact in general international litigation.[1] The distinction, however, takes on a particular significance in the face of a rising practice to plead and prove points of international law before investment

---

[1] The distinction is only applicable in international legal regimes which are equipped with an appellate system such as the WTO dispute settlement system.

tribunals through party-appointed legal expertise.² Instead of being scrutinised to assess its consequences on the system, this well-established practice is taken notice of, matter of factly, without much questioning of its legal basis or legitimacy, at most noticing its 'oddness' or 'strangeness'.³ And yet, especially in a civil lawyer's eyes, the trend does not seem consistent with the ancient adage *iura novit curia* according to which the judge 'knows' the applicable law while the parties have to prove, including through expert witnesses, the facts of the case.⁴ Legal experts, acting as party-appointed witnesses, whether they testify before the tribunal or simply provide a written statement, become, from a procedural point of view, a means of evidence of the applicable law. Even within common law systems which tend to be more adversarial and in which the *iura novit curia* is not applied systematically, it is commonly admitted that 'expert testimony is used [...] to demonstrate facts that could not be demonstrated to a factfinder without some special skill or discipline'.⁵ But international law, even in its customary form, is not a fact that must be proved but a law that must be applied to given facts.

The maxim *iura novit curia* produces most of its effects in the context of due process of law requirements as it answers the question whether the adjudicator can raise on her own motion legal arguments that have not been put forward by the parties.⁶ It thus regulates the powers of the adjudicator as to the determination of the law. But it can also be relevant to determine whether the parties must only argue the applicable law in their submissions, or whether they can go as far as to plead and prove it through recourse to legal expert witnesses. It must however be conceded that the difference between proving and arguing, which is applicable in some legal systems,⁷ is based on the existence of rules of admissibility of

---

² A Newcombe, 'The Strange Case of Expert Legal Opinions in Investment Treaty Arbitrations' (*Kluwer Arbitration Blog*, 18 March 2010). <http://arbitrationblog.kluwerarbitration.com/2010/03/18/the-strange-case-of-expert-legal-opinions-in-investment-treaty-arbitrations/> accessed 1 June 2022.
³ ibid.
⁴ Relying on the law of procedure in France and Switzerland, see C Jarrosson, 'L'expertise juridique' in C Reymond (ed), *Liber amicorum Claude Reymond: Autour de l'arbitrage* (Litec Paris 2004) 127–51. *Da mihi factum dabo tibi jus* is the other formulation of the same principle.
⁵ TE Baker, 'The Impropriety of Expert Witness Testimony on the Law' (1992) 40 UKanLRev 325, 331.
⁶ JDM Lew, 'Iura Novit Curia and Due Process' (Queen Mary Law Research Paper Series No 72/2010, 1 January 2011) <http://dx.doi.org/10.2139/ssrn.1733531> accessed 1 June 2022; M Kurkela & S Turunen, *Due Process in International Commercial Arbitration* (OUP 2010) 178 ff.
⁷ Such as the Canadian legal system.

evidence. International law does not impose limitations on admissibility of evidence: 'International tribunals ... have generally had the power to decide for themselves what is admissible as evidence and have taken a liberal approach to the matter'.[8] Therefore, the question whether a customary rule must be treated as fact or law for evidentiary purposes is more an issue of legitimacy than of legality.

This chapter will retain a formalist approach of that source of law which will then be completed by a more realist appraisal of the practice allowing to encompass sociological justifications, which may better account for the increase in the recourse to legal experts on international law issues in investment arbitration. Part 2 will present and comparatively assess the abundance of the recourse in investment arbitration to legal witnesses on issues of international law; Part 3 will then proceed to a theoretical analysis which will test the hypothesis according to which recourse to international law witnesses in investment arbitration could be justified when dealing with customary international law; it will appear that, at most, customary norms may have been the Trojan horse of the recourse to international law experts in investment arbitration because international law witnesses are seldom relied on for the purposes of ascertaining the contents or even the meaning of customary international law. Since the theoretical hypothesis does not pass the empirical test, Part 4 will offer an alternative justification that has more to do with the sociology of investment law and with its constant search for legitimacy than with any formal analysis of the sources of law.

2 The Puzzling Practice of Extensive Use of International Law Expert Witnesses in Investment Arbitration

2.1 A Well-Established Practice of Legal Opinions in Investment Arbitration

There is a growing recourse to legal experts, generally party-appointed expert witnesses, for the purposes of establishing the contents or the meaning of a given international law norm in investment arbitration. Far from receding, the practice is so frequent that a database on international investment arbitration provides the possibility to search for cases by the names of experts who provided a legal opinion,[9] notwithstanding the fact that the

---

[8] CF Amerasinghe, *Evidence in International Litigation* (Martinus Nijhoff 2005) 164.
[9] Italaw, 'Expert (Legal Opinion)' (*Italaw*, 2022) <www.italaw.com/browse/expert-legal-opinions> accessed 1 June 2022.

contents of many of the opinions have not been made public and can only be used to the extent that they are cited within the award. These legal 'witnesses' are either general authorities recognised in international law or experts of international investment law who may act as counsel or even arbitrators in other cases.[10] Their identification in the awards is not always consistent: they are oftentimes simply presented as authors of 'legal opinions' and, as such, they may be distinguished, in the same award, from 'witnesses' and 'expert opinions'.[11] In other cases, among experts on international law, a difference is established, mainly for fees and expenses purposes, between 'consulting experts' and 'testifying experts'.[12] In the same case, the individual contribution of experts of international law can be labelled 'opinion', 'legal opinion' or 'expert opinion', which are all introduced under a general heading of 'witnesses' testimony'. The latter, thus, conflates all types of witnesses, whether they are experts in international law, domestic law or of technical matters.[13] They can more generally be included in a wider category of expert witnesses which includes three types of experts: international law experts, national law experts and quantum/industry experts.[14]

The battle of legal experts on issues of international law started with the *Loewen* case, in which Christopher Greenwood and Sir Ian Sinclair, besides other legal experts, wrote legal opinions for the two parties.[15] But the *Yukos* arbitration case is one of the most salient examples of a battle of experts on international law issues, even though many of the opinions by international law experts also related to aspects of comparative constitutional law, on the conclusion of treaties, or on the comparative law of foreign relations.[16] Overall, many legal opinions deal with issues of domestic law

---

[10] M Langford, D Behn & R Lie, 'The Revolving Door in International Investment Arbitration' in A Føllesdal & G Ulfstein, *Judicialization of International Law: A Mixed Blessing?* (OUP 2018) 145–6.

[11] *Jan de Nul v Egypt* (Award of 6 November 2008) ICSID Case No ARB/04/13, 27.

[12] *Siag v Egypt* (Award of 1 June 2009) ICSID Case No ARB/05/15, 165–6.

[13] *Yukos Universal Ltd v Russia* (Interim Award on Jurisdiction and Admissibility of 30 November 2009) UNCITRAL, PCA Case No 2005–04/AA227, 46 ff.

[14] Langford & ors (n 10) 145–6.

[15] *Loewen Group, Inc and Raymond L Loewen v USA* (Award of 26 June 2003) ICSID Case No ARB(AF)/98/3.

[16] *Yukos Universal Ltd v Russia*; see also, among others, the awards in *Pezold v Zimbabwe* (Award of 28 July 2015) ICSID Case No ARB/10/15; see also in *Chevron* where the expert opinions of J Paulsson & NJ Schrijver were not made public, nor were they referenced in the final award, in *Chevron Corporation and Texaco Petroleum Corporation v Ecuador* (Award of 31 August 2011) UNCITRAL, PCA Case No 34877. Notice, however, that in the *Pezold* case, the majority of the experts were 'quantum experts' who had to assess the damage as a matter of fact. Their expertise was not in international law issues.

which the members of the tribunal may not be familiar with and which are, at least formally, applied as mere facts in the dispute[17] or as issues of financial assessment.[18] But a great number tackle issues of international law for which it could be expected that the tribunal has the required expertise.[19]

This practice is quite unique and specific to investment arbitration. It is inexistent before international courts and tribunals.[20] It must be stressed, however, that this scarcity of the practice is not the result of an exclusionary rule since the admissibility of evidence in international law is as liberal before investment tribunals as before any other international court or tribunal.[21] Nothing precludes the parties from presenting expert witnesses on international law before the International Court of Justice (ICJ), for instance, except for a sense of impropriety in front of a court which is composed of at least 15 highly reputed experts of international law. Articles 50 and 51 of the ICJ Statute refer to the recourse to experts without distinguishing between the types of experts or the issues on which they can be called upon. Rule 57 of the ICJ relates the presentation of witnesses and experts to 'any evidence' that a party wishes to produce, thus linking evidence – and factual matters – to the appointment and approval by the Court of expert witnesses. However, the relationship is implicit and the appointment of experts is not limited by an objective of evidence production. Equally, if not even more clearly, nothing in the ICSID rules seems to limit the appointment – by the parties or the tribunal – of experts.[22]

---

[17] Thus, for instance, Alain Pellet, Martti Koskenniemi and Georg Nolte provided opinions on the provisional application of treaties in, respectively, French, Finnish and German constitutional law in the Yukos case *Yukos Universal Ltd v Russia* (Interim Award on Jurisdiction and Admissibility of 30 November 2009) UNCITRAL, PCA Case No 2005-04/AA227 [323–4]. In the same series of cases, several experts of Russian constitutional law were presented for the same domestic law issues.

[18] See, for example, the legal opinion of Alejandro Arraez in *Victor Pey Casado v Chile* (Opinion of Alejandro Arraez and Associates of 3 September 2002) ICSID Case No ARB/98/2.

[19] In the Yukos case for instance, the international law experts outnumbered the technical and the domestic law experts.

[20] See, *infra*, rare cases of expert opinions for the purposes of establishing a customary rule.

[21] On the liberal approach of evidence in international litigation, see Amerasinghe (n 8) and D Sandifer, *Evidence Before International Tribunals* (UVA Press 1975); but also, underlining the difficulties arising from an excessively liberal approach, C Brower, 'Evidence Before International Tribunals: The Need for Some Standard Rules' (1994) 28(1) Int'l L 47.

[22] While Rule 35 on 'Examination of Witnesses and Experts' is limited to the examination before the Tribunal, Rule 36 does refer to the admission of 'evidence given by a witness or expert', ICSID Rules of Procedure for Arbitration Proceedings (Arbitration Rules) (adopted 25 September 1967, entered into force 1 January 1968) rules 35–6 (hereinafter ICSID Arbitration Rules).

In fact, the rules tackle the situation of witnesses and that of experts in the same provisions, thus suggesting that there is no procedural difference between the two categories. The 2013 United Nations Commission on International Trade Law (UNCITRAL) Arbitration Rules provide a more detailed regime for the expert witnesses appointed by the parties. Encompassed in a section on 'evidence', Article 27 refers to 'witnesses, including expert witnesses who are presented by the parties to testify ... on any issue of fact or expertise'.[23] The formulation suggests that an expert contribution could be on issues other than of fact. Nothing in the applicable procedural rules seem to limit the appointment by the parties of international law experts as expert witnesses.

The scarcity of legal experts before international tribunals is thus the result of parties' self-restraint, rather than of any regulation by international tribunals. Before the ICJ, the instances in which the parties have introduced expert witnesses on issues of law are very rare. Most of the legal testimonies deal with issues of domestic law which are seen by international judges as issues of fact that can be proved by recourse to expert witnesses.[24] That analysis is applicable to other international tribunals, including the WTO dispute settlement in which, however adversarial the proceedings,[25] the parties do not appoint legal expert witnesses on issues of international law, as they would appoint expert witnesses on issues of domestic law or on technical matters. The only

---

[23] UNCITRAL, 'Arbitration Rules of the United Nations Commission on International Trade Law' (15 December 1976) UN Doc A/31/98, 31st Sess Supp No 17, as amended in 2010 (A/RES/65/22) and 2013 (A/RES/68/109), Art 27 (UNCITRAL Rules).

[24] See, for example, *Right of Passage over Indian Territory (Portugal v India)* (Observations and submissions of the Government of the Portuguese Republic on the Preliminary Objections of the Government of India) [1957] VIII ICJ Rep 629, in which Portugal submitted the written testimony of a Chicago University Professor of Comparative Law in order to prove the existence of a general principle of law. But given that the Court identified a local custom in the case, it did not need consider the elements referring to a possible general principle of law. The scope of the analysis does not extend however to legal expertise on issues of domestic law as such that investment tribunals encounter very frequently. Because of its procedural status as a fact, domestic law before the international adjudicator may more legitimately be subject to legal expertise than international law itself. When in the logical position of a fact, domestic law cannot be covered by the *jura novit curia* principle. J Hepburn holds a different position in considering that in investment arbitration disputes the principle *iura novit curia* should apply not only to international law but also to domestic law because it is a matter of law, see J Hepburn, *Domestic Law in International Investment Arbitration* (OUP 2017) 120–37.

[25] Discussing the relative weight of 'adversarialism' v 'inquisitorialism', see J Pauwelyn, 'The Use of Experts in WTO Dispute Settlement' (2008) 51(2) ICLQ 325, 327.

way through which a legal opinion can be taken into account is through the *amicus curiae* brief.[26]

That the practice of appointing as expert witnesses international law scholars has not emerged does not mean, however, that parties before the ICJ or any other international tribunal do not rely on expert opinions of highly recognised international law experts. They do so by taking into consideration the parties' submissions and pleadings: highly recognised and respected authorities in international law are incorporated within the counsel team of each party, and are not introduced by the parties as 'objective' expert witnesses.

2.2 The Influence of Commercial Arbitration and of Domestic Courts

The trend towards legal testimonies on international law issues may well stem from a conflation of litigation methods by actors involved both in commercial and investment arbitration: in the former, a handful of arbitrators are not expected to know the dozens of applicable domestic legal systems that may be involved in the disputes to which they are appointed. The American Law Institute/International Institute for the Unification of Private Law (ALI/UNIDROIT) principles provide for instance that 'the court may appoint an expert to give evidence on any relevant issue for which expert testimony is appropriate, including foreign law',[27] thus

---

[26] Within the WTO dispute settlement system, opinions of legal experts can be encountered under the form of an *amicus curiae'* submission; see, for example, the *amicus curiae* of Robert Howse in WTO, *United States – Measures Concerning the Importation, Marketing and Sale of Tuna and Tuna Products – Report of the Appellate Body* (16 May 2012) WT/DS381/AB/R [8]. At the appellate level, and given the Appellate Body's limited scope of review, that an *amicus curiae* brief deal exclusively with issues of law is even an admissibility requirement, WTO, *European Communities – Measures Affecting Asbestos and Asbestos-Containing Products – Communication of the Appellate Body* (8 November 2000) WT/DS135/9 [7(c)].

[27] Article 22.4 of the ALI/Unidroit principles:

> The court may appoint an expert to give evidence on any relevant issue for which expert testimony is appropriate, including foreign law.
> 22.4.1 If the parties agree upon an expert the court ordinarily should appoint that expert.
> 22.4.2 A party has a right to present expert testimony through an expert selected by that party on any relevant issue for which expert testimony is appropriate.
> 22.4.3 An expert, whether appointed by the court or by a party, owes a duty to the court to present a full and objective assessment of the issue addressed.

See ALI & UNIDROIT, 'ALI/UNIDROIT Principles of Transnational Civil Procedure' (*UNIDROIT*, 2006) Art 22.4 <www.unidroit.org/instruments/civil-procedure/ali-unidroit-principles/> accessed 1 June 2022.

extending the scope of the expertise beyond factual matters.[28] That is consistent with the predominant common law conception of foreign law as a matter of fact, even when it is the applicable law.[29] As such, it can be submitted to a legal expert. That conception is not bluntly incompatible with the way things stand in civil law systems: foreign law is considered as law if it is the applicable law, but it can still be proved through recourse to party-appointed experts.[30] Thus, in commercial arbitration, the practice of party-appointed experts is widespread and justified as a means to prove domestic law with which the arbitral tribunal is not familiar.[31] However, there is less basis for an investment tribunal to rely on expert witnesses on issues of law when the applicable law is public international law.

The practice of appointing legal experts to establish international law rules may also result from the influence exerted by some domestic legal systems on investment arbitration. The use of legal experts to elucidate the contents of domestic law is inexistent or very rare before domestic jurisdictions, even in common law systems in which the adage *iura novit curia* is generally inapplicable, at least in civil proceedings.[32] In the United States, for instance, the recourse to legal expert witnesses to establish the meaning of domestic law is harshly criticised in the rare occasions where it has appeared.[33] In civil law systems, legal expertise on domestic law is not even conceivable anywhere else than in the parties' submissions.[34] However, some legal systems have seen the emergence of 'law expertise' within the judicial experts category for the purposes of establishing the

---

[28] G Cordero Moss, 'Tribunal's Power v Party Autonomy' in P Muchlinski, F Ortino & C Schreuer (eds), *Oxford Handbook of International Investment Law* (OUP 2008) 1235.

[29] OC Sommerich & B Busch, 'The Expert Witness and the Proof of Foreign Law' (1953) 38 Cornell LRev 125, 128.

[30] On the ambiguous status of foreign law between the position of fact and that of law in civil law systems, see H Muir Watt & M Creach, 'Expertise sur la teneur du droit étranger' [2016] *Répertoire de droit international* (Dalloz 2016) 12.

[31] Even here, one would expect them to be appointed on the basis of their knowledge of the domestic law involved on a case-by-case basis. Such a guiding principle would probably avoid the concentration of all cases in the hands of a few arbitrators whose knowledge of the applicable law is only fictional and who cannot but rely on the legal witnesses on issues of domestic law.

[32] See, for instance, Joined Cases C-430/93 & C-431/93 *Jeroen van Schijndel and Johannes Nicolaas Cornelis van Veen v Stichting Pensioenfonds voor Fysiotherapeuten* [1995] ECLI:EU:C:1995:185, Opinion of Mr Advocate General Jacobs [33], citing FA Mann, 'Fusion of the Legal Professions?' (1977) 93 LQR 367, 369.

[33] SI Friedland, 'Expert Testimony on the Law: Excludable or Justifiable?' (1983) 37 U Mia L Rev 451; Baker (n 5) 331.

[34] Jarrosson (n 4) 130.

specific and technical legal rules applicable to a profession,[35] while others use the *amicus curiae* proceeding as a means to provide legal expertise on domestic law.[36] But these developments confirm that issues of domestic law are not expected to be 'proved' through expertise. On the contrary, party-appointed legal experts on issues of foreign law are frequent, especially in common law systems in which foreign law is considered as a matter of fact even when it is the applicable law chosen by the parties.[37] However, it seems that even for the establishment of foreign law purposes, national judges aim at limiting their reliance on party-appointed legal experts for the establishment of points of law, even foreign law. They do so through the development of cooperation procedures between their respective institutions.[38]

The situation seems different when it comes to the recourse, before domestic tribunals, to legal experts to establish points of international law, even when the latter is part of the applicable law. There seems, however, to exist a sharp contrast between civil law and common law systems. On the one hand, the practice of expert witnesses on international law issues has not developed in civil law systems: the only way that 'law expertise' can be provided to the judge is through the *amicus curiae* mechanism.[39] The specific category of 'law expertise' that exists in some European countries does not seem to apply to general questions of law such as issues of international law. On the other hand, common law tribunals admit legal

---

[35] According to a report on European judicial systems, the 'law expertise' is admitted in at least 10 European countries (Estonia, Germany, Greece, Ireland, Malta, Netherlands, Norway, Poland, Russian Federation, Turkey), see CEPEJ, 'European Judicial Systems – Edition 2014 (2012 data): Efficiency and Quality of Justice' (*EEEI*, 9 October 2014) 441 ff <https://experts-institute.eu/wp-content/uploads/2018/03/extract-rapport-2014-en.pdf> accessed 1 June 2022.

[36] The old institution of the *amicus curiae* in the common law systems has always been used as a type of legal expertise. That is now also the case in some civil law systems in which the *amicus curiae* has been introduced. That is the case in France, for example, where the *amicus curiae* had been introduced in the 1990s. D Mazeaud, 'L'expertise de droit à travers l'*amicus curiae*' in MA Frison-Roche & D Mazeaud (eds), *L'expertise* (Dalloz 1995) 109, 118; H Muir Watt & M Creach, 'Notion d'expertise' [2016] *Répertoire de droit international* (Dalloz 2016) 10.

[37] Sommerich & Busch (n 29) 128. Even in systems in which the applicable foreign law is not considered as a pure matter of fact, the tribunals tend to treat it procedurally as a fact that must be established (Watt & Creach (n 30) 12).

[38] MJ Wilson, 'Demystifying the Determination of Foreign Law in US Courts: Opening the Door to a Greater Global Understanding' (2011) 46(5) Wake Forest LRev 887.

[39] Frison-Roche & Mazeaud (n 36) 109, especially at 11; R Encinas de Munagorri, 'L'ouverture de la Cour de cassation aux *amici curiae*' [2005] RTD civ 88.

expertise for the purposes of establishing the content of customary international law.[40] In the United States, for instance, a combination of domestic US rules of civil procedure and of the law of evidence has led to the conclusion that 'the court can receive expert testimony [on international law] but need not do so'.[41] This is related to a tradition of strong reliance on international law scholarship for the proof of customary norms.[42] Thus, expert affidavits are generally admitted by domestic courts for purposes of ascertaining customary international law.[43] They may, however, be deemed to 'lack the evidentiary value as proof of a [given] customary international law' rule.[44] That practice of relying on expert affidavits to determine the content of international law rules has also been recently observed as rising in Canadian case law, notwithstanding controversy as to the admissibility of legal expertise on issues of international law and as to the consequences at the appellate level of treating international law as a fact that is proved through expertise.[45]

It seems that it is under the influence of both this common law practice relating to international law and the commercial arbitration practice relating to foreign law that the recourse to legal experts on international law has emerged in investment arbitration: in the *Loewen* case, for example, both the government of the United States as the respondent and the Canadian investor may have found it natural to provide legal opinions from eminent international law experts for the purposes of ascertaining the content of a customary rule. But, it is not so much the mere emergence of the practice in regard to customary law, rather the generalisation beyond customary law that is puzzling.

---

[40] HJ Maier, 'The Role of Experts in Proving International Human Rights Law in Domestic Courts: A Commentary' (1996) 25 GaJInt'l & CompL 205, 212; HW Baade, 'Proving Foreign and International Law in Domestic Tribunals' (1978) 18(4) VaJInt'l L 619, 626. See, however, early cases in which the US Supreme Court had another position: 'Foreign municipal laws must indeed be proved as facts, but it is not so with the law of nations' *The Scotia*, 81 US 170 (1871) 188.

[41] Baade (n 40) 627.

[42] For a variety of examples of reliance on international law doctrine from several jurisdictions, see C Ryngaert & D Hora Siccama, 'Ascertaining Customary International Law: An Inquiry into the Methods Used by Domestic Courts' (2018) 65 NILR 1, 15 ff.

[43] ibid 15.

[44] *Flores v Southern Peru Copper Corp*, 414 F.3d 233 (2d Cir 2003) [86].

[45] G van Ert, 'The Admissibility of International Legal Evidence' (2005) 84 CanBar Rev 31, 31–46; G van Ert, 'The Reception of International Law in Canada: Three Ways we Might Go Wrong' (*Canada in International Law at 150 and Beyond* Paper No 2, 2018) <www.cigionline.org/sites/default/files/documents/Reflections%20Series%20Paper%20no.2web.pdf> accessed 1 June 2022.

3 The Specificity of Customary Norms as a Possible Justification

The question that needs to be answered is whether recourse to legal experts on issues of international law is justified when it is used for the discussion of the constitutive elements of a customary norm. Indeed, from a formalist perspective, before the establishment of the norm, the latter are factual elements that must be proved by the parties.

3.1 The Formalist Analysis: The Constitutive Elements of Custom as Facts That Must Be Proved

The specific nature of customary norms as regards the distinction of fact and law may thus provide a possible formalist explanation for the development of the practice of expert witnesses on international law issues. Customary rules are legal elements once they have been established through adjudication. But while in the process of being ascertained, their constitutive elements are nothing more than facts that have to be proved before the judge. Both practice and *opinio juris* are facts as long as they have not been recognised as being constitutive of a legal rule;[46] *opinio juris* is specific only in that it is an immaterial and psychological fact as opposed to practice, which is material. That the constitutive elements of customary rules are factual elements that must be proved can be drawn from the language of the ICJ as well as of the International Law Commission (ILC), which both use the language of fact-finding and evidence.[47] According to the ICJ, 'the Party which relies on a custom […] must prove that this custom is established […]'.[48] In its Conclusions and Commentaries on Identification of Customary International Law, the ILC underlines that the word 'evidence' is used as a 'broad concept relating to all the materials that may be considered as a basis for the identification of customary international law', and not in a 'technical sense'.[49] Such a cautious

---

[46] The immaterial or psychological nature of the *opinio juris* has led some scholars to consider it as a 'normative' element, while the practice is the only 'factual element' (J Kokott, *The Burden of Proof in Comparative and Human Rights Law: Civil and Common Law Approaches with Special Reference to the American and German Legal Systems* (Kluwer Law International 1998) 225).

[47] For an analysis of the constitutive elements of custom as factual elements, see S El Boudouhi, *L'élément factuel dans le contentieux international* (Bruylant 2013) 267–75.

[48] *Rights of Nationals of the United States of America in Morocco (France v USA)* (Judgment) [1952] ICJ Rep 176, 200.

[49] ILC, 'Draft Conclusions on Identification of Customary International Law, with Commentaries' (30 April–1 June and 2 July–10 August 2018) UN Doc A/73/10, reproduced in [2018/II – Part Two] YBILC 117, 127, fn 680.

approach aims at setting aside any exclusionary rules that would derive from other legal systems, but the reference to 'evidence' as well as the use of the word 'prove' point nevertheless to the factual nature of the constitutive elements which are submitted to the burden of proof.[50]

Relying on expert testimony for the purposes of ascertaining practice and *opinio juris* can be accounted for in that

> [a]ccess to the norms of traditional customary international law is supposed to require that the facts of national practice and decision be discovered, interpreted and described in much the same manner as a sociologist or anthropologist collects and characterizes other facts of human activity.[51]

The distinction that is made in the US law between adjudicative and legislative facts may well be relevant for the analysis of customary international law: the constitutive elements of a customary norm could be compared to 'legislative facts' that may, but must not, be proved through recourse to legal expert witnesses.[52] Even in this latter case, it may be argued that expert witnesses may not need to be legal experts, at least not international law experts, but experts of the field in which the alleged customary norm emerges. Thus, in the *South West Africa* cases, the ICJ heard several expert testimonies of renowned scholars provided by South Africa as evidence. Among them, Professor ST Possony, from Stanford University, provided expertise in political history for the purposes of discarding the existence of a customary rule on racial discrimination.[53] Since the expert testimony deals with the facts on which a customary rule would be based, it need not be a legal expertise. The constitutive elements in that case were to search in the general practice of international relations rather than in a legal practice.[54] But the recourse to the expertise was justified in that it could, by providing elements of practice within international relations, help the adjudicator determine what the applicable rule is. When it comes to investment arbitration, even the cases which could be expected to give rise to a genuine expert opinion

---

[50] *Cargill, Inc v Mexico* (Award of 18 September 2009) ICSID Case No ARB(AF)/05/2 [273].
[51] For an analogy between legislative facts in US law and constitutive elements of CIL, see Maier (n 40) 209.
[52] Baade (n 40) 626–7.
[53] *South West Africa Cases (Ethiopia v South Africa; Liberia v South Africa)* (Judgment) [1966] ICJ Rep 6, 7, 10; see also, in the same case, *South West Africa Cases (Ethiopia v South Africa; Liberia v South Africa)* (Pleadings, *South West Africa*, vol XI) 643–708.
[54] The same reasoning could be applied to general principles of law on which expert witnesses could be called to testify on issues of comparative law for the purposes of proving the existence of a general principle of law. See for instance the *Right of Passage over Indian Territory (Portugal v India)* (Judgment) [1960] ICJ Rep 6.

on the contents of a given customary norm prove to go well beyond that assessment of the contents of the law.[55] No example was found in which an expert legal opinion was used for the purposes of the determination or the interpretation of a customary rule. That may well be due to the fact that the recourse to customary law in international investment law remains mostly ancillary and is not seen as a decisive factor.

Moreover, in most investment arbitration cases, the customary rules that are invoked do not lie simply in the practice of international relations, but rather in treaty rules or rules which exist in other legal systems. Thus, because the constitutive elements of the customary norms invoked in investment law are other norms of international law – bilateral investment treaties, multilateral treaties – the testimony of experts on issues of international law may appear justified. Experts in political history, international relations or geography could certainly not bring a useful testimony as to the correct understanding of the rule of denial of justice, for example.

This could seem consistent with the ILC's approach which has established in Conclusion 14 of its *Draft Conclusions on the Identification of International Law* that 'teachings of the mostly highly qualified publicists of the various nations may serve as a subsidiary means for the determination of rules of customary international law'.[56] If legal expert testimonies are considered as live or ad hoc testimonies of the 'most highly qualified publicists', then their contribution would be accounted for by Conclusion 14 of the ILC Draft Conclusions. While the provision does not deal with the procedural status of expert testimonies, they could well be considered as subsidiary means to establish a customary rule. To come to that conclusion, the ILC relied not only on ICJ case law[57] but also on the American Supreme Court which had considered since its very first recognition of customary international law that the work of 'jurists and commentators ... provide trustworthy evidence of what the law really is'.[58] The ILC does

---

[55] Because it required an assessment of the contents of the denial of justice principle in international law, the *Loewen* case could have given rise to a genuine expert opinion dealing with practice and *opinion juris* as factual constitutive elements of a customary principle. And yet, the opinion dismisses the practice and *opinio juris* part rather expeditiously while focusing on legal characterisation of the facts (*Loewen Group, Inc and Raymond L Loewen v USA* (Opinion of Richard B Bilder (on international law governing state responsibility for treatment of foreign investors) of 16 March 2001) ICSID Case No ARB(AF)/98/3 [34]).

[56] ILC, 'Draft Conclusions on Identification of Customary International Law, with Commentaries' (30 April–1 June and 2 July–10 August 2018) UN Doc A/73/10, reproduced in [2018/II – Part Two] YBILC 117, 150.

[57] SS *'Lotus' (France v Turkey)* (Judgment) [1927] PCIJ Series A No 10, 27 & 30.

[58] *The Paquete Habana*, 175 US 677 (1900) 700.

not, however, distinguish the specific situation where the 'highly qualified publicists' are introduced in the proceedings as expert witnesses from the general situation in which the teachings of those experts would be relied on in the written proceedings. It seems that the reference to the 'highly qualified publicists' in Conclusion 14 is redundant with Article 38(1)(d) of the ICJ Statute: the opinion of 'highly recognized publicists' is not more useful to establish customary rules than it is to determine any other rule of international law. In other words, it is not the specificity of customary rules which accounts for the reference by the ILC to this subsidiary means of establishing international law. At no point does the ILC mention that the specific nature of customary law makes the contribution of 'highly recognized publicists' especially relevant or more relevant than for treaty law for instance. Thus, if the recourse to legal expert testimonies were to be analysed as a subsidiary means for the determination of customary international law, it would be on the basis of Article 38(1)(d) of the ICJ Statute. This may explain the discussion of legal doctrine in the parties' and tribunals' reasoning on the substance, but it does not provide a clear basis for the procedural status – as expert witnesses – of that legal doctrine in the proceedings.

As to the interpretation of customary international law, the recourse to expert witnesses would be justified if it were to be admitted that interpreting amounts to establishing new constitutive elements.[59] If, on the contrary, interpretation of customary law is considered as a different cognitive process based not on the establishment of constitutive elements but on teleological and systemic reasoning,[60] then there would not be any need to rely on the live or ad hoc testimony of a legal expert to establish the meaning of a customary rule. The adjudicating authority as well as the parties' counsel are expected to be self-sufficient in teleological and systemic legal reasoning. While 'highly recognized publicists' could still be relied on as subsidiary means of establishing international law, that would have nothing to do with the specific need of establishing the constitutive elements of a customary rule. In other words, legal expertise as a means of proving

---

[59] While it is not the place here to discuss whether interpretation of an existing rule can amount to ascertaining new constitutive elements, that could be argued where the 'interpretation' amounts to a new rule of customary international law. For instance, asking whether State immunity must be understood as applying to jus cogens violations could be a matter of interpretation but it is in fact about identifying a new rule of customary law according to which *jus cogens* violations constitute an exception within the general rule of State immunity.

[60] P Merkouris, 'Interpreting the Customary Rules on Interpretation' (2017) 19 ICLR 126.

the existence of an international rule would apply to the establishment of customary rules but not to their interpretation, which is not to be treated differently from the interpretation of any other rule of international law.

3.2 Testing the Hypothesis in Investment Arbitration Practice: The Proof of Customary Norms as the Trojan Horse of Legal Expertise on International Law

Taking customary international law seriously would entail presenting evidence of its constitutive elements when its contents or its interpretation are discussed among the parties. One could intuitively, and naively, expect that many international law expert opinions in investment arbitration deal with contested customary rules of investment law. That expectation stems from the observation of what happens elsewhere: while the practice of expert testimonies on issues of customary law has not been developed before the ICJ,[61] the case law of the world court shows that there is room for improvement when it comes to providing 'evidence' of the existence of customary rules since it 'rarely presents a documented examination of a broad cross-section of the international community's members'.[62] That usually results in scholarly discussions following statements of the ICJ on the existence or the inexistence of customary norms.[63] The ICJ is thus regularly criticised for not providing sufficient proof of the practice or *opinio juris* it relies on to declare the existence or inexistence of customary rules.[64] Thus, one could expect that if expert witnesses on issues of law were – in an unforeseeable future – to become common practice before the ICJ, that would certainly have to be on elusive and moving aspects of customary law, rather than on issues of treaty interpretation, for example. In that regard, investment arbitration could be expected to be the laboratory for innovative examination of evidence of difficult customary law questions. Could investment arbitration succeed where the ICJ seems to fail?

An examination of the opinions requested from legal expert witnesses shows that there is no reason for such hope. The necessity to prove the

---

[61] However, see Section 2.1.
[62] J Charney, 'Universal International Law' (1993) 87(4) AJIL 529, 537.
[63] S Talmon, 'Determining Customary International Law: The ICJ's Methodology between Induction, Deduction and Assertion' (2015) 26(2) EJIL 417.
[64] See *Ahmadou Sadio Diallo (Republic of Guinea v Congo)* (Preliminary Objections) [2007] ICJ Rep 582 (*Diallo* case) on whether over thousands of BITs can be interpreted as *opinio juris* giving rise to a new customary rule.

existence of a customary rules may appear, at best, as the Trojan horse of the recourse to legal experts for the purposes of adjudicating an issue of international law. Indeed, the recourse to legal experts on issues of international law goes well beyond the proof of customary rules, and in fact is seldom justified by the needs of ascertainment or interpretation of the latter. There is no correlation between the recourse to legal expert witnesses and the need to prove the existence of a customary rule of international law. No expert opinion on international law seems to have been required with the purpose of helping the tribunal assess the existence of a customary rule. That is mainly due to the fact that investment tribunals very seldom, if ever,[65] assess by themselves the existence of a customary rule. *Pope and Talbot v Canada* is a case in which the reliance by the parties and the Tribunal on international law expert opinions could have been useful. It could have balanced the rather egregious reasoning of the Tribunal which discarded the requirement of *opinio juris* to conclude whether a new customary rule existed.[66] But the practice of resorting to international law experts had not developed then and no expert opinions on international law were presented by the parties. But even since the emergence of the expert legal opinions, it seems that the rare cases in which there is discussion by the tribunal of the content of a given customary norm, be it for its determination or for its interpretation, are not the ones for which the parties deem it necessary to present expert witnesses on international law. For purposes of determination of content of a given customary rule, investment tribunals thus rely exclusively on principles formerly set by other international courts or the legal doctrine. In *ADC v Hungary*, international law expert witnesses could have been deemed necessary to help the Tribunal determine the standard of compensation for an unlawful expropriation as a customary norm the limits of which could have been discussed. Instead, in order to determine the standard of damages, the Tribunal simply relied on a wide amount of documentary authorities – ie established case law of the ICJ and highly recognised legal doctrine, rather than on expert witnesses, which had not been produced by the parties otherwise than in their legal submissions.[67] *Mondev* is one of the rare

---

[65] OK Fauchald, 'The Legal Reasoning of ICSID Tribunals – An Empirical Analysis' (2008) 19(2) EJIL 301, 311.

[66] *Pope & Talbot Inc v Canada* (Award in Respect of Damages of 31 May 2002) UNCITRA [62]; P Dumberry, *The Formation and Identification of Rules of Customary International Law in International Investment Law* (CUP 2018) 141.

[67] *ADC Affiliate Ltd et al v Hungary* (Award of 2 October 2006) ICSID Case No ARB/03/16, [479 ff].

investment cases which explicitly discusses, for interpretive and not ascertainment purposes, the constitutive elements of custom, and especially *opinio juris*.[68] And yet, no international law expert witnesses were presented by the parties on that matter,[69] possibly due to the authority and reputation of the highly recognised expertise of the three arbitrators.[70] Similarly, in *Sempra v Argentina*, the opinions of international law witnesses could have been deemed necessary because what was involved was a general rule of international law, ie, the state of necessity. The establishment of the conditions and limits of such a rule could well have called for the objective, if not independent, opinion of international law expert witnesses to assess the State practice and *opinio juris* on that matter, independently from the facts of the case.[71] However, and because the debate on the contents on the state of necessity rule is considered to have been settled in a final manner by the ILC, what was expected from legal experts' opinions was a more general view on the way the treaty rule should be articulated with the customary rule to determine which of the two should prevail, the customary norm setting a higher threshold for the state of necessity to be successfully invoked by the State. In other words, the expert opinions did not deal with the factual question of the contents of the customary rule of state of necessity, but rather with a purely legal question of interpretation of a treaty provision in light of a similar customary rule and of legal characterisation of the financial crisis in Argentina in that regard.[72] As to the *Yukos* series in which a great number of eminent international law expert witnesses appeared, none of the issues involved by the opinions covered customary international law. Most of the substance of the opinions dealt with comparative constitutional law applied to the law of treaties.[73] Once

---

[68] *Mondev International Ltd v USA* (Award of 11 October 2002) ICSID Case No ARB(AF)/99/2, 110–13.
[69] Legal experts, among which a US judge, were heard in that case as witnesses on issues of domestic law.
[70] Sir Ninian Stephen, Stephen Schwebel and James Crawford.
[71] *Sempra Energy v Argentina* (Award of 28 September 2007) ICSID Case No ARB/02/16 and ARB/03/02.
[72] See opinions of José Alvarez (for the investor) and Anne-Marie Slaughter and William Burke-White (for Argentina) in *Sempra* and *Camuzzi*; *Sempra Energy v Argentina* (Opinion of José E Alvarez of 12 September 2005) ICSID Case No ARB/02/16 [46 ff]; *Sempra Energy v Argentina* (Opinion of Anne-Marie Slaughter and William Burke-White of 19 July 2005) ICSID Case No ARB/02/16 [19 ff, 46 ff]; *Camuzzi v Argentina International SA* (Opinion of José E Alvarez of 12 September 2005) ICSID Case No ARB/03/02 [46 ff]; *Camuzzi International SA v Argentina* (Opinion of Anne-Marie Slaughter and William Burke-White of 19 July 2005) ICSID Case No ARB/03/02 [19 ff, 46 ff].
[73] *Yukos Universal Ltd v Russia*.

more, the extensive resort to legal experts in that case does not seem justified by the need to prove the existence nor the interpretation of a given customary norm.

The preliminary conclusion that can be drawn from these observations is that customary international law in investment arbitration has not yet reached the point where the parties would see it as the issue that is worth investing on several costly testimonies by international law experts. Despite the wishes of reputed scholars which have not been confirmed by the ICJ,[74] the potentialities of customary law have not yet been fully realised in investment arbitration. Its scope remains mainly interpretative when it comes to the settlement of disputes, which are almost exclusively based on treaty rules.

4   The Realist Appraisal: The Paradox of the Struggle for Legitimacy

The paradox of the struggle for legitimacy lies in the following: on the one hand, expert witnesses on international law issues are appointed to give more moral weight to the decision of arbitral tribunals whose legitimacy has often been discussed. The conclusion that can be drawn from the above analysis on the recourse to international law experts for the purposes of establishing or interpreting customary rules is that the search for more legitimacy is the rationale of that practice, rather than a genuine need of technical expertise. The practice could have been justified by procedural or technical reasons regarding customary rules. On the other hand, the abundance of the recourse to expert witnesses, the uniqueness of which sets apart investment arbitration from other international dispute settlement systems, may contribute to enhancing the legitimacy crisis. Presenting expert witnesses on issues of international law aims at weighing on the tribunal's decision-making process through authoritative opinions. But that adds further complexity and cost to proceedings for which the costs are one of the controversial aspects.[75] In that regard, it

---

[74] AF Lowenfeld, 'Investment Agreements and International Law' (2003) 42 ColumJ Transnat'l L 123; SM Schwebel, 'The Influence of Bilateral Investment Treaties on Customary International Law' (2004) 98 ASIL Proc 27; JE Alvarez, 'A Bit on Custom' (2009) 42 NYU JIntlL & Pol 17; but see the decision of the International Court of Justice in the *Diallo Case*.

[75] In the discussions within UNCITRAL Working Group III on the Reform of ISDS, costs are one of the major issues that have been raised. Arguing that recourse to legal expert testimonies entails more costs and complexity than integrating the given experts within the team

would be interesting to see if the practice of legal expert testimonies would be as abundant with a quasi-permanent court of investment disputes as set out in the EU-Canada CETA or in the hypothetical multilateral investment court that is being discussed at UNCITRAL since 2017.

Given that it is not justified by the nature of the norms invoked, ie by customary nature of the involved norms, the frequent recourse to expert witnesses in investment arbitration has to be accounted for by other considerations. The fact that this trend is unique in international litigation and exclusive to investment arbitration raises the question of the features of that field that have led to its development. The experts are party appointed but, unlike parties' counsels, they are presented as objective observers.[76] The appointment of legal experts on international law issues by the parties may aim at more authority of the point of view that is defended, as if the authority of the arbitrators, as opposed to that of other 'institutionalized' members of international tribunals, were deemed insufficient and needed to be buttressed by opinions of other legal experts, whatever the expertise in international law of the arbitrators. The 'orator-like role' of these specific witnesses has been pointed out as being 'part of a symbolic strategy'[77] which aims at bringing more legitimacy to the process. This can be compared with the role of *amicus curiae* before some domestic tribunals who do not otherwise admit expert witnesses on issues of domestic law: they have been described as 'experts of prestige',[78] the difference being here that these expert opinions are paid for.

It is somehow ironic that the efforts towards more legitimacy could result in exactly the opposite situation where the legitimacy could be more fragile with the extensive recourse to party appointed legal experts on international law. According to the above distinction between issues of fact, subject to expertise, and issues of law, reserved to the tribunal, relying on expert witnesses for the purposes of clarifying issues of international law amounts for the arbitral tribunal to acting as a mere umpire between

---

of the parties' counsel, see DF Donovan, 'Re-examining the Legal Expert in International Arbitration' in HKIAC (ed), *International Arbitration: Issues, Perspectives and Practice: Liber Amicorum Neil Kaplan* (Wolters Kluwer 2019) ch 11; and

B Berger, 'The Use of Experts in International Arbitration: Specific Issues Relating to Legal Experts' in S Besson & H Frey (eds), *Expert Evidence: Conflicting Assumptions and How to Handle them in Arbitration* (Juris Publishing 2021) ch 6.

[76] Note, however, that just as it has happened that an *ad hoc* judge can decide against the appointing party before the ICJ, it can also happen that an expert witness may testify against the appointing party at least partially. See the case of Schearer in *Siag v Egypt* [474].

[77] Langford & ors (n 10) 145–6.

[78] Mazeaud (n 36) 109, especially at 11.

the parties, rather than as a proactive adjudicative authority, to a degree that is not encountered even in common law systems. It has already been pointed out in another context that relying heavily on party appointed legal experts 'adds an adversarial spin to the proceedings'.[79] It makes the system appear as an inherently adversarial system in which even the applicable law is subject to assessment by the parties and their appointed expert testimonies.

The trend ultimately raises the question of the type of legal expertise that is required from investment arbitrators. It has been stated, in the context of commercial arbitration and in relation with foreign law, that the *iura novit arbiter* principle raises the question of the 'burden of education' to determine 'how the arbitrators are to gain the necessary expertise in the applicable material law to fulfil their mission to resolve the dispute in accordance with it'.[80] Since investment arbitration is deeply embedded in public international law, members of arbitral tribunals are expected to have enough knowledge of international law for the recourse to legal experts as objective experts on international law issues not to be necessary. It is, however, striking that legal experts on points of international law are used even before arbitrators whose expertise in international law is not to be doubted, such as highly recognised public international law academics or former judges, and until recently, current[81] judges of the ICJ. The added value of such expertise is yet to be proven given that it is easy for the 'experts' sitting on the arbitral tribunal to discard it using the same type of legal reasoning but with a more authoritative position. This is what happened for instance in the *CME Czech Republic BV* where the Tribunal considered that the opinion of Professor Schreuer is 'inconsistent with the general principles of international law found by the Tribunal'.[82] Thus, the

---

[79] Wilson (n 38) 909.
[80] Kurkela & Turunen (n 6) 178 ff.
[81] ICJ, 'Speech by HE Mr Abdulqawi A Yusuf, President of the International Court of Justice, on the occasion of the Seventy-Third Session of the United Nations General Assembly' (*Statements by the President*, 25 October 2018) 12 <www.icj-cij.org/public/files/press-releases/0/000-20181025-PRE-02-00-EN.pdf> accessed 30 July 2022: 'Members of the Court have come to the decision, last month, that they will not normally accept to participate in international arbitration. In particular, they will not participate in investor-State arbitration or in commercial arbitration'.
[82] *CME Czech Republic BV v Czech Republic* (Final Award of 14 March 2003) UNCITRAL [§ 452]: the 'legal expert' on international law, prof Schreuer, presented legal arguments which were easily set aside by the tribunal (composed of W Kühn, I Brownlie & S Schwebel). This disqualification of the opinion as 'unsustainable in fact and law' could be attributed to the fact that the arbitrators and the expert had the same legal skills. That was not the case of the other legal witnesses presented for purposes of interpreting domestic law in the same case.

international adjudicator, even in investment arbitration, whether judge or arbitrator, should be 'the sole authority on the law and its interpretation'.[83] But that cannot, however, be more than a matter of impropriety since there exist no exclusionary rules of evidence.

What adds to the legitimacy crisis relating to expert witnesses on international law is not only the fact that they are 'interrogated' on issues of international law, which the tribunal should be familiar with, but also the extent and scope of their opinion. While we have seen that these expert witnesses do not fit in any given procedural category, one cannot ignore the limitation that is usually imposed on expert opinions before tribunals, be they international or national; the expert is usually not expected to apply the law to the facts of the case but only to bring clarifications on some – usually factual – aspects of the dispute. Expert witnesses do not fulfil the same function as counsels whose mission is to provide a convincing legal characterisation of facts. In investment arbitration, on the contrary, it appears in some cases that there is no substantive difference between expert witnesses and the counsel of the parties, except for the pretence to objectivity of individuals, whatever their eminence and integrity, who are paid by the parties to support their point of view.[84] In many cases, the questions that are asked to the legal expert amount to the very same ones that the Tribunal is expected to settle in the award. What is often asked of the legal experts is not an exposition or a clarification on the content of a given rule of international customary law, or even of treaty law, but rather the application of a given rule to the particular facts of the case. This has been observed in cases in which the international law expert witnesses in investment arbitration intervened on 'pedestrian' points[85] that did not require for a clarification of a well-established rule but rather for the application of the rule to the facts of the case. Thus, in *Chevron v Ecuador*, the legal expert Jan Paulsson is asked 'by counsel for Chevron to opine on whether the Lago Agrio litigation has rendered Ecuador responsible for a denial of justice under public international law'.[86] The same exhaustive opinion on all legal and factual aspects of the case was given by Bilder in his opinion on *Loewen*: instead of simply interpreting the North American

---

[83] Baker (n 5) 362.
[84] Expert witnesses, unlike the parties, are cross-examined but legal expert witnesses also have the same rights to due process as the parties since they are often presented along each submission of the parties.
[85] Langford & ors (n 10) 316.
[86] *Chevron Corporation and Texaco Petroleum Corporation v Ecuador (II)* (Opinion of Jan Paulsson of 12 March 2012) PCA Case No 2009–23 [8].

Free Trade Agreement (NAFTA) provisions which were discussed, or simply clarifying the contents of the denial of justice principle from a customary law perspective, as could be expected from a genuine legal expert testimony, the expert opinion dwells on the legal characterisation of each fact of the case so as to come to the conclusion that the principle had not been violated by the American judges. In other words, the expert witness is asked to do the same legal characterisation of facts that the counsel and the tribunal must do, instead of being simply called to clarify the content of a norm, as expert witnesses are usually expected to do without interfering with the adjudicatory function of the tribunal, at least, as conceived in systems in which experts are judge-appointed.[87] The request of opinion may not concern the whole dispute but nevertheless the expert witness is systematically asked to assess the facts of the case in light of their legal expertise, ie to adjudicate the situation *in lieu* of the tribunal, even though the latter is not bound by the opinions.[88] And yet, even in common law systems, the expert testimony is inadmissible according to the rules of evidence if it goes as far as applying the disputed international law rule to the facts of the case.[89]

5 Conclusion

At a time where there is concern about ISDS and reform proposals, it is doubtful that the practice of party appointed experts on international law issues meets the legitimacy requirements that many States and civil society have voiced over the last years. One hypothesis that could justify such a practice is where such expert witnesses would intervene exclusively on issues of customary international law which may call for international

---

[87] While such a restriction of the scope of the expertise is not explicit in international law, the International Court of Justice is however cautious so as to ask very specific factual questions the answer to which will not prejudge its legal characterisation of the facts of the case. See, for example, *Maritime Delimitation in the Caribbean Sea and the Pacific Ocean (Costa Rica v Nicaragua)* (Order of 31 May 2016) [2016] ICJ Rep 235 (appointment of experts).

[88] An example of a situation where the request of opinion did not cover the whole dispute but only one aspect on which the expert had to assess and legally characterise the facts of the case: *Ecuador v USA* (Expert Opinion of Prof Alain Pellet of 23 May 2012) PCA Case No 2012-5 [39]. Yet, even though covering only part of the whole dispute, the opinion is drafted as if it were part of a judicial opinion.

[89] From a decision of the Canadian Federal Court: *Boily v HMTQ* 2017 FC 1021 [25]: 'Prothonotary Morneau, Mr. Boily and the Crown all agree that pages 10 to 12 of the Report (at least in part) provide an opinion on the relevant international law *as it applies to Mr. Boily's case*. This type of legal analysis cannot be the subject of expert evidence and was rightfully deemed inadmissible by Prothonotary Morneau' (emphasis added).

legal expertise for the ascertainment of the legal rules. Since the ascertainment requires an assessment of practice and *opinio juris* as constitutive factual elements, it could be reasonably expected that the parties and the tribunal rely on the objective opinions of expert witnesses. While such a hypothesis remains a desirable evolution in investment arbitration, which would make the assessment of customary rules more accurate than that of the ICJ, the role of customary international law within investment arbitration remains for now limited in that regard. That does not mean, however, that the role of custom in investment law has become irrelevant as was suggested by the Organisation for Economic Cooperation and Development (OECD) a few years ago,[90] but rather that it is not seen by the parties as decisive enough as to call for the appointment of one or several expert witnesses for the purposes of establishing its contents. The recourse to expert witnesses on issues of international law could thus become in the future an indicator of the importance of customary rules: if the tribunal were to examine the application of a customary norm that is not only of interpretative value, chances are that parties would provide expert witnesses discussing that point.

---

[90] OECD, '"Indirect Expropriation" and the "Right to Regulate" in International Investment Law' (OECD Working Papers on International Investment 2004/04, 2004) 2; P Dumberry, 'Are BITs Representing the "New" Customary International Law in International Investment Law' (2010) 28 Penn State Int Law Rev 675, 697.

3

The Identification of Customary International Law and International Investment Law and Arbitration

State Practice in Connection with Investor-State Proceedings

DIEGO MEJÍA-LEMOS

1 Introduction

State practice in support of general rules governing the identification of customary international law (CIL), a subset of secondary rules of general international law epitomised by the so-called 'two-element approach' to CIL identification, is often neglected. Nevertheless, its nature and significance raise important issues. As with other secondary rules, decisions of international courts and tribunals are often uncritically assumed to be a sufficient basis for rules governing CIL identification. Yet, despite their varying degrees of authoritativeness, such decisions are not a sufficient, let alone a necessary, condition for establishing general rules on CIL identification. By contrast, State practice remains a necessary condition to establish the existence and content of that subset of rules, as with any other international law rules.[1]

These issues not only arise as a matter of general international law, but also where sub-systems of particular international law are applied. Paramount among those sub-systems is international investment law. Insofar as international arbitration remains the preferred method for the settlement of foreign investment disputes, post-award proceedings commenced before domestic courts afford an important, though heretofore insufficiently explored, opportunity to enquire into actual general practice on CIL identification, attributable to State organs from different branches of government, participating in such proceedings in various capacities.

---

[1] ILC, 'Draft Conclusions on Identification of Customary International Law, with Commentaries' (30 April–1 June and 2 July–10 August 2018) UN Doc A/73/10, reproduced in [2018/II – Part Two] YBILC 122 (hereinafter 'Draft Conclusions on CIL Identification') 124 [4] (noting at the outset of that '[t]he draft conclusions reflect *the approach adopted* by *States*, as well as by international courts and organizations and most authors' (emphasis added)).

This chapter, based on a survey of selected State practice in connection with post-award proceedings, examines how the interplay between general international law and international investment law may have a bearing on the understanding of major general rules governing CIL identification. The body of practice on which the chapter focuses is not only confined to practice of judicial organs in the form of decisions by domestic courts hearing post-award proceedings, but also of executive organs, in the form of pleadings by States appearing in post-award proceedings. The aforementioned surveyed State practice is analysed through the prism of selected literature, decisions of international courts and tribunals, including those of the International Court of Justice (ICJ), and, in particular, to an extensive extent, the work of the International Law Commission (ILC) on CIL Identification,[2] including the reports of the ILC Special Rapporteur on this subject, notably as discussed by States.

The remainder of this chapter is divided into four parts. Part 2 examines the nature and significance of State practice in connection with proceedings before domestic courts, with a particular reference to post-award proceedings in the field of international investment law and arbitration. It discusses, in greater detail, various general issues concerning the primacy of State practice over decisions of international courts and tribunals, despite the latter's often prevailing role in analyses of CIL, and the various roles State practice may play, in the form of domestic court decisions or conduct in connection with domestic court proceedings. Part 3 proceeds in two sections. The first section provides an overview of uses of ICJ Statute Article 38(1) by investor-State arbitral tribunals and, more importantly, by States in connection with those proceedings. The second section analyses actual instances of State practice in connection with post-award proceedings. It shows how that practice may have an impact on the overarching question of whether secondary rules on CIL identification have a basis in actual State practice. This is also raised in the practice discussed in the first section. Part 4 concludes with some suggestions for further research.

2 State Practice in Connection with Proceedings Before Domestic Courts: Nature and Significance

This part examines the nature of State practice in the form of judicial decisions, addressing, among others, the questions of whether and to what extent a decision by a domestic court may be seen separately or

[2] ibid.

concurrently regarded as a constitutive element of custom, be it practice and/or acceptance as law, under ICJ Statute Article 38(1)(b), and/or as a subsidiary means, under ICJ Statute Article 38(1)(d),[3] respectively. This part further examines the nature of other State practice in connection with proceedings before domestic courts.

While, as mentioned in Part 1, decisions of international courts and tribunals tend to be the exclusive or, if not so, the preferable basis for CIL identification,[4] they may only constitute a subsidiary means for the determination of CIL rules, among other rules of international law.[5] By contrast, decisions of domestic courts may play a twofold role[6] in two spheres: internally, with respect to a custom and any resulting CIL rule(s), they may constitute general practice and/or acceptance as law in support thereof (as constitutive elements of that custom, both at its formative stage and, once in force, as requirements to identify any resulting CIL rule(s), under the 'two-element approach'); and externally, with respect to any existing CIL rule(s) to whose creation they did not contribute, they may constitute a subsidiary means for the determination of the existence, scope and/or content of any such other CIL rule(s).[7]

Hence, in contrast to decisions of domestic courts, which may play up to three roles (ranging from the formation of either constitutive element of

---

[3] ILC, 'Identification of Customary International Law: Statement of the Chairman of the Drafting Committee, Mr Mathias Forteau (Statement of the Chairman, 29 July 2015) 16–17 <https://legal.un.org/ilc/documentation/english/statements/2015_dc_chairman_statement_cil.pdf> accessed 15 January 2022 ('it is important to recognize the dual function played by decisions of national courts with regard to customary international law, that is, both as a form of State practice and/or evidence of *opinio juris* […] and as a subsidiary means for the determination of customary rules').

[4] This tendency is reflected in some of the concerns expressed by ILC members during the plenary sessions; ibid 15 ('during the debate in the Plenary, several members cautioned against elevating decisions of national courts, in terms of their value for identifying rules of customary international law, to the same level of those of international courts and tribunals, which in practice play a greater role in this context').

[5] M Wood, 'Third Report on Identification of Customary International Law' (27 March 2015) UN Doc A/CN.4/682, 41–2 [59].

[6] ibid 42 [58] (noting '[d]ecisions of national courts may play a dual role in relation to customary international law: not only as State practice, but also as a means for the determination of rules of customary international law').

[7] These three roles are specifically stated in this order by the ILC. Fourth report on identification of customary international law by M Wood, 'Fourth Report on Identification of Customary International Law' (8 March 2016) UN Doc A/CN.4/695, 3 [8] (referring to 'the Commission's treatment of national court decisions in the present topic as both a form of State practice or evidence of acceptance as law (*opinio juris*), and as a subsidiary means for determining the existence or content of customary international law').

custom, to the identification of ensuing CIL rules and to other determinations), decisions of international courts and tribunals may only play the role of serving as a subsidiary means for the determination of CIL,[8] let alone their role, if any, as 'material source' for certain CIL rules, with whose creation they may be deemed to be so associated. And, even in their capacity as subsidiary means, there are limitations to the weight decisions of international courts and tribunals can have with respect to CIL determinations. The United States of America, for instance, points out in a commentary on the ILC's work on CIL Identification, that '[e]ven the International Court of Justice does not offer interpretations of customary international law that are binding on all States'.[9] Furthermore, the United States observes, 'a tribunal might accept without analysis that a rule is customary based on nothing more than the absence of a dispute between the parties'.[10] And, relatedly, the United States points to the fact that State practice in connection with proceedings before international courts and tribunals – as might also happen before domestic courts, may have to be weighed in view of 'the context of litigation, [in which] States may choose to assert or decline to contest that rules are customary in nature for reasons of litigation strategy rather than out of a thorough assessment that such rules are customary in nature'.[11] In sum, this comparatively limited role of decisions of international courts and tribunals renders more incomprehensible the tendency to overlook decisions of domestic courts.

Decisions of courts of States, often interchangeably referred to as 'domestic', 'internal' or 'national', and the questions of whether and in what forms they constitute State practice for the purposes of custom formation, its evidence, and, latterly, the identification of resulting CIL rules, have given rise to various questions, addressed by States themselves,[12] international courts and tribunals, and the ILC.

---

[8] This role may comprise instances where a State relies on a decision of an international court or tribunal in support of its own identification of practice in support of a given rule. This is illustrated by Belgium's reference to a decision of the ICTY referring for CIL identification purposes to a statute which it regards as showing that legislative practice is a form of state practice, under ICJ Statute Article 38(1)(b). Belgium, 'Observations de la Belgique sur le sujet "formation et détermination du droit international coutumier"' (66th United Nations General Assembly, 6th Commission, 2014) 1–2 [4] <https://legal.un.org/ilc/sessions/66/pdfs/french/icil_belgium.pdf> accessed 11 February 2022.

[9] USA, 'Comments from the United States on the International Law Commission's Draft Conclusions on the Identification of Customary International Law as adopted by the Commission in 2016 on First Reading' (70th United Nations General Assembly, 6th Commission, 2018) 18 <https://legal.un.org/ilc/sessions/70/pdfs/english/icil_usa.pdf> accessed 11 February 2022.

[10] ibid.

[11] ibid.

[12] Belgium (n 8) 1 [2].

Furthermore, decisions of domestic courts have been widely recognised as a form of State practice, as evidenced in decisions of both national and international courts and tribunals alike.[13] To the extent that decisions, like other similar forms of conduct, are verbal in nature, the question of their character as a form of State practice overlaps with the debate over whether practice can only consist in 'physical' acts or may also comprise 'verbal acts'. While a detailed discussion of this problem exceeds the scope of this part, it suffices to observe that the ILC has concluded that there is sufficient support in State practice and decisions of international courts and tribunals to hold that verbal acts may constitute State practice. This proposition has found support among States, as evidenced in their comments, and elicited the interest of some of them. Israel, for instance, agrees with the inclusion of verbal acts as State practice, with some *caveats*,[14] and suggests that it be defined as 'verbal conduct (whether written or oral) [...] when such conduct itself is regulated by the alleged customary rule'.[15]

Having observed this, the key factor for a domestic judicial decision to constitute an instance of state practice of a given State is that that decision emanate from a (judicial) organ of that State. Hence, attributability, as opposed to other properties of decisions often discussed, such as quality of reasoning or finality,[16] is essential. Some States have argued in favour of a more stringent criterion, requiring not only attributability to any judicial organ, but a certain (high) position in a given State's judicial hierarchy. Israel, for instance, considers that 'only high courts' final and

---

[13] *Prosecutor v Ayyash et al* (Interlocutory Decision on the Applicable Law: Terrorism, Conspiracy, Homicide, Perpetration, Cumulative Charging) STL-11-01/I/AC/R176bis (16 February 2011) [102–4] ('the behaviour of States [...] decisions by national courts'); *Natoniewski v Federal Republic of Germany* (29 October 2010) Poland Supreme Court, Ref No CSK 465/09, reproduced in (2010) 30 Polish YB Intl Law 299, 299–303 ('relevant legal materials [...] include [...] decisions of national courts'). These decisions are discussed in M Wood, 'First Report on Formation and Evidence of Customary International Law' (17 May 2013) UN Doc A/CN.4/L.663, 133 [75] & 136 [85].

[14] Israel, 'ILC Draft Conclusions on Identification of Customary International Law – Israel's Comments and Observations' (70th United Nations General Assembly, 6th Commission, 2018) 14 [34] <https://legal.un.org/ilc/sessions/70/pdfs/english/icil_israel.pdf> accessed 11 February 2022 (ie, 'only what states "do" rather than what they "say" matters most'.)

[15] ibid (original emphasis omitted).

[16] That finality is not an essential element is reflected in the very definition of the term 'decisions of national courts', as understood by the ILC's Drafting Committee. See ILC, 'Statement of the Chairman of the Drafting Committee, Mr. Gilberto Saboia' (Statement of Chairman, 7 August 2014) 13 <https://legal.un.org/ilc/sessions/66/pdfs/english/dc_chairman_statement_identification_of_custom.pdf> accessed 15 January 2022 ('[t]he words 'decisions of national courts' are to be understood broadly, as covering not only final judgments of courts, but also relevant interlocutory decisions'). The absence of a finality

definitive decisions (ie, that cannot be further appealed) should be taken into account'.[17] Nevertheless, this proposed criterion may be an overstatement, if it concerns the necessary conditions for a decision to constitute State practice, and may be best portrayed as a criterion for attributing weight to the respective decision, without denying its character as a form of State practice, provided that it be attributable and remain in force (ie, if not final, at least not reversed on appeal or cassation).[18] In sum, as the ILC concludes, '[d]ecisions of national courts at all levels may count as State practice', without prejudice, as discussed above, to recalling that 'it is likely that greater weight will be given to the higher courts'.[19]

Other factors which may be of relevance include the nature[20] and subject-matter of the alleged CIL rule at issue.[21] For example, Israel has suggested that 'decisions of higher national courts [...] would only

---

requirement has prompted some disagreement on the part of states, as exemplified by Israel's proposition that 'acts (laws, judgments etc.) must be final and conclusive in order to qualify as evidence of CIL'. Israel (n 14) 6 [20] (adding 'definitive'; original emphasis omitted).

[17] Israel (n 14) 7 [23] (original emphasis omitted.)

[18] New Zealand, 'Draft Conclusions on the Identification of Customary International Law adopted by the International Law Commission (A/71/10 at Chapter 5): Comments by the Government of New Zealand' (70th United Nations General Assembly, 6th Commission, 2018) 5 [18] <https://legal.un.org/ilc/sessions/70/pdfs/english/icil_new_zealand.pdf> accessed 11 February 2022 ('it is very difficult to imagine a situation in which a decision that has been overruled by a higher court could still be relied upon as State practice in this context'). Israel appears to take a strict approach in this regard across various issues, which may explain why it would not be inclined to entertain the idea of factoring in an organ's judicial hierarchy into the decision's weight rather than denying its character as state practice altogether (thus not giving effect to its attributability). Israel, for instance, opposes draft conclusion 3's statement that 'statements made casually [...] carry less weight', since, in its view, it 'does not fully consider the issue of proper authorization of State officials'. Israel (n 14) 8 [25] (original emphasis omitted.) Special Rapporteur Wood, in his suggestions in response to comments by states, aptly notes that 'decisions of higher courts should in general be accorded greater weight; and where a lower court decision has been overruled by a higher court on the relevant point, the evidentiary value of the former is likely to be nullified', ILC, 'Identification of Customary International Law: Comments and Observations Received From Governments' (14 February 2018) UN Doc A/CN.4/716, 26 [56]; A decision must also not 'remain unenforced', see Draft Conclusions on CIL Identification (n 1) 128 [5].

[19] Draft Conclusions on CIL Identification (n 1) 134 [6].

[20] The nature of the alleged CIL rule was exemplified in the ILC's discussion by 'prohibitive rules'. It may be argued that the character of as a rule as a primary or secondary rule is another aspect of its nature that might be equally taken into account. Draft Conclusions on CIL Identification (n 1) 128 [4] (noting that 'where prohibitive rules are concerned, it may sometimes be difficult to find much affirmative State practice').

[21] ibid 127 [3] (on 'the need to apply the two-element approach while taking into account the subject matter that the alleged rule is said to regulate').

constitute practice or *opinio juris* in and of themselves when the issue in question concerns the conduct or view of judicial bodies (such as the dismissal of a lawsuit by reason of immunity)'.[22] Israel's suggested criterion of a concordance between a State organ's scope of competence, in this case a judicial one, and the purported CIL rule's subject-matter, appears reasonable. In particular, this criterion lends further support to the suitability of decisions of national courts as practice in support of secondary rules of CIL. In fact, secondary rules, such as those on immunity, tend to fall within the purview of judicial organs, thus paving the way for relying on their decisions in order to establish State practice in support of secondary rules on CIL identification.

Decisions of domestic courts may constitute a form of acceptance as law, as well, as seen in decisions of international and national courts and tribunals alike.[23] In its aforementioned work, the ILC had relied on domestic court decisions to establish the existence of acceptance as law.[24] Furthermore, not only may decisions of domestic courts constitute a form of evidence of acceptance as law in themselves, but they may also contain other separate forms of such evidence, such as 'public statements made on behalf of States'.[25]

The assessment of whether and to what extent domestic court's decisions express (or evidence, as the case may be) the acceptance as law on the part of the respective State raises important and, to a certain extent, unresolved, issues. Latterly, among other criteria, ILC Special Rapporteur Wood calls for a cautious analysis as to whether, in the words of Moremen, whom he cites approvingly, acceptance as law presumably

---

[22] ibid (original emphasis omitted).
[23] *Jurisdictional Immunities of the State (Germany v Italy: Greece intervening)* (Judgment) [2012] ICJ Rep 99, 135 [77] (relying on 'the positions taken by States and the jurisprudence of a number of national courts which have made clear that they considered that customary international law required immunity'); *Prosecutor v Ayyash et al* (Interlocutory Decision on the Applicable Law: Terrorism, Conspiracy, Homicide, Perpetration, Cumulative Charging) [100]. These decisions are discussed in M Wood, 'Second Report on Identification of Customary International Law' (22 May 2014) UN Doc A/CN.4/L.672 (hereinafter 'Second Report'), 61 [76(b)].
[24] ILC, 'Formation and Evidence of Customary International Law: Elements in the Previous Work of the International Law Commission that Could be Particularly Relevant to the Topic' (Memorandum by the Secretariat, 14 March 2013) UN Doc A/CN.4/659, 155 [29] (noting that '[t]he Commission has relied upon a variety of materials in assessing the subjective element for the purpose of identifying a rule of customary international law', and referring to, among others, 'pronouncements by municipal courts').
[25] Draft Conclusions on CIL Identification (n 1) 141 [5] ('[d]ecisions of national courts may also contain such statements when pronouncing upon questions of international law').

expressed in a given domestic court's decision 'derives from international law, from domestic law, or from domestic auto-interpretation of international law'.[26]

The conduct of States in connection with proceedings commenced before domestic courts is also a form State practice, along other forms of 'executive' State practice, so-called since it emanates from organs belonging to the executive branch of a government, as opposed to its 'legislative' or 'judicial' branches (following Montesquieu's tripartite model of governmental functions). The attributability of a conduct to a State organ, as opposed to that conduct's connection with the proceedings, remains the key to the characterisation of that conduct as a form of State practice. This implies, among others, that conduct not attributable to a State, even if it is performed in connection with proceedings before domestic courts, and has an actual bearing on the questions of international law raised in those proceedings, does not constitute a form of State practice. As Special Rapporteur Wood aptly observes,

> while individuals and non-governmental organizations can indeed 'play important roles in the promotion of international law and in its observance' (for example, by encouraging State practice by bringing international law claims in national courts or by being relevant when assessing such practice), their actions are not 'practice' for purposes of the formation or evidencing of customary international law.[27]

This statement by the Special Rapporteur finds support among States commenting upon his work, as exemplified by Singapore's comments to similar effects.[28] Singapore expressly confines 'practice that contributes to the formation, or expression of rules of customary international law' to that of States, to the explicit exclusion of that of 'non-State actors'.[29]

---

[26] M Wood, 'Second Report' (n 23) 61 [76(b)], quoting PM Moremen, 'National Court Decisions as State Practice: A Transnational Judicial Dialogue?' (2006) 32 NCJInt'l L& ComReg 259, 274.

[27] ibid 32–3 [45].

[28] Singapore, 'Response of the Republic of Singapore to the International Law Commission's Request for Comments and Observations on the Draft Conclusions on Identification of Customary International Law' (70th United Nations General Assembly, 6th Commission, 2018) 2 [5] <https://legal.un.org/ilc/sessions/70/pdfs/english/icil_singapore.pdf> accessed 11 February 2022 (noting her agreement with the general proposition 'that the conduct of non-State actors, such as non-governmental organisations, transnational corporation and private individuals, is not practice that contributes to the formation, or expression of rules of customary international law).

[29] ibid 2 [5] (noting conduct of 'non-State actors' may not deemed such practice).

3 State Practice in Connection with Investor-State Dispute Settlement Proceedings and CIL Identification: The Interaction between Award and Post-Award Practice

This part provides a survey of practice of identification of CIL in connection with investor-State dispute settlement proceedings (ISDS) under a number of international investment agreements (IIAs). The practice surveyed not only studies that of ISDS arbitral tribunals, in the form of their decisions at various stages of the proceedings and, where applicable, of post-award proceedings before international law organs, such as International Centre for Settlement of Investment Disputes (ICSID) annulment committees, but also examines the practice of States in connection with those proceedings. The latter body of practice comprises not only submissions which are widely regarded as forms of State practice in connection with ISDS proceedings, epitomised by submissions pursuant Article 1128 of the North American Free Trade Agreement (NAFTA), but also practice of State pleadings before domestic courts, in post-award proceedings, where applicable. This part proceeds in two sections.

3.1 State Practice in Connection with CIL Identification in Investor–State Dispute Settlement Proceedings

This section examines the practice of ISDS arbitral tribunals and ICSID annulment committees, on one hand, and that of States, most prominently in the form of NAFTA Article 1128 submissions and submissions of a similar nature under other IIAs, on the other hand. A key criterion for the identification of this practice has been the reliance, whether explicit or implicit, on ICJ Statute Article 38(1), including its subparagraph (b), concerning CIL identification.

There is a set of instances of State practice questioning the widespread tendency towards CIL identification merely based on the findings of international courts and tribunals. Notably, these various instances of State practice place emphasis on the role of the two-element approach as a criterion for determining whether and to what extent CIL identification on the basis of decisions of international courts and tribunals is permissible. In her application for annulment of the award in *CMS Gas Transmission Company v The Argentine Republic*, Argentina invoked ICJ Statute Article 38(1)(d) to argue that 'even if the cited references were correct and sufficiently supported, that would not cure the Tribunal's failure to express its reasoning, since the authorities and the case law are secondary sources of international law'.³⁰ In its NAFTA Article 1128 submission in *Eli Lilly and Company v Government of Canada*, Canada specifically stated that 'the NAFTA Parties have repeatedly asserted their agreement that the decisions of international investment tribunals are not a source of State practice or *opinio juris* for the purpose of establishing a new customary norm'.³¹ As Canada noted more specifically in *Bear Creek Mining Corporation v Republic of Peru*,

> [t]he decisions and awards of international courts and tribunals do not constitute instances of State practice for the purpose of proving the existence of a customary norm and are only relevant to the extent that they include an examination of State practice and *opinio juris*.³²

El Salvador, in its non-disputing party submission in *Spence International Investments et al v The Republic of Costa Rica*, having recalled the Dominican Republic-Central America Free Trade Agreement (CAFTA-DR) parties' reliance on the two-element approach to CIL identification, further observed that, 'while decisions of arbitral tribunals that discuss State practice might be useful as evidence of the State practice they discuss, arbitral decisions can never substitute for State practice as the *source* of customary international law', adding that CIL identification claims so substantiated are even more tenuous where those decisions 'themselves contain no analysis of State practice or *opinio juris*'.³³ Indeed, as Canada observed in a response to NAFTA Article 1128 submissions in *Mesa Power Group LLC v Government of Canada*, 'the awards of investment tribunals do not qualify as state practice for the purposes of proving the existence of a rule of customary international law'.³⁴ In its observations regarding the Award on Jurisdiction and Merits issued by the *Bilcon of Delaware v Canada* Tribunal, Canada challenged that Tribunal's assessment of CIL in connection with its interpretation of NAFTA Article 1105 on grounds that, as 'all three NAFTA parties have consistently agreed, decisions of arbitral tribunals can describe

---

³⁰ *CMS v Argentina* (Application for Annulment and Request for Stay of Enforcement of Arbitral Award of 8 September 2005) ICSID Case No ARB/01/8 [62] fn 48.
³¹ *Eli Lilly and Company v Canada* (Observations on Issues Raised in 1128 Submissions of the United States and Mexico of 22 April 2016) Case No UNCT/14/2 [24].
³² *Bear Creek Mining Corporation v Peru* (Submission of Canada pursuant to Article 832 of the Canada-Peru Free Trade Agreement of 9 June 2016) ICSID Case No ARB/14/21 [10].
³³ *Spence International Investments, et al v Costa Rica* (Non-Disputing Party Submission of The Republic of El Salvador of 17 April 2015) ICSID Secretariat File No UNCT/13/2 [6].
³⁴ *Mesa Power Group LLC v Canada* (Response to 1128 Submissions of 26 June 2015) PCA Case No 2012–17 [2(ii)].

and examine customary international law, but they are not themselves a source of customary international law'. More specifically, and like El Salvador, Canada argued that '[t]he decisions upon which the *Bilcon* majority relied, and in particular, the decision of the Tribunal in *Merrill and Ring v Canada*, do not conduct the required analysis of customary international law'.[35] Conducting a similar analysis of the soundness of an arbitral tribunal's identification of CIL, the United States argued in *ADF Group Inc v United States of America* that

> [c]ontrary to the *Pope* tribunal's suggestion that the sheer number of BITs could evidence the existence of a rule of customary international law, all three NAFTA Parties agree that State practice alone – without a showing of *opinio juris* – cannot give rise to a rule of customary international law'.[36]

In particular, the United States rejected the above mono-elemental approach, which satisfies itself with the proposition that the growing set of BITs amounts to CIL on foreign investment, as it specifically argued that, '[b]ecause the *Pope* tribunal made no effort to determine the existence of *opinio juris*, its reasoning as to the BITs and customary international law is faulty'.[37] This echoes Canada's proposition to a similar effect.[38] Furthermore, this is consistent with the United States' emphasis on the need for establishing 'the twin requirements of State practice and *opinio juris*', as discussed in the ILC's Second Report on CIL Identification.[39] The aforementioned denials of, or qualifications of the limited relevance of, CIL identification solely based on decisions of international courts and tribunals is not without prejudice to their role in aid of treaty interpretation. In this vein, the Tribunals in *Sempra Energy International v The Argentine Republic* and *Camuzzi International SA v The Argentine Republic* noted that arbitral tribunals partake in treaty interpretation, which 'is not the exclusive task of States', contrary to what Argentina had argued, since interpretation 'is precisely the role of judicial decisions as a source of

---

[35] *Mesa Power Group LLC v Canada* (Observations on the Award on Jurisdiction and Merits in *William Ralph Clayton, William Richard Clayton, Douglas Clayton, Daniel Clayton and Bilcon of Delaware, Inc v Canada* of 14 May 2015) PCA Case No 2012–17 [17].

[36] *ADF Group Inc v USA* (Final Post-Hearing Submission of Respondent United States of America on Article 1105(1) and *Pope & Talbot* of 1 August 2002) Case No ARB(AF)/00/1, 4.

[37] ibid.

[38] *Loewen Group, Inc and Raymond L Loewen v USA* (Second Submission of the Government of Canada Pursuant to NAFTA Article 1128 of 27 June 2002) ICSID Case No ARB(AF)/98/3 [11], discussed below.

[39] *Mercer International Inc v Canada* (Submission of the United States of America of 8 May 2015) ICSID Case No ARB(AF)/12/3 [19].

international law in Article 38(1) of the Statute of the International Court of Justice, to which the Respondent refers'.[40]

There are other instances of State practice which focus on the very question of the legal basis and content and scope of the two element approach to CIL identification as such. The following instances are notable for their implicit and explicit reliance on ICJ Statute Article 38(1), particularly its subparagraph (b).

Some instances of State practice rely on ICJ Statute Article 38(1)(b) implicitly. In a submission pursuant to Article 10.20.2 of the CAFTA-DR in *Michael Ballantine and Lisa Ballantine v The Dominican Republic*, the United States noted that 'Annex 10-B to the CAFTA-DR addresses the methodology for interpreting customary international law rules covered by the agreement', and added that '[t]his two-element approach – State practice and *opinio juris* – is "widely endorsed in the literature" and "generally adopted in the practice of States and the decisions of international courts and tribunals, including the International Court of Justice".[41]

Other instances of State practice explicitly invoke ICJ Statute Article 38(1)(b). In *Lone Pine Resources Inc v Government of Canada*, Canada, referring to the NAFTA parties' respective NAFTA Article 1128 submissions, specifically indicated that the NAFTA parties' understanding as to the applicability of the two-element approach, including as to the burden of proving each constitutive element, 'finds its source in Article 38 of the Statute of the International Court of Justice'.[42] Similarly, and more specifically, Canada argued in *Eli Lilly and Company v Government of Canada* that, '[p]ursuant to Article 38(1)(b) of the Statute of the International Court of Justice, customary international law has two constitutive elements: (1) extensive, uniform and consistent general practice by States; and (2) belief that such practice is required by law (*opinio juris*)'.[43] In its NAFTA Article 1128 submission in *Loewen Group, Inc and Raymond L. Loewen v*

---

[40] *Sempra Energy v Argentina* (Decision on Objections to Jurisdiction of 11 May 2005) ICSID Case No ARB/02/16 [147]; *Camuzzi International SA v Argentina* (Decision on Objections to Jurisdiction of 11 May 2005) ICSID Case No ARB/03/2 [135] (notably where 'tribunals [are] called to settle a dispute, particularly when the question is to interpret the meaning of the terms used in a treaty').

[41] *Michael Ballantine and Lisa Ballantine v Dominican Republic* (Submission of the United States of America of 22 September 2017) PCA Case No 2016–17 [19].

[42] *Lone Pine Resources Inc v Canada* (Observations of the Government of Canada on the Issues Raised in the Memorials Submitted by the United States of America and Mexico by Virtue of NAFTA Article 1128 of 22 September 2017) Case No UNCT/15/2 [8].

[43] *Eli Lilly and Company v Canada* (Post-Hearing Submission of 25 July 2016) Case No UNCT/14/2 [46].

The United States of America, Mexico, quoting ICJ Statute Article 38(1)(b), started its analysis of CIL identification by stating that 'Article 38 of the Statute of the International Court of Justice describes customary international law'.[44] More specifically, Canada submitted, 'Article 38(1)(b) of the ICJ Statute identifies the two essential elements of custom: practice and *opinio juris*'.[45] Indeed, Canada argued, 'the provisions at issue in this case contained in the more than 1800 BITs and in the ICSID Convention in existence have not been transformed into rules of customary international law consistent with Article 38(1)(b) of the ICJ Statute'.[46]

The question of the significance of a proper determination of the relevant source of law, particularly where CIL rules are arguably involved, has also been addressed in the surveyed practice. The Annulment Committee in *Venezuela Holdings, BV, and others v The Bolivarian Republic of Venezuela* found that the BIT at issue, which contained an 'explicit reference ... to 'the general principles of international law' ... is presumably to be understood as pointing in turn to one of the sources of law enumerated in Article 38(1) of the Statute of the International Court of Justice'. In that Annulment Committee's view, '[i]t is the Tribunal which makes its own addition to the Treaty list by adding in a mention of customary international law'.[47] For this Annulment Committee,

> the Tribunal gives no indication of where it derives the authority to make what looks like a modification – or indeed an expansion – of the source rules laid down in the Article, nor does the Tribunal state what criterion it has in mind to use in order to decide (when the case arises) whether or not to 'include customary international law'.[48]

Such an 'expansion', this Annulment Committee observed, can be evidenced by the fact that '[i]n Article 38(1) of the ICJ Statute, the sub-paragraph referring to "international custom" stands separate and distinct from the sub-paragraph referring to "general principles".[49] Based on the above considerations, this Annulment Committee found that

---

[44] *Loewen Group, Inc and Raymond L Loewen v USA* (Second Submission of the United Mexican States of 9 November 2001) ICSID Case No ARB(AF)/98/3, 2.
[45] *Loewen Group, Inc and Raymond L Loewen v USA* (Second Submission of the Government of Canada pursuant to NAFTA Article 1128 of 27 June 2002) (n 38) [12].
[46] ibid [11].
[47] *Venezuela Holdings v Venezuela* (Decision on Annulment of 9 March 2017) ICSID Case No ARB/07/27 [159] (adding 'the exclusive sources of law for the determination of the dispute brought to arbitration are those listed *in extenso* in Article 9(5) of the BIT').
[48] ibid.
[49] ibid [159] fn 180.

[t]he Tribunal manifestly exceeded its powers to the extent that it held that general international law, and specifically customary international law, regulated the determination and assessment of the compensation due to the Mobil Parties for the expropriation of their investment in the Cerro Negro Project, in place of the application of the provisions of the BIT.[50]

Indeed, this Annulment Committee emphasised that the aforementioned shortcomings were 'so seriously deficient both in their reasoning and in the choice and application of the appropriate sources of law under the governing Bilateral Investment Treaty as to give rise to grounds for annulment under Article 52(1) of the ICSID Convention'.[51] In particular, this Annulment Committee concluded, 'the "manifest" nature of this failure is shown by the inadequacies in the Tribunal's reasoning for the choice of applicable law, in both its positive (the law chosen) and negative (the law rejected) aspects'.[52] The aforementioned conclusions led to this Annulment Committee's decision to partly uphold 'the request for the annulment of the portion of the Award dealing with compensation for the expropriation of the Cerro Negro Project'.[53] This Annulment Committee's reasoning is notable not only for its materiality to the decision, but also for its reliance on the categories set out in ICJ Statute Article 38(1), and, in particular, the significance of specifically basing findings on custom as a source of law separate from general principles of law, even though CIL typically contains general principles.

The significance of not only finding State practice of reliance on ICJ Statute Article 38(1)(b), but also of establishing this practice is not engaged in by virtue of a conventional legal obligation under the ICJ Statute, is exemplified by the United States challenge of reliance on the ICJ Statute qua treaty. The United States, in *ADF Group Inc v United States of America*, stated that 'there is no basis in international law for the *Pope* tribunal's analysis of the phrase "international law" in Article 1105(1) based solely on the reference to that term in the Statute of the International Court of Justice, a treaty not related to the NAFTA'. In this vein, the United States submitted, 'context includes the text of the treaty and certain related instruments, but does not include unrelated treaties'.[54] Indeed, the United States argued, '[c]ontrary to the *Pope* tribunal's approach, Article 38 does

---

[50] ibid [188(a)].
[51] ibid [189].
[52] ibid.
[53] ibid [196(3)].
[54] *ADF Group Inc v USA* (Post-Hearing Submission of Respondent United States of America on Article 1105(1) and *Pope & Talbot* of 27 June 2002) Case No ARB(AF)/00/1, 13, fn 31.

not purport to define the term 'international law' in any event'.[55] While the United States focused on its understanding of the purpose of ICJ Statute Article 38(1), and did not place emphasis on the absence of an obligation to apply it *qua* treaty to CIL identification in connection with proceedings under NAFTA, the observation that the ICJ Statute is 'unrelated' to the NAFTA does raise the question of the legal basis for applying ICJ Statute Article 38(1) outside ICJ proceedings, an issue to which the following section turns.

3.2 State Practice in Connection with Post-Award Proceedings

This section provides an overview of selected features of the surveyed State practice. It shows how domestic courts and States that are parties to post-award proceedings before those courts approach CIL identification, relying on ICJ Statute Article 38(1)(b). As mentioned in the conclusion to the previous section, there is a genuine need for identifying the legal basis for applying ICJ Statute Article 38(1)(b) outside ICJ proceedings, including, if any, *qua* a statement reflecting any CIL rules on CIL identification.

The instances discussed in greater detail below happen to particularly relate to Argentina's challenge of ISDS arbitral decisions before Belgian and German courts, and form the focus of this section. They add to domestic decisions adopted in various jurisdictions in connection with ISDS proceedings and, broadly, other international arbitrations involving States as respondents. Without entering into a fuller survey and discussion of such decisions, two cases are worthy of mention.

In *Swissbourgh Diamond Mines (Pty) Limited & 8 ors v Kingdom of Lesotho*, the Supreme Court of Singapore's Court of Appeal made a number of observations concerning the nature of ISDS proceedings and the interplay of treaty and custom within international investment law's hybrid framework. This judgment decided an appeal against a decision adjudicating on a setting aside application challenging an award made by an *ad hoc* international arbitration tribunal constituted under the auspices of the Permanent Court of Arbitration and seated in Singapore pursuant to Art 28 of Annex 1 to the Protocol on Finance and Investment of the Southern African Development Community.[56] The Court of Appeal

---

[55] ibid.
[56] *Swissbourgh Diamond Mines (Pty) Limited & ors v Kingdom of Lesotho* (27 November 2018) Court of Appeal of the Supreme Court of Singapore, Civil Appeal No 149 of 2017 [2018] SGCA 81 [2].

made a number of relevant, general, propositions, namely, that '[i]nternational investment law is a hybrid legal construct uniquely placed at the crossroads of domestic and international law and of private and public law', and that '[t]he dispute resolution mechanisms and substantive rules of investment protection provided for in the growing body of investment treaties enable such investors to bring proceedings against host States for alleged breaches of investment treaty obligations'.[57] Furthermore, and with particular reference to CIL's place in ISDS proceedings, the Court of Appeal observed that

> [w]hile these treaties are unusual in the sense that States party to them undertake obligations that may be enforced by private individuals, this is generally subject to the qualification that an investor would not be permitted to bring a claim against the State unless certain jurisdictional requirements provided for either under the treaty or as a matter of customary international law are first satisfied.[58]

In *Democratic Republic of the Congo and others v FG Hemisphere Associates LLC*, the Court of Final Appeal of the Hong Kong Special Administrative Region considered the customary status of rules on absolute or restrictive immunity.[59] While the Court of Final Appeal found that '[w]hether the state immunity available in the courts of Hong Kong is absolute or restrictive is a question of common law', and that '[t]he correct answer does not depend on it being a rule of customary international law',[60] it made a number of findings concerning the nature of CIL. Paramount among those findings are the Court of Final Appeal's propositions that 'there may well be areas in which ... international custom proves more important than treaties',[61] and, crucially for this chapter's purposes, that 'a rule of domestic law in any given jurisdiction may happen to result from a rule of customary international law or it may happen to precede and contribute to the crystallisation of a custom into a rule of customary international law'.[62]

Turning to the cases in post-award ISDS proceedings initiated by Argentina before Belgian and German courts, a more in depth analysis

---

[57] ibid [1].
[58] ibid.
[59] *Democratic Republic of the Congo and ors v FG Hemisphere Associates LLC* (8 June 2011) Court of Final Appeal of the Hong Kong Special Administrative Region, FACV Nos 5, 6 & 7 of 2010.
[60] ibid [68].
[61] ibid [119].
[62] ibid [68].

is warranted, particularly of Argentina's arguments before the Belgian Court of Cassation.

In *K v The Argentine Republic*, the Third Chamber of Germany's Federal Constitutional Court's Second Senate adjudicated on two constitutional complaints initiated by the Republic of Argentina.[63] The Chamber made a number of observations concerning the nature of CIL, which are worthy of analysis. Among others, the Chamber observed, '[g]eneral rules of international law are rules of universally applicable customary international law, supplemented by the traditional general legal principles of national legal orders', and, crucially, that '[w]hether a rule is one of customary international law, or whether it is a general legal principle, emerges from international law itself, which provides the criteria for the sources of international law'.[64] The latter proposition is notable for aptly emphasising the role of international law as legal regulation of the conditions for existence of a source of law, including as to CIL-identification.

Furthermore, the Chamber applied the two-element approach to its analysis of the customary status of the rules on state of necessity. Indeed, having stated that the '[i]nvocation of state necessity is recognised in customary international law in those legal relationships which are exclusively subject to international law', the Chamber, however, found 'there is no evidence for a state practice based on the necessary legal conviction (*opinio juris sive necessitatis*) to extend the legal justification for the invocation of state necessity to relationships under private law involving private creditors'.[65]

The Chamber, more specifically, went on to address each of the elements of custom, making a number of relevant general propositions in its process of CIL-ascertainment.

As for State practice, the Chamber observed, '[a] general legal principle cannot be verified absent a corresponding embodiment in actual legal practice'.[66] This general observation was preceded by the Chamber's discussion of the value of international decisions.

The Chamber noted that '[t]he practice of international courts does not constitute an adequate basis for the recognition of an objection of state necessity towards private individuals'.[67] The Chamber made this

---

[63] *K v Argentina* (8 May 2007) German Federal Constitutional Court, Order of the Second Senate, 2 BvM 1/03 [1–95].
[64] ibid [31].
[65] ibid [33].
[66] ibid [63].
[67] ibid [49].

observation having acknowledged that 'the rulings of international tribunals have always been used as indicators of the existence of customary international law',[68] and, more specifically,

> [t]he rulings of international courts are, as a rule, major indications that certain rules of international law are anchored in customary law because – frequently in contrast to rulings of national courts – they deal with the qualification and application of specific norms under international law.[69]

The Chamber's use of the words 'indications' and 'indicators' correctly characterises the role of international decisions in CIL-identification, importantly avoiding a conflation between law-making and law-ascertaining roles, insofar as international courts and tribunals are concerned. The Chamber added that

> [w]hilst courts such as the International Court of Justice or the International Tribunal for the Law of the Sea are, as a rule, restricted by their charters to settling those international-law matters which relate to relations between two or more states or other subjects of international law, international tribunals may also deal with cases which relate to economic disputes between states and private individuals.[70]

The Chamber further specified the conditions under which international decisions may be considered appropriate *'indicia'*. Indeed, the Chamber observed, 'disputes, [in which] the ruling was consequently based on the international-law relationship between two states' lead to international decisions which are unsuitable as *indicia* of State practice, since such 'purely international proceedings cannot be used as *indicia* in the assessment of state practice concerning the direct defence of state necessity vis-à-vis private persons for the direct disputes in front of national courts that are customary today'.[71] Crucially for the Chamber's final finding, it observed that ICSID decisions, despite involving 'claimants ... [which] were legal entities subject to private law ... [n]onetheless, ... do not provide any indications of the transferability of a plea of state necessity to private-law relations'.[72] The Chamber emphasised that this distinction followed, among others, from the legal position of investors under international investment agreements, which the Chamber characterised as comprising 'an obligation ...

[68] ibid.
[69] ibid.
[70] ibid.
[71] ibid [59].
[72] ibid [50].

which is owed not directly to the private applicant, but to his or her home state, although the protective purpose of the agreement targets the interests of private investors'.[73]

Having delimited the proper place of international decisions in CIL-identification, the Chamber did conduct '[a]n inspection of national case-law on the question of state necessity [which] also fails for lack of agreement to suggest that the recognition of state necessity impacting on private-law relationships is established in customary law'.[74] The Chamber also considered scholarship on the question of relevant State practice, concluding that, although

> scholarly literature takes the view, in agreement with international and national case-law, that necessity is recognised by customary law ... [t]he relevant literature also distinguishes, however, between recognition in relations between states on the one hand and recognition as a legal justification in relations with private individuals on the other.[75]

In sum, 'as the evaluation of state practice undertaken to verify customary law has revealed',[76] the Chamber concluded, 'there is no rule under international customary law which recognises the transferability of the defence of necessity from relationships under international law to relationships under private law'.[77]

As for acceptance as law, the Chamber noted that, while

> [t]he ILC Articles on State Responsibility [(ASR)] ... [which] also [cover] state necessity under international law ... [were] accepted by the United Nations General Assembly on 12 December 2001 [t]his, however, leads neither *eo ipso* to customary-law application, nor to legally binding application for another reason, but may serve as an indication of a legal conviction as is necessary to form customary law.[78]

This observation, although not preventing the Chamber from otherwise recognising the character of the ASR as codificatory of customary international law,[79] is notable for confining the role of UN General Assembly resolutions to the role of evidence, and not in themselves constitutive, of *opinio juris*.

---

[73] ibid [51].
[74] ibid [61].
[75] ibid [62].
[76] ibid [63].
[77] ibid [64].
[78] ibid [33].
[79] ibid.

In *Argentine Republic v NMC Capital*, Argentina appeared before the Court of Cassation of Belgium.[80] Argentina claimed that the decision it impugned had violated the customary rule of *ne impediatur legatio*. In particular, Argentina argued, the impugned decision had breached the 'rule of customary international law binding at the very least on the Argentine Republic and the Kingdom of Belgium by virtue of which the immunity from execution of which diplomatic missions of a foreign State benefit must be the object of a specific waiver'.[81] By failing to acknowledge the 'autonomous character of the immunity from execution of bank accounts of foreign diplomatic missions', Argentina concluded, the impugned decision had breached various treaty provisions including, specifically, ICJ Statute Article 38(1)(b).[82]

Argentina elaborated on her view that ICJ Statute Article 38(1)(b) had been specifically breached. In order to make better sense of this part of Argentina's argument, it is worth bearing in mind the distinction between primary and secondary rules.

First, Argentina had maintained that

> the immunity from execution of which the bank accounts of a diplomatic mission benefit results from the international customary rule *ne impediatur legatio* which seeks to guarantee the efficient accomplishment of the functions of diplomatic missions, independently of the general immunity from execution of which foreign States benefit.[83]

Secondly, Argentina argued, 'the binding force of this international custom as source of international law is consecrated by article 38, § 1st, b), of the Statute of the International Court of Justice, annexed to the Charter of the United Nations of 26 June 1945'.[84] For Argentina, the violation of ICJ Statute Article 38(1)(b), resulted, more specifically, from the fact that 'the judgement decides that there does not exist international custom by virtue of which the immunity of execution of which the bank accounts of diplomatic missions of a foreign State benefit should be the object of specific waiver'.[85] The judgment, Argentina maintained, had failed to acknowledge the specificity of the waiver since

---

[80] *Argentina v NMC Capital* (22 November 2012) Court of Cassation of Belgium, C.11.0688.F/1.
[81] ibid 3 (author's translation from the original French).
[82] ibid 14 (namely, Articles 3, 22 and 25 of the Vienna Convention of 1961; Articles 1 and 31 of the Vienna Convention of 1969; and Article 32 of the European Convention on Immunity of States).
[83] ibid 13.
[84] ibid 16.
[85] ibid.

it deducts that the general waiver of the claimant to her immunity from execution with regard to the defendant necessarily implies a waiver of her immunity from execution as it concerns to the bank accounts of her diplomatic mission in Belgium, notwithstanding that this latter immunity from execution had not been the object of a specific waiver.[86]

In sum, Argentina concluded, by reason of its failure to require a specific waiver, 'the judgement breaches the aforementioned international custom [...] as well as of article 38, § 1st, b) of the Statute of the International Court of Justice'.[87]

The Court of Cassation considered that Argentina's ground for cassation, as formulated above, was 'well-founded'.[88] The Court of Cassation considered that the judgment had not verified 'that the sums seized were destined to aims other than the functioning of the diplomatic mission of the claimant'.[89] Furthermore, the Court of Cassation observed that the judgment in deciding

> that the general waiver [...] extends to properties of this diplomatic mission, including its bank accounts, without requiring an express and special waiver concerning these properties, violates Articles 22, 3, and 25 of the Vienna Convention of 18 April 1961 and the international customary rule of *ne impediatur legatio*.[90]

While the Court of Cassation refrained from explicitly discussing Argentina's claim of violation of ICJ Statute Article 38(1)(b), the Belgian Attorney General, in an opinion regarding Argentina's request for cassation, agreed with Argentina's claim as to the existence and content of the CIL rule of *ne impediatur legatio*.[91] In the opinion, the Belgian Attorney General, like Argentina, invoked ICJ Statute Article 38(1)(b), and referred generally to 'the constitutive elements of custom: (1) repetition during a sufficient period of time and within the framework of certain acts or behaviours called precedents, and (2) the *opinio juris sive necessitatis*'.[92]

That the Court of Cassation was silent on Argentina's argument that ICJ Statute Article 38(1)(b) had itself been breached does not indicate a refusal to discuss that provision. In another decision also involving

---

[86] ibid 16–17.
[87] ibid 17.
[88] ibid 18 (consequently, the Court of Cassation declined to entertain Argentina's second cassation ground).
[89] ibid 18.
[90] ibid 18.
[91] Belgium (n 8) 3 [8].
[92] ibid.

Argentina, the Court of Cassation analysed ICJ Statute Article 38(1)(b). In *NML Capital v Argentine Republic*,[93] the Court of Cassation stated that

> [b]y virtue of article 38, § 1st, b), of the Statute of the International Court of Justice, annexed to the Charter of the United Nations of 26 June 1945, the International Court of Justice, the mission of which is to settle in accordance with international law the disputes which are submitted thereto, applies international custom as proof of a practice generally accepted as being law.[94]

In particular, it rejected the fourth strand of the second ground for cassation in support of which NMC Capital alleged that the impugned decision had violated Article 38(1)(b), ICJ Statute,[95] for

> it does not result from this provision that the state judge who identifies and interprets an international customary rule is obliged to verify, in his decision, the existence of a general practice, admitted by a majority of states, which would be the origin of this customary rule.[96]

This statement, at first, appears to deny the applicability of the two-element approach, since the rule whose identification is at issue is expressly characterised as one of CIL. Yet, it might be construed as partially accurate, to the extent that ICJ Statute Article 38(1)(b) *qua* treaty provision is, indeed, only binding on the ICJ as such. Furthermore, as Belgium observed with respect to this particular decision, in the decision whose cassation was sought, 'the Court of Appeals, notably invoking a jurisprudence of the Court of Cassation confirming the existence of an international custom, sufficiently responded to the question'.[97]

In *Partenreederei MS "Neptun" GmbH & Co KG v Arquimedes Lazaro R*,[98] the Court of Cassation rejected the recourse of cassation, including in particular the third ground of cassation, whereby the applicant adduced that Article 38(1)(b), ICJ Statute, had been violated by the

---

[93] *NML Capital v Argentine Republic* (11 December 2014) Court of Cassation of Belgium, C.13.0537.
[94] ibid 28.
[95] ibid 29 (denying the ground of cassation, since it 'entirely relies on the contrary holding', namely that an international custom had been 'illegally' identified).
[96] ibid 28–9.
[97] Belgium, 'Observations de la Belgique sur le sujet "détermination du droit international coutumier"' (67th United Nations General Assembly, 6th Commission, 2015) 1 <https://legal.un.org/ilc/sessions/67/pdfs/french/icil_belgium.pdf> accessed 11 February 2022 (author's translation from the French original.)
[98] *Partenreederei MS "Neptun" GmbH & Co KG v Arquimedes Lazaro R* (14 January 2005) Court of Cassation of Belgium, C.03.0607.N.

decision impugned,[99] for the claimant 'wrongly assumed that the formula "international custom" employed by the appeals judges refers to an international custom as source of international law in the sense of Article 38 of the Statute of the International Court of Justice'.[100] This response not only did not address the content of ICJ Statute Article 38(1)(b), like the Court of Cassation's observation in *NML Capital v Argentine Republic*, but also went on to deny that the custom at issue was an international custom at all, unlike the custom involved in *NML Capital v Argentine Republic*.

The above instances of practice add to cases, also before the Belgian Court of Cassation, in which ICJ Statute Article 38 is invoked by the parties, but not dealt with in the decision, as illustrated by *JPA and consorts v Kingdom of the Netherlands and De Nederlandsche Bank*,[101] where Article 38(1)(b) was relied upon by the claimant.[102]

It is worth noting that the aforementioned instances of State practice are also in addition to a growing body of provisions in bilateral investment agreements in which general rules on CIL identification are expressly stated. While a discussion of the value of this practice is beyond the scope of this chapter, which has focused on practice in connection with post-award proceedings, it is worth bearing in mind that the following provisions in bilateral investment treaties specifically refer to the 'two-element approach': Article 5(2), China/Mexico BIT (2008); footnote 6 to Article 4(1), Singapore/Colombia BIT (2013); footnote 4 to Article 3(1), Burkina Faso/Singapore BIT (2014); footnote 1 to Article 4(2), Mexico/Singapore BIT (2009); footnote 6 to Article 4(1), Singapore/Colombia BIT (2013); and footnote 4 to Article 3(1), Burkina Faso/Singapore BIT (2014), among others.

To sum up, the aforementioned proceedings before the Belgian Court of Cassation are noteworthy. They involve practice in connection with national judicial proceedings by executive organs of both the Argentine and Belgian States. In particular, these forms of executive State practice are notable for their direct relevance to the content of the two-element

---

[99] ibid 7–8 (arguing, among others, 'the appeal judges have violated international law, and more precisely the notion of international custom, as defined in Article 38 of the Statute of the International Court of Justice'; author's translation from the original French).

[100] ibid 10 (concluding that, among others, by 'relying on a wrong reading of the judgment, the [cassation] ground, in this branch, fails as a matter of fact'; author's translation from the original French).

[101] *JPA & consorts v Kingdom of the Netherlands & De Nederlandsche Bank* (23 October 2015) Court of Cassation of Belgium, C.14.0322.F.

[102] ibid 15.

approach, as a secondary rule treated distinctly from the CIL rule at issue (in this instance also secondary rule, on immunity from execution). Indeed, both the Argentine State in its pleadings, and the Belgian State through the Attorney General's opinion, were in agreement as to the applicability and violation of the two-element approach, and both invoked ICJ Statute Article 38(1)(b), thus showing that, at the very least, this provision has a significance not *qua* treaty provision (the only issue actually explicitly touched upon in the Court of Cassation's respective decision), but as a statement of the two-element approach. Therefore, these two instances of actual State practice lend support to the ILC's statement of the two-element approach. And, together with the aforementioned, growing, instances of investment treaty practice, they show the potential of international investment law and arbitration as a sub-system of particular international law which contributes to the strengthening of key secondary rules of general international law, such as those governing CIL identification, including the two-element approach, which lies at the core of CIL identification.

4 Some Concluding Reflections

This chapter has investigated the significance of the surveyed State practice, with a particular focus on some of the wider implications it might have with respect to broader debates on CIL identification. Notably, it has shown that the very question of the applicability and content of ICJ Statute Article 38(1)(b), and the two-element approach to CIL identification, which is associated to this provision, have been raised and addressed with increasing sophistication by States in connection with ISDS proceedings.

This practice also shows that, to a certain extent, arguments about the applicability and scope of the two-element approach, the main basis for CIL identification, as opposed to the interpretation of previously identified CIL rules, has some hermeneutic dimensions. Such hermeneutic dimension raises questions calling for further research including the extent to which that dimension is a form of interpretation on an equal footing with CIL, let alone treaty, interpretation, in particular a form of 'existential' interpretation – blurring the distinction between identification and interpretation, or rather an exercise in 'characterisation' –in the same sense as private international law proceeds when categorising certain rules.

Furthermore, a bidirectional interaction between general international law and international investment law has been observed, insofar as State practice in connection with the latter sheds light on the former.[103] This departs from the common view that only general international law has an impact on sub-systems of particular international law. This interplay is highly significant, since it adds to the basis in actual State practice of general secondary rules. The potential for wider contributions of State practice in post-award proceedings with respect to secondary rules of general international law is thus worthy of further research.

---

[103] Cf D Mejía-Lemos, 'General International Law and International Investment Law: A Systematic Analysis of Interactions in Arbitral Practice' in J Chaisse *et al* (eds), *Handbook of International Investment Law and Policy* (Springer Singapore 2020).

4

Assessing Damages in Customary International Law

The Chorzów's Tale

JOSÉ MANUEL ÁLVAREZ-ZARATE*

1 Introduction

International Investment Agreements (IIAs)[1] regulate the basic treatment and protection of foreign investors and their investments in cases of expropriation where an adequate compensation based on the investment's value has been provided.[2] They do not, however, regulate compensation for other substantive protections granted to investors. This includes, for instance, the fair and equitable treatment (FET), the minimum standard of treatment (MST) or the prohibition of discrimination. In the absence of a conventional standard of compensation in assessing the value of damages to be paid to an alien for international wrongful acts of States, today, there is a common understanding among arbitral tribunals that customary international law (CIL) is a valuable source to apply. Nevertheless, determining the amount to be paid for damages, through an application of the relevant CIL rules, is far from a simple task since tribunals are faced with assessing the evidence provided by the parties, if any, and taking a

---

* Thanks to Mariana Puentes and Sofia Urrea for their invaluable research assistance. However, the responsibility of this narrative is solely of the author.
[1] In this chapter the term IIA and BITs are used with interchangeably.
[2] For example: USTR, '2012 U.S. Model Bilateral Investment Treaty' (*USTR*, 2012) Art 6 <https://ustr.gov/sites/default/files/BIT%20text%20for%20ACIEP%20Meeting.pdf> accessed 25 July 2022 '2. The compensation referred to in paragraph 1(c) shall: (...) (b) be equivalent to the fair market value of the expropriated investment immediately before the expropriation took place ("the date of expropriation")'; and, Germany, 'Germany Model Treaty -2008' (*German Government*, 2008) Art 4 <https://investmentpolicy.unctad.org/international-investment-agreements/treaty-files/2865/download>: 'Such compensation must be equivalent to the value of the expropriated investment immediately before the date on which the actual or threatened expropriation, nationalization or other measure became publicly known'; see, UNCTAD, 'Expropriation: UNCTAD series on Issues in International Investment Agreements II' (*UNCTAD*, 2012) UN Doc UNCTAD/DIAE/IA/2011/7.

position on the existence and content of the CIL rule.³ Thus, a myriad of important questions arise, both for the parties to argue and for the tribunals to determine the connection to such CIL rules in a concrete case. For instance, where should tribunals look for the existence of an invoked CIL rule and should it be identified? When did the rule emerge as a result of the practice of States and how can it be interpreted?

Despite recognising the Herculean task of establishing the generality of State practice and *opinio juris* of a CIL rule for damages in international investment law, some commentators maintain that for practical reasons international tribunals: (i) often find it in the International Law Commission's (ILC) Articles on the Responsibility of States for Internationally Wrongful Acts (ARSIWA) simply because there is no better legal source for guidance; (ii) oftentimes, they also turn to decisions of courts and other tribunals that, in their view, have established the content of these customary rules;⁴ and, (iii) draw inspiration from UN General Assembly (UNGA) resolutions.⁵ In the latter case, for example, some authors frame the discussion of the CIL rule for the standard of compensation as 'appropriate compensation' by utilising its articulation in the 1962 UNGA Resolution No 1803, relating to the 'Permanent Sovereignty over Natural Resources', to assert the existence of *opinio juris*,⁶ which bears a resemblance to one of the elements of CIL. However, as 'evidenced by the process of elaboration of this instrument ... the classical doctrine [on compensation] does not represent the general consensus of States and consequently cannot be considered as a rule of customary law'.⁷

---

³ S Ripinsky & K Williams, *Damages in International Investment Law* (BIICL 2008) 26, 31.
⁴ ibid; in the view of these authors, in particular, the judgment in the *Case Concerning the Factory at Chorzów (Germany v Poland)*, (Merits), PCIJ, Judgment 13 of September 1928, PCIJ Series A No 17 (*Chorzów Factory, Chorzów or Chorzów Factory* (Indemnity)).
⁵ Ripinsky & Williams (n 3) 27. As for the use of ILC, 'Draft Articles on Responsibility of States for Internationally Wrongful Acts with Commentaries' (23 April–1 June and 2 July–10 August 2001) UN Doc A/56/10, reproduced in [2001/II – Part Two] YBILC 31 (ARSIWA). These commentators said that neither of the parties challenged the customary status of a particular rule. As a matter of practice, arbitral tribunals tend to treat the Articles without scrutiny as evidence and as general reflection of international custom. This assertion might be applicable to cases decided after 2001, but not to cases decided before the ARSIWA were approved by the UN.
⁶ I Marboe, *Calculation of Compensation and Damages in International Investment Law* (2nd ed, OUP 2017) 46–7, where it was said that 'The UN General Assembly Resolution No 1803 relating to the Permanent Sovereignty over Natural Resources of December 1962 can be regarded as the last expression of a common *opinio juris* of the international community on this question'.
⁷ E Jiménez De Aréchaga, 'International Law in the Past Third of a Century' (1978) 159 RdC 1, 301.

The *Chorzów Factory* case has been widely commented on and is still referenced by international courts[8] to follow the full reparation principle for reparations as in *Chorzów* and to expand on cases when there is 'uncertainty about the extent of the damage caused' to say that it should be taken into 'account of equitable considerations'[9] and 'to make reparation in and adequate form' where 'compensation should not, however, have a punitive or exemplary character.'[10] However, there is a persistent narrative perpetuated by some investment tribunals, after 2001, that some of the rules on the assessment of compensation interpreted in *Chorzów* are CIL, or that this case itself is CIL.[11] This is not necessarily an accurate reflection of the existing normative *status quo*, because the rules described in the case did not automatically achieve CIL status. Nevertheless, *Chorzów* is still being used as a jurisprudential golden standard for applying 'recognised' CIL rules when assessing damages, and is often invoked to assert that when expropriations do not follow the rules provided in the treaty,[12]

---

[8] *Armed Activities on the Territory of the Congo (Congo v Uganda)* (Judgment) [2005] ICJ Rep 168, the Court observes that it is well established in general international law that a State which bears responsibility for an internationally wrongful act is under an obligation to make full reparation for the injury caused by that act; see also, *Chorzów Factory* (Indemnity); *Case Concerning the Gabčíkovo-Nagymaros Project (Hungary/Slovakia)* (Judgment) [1997] ICJ Rep 7; *Avena and Other Mexican Nationals (Mexico v USA)* (Judgment) [2004] ICJ Rep 12 [259]; and *Armed Activities on the Territory of the Congo (Congo v Uganda)* (Reparations) 2022 <www.icj-cij.org/public/files/case-related/116/116-20220209-JUD-01-00-EN.pdf> accessed 1 August 2022 (the Court recalls that 'reparation must, as far as possible, wipe out all the consequences of the illegal act' (*Chorzów Factory* (Indemnity) [21]) [259]); also, *Ahmadou Sadio Diallo (Republic of Guinea v Congo)* (Merits) [2010] ICJ Rep 639 [161]; *Ahmadou Sadio Diallo (Republic of Guinea v Congo)* (Compensation) [2012] ICJ Rep 324 [13]; Certain Activities Carried Out by Nicaragua in the Border Area (Costa Rica v Nicaragua) (Compensation) [2018] ICJ Rep 15 [29] ('Before turning to the consideration of the issue of compensation due in the present case, the Court will recall some of the principles relevant to its determination. It is a well-established principle of international law that "the breach of an engagement involves an obligation to make reparation in an adequate form"').

[9] *Congo v Uganda*. (Judgment of Reparations) [2022] ICJ 106.

[10] Costa Rica v Nicaragua (Compensation) [2018] ICJ 29-30.

[11] For example: *SD Myers Inc v Canada* (Partial Award of 13 November 2000) UNCITRAL [331]; *Metalclad v Mexico* (Award of 30 August 2000) ICSID Case No ARB(AF)/97/1 [122]; *ADC Affiliate Limited v Hungary* (Award of 2 October 2006) ICSID Case No ARB/03/16 [480, 483–4]; *Stati & ors v Kazakhstan* (Award of 19 December 2013) SCC Case No V116/2010 [1462–3]; *Houben v Burundi* (Award 12 January 2016) ICSID Case No ARB/13/7 [218, 220–1]; *Tethyan Copper v Pakistan* (Award of 12 July 2019) ICSID Case No ARB/12/1 [278, 280]; *Watkins Holdings v Spain* (Award 21 January 2020) ICSID Case No ARB/15/44 [673, 677].

[12] For a summary of the discussion on lawful and unlawful expropriation, see SR Ratner, 'Compensation for Expropriations in a Word of Investment Treaties: Beyond the Lawful/Unlawful Distinction' (2017) 111(1) AJIL 7.

ie when compensation to the investor is not promptly paid, it subsequently becomes an illegal expropriation.[13]

However, a closer reading of *Chorzów* reveals that this judgment did not state that neither the rules of full compensation, nor the one applied for the illegal taking of German interests in Upper Silesia, provided in its decision to assess the quantum of damages were CIL. The famous passage in page 47 of the decision, which has been invariably quoted by tribunals and scholars, could not be considered an assertion of CIL.

2 The *Chorzów* Narrative

The lack of guidance from primary investment protection norms in assessing damages has led to discussions in the academia[14] and international investment arbitral tribunals,[15] where it has been claimed that in the absence of a conventional norm to assess the amount of the reparation for the investor, CIL must be applied. Although this claim might be correct, there has been a lack of explanation in the realms of investment literature and arbitral decisions about the moment when the customary rule for the assessment of damages, and the standard of full reparation, were formed. Subsequently, the *Chorzów* case has emerged as an initial point of reference for many scholars and arbitral tribunals, who have created a storyline claiming that this case represents CIL in the assessment of damages.[16] The language of the often-cited passage states that

---

[13] For example: *Unión Fenosa v Egypt* (Award of 31 August 2018) ICSID Case No ARB/14/4 [10.96]; *Tethyan Copper* [278, 280]; *ConocoPhillips v Venezuela* (Award of 8 March 2019) ICSID Case No ARB/07/30 [207–17]; and, *Watkins Holdings v Spain* [673, 677].

[14] ZC Reghizzi, 'General Rules and Principles on State Responsibility and Damages in Investment Arbitration: Some Critical Issues' in A Gattini, A Tanzi & F Fontanelli (eds), *General Principles of Law and International Investment Arbitration* (Brill 2018) 69; MH Mendelson, 'Compensation for Expropriation: The Case Law' (1985) 79(2) AJIL 414, 418; M Shaw, *International Law* (6th ed, CUP 2006) 801; DA Desierto, 'The Outer Limits of Adequate Reparations for Breaches of Non-Expropriation Investment Treaty Provisions: Choice and Proportionality in Chorzòw' (2017) 55(2) ColumJ Transnat'l L 395, 407–8.

[15] For example: *Foresight v Spain* (Award of 14 November 2018) SCC Case No V2015/150 [434–6]; *Masdar Solar v Spain* (Award of 16 May 2018) ICSID Case No ARB/14/1 [549]; *Novenergia II v Spain* (Final Award of 15 February 2018) SCC Case No 2015/063 [807–9]; *OperaFund v Spain* (Award of 6 September 2019) ICSID Case No ARB/15/36 [609].

[16] S Marks, 'Expropriation: Compensation and Asset Valuation' (1989) 48(2) CLJ 170, 171; J Neill, '*Chorzów Factory* and Beyond: Case Law Update' (*Landmark Chambers*, August 2018) <www.landmarkchambers.co.uk/wp-content/uploads/2018/08/Presentation-JN-Chorzow-Factory.pdf> accessed 1 June 2022; T Yamashita, 'Investors in the Formation of Customary International Law' in S Droubi & J d'Aspremont (eds), *International Organisations, Non-State Actors, and the Formation of Customary International Law*

> [T]he essential principle contained in the actual notion of an illegal act – a principle which seems to be established *by international practice* and in particular by the decisions of *arbitral tribunals* – is that reparation must, as far as possible, wipe-out all the consequences of the illegal act and re-establish the situation which would, in all probability, have existed if that act had not been committed.[17]

Firstly, the language used in this passage did not explicitly say that it was interpreting or applying CIL rules. Secondly, if that passage is intended to be interpreted as a statement of the Permanent Court of International Justice (PCIJ) about the CIL in 1928, a closer look shows that contrary to what the judgment said, as will be seen further on, prior to the *Chorzów* case neither *international practice* nor *arbitral tribunals* have consistently applied the full reparation principle and its means to assess the damages suffered by an injured alien.

So, from where has this narrative – which considers *Chorzów* as the distillation of the CIL on the assessment of damages – been conceived? Looking at the doctrine and cases, from 1928 to present, one can find that the *Chorzów* case especially rose to prominence after the adoption of the 2001 ARSIWA.[18] Special Rapporteur James Crawford quoted it when commenting on Article 36 ARSIWA regarding compensation.[19] At that time, there was also the boom of Investor-State dispute settlement (ISDS) cases against Latin American countries, where many arbitrators that had no prior experience or knowledge in public international law were thrust onto the ISDS scene.[20] Such reasons may have facilitated the post-2001 diversion of arbitral decisions from the previously established doctrine and cases, where *Chorzów* has increasingly been featured prominently as a reference of a principle of law in assessing

---

(Manchester University Press 2020) 396; R Cox Alomar, 'Investment Treaty Arbitration in Cuba' (2017) 48(3) U Miami Inter-Am L Rev 1, 30, 45; CM López Cárdenas, *La desaparición forzada de personas en perspectiva histórico jurídica: su origen y evolución en el ámbito internacional* (Editorial Universidad del Rosario 2017) 280.

[17] *Chorzów Factory* (Indemnity), [47] (emphasis added).
[18] F Torres, 'Revisiting the *Chorzów Factory* Standard of Reparation – Its Relevance in Contemporary International Law and Practice' (2021) 90(2) Nord J Intl L 190, 191.
[19] J Crawford, *The International Law Commission's Articles on State Responsibility: Introduction, Text and Commentaries* (CUP 2002) 218–30.
[20] JM Álvarez-Zárate & DM Beltrán, 'Desafíos del arbitraje de inversión en los sectores minero-energético en América Latina' in LFM Castillo & C Villanueva (eds), *Anuario iberoamericano en Derecho de la Energía, Vol. II, Regulación de la transición Energética* (Universidad Externado de Colombia 2019) 261; JM Álvarez-Zárate, 'Legitimacy Concerns of the Proposed Multilateral Investment Court: Is Democracy Possible?' (2018) 59(8) BCLRev 2765.

damages.[21] These same post-2001 international arbitral decisions also relied on *Chorzów* as a legal source, because of the prestige of the PCIJ. In essence, the invocation of the *Chorzów* 'precedent' functioned on two levels. One, by invoking it, investment tribunals hoped that this would by 'association' bestow, somehow, an authority, or *gravitas*, behind their reasoning on assessment of damages. Two, the *Chorzów* case was a focal point in their argument that, under international investment law, CIL perhaps provided the rules for assessment of damages for responding to the so-called "illegal" expropriations where a payment was not made promptly. As a result, this narrative needs to be questioned to demystify the *Chorzów* judgment as a custom-making moment, where supposedly custom was interpreted in the decision and the rules for illegal takings[22] were created. Yet, in reality, CIL cannot be found nor identified in this decision.

This narrative implies that the decision was a custom-making moment,[23] where, back in 1928, the Court identified the already crystalised international custom to measure damages for international wrongs and that it interpreted the contended CIL with authority in the way it did so. However, no crystallised custom was revealed in the

---

[21] For example: C Eagleton, 'Measure of Damages in International Law' (1929) 39(1) YLJ 52; AJIL, 'Article 27. Violation of Treaty Obligations' (1935) 29 AJIL Supp 1077, 1080; A Herrero Rubio, 'Curso De 1955 De La Universidad De Valladolid en Vitoria' (1956) 9(1/2) REDI 281, 285; E Vitta, 'Responsabilidad De Los Estados' (1959) 12(1/2) REDI 11, 27–8; International Organization, 'International Court of Justice' (1959) 13(3) Int'l Org 446; OECD, 'Draft Convention on the Protection of Foreign Property' (1967) 7 ILM 117; SD Metzger, 'Property in International Law' (1964) 50(4) VaLRev 594, 600; GW Haight, 'International Organizations OECD Resolution on the Protection of Foreign Property' (1968) 2(2) Int'l L 326, 327; CQ Christol, 'International Liability for Damage Caused by Space' (1980) 74(2) AJIL 346, 352; N Kaufman Hevener & SA Mosher, 'General Principles of Law and the UN Covenant on Civil and Political Rights' (1978) 27(3) ICLQ 596, 598; G Handl, 'The Environment: International Rights and Responsibilities' (1980) 74 ASIL Proc 222, 233; JR Crook, 'Applicable Law in International Commercial Arbitration: The Iran-U.S. Claims Tribunal Experience' (1989) 83(2) AJIL 278, 303; JM Selby, 'State Responsibility and the Iran-United States Claims Tribunal' (1989) 83 ASIL Proc 240, 245; YN Kly, 'Human Rights, Aboriginal Canadians and Affirmative Action' (1992) 24(4) Peace Research 33, 37; and *Aloeboetoe et al v Suriname*, IACtHR (Reparations and Costs, Judgment of 10 September 1993) IACHR Series C no 15, 11.

[22] For the different meanings of illegal takings see, M Żenkiewicz, 'Compensable vs. Non-Compensable States' Measures: Blurred Picture Under Investment Law' (2020) 17(3) MJIEL 362.

[23] J d'Aspremont. 'The Custom-Making Moment in Customary International Law' in P Merkouris, J Kammerhofer & N Arajärvi (eds), *The Theory, Practice, and Interpretation of Customary International Law* (CUP 2022).

decision, but still, the *Chorzów* case has been utilised for different purposes by arbitral tribunals under the contour of that authoritative narrative. In order to cast a critical eye on whether this narrative stands up to scrutiny, three different periods with regards to damages in international law will be examined. The following sub-sections will seek to determine whether the CIL rules on assessing damages existed in these periods and whether a custom-making moment had emerged. These three periods are: (i) prior to the *Chorzów* judgment, ie prior to 1928; (ii) from 1928 to 2001, ie between *Chorzów* and the adoption of the ARSIWA; and (iii) from 2001 to present. A point that needs to be mentioned here, and to which we shall return, is that in these last two periods the *Chorzów* case was interpreted by arbitral tribunals and academia in a variety of different ways.

2.1 Damages before the Chorzów Decision in 1928

In 1929, Clyde Eagleton wrote that little attention was devoted by writers 'to the measure of damages in international law; and the paucity of doctrine and precedent has embarrassed recent attempts to codify the law relating to the responsibility of states'.[24] Also, he saw that no consistent practice existed in these words.

> [B]ecause of the divergencies of theory which underlie the measuring of damages, which, indeed, lie at the foundation of international responsibility, it is contended, however, that, because of contrariety of opinion, and the difficulties of statement, no effort should be made to state rules as to the measure of damages.[25]

A closer look at the arbitral and mixed claims commissions' practice before 1928 confirms Eagleton's assertions, ie, that the *Chorzów* decision was not the alleged custom-making moment and that the PCIJ could not have relied on earlier cases in identifying CIL rules for the assessment of damages, for the simple reason that prior practice was vastly inconsistent in the means and methods employed in determining the amount of reparation. This simple verification contradicts the narrative that a full reparation standard was customarily applied before 1928 to determine the amount of compensation in international claims; least of all, in expropriations to 'wipe-out all the consequences of the wrongful act and re-establish

---

[24] Eagleton (n 20) 52.
[25] ibid 75.

the situation which would, in all probability, have existed if that act had not been committed'.[26]

The pleadings of States before mixed commissions and arbitral tribunals is a veritable treasure trove of variety for the proposed means of reparations for different kinds of breaches of international obligations. Sometimes, discussions were on the different ways to provide reparations, such as in the *Delagoa* case (1900),[27] where Portugal proposed two different means that could be acceptable. The *compromis*, which granted the tribunal its jurisdiction and determined its scope, was concerned exclusively with the form and measure of the compensation for a cancelled railway concession. At no time was there any question raised on the validity of the act of expropriation itself, as to verify whether this was legal or not.[28]

In the Spanish Treaty Claims Commission of 1901, Rule 9 required proof to sustain an award.[29] Consequently, injuries were assessed by the value of the property, ie, the market price of the houses, machinery, furniture, and buildings with affidavits, which would include further explanation.[30] In this commission, the method for calculation of damages was not a debated issue, but only the property subject to reparation.

---

[26] Some cases before 1928 decided to award *lucrum cessans*. For a thoughtful description of the cases and the evolution in private law and influence in international law see, HE Yntema, 'The Treaties with Germany and Compensation for War Damage. IV: The Measure of Damages in International Law' (1924) 24(2) ColumLRev 134, 153, where Yntema states that 'there is a duty to make complete compensation ... The only limitations upon this duty spring from evidential or equitable considerations ... The compensation must be reasonably adjusted to the particular circumstances of the individual case'.

[27] 'In this relation it is proper to advert to the note of Senhor Barros Gomes, in which he stated that there were two ways in which an arrangement could then be made with the Portuguese company that would protect the interests of the share and bondholders. One of these ways was the acceptance by the company of the tariff of rates proposed by the government of the Transvaal; the other, a radical alteration of the concession, which would produce the same result (...)' *Delagoa Bay Railway* (1900) published in JB Moore (ed), *History and Digest of the International Arbitrations to Which the United States Has Been a Party*, Vol 2 (US GPO 1898) 1865.

[28] ILC, 'Report on International Responsibility by Mr FV Garcia-Amador, Special Rapporteur' (20 January 1956) UN Doc A/CN.4/96, 173–231.

[29] Spanish Treaty Claims Commission, *Rules and Regulations of Practice and Procedure: Adopted and Amended from Time to Time by the Comission, Together with a Copy of the Organic Act and Other Papers* (US GPO 1902) 4, Rule 9 ('All facts necessary to sustain an award and all special facts, proof of which is required by the Commission, must be established by evidence and not otherwise').

[30] ibid 62 (on the market price) & 454 (on the question of damages that must be actual and direct, and not remote or prospective).

In the *Janes* Claim (1926), the Claims Commission awarded damages, not because the amount 'corresponded to the injury' caused by the original harm, but because the respondent Government had been guilty of an 'international delinquency' in failing to measure up to 'its duty of diligently prosecuting and properly punishing the offender'.[31]

In the *Lorenzo A Oliva* case, large damages were claimed for future profits that could have been achieved during the concession granted to the claimant for the construction of a pantheon in Caracas cemetery because the claimant's wrongful expulsion from Venezuela. In awarding damages for the claimant's expulsion, and for the loss sustained on account of the interference with his concession, 'Umpire Ralston disallowed the claim for estimated profits'.[32] Other cases, such as the *Alabama*, *Montijo* or *Cotesworth*, also merit mention, as they demonstrate the multifarious approaches used in assessing damages.[33]

Thus, upon reviewing the case-law preceding the 1928 *Chorzów* judgment, it is clear that in some of the most well-known cases, arbitral tribunals did not consistently follow the full reparation principle, unlike what the *Chorzów* judgment may lead one to believe, nor did they state that any breach of an engagement would transform an expropriation into an illegal one.[34] This makes both the claims that there was a constant line of international precedents applying the principle of full reparation, and that a CIL rule was applied by the PCIJ to decide *Chorzów*, baseless or shaky at best.

A similar lack of evidence exists with respect to the assertion of arbitral tribunals that the principle of full reparation forms part of the applicable international law in cases where no prompt payment by the State has occurred. This principle was infrequently applied, and a contextual reading

---

[31] ILC (n 28) 213, referring to General Claims Commission (US & Mexico), *Opinions of Commissioners Under the Convention Concluded on 8 September 1923 Between the United States and Mexico*, Vol 1 (US GPO 1927) 108.

[32] See, *Oliva case (Italy) v Venezuela* (1903), published in MM Whiteman, *Damages in International Law*, Vol III (US GPO 1943)1865–6.

[33] See, for example: *Alabama Claims of USA v UK* (Ad hoc Award of 14 September 1872) published in JB Moore (ed), *History and Digest of the International Arbitrations to Which the United States Has Been a Party*, Vol 1 (US GPO 1898) 543, 658–9; *Montijo (USA) v Colombia* (Award of 10 April 1875) published in JB Moore (ed), *History and Digest of the International Arbitrations to Which the United States Has Been a Party*, Vol 2 (US GPO 1898) 1421, 1444–5; *Cotesworth & Powell (UK) v Colombia* (Award of November 1875) published in JB Moore (ed), *History and Digest of the International Arbitrations to Which the United States Has Been a Party*, Vol 2 (US GPO 1898) 2050–85; and the *Delagoa case* 1865.

[34] See *Chorzów Factory* (Indemnity) [29,47].

of *Chorzów* lends no real support to this assertion. More specifically, in *Chorzów*, the PCIJ interpreted Article 6 of the Geneva Convention[35] as providing a clear prohibition of the liquidation of German interests in Upper Silesia.[36] Commenting on the case, Manley O Hudson observed that the Court stated that Poland's action was not an expropriation to render which lawful only the payment of fair compensation would have been wanting, 'but a seizure of property which could not be lawfully expropriated even against compensation'.[37] So, the result of the seizure in this case was to create an 'obligation to restore the undertaking and, if this be not possible, to pay its value at the time of indemnification'.[38] Thus, because Poland seized German interests it behaved contrary to international law, since the legal course of action was to expropriate, not seize, property, according to *Chorzów's* interpretation of the Geneva Convention. From this, many arbitral tribunals have extrapolated that expropriating with no prompt compensations is illegal,[39] ie, in direct violation of an obligation enshrined in an international treaty. However, this may be an oversimplification. As Herz correctly noted as early as 1941, even if the compensation was provided with a delay, this does not render an expropriation automatically illegal because 'in practice deferred payments have frequently

---

[35] German–Polish Convention regarding Upper Silesia (Germany & Poland) (adopted 15 May 1922) Art 6 (Geneva Convention). Poland may expropriate in Polish Upper Silesia enterprises belonging to large-scale industry, including deposits, and frank rural property, in accordance with the provisions of Articles 7 to 23. Subject to these provisions, the property, rights and interests of German nationals or companies controlled by German nationals cannot be liquidated in Polish Upper Silesia.

[36] 'It should first of all be observed that whereas Head II is general in scope and confirms the obligation of Germany and Poland in their respective portions of the Upper Silesian territory to recognize and respect rights of every kind acquired before the transfer of sovereignty, by private individuals, companies or juristic persons, Head III only refers to Polish Upper Silesia and establishes in favour of Poland a right of expropriation which constitutes an exception to the general principle of respect for vested rights' *German Interests in Polish Upper Silesia* (Germany v Poland) (Merits) [1926] PCIJ Series A No 7 [21]; '(…) As these rights related to the Chorzow factory and were, so to speak, concentrated in that factory, the prohibition contained in the last sentence of Article 6 of the Geneva Convention applies in respect of them. Poland should have respected the rights held by the Bayerische under its contracts with the Obserschlesische, been contrary to Article 6 and the following articles of the Geneva Convention' *German Interests in Polish Upper Silesia* (Germany v Poland) (Merits) [1926] PCIJ Series A No 7 [44].

[37] MO Hudson, 'The Seventh Year of the Permanent Court of International Justice' (1929) 3(1) AJIL 1, 23.

[38] ibid 23.

[39] *ADC Affiliate Limited v Hungary* [481–4, 493]; *Siemens AG v Argentina* (Award of 7 February 2007) ICSID Case No ARB/02/8 [352]; *Vivendi (I) v Argentina* (Final Award of 20 August 2007) ICSID Case No ARB/97/3 [8.2.3].

been accepted or agreed upon, the fact that interest has usually been paid for the delay seems to corroborate this rule'.[40]

2.2 Damages after Chorzów and until 2001

After the *Chorzów* decision, there remained a lack of consensus among scholars and tribunals about the assessment of damages. For example, on the problem of compensation of expropriations and requisitions, Bin Cheng asserted that, according to the *Upton* case, compensation was indispensable and that the duty to compensate has been 'either based upon respect for private property'[41] or, as the *Norwegian Ships* case provided, 'upon enrichment of the community at the expense of isolated individuals'.[42]

In 1938, LH Woolsey recognised that 'international commissions have not followed definite rules' in assessing indemnity, because they have 'treated each case according to its peculiar circumstances and considered several standards of value in reaching the final result'.[43] He also made a distinction between just compensation related to lawful expropriations and damages for tortious actions, where '[i]t is clear that damages might be more comprehensive than just compensation for property taken'.[44] For Woolsey, 'the distinction between lawful and unlawful dispossession is commented upon by the Permanent Court of International Justice in the *Chorzów Factory* case'.[45] Other authors have claimed that the PCIJ held the principle of full compensation, but such decisions were regarding the interpretation of a specific treaty, thus it was not a *dictum* where a general rule was identified.[46] Given the different views between various authors and tribunals, it cannot reasonably be argued that there was a consensus on the assessment of damages.[47]

---

[40] JH Herz, 'Expropriation of Foreign Property' (1941) 35(2) AJIL 243, 243–62; Herz gave as examples: the *Savage* case (1865) published in JB Moore (ed), *History and Digest of the International Arbitrations to Which the United States Has Been a Party*, Vol 2 (US GPO 1898) 1855–7, *Norwegian Shipowners' Claims (Norway v USA)* (Award of 13 October 1922) I RIAA 307, and the *Chorzów Factory*.

[41] B Cheng, *General Principles of Law: As Applied by International Courts and Tribunals* (Stevens 1953) 47.

[42] ibid.

[43] LH Woolsey, 'The Expropriation of Oil Properties by Mexico' (1938) 32(3) AJIL 519, 524.

[44] ibid ('where property has been taken by expropriation proceedings or by tortious action, international law imposes the duty of making adequate reparation').

[45] ibid.

[46] PS Wilde Jr, 'El Derecho Internacional y el Petróleo Mexicano' (1940) 7(26(2)) Trimestre Económico 271, 271–90.

[47] R Dolzer, 'New Foundations of the Law of Expropriation of Alien Property' (1981) 75(3) AJIL 553, 553–89.

This is buttressed by the jurisprudence of the period. During this, there were different kinds of cases, such as those before the Iran-U.S. Claims Tribunal (IUSCT), contractual cases, and some (although not too many) ISDS cases, which dealt with assessing damages. A common theme in all of these was that the tribunals involved did not consider *Chorzów* as either reflecting CIL or providing guidance on how to identify the relevant CIL rules. In furtherance to this, out of 28 public cases reviewed for this piece, not even one held that there were illegal expropriations in play.[48] Eight cases did not make an analysis on damages,[49] 13 cases did not even mention CIL or *Chorzów*,[50] three mentioned *Chorzów* on the assessment,[51]

---

[48] For this chapter we reviewed 28 out of 31 cases between 1928 and 2001, two of which are not public: *Guadalupe Gas Products Corporation v Nigeria* (Award of 22 July 1980) ICSID Case No ARB/78/1; *Biedermann v Kazakhstan* (Award of 1 January 1999) SCC Case No 97/1996.

[49] *Holiday Inns SA & ors v Morocco* (Order Taking Note of the Discontinuance 17 October 1978) ICSID Case No ARB/72/1; *Reynolds Jamaica Mines Limited and Reynolds Metals Company v Jamaica* (Order Taking Note of the Discontinuance of 12 October 1977) ICSID Case No ARB/74/4; *Kaiser Bauxite Company v Jamaica* (Decision on Jurisdiction and Competence of 6 July 1975) ICSID Case No ARB/74/3; *Gabon v Société Serete SA* (Order Taking Note of the Discontinuance Issued by the Tribunal of 27 Feb 1978) ICSID Case No ARB/76/1; *SEDITEX Engineering v Madagascar* (Settlement by the Parties of 20 June 1983) ICSID Case No CONC/82/1; *Swiss Aluminium Limited & Icelandic Aluminium Company Limited v Iceland* (Order of the Secretary-General Taking Note of the Discontinuance of 6 March 1985) ICSID Case No ARB/83/1; *Tesoro Petroleum Corporation v Trinidad and Tobago* (Report of the Conciliation Commission of 27 November 1985) ICSID Case No CONC/83/1; and, *Colt Industries Operating Corporation v Republic of Korea* (Order Taking Note of the Discontinuance of 3 August 1990) ICSID Case No ARB/84/2.

[50] *Adriano Gardella SpA v Côte d'Ivoire* (Award of 29 August 1997) ICSID Case No ARB/74/1; *AGIP SpA v Congo* (Award of 30 November 1979) ICSID Case No ARB/77/1; *Klöckner Industrie-Anlagen GmbH & ors v Cameroon & Société Camerounaise des Engrais* (Award of 21 October 1983) ICSID Case No ARB/81/2; *Amco Asia Corporation & ors v Indonesia* (Award of 20 November 1984) ICSID Case No ARB/81/1; *Société Ouest Africaine des Bétons Industriels v Senegal* (Award of 25 February 1988) ICSID Case No ARB/82/1; *SARL Benvenuti & Bonfant v Congo* (Award of 8 August 1980) ICSID Case No ARB/77/2; *LETCO v Liberia* (Award of 31 March 1986) ICSID Case No ARB/83/2; *Atlantic Triton Company Limited v People's Revolutionary Republic of Guinea* (Award of 21 April 1986) ICSID Case No ARB/84/1; *American Manufacturing & Trading, Inc v Republic of Zaire* (Award of 21 February 1997) ICSID Case No ARB/93/1; *Saar Papier Vertriebs GmbH v Poland* (Final Award of 16 October 1995) UNCITRAL; *Fedax NV v Venezuela* (Award of 9 March 1998) ICSID Case No ARB/96/3; *Sedelmayer v Russia* (Arbitration Award of 7 July 1998) SCC; *Maffezini v Spain* (Award of 13 November 2000) ICSID Case No ARB/97/7; *Vivendi (I) v Argentina* (Award of 21 November 2000) ICSID Case No ARB/97/3; and *Wena Hotels v Egypt* (Award of 8 December 2000) ICSID Case No ARB/98/4.

[51] *Southern Pacific Properties (Middle East) Limited v Egypt* (Award of 20 May 1992) ICSID Case No ARB/84/3; *SD Myers Inc v Canada* (Partial Award I); *SD Myers Inc v Canada* (Second Partial Award of 21 October 2002) UNCITRAL; *Metalclad v Mexico*.

and three (with *Metalclad* falling under both these last categories) mentioned CIL within the context of damages' assessment.[52]

In 1992, in the *Southern Pacific Properties v Egypt* case, no reference was made to CIL, and *Chorzów* was referred to in regard to the application of the Discounted Cash Flow (DCF) method to assess the damages. Following the *Amoco* case, the Tribunal considered that DCF method was not appropriate for determining fair compensation in this case, because of the lack of operational time that would result from awarding 'possible but contingent and undeterminate damage which, in accordance with the jurisprudence of arbitral tribunals, cannot be taken into account',[53] and then held that 'no reparation for speculative or uncertain damage can be awarded'.[54]

From the above, one can see that none of these cases said that *Chorzów* was CIL, but there was some rudimentary consistency among certain arbitral tribunals, which held in broad strokes that the *Chorzów* case contained some principles. The tribunals understood such principles in varying ways: as a principle without qualification to award the costs of the investment, such as in *Metalclad v Mexico*;[55] or stated as a principle of international law as *Myers v Canada* held;[56] or, as *Amoco v Indonesia* stated, full compensation is a general principle of law 'which may be considered as a source of international law', with *Chorzów* functioning as 'the basic precedent in this respect'.[57] However, in other cases, a different line was followed, as for instance in *Mobil Oil Corporation*, where the Tribunal was of the view that the investor was 'entitled under the principles of customary international to *appropriate compensation*'.[58]

---

[52] *Mobil Oil Corporation & ors v New Zealand* (Decision on Liability of 6 January 1988) ICSID Case No ARB/87/2; *AAPL v Sri Lanka* (Final Award of 27 June 1990) ICSID Case No ARB/87/3; *Metalclad v Mexico*.
[53] *Southern Pacific Properties (Middle East) Limited v Egypt* [189]; *Chorzów Factory* (Indemnity) [51].
[54] ibid [189].
[55] *Metalclad v Mexico* [122].
[56] *SD Myers v Canada* (Partial Award I) [331].
[57] *Amco Asia Corporation & ors v Indonesia* [267].
[58] *Mobil Oil Corporation & ors v New Zealand* [3.4] (emphasis added); see also, *Amoco International Finance Corp v Iran* (Partial Award (Award No 310-56-3) of 14 July 1987) IUSCT Case No 56 [191] (emphasis added), in [113] this case also states that *Chorzów* contained principles of international law generally accepted for the treatment of foreigners.

2.3 Damages from 2001 until Present

Examining the cases relating to assessment of damages post-adoption of the ARSIWA, it seems that the *Chorzów* case has served as a means for tribunals and scholars to make different kinds of claims regarding the standard of compensation, and its assessment and application under CIL. So much so, in fact, that the *Chorzów* standard has been seen by some not only as a reflection of CIL, but 'as a static set of uncontested rules that can be applied automatically and deductively in granting redress whenever an international wrongful act takes place'.[59] Despite this, what is striking is that such statements are not supported by delving deeper into the matter or providing any further evidence other than merely quoting the *Chorzów* judgment. Several scholars have fallen in line with this view, assenting to this conception of the narrative.[60] Some also claim, in relation to the so-called illegal expropriations, that 'the standard of compensation is found, not in the applicable ... BIT, but rather in customary international law under the rubric of the widely reputed *Chorzów Factory* rule'.[61]

However, more established authors currently recognise in *Chorzów* a general principle of law as opposed to a CIL rule, expressing that 'the guiding principle is that reparation must, as far as possible, restore the situation that would have existed had the illegal act not been committed, expressed in the *Chorzów Factory case*'[62] and that '[u]nder this principle, damages for a violation of international law have to reflect the damage actually suffered by the victim'.[63] As a source of international law, general principles of law have been recognised as a legal basis for international legal principles relating to foreign investment. As Sornarajah notes, '[t]he principle that compensation must be paid is itself said to be a general principle of law'.[64]

As already mentioned, cases after 2001 show that many arbitral tribunals have resorted to, and argued that the *Chorzów* judgment reflects CIL[65] without giving reasons why this is so while others do not even

---

[59] Torres (n 17) 227.
[60] Marks (n 15) 171; Neill (n 15); Yamashita (n 15) 396; López Cárdenas (n 15) 280.
[61] Cox Alomar (n 15) 45; see also, JW Salacuse, *The Law of Investment Treaties* (OUP 2010) 254–5, who says that, in *Chorzów*, the PCIJ 'stated that, according to customary international law, if a state has committed a wrong it is liable to pay reparations'.
[62] R Dolzer & C Schreuer, *Principles of International Investment Law* (2nd edn, OUP 2012) 294.
[63] ibid 295.
[64] M Sornarajah, *The International Law on Foreign Investment* (3rd edn, CUP 2010) 85.
[65] For example: *ADC Affiliate Limited v Hungary* [480, 483–4]; *Siemens AG v Argentina* [349, 353]; *Stati & ors v Kazakhstan* [1462–3]; *OAO Tatneft v Ukraine* (Award on the Merits

ASSESSING DAMAGES IN CUSTOMARY INTERNATIONAL LAW 85

mention it at all.[66] For example, in some tribunals when the IIAs do not provide a rule for illegal takings, the tribunal is required to apply the default standard contained in '[t]he customary international law standard for the assessment of damages resulting from an unlawful act is set out in the decision of the PCIJ in the *Chorzów Factory* case ...'.[67] Similarly, 'for purposes of determining the compensation' the tribunal must assess this, 'which is governed by customary international law as reflected in *Factory at Chorzów*'.[68] For others, 'it is appropriate for the Tribunal to apply the standard of reparation found in customary international law. The claimants correctly cite, and the respondent does not dispute, the full reparation standard articulated in *Chorzów*'.[69] Or, when tribunals conflate two sources of international law, principles and CIL, by interpreting them as being the same, they quote *Chorzów*, where '[i]t is these well-established principles that represent customary international law, including for breaches of international obligations under BITs, that the Tribunal is bound to apply'.[70]

Most of the cases that state *Chorzów* is CIL have ignored the basic requisites for custom, State practice and *opinio juris*, distilled from Article 38(1) (b) 1920 Statute of the PCIJ.[71] Additionally, and perhaps most importantly, these cases have ignored that according to Article 59 of the PCIJ Statute, decisions 'of the Court [have had] no binding force except between the

---

of 29 July 2014) PCA Case No 2008-8 [540]; *Gold Reserve Inc v Venezuela* (Award of 22 September 2014) ICSID Case No ARB(AF)/09/1 [678–9]; *British Caribbean Bank v Belize* (Award of 19 December 2014) PCA Case No 2010-18 [288, 293]; *Vivendi (II) v Argentina* (Award of 9 April 2015) ICSID Case No ARB/03/19 [27]; *AWG Group v Argentina* (Award of 9 April 2015) UNCITRAL [27]; *Houben v Burundi* [218, 220–1]; *Crystallex International Corporation v Venezuela* (Award of 4 April 2016) ICSID Case No ARB(AF)/11/2 [846]; *Burlington Resources Inc v Ecuador* (Decision on Reconsideration and Award of 7 February 2017) ICSID Case No ARB/08/05 [160, 177]; *Unión Fenosa v Egypt* [10.96]; *Tethyan Copper* [278, 280]; *Watkins Holdings v Spain* [673, 677].

[66] *Adriano Gardella SpA v Côte d'Ivoire*; *AGIP SpA v Congo*; *Klöckner Industrie-Anlagen GmbH & ors v Cameroon & Société Camerounaise des Engrais*; *Amco Asia Corporation & ors v Indonesia*; *Société Ouest Africaine des Bétons Industriels v Senegal*; *SARL Benvenuti & Bonfant v Congo*; *LETCO v Liberia*; *Atlantic Triton Company Limited v People's Revolutionary Republic of Guinea*; *American Manufacturing & Trading, Inc v Republic of Zaire*; *Saar Papier Vertriebs GmbH v Poland*; *Fedax NV v Venezuela*; *Sedelmayer v Russia*; *Maffezini v Spain*; *Vivendi (I) v Argentina*; and *Wena Hotels v Egypt*.

[67] *ADC Affiliate Limited v Hungary* [483–4].
[68] *Siemens AG v Argentina* [353].
[69] *Watkins Holdings v Spain* [673].
[70] *Gold Reserve Inc v Venezuela* [678].
[71] Statute of the Permanent Court of International Justice (adopted 16 December 1920, entered into force 8 October 1921) 6 LNTS 389, Art 38(1)(b) (PCIJ Statute).

parties and in respect of that particular case'.[72] So, its jurisprudence did not create international law nor was it a source of law in 1928; contemporarily, it is likewise not the case as the 1945 ICJ Statute basically replicates the same rules of 1920 PCIJ Statute.[73]

3   Concluding Remarks

The different and flexible interpretations given to *Chorzów* might be explained because it was written by way of general statements, which referred to the principles of law and international law that had supposedly been constantly applied in the international cases preceding it. So, despite the fact that the Court did not explicitly mention *any* of these previous cases that established such rules, subsequent cases have blindly trusted those general statements, thus ignoring that the principles of reparation in *Chorzów* were already enshrined in the Geneva Convention.[74] Further, as has been demonstrated, the principle of full reparation was not previously provided for nor consistently applied in prior arbitral practice as *Chorzów* had claimed. However, being a sound judgment, after *Chorzów*, the principle of full reparation was used more frequently by arbitral tribunals.

Thus, tribunals and commentators assembled the story of *Chorzów* by conflating rules that were intended to serve different purposes. For example, those rules for the determination of the amount of compensation as provided in *Chorzów*, being simultaneously placed together with the principle of international responsibility[75] and the obligation of reparation for

---

[72] The Statute of the International Court of Justice (adopted 26 June 1945, entered into force 24 October 1945) 33 UNTS 993, Arts. 38 & 59 have equal language as the PCIJ Statute, Art 38(4), which provide that the Court '[S]hall apply: (4) Subject to the provisions of Article 59, judicial decisions and the teachings of the most highly qualified publicists of the various nations, as subsidiary means for the determination of rules of law'.

[73] ICJ Statute, Art 38(1) reads as follows: '1. The Court, whose function is to decide in accordance with international law such disputes as are submitted to it, shall apply: (a) international conventions, whether general or particular, establishing rules expressly recognised by the contesting States; (b) international custom, as evidence of a general practice accepted as law; (c) the general principles of laws as recognised by civilized nations; (d) subject to the provisions of Article 59, judicial decisions and the teachings of the most highly qualified publicists'.

[74] German–Polish Convention regarding Upper Silesia, Art 22, 'Completion of the expropriation within the meaning of Article 10, paragraph 2, and Article 15, paragraph 1, paragraph 2, includes, among other things, the payment of the fixed indemnity; it does not imply the termination of a lawsuit brought before the German-Polish Mixed Arbitral Tribunal relating to a more extensive claim for damages, or of a procedure relating to the admissibility of expropriation'.

[75] *ADC Affiliate Limited v Hungary* [480–4]; *Siemens AG v Argentina* [349–50, 355]; *Stati & ors v Kazakhstan* [1462–3]; *OAO Tatneft v Ukraine* [540]; *Gold Reserve Inc v Venezuela*

wrongful acts, which were considered in the judgment to be principles of international law.[76] A close look at the judgment shows that these are rules that need to be applied in different times; first, when finding whether the State is responsible for breaching an international obligation and, second, at the time of assessing the amount for reparation.[77]

At present, many arbitral tribunals do not explain why *Chorzów* is CIL, nor if it is being applied as a general principle of law. Mostly, the technique used by these tribunals has consisted of merely quoting the passages of *Chorzów* that contain such assertions.[78] In other cases, tribunals will occasionally interpret the rules regarding international responsibility contained in *Chorzów* to assert that they are CIL in order to apply them when determining the amount of compensation in a case.[79] By 1928, it is arguable that there was constant international practice in the application of the principle of full reparation or that the method to determine the amount of compensation, as stated by *Chorzów*, had been well developed.

Reasons for the lack of contemporary explanation could be attributed to the recognition of the authority of the World Court, or perhaps because the ARSIWA cites the *dicta* of the case. Also, such confidence in the narrative, that the *Chorzów* case established the rules for assessing the damage in a case, may have surged because this judgment had explicitly asserted that these rules were internationally recognised.[80]

[678–9]; *British Caribbean Bank v Belize* [288, 293]; *AWG Group v Argentina* [27]; *Crystallex International Corporation v Venezuela* [847–8]; *Unión Fenosa v Egypt* [10.96]; *Watkins Holdings v Spain* [673, 677].

[76] *Amco Asia Corporation & ors v Indonesia* [266–8, 281]; *SD Myers Inc v Canada* (Partial Award I) [311, 315]; and *Gold Reserve Inc v Venezuela* [678, 681].

[77] ('[I]t is a principle of international law that the reparation of a wrong may consist in an indemnity corresponding to the damage which the nationals of the injured State have suffered as a result of the act which is contrary to international law') & ('it is a principle of international law, and even a general conception of law, that any breach of an engagement involves an obligation to make reparation') *Chorzów Factory* (Indemnity) [27, 29].

[78] See *Chorzów Factory* (Indemnity) [47].

[79] *Amco Asia Corporation & ors v Indonesia* [281]; *SD Myers Inc v Canada* (Partial Award I) [311, 315]; *SD Myers Inc v Canada* (Dissenting Opinion of Professor Bryan P Schwartz of 30 December 2002) UNCITRAL [12–14]; and *Gold Reserve Inc v Venezuela* [678, 681].

[80] '(...) [T]he Court observes that it is a principle of international law, an even a general conception of law, that any breach of an engagement involves an obligation to make reparation (...)' & '[t]he essential principle contained in the actual notion of an illegal act – *a principle which seems to be established by international practice and in particular by the decisions of arbitral tribunals...*' *Chorzów Factory* (Indemnity) [29, 47] (emphasis added).

Following this line of argument, the principle of full reparation and the distinction between legal and illegal expropriation emerges where some tribunals and case laws claim that these would form part of CIL.[81] This claim has had important effects on matters pertaining to the applicable law, especially when discussing the date for the assessment of damages and the standard of reparation.

To summarise, the narrative built around *Chorzów* has some inconsistencies, mostly (i) because the decision has been taken out of context by some in academia, and by investment arbitration tribunals alike, when assessing damages;[82] (ii) because the *Chorzów* ruling does not cite the legal sources that, without doubt, would allow them to affirm that the full reparation principle was applied consistently by claims commissions and arbitral tribunals before 1928, and that the counterfactual method to assess damages were CIL;[83] (iii) the ruling did not categorically say, neither show, that CIL had been applied to the case as a legal source,[84] but this has not prevented many investment arbitral awards after 2001 from claiming that *Chorzów* is CIL;[85] and (iv) the context in which the judgment ruled upon the international illegal act, ie by breach of the

---

[81] *Yukos Universal Ltd v Russia* (Final Award of 18 July 2014) UNCITRAL, PCA Case No 2005-04/AA227 [1581-4, 1758-69, 1826-7]; *Tidewater v Venezuela* (Award of 13 March 2015) ICSID Case No ARB/10/5 [140-6, 159-63]; and, *Quiborax v Bolivia* (Award of 16 September 2015) ICSID Case No ARB/06/2 [240-55, 325-30, 343-7, 370-85].

[82] M. Sornarajah (n 68) 425.

[83] In the *Chrozów Factory* Indemnity decision, no reference was made either to a legal source (aside from the Upper Silesian Treaty of 1922) or any previous jurisprudence nor arbitral cases. Regarding the latter, it is generally mentioned by the Court as 'decisions of arbitration tribunals' without specifying which ones. *Chorzów Factory* (Indemnity) [68, 79, 125, 155].

[84] Instead, the judgment said that: 'The essential principle contained in the actual notion of an illegal act – a principle which seems to be established by international practice and in particular by the decisions of arbitral tribunals – is that reparation must, as far as possible, wipe out all the consequences of the illegal act and re-establish the situation which would, in all probability, have existed if that act had not been committed' *Chorzów Factory* (Indemnity) [47].

[85] For example: *ADC Affiliate Limited v Hungary* [480, 483-4]; *Siemens AG v Argentina* [349, 353]; *Stati & ors v Kazakhstan* [1462-3]; *OAO Tatneft v Ukraine* [540]; *Gold Reserve Inc v Venezuela* [678-9]; *British Caribbean Bank v Belize* [288, 293]; *Vivendi (II) v Argentina* [27]; *AWG Group v Argentina* [27]; *Houben v Burundi* [218, 220-1]; *Crystallex International Corporation v Venezuela* [846]; *Burlington Resources Inc v Ecuador* [160, 177]; *Unión Fenosa v Egypt* [10.96]; *Tethyan Copper* [278, 280]; *Watkins Holdings v Spain* [673, 677].

Geneva Convention, is overlooked by those who argue that in the context of Bilateral Investment Treaty (BIT) claims, there are illegal expropriations[86] to justify awarding damages with a different date that that provided by the BIT.[87]

---

[86] A discussion on illegal expropriation can be find in *Quiborax v Bolivia* (Partially Dissenting Opinion of Brigitte Stern of 7 September 2015) ICSID Case No ARB/06/2 [28–9] 'The majority attempts to justify its approach based on what is referred to as a careful analysis of the *Chorzów* case as well as on the position adopted by 'several investment arbitration tribunals' (…) In my view, a careful analysis of *Chorzów* does not support the approach of the majority and it cannot be contested that there are extremely few awards having adopted an ex post analysis as has been used here. (…)'.

[87] At the date of the expropriation. See, for example: Agreement Between Japan and Georgia for the Liberalisation, Promotion and Protection of Investment (Japan & Georgia) (adopted 29 January 2021, not yet in force) Art 11, (Expropriation and Compensation) '2. The compensation shall be equivalent to the fair market value of the expropriated investment *at the time* when the expropriation was publicly announced or when the expropriation occurred, whichever is earlier. The fair market value shall not reflect any change in value occurring because the expropriation had become known earlier' (emphasis added); Agreement Between The Government of the State of Israel and The Government of the United Arab Emirates on Promotion and Protection of Investments (Israel & UAE) (adopted 20 October 2020, not yet in force) Art 6 (Expropriation and Compensation) '2. The compensation shall: (…) (b) be equivalent to the fair market value of the expropriated investment immediately before the expropriation took place (…)'; Agreement Between The Government of Hungary and The Government of The Kyrgyz Republic for the Promotion and Reciprocal Protection Of Investments (Hungary & Kyrgyzstan) (adopted 29 September 2020, entered into force 10 April 2022) Art 6, (Expropriation) '1. (…) Such compensation shall amount to the market value of the investment expropriated immediately before expropriation or impeding expropriation became public knowledge (whichever is earlier) (…)'.

PART II

The Interpretation of Secondary Rules
in International Investment Law

5

Uses of the Work of International Law Commission on State Responsibility in International Investment Arbitration

SOTIRIOS-IOANNIS LEKKAS[*]

1 Introduction

The Articles on State Responsibility for Internationally Wrongful Acts ('ARSIWA') constitute an experiment in international law-making. Unlike other successful projects of the International Law Commission ('ILC'), such as its work on the law of treaties and diplomatic and consular relations, the ARSIWA have not yet led to the adoption of a multilateral treaty.[1] Yet, their text is cited commonly as the authoritative statement of the law on State responsibility with investment tribunals being by far their most frequent users. To put this into perspective, in a 2017 report to the UN General Assembly, the UN Secretariat identified 392 publicly available decisions of various bodies which make reference to the ARSIWA including those of the ICJ, the ICC, the WTO, international and hybrid criminal tribunals, and human rights courts and treaty bodies.[2] Although the report does not provide a specific number for investment arbitrations,

---

[*] Postdoctoral Researcher, Department of Transboundary Legal Studies, University of Groningen (email: s.i.lekkas@rug.nl). This chapter is based on research conducted in the context of the project 'The Rules of Interpretation of Customary International Law' ('TRICI-Law'). This project has received funding from the European Research Council (ERC) under the European Union's Horizon 2020 Research and Innovation Programme (Grant Agreement No 759728).

[1] ILC, 'Draft Articles on Responsibility of States for Internationally Wrongful Acts with Commentaries' (23 April–1 June and 2 July–10 August 2001) UN Doc A/56/10, reproduced in [2001/II – Part Two] YBILC 31 (ARSIWA); for a useful list of multilateral treaties originating from ILC works, see H Owada, 'The International Law Commission and the Process of Law-Formation' in *Making Better International Law: The International Law Commission at 50* (UN 1998) 167, 172.

[2] UNGA, 'Responsibility of States for Internationally Wrongful Acts: Compilation of Decisions of International Courts, Tribunals and Other Bodies, Report of the Secretary-General, Addendum' (20 June 2017) A/71/80/Add.1.

it records 264 arbitral decisions referencing ARSIWA (72.5%) with investment tribunals accounting for the majority of these references.[3] At the same time, the interpretation and/or application of ARSIWA is one of the most common issues arising in investment arbitration. In numerical terms, 444 cases have led to a decision since 2000 including cases in which no issues of responsibility arose or in which the reasoning of the decision is not public.[4] The present study has traced at least 200 decisions issued in the same period citing ARSIWA or its previous versions. The extent of the practice attests to the central importance of the formally unwritten law of State responsibility and its interpretation in investment proceedings. Indeed, investment tribunals refer to this body of law to determine a variety of key issues including whether the acts forming the basis of the claim belong to the respondent state, what are the consequences of a finding against the respondent state, or whether there are circumstances precluding a finding against the respondent state or calling for mitigation. The sheer volume of the practice also raises broader questions about the ways in which investment tribunals engage with the identification and development of unwritten international law, that is, customary international law and general principles of law.

This chapter examines and also critically assesses the methods which investment tribunals explicitly or implicitly employ when using the ARSIWA in order to identify rules of general international law on State responsibility and determine their content. It does so by building upon, and adding to, the work of the UN Secretariat.[5] Section 2 introduces the problem

---

[3] ibid. The present study has identified 150 relevant decisions of investment tribunals up to and including 2016 and additional 19 decisions during 2017 (ie 55–65% of the reported arbitral awards).

[4] On the total number of investment arbitrations leading to a decision since 2000, see: UNCTAD, 'Investment Dispute Settlement Navigator' (*UNCTAD Investment Policy Hub*, 31 December 2019) <https://investmentpolicy.unctad.org/investment-dispute-settlement/> accessed 10 May 2021.

[5] UNGA, 'Responsibility of States for Internationally Wrongful Acts: Compilation of Decisions of International Courts, Tribunals and Other Bodies, Report of the Secretary-General' (1 February 2007) UN Doc A/62/62; complemented by UNGA, 'Responsibility of States for Internationally Wrongful Acts: Compilation of Decisions of International Courts, Tribunals and Other Bodies, Report of the Secretary-General' (17 April 2007) UN Doc A/62/62/Add.1; UNGA, 'Responsibility of States for Internationally Wrongful Acts: Compilation of Decisions of International Courts, Tribunals and Other Bodies, Report of the Secretary-General' (30 April 2010) UN Doc, A/65/76; UNGA, 'Responsibility of States for Internationally Wrongful Acts: Compilation of Decisions of International Courts, Tribunals and Other Bodies, Report of the Secretary-General' (30 April 2013) UN Doc A/68/72; UNGA, 'Responsibility of States for Internationally

of ARSIWA's lack of formal status and its implications for the use of ARSIWA in international adjudication. Section 3 surveys whether and how investment tribunals justify their reliance on ARSIWA. Section 4 highlights the variety of ways in which ARSIWA are used in the process of the determination of the content of applicable rules of law. Section 5 discusses the outcomes of this survey against the analytical backdrop of the unity of the law on State responsibility and the law relating to sources of international law. The chapter argues in favour of a principled use of ARSIWA in investment proceedings based on the distinction between the ascertainment of the legal status of a normative proposition contained therein and the determination of the content of a normative proposition whose status is undisputed.

2 Formal Status of ARSIWA and Its Methodological Corollaries

From a 'formal' perspective, the ARSIWA, as a document originating from the International Law Commission, does not possess any binding force.[6] In terms of the Statute of the ICJ, the ARSIWA constitutes 'teachings of the most qualified publicists' that can be used as 'subsidiary means for the determination of rules of law'.[7] Yet, in fact, international courts and tribunals tend to attach to ARSIWA much more weight than the label of 'teachings' would normally suggest and often treat them as uncontroversial statements of applicable rules of law.[8] This section briefly maps out the available justifications and methodologies for the use of ARSIWA in investment arbitration and points out why the practice of investment tribunals matters.

Wrongful Acts: Compilation of Decisions of International Courts, Tribunals and Other Bodies, Report of the Secretary-General' (21 April 2016) UN Doc A/71/80; UNGA, 'Responsibility of States for Internationally Wrongful Acts: Compilation of Decisions of International Courts, Tribunals and Other Bodies, Report of the Secretary-General' (26 April 2017) UN Doc A/72/81; UNGA, 'Responsibility of States for Internationally Wrongful Acts: Compilation of Decisions of International Courts, Tribunals and Other Bodies, Report of the Secretary-General' (23 April 2019) UN Doc A/74/83.

[6] Eg WTO, *United States – Measures Affecting the Cross-Border Supply of Gambling and Betting Services – Report of the Panel* (10 November 2004) WT/DS285/R [6.128].

[7] Statute of the International Court of Justice (adopted 26 June 1945, entered into force 24 October 1945) 33 UNTS 993, Art 38(1)(d) (ICJ Statute); D Caron, 'The ILC Articles on State Responsibility: The Paradoxical Relationship between Form and Authority' (2002) 96 AJIL 857, 857.

[8] Eg R Sloane, 'On the Use and Abuse of Necessity in the Law of State Responsibility' (2012) 106 AJIL 447, 452.

To start, investment tribunals are constituted for the settlement of a dispute between a State and a national of another State arising out of an investment which the parties have consented to submit to arbitration.[9] Whether investment tribunals can apply in this context also other rules of international law including customary international law and general principles of law is a procedural issue.[10] Relevant procedural rules commonly uphold in the first place the autonomy of the parties to determine the applicable law,[11] but provide residually for the application of 'applicable rules of international law' in the absence of an agreement or when the tribunal determines such law to be appropriate.[12] Besides, even when the rules of general international law are not deemed directly applicable to a specific issue, a tribunal might decide to take them into account as relevant rules for the interpretation of the applicable IIA.[13] Questions of identification of the international law on State responsibility arise against this procedural background. By implication, investment tribunals turn to ARSIWA for the purposes of identifying rules of international law external to the IIA in question or otherwise applicable to the case. Accordingly, investment tribunals tend to justify their reliance on ARSIWA by using

---

[9] Eg C Schreuer, 'Investment Disputes' [2013] MPEPIL 517 [1].
[10] Eg O Spielmann, 'Applicable Law' in P Muchlinski, F Ortino & C Schreuer (eds), *The Oxford Handbook of International Investment Law* (OUP 2008) 89, 90.
[11] Eg C Schreuer & ors, *The ICSID Convention: A Commentary* (2nd edn, CUP 2009) 557; D Caron & L Caplan, *The UNCITRAL Arbitration Rules: A Commentary* (2nd edn, OUP 2013) 112.
[12] R Dolzer & C Schreuer, *Principles of International Investment Law* (2nd edn, OUP 2012) 288; eg ICSID Convention, Art 42(1); United Nations Commission on International Trade Law (UNCITRAL), 'Arbitration Rules of the United Nations Commission on International Trade Law' (15 December 1976) UN Doc A/31/98, 31st Session Supp No 17, Art 35(1) (UNCITRAL Rules); International Chamber of Commerce (ICC), '2021 Arbitration Rules and 2014 Mediation Rules' (*ICC*, November 2020) Art 21(1) <https://iccwbo.org/content/uploads/sites/3/2020/12/icc-2021-arbitration-rules-2014-mediation-rules-english-version.pdf> accessed 10 May 2021; Arbitration Institute of the Stockholm Chamber of Commerce (SCC), '2017 Arbitration Rules' (*SCC*, 1 January 2020) Art 27(1) <https://sccinstitute.com/media/1407444/arbitrationrules_eng_2020.pdf> accessed 10 May 2021; North American Free Trade Agreement (NAFTA) (adopted 17 December 1992, entered into force 1 January 1994) 32 ILM 289, Art 1131(1) as maintained by Art 14.D.9; Agreement Between the United States of America, the United Mexican States, and Canada (adopted 10 December 2019, entered into force 1 July 2020); The Energy Charter Treaty (adopted 17 December 1994, entered into force 16 April 1998) 2080 UNTS 95, Art 26(6).
[13] Vienna Convention on the Law of Treaties (adopted 23 May 1969, entered into force 27 January 1980) 1155 UNTS 331, Art 31(3)(c); eg *Al Tamimi v Oman* (Award of 3 November 2015) ICSID Case No ARB/11/33 [321–3] (US-Oman Free Trade Agreement/ARSIWA (n 1) Art 5); *Windstream v Canada* (Award of 27 September 2016) PCA Case No 2013–22 [233] (NAFTA, Art 1503(2)/ARSIWA (n 1) Art 5).

the terminology of 'formal' sources of international law, albeit with varying degrees of sophistication.

In the first place, the well-recorded discrepancy between the 'formal' status of ARSIWA as a source of law and their effective 'authority' in the context of investment arbitration calls for a more detailed survey into how investment tribunals justify their use of ARSIWA.[14] With respect to customary international law, the ILC has opined – in a somewhat self-aggrandising manner – that 'a determination by the Commission affirming the existence and content of a rule of customary international law may have particular value, as may a conclusion by it that no such rule exists'.[15] This is so notwithstanding the fact that the ILC outputs cannot constitute evidence of State practice or *opinio juris* in and of themselves, as they do not originate directly, or even indirectly, from States.[16] Moreover, as the late Judge Crawford recounts, the ARSIWA 'have been derived from cases, from practice, and from often unarticulated instantiations of general legal ideas'.[17] This implies that the ARSIWA are not necessarily a monolith from the perspective of sources of international law. Even assuming that some normative propositions included in the ARSIWA do not strictly adhere to the standards of identification of customary international law, tribunals might still have recourse to them as articulations of underlying general principles of law.[18] In a nutshell, there are multiple justifications available to investment tribunals for their use of ARSIWA.

Besides, apart from *why* investment tribunals rely so much on ARSIWA, a closely related question is also *how* they make use of ARSIWA. In their final form, the ARSIWA consist of provisions articulated in prescriptive

---

[14] Caron (n 7) 858.
[15] ILC, 'Draft Conclusions on Identification of Customary International Law, with Commentaries' (30 April–1 June and 2 July–10 August 2018) UN Doc A/73/10, reproduced in [2018/II – Part Two] YBILC 122 (hereinafter CICIL), Commentary to Part Five [2]; *compare* CICIL, Commentary to Conclusion 1 [5] fn 112.
[16] ibid, Conclusion 4.
[17] J Crawford, 'The International Court of Justice and the Law of State Responsibility' in CJ Tams & J Sloan (eds), *The Development of International Law by the International Court of Justice* (OUP 2013) 71, 74.
[18] ICJ Statute, Art 38(1)(c); on the argument that the principles comprising the law of State responsibility constitute general principles of law; cf, eg, CT Kotuby & LA Sobota, *General Principles of Law and International Due Process: Principles and Norms Applicable in Transnational Disputes* (OUP 2017) 143–56; M Đorđeska, *General Principles of Law Recognized by Civilized Nations (1922–2018): The Evolution of the Third Source of International Law through the Jurisprudence of the Permanent Court of International Justice and the International Court of Justice* (Brill 2020) 393–7.

terms much like the draft of a treaty.¹⁹ It could be argued that an international court or tribunal having recourse to them should approach them in a way akin to any document having binding effect.²⁰ In so doing, the court or tribunal should follow a methodology that builds upon the rules of treaty interpretation but also accounts for the fact that the ARSIWA do not originate directly from States but from a technical body of the UN.²¹ However, the traditional perception of ILC outputs as 'teachings' is inimical to according any particular value to the views of the ILC as such, the ILC being a body of legal experts not of representatives of States.²² Rather, a decision-maker should focus on the evidence that the ILC adduces for the existence of a rule and reconstruct the content of the rule in question on the basis of that evidence.²³ In more practical terms, the ILC outputs on the topic not only encompass the ARSIWA and their accompanying commentaries, but also a multitude of documents including the previous reports of the Commission, comments by governments, the summary records of discussions within the plenary including the reports of drafting committees, and the reports of the special rapporteurs.²⁴ A combined reading of these documents reveals 'titanic disagreements' on virtually all issues, which are imprinted in the carefully balanced language of the final text.²⁵ In this respect, the traditional label of 'teachings' provides little guidance as to how to navigate

---

[19] Caron (n 7) 866; Sloane (n 8) 452.

[20] G Abi-Saab, 'La Commission du Droit International, la codification et le processus de la formation de droit international' in *Making Better International Law: The International Law Commission at 50* (UN 1998) 181, 196.

[21] G Gaja, 'Interpreting Articles Adopted by the International Law Commission' (2015) 85 BYBIL 10, 17–20.

[22] Caron (n 7) 868–9; cf, eg, CICIL (n 15) Commentary to Conclusion 14 [3]; more vaguely, ILC, 'Second Report on General Principles of Law by Marcelo Vázquez-Bermúdez, Special Rapporteur' (9 April 2020) UN Doc A/CN.4/741 [179] ('caution is needed when drawing upon writings, as their value for determining the existence of a rule of international law may vary').

[23] Caron (n 7) 867; cf *The Paquete Habana*, 175 US 677 (1900) 700; cited with approval in CICIL (n 15) Commentary to Conclusion 14 [3] ('Such works are resorted to by judicial tribunals, not for the speculations of their authors concerning what the law ought to be, but for trustworthy evidence of what the law really is').

[24] For an overview, see ILC, 'Analytical Guide to the Work of the International Law Commission' (*ILC*, 14 April 2020) <https://legal.un.org/ilc/guide/9_6.shtml#top> accessed 10 May 2021.

[25] J Crawford, 'Investment Arbitration and the ILC Articles on State Responsibility' (2010) 25 ICSID Rev 127, 129; also, eg A Pellet, 'The ILC's Articles on State Responsibility for Internationally Wrongful Acts and Related Texts' in J Crawford, A Pellet & S Olleson (eds), *The Law of International Responsibility* (OUP 2010) 75, 87.

through all these materials in determining applicable rules of law, as it treats all these materials indistinctly.[26]

In this context of contestation, the premise of this study is that the practice of investment tribunals, as the most frequent users of ARSIWA, can further elucidate the connections between the ARSIWA and the framework of sources of international law, and shed light on the methodology for their proper use. As a preliminary point, the practice of investment tribunals regarding ARSIWA has been paralleled to 'a drowning man ... grab[bing] a stick in the sea in the hope of having certainty'.[27] More fundamentally, it has been argued that the power of the international judge to resolve an international dispute necessarily entails a certain degree of discretion as to the identification of applicable rules and the determination of their content.[28] Hence, the tendency of investment to rely on ARSIWA could be dismissed as an instantiation or corollary of such discretion or 'expediency' in international judicial decision-making.[29] Yet, whilst it is arguable that international judges enjoy more leeway than domestic ones in identifying and determining the content of applicable rules of law, they are not entirely uninhibited by any rules or principles.[30] In resolving competing claims as to the identification and determination of the content of rules of State responsibility, investment tribunals have the incentive –and often do– justify thoroughly their legal findings.[31] Apart from dispelling any impression of bias or arbitrariness, investment tribunals have the strong incentive to pre-empt the annulment of the award or to prevent any domestic obstacles in the implementation of their decision.[32] Therefore, the practice of investment tribunals engaging with ARSIWA cannot be reduced easily to mere expediency, but could

---

[26] Caron (n 7) 869.
[27] Crawford (n 25) 128.
[28] cf, on the general point, M Bedjaoui, 'Expediency in the Decisions of the International Court of Justice' (2000) 71 BYBIL 1, 5.
[29] ibid 4–5; see, critically, Caron (n 7) 866.
[30] cf, on the opposite view, J d'Aspremont, 'The Idea of 'Rules' in the Sources of International Law' (2014) 84 BYBIL 103, 126–7.
[31] cf, on the general point, C Kessedjian, 'Le tiers impartial et indépendant en droit international: Juge, arbitre, médiateur, conciliateur – Cours général de droit international' (2019) 403 RdC 56, 504.
[32] Convention on the Settlement of Investment Disputes Between States and Nationals of Other States (adopted 18 March 1965, entered into force 14 October 1966) 575 UNTS 159, Art 52 (hereinafter ICSID Convention); on available proceedings see, eg, F Baetens, 'Keeping the Status Quo or Embarking on a New Course? Setting Aside, Refusal of Enforcement, Annulment and Appeal' in A Kulick (ed), *Reassertion of Control over the Investment Treaty Regime* (CUP 2017) 103, 105–13.

constitute evidence of existing or emerging rules or principles, or at least, good practices, for the identification and interpretation of applicable rules of unwritten international law.

3   Patterns of Justification for the Use of ARSIWA in International Investment Arbitration

At first glance, a majority of investment tribunals give specific reasons for relying on ARSIWA, albeit a significant number of tribunals are silent on the matter. In purely quantitative terms, out of a sample of 205 decisions surveyed for the purposes of this study, 144 provide separately a justification for their reliance on ARSIWA or its previous versions. Conversely, 61 decisions cite the ILC Articles without explicitly providing a reason for doing so. On the one hand, the significant number of decisions that lack any justification for reliance on ARSIWA give support to the argument that the distinction between identification and determination of content is not water-tight not only in theory but also in practice.[33] However, a closer look at the reasoning of the tribunals depicts a much more diverse and nuanced picture than a numerical presentation suggests. In some cases, the tribunals' stance towards the nexus between ARSIWA and the sources of international law becomes apparent from the context of the reference or the decision notwithstanding the lack of an *expressis verbis* or clear-cut justification. On the other hand, the tribunals provide a wide variety of justifications which do not always consist of a clear link between the ARSIWA and the 'formal' source of the applicable rule. Besides, the same decision might follow different lines of reasoning with respect to different provisions of ARSIWA or rely on ARSIWA only partly for the identification of applicable rules on State responsibility.[34] Mindful of these difficulties, the present subsection attempts to flag up common patterns in the ways in which investment tribunals justify their reliance on ARSIWA, whereas the following subsection focuses on how they use ARSIWA for the determination of the content of the applicable rule.

From the outset, tribunals recognise that the ARSIWA have no formally binding status as such either implicitly or, less often, explicitly.[35] However,

---

[33] On the theoretical point: J d'Aspremont, 'Three International Lawyers in a Hall of Mirrors' (2019) 32 LJIL 367, 369–72.
[34] Compare, eg, fns 49/68 and fns 58/69 and the text accompanying them.
[35] See eg *Noble Ventures Inc v Romania* (Award of 12 October 2005) ICSID Case No ARB/01/11 [69]; *F-W v Trinidad and Tobago* (Award of 3 March 2006) ICSID Case No ARB/01/14

remarkably, this survey has found only one award that explicitly characterises the ARSIWA – and, particularly, the ILC's Commentary – as 'works of highly qualified writers',[36] despite this characterisation being relatively uncontroversial in theory with respect to works of the ILC.[37] The underlying reason for this discrepancy seems to be the ensuing discrepancy between the relative value which such sources are to be accorded generally in the determination of applicable rules according to the ICJ Statute and the effective authority of ARSIWA in the context of investment arbitration.

In the first place, tribunals use the ARSIWA in the process of identifying rules stemming from customary international law. In most cases, investment tribunals affirm the applicability of ARSIWA, because they 'reflect',[38] 'codify',[39] 'state',[40] 'restate',[41] 'express',[42] 'formulate',[43] 'articulate',[44] 'represent',[45] or 'are declaratory of'[46] rules or principles of customary international law on State responsibility. Very often, these findings are couched in axiomatic terms without any further explanation or are reasoned in such vague terms so as to amount to little more than assertions.[47] When they do reason such findings, tribunals tend to uphold the authority of ARSIWA because of the evidence they rely upon,[48] their particular

---

[202]; *Sempra Energy v Argentina* (Award of 28 September 2007) ICSID Case No ARB/02/16 [344]; *Al-Bahloul v Tajikistan* (Final Award of 8 June 2010) SCC Case No V 064/2008 [42]; *Rompetrol v Romania* (Award of 6 May 2013) ICSID Case No ARB/06/3 [189]; *Tidewater v Venezuela* (Annulment of 27 December 2016) ICSID Case No ARB/10/5 [144].

[36] *Merrill & Ring v Canada* (Award of 31 March 2010) ICSID Administered Case No UNCT/07/1 [203].

[37] See, eg, RY Jennings, 'The Progressive Development of International Law and its Codification' (1947) 24 BYBIL 301, 308; M Lachs, 'Teachings and Teaching of International Law' (1976) 151 RdC 164, 224–5; but see CICIL (n 15) Commentary to Conclusion 14 [5] fn 112.

[38] Eg *CMS v Argentina* (Annulment of 25 September 2007) ICSID Case No ARB/01/8 [121].

[39] Eg *Total SA v Argentina* (Decision on Liability of 27 December 2007) ICSID Case No ARB/04/01 [220].

[40] Eg *EnCana v Ecuador* (Award of 3 February 2006) UNCITRAL, LCIA Case No UN3481 [154].

[41] Eg *Nykomb v Latvia* (Arbitral Award of 16 December 2003) SCC Case No 118/2001, 38.

[42] Eg *Unión Fenosa v Egypt* (Award of 31 August 2018) ICSID Case No ARB/14/4 [8.2].

[43] Eg *ADF Group Inc v USA* (Award of 9 January 2003) ICSID Case No ARB(AF)/00/1 [166].

[44] Eg *Teinver v Argentina* (Award of 21 July 2017) ICSID Case No ARB/09/1 [1089].

[45] Eg *Paushok v Mongolia* (Decision on Jurisdiction of 28 April 2011) UNCITRAL [576].

[46] Eg *Vivendi (I) v Argentina* (Annulment of 3 July 2002) ICSID Case No ARB/97/3 [96].

[47] Eg *Metalclad v Mexico* (Award of 30 August 2000) ICSID Case No ARB(AF)/97/1 [73]; *Unglaube v Costa Rica* (Award of 16 May 2002) ICSID Case No ARB/08/1 & ICSID Case No ARB/09/20 [320].

[48] Eg *ConocoPhillips v Venezuela* (Decision on Jurisdiction and Merits of 3 September 2013) ICSID Case No ARB/07/30 [339]; *Bilcon v Canada* (Decision on Damages of 10 January 2019) PCA Case No 2009-04 [197]; *Novenergia II v Spain* (Final Award of 15 February 2018) SCC Arbitration 2015/063 [807].

drafting process,[49] or their subsequent reception in practice.[50] In this latter respect, several tribunals have taken note of the fact that the General Assembly has annexed ARSIWA to a resolution and commended them to the consideration of States.[51] Other tribunals refer to the pronouncements of other international courts or investment tribunals finding that certain provision of ARSIWA reflect customary international law.[52] Whatever the specific line of reasoning, the common thread between these decisions is the finding that ARSIWA or a specific provision has decisive value for the identification of customary international law on this matter. In practical terms, the normative propositions contained in ARSIWA are treated as having the status of – or, more precisely, as materially identical with – rules of customary international law.

Second, a significant number of decisions use ARSIWA as means to identify rules of general application without explicitly utilising the terminology of customary international law. On the one hand, there are decisions mentioning ARSIWA in the context of identification of general principles of law. In this respect, tribunals usually declare that certain provision of ARSIWA or a statement in the Commentary is generally recognised in domestic legal systems without engaging in any detailed comparative examination or independently assessing its transposability in international law.[53] On the other hand, quite often, tribunals turn to ARSIWA as means for the identification of international law without deciding or clarifying what is the particular status of the underlying rules. In most cases, it is impossible to discern whether there are any legal reasons for such ambiguity or whether it is just a product of idiosyncratic

---

[49] Eg *ADM v Mexico* (Award of 21 November 2007) ICSID Case No ARB(AF)/04/05 [116].
[50] cf, more generally, CICIL (n 15) Commentary to Part Five [2].
[51] Eg *Jan de Nul v Egypt* (Decision on Jurisdiction of 16 June 2006) ICSID Case No ARB/04/13 [89]; *Saipem v Bangladesh* (Decision on Jurisdiction and Provisional Measures of 21 March 2007) ICSID Case No ARB/05/07 [148]; *Hamester v Ghana* (Award of 18 June 2010) ICSID Case No ARB/07/24 [171]; *Electrabel v Hungary* (Decision on Jurisdiction and Liability of 30 November 2012) ICSID Case No ARB/07/19 [7.60].
[52] Eg *Tatneft v Ukraine* (Decision on Merits of 29 July 2014) UNCITRAL [540]; *El Paso Energy International Company v Argentina* (Award of 31 October 2011) ICSID Case No ARB/03/15 [617]; *ConocoPhillips v Venezuela* [339].
[53] Eg *Gemplus v Mexico* (Award of 16 June 2010) ICSID Cases Nos ARB(AF)/04/3 & ARB(AF)/04/4 [11.12] (ARSIWA (n 1) Art 39); *El Paso v Argentina* [621–3] (ARSIWA (n 1) Art 25(2): as an alternative basis alongside custom); *EDF v Argentina* (Award of 11 June 2012) ICSID Case No ARB/03/23 [1302–4] (duty to mitigate– ARSIWA (n 1) Art 31); *Desert Line v Yemen* (Award of 6 February 2008) ICSID Case No ARB/05/17 [289]; on the identification of general principles of law, see ILC (n 22) [112].

drafting.⁵⁴ However, in some cases, the context of the decision reveals deeper concerns about the applicability of the rules on State responsibility reflected in ARSIWA in the investor-State context.⁵⁵ So, for instance, in the *Jan de Nul* Award, the Tribunal declared that the General Assembly resolution, to which ARSIWA are annexed, 'is considered as a statement of customary international law on the question of attribution for purposes of asserting the responsibility of *a State towards another State*'.⁵⁶ Despite this finding, it held that ARSIWA was 'applicable *by analogy* to the responsibility of States towards private parties'.⁵⁷ A similar issue arose in *Vestey* where Venezuela argued that the principle of full reparation reflected in Art 31 ARSIWA was inapplicable in the case of unlawful expropriation.⁵⁸ In response, the Tribunal held that 'while the ILC Articles govern a State responsibility vis-à-vis another State and not a private person, it is generally accepted that the key provisions of the ILC, such as Article 31(1) *can be transposed* in the context of the investor-State disputes.'⁵⁹ Relying on judicial decisions applying the principle of full reparation in the context of expropriation,⁶⁰ the Tribunal concluded that 'Venezuela must provide full reparation under customary international law'.⁶¹ In all these cases, tribunals treat ARSIWA as definitive statements of applicable rules of law, albeit with some ambiguity as to the precise source of such rules. Apart from general principles of law common to domestic laws, it is not apparent whether tribunals apply customary international law or refer to an altogether different category of general principles of law emanating from within international law.⁶²

Another strand of decisions seems to take into account the parties' mutual reliance on ARSIWA in their submissions so as to affirm their

---

⁵⁴ Eg *Saint-Gobain v Venezuela* (Decision on Liability and Quantum of 30 December 2016) ICSID Case No ARB/12/13 [448] (ARSIWA (n 1) Art 8); *Ares v Georgia* (Award of 26 February 2008) ICSID Case No ARB/05/23 [8.3.3] (ARSIWA (n 1) Art 15).
⁵⁵ cf, eg, K Hobér, 'State Responsibility and Attribution' in P Muchlinski, F Ortino & C Schreuer (eds), *The Oxford Handbook of International Investment Law* (OUP 2008) 549, 552.
⁵⁶ *Jan de Nul v Egypt* (Award of 6 November 2008) ICSID Case No ARB/04/13 [156] (emphasis added); also, in the exact same terms, *Masdar Solar v Spain* (Award of 16 May 2018) ICSID Case No ARB/14/1 [167].
⁵⁷ ibid (emphasis added).
⁵⁸ *Vestey v Venezuela* (Award of 15 April 2016) ICSID Case No ARB/06/4 [323].
⁵⁹ ibid [326] (emphasis added).
⁶⁰ ibid [329].
⁶¹ ibid [331]; see, along similar lines, *Rompetrol v Romania* [189–90].
⁶² As to the latter concept, see ILC (n 22) [171].

applicability in the proceedings. Notably, some tribunals appear to treat the parties' agreement as the sole basis for the application of a provision of ARSIWA in the proceedings without any finding on whether such provision actually reflects a rule stemming from a 'formal' source of international law.[63] So, for instance, in *EDF*, the Tribunal found it unnecessary to take a position on 'the theoretical question of how far the various aspects of ILC Article 25 codifi[ed] customary defenses related to necessity'.[64] The Tribunal took note that 'both sides in this arbitration stipulate[d] that the Tribunal's analysis should take as applicable legal norms the State of Necessity defen[c]e presented by the contours articulated in ILC Article 25' and found that 'the standards urged by both sides, as providing applicable norms'.[65] In these cases, the emphasis of tribunals seems to be on the relevance of party autonomy for the determination of applicable law rather than its identification on the basis of the relevant rules of international law. Yet, it could be argued that the parties' agreement has only evidentiary value as to the status of the rule reflected in certain provision of ARSIWA so as to obviate the need for further independent analysis.[66] So, for instance, the annulment committee in *Continental Casualty* upheld the legal findings of the Tribunal on applicable law on the basis that 'it was not disputed by either party that Article 25 of the ILC Articles codified the customary international law principles, and the Tribunal proceeded on this basis'.[67]

This overview shows that investment tribunals tend to justify their reliance on ARSIWA by using the terminology of 'formal' sources of international law. However, although the vocabulary of 'formal' sources is used or alluded to, it can be concluded that investment tribunals do not seem to treat ARSIWA as a monolith in the process of identification of

---

[63] cf, eg, *Suez, Sociedad General de Aguas de Barcelona SA, and Vivendi Universal SA v Argentina* (Decision on Annulment of 5 May 2017) ICSID Case No ARB/03/19 [289] (*Suez v Argentina* (Annulment)); *Staur Eiendom v Latvia* (Award of 28 February 2020) ICSID Case No ARB/16/38 [311]; also, similarly, *Teinver v Argentina* [702, 721 & 1044].

[64] *EDF v Argentina* [1167].

[65] ibid [1168–9].

[66] cf, e.g., *Biwater Gauff v Tanzania* (Award of 24 July 2008) ICSID Case No ARB/05/22 [479]; *Pezold v Zimbabwe* (Award of 28 July 2015) ICSID Case No ARB/10/15 [624]; *Victor Pay Casado v Chile* (Resubmission Award of 13 September 2016) ICSID Case No ARB/98/2 [203–4].

[67] *Continental Casualty v Argentina* (Decision on the Application for Partial Annulment, and the Application for Partial Annulment of 16 September 2011) ICSID Case No ARB/03/9 [114]; *EDF v Argentina* (Decision on Annulment of 5 February 2016) ICSID Case No ARB/03/23 [329].

applicable rules. In most cases, tribunals accord ARSIWA decisive value in the process of identification of rules of customary international law on State responsibility. Other tribunals evoke the terminology of general principles of law or are ambiguous in this respect. What is more, tribunals usually avoid wide-ranging conclusions and focus on whether a specific provision of ARSIWA reflects an applicable rule. That said, a noteworthy insight gained from the empirical analysis is that these variations are not limited to certain parts or provisions of ARSIWA. Rather, they exist with respect to a variety of issues such as the rules on attribution of conduct, the breach of an international obligation, the circumstances precluding wrongfulness, or the provisions relating to reparation and implementation of responsibility.

4 Patterns of Interpretation in the Use of ARSIWA in International Investment Arbitration

4.1 Content-Determination Pursuant to the 'Text' of ARSIWA

Whether they provide a justification or not, tribunals rely on ARSIWA primarily as means to determine the content of applicable rules on State responsibility. In the case of treaties, the determination whether a text or statement has the formal hallmark of a treaty entailing binding obligations, on the one hand, and the determination of the meaning of a binding treaty provision, on the other, clearly involves different considerations so much so that it is possible to speak of two distinct juridical operations governed by different rules.[68] However, the ARSIWA are not a treaty. As we have seen, tribunals justify their applicability in investment arbitration as expressions of unwritten international law, that is, customary international law or, less often, general principles of law. In this respect, it has been maintained in theory that it is impossible to identify a rule of unwritten international law without, at the same time, determining its content.[69] Conversely, rules of unwritten law are not amenable to interpretation, this operation presupposing the existence of a text.[70] As a corollary, the

---

[68] *Compare* VCLT, Art 2(1)(a); eg *Aegean Sea Continental Shelf (Greece v Turkey)* (Jurisdiction) [1978] ICJ Rep 3 [96]; *Maritime Delimitation and Territorial Questions (Qatar v Bahrain)* (Jurisdiction and Admissibility) [1994] ICJ Rep 112 [23]; *with* VCLT, Arts 31–3; e.g., *Arbitral Award of 31 July 1989 (Guinea-Bissau v Senegal)* [1991] ICJ Rep 53 [48].
[69] M Bos, *A Methodology of International Law* (Asser 1984) 109.
[70] T Treves, 'Customary International Law' [2006] *MPEPIL* [2].

determination of the content of a rule depends on the very same means as the identification of a rule and requires the establishment of State practice and *opinio juris* or of recognition and transposability, as the case may be.[71] This section (and the subsections that comprise it) shows that these theoretical considerations can explain the practice of investment tribunals relating to ARSIWA only partially. Although decisions differ to a large extent as to how they use ARSIWA in the determination of the content of applicable rules, it is possible to discern certain trends. One discernible trend that is not easily reconcilable with these considerations is investment tribunal's emphasis on a 'textualist' approach when using ARSIWA to determine the content of applicable rules on State responsibility.

To start with, the role of interpretation in determining the content of applicable rules of State responsibility is not usually pronounced and intertwines with the ways in which tribunals use ARSIWA in this process. According to the classification laid down in Art 38(1) ICJ Statute, ILC works constitute 'subsidiary means for the determination of rules of law'.[72] Albeit investment tribunals never refer to this categorisation explicitly (but for one singular exception),[73] some of them effectively use ARSIWA as such by merely citing them to support a determination that certain normative proposition found in judicial pronouncements or other sources reflects a rule of international law.[74] These tribunals seem to treat ARSIWA indistinctly as secondary evidence in the determination of unwritten international law without any methodological explanation as to the steps followed in this process.

However, in many cases, the ways in which tribunals engage with ARSIWA in the process of determination of applicable rules goes beyond indirect reliance. Most notably, there is an abundance of decisions in which tribunals proceed to apply provisions of ARSIWA as self-explanatory to the facts of the case. Thus, for instance, many tribunals quote Article 4 ARSIWA as a representation of applicable law and continue to determine whether a person or an entity is a State organ or not relying on the

---

[71] CICIL (n 15) Conclusion 2; ILC (n 22) [112 & 171].
[72] See fns 7 and 35.
[73] See fn 36.
[74] See, eg *LESI v Algeria* (Award of 10 January 2005) ICSID Case No ARB/03/08 [19(ii)] (non-attribution of conduct of private individuals); *Claimant v Slovakia* (Award of 5 March 2011) ad hoc Arbitration [197]; *Pac Rim v El Salvador* (Award of 14 October 2016) ICSID Case No ARB/09/12 [5.62] (non-opposability of domestic law as justification for non-performance of an international obligation); *Olin v Libya* (Final Award of 25 May 2018) ICC Case No 20355/MCP [472–4] (principle of full reparation); *Achmea (I) v Slovakia* (Final Award of 7 December 2012) PCA Case No 2008–13 [334] (award of interest).

characterisation provided in the domestic law of the relevant State.[75] Similarly, tribunals have applied without any discussion a variety of provisions of ARSIWA including those on attribution of conduct,[76] on the time of the breach,[77] on circumstances precluding wrongfulness,[78] and on reparation.[79] In the same vein, tribunals often identify in a provision of ARSIWA an applicable rule of law and then refer to judicial pronouncements as means to determine the meaning of that provision. To illustrate this point, in the *Jan de Nul* award on the merits, the Tribunal considered ILC's provision that a given conduct is considered an act of State 'if the person or group of persons is in fact acting on the instructions of, or under the direction or control of, that State in carrying out the conduct'.[80] After characterising ARSIWA 'a statement of customary international law', it proceeded to further clarify the meaning of the provision.[81] The Tribunal held that '[i]nternational jurisprudence is very demanding in order to attribute the act of a person or entity to a State, as it requires both a general control of the State over the person or entity and a specific control of the State over the act the attribution of which is at stake; this is known as the "effective control" test', citing in support the findings of the ICJ in *Nicaragua*.[82] Subsequent awards reproduce the *Jan de Nul* formula more

---

[75] Eg, *ADF Group v USA* (Award of 9 January 2003) ICSID Case No ARB(AF)/00/1 [166]; *Oostergetel v Slovakia* (Final Award of 23 April 2012) UNCITRAL [151 & 155]; *Bosh v Ukraine* (Award of 25 October 2012) ICSID Case No ARB/08/11, 3 [16]; *Levi v Peru* (Award of 26 February 2014) ICSID Case No ARB/10/17 [157-8]; *Awdi v Romania* (Award of 2 March 2015) ICSID Case No ARB/10/13 [323]; *Infinito Gold v Costa Rica* (Decision on Jurisdiction of 4 December 2017) ICSID Case No ARB/14/5 [198]; *Casinos Austria v Argentina* (Decision on Jurisdiction of 29 June 2018) ICSID Case No ARB/14/32 [288]).

[76] Eg, *Masdar Solar v Spain* [168-9] (ARSIWA (n 1) Arts 4, 5 & 8); *Kardassopoulos v Georgia* (Decision on Jurisdiction of 6 July 2007) ICSID Case No ARB/05/18 [190] (ARSIWA (n 1) Art 7); *Cengiz v Libya* (Final Award of 7 November 2018) ICC Case No 21537/ZF/AYZ [424-5] (ARSIWA (n 1) Art 10); *Bilcon v Canada* (Decision on Jurisdiction and Liability of 17 March 2005) PCA Case No 2009-04 [321-2] (ARSIWA (n 1) Art 11).

[77] Eg *Mondev International Ltd v USA* (Award of 11 October 2002) ICSID Case No ARB(AF)/99/2 [58] (ARSIWA (n 1) Art 14(1)); *El Paso v Argentina* [515] (ARSIWA (n 1) Art 15).

[78] Eg *Sempra Energy v Argentina* [246] (ARSIWA (n 1) Art 23); *Pezold v Zimbabwe* [657] (ARSIWA (n 1) Arts 25(2)(b) & 26).

[79] Eg *Armas v Venezuela* (Final Award of 26 April 2019) PCA Case No 2013-3 [476-7] (ARSIWA (n 1) Art 31); *Innogy v Spain* (Decision on Jurisdiction, Liability and Certain Issues of Quantum of 30 December 2019) ICSID Case No ARB/14/34 [685] (ARSIWA (n 1) Art 35); *ADM v Mexico* [281] (ARSIWA (n 1) Art 36).

[80] ARSIWA (n 1) Art 8.

[81] *Jan de Nul* (Award) [156 & 172].

[82] ibid [173] citing *Military and Paramilitary Activities in and against Nicaragua (Nicaragua v USA)* (Merits) [1986] ICJ Rep 16 [113 & 115].

or less *verbatim*,[83] even though the 'general control' prong of the test does not feature explicitly in the text of Article 8 ARSIWA, its Commentary or the pronouncements of the ICJ after *Nicaragua*.[84]

In these two groups of cases, it is difficult to discern what precise juridical operation is at play, but two alternatives are conceivable from an analytical perspective. On the one hand, the lack of any separate analysis on the content of the applicable rule is suggestive of the absence of an intermediate step between identification of a rule of customary international law or general principle of law and its application.[85] Similarly, the reliance on judicial pronouncements can be construed as an extension of the determination of State practice/*opinio juris* or recognition/transposability, as the case may be, albeit implicitly and on the basis of secondary evidence.[86] After all, judicial decisions, much like ARSIWA, constitute 'subsidiary means' for the determination of applicable rules.[87] On the other hand, these tribunals not even purport to determine the content of the applicable rule on State responsibility through an independent analysis of State practice and *opinio juris* or a comparative survey. Rather, they proceed to apply the formulations of the ILC to the facts of the case as if they were a binding text.

In this respect, the conciseness of analysis can also be construed as an emanation of a textual approach towards ARSIWA in a way that parallels known approaches of treaty interpretation. In other words, the tribunals' line of reasoning consists conceivably of the application of the terms of a provision whose source of legal validity (CIL or general principle of law) has already been determined, because they deem its ordinary meaning sufficiently clear.[88] To illustrate this point, in *Tulip*, the Tribunal examined whether the termination of a contract by a company owned

---

[83] Eg, *Hamester v Ghana* [179]; *White Industries v India* (Final Award of 30 November 2011) UNCITRAL [8.1.7 & 8.1.10–7]; *Almås v Poland* (Award of 27 June 2016) PCA Case No 2015-13 [268–72]; *Gavrilović v Croatia* (Award of 26 July 2018) ICSID Case No ARB/12/39 [828].

[84] ARSIWA (n 1) Commentary to Art 8 [1–2 & 7]; see, eg, *Application of the Convention on the Prevention and Punishment of the Crime of Genocide (Bosnia and Herzegovina v Serbia and Montenegro)* (Judgment) [2007] ICJ Rep 43 [400].

[85] A Gourgourinis, 'The Distinction between Interpretation and Application of Norms in International Adjudication' (2011) 2 JIDS 31, 34–6.

[86] CICIL (n 15) Conclusion 13; ILC (n 22) [181].

[87] ICJ Statute, Art 38(1)(d).

[88] cf, eg, *Arbitral Award of 31 July 1989* [48]; also, *Competence of the General Assembly for the Admission of a State to the United Nations* (Advisory Opinion) [1950] ICJ Rep 4, 8; *South West Africa Cases (Ethiopia v South Africa; Liberia v South Africa)* (Preliminary Objection) [1962] ICJ Rep 319, 336.

predominantly by a State agency was attributable to Turkey. The Tribunal accepted that 'the ILC Articles constitute a codification of customary international law with respect to the issue of attribution of conduct to the State'.[89] Turning to Article 8 ARSIWA, the Tribunal focused on its text and decided that '[p]lainly, the words "instructions", "direction" and "control" are to be read disjunctively'.[90] The fact that a State agency owned the majority share of the company in question entailed that the company was under the control of the Turkish State in the sense that Turkey was capable of exercising a degree of control to implement governmental policies.[91] Nonetheless, the Tribunal held that such control was insufficient for attribution, because, according to the ILC's Commentary, the State must 'us[e] its ownership interest in or control of a corporation in order to achieve a particular result'.[92] In the subsequent annulment decision in *Tulip*, the committee clarified that 'the tribunal, in *interpreting* Article 8, took into account the ILC Commentary' and upheld the analysis of the Tribunal finding that '[it] correctly *interpreted* Article 8'.[93] Such textual analysis of ARSIWA with reference to the ILC Commentary as an authoritative interpretative aid is most common in the practice of investment tribunals, even if they are not always as explicit as the *Tulip* committee when justifying their methodological choices.[94] Therefore, there is evidence to suggest that such 'textualist' approach constitutes essentially an interpretative operation.

Along similar lines, it is possible to argue that tribunals frame their reliance on previous case law in terms of interpretation because such previous pronouncements only purported to interpret rules whose existence was undisputed. So, for instance in *El Paso*, Argentina argued that the Tribunal exceeded its powers by relying on case law to determine the applicable standard of reparation under the law on State responsibility, despite judicial decisions' lack of binding status beyond the confines of a specific case.[95] The annulment committee dismissed this claim on the basis that '[a]rbitral tribunals must resort to different methods of

---

[89] *Tulip v Turkey* (Award of 10 March 2014) ICSID Case No ARB/11/28 [281].
[90] ibid [303].
[91] ibid [307–8].
[92] ibid [306] citing ARSIWA (n 1) Commentary to Art 8 [6].
[93] *Tulip v Turkey* (Decision on Annulment of 30 December 2015) ICSID Case No ARB/11/28 [187–8] (emphasis added).
[94] Eg *Pezold v Zimbabwe* [448]; *Electrabel v Hungary* [7.109 & 7.113]; *Saint-Gobain v Venezuela* [450].
[95] cf, explicitly, *El Paso Energy International Company v Argentina* (Decision on Annulment of 22 September 2014) ICSID Case No ARB/03/15 [214].

interpretation to decide the dispute' before them and, in the event, the tribunal relied on previous case law only 'to be helped in its interpretation'.[96] More generally, tribunals seem to single out a provision of ARSIWA as the embodiment of an unwritten rule, whilst the reference to international jurisprudence only comes after this determination without justification, as if it were only an interpretative aid.

4.2   Content-Determination through the Application of Means Akin to Treaty Interpretation

Apart from such textual approach, it is not uncommon for tribunals to invoke or evoke other interpretative principles commonly used in the process of treaty interpretation. First, a few tribunals have recourse to materials produced in the long preparatory process of ARSIWA as another means to determine the content of the applicable rules on State responsibility. Second, investment tribunals often refer to means of interpretation applied to treaties focusing on the context or object and purpose of ARSIWA.

References to the discussions within the ILC leading up to the adoption of ARSIWA are not particularly frequent in investment decisions. In some cases, tribunals rely on the record of discussions in order to determine whether the silence of ARSIWA also implies a determination by the ILC that certain concept or proposition does not form part of international law.[97] Thus, in *Alghanim*, the investor invoked the distinction between 'obligations of conduct' (ie those that prescribe or proscribe a specific conduct) and 'obligations of result' (ie those that require the achievement of a specific result irrespective of the conduct adopted) that appeared in previous drafts of ARSIWA.[98] The Tribunal took note of the critical stance of the last Special Rapporteur and the deletion of the distinction from the final draft of ARSIWA and concluded that the distinction did not form part of customary international law.[99] Furthermore, in other cases, tribunals purport to rely on the preparatory works of ARSIWA as a means to interpret a provision of ARSIWA. For instance, in the *LG&E* decision, the Tribunal

---

[96] ibid [216].
[97] Eg *Loewen Group, Inc and Raymond L Loewen v USA* (Award of 26 June 2003) ICSID Case No ARB(AF)/98/3 [149] (exhaustion of local remedies as a substantive defence); *Salini v Argentina* (Decision on Jurisdiction of 23 February 2018) ICSID Case No ARB/15/39 [85] (doctrine of extinctive prescription).
[98] *Alghanim v Jordan* (Award of 14 December 2017) ICSID Case No ARB/13/38 [302].
[99] ibid.

started from the determination that Article 25 ARSIWA reflects the standard of necessity in international law.[100] It, then, proceeded to discuss each of the elements of Article 25 ARSIWA referring exclusively to the opinions of the ILC Special Rapporteurs and other individual members of the ILC.[101] From a methodological perspective, it is possible to maintain that these tribunals merely examine all available secondary evidence without endorsing any firm distinction between identification and determination of the content of the applicable rule.[102] However, in cases like the *LG&E*, the analysis clearly emphasises the intention of the ILC in adopting certain provision rather than the evidence upon which the ILC relied. For this reason, these findings are not easily explicable under the mainstream view on the identification of customary international law or general principles of law.[103] Rather, these tribunals seem to resort to the record of discussions of the ILC more as an interpretative aid in a way that parallels the use of *travaux préparatoires* in the context of treaty interpretation.

More conspicuously, investment tribunals often refer to interpretative principles which pertain to the 'the spirit, purpose and context of the clause or instrument in which the words are contained'.[104] The Tribunal's approach in *Devas* relating to the attribution of conduct of a State-owned company to India provides a very illustrative example. In this case, the Tribunal noted that the text of Article 8 ARSIWA only mentioned 'persons or group of persons', but made no reference to 'entities' like, for instance, Article 5 ARSIWA establishing also a rule of attribution of conduct.[105] Nonetheless, the Tribunal considered that 'it is generally recognized in modern legal systems that "person" includes not only a natural person but also a legal person' and that several Institutes of Internal Auditors (IIAs) included corporations in their definition of 'persons'.[106] In methodological terms, the Tribunal referred to other rules of international law, which it deemed relevant for the interpretation of the rule reflected in ARSIWA, in a way akin to the context of a treaty.[107] Furthermore, the

---

[100] *LG&E v Argentina* (Decision on Liability of 3 October 2006) ICSID Case No ARB/02/1 [245].
[101] ibid [249-59].
[102] See text accompanying fns 24-6.
[103] cf text accompanying fns 22-3, 72-4, & 85-7.
[104] cf *Arbitral Award of 31 July 1989* [48]; *South West Africa Cases* 336.
[105] *Devas v India* (Decision on Jurisdiction and Merits of 25 July 2016) PCA Case No 2013-09 [278].
[106] ibid [278]-[279].
[107] cf VCLT, Art 31(3)(c); for a similar approach see: *Sempra Energy v Argentina* [353] ('[Article 25(2)(b) ARSIWA] is of course the expression of a general principle of law devised to prevent a party from taking legal advantage of its own fault').

Tribunal remarked that 'it would make no sense to impose a restrictive interpretation that would allow a State to circumvent the rules of attribution by sending its direction or instruction to a corporate entity rather than a physical person or group of physical persons'.[108] Instead, it opted for a different interpretation noting that even in the case of corporations the instructions or direction would be received and acted upon by natural persons (ie the directors and agents of the corporation).[109] From a doctrinal viewpoint, the Tribunal chose out of two available interpretations the one that gave full effect to Article 8 ARSIWA in what appears to be a straightforward application of the interpretative principle of effectiveness (*ut res magis valeat quam pereat* or *effet utile*).[110]

Moreover, several tribunals often proceed to construct provisions of ARSIWA on the basis of broader considerations, which they deem as cross-cutting in the law of State responsibility. For instance, several tribunals invoke the stability of international obligations as a stepping stone for a restrictive interpretation of the customary defence of necessity.[111] Another set of illustrative decisions declare that the purpose of an award of interest under Article 38 ARSIWA is to 'ensure full reparation' and proceed to award compound interest.[112] This is so notwithstanding the fact that Article 38 ARSIWA is silent on the matter and the ILC Commentary clearly favours the award of simple interest.[113] These findings seem to evoke the object and purpose or the *ratio* of ARSIWA or of specific provisions in order to determine the meaning of the applicable rule in a way that parallels known approaches to treaty interpretation.[114] The common thread that binds all these pronouncements together is the blending of a literal reading of ARSIWA with contextual

---

[108] *Devas v India* [280].
[109] ibid.
[110] cf, eg, *Application of the International Convention on the Elimination of All Forms of Racial Discrimination (Georgia v Russian Federation)* (Preliminary Objections) [2011] ICJ Rep 70 [133]; *Free Zones of Upper Savoy and the District of Gex (France/Switzerland)* (Order) [1929] PCIJ Ser A No 22, 13.
[111] Eg *Suez v Argentina* (Annulment); *AWG Group v Argentina* (Decision on Liability of 30 July 2010) UNCITRAL [249]; *EDF v Argentina* (Award) [1171].
[112] Eg *Quiborax v Bolivia* (Award of 16 September 2015) ICSID Case No ARB/06/2 [514 & 520–4]; *Crystallex v Venezuela* (Award of 4 April 2016) ICSID Case No ARB(AF)/11/2 [932 & 935]; *Hrvatska Elektropriveda v Slovenia* (Award of 17 December 2017) ICSID Case No ARB/05/24 [539–40]; *Teinver v Argentina* [1120–1 & 1125]; on a similar approach in relation to the rules of attribution: *F-W v Trinidad and Tobago* [200].
[113] ARSIWA (n 1) Commentary to Art 38 [8].
[114] cf, eg, R Gardiner, *Treaty Interpretation* (2nd edn, OUP 2015) 215–21; *LaGrand (Germany v United States)* (Judgment) [2001] ICJ Rep 466 [102].

or teleological considerations that mirrors the process dictated by the rules of treaty interpretation.

4.3 Interpretation of the Law on State Responsibility and Its 'Rule-ness' in International Investment Arbitration

It has been shown so far that it is not uncommon for investment tribunals to hold explicitly or implicitly, through the use of relevant methods, that the determination of the content of the applicable rules of State responsibility also requires a process of interpretation notwithstanding its unwritten character.[115] A further question that arises is whether the practice of investment tribunals evidences the existence of rules or principles governing this process.

Remarkably, some decisions not only accept that the determination of the content of rules of State responsibility also involves interpretation, but they also clearly suggest that such process is governed by relevant rules or principles of international law. The award on jurisdiction in *ST-AD* is telling as to this general point. In this case, the Tribunal enunciated that 'every rule … of international law must be interpreted in good faith'.[116] Applying this rule of interpretation to the requirement of exhaustion of local remedies under customary international law,[117] the Tribunal found that '[t]his rule is interpreted to mean that applicants are only required to exhaust domestic remedies that are available and effective'.[118] Similarly, several decisions relating to the customary defence of necessity, which is articulated in Article 25 ARSIWA, raise explicitly the issue of interpretation.[119] Most notably, in *Enron*, the annulment committee censured parts of the award discussing whether measures taken by Argentina were the only way to address the economic crisis constituting the situation of necessity and whether Argentina contributed to that crisis.[120] According to the committee, the 'only way' and 'non-contribution' requirements spelled out in Articles 25(1)(a) and 25(2)(b) ARSIWA, respectively, were

---

[115] cf, e.g., P Merkouris, 'Interpreting the Customary Rules on Interpretation' (2017) 19 ICLR 126, 134–6.
[116] *ST-AD v Bulgaria* (Decision on Jurisdiction of 18 July 2013) PCA Case No 2011–06 [364].
[117] ibid citing, among other sources, ARSIWA (n 1) Art 44(b).
[118] ibid [365].
[119] Eg *Impregilo v Argentina* (Award of 21 June 2011) ICSID Case No ARB/07/17 [341–57]; *Unión Fenosa v Egypt* [860] ('a common-sense interpretation').
[120] *Enron v Argentina* (Decision on Annulment of 30 July 2010) ICSID Case No ARB/01/3 [369–92].

'capable of more than one interpretation'.[121] The committee held that the Tribunal 'was necessarily required, either expressly or *sub silentio*, to decide or assume the correct interpretation in order to apply the provision to the facts of the case'.[122] It, thus, concluded that the Tribunal committed an annullable error by not laying down its own interpretation of these requirements.[123] Inversely, in *EDF*, the annulment committee admitted as a matter of principle that the 'the concept of "only means" is open to more than one interpretation'.[124] It held that '[i]n the light of the principle that necessity is an exceptional plea which must be strictly applied (a principle expressly stated in paragraph 1171 of the Award), ... "only" means "only"; it is not enough if another lawful means is more expensive or less convenient'.[125] Although the committee held that failure to elaborate on the issue of interpretation did not constitute an annullable error, it nonetheless recognised the application of a principle or rule of interpretation to the customary rule of necessity according to which 'exceptions to general principles are to be interpreted restrictively'.[126]

By contrast, some decisions eschew a precise determination as to the content of the applicable rule of State responsibility by limiting themselves to taking note of the parties' stance in the proceedings. In some cases, the lack of an independent analysis on the content of the applicable rule seems to be elicited by factual or evidentiary considerations. So, in *Inmaris*, the Tribunal identified the applicable rule in Article 31(1) ARSIWA that provides for 'the obligation to make full reparation for the injury caused by the internationally wrongful act'.[127] As to the issue of causation, Ukraine proposed two tests, namely, one based on proximity and another based on foreseeability.[128] The Tribunal declined to determine the applicable test finding that the relevant acts caused harm to the investor 'under either standard discussed by the respondent'.[129]

---

[121] ibid [369 & 386].
[122] ibid [386].
[123] ibid [377 & 386].
[124] *EDF v Argentina* (Annulment) [335]; similarly, *Suez v Argentina* (Annulment) [290].
[125] *EDF v Argentina* (Annulment) [335].
[126] On this principle: *Aegean Sea Continental Shelf (Greece v Turkey)* (Judgment) [1978] ICJ Rep 62, Separate Opinion of Judge de Castro [17] citing M Habicht, *Analysis of the Treaties in Post-War Treaties for the Pacific Settlement of International Disputes*, Part II (HUP 1931) 1000; see also, A Solomou, 'Exceptions to a Rule Must be Narrowly Construed' in J Klinger, Y Parkhomenko, & C Salonidis (eds), *Between the Lines of the Vienna Convention?* (Kluwer 2019) 359 ff.
[127] *Inmaris v Ukraine* (Award of 1 March 2012) ICSID Case No ARB/08/8 [381].
[128] ibid [381].
[129] ibid.

However, in other decisions, the agnostic stance towards interpretation appears to stem from legal considerations. To give an illustrative example, in *Suez* annulment decision, the crucial issue was whether the Tribunal failed to apply the proper law, in the event, Article 25 ARSIWA on the state of necessity. The committee conceded as a matter of principle that the 'only way' and 'non-contribution' requirements appearing in Article 25 ARSIWA 'are indeed susceptible to a certain degree of interpretation'.[130] However, it emphasised that no party raised any issue of interpretation in the proceedings before the Tribunal. On this basis, the committee concluded that 'an interpretation issue that was not raised by the Parties cannot be considered "outcome-determinative" with the consequence that a failure to address such issue would amount to a manifest excess of powers under Article 52(1)(b)'.[131]

The committee's reasoning in *Suez* echoes other annulment decisions that distinguish between 'disregarding the proper law', which constitutes an annullable error, from 'misapplication of the proper law', which does not.[132] In the case of applicable treaty provisions, annulment committees also occasionally examine whether tribunals disregarded any applicable rules of interpretation, despite allowing them ample deference as to the application of such rules in the specific case.[133] The *Suez* case raises the question whether and how this distinction can be applied with respect to applicable rules of unwritten international law, such as those under the law of State responsibility. In this respect, as has been shown, the *Enron* annulment decision clearly suggests that a tribunal must pay some regard, either explicitly or *sub silentio*, to the principles upon which it bases its determination of the content of the applicable rules of unwritten international law.[134] What is more, the *EDF* committee traced back the interpretative principle applied by the Tribunal despite finding that this was beyond the scope of annulment review.[135] By contrast, whilst acknowledging a distinction between identification of applicable rules of unwritten law and their interpretation, the *Suez* committee relied exclusively on the parties' stance in the underlying proceedings to decide whether an issue

---

[130] *Suez v Argentina* (Annulment) [290].
[131] ibid [291]; similarly, *Suez & Interagua v Argentina* (Decision on Annulment of 14 December 2014) ICSID Case No ARB/03/17 [183–4].
[132] Schreuer & ors (n 11) 959–64; see, eg, *Teinver v Argentina* (Decision on Annulment of 29 May 2019) ICSID Case No ARB/09/1 [60].
[133] cf, most notably, *Industria Nacional de Alimentos (Luccetti) v Perú* (Decision on Annulment of 5 September 2007) ICSID Case No ARB/03/4 [113 &116].
[134] See text accompanying fns 120–3.
[135] See text accompanying fns 124–6.

of interpretation was 'outcome-determinative'. In this way, it remained entirely agnostic as to the existence of rules or principles of interpretation of unwritten international law.

To summarise, investment tribunals employ an array of methods in the course of determining applicable rules on unwritten international law on State responsibility. At the crux of these diverse approaches seems to lay a latent, or sometimes explicit, distinction at an analytical level between the identification of applicable rules on State responsibility and their interpretation with ARSIWA operating as the focal point. This distinction is not merely a theoretical one, but it has both substantive and procedural implications. First, the use of ARSIWA as an object of interpretation has allowed investment tribunals to develop the law on State responsibility in ways that contradict, or cannot be inferred from, the evidence adduced by the ILC. The award of compound interest in investment arbitration is a case in point. Second, a comparative survey between investment awards reveals that new divisions have spun out as to the choice of the proper means of interpretation. The cases on the content of the necessity defence are paradigmatic. Third, the casting of disputes on the content of the law on State responsibility in terms of interpretation by reference to ARSIWA has also played a role in the context of annulment proceedings. In this respect, the division between annulment committees is not so much whether customary international law or general principles of law on State responsibility can be interpreted; annulment committees readily accept this point. Rather, the main point of contention seems to be the existence and interplay of applicable interpretative rules or principles so as to enable annulment review, delineate its scope, and determine its operation.

5   Interpretation as a Balancing Exercise between Centrifugal Forces in International Investment Arbitration and the Unity of Law on State Responsibility

The previous section has identified a variety of ways in which investment tribunals use ARSIWA in determining applicable rules on State responsibility. In the main, investment tribunals favour a formalist approach: they tend to justify their reliance on ARSIWA as means to determine the applicable rules on State responsibility on the basis of the rules on the identification of international law. Moreover, many investment tribunals go even further and proceed to apply, explicitly or implicitly, (meta-)rules or (meta-)principles of interpretation on ARSIWA in order to determine the content of the applicable rule. At the same time, some decisions remain agnostic with regards to the issue of interpretation. This section argues that the fundamental consideration of the unity of the law on State responsibility militates in favour of its uniform application and against a case-by-case approach. The theory of sources of international law provides several footholds for the interpretation of rules of unwritten international law.

To start, the fundamental premise of the law on State responsibility is its unity: '*every* internationally wrongful act of a state entails the international responsibility of that state'.[136] Yet, an agnostic approach as to the methodology for the determination of the content of the applicable rule can severely distort its content. To illustrate this point, in *Bayindir*, the Tribunal referred to 'the international rules of attribution reflected in Articles 4, 5 and 8 [ARSIWA]', which it found applicable 'as expressing current customary international law'.[137] In its analysis on Article 8 ARSIWA, the Tribunal held:

> the Tribunal is aware that the levels of control required for a finding of attribution under Article 8 in other factual contexts, such as foreign armed intervention or international criminal responsibility, may be different. It believes, however, that the approach developed in such areas of international law is not always adapted to the realities of international economic law and that they should not prevent a finding of attribution if the specific facts of an investment dispute so warrant.[138]

In the specific case of Article 8 ARSIWA, the ICJ has ruled that the 'effective control' test cannot be displaced in the absence of an applicable *lex specialis*.[139] Yet, at first glance, the *Bayindir* panel was not obligated to follow the ICJ's ruling and an inductive examination of the available primary and secondary evidence at the time would have led to conflicting results.[140] What is striking in this award is that the Tribunal put aside the much debated 'effective control' test purporting that it is a factual issue pertaining to the application of the customary rule. This enabled

---

[136] ARSIWA (n 1) Art 1 (emphasis added); on the notion of unity, see eg A Nollkaemper, 'Constitutionalization and the Unity of the Law of International Responsibility' (2009) 16 IJGLS 535, 536.
[137] *Bayindir v Pakistan* (Award of 27 August 2009) ICSID Case No ARB/03/29 [113] & fn 19.
[138] ibid [130].
[139] *Application of the Convention on the Prevention and Punishment of the Crime of Genocide* [401] and text accompanying fns 80–4.
[140] See, notably, *Maffezzini v Spain* (Decision on Jurisdiction of 25 January 2000) ICSID Case No ARB/97/7 [77–82]; *Tadić* (Judgment) IT-94-1-A, AC (15 July 1999) [117–20]; ARSIWA (n 1) Commentary to Art 8 [5].

the Tribunal to infuse its analysis of the content of the applicable rule of responsibility with asides about the speciality of international economic law in a way that runs counter to the fundamental consideration of the unity of the law on State responsibility.[141] The *Bayindir* award stands out as an outlier, investment tribunals accepting this premise virtually unanimously. Accepting the premise of the unity of the law on State responsibility, which the ICJ has upheld as a rule of customary international law, militates against a case-by-case approach and reveals the need for a consistent methodology for the determination of the content of rules on State responsibility.[142]

Consistently with the mainstream approach concerning the sources of international law, the determination of the applicable rules of the law on State responsibility must take place in principle on the basis of an inductive examination of all available evidence.[143] However, at the same time, a purely inductive approach towards the identification of unwritten international law has certain limitations. So, with respect to the identification of customary international law, the ILC has concluded that 'the two-elements approach does not preclude an element of deduction as an aid' particularly 'when considering possible rules of customary international law that operate against the backdrop of rules framed in more general terms that themselves derive from and reflect a general practice accepted as law or when concluding that possible rules of international law form part of an "indivisible regime"'.[144] More emphatically, the current special rapporteur on general principles of law has opined that 'deduction is … the main criterion to establish the existence of a legal principle that has a general scope'.[145] The fact that the ILC perceives deduction as part and parcel of the process of identification of a rule of unwritten international law is somewhat less relevant. The key point is the acknowledgment of a juridical operation analytically distinct from induction that consists of the determination of the content of the applicable rule on the basis of an inference from a normative proposition whose status is undisputed.

To illustrate this point, according to the ILC, the provisions of ARSIWA relating to the content of State responsibility are 'without prejudice to any

---

[141] Eg S Olleson, 'Attribution in Investment Treaty Arbitration' (2016) 31 ICSID Rev 457, 481–2.
[142] See *Legal Consequences of the Separation of the Chagos Archipelago from Mauritius in 1965* (Advisory Opinion) [2019] ICJ Rep 95 [177].
[143] Caron (n 7) 867.
[144] CICIL (n 15) Commentary to Art 2 [5].
[145] ILC (n 22) [168].

right, arising from the international responsibility of a State, which may accrue directly to any person or entity other than a State.'[146] Nonetheless, investment tribunals commonly apply the rules on reparation reflected in ARSIWA, even if this involves an element of interpretation as an intermediate step.[147] Notably, in *Quiborax*, the issue arose whether investment tribunals can issue a declaratory award as a form of reparation. The Tribunal referred to Articles 34 and 37 ARSIWA and enunciated that ARSIWA 'restate customary international law and its rules on reparation have served as guidance to many tribunals in investor-State disputes'.[148] It specified that 'the remedies outlined by the ILC Articles may apply in investor-State arbitration depending on the nature of the remedy and of the injury which it is meant to repair.'[149] In this respect, it cautioned that 'some types of satisfaction as a remedy *are not transposable* to investor-State disputes'.[150] In particular, it held that 'the type of satisfaction which is meant to redress harm caused to the dignity, hono[u]r and prestige of a State, is not applicable in investor-State disputes.'[151] The Tribunal concluded, thus, that '[t]he fact that some types of satisfaction are not available does not mean that the Tribunal cannot make a declaratory judgment as a means of satisfaction under Article 37 [ARSIWA], if appropriate'.[152] In practical terms, the tribunal essentially engaged in the interpretation of Article 37 ARSIWA as a rule of customary international law referring expressly to its wording and its object and purpose. Whether it did so in order to determine its transposability in the context of investor-State arbitration or whether it interpreted it as a directly applicable rule of customary international law is less relevant for practical purposes.

The important point is that the determination of the applicable rules of State responsibility is composed of two analytically distinct operations with ARSIWA being at the crux of the analysis. On the one hand, the determination of the status of a normative proposition contained in ARSIWA involves an inductive analysis of evidence.[153] In this respect, the practice of investment tribunals is an unambiguous attestation that

---

[146] ARSIWA (n 1) Art 33(2) & Commentary to Art 28 [3].
[147] See text accompanying fns 63–6.
[148] *Quiborax v Bolivia* [555].
[149] ibid.
[150] ibid [555] (emphasis added).
[151] ibid [559].
[152] ibid [560].
[153] CICIL (n 15) Commentary to Art 2 [5].

ARSIWA enjoy a *'présomption de positivité'*.[154] In practical terms, challenging the status of most normative propositions contained in ARSIWA would require evidence indicating lack of generality of practice/*opinio juris* or recognition, as the case might be. On the other hand, the determination of the content of a normative proposition contained in ARSIWA also involves an element of interpretation. Specifically, it involves criteria that parallel the process of treaty interpretation. The key difference is that the intention of the drafters of ARSIWA – that is, the ILC – is less relevant in this process because the formal foundation of the normative propositions contained therein is only the *consuetudo* of States.[155] In practical terms, this is reflected in the findings of investment tribunals emphasising the text, context, and object and purpose of ARSIWA or a specific provision at the expense of the multitude of materials leading up to their adoption or even, in case of inconsistency, the ILC Commentary.[156] Therefore, the process of interpretation is not an unprincipled process, even if the relevant principles and their interaction are still in a process of elaboration and refinement (not unlike the rules of treaty interpretation before the adoption of the Vienna Convention on the Law of Treaties (VCLT)).

To recap, the premise of the law on State responsibility is inimical to an agnostic approach with respect to the identification and interpretation of the rules on State responsibility. The crucial normative concern is the unmaking of the law on State responsibility through its blending with considerations special to specific sub-systems, in this case, international investment law. In this respect, adherence to ARSIWA is only a starting point. Rather, the key point is that the determination of the applicable rules on State responsibility on the basis of ARSIWA is also a principled process to which interpretation is an inextricable part.

6 Conclusion

Undeniably, investment tribunals spearhead the consolidation of the general law of State responsibility through their widespread endorsement of ARSIWA. This comparative analysis of the use of ARSIWA in investment arbitration has shown that the discrepancy between the current form of

---

[154] Eg A Pellet, 'L'adaptation du droit international aux besoins changeants de la société internationale' (2007) 329 RdC 9, 40; also, M Paparinskis, 'Investment Treaty Arbitration and the (New) Law of State Responsibility' (2013) 24 EJIL 617, 618.
[155] See text accompanying fns 20–1.
[156] See text accompanying fns 88–96 & 104–19.

ARSIWA and their effective authority should not be overstated. In the main, investment tribunals do justify their reliance on ARSIWA using the vocabulary of the sources of international law. In fact, the formal status of most normative propositions contained in ARSIWA has been tested and analysed from every possible angle by hundreds of investment panels. Whilst admittedly this has led to divergent views as to theoretical points, the preponderance of decisions converges into treating ARSIWA as authoritative statements on the law on State responsibility.

What emerges as a new challenge is ensuring the uniformity of the law on State responsibility within this context of pervasive use. The focus of States, investors, and tribunals seems to have moved away from 'grand questions of principle' towards 'the boring small print' of responsibility rules like the meaning of control, contribution, injury, causation, or damage.[157] In this respect, the traditional approaches on the identification of customary international law and general principles of law have certain limitations. This survey has shown that investment tribunals are increasingly aware that, through their use and elaboration of ARSIWA, they are engaging in the interpretation of the formally unwritten law on State responsibility. The realisation that interpretation is also a principled process guided by international law will ensure the unity and consistent development of the law on State responsibility even within the specialised context of investment arbitration.

In fact, this survey has shown that elements of such a principled methodology are already present in the practice of investment tribunals, even if in incipient form. In the first place, the determination that a normative proposition contained in ARSIWA reflects a rule of customary international law or a general principle of law is only a starting point. This determination entails that the ordinary meaning of the terms of ARSIWA is important in specifying the content of the formally unwritten rule. In this respect, tribunals seem mindful that this is essentially an interpretative endeavour guided by considerations of good faith. Second, another overarching consideration is that rules on State responsibility do not exist in a vacuum but form part of an internally coherent law of State responsibility that should be deemed compatible with the rules and principles of international law which this law is meant to make operational. As a corollary, whilst tribunals tend to confirm the status of a normative proposition contained in ARSIWA in a piecemeal fashion (ie for each provision separately), this does not constitute the end of the analysis. Tribunals also

---

[157] M Paparinskis, 'The Once and Future Law of State Responsibility' (2020) 114 AJIL 618, 625.

take into account the immediate and broader context of each provision alongside the object and purpose of the entirety of ARSIWA and of each provision within the broader system of ARSIWA when clarifying its content. Third, tribunals seem also to appreciate that the anticipated outcome of this innately interpretative exercise is not the determination of the intention of the drafters of ARSIWA, but the concretisation of rules and principles emanating from the legally relevant conduct of States. Whilst they seem to accord particular value to an ILC's determination denying binding status to a certain normative proposition, they use materials produced in the run-up to the adoption of ARSIWA only exceptionally and in a supplementary fashion in the context of the interpretation of a normative proposition contained in the ARSIWA.

6

Revisiting the Availability of Countermeasures in Investment Arbitration

ANNA VENTOURATOU

1 Introduction

The Articles on the Responsibility of States for Internationally Wrongful Acts (ARSIWA) were intended as the International Law Commission's (ILC) 'permanent contribution to general international law'.[1] As such, the provisions enshrined therein, including the 'circumstances precluding wrongfulness' under Part I, Chapter 5, are in principle binding on, and applicable to, all States[2] (generality *ratione personae*) and apply to the whole field of international obligations of States,[3] regardless of their content or source[4] (generality *ratione materiae*). This chapter discusses whether, despite this *prima facie* general applicability, a responding State may be precluded from invoking the customary defence of

---

[1] ILC, 'Summary Record of the 2587th Meeting' (15 June 1999) UN Doc A/CN.4/SR.2587 [46]. *Contra* see, eg D Caron, 'The ILC Articles on State Responsibility: The Paradoxical Relationship between Form and Authority' (2002) 96 AJIL 857; R Sloane, 'On the Use and Abuse of Necessity in the Law of State Responsibility' (2012) 106 AJIL 447, 452–3; M Paparinskis, 'Investment Arbitration and the Law of Countermeasures' (2009) 79 BYBIL 264, 318. The present chapter embarks on the assumption that such defences are indeed of a customary nature and does not engage further with this criticism.

[2] B Cheng, 'Some Remarks on the Constituent Element(s) of General (or So-Called Customary) International Law' in A Anghie & G Sturgess (eds), *Legal Visions of the 21st Century: Essays in Honour of Judge Christopher Weeramantry* (Kluwer 1998) 379–80; A Gourgourinis, 'General/Particular International Law and Primary/Secondary Rules: Unitary Terminology of a Fragmented System' (2011) 22 EJIL 993, 1010 ff. See also ILC, 'Draft Articles on the Law of Treaties with Commentaries' (4 May–19 July 1966) UN Doc A/CN.4/191, reproduced in [1966/II] YBILC 187, 246 [5].

[3] ILC, 'Draft Articles on Responsibility of States for Internationally Wrongful Acts with Commentaries' (23 April–1 June and 2 July–10 August 2001) UN Doc A/56/10, reproduced in [2001/II – Part Two] YBILC 31 (ARSIWA Commentary), general commentary [5]; see also, J Crawford, 'The ILC's Articles on Responsibility of States for Internationally Wrongful Acts: A Retrospect' (2002) 96 AJIL 874, 879.

[4] See similarly F Paddeu, *Justification and Excuse in International Law: Concept and Theory of General Defences* (CUP 2018) 16 fn 58.

countermeasures in the context of an investment dispute. It identifies and assesses four factors potentially affecting the availability of countermeasures in investment arbitration: the jurisdictional constraints of the arbitral tribunal, limitations in the law applicable to the dispute, the interpretation of the investment protection treaty in question, and potential limitations to the scope of application of the defence under customary international law.

The jurisdiction of an arbitral tribunal and the law applicable to the dispute are defined by the claim and the treaty in question. The tribunal's jurisdiction extends only to rulings on the matters raised by the claimant (*non ultra petita*), based on interpretation and application of the treaty at hand.[5] Nonetheless, many investment treaties authorise the tribunal to decide the issues in dispute, not only on the basis of the treaty itself, but also of 'applicable rules of international law'.[6]

The first task for the tribunal is to determine whether countermeasures are such 'applicable rules'. This is an interpretative task. The tribunal through interpretation of the investment treaty in question will need to ascertain whether countermeasures as a defence are, explicitly or implicitly, displaced in the context of disputes arising thereunder. For example, the treaty in question may contain rules that constitute *lex*

---

[5] Clauses on the settlement of disputes between an investor and a host State in BITs usually read '[t]his Article shall apply to ... a dispute ... arising out of an alleged breach of an obligation ... under ... this Treaty' or '[d]isputes with regard to an investment which arise within the terms of this Agreement ...'; see eg, India, 'Model Text for the Indian Bilateral Investment Treaty' (*Indian Ministry of Finance*, 14 January 2016) Art 14 <https://dea.gov.in/sites/default/files/ModelBIT_Annex_0.pdf> accessed 1 June 2022; Canada, '2004 Model Agreement for the Promotion and Protection of Investments' (*Canadian Government*, 2004) Art 22 <https://investmentpolicy.unctad.org/international-investment-agreements/treaty-files/2820/download> accessed 1 June 2022 (hereinafter 'Canada Model BIT'); Agreement Between the Government of the United Kingdom of Great Britain and Northern Ireland and the Government of the Republic of Argentina for the Promotion and Protection of Investments (UK & Argentina) (adopted 11 December 1990, entered into force 19 February 1993) Art 8.

[6] It is not uncommon in international law to have a court or tribunal vested with limited jurisdiction, whilst having no limits on the rules of international law that it may apply in settling disputes properly brought before it. See eg United Nations Convention on the Law of the Sea (adopted 10 December 1982, entered into force 16 November 1994) 1833 UNTS 397, Arts 288(1) & 293(1) (UNCLOS); North American Free Trade Agreement (NAFTA) (adopted 17 December 1992, entered into force 1 January 1994) 32 ILM 289, Arts 1116–17, 1120 & 1131(1); Art 14.D.3,14.D.9 Agreement between the United States of America, the United Mexican States, and Canada (adopted 10 December 2019, entered into force 1 July 2020) <https://ustr.gov/trade-agreements/free-trade-agreements/united-states-mexico-canada-agreement/agreement-between> accessed 1 June 2022 (USMCA).

specialis to the defence of countermeasures under general international law. In such cases, the special provisions prevail over the general, to the extent that they regulate the same subject matter in a different manner.[7] Moreover, it has been argued that the conferral of substantive, direct rights to investors through investment protection treaties implies the non-applicability of the defence of countermeasures. If countermeasures are taken in response to a prior internationally wrongful act of the investor's home State, then the defence can only preclude the wrongfulness of a temporary non-performance of obligations owed to such State and not of obligations owed directly to the investor, which would, essentially, be a third party to such dispute. In this context, the tribunal shall also take into consideration any relevant rules of international law applicable between the parties,[8] such as the rules under customary international law on the protection of aliens and the institution of diplomatic protection, which may inform the content of relevant treaty provisions.

If the defence is, following this interpretative exercise, found to be applicable to an investment dispute, then the arbitral tribunal is further faced with two jurisdictional considerations. Firstly, the application of countermeasures may require examination of rights and obligations that fall, *prima facie*, outside its subject matter jurisdiction as established in that dispute, or even outside its jurisdictional field in general.[9] The tribunal would have to determine whether a prior internationally wrongful act has been committed, which would probably constitute a breach of an obligation outside the investment treaty under consideration, and thus, outside the jurisdictional limits of the arbitral tribunal. Secondly, the prior internationally wrongful act would be committed by the State of nationality of the investor and not the investor itself. This raises a *Monetary Gold*-like[10]

---

[7] See rule codified in ARSIWA, Art 55.
[8] See Vienna Convention on the Law of Treaties (adopted 23 May 1969, entered into force 27 January 1980) 1155 UNTS 331, Art 31(3)(c).
[9] ie, the general class of cases in respect of which a court exercises and is entitled to exercise its functions, G Fitzmaurice, 'The Law and Procedure of the International Court of Justice: International Organizations and Tribunals' (1952) 29 BYBIL 1, 40–2. Also known as 'foundational jurisdiction' or outer limits/jurisdictional boundaries of the court or tribunal, see Y Shany, 'Jurisdiction and Admissibility' in C Romano, K Alter & Y Shany (eds), *The Oxford Handbook of International Adjudication* (OUP 2013) 782; A Broches, 'The Convention on the Settlement of Investment Disputes between States and Nationals of Other States' (1973) 136 RDC 333, 351.
[10] *Case of the Monetary Gold Removed from Rome in 1943* (Preliminary Question) [1954] ICJ Rep 19 (Monetary Gold) 32; A Grotto, 'Monetary Gold Arbitration and Case' [2008] MPEPIL 175. For the applicability of the principle in investment arbitration see *Larsen v Hawaiian Kingdom* (Award of 5 February 2001) UNCITRAL, 119 ILR 566, 588 [11.8–11.24].

consideration regarding the personal jurisdiction of the arbitral tribunal, as the author of the act would not be a party to the proceedings.

This chapter addresses the considerations above in two substantive sections. Section 2 provides an overview of the tribunals' reasoning and the parties' arguments in the relevant investment case law. All tribunals that have been seized of this matter rejected the arguments of the respondent on the defence of countermeasures but diverged significantly in terms of reasoning. Thus, arbitral tribunals so far have not provided a definite and consistent answer to the applicability of the defence. Section 3 critically assesses the approach of the tribunals to the application of the *lex specialis* principle, to the nature of investors' rights under investment protection treaties and to the limits of their jurisdiction *ratione materiae* and *personae*. This chapter argues that the defence of countermeasures under customary international law is indeed applicable in the context of investment disputes and that arbitral tribunals have the power to examine all the requirements of the defence in order to rule on its applicability in a given case.

2 Countermeasures in Investment Case Law: The US–Mexico Sugar War and the Ambivalent Arbitral Practice

The defence of countermeasures in the context of investment arbitration was primarily discussed in three North American Free Trade Agreement (NAFTA)-based[11] disputes: *Archer Daniels Midland Company and Tate & Lyle Ingredients Americas, Inc v Mexico* (*ADM*), *Corn Products International, Inc v Mexico* (*CPI*) and *Cargill, Inc v Mexico* (*Cargill*).[12] All three disputes arose in the context of the same broader situation of tension between the US and Mexico, which involved proceedings not only before these arbitral tribunals, discussed in this chapter, but also before the WTO Dispute Settlement System[13] and NAFTA.[14]

---

[11] North American Free Trade Agreement (adopted 17 December 1992, entered into force 1 January 1994) 32 ILM 289 (NAFTA).
[12] *ADM v Mexico* (Award of 21 November 2007) ICSID Case No ARB/(AF)/04/5 [110–80] (*ADM*); *Corn Products v Mexico* (Decision on Responsibility of 15 January 2008) ICSID Case No ARB/(AF)/04/1 [144–91] (*CPI*); *Cargill, Inc v Mexico* (Award of 18 September 2009) ICSID Case No ARB(AF)/05/2 (*Cargill*).
[13] WTO, *Mexico – Anti-Dumping Investigation of High Fructose Corn Syrup from the United States – Report of the Panel* (28 January 2000) WT/DS132/R; WTO, *Mexico – Tax Measures on Soft Drinks and Other Beverages – Report of the Panel* (7 October 2005) WT/DS308/R; WTO, *Mexico – Tax Measures on Soft Drinks and Other Beverages – Report of the Appellate Body* (6 March 2006) WT/DS308/AB/R (*Mexico – Soft Drinks*).
[14] For an overview of the dispute settlement proceedings see JJ Losari & M Ewing-Chow, 'Legitimate Countermeasures in International Trade Law and Their Illegality in

The disagreement started with the US imposing measures, which restricted the access of Mexico's surplus sugar produce to the US market. It further escalated by the subsequent failure of the US to take part in the NAFTA dispute settlement proceedings initiated by Mexico with respect to the market restrictions, by blocking the appointment of panelists contrary to NAFTA Chapter Twenty. Mexico proceeded with a series of measures aiming to protect its domestic sugar industry, including a 20% tax on soft drinks using sweeteners which were primarily used by US companies. In response to the US claims that the tax was in breach of its NAFTA obligations, Mexico invoked the defence of countermeasures under general international law, claiming that the tax was lawfully introduced in response to prior violations by the US of its NAFTA obligations regarding the access of Mexican-produced sugar to the US market and dispute settlement proceedings. Three (redacted) awards were issued on this matter by tribunals constituted under the NAFTA dispute settlement provisions.

Even though all three disputes were based on the same factual matrix and the same legal instrument, the three awards have significant differences in terms of reasoning. The proceedings for all three cases took place largely in parallel. The Tribunals in *ADM* and *CPI* were unaware of each other's findings and there are no cross-references between the two awards or engagement with each other's reasoning. The Tribunal in *Cargill* received the *ADM* award during its deliberations along with comments from both sides.[15] Thus, the *Cargill* Tribunal had the opportunity to take into consideration the reasoning of the Tribunal in *ADM* and engage with its findings on the defence of countermeasures.[16]

All disputes were submitted to arbitration pursuant to NAFTA Chapter Eleven,[17] for alleged violations of, *inter alia*, the national treatment and expropriation provisions of NAFTA by Mexico.[18] The kind of claims that may be submitted to investor-State arbitration under Article 1120 NAFTA are specified in Articles 1116 and 1117, which accordingly, along with the application of the claimant, establish the scope of jurisdiction of

---

International Investment Law' in P Pazartzis & M Gavouneli (eds), *Reconceptualising the Rule of Law in Global Governance, Resources, Investment and Trade* (Bloomsbury 2016) 413 ff; J Pauwelyn, 'Editorial Comment: Adding Sweeteners to Softwood Lumber: The WTO–NAFTA "Spaghetti Bowl" Is Cooking' (2006) 9 JIEL 197, 198–9.

[15] *Cargill* [45–51].
[16] *Cargill* [380, 410–19].
[17] NAFTA, Art 1120.
[18] NAFTA, arts 1102 & 1110.

the arbitral tribunals.[19] Moreover, the tribunals were constituted under the auspices of the International Centre for Settlement of Investment Disputes (ICSID). Under Article 42(1) ICSID Convention, a tribunal should 'decide a dispute in accordance with such rules of law as may be agreed by the parties.'[20] In turn, Article 1131(1) NAFTA provides that '[a] Tribunal established under this Section shall decide the issues in dispute in accordance with this Agreement and applicable rules of international law.' Thus, the parties to NAFTA have agreed that general international law is, in principle, within the law that a NAFTA tribunal may apply in the determination of a dispute before it. The provisions on jurisdiction and applicable law were relevant to the discussion of the tribunals regarding the availability of countermeasures to investment arbitration and their power to examine the customary requirements of the defence.

The present section discusses the relevant analysis of the tribunals in the cases of *ADM*, *CPI* and *Cargill*. It outlines the tribunals' approach to the application of the *lex specialis* principle, the customary requirements for successful invocation of countermeasures, the nature of investors' rights under investment treaties and the limits of their jurisdiction *ratione materiae* and *ratione personae*.

2.1 Countermeasures under General International Law and the lex specialis Principle

An arbitral tribunal would, first of all, have to decide whether the customary defence of countermeasures is an '*applicable* rule … of international law' within the meaning of Article 1131(1) NAFTA. Even if NAFTA empowers, in principle, arbitral tribunals to apply rules of international law that are not explicitly included in the text of NAFTA itself, tribunals must still investigate whether NAFTA contains any rules that constitute *lex specialis*, and thus, apply to the exclusion of the relevant rules under general international law. The challenge is, first, to identify whether there is indeed a relationship of *lex specialis/lex generalis* between the two rules and, second, to determine the extent to which the two rules are co-extensive and mutually exclusive. According to the ILC, for the *lex specialis* to displace the relevant *lex generalis*, it is not enough that the same subject matter is covered by the two rules, but there must be an actual inconsistency

---

[19] NAFTA, Art 1120.
[20] Convention on the Settlement of Investment Disputes Between States and Nationals of Other States (adopted 18 March 1965, entered into force 14 October 1966) 575 UNTS 159, Art 42(1).

between the two rules – a genuine conflict of norms.[21] The general rule is displaced only to the extent of the inconsistency with the treaty specific rule, whilst other aspects continue to operate in a residual fashion.[22] The tribunal in *ADM* was the only one of the three that discussed the NAFTA applicable law clause, explored the interaction of the defence of countermeasures under general international law with the NAFTA provisions and examined the application of the *lex specialis* principle in order to discern whether countermeasures can be invoked in the context of a NAFTA Chapter Eleven dispute.

The Tribunal began its analysis by reference to Article 1131(1) NAFTA. Although this provision pertains to the law applicable to the dispute, the Tribunal examined its content to determine whether it has '*jurisdiction* to decide on the validity of the defense'.[23] This shows the close relationship between the jurisdiction of an adjudicative body and the law that it may apply in the exercise of such jurisdiction. The Tribunal confirmed that Article 1131(1) NAFTA 'includes the application of rules of customary international law with respect to claimed breaches [of NAFTA provisions]'.[24] This finding confirms that the Tribunal has, indeed, the power to examine and apply customary international law, including the defences under the general international law on State responsibility, but only in the context of deciding the specific claims of breaches that are properly brought before it on the basis of the relevant jurisdictional clause.

Having established that customary defences are *prima facie* applicable to the dispute at hand in accordance with the NAFTA applicable law clause, the Tribunal proceeded to examine whether NAFTA otherwise excludes the application of countermeasures. The claimants have argued that NAFTA includes certain provisions that constitute *lex specialis* to the customary defence of countermeasures, which is, therefore, excluded in accordance with Article 55 ARSIWA.

According to the claimants, NAFTA

> Chapters Nineteen and Twenty establish the regime for dispute resolution that governs the 'existence of an internationally wrongful act' and the 'content' of the international responsibility of the Parties in the event of a

---

[21] ARSIWA, Art 55, commentary [4]; ILC, 'Report on Fragmentation of International Law: Difficulties Arising from the Diversification and Expansion of International Law, Finalised by Martti Koskenniemi' (13 April 2006) UN Doc A/CN.4/L.682 [23–5] (Fragmentation Report).
[22] ARSIWA, Art 55, commentary [2].
[23] *ADM* [111] (emphasis added).
[24] ibid.

breach of their obligations under the NAFTA ... In other words, by signing the NAFTA, the Parties have deliberately forgone the residual right to take countermeasures under customary law.[25]

In response to this argument, the Tribunal acknowledged that the NAFTA indeed offers a form of *lex specialis* to supplement the standards of customary international law on a number of issues such as the treatment of aliens and diplomatic protection.[26] This '*express* content'[27] of the NAFTA, which clearly deviates from – or rather, goes beyond – the relevant rules of customary international law, constitutes *lex specialis* and is applicable to the exclusion of the relevant customary rules. However, according to the Tribunal, customary international law 'continues to govern all matters not covered' by the NAFTA provisions. To this end, it found that 'Chapter Eleven [NAFTA] neither provides nor specifically prohibits the use of countermeasures. Therefore, the question of whether the countermeasures defence is available to the Respondent is not a question of *lex specialis*, but of customary international law.'[28] The Tribunal confirmed that the only reference to countermeasures in the NAFTA was as a means of penalty for non-compliance with a decision rendered in a Chapter Twenty State-to-State arbitration.[29] In that case, no such decision has been rendered. Accordingly, it found that countermeasures can be invoked as a defence in a Chapter Eleven dispute subject to the conditions specified in general international law.[30] In other words, the silence of Chapter Eleven on the issue of countermeasures was interpreted as implicit acceptance of the relevant rules of general international law.

2.2 The Nature of Investors' Rights under Investment Protection Treaties

The arbitral tribunals were faced with an additional question in deciding the applicability of the customary defence of countermeasures to disputes under Chapter Eleven NAFTA. A responding State would invoke the defence of countermeasure as a response to a prior internationally wrongful act by the State of nationality of the investor. Nonetheless, that State is not a party to the dispute. It is rather the investor, a private individual, that

---

[25] *ADM* [114].
[26] *ADM* [117–18].
[27] *ADM* [119] (emphasis added).
[28] *ADM* [120].
[29] *ADM* [122]; cf NAFTA, Art 2019.
[30] *ADM* [123].

takes part in the proceedings under Chapter Eleven. The tribunals discussed the nature of investors' rights under Chapter Eleven and whether such nature affects the applicability of the defence of countermeasures under general international law to investor-State disputes.

The claimants argued that investors under Chapter Eleven NAFTA

> are vested with *direct independent* rights and ... are immune from the legal relationship between the Member States. The investor's cause of action is grounded upon substantive investment obligations which are owed to it directly. A breach of these obligations does not therefore amount to a breach of an inter-state obligation; thus the general rules of state responsibility – including those regarding the circumstances precluding wrongfulness – cannot be presumed.[31]

In other words, countermeasures cannot be invoked as a defence to justify non-performance of obligations under Chapter Eleven, because such obligations are owed to the investors directly and not their State of nationality. According to this argument, the investor is a third party to the dispute between its State of nationality and the responding host State.

Mexico, on the other hand, argued that obligations under NAFTA, including Chapter Eleven, are owed only to the State of the investors' nationality. According to this line of argument, investors are either 'stepping into the shoes and asserting the rights of their home State' when initiating arbitration (derivative theory) or are 'vested only with an exceptional procedural right to claim State responsibility' (intermediate theory).[32] The relevant substantive obligations remain always inter-State, and thus, the defence of countermeasures can be properly invoked against the State of nationality for prior internationally wrongful acts that it has committed.

Indeed, under customary international law, countermeasures 'must be directed against' a State which is the author of the internationally wrongful act.[33] Accordingly, the wrongfulness of an act taken as countermeasure is precluded only with respect to obligations owed to the responsible State and not obligations owed to another party.[34] On the other hand, as stipulated in the ILC Commentary to Article 49 ARSIWA, a countermeasure can affect the interests of third parties as an 'indirect or collateral effect'.[35]

---

[31] *ADM* [162] (emphasis added).
[32] *ADM* [163].
[33] ARSIWA, Art 49 & commentary [4]; *Gabčíkovo-Nagymaros Project (Hungary/Slovakia)* (Judgment) [1997] ICJ Rep 7 (*Gabčíkovo-Nagymaros*) [83]; *CPI* [163].
[34] ibid.
[35] *CPI* [164]; ARSIWA, commentary to Art 49 [5].

Thus, it must be determined whether an investor under NAFTA 'has rights of its own, distinct from those of the State of its nationality, or merely interests.'[36]

In *ADM*, the Tribunal sided with the view that investment rights are derivative and thus countermeasures can indeed be invoked as a defence by the responding State as they do not affect 'individual substantive rights'.[37] It found that

> the proper interpretation of the NAFTA does not substantiate that investors have individual rights as alleged by the Claimants. Nor is the nature of investors' rights under Chapter Eleven comparable with the protections conferred by human rights treaties. Chapter Eleven may share ... with human rights treaties the possibility of granting to non-State actors a procedural right to invoke the responsibility of a sovereign State before an international dispute settlement body. But the fundamental difference between Chapter Eleven of the NAFTA and human rights treaties in this regard is ... that Chapter Eleven *does not provide individual substantive rights for investors*, but rather complements the promotion and protection standards of the rules regarding the protection of aliens under customary international law.[38]

According to the Tribunal, the substantive obligations under Chapter Eleven remain inter-State providing the standards by which the conduct of the NAFTA Party towards the investor will be assessed in the arbitration.[39] These substantive obligations cannot be waived by the investors.[40] They are binding by virtue of the agreement between the State parties to the treaty. Moreover, according to the Tribunal, these obligations are complemented by customary international law to the extent that it is not displaced by the *lex specialis* of the treaty.[41] On the contrary, the right of investors to trigger arbitration against the host State is a purely procedural one.[42] Investors are given the 'exceptional right of action through arbitration that would not otherwise exist under international law'[43] and

---

[36] CPI [165].
[37] ADM [127, 173–9]; cf *ADM v Mexico* (Concurring Opinion of Arthur W Rovine of 20 September 2007) ICSID Case No ARB(AF)/04/05, who strongly supported that Chapter Eleven NAFTA investor rights belong to the investor and cannot be suspended or eliminated by countermeasures taken against the investor's home State.
[38] ADM [171] (emphasis added).
[39] ADM [173].
[40] ADM [174].
[41] ibid.
[42] ADM [173].
[43] ibid.

it is a right that they may choose to exercise or waive, at their own discretion. When an investor files a request for arbitration, it accepts a standing offer by the host State and creates a direct legal relationship in the form of an arbitration agreement.[44] This is the only direct relationship under international law. The relationship between the State of nationality and the host State remains unchanged.

By contrast, the tribunals in *CPI* and *Cargill* took a very different approach to this issue. They found that rights under Chapter Eleven NAFTA are not merely procedural.[45] Rather 'NAFTA confers upon investors substantive rights separate and distinct from those of the State of which they are nationals.'[46] The Tribunal in *CPI* put emphasis on the interpretation of the relevant treaty provisions. It held that individuals and corporations can also hold rights under international law and that when such rights are said to be derived from a treaty 'the question will be whether the text of the treaty reveals an intention to confer rights not only upon the Parties thereto but also upon individuals and/or corporations.'[47] In the case of NAFTA, the Tribunal found that the parties' intention was to confer substantive rights directly upon investors.[48] This was, according to the Tribunal, evident from the language of the treaty and from the fact that procedural rights are also conferred upon the investors.[49] The Tribunal observed that '[t]he notion that Chapter XI conferred upon investors a right, in their own name and for their own benefit, to institute proceedings to enforce rights which were not theirs but were solely the property of the State of their nationality is counterintuitive.'[50]

Further to this textual interpretation of NAFTA, the Tribunal in *CPI* referred to the rights of aliens under customary international law. It argued that 'the notion that in diplomatic protection cases the State was asserting a right of its own' was just a fiction, which was only necessary because procedurally individuals could not bring an international claim.[51] It further argued that this fiction did not reflect the substantive reality, something that is evident 'not only in the juristic writing but also in various rules of law surrounding diplomatic protection claims' such as the rule on exhaustion

---

[44] *ADM* [174].
[45] *Cargill* [424].
[46] *CPI* [167].
[47] *CPI* [168].
[48] *CPI* [168–9].
[49] *CPI* [169].
[50] ibid.
[51] *CPI* [170].

of local remedies and the doctrine of continuing nationality.[52] According to the Tribunal, if the rights were rights of the State itself, then there wouldn't be a requirement to bring a case first before domestic courts, as is the case with other international obligations owed directly to the State. Similarly, if an injury to the national is a violation of the rights of the State, then the victim's nationality after the date of the injury would not be of legal relevance. Thus, the Tribunal implies that even under customary international law, the substantive rights of investors are essentially direct. Accordingly, the investor 'is a third party in any dispute between its own State and another NAFTA Party and a countermeasure taken by that other State against the State of nationality of the investor cannot deprive that investor of its rights.'[53]

The Tribunal in *Cargill* provided a different reasoning in support of its finding that investors' rights under NAFTA are substantive. It drew a distinction between those rights and diplomatic protection under general international law. According to the Tribunal, 'in the case of diplomatic espousal ... the claim is *owned* by the espousing State and the espousing State *is the named party*. Moreover, the operative paragraph of the resulting award reciting the decision of the tribunal names the espousing State, and not the national'.[54] Conversely, in the case of investment arbitration under NAFTA Chapter Eleven, the investor *itself* initiates proceedings, is the named party to such proceedings and is named in the dispositive of the award.[55] The Tribunal held that the origin of the rights should not be confused with the holder of the rights: 'That the origin of individual rights may be found in the act of a sovereign, or in the joint act of sovereigns, does not negate the existence of the rights conferred'.[56] It thus concluded that countermeasures cannot afford a defence in respect of a claim asserted under Chapter Eleven by a national of the allegedly offending State.[57]

2.3 *The Customary Requirements for a Lawful Countermeasure and the Jurisdictional Limits of Arbitral Tribunals*

The tribunals in their analysis regarded Articles 22 and 49–53 ARSIWA 'as an authoritative statement of customary international law on countermeasures'.[58] Article 49 ARSIWA provides that an injured State may take

---

[52] *CPI* [170–3].
[53] *CPI* [176].
[54] ibid.
[55] *Cargill* [425].
[56] *Cargill* [426].
[57] *Cargill* [429–30].
[58] *ADM* [125–6]; *CPI* [145–9].

countermeasures, in the form of limited and temporary non-performance of international obligations, against a State which is responsible for an internationally wrongful act, in order to induce compliance of that State with its international obligations. Article 51 ARSIWA further provides the requirement of proportionality, ie, that the effects of the countermeasure must be commensurate with the injury suffered taking into account the gravity of the internationally wrongful act and the rights in question. The tribunals also referred to the findings of the International Court of Justice (ICJ) in *Gabčikovo-Nagymaros*,[59] which establishes the same criteria as those codified by the ILC.[60] The analysis of the tribunals implies acceptance of these criteria as part of the customary law on countermeasures.[61]

The first requirement under customary international law, ie the existence of a prior internationally wrongful act, is also the most interesting in the context of investor-State dispute settlement (ISDS). The arbitral tribunals would have to determine whether such a prior breach has taken place in order to rule on the applicability of the defence. This raises important jurisdictional questions in cases where this prior breach is outside the limits of the tribunal's subject matter jurisdiction.

First of all, as confirmed by the Tribunal in *CPI*, 'the requirement of a prior violation of international law is an absolute precondition of the right to take countermeasures'.[62] Mexico had argued that to succeed in its countermeasures defence under customary international law, it did not need to prove that the US had indeed violated its obligations but rather that at the time of taking the countermeasure and while it was in place, it had 'a genuine belief that it had a reasonable prospect of succeeding in establishing that the United States was in breach, should that question

---

[59] *Gabčikovo-Nagymaros* [82 ff].
[60] Note the feedback loop (inter-temporal twist) between the work of the ILC and the findings of the ICJ. The ICJ in *Gabčikovo-Nagymaros* relies, among others, upon the work of the ILC and the rules on countermeasures as were codified in Articles 47 to 50 of the Draft Articles on State Responsibility (1996), see *Gabčikovo-Nagymaros* [83]. A few years later, the ILC refers back to the findings of the Court in *Gabčikovo-Nagymaros* in its commentary to the relevant articles to support its conclusions codified therein, see commentary to Art 49 [2]; commentary to Art 51 [4]; see on this matter eg Sloane (n 1) 452–3; Paparinskis (n 1) 318. The Tribunal in *ADM*, oddly, refers to both sources, as separate authorities, in order to lay down the requirements for a lawful countermeasure under customary international law.
[61] It is interesting to note that neither the parties nor the tribunals referred to the procedural requirements of countermeasures enshrined in Art 52 ARSIWA.
[62] *CPI* [185].

come before a competent tribunal.'[63] Accordingly, the Tribunal would not need exceed the limits of its jurisdiction as it could decide on whether Mexico had such genuine belief without examination of the actions of the US *per se*. The Tribunal rejected this argument as an attempt by Mexico to 'square the circle', confirming that the jurisdictional concern cannot be easily avoided.[64]

The Tribunal in *ADM* found on this matter that it 'has no jurisdiction to decide whether the United States breached any of its international obligations under Chapter Three or Chapter Twenty of the NAFTA.'[65] The Tribunal recalled that it was established under Chapter Eleven for the settlement of an investment dispute, comprising allegations of violations by the respondent of Articles 1102, 1106 and 1110 NAFTA. Thus, it had no jurisdiction to decide whether the US breached any of its international obligations complained by Mexico, since those were prescribed under NAFTA Chapters Three, Seven and Twenty.[66] Mexico argued that the jurisdiction of the Tribunal entailed the power to examine its argument on countermeasures as this was invoked as a defence precluding its international responsibility,[67] but the Tribunal rejected this line of reasoning.

Interestingly, the Tribunal found that it had jurisdiction to examine the rest of the customary requirements of countermeasures. It stipulated that '[b]oth parties agree that the Tribunal has jurisdiction to decide any defense under Chapter Eleven, including a countermeasures defense'.[68] Thus, the Tribunal acknowledged the nature of countermeasures as a defence and its jurisdiction to rule on applicable defences but still found that its power does not extend to *all* the customary requirements of such defence. Accordingly, the Tribunal proceeded to examine whether Mexico's tax measure was taken in response to the alleged US violations, aimed at inducing the US to comply with the NAFTA obligations that it has allegedly breached and was proportionate to such aim, without first establishing that a prior internationally wrongful act has taken place. It found that Mexico's measure did not meet these requirements and rejected the countermeasures defence on that basis, thereby circumventing the jurisdictional considerations.

[63] *CPI* [184].
[64] *CPI* [185].
[65] *ADM* [128].
[66] *ADM* [127–9].
[67] *ADM* [129–30].
[68] *ADM* [132].

The Tribunal in *CPI* reached a similar conclusion regarding the limits of its jurisdiction. In an *obiter dictum*,[69] it held that it would not have the jurisdiction to determine whether Mexico's allegations against the US were well-founded or not, because 'the United States is not a party to these proceedings and the Tribunal does not have jurisdiction to determine whether any provision of the NAFTA falling outside Chapter XI has been violated'.[70] The Tribunal here raises not only the issue of jurisdiction *ratione materiae*, discussed in *ADM*, but also a concern regarding the limits of its personal jurisdiction. It makes a *Monetary Gold*-like argument,[71] implying that it may not determine the legal interests of a non-party to the dispute (the US) without its consent.[72]

3 Evaluating the Tribunals' Approach: Treaty Interpretation, Customary Law and General Principles of International Adjudication

It becomes evident from the analysis above that tribunals have adopted opposing views on issues crucial to the applicability of the customary defence of countermeasures to investor-State disputes. Despite the inconsistencies, through their reasoning and analysis we can identify the main questions and opposing arguments regarding the applicability of defence. This section evaluates the tribunals' reasoning and discusses the availability of countermeasures to responding States in ISDS in view of the customary rules of treaty interpretation, the *lex specialis* principle and general principles of international adjudication.

3.1 *The* Lex Specialis *Principle: Revisiting the Interaction of Countermeasures with Investment Protection Treaties*

As discussed in Section 2, only the Tribunal in *ADM* examined how the defence of countermeasures under customary international law interacts with the NAFTA provisions and whether it is displaced by a *lex specialis*. The

---

[69] The Tribunal had already rejected the applicability of the defence of countermeasures on the basis that investors' rights are direct and independent but still proceeded to discuss whether it would have jurisdiction to examine the prior internationally wrongful act as it was 'a matter which was the subject of much debate … on which it is necessary to say something' see *CPI* [180].
[70] *CPI* [182].
[71] See fn 11.
[72] Paparinskis (n 1) 337–8.

analysis in *ADM* confirms, in the first place, the applicability by default of the general international law on State responsibility, including the circumstances precluding wrongfulness, to treaty-based claims. The Tribunal's analysis on the issue of *lex specialis* suggests that the absence of *explicit* derogation must be regarded as a continuation, or rather, an implicit acceptance of the existing rules under general international law. The silence of NAFTA on the issue of countermeasures as a defence was interpreted as implicit acceptance of its applicability to disputes arising thereunder.

This approach is in line with the general 'presumption against normative conflict' in international law.[73] As explained by the Arbitral Tribunal in the *Georges Pinson* case:

> Toute convention internationale doit être réputée s'en référer tacitement au droit international commun, pour toutes les questions qu'elle ne résout pas elle-même en termes exprès et d'une façon différente.[74]

The ICJ has also adopted the same approach on the applicability of general international law to treaty claims. In the case of *ELSI*, the ICJ Chamber discussed whether the customary rule of exhaustion of local remedies for the exercise of diplomatic protection was applicable, even though the compromissory clause in question made no reference to such prerequisite for submission of a dispute to the Court. It held that it was 'unable to accept that an important principle of customary international law should be held to have been *tacitly* dispensed with, *in the absence of any words making clear an intention to do so*'.[75] Nonetheless, the Court admitted that the parties could indeed deviate from the customary rule. As Sir Frank Berman points out '[a]s a matter of abstract logic, it is perfectly conceivable that a pair of Contracting States might wish to displace the general law in their mutual relations; very often that is the whole purpose of a bilateral treaty.'[76] The Court suggested, however, through its reasoning, that this should be clearly discernible from the text of the treaty and cannot be presumed. The Tribunal in *ADM* seems to adopt the same approach. General international law, including the defence of countermeasures,

---

[73] ILC, 'Fragmentation Report' (n 21) [37–8].
[74] *Georges Pinson* case (*France/United Mexican States*) (Award of 13 April 1928) 5 UNRIAA 329, 422, which translates as follows: 'Every international convention must be deemed tacitly to refer to the common international law for all the questions which it does not itself resolve in express terms and in a different way'.
[75] *Elettronica Sicula SpA (ELSI)* (*USA v Italy*) (Judgment) [1989] ICJ Rep 15 [50] (emphasis added).
[76] F Berman, 'Treaty "Interpretation" in a Judicial Context' (2004) 29 YaleJIntlL 291, 319.

applies by default to all international disputes, subject to the application of the *lex specialis* principle, which dictates that a special provision shall prevail, to the extent that it clearly derogates from general international law. Thus, the premise of the Tribunal's reasoning in *ADM* is consistent with the customary rules of interpretation and the *lex specialis* principle. Chapter Eleven NAFTA does not seem to preclude the applicability of countermeasures to disputes arising thereunder.

Nevertheless, Chapter Twenty NAFTA establishes a *lex specialis* that displaces at least some countermeasures: those in response to violations of NAFTA itself. As evidenced also by the Tribunal's reasoning in *ADM*, countermeasures in international law have a 'dual' character, which is already reflected in their double appearance in both Articles 22 and 49 to 54 ARSIWA: they constitute a means of implementing international responsibility and at the same time a defence against a claim of breach.[77] NAFTA indeed specifies the means by which international responsibility may be implemented for breaches of its own provisions by one of its parties. In such cases the parties may resort to the dispute settlement provisions of the NAFTA as well as the provisions on suspension of benefits ('countermeasures' under NAFTA aiming to induce compliance with a panel decision).[78] These provisions constitute *lex specialis* with respect to *some* countermeasures: those in response to a prior breach of the same treaty. The do not, however, preclude *all* countermeasures.[79] If, for example, the respondent argued that non-performance of its NAFTA obligations was in response to prior violations of another State party in the field of human rights or environmental protection, this scenario would not be covered by the dispute settlement or the suspension of benefits provisions of the NAFTA, and thus, it wouldn't be governed by the *lex specialis*. *Lex specialis* prevails over the relevant *lex generalis* only to the extent that the two rules are co-extensive and in genuine conflict.[80] Aspects of the *lex generalis* that are not derogated from continue to apply by default in the relations between the parties.

---

[77] Countermeasures as a 'sword' (invocation of responsibility for breaches of the investment protection regime) and as a 'shield' (defence against a claim of breach), see Paparinskis (n 1) 270.

[78] NAFTA, Arts 2004 & 2019.

[79] Similarly, in the case of the WTO, Arts. 22 and 23 of the Dispute Settlement Understanding (DSU) provide for WTO-mandated suspension of concessions and the obligation to have recourse to the DSU instead of taking unilateral action in order to seek redress for any alleged breach. These provisions – in and of themselves – exclude the application of some countermeasures under general international law (unilateral countermeasures as far as breaches of the WTO Agreements themselves are concerned) but not others.

[80] See (n 21).

The Tribunal referred to the provisions on countermeasures under Chapter Twenty and stipulated that since there has been no panel decision under Chapter Twenty the provisions on suspension of benefits were inapplicable. But it did not acknowledge that the dispute settlement arrangements under Article 2004 NAFTA establish a *compulsory* procedure that displaces other unilateral means for the implementation of responsibility with respect to NAFTA violations. Article 2004 provides that 'the dispute settlement provisions of this Chapter *shall* apply with respect to the avoidance or settlement of *all* disputes between the Parties regarding the interpretation or application of this Agreement or *wherever* a Party considers that an actual or proposed measure of another Party is or would be inconsistent with the obligations of this Agreement …'.[81] Unilateral countermeasures in the form of suspension of obligations under another NAFTA chapter in order to induce compliance with NAFTA Chapter Twenty are incompatible with this provision.

In *ADM*, Mexico invoked the defence of countermeasures under general international law with respect to the US breaches of NAFTA itself. In principle, this situation would indeed be regulated by the *lex specialis*, ie, the NAFTA provisions on State-to-State dispute settlement. The Tribunal introduced an artificial distinction between different chapters of the same instrument and stipulated that only in Chapter Twenty we find any reference to countermeasures, whilst the dispute at hand was brought before it under Chapter Eleven.[82] However, this argument, on its own, is not convincing. In principle, any grievances against the State of nationality of the investor for alleged breaches of the NAFTA are subject to the dispute settlement provisions of Chapter Twenty and cannot be presented before a Chapter Eleven tribunal through the defence of countermeasures. This approach is in line with the principle of effective interpretation:[83] the tribunal should not read a treaty in a manner that leads its provisions (in this case, the dispute settlement provisions under Chapter Twenty) to redundancy or inefficiency.[84]

---

[81] NAFTA, Art 2004 (emphasis added).
[82] See *ADM* [123]: 'Countermeasures may serve as a defence under a Chapter Eleven case, as this is a matter not specifically addressed in Chapter Eleven'.
[83] See, eg, *Corfu Channel (United Kingdom v Albania)* (Merits) [1949] ICJ Rep 4, 24; *Dispute Regarding Navigational and Related Rights (Costa Rica v Nicaragua)* (Judgment) [2009] ICJ Rep 213 [52]; *Application of the International Convention on the Elimination of All Forms of Racial Discrimination (Georgia v Russian Federation)* (Preliminary Objections) [2011] ICJ Rep 70 [133–4].
[84] ILC (n 2) 219, commentary to Arts 27–8 [6].

The Tribunal's findings in *ADM* were probably motivated, albeit implicitly, by another factual aspect of the dispute. As the respondent submitted before the Tribunal, the means described in NAFTA Chapter Twenty for implementing the international responsibility of the US were not available to Mexico, as the US had blocked Mexico's access to a NAFTA panel.[85] This very fact constituted one of the breaches of NAFTA complained of by Mexico. Therefore, neither the dispute settlement nor the countermeasures' provisions under NAFTA were *actually* available to Mexico in that case. In the words of Mexico, 'a State party cannot be bound by a *lex specialis* that has proved impossible to invoke'.[86] The Tribunal, through its findings, seems to implicitly side with this argument. This approach can also be justified on the basis of general principles of international law. The principle of law expressed in the maxim *ex iniuria jus non oritur* dictates that unlawful conduct cannot modify the law applicable in the relations between the parties, or, in other words, that States should not benefit from their own wrong.[87]

3.2 *The Question of Independent Rights: Revisiting the Power of Host States to Suspend Investors' Rights in Response to Conduct of Their Home State*

Regarding the nature of the rights of investors, the analysis of the tribunals, discussed above, is twofold. In the first instance it seems that they interpret the NAFTA to discern whether the rights enshrined therein are directly ascribed to the investor or derivative of the inter-State relationship. Through this first limb of analysis, they seem to suggest that the issue of the nature of investors' rights is not a theoretical question to be determined *in abstracto*. As it has been pointed out by Paparinskis,

> the nature of the rights is not an abstract and irrebutable *a priori* proposition, and as a rule of *jus dispositivum* is open to amendment or reinterpretation, in particular through subsequent agreement and practice. ... The nature of investors' rights may at least in principle differ in different investment treaty rules, having important consequences for the applicability of countermeasures.[88]

However, the second part of their reasoning traces the nature of investors' rights back to customary international law. For example, the analysis

---

[85] *ADM* [115].
[86] ibid.
[87] *Gabčíkovo-Nagymaros* [133]; *Jadhav (India v Pakistan)* (Judgment) [2019] ICJ Rep 418 [64].
[88] Paparinskis (n 1) 335.

in *ADM* suggests that investment treaties are simply an extension of the customary rules regarding the protection of aliens, which are already binding on all States. According to the Tribunal, although the institution of diplomatic protection is displaced by the establishment of a different dispute settlement mechanism for the implementation of responsibility under investment treaties, the nature of the substantive obligations regarding the protection of aliens, that already existed under customary international law, remains unaffected by the addition of further obligations in investment treaties. Although the Tribunal did not expressly characterise it as such, its reasoning was in essence an interpretation of the obligations under NAFTA in view of relevant rules of customary international law. The Tribunal in *CPI*, although it reached a different conclusion, followed a similar approach. First, it offered an interpretation of the NAFTA and argued that it confers direct rights to the investors. Then, it further buttressed this argument by recourse to customary international law. According to the Tribunal, evidence suggests that even under the traditional institution of diplomatic protection, where the State is the one bringing the investor's claim to the international plane, the rights are in reality owned by the investor. Accordingly, the NAFTA provisions, read in light of customary international law, suggest that investors' rights are independent from their home State. In *Cargill*, the Tribunal had recourse to the customary law on diplomatic protection in the context of an *a contrario* argument. It argued that diplomatic protection is diametrically different to contemporary investment arbitration and that such differences lead to the conclusion that today investors' rights under investment treaties are direct, whereas under customary international law and the rule on diplomatic protection, they remained tied to the State of nationality.

It emerges from the above that all three tribunals are using the same evidence relating to the protection of aliens and the institution of diplomatic protection under customary international law, but reach very different interpretative results. It becomes evident that there is a lack of methodology in the deductive reasoning of tribunals which leads to conflicting conclusions and inconsistencies in terms of reasoning.

In evaluating the evidence and arguments raised in the three cases above, there is nothing to suggest that the rights of investors are detached from their State of nationality. The default applicability of customary international law, discussed in the previous sub-section, suggests that substantive obligations assumed by States under investment treaties are simply in addition to the existing customary obligations and they do not alter their scope and nature if such change is not explicitly provided for. Thus, only the procedural aspects of implementation of international responsibility are affected by current investment treaties that provide for investor-State arbitration without the involvement of the State of nationality.

Moreover, under customary international law, obligations assumed by States which have individuals are beneficiaries and are considered non-derogable are listed in Article 50 ARSIWA as obligations that cannot be affected by countermeasures. The tribunals failed to provide evidence that such list under customary international law has been expanded and also failed to take this list into consideration in interpreting the provisions of the investment treaty in question.

Lastly, other provisions that are typically included in investment protection treaties further suggest that the protection of investors is not immune from changes in the relationship between the host State and the State of nationality. Most pertinently, the 'security exception', which is included in a number of bilateral and multilateral investment protection treaties, including NAFTA,[89] often stipulates, among others, that nothing in the text of the agreement should be construed 'to prevent any Party from taking any actions that it considers necessary for the protection of its essential security interests ... taken in time of war or other emergency in international relations'.[90] It becomes evident that under this clause, an emergency in the relations between the home State of the investor and the host State would justify the taking of measures that are *prima facie* incompatible with the obligations of the host State under the investment agreement. In other words, through no fault of its own, the investor may have to suffer the consequences of the deterioration of the relations between the two States to the extent that the essential security interests of the host state are at risk. Countermeasures taken in response to a prior internationally

---

[89] See on national security, NAFTA, Art 2102.
[90] (emphasis added) see, eg, The Energy Charter Treaty (adopted 17 December 1994, entered into force 16 April 1998) 2080 UNTS 95, Art 24; Canada Model BIT (n 5); Agreement Between the Government of the Republic of Korea and the Government of Japan for the Liberalisation, Promotion and Protection of Investment (Japan & Korea) (adopted 22 March 2002, entered into force 1 January 2003) Art 16; Agreement Between Japan and the Socialist Republic of Viet Nam for the Liberalization, Promotion and Protection of Investment (Japan & Vietnam) (adopted 14 November 2003, entered into force 19 December 2004) Art 15; Agreement Between Japan and the Republic of Chile for a Strategic Economic Partnership (Japan & Chile) (adopted 27 March 2007, entered into force 3 September 2007) Art 193; Agreement Between New Zealand and Singapore on a Closer Economic Partnership (New Zealand & Singapore) (adopted 14 November 2000, entered into force 1 January 2001) Art 76; Agreement Between Japan and the Republic of the Philippines for an Economic Partnership (Japan & Philippines) (adopted 9 September 2006, entered into force 11 December 2008) Art 99.

wrongful act of the State of nationality of an investor may affect the interests of the latter in a similar fashion.

3.3 Countermeasures as a Response to a Prior Internationally Wrongful Act: Revisiting the Limits of Arbitral Tribunals' Subject Matter and Personal Jurisdiction

As seen in the analysis of the case law above, the arbitral tribunals that have been seized with the issue of the applicability of countermeasures in investment disputes so far have taken a restrictive approach to the limits of their subject matter and personal jurisdiction. They require that the indispensable incidental matter which arises in the context of an applicable defence, ie, the existence of a prior internationally wrongful act in the case of countermeasures, would also fall within their scope of jurisdiction if it was brought before them as an independent claim, in order to proceed to its examination. This essentially means that very few countermeasures, if any at all, could properly be examined by an arbitral tribunal: those that consist of the non-performance of obligations arising under the same investment treaty.

The WTO adjudicative bodies have also taken a similar approach to this issue. In the case of *Mexico – Soft Drinks*, which was adjudicated in the context of the same broader US-Mexico dispute, the panel and Appellate Body argued that their jurisdiction *ratione materiae* does not entail the power to examine a prior internationally wrongful act that constitutes violation of rules other than the WTO covered agreements. According to the AB, WTO adjudicative bodies cannot 'become adjudicators of non-WTO disputes', as this is not their function as intended by the DSU.[91]

This approach introduces a *Monetary Gold*-like consideration with regards to jurisdiction *ratione materiae*.[92] The arbitral tribunals examined above, as well as the WTO adjudicative bodies, seem to suggest that 'to adjudicate upon the international responsibility of [a State] without its consent [on that particular matter] would run counter to a well-established

---

[91] *Mexico – Soft Drinks* [56, 78].
[92] See pertinently P Tzeng, 'The Doctrine of Indispensable Issues: Mauritius v United Kingdom, Philippines v China, Ukraine v Russia, and Beyond' (*EJIL:Talk!*, 14 October 2016) <www.ejiltalk.org/the-doctrine-of-indispensable-issues-mauritius-v-united-kingdom-philippines-v-china-ukraine-v-russia-and-beyond/> accessed 1 June 2022; P Tzeng, 'Investments on Disputed Territory: Indispensable Parties and Indispensable Issues' (2017) 14 Braz J Int Law 121.

principle of international law ... namely, that [an adjudicative body] can only exercise jurisdiction over a State with its consent.'[93]

In the case of ISDS, we are also faced with a more traditional *Monetary Gold*-like consideration: the investor's State of nationality, who is the author of the alleged internationally wrongful act, is absent from the proceedings. This raises a problem regarding the scope of the arbitral tribunal's jurisdiction *ratione personae*, as it is called to discuss the international responsibility of a non-participating State.

3.3.1 The Case for an Expansive Approach to the Jurisdiction of Arbitral Tribunals: The Approach of the ICJ

In its 2020 International Civil Aviation Organisation (ICAO) Council judgments,[94] the ICJ expressly endorsed an expansive approach to the jurisdiction of adjudicative bodies in the context of applicable defences. The applicants (Saudi Arabia, Bahrain, United Arab Emirates and Egypt, also known as 'the Quartet') challenged the decision of the ICAO Council to uphold its jurisdiction over Qatar's claims relating to the Quartet's aviation restrictions against Qatar-registered aircrafts. The Quartet had argued that the 'ICAO Council lacked jurisdiction under the Chicago Convention since the real issue in dispute between the Parties involved matters extending beyond the scope of that instrument, including whether the aviation restrictions could be characterised as lawful countermeasures under international law'.[95] The Council rejected this preliminary objection. The respondents instituted an appeal from the Council's decision on jurisdiction before the ICJ under Article 84 of the Chicago Convention. The ICJ, in its judgment, found that the ICAO Council did not err in rejecting the Quartet's assertion and rejected the applicant's grounds of appeal.

In its judgment, the Court stipulated that 'the integrity of the Council's dispute settlement function would not be affected if the Council examined issues outside matters of civil aviation for the *exclusive* purpose of deciding a dispute which falls *within* its jurisdiction ... Therefore, a possible need for the ICAO Council to consider issues falling outside the scope of

---

[93] *Monetary Gold*, 32 (paraphrased).
[94] *Appeal Relating to the Jurisdiction of the ICAO Council under Article II, Section 2, of the 1944 International Air Services Transit Agreement (Bahrain, Egypt and United Arab Emirates v Qatar)* (Judgment) [2020] ICJ Rep 172; *Appeal Relating to the Jurisdiction of the ICAO Council under Article 84 of the Convention on International Civil Aviation (Bahrain, Egypt, Saudi Arabia and United Arab Emirates v Qatar)* (Judgment) [2020] ICJ Rep 81 (hereinafter *2020 ICAO Council Judgments*)
[95] *2020 ICAO Council Judgments* [24].

the Chicago Convention *solely* in order to settle a disagreement relating to the interpretation or application of the Chicago Convention would not render the application submitting that disagreement to it inadmissible.'[96] In other words, the ICJ confirmed that the ICAO Council's jurisdiction entails the power to decide an indispensable incidental matter in the context of the defence of countermeasures in order to discharge its function under the Chicago Convention.

The findings of the Court in 2020 are in line with previous jurisprudence. The PCIJ, already in 1927, famously pronounced in *Factory at Chorzów* that 'reparation ... is the indispensable complement of a failure to apply a convention ... Differences relating to reparations ... are consequently differences relating to its application'.[97] The power of an adjudicative body to examine a defence along with all issues indispensable to determine its applicability in the case before it follows from the 'principle that jurisdiction to determine a breach implies jurisdiction to award compensation',[98] or more generally, to rule on the content of a State's international responsibility. The applicability of a defence under the law of State responsibility determines whether the responding State bears international responsibility and the ensuing consequences. Thus, incidental findings in the context of a respondent's defence are indispensable for the adjudicative body to exercise its function.

This approach is also in line with the principle elaborated by the ICJ in the *Nuclear Tests* case. The Court confirmed that an adjudicative body 'is fully empowered to make whatever findings may be necessary' in order 'to ensure that the exercise of its jurisdiction over the merits, if and when established, shall not be frustrated' and 'to provide for the orderly settlement of all matters in dispute'.[99] Accordingly, the competence of an adjudicative body to examine all indispensable incidental issues in the context of an applicable defence is part of its inherent powers deriving from its 'mere existence ... as a judicial organ established by the consent of States, and is conferred upon it in order that its basic judicial functions may be safeguarded.'[100]

Importantly, the approach of the ICJ suggests that the limited or specialised jurisdictional field of an adjudicative body, ie, the general class of cases in respect of which it exercises and is entitled to exercise

---

[96] ibid [61] (emphasis added).
[97] *Factory at Chorzów (Germany v Poland)* (Jurisdiction) [1927] PCIJ Ser A No 9, 21.
[98] J Crawford, *State Responsibility – The General Part* (CUP 2013) 599.
[99] *Nuclear Tests Case (Australia v France)* (Judgment) [1974] ICJ Rep 253 [23].
[100] ibid.

its functions,[101] does not affect the power to rule on such indispensable incidental issues in the context of defences. The function of an international adjudicative body, regardless of its character as general (such as the ICJ, which may, in principle and subject to the parties' consent, exercise jurisdiction over *all* issues of international law, as outlined in Article 36 its Statute) or specialised (such as an investment arbitral tribunal or the WTO panels and Appellate Body), is to decide the case that is brought before it in accordance with its statute and rules of procedure. To discharge this function, it may need to examine rights and obligations that are necessarily implicated by the main claim before it. The findings of the ICJ in the *2020 ICAO Council* case discussed above clearly support this argument. The ICJ confirmed that the ICAO Council, a specialised dispute settlement body, has the power to examine indispensable incidental issues for the purpose of deciding a case properly brought before it.[102]

Moreover, the argument that courts of general competence can have an expansive understanding of their jurisdiction whereas specialised courts should exercise self-restraint seems to imply, essentially, a difference in the competency, adequacy or suitability of such court to determine a wider spectrum of issues under international law. Naturally, the competency of the court can only be assessed by reference to its members. In other words, this argument seems to imply that the judges (and not the court) are in one case more 'competent' to determine all issues of international law than in the other. In international dispute settlement, as we know it today, this assumption cannot be easily substantiated. Although the professional and academic backgrounds of arbitrators vary, we cannot disregard the fact that several of them are highly specialised in general public international law and have even served as judges in other international adjudicative *fora*.[103] When broader matters of international law are implicated in the dispute in question, the arbitral panel should comprise

---

[101] See (n 9).
[102] *2020 ICAO Council Judgments* [61] (emphasis added).
[103] Eg, many judges of the International Court of Justice have participated ('moonlighted') as arbitrators in international investment disputes or as members of ICSID annulment committees, until ICJ's decision to restrict the practice of allowing members to serve in arbitral tribunals. ICJ members have decided that they 'will not normally accept to participate in international arbitration' and, 'in particular, they will not participate in investor–state arbitration or in commercial arbitration', see ICJ, 'Speech by HE Mr Abdulqawi A Yusuf, President of the International Court of Justice, on the occasion of the Seventy-Third Session of the United Nations General Assembly' (Statements by the President, 25 October 2018) <www.icj-cij.org/public/files/press-releases/0/000-20181025-PRE-02-00-EN.pdf> accessed 1 June 2022.

individuals that possess the necessary knowledge. This is a matter that relates to the selection of arbitrators in any given case.

3.3.2 Countermeasures *vs* Counterclaims

The tribunals' narrow approach to jurisdiction *ratione materiae* brings to mind the requirements for the admissibility of counter-claims.[104] Article 46 of the ICSID Convention provides that 'except as the parties otherwise agree, the Tribunal shall, if requested by a party, determine any incidental or additional claims or counter-claims arising directly out of the subject matter of the dispute provided that they are *within the scope of the consent* of the parties *and are otherwise within the jurisdiction of the Centre.*'

Indeed, there is a reasonable analogy to be drawn between the requirements on the admissibility of a counterclaim and an adjudicative body's jurisdiction to examine the defence of countermeasures. Given that countermeasures are a lawful reaction to a prior internationally wrongful act, a responding State can always claim that its action was in response to the wrongful act of the applicant regardless of whether the court or tribunal would be able to rule on the wrongfulness of such act as an independent claim or counterclaim. This could constitute a back door for entertaining claims that would otherwise be inadmissible.

However, in the case of countermeasures, the respondent will not have an independent verdict on the actions of the applicant. The court's finding of a prior breach will only constitute part of its reasoning to determine the case brought before it by the applicant. This was clearly stipulated by the ICJ in the *2020 ICAO Council* judgment: incidental findings are made by an adjudicative body 'for the *exclusive* purpose of deciding a dispute which falls *within* its jurisdiction'.[105] As Judge Higgins conceded in her, otherwise very critical, separate opinion to the *Oil Platforms* judgment, the *non ultra petita* rule 'does not operate to preclude the Court from dealing with certain other matters "in the reasoning of its Judgment, should it deem this necessary or desirable"'.[106]

---

[104] *Oil Platforms (Iran v USA)* (Counter-Claim, Order of 10 March 1998) [1998] ICJ Rep 203 [33]; *Armed Activities on the Territory of the Congo (Congo v Uganda)* (Counter-Claims, Order of 29 November 2001) [2001] ICJ Rep 678 [35]; *Jurisdictional Immunities of the State (Germany v Italy)* (Counter-Claim, Order of 6 July 2010) [2010] ICJ Rep 310 [14].

[105] *2020 ICAO Council Judgments* [61].

[106] *Oil Platforms (Iran v USA)* (Merits) [2003] ICJ Rep 161, Separate Opinion of Judge Higgins 225 [14], citing *Arrest Warrant of 11 April 2000 (Congo v Belgium)* (Judgment) [2002] ICJ Rep 3, 19 [43].

Moreover, an incidental finding would normally not appear in the judgment's *dispositif*.[107] The findings of an adjudicative body may still be an authoritative affirmation of the applicant's wrongdoing but incidental findings dependent on the principal claim in the dispute cannot generate any rights to remedies. This is a key difference which suggests that *Monetary Gold*-like considerations and analogies with the rules on counterclaims are misplaced.

4   Concluding Remarks

Economic restrictions, or the threat thereof, have always been a core foreign policy tool,[108] used to enforce international rules, react to illegality, prevent conflict, respond to emerging or current crises or exert pressure towards a change in policy or activity. To the extent that such restrictions are, *prima facie*, inconsistent with a State's international obligations, and not lawful (yet unfriendly) acts of retorsion, their imposition must be justified on the basis of an applicable defence, or it will prompt the consequences of international responsibility.[109] It is thus essential to clarify whether and under what conditions, restrictions that affect the rights of foreign investors are allowed under the provisions of current investment protection treaties and customary international law.

Given the importance of foreign investment for both the destination and the origin State in terms of economic growth and productivity, and the prime role of investment protection commitments in the bilateral relations of States, the imposition of restrictions affecting the rights of foreign investors can be a powerful tool for the enforcement of the international rule of law. The defence of countermeasures under customary international law recognises the right of States to react to a breach of international obligations by temporarily suspending its own obligations towards the responsible State in order to induce compliance with international law. This chapter discussed whether this customary defence can be invoked in the context of relevant arbitral proceedings in order to

---

[107] cf *Oil Platforms* where the finding on applicable defence was included in the judgment's *dispositif*. See relevantly *Oil Platforms* (Merits) Declaration of Judge Koroma 223 [4], Dissenting Opinion of Judge Al-Khasawneh 266 [9].

[108] D Cohen & Z Goldman, 'Like It or Not, Unilateral Sanctions Are Here to Stay' (2019) 113 AJIL Unbound 146, 147.

[109] See A Tzanakopoulos, 'We Who Are Not as Others: Sanctions and (Global) Security Governance' in R Geiß & N Melzer (eds), *The Oxford Handbook of the International Law of Global Security* (OUP 2021) 779.

preclude the wrongfulness of restrictions that are *prima facie* contrary to a State's investment protection obligations. In other words, it aimed to clarify whether suspension of investment protection can be used as a tool to exert pressure on a State that violates international law.

This chapter demonstrated that the defence of countermeasures under general international law is applicable by default to investment disputes, unless interpretation of the investment treaty in question suggests otherwise. On the nature of investors' rights, on which much ink has been spilled in the academic literature, it was argued that they are not detached from the inter-State relations of the home and the host State. Customary international law on the protection of aliens and the institution of diplomatic protection informs the content of current investment treaties and suggests that the protections enshrined therein are an extension of such customary law, complemented by a procedural right to initiate proceedings without the involvement of the State of nationality. The text and context of investment treaties provides further support to this argument. Lastly, this chapter demonstrated that the power of an adjudicative body to rule on all indispensable incidental matters that arise in the context of an applicable defence is inherent. Findings on such incidental matters form part of the reasoning of the tribunal and have no independent legal force. Thus, the limited scope of an arbitral tribunal's subject matter jurisdiction and the absence of the State of nationality of the investor from the proceedings do not preclude the examination of the defence of countermeasures.

In view of the above, this chapter concludes that the customary defence of countermeasures is indeed available to responding States in international investment proceedings. A host State is entitled under general international law to react to another State's breach of an international obligation by temporarily suspending its protection of the latter's investors within its territory, in accordance with the requirements for a lawful countermeasure under customary international law. Such countermeasures can be a powerful arrow in the quiver of States that can be used to ensure the effective implementation of international responsibility.

7

Investment Tribunals, the Duty of Compensation in Cases of Necessity

A Customary Law Void?

FEDERICA I PADDEU

1 Introduction

According to Article 27(b) of the Articles on the Responsibility of States for Internationally Wrongful Acts (ARSIWA), the successful invocation of a defence is 'without prejudice ... to the question of compensation for any material loss caused by the act in question'.[1] The Commentary to this provision clarifies that this compensation is not part of the framework of reparation: it is not, in short, one of the obligations arising out of the wrongful act.[2] It concerns, instead, the question whether a State invoking a defence 'should nonetheless be expected to make good any material loss suffered by the State directly affected'.[3] Material loss, the Commentary continues, is a narrower concept than damage as it concerns only the adjustment of losses that may occur when a party relies on a defence.

Beyond this, the Commentary gives little guidance as to when such a duty could be owed. It states that in certain situations a duty of compensation 'is a proper condition' for allowing reliance on a defence, as otherwise a State might shift the burden of protecting its own interests onto other 'innocent' third parties.[4] By way of example, it notes that Hungary accepted this principle when relying on the plea of necessity in *Gabčíkovo-Nagymaros*.[5] But the Commentary does not say in respect of which defences, and in what circumstances, compensation will be due.

---

[1] ILC, 'Draft Articles on Responsibility of States for Internationally Wrongful Acts with Commentaries' (23 April–1 June and 2 July–10 August 2001) UN Doc A/56/10, reproduced in [2001/II – Part Two] YBILC 31 (ARSIWA).
[2] ibid, Commentary to Art 27(b) [4].
[3] ibid.
[4] ibid [5].
[5] ibid.

Indeed, it does not say that compensation is due in cases of necessity; it only notes that Hungary offered compensation when invoking necessity. Indeed, the Commentary clarifies that it 'does not attempt to specify in what circumstances compensation should be payable'.[6] The most that it offers, by way of guidance, is that it will be for the parties involved to agree on any possible compensation.[7]

It is not unusual for parties who benefit from the plea of necessity to offer compensation to affected parties. Hungary, as noted by the ILC, did it in *Gabčíkovo-Nagymaros* and, more recently, Bolivia may be seen as having made a similar offer in an investment arbitration.[8] But such instances are certainly not the norm. In most instances, no offer of compensation will be forthcoming and, consequently, there will be no agreement between the parties. What happens, then, when the parties do not agree on any possible compensation for material loss? What happens when, as has most often been the case in practice, the State invoking a defence rejects that it owes compensation to the affected party? It is precisely here that the question whether compensation is owed, as a matter of obligation, arises.

For the most part, investment tribunals have had to address situations in which offers of, or agreements on, compensation for material loss caused by acts adopted in a state of necessity have not been forthcoming. At least four different States have relied on the defence of necessity to *justify*,[9] and thus, render lawful conduct incompatible with their obligations under bilateral investment treaties.[10] In all cases the claimants have appealed to ARSIWA Article 27(b) and argued that, notwithstanding the necessity defence, respondents were required to compensate them for the

---

[6] ibid [6].
[7] ibid.
[8] *South American Silver v Bolivia* (Award of 22 November 2018) PCA Case No 2013–15 [535].
[9] These are Argentina, in the various disputes brought against it by investors in the wake of the financial crisis of the early 2000s, many of which will be considered in this article; Bolivia in *SAS v Bolivia* (Award of 22 November 2018) PCA Case No 2013–15; Egypt in *Unión Fenosa v Egypt* (Award of 31 August 2018) ICSID Case No ARB/14/4; and Zimbabwe in *Pezold v Zimbabwe* (Award of 28 July 2015) ICSID Case No ARB/10/15; *Bernardus Henricus Funnekotter v Zimbabwe* (Award of 22 April 2009) ICSID Case No ARB/05/6.
[10] These are, at least, the awards available publicly. There is information that an additional State, Ukraine, invoked the necessity plea in an investment arbitration, but the award has not been published. For an overview, see, D Charlotin, 'Revealed: Tribunal in *JKX v Ukraine* Awarded Nearly 12 Million USD for Arbitrary Measures and Breach of Free Transfer Clause; Ukraine's Necessity Defence was Rejected' (*International Arbitration Reporter*, 29 June 2020) <www.iareporter.com/articles/revealed-tribunal-in-jkx-v-ukraine-awarded-nearly-12-million-usd-for-arbitrary-measures-and-breach-of-free-transfer-clause-ukraines-necessity-defence-was-rejected/> accessed 10 May 2021.

material loss suffered as a result of the allegedly justified measures. All States denied owing such compensation.

Are these States *required* to compensate claimants for the loss caused by their justified, and therefore lawful, conduct? Absent the parties' agreement, an obligation to make compensation in these circumstances requires a basis in positive law. This compensation, as the ILC Commentary to Article 27 clarifies,[11] is not a form of reparation; after all, there has been no wrongful act. So, it cannot be based on the obligation to make reparation that arises for States as a consequence of a wrongful act. It must have a discrete legal source. Investment tribunals, deciding in accordance with international law needed, therefore, to identify a positive law basis for the respondent's duty to compensate material loss resulting from acts justified by necessity.

A duty of compensation could be found in the relevant applicable treaty: the treaty may specifically provide for this.[12] Investment tribunals have also interpreted such a duty from the purpose of the Bilateral Investment Treaties (BITs) themselves. Thus, the Tribunal in *BG Group* found that a duty of compensation in these circumstances could be required by the UK–Argentina BIT.[13] But this is relatively rare. Most treaties do not make provision for compensation in relation to emergency measures and, when they do, they often provide for compensation in only a limited range of cases. In all other cases, therefore, a tribunal will need to look to other sources of international law: customary law or general principles of law. The focus of this chapter is the tribunals' engagement with customary international law in their assessment of the existence of an obligation to

---

[11] ARSIWA (n 1) Commentary to Art 27(b) [4].
[12] See, eg, Art 5, Agreement between the Federal Republic of Germany and Brunei Darussalam concerning the Encouragement and Reciprocal Protection of Foreign Investments (Brunei & Germany) (adopted 30 March 1998, entered into force 15 June 2004) Art 5, which states:
   Without prejudice to Paragraph 1 of this Article ["national crisis clause"], nationals and companies of one Contracting Party who in any of the situations referred to in that Paragraph suffer damages or losses in the territory of the other contracting Party resulting from:
   (a) requisitioning of their property by its forces or authorities, or
   (b) destruction of their property by its forces or authorities which was not caused in combat action or was not required by the necessity of the situation, shall be accorded restitution or fair and adequate compensation.

This provision is quoted in F Franke, 'The Custom of Necessity in Investor-State Arbitrations' in R Hofmann & CJ Tams (eds), *International Investment Law and General International Law* (Nomos 2011) 156 fn 203.
[13] *BG Group v Argentina* (Final Award of 24 December 2007) UNCITRAL [409].

make compensation for material loss caused by acts justified under the plea of necessity. As will be seen, tribunals have reached opposite conclusions on the existence of a duty of compensation. However, they all share in common one feature: an omission to engage with the method of customary law identification. Some tribunals assert the existence of the duty, others derive it from the elements of the customary defence of necessity, yet others still simply name-check precedents and general principles of law. But none of these awards provided *any* evidence of practice and *opinio juris* in relation to this duty.

In addition to this introduction, the chapter proceeds in three steps. Section 2 provides an overview of the investment case law. It will review the range of conclusions reached by different investment tribunals and, in so doing, focus on the reasoning deployed to reach those conclusions. It will show that, whether they accept or reject the existence of a duty of compensation, their reasoning does not involve any engagement with the elements of customary law. At most, tribunals offer vague references to previous precedents and case law, and never once to State practice and *opinio juris*. Section 3 will then focus on analysis: it reviews the available practice and *opinio juris*, limited as it is, and assesses the precedents invoked in support of the duty of compensation by these tribunals. As will be seen, the practice is scant and inconsistent and the precedents invoked are at best equivocal as to the existence of a duty of compensation. If States have expressed any *opinio* in this regard this is an *opinio non juris*: there is *no* customary obligation to make compensation in cases of necessity. Section 4 concludes.

Two clarifications are necessary before proceeding. First, this chapter takes an orthodox approach to the identification of customary law, in line with the so-called 'two element theory' followed by the ILC in its recent work on customary law and supported by States in connection with that work.[14] In light of this, it will focus first and foremost on identifying existing practice and *opinio juris* of States in respect of the duty of compensation. The article will also take into account the case law of international tribunals. This is because while international courts and tribunals do not have a formal role in the development of international law, in practice, decisions of international tribunals can influence the development of

---

[14] UNGA, 'Identification of Customary International Law' (11 January 2019) UN Doc A/RES/73/203; see also ILC, 'Draft Conclusions on Identification of Customary International Law, with Commentaries' (30 April–1 June and 2 July–10 August 2018) UN Doc A/73/10, reproduced in [2018/II – Part Two] YBILC 122, 122–56.

international law, including the law of State responsibility and the law of investment protection.[15] Second, this chapter will take necessity *as a justification*, namely, as a defence which renders conduct lawful, and not as an excuse, namely, as a defence which excludes the consequences of a wrongful act.[16] The reasons for this choice are that the majority of States who support this defence at international law classify it as a justification, and that States have invoked it in international courts and tribunals as such.[17]

2   Investment Tribunals and the Duty of Compensation

Several States have invoked the plea of necessity in investment treaty arbitration. In most (if not all) of these instances, the parties have addressed the question of compensation in the event that the State's plea of necessity was successful. Likewise, in most instances, tribunals have addressed the duty of compensation in *obiter* only: respondents' plea of necessity having been unsuccessful on other, often multiple, grounds. Many tribunals have not addressed the question of compensation at all: having rejected the plea of necessity on other grounds, there was no need to consider this issue.[18]

---

[15] On this see, generally, H Lauterpacht, The Development of International Law by the International Court (Stevens & Sons 1958); P Daillier, 'The Development of the Law of Responsibility through the Case Law' in J Crawford, A Pellet & S Olleson (eds), The Law of International Responsibility (OUP 2010); CJ Tams & J Sloan (eds), The Development of International Law by the International Court of Justice (OUP 2012); C Schreuer, 'The Development of International Law by ICSID Tribunals' (2016) 31(3) ICSID Rev 728; CJ Tams, 'The Development of International Law by the International Court of Justice' in E Cannizzaro & ors (eds), *Decisions of the ICJ as Sources of International Law?* (International and European Papers Publishing 2018).

[16] If necessity were an excuse, the duty of compensation would be encompassed by the obligation to make reparation. After all, in this case, the State invoking the defence would have committed an internationally wrongful act. However, it would be a limited form of reparation: only for material loss. Necessity would then operate as a partial excuse: it would exclude some, but not all, consequences of the wrongful act for the invoking State. Note that this solution is not as simple as it might at first appear. As a matter of practice, it faces the difficulty that States do not support or invoke necessity as an excuse. As a matter of theory, it faces the difficulty of providing a principled basis for the distinction between total excuses and partial excuses. For a discussion of this issue, see: F Paddeu, *Justification and Excuse in International Law: Concept and Theory of General Defences* (CUP 2018) 81–6.

[17] F Paddeu, 'The Impact of Investment Arbitration in the Development of State Responsibility Defences' in R Hofmann, S Schill & CJ Tams (eds), *ICSID at 50: Investment Arbitration as a Motor of General International Law* (Edward Elgar, forthcoming) <https://papers.ssrn.com/sol3/papers.cfm?abstract_id=2865718> accessed 10 May 2022.

[18] Eg *von Pezold* [624–68].

Tribunals' approaches to the duty of compensation have varied significantly, covering the full range of possibilities: some have accepted the existence of this duty, others have denied it, and others still have not taken a position. They have all had in common, however, minimal or no engagement with the evidence of the (potential) positive law source of this duty. In particular, none of these tribunals have applied the orthodox method (or any other method, for that matter) for the identification of customary law: tribunals have instead resorted to simple assertions, deductions, and denials. The next four sections review the different approaches taken by investment tribunals.

2.1 Assertions

Some tribunals have asserted the existence of a duty of compensation. When a tribunal asserts a rule, it provides no reasoning (inductive or deductive as it may be) in support of the stated rule.[19] To use Stefan Talmon's words, asserting customary rules is like pulling rabbits out of a hat.[20] To be sure, assertion is not a method for the identification of customary rules: it 'is a way of stating a conclusion.'[21] For the most part, investment tribunals have not simply 'pulled' the duty of compensation from out of a hat. But their reasoning in support of this duty is often unsuitable, and where available it is so thin as to provide no support at all.

The Tribunal in *CMS v Argentina* held that Article 27(b) 'establishe[d] the appropriate rule of international law on this issue' and that it was 'the meaning of international law or the principles governing most domestic legal systems' that a party invoking necessity owed compensation.[22] These seem to be references to customary law and general principles of law as the potential source of the duty of compensation. Reliance on each of these two sources is, however, insufficient. As to general principles, these are referred to in two paragraphs,[23] and in neither case are references provided. As to customary law, the tribunal provided no evidence

---

[19] S Talmon, 'Determining Customary International Law: The ICJ's Methodology between Induction, Deduction and Assertion' (2015) 26 *EJIL* 417, 434.
[20] ibid.
[21] O Sender & M Wood, 'The International Court of Justice and Customary International Law: A Reply to Stefan Talmon' (*EJIL:Talk!*, 30 November 2015) <www.ejiltalk.org/the-international-court-of-justice-and-customary-international-law-a-reply-to-stefan-talmon/> accessed 10 May 2022; See also Merkouris, 'Interpreting the Customary Rules on Interpretation' (2017) 19 ICLR 126, 137.
[22] *CMS v Argentina* (Award of 12 May 2005) ICSID Case ARB/01/8 [390].
[23] ibid [388, 390].

of practice or *opinio juris*, and simply mentioned the cases of *Orr and Laubenheimer*,[24] *General Company of the Orinoco River*,[25] *Bulgarian Property*,[26] and *Gabčíkovo-Nagymaros*[27] as precedents. To be sure, tribunals can (and do) contribute to the development of the law: but once these cases are considered in detail, it will become apparent that these decisions do not unequivocally support a duty of compensation. The award was indeed subsequently annulled, among others, due to a manifest error of law in relation to Article 27(b): as the Annulment Committee explained, this provision did not impose a duty of compensation; it was simply a without prejudice clause.[28]

The Tribunals in *Enron* and *Sempra* both noted that Article 27(b) was vague and, in line with the Commentary to this provision, that whether compensation was due in these circumstances was a matter that must be decided by the parties. Both Tribunals added that absent agreement between the parties 'this determination is to be made by the Tribunal to which the dispute has been submitted.'[29] The reasoning is not entirely clear, but it is plausible to read these awards as endorsing a duty of compensation in cases of necessity: compensation is either agreed between the parties or decided by the tribunal. The tribunals do not clarify, however, what is the source of their power to determine (and impose the payment of) compensation. Neither tribunal ultimately went on to make the determination since both rejected the Argentine defence.

The Tribunal in *South American Silver v Bolivia* was even briefer on this point. In a dispute concerning the payment of compensation for an expropriation, the Tribunal stated:

> It is clear that Bolivia's state-of-necessity [sic] defense was not designed to excuse the non-payment of compensation for the expropriation, nor could it, since the invocation of this defense does not preclude the payment of compensation by the State for the damage effectively resulting from acts attributable to it.[30]

---

[24] *Orr and Laubenheimer and the Post-Glover Electric Company* (1900) 15 RIAA 33.
[25] *Company General of the Orinoco* (1905) 10 RIAA 184.
[26] League of Nations, 'Report of the Commission of Enquiry on the Incidents on the Frontier between Bulgaria and Greece, Doc No C.727.M.270.1925.VII (Annex 815)' (1926) 7 LNOJ 196.
[27] *Case Concerning the Gabčíkovo-Nagymaros Project (Hungary/Slovakia)* (Judgment) [1997] ICJ Rep 7.
[28] *CMS v Argentina* (Annulment of 25 September 2007) ICSID Case No ARB/01/8 [146–7].
[29] *Enron v Argentina* (Award of 22 May 2007) ICSID Case No ARB/01/3 [345]; *Sempra Energy v Argentina* (Award of 28 September 2007) ICSID Case No ARB/02/16 [394].
[30] *South American Silver* [535, 620].

There is some ambiguity in this statement. The passage uses the language of Article 27(b) (compensation is not precluded), seemingly going no further than this provision: the successful invocation of a defence is without prejudice to the question of compensation. But the passage can also be interpreted as going beyond Article 27(b); supporting a duty of compensation in (at least some) cases of necessity. The Tribunal first states that the plea of necessity cannot apply to deny compensation for expropriation: this is not what the plea was 'designed' to do. The plea of necessity cannot be invoked when the relevant primary rule excludes its invocation, implicitly or explicitly.[31] Arguably, the situation of necessity is already catered to by the primary rule on expropriation, as it is necessity that justifies the taking of the property. Necessity cannot do double work, as it were, it cannot justify the taking *and* justify the denial of compensation. The plea cannot thus be invoked as Bolivia has done. So far, so plausible. The tribunal then appears to go further. Even if necessity were applicable to this situation, it says, the plea could not deny compensation for expropriation. In short, a successful invocation of the plea would still involve an obligation to pay compensation for the expropriation. If this were the correct interpretation of the Tribunal's statement, it would be no more than an assertion that compensation was due even in cases of successful invocation of the plea – at least, in some of these cases (expropriation). The Tribunal provides no evidence of a positive law source, let alone of customary law, for this duty in the award.

2.2 Deductions

Other tribunals have obviated the need to provide a positive law basis to the duty of compensation, by grafting this obligation to the customary rule of necessity itself. They have done this by interpreting the rule on compensation as *including* a duty of compensation as one of its requirements. If the plea of necessity is recognised in customary law, and the duty of compensation is inherent in the plea, then it follows that the duty of compensation is also part of customary law. This is the case of the awards of the Tribunal and annulment committee in *EDF v Argentina*.

The *EDF* Tribunal stated that to succeed in its invocation, Argentina had to demonstrate:

> three key elements of ILC Articles 25 and 27: (i) that the wrongful act was the only way to safeguard Argentina's essential interest under Article 25 (1)(a);

---

[31] ARSIWA (n 1) Art 25(2)(a) & Commentary to Art 25 [19].

(ii) that Respondent did not contribute to the situation of necessity; and (iii) that Respondent did not return to the pre-necessity *status quo* when possible, or compensate Claimants for damage suffered as a result of the relevant measures.[32]

It further explained that even if Argentina were successful in invoking the plea, this did not '*per se* preclude payment of compensation to the injured investor for any damage suffered as a result of the necessity measures enacted by the State.'[33] Having contributed to the situation of necessity, and having failed to re-establish the *status quo*, Argentina's defence failed.[34]

In annulment proceedings, Argentina claimed that the Tribunal had 'invented' this additional element.[35] The Annulment Committee, however, endorsed the Tribunal's finding. According to the Committee, this requirement had not been invented by the Tribunal, but was rather reflective of 'what is inherent in the very concept of necessity'.[36] By this, the Committee meant its temporary character: 'If a departure from a legal obligation can be justified by a state of necessity, it can be justified for only so long as that state of necessity exists'[37] – an argument also adduced by the Tribunal in *CMS*. In short, since the plea of necessity is only temporary, *therefore*, compensation is due.

Panos Merkouris has argued that deductive methods may be applied to the interpretation of customary rules the existence of which has already been established.[38] The Committee's approach could be viewed in this light, as proceeding either teleologically or by necessary implication to deduce the existence of a duty of compensation from the (established) rule of necessity. Leaving aside the doctrinal question whether interpretation of customary rules differs from their identification, it seems a step too far to accept that additional obligations may be inferred, by deduction, from established customary rules: especially where the practice supporting that rule does not provide evidence in respect of that specific obligation (as will be seen below). At any rate, even if this method were found to be in line with the generally accepted method for customary law identification, the

---

[32] *EDF v Argentina* (Award of 11 June 2012) ICSID Case No ARB/03/23 [1171].
[33] ibid [1177].
[34] ibid [1181].
[35] *EDF v Argentina* (Decision on Annulment of 5 February 2016) ICSID Case No ARB/03/23 [291, 325].
[36] ibid [330].
[37] ibid.
[38] Merkouris (n 21) 137.

conclusion the Committee reaches is a *non sequitur*. The temporariness of the plea (which is only a contingent feature)[39] concerns compliance with the obligation. In principle, defences do not strike down the rule at issue, which remains in force throughout the period that the defence subsists.[40] But the State's obligation to comply with the rule is set aside throughout the period in which the facts giving rise to the defence continue to exist. Once these facts come to an end, the obligation is 'restored', as it were, and the State must resume compliance with it.[41] If it does not, then the State will be *pro tanto* responsible for the violation of the obligation from the moment when the defence ceased.[42] Take the following example. Due to a situation of necessity which arose on 10 February 2020, State A was unable to comply with its treaty obligation to deliver 10 tonnes of rice on the first day of every month to State B. Say, then, that the situation of necessity ended on 15 July 2020. State A would be required on 1 August to deliver 10 tonnes of rice to State B. If it failed to deliver those on 1 August, then State A would be responsible *as from 1 August* for the failure to comply with its obligation to State B. The defence is temporary in that it can only justify State A's failure to comply with its obligation for the five months of March, April, May, June, and July. Indeed, throughout this time, State A's obligation to deliver is in abeyance due to the situation of necessity. But the plea's temporary character, which concerns the return to compliance *after* the defence has ended, has nothing to do with the question of compensation for material loss, which concerns the allocation of the losses generated *during* the situation of necessity (ie, during the period when the State was justified in not complying with the obligation). In the example above, a duty of compensation would relate to the loss caused to State B as a result of A's failure to deliver the required amount of rice for the five months between the start (on 10 February) and the end (15 July) of the situation of necessity.

---

[39] The temporary character of a defence is not 'inherent' in any defence (not even in the plea of necessity), and it is rather contingent on (i) the underlying obligation and (ii) on the characteristics of the specific situation. Indeed, as ARSIWA (n 1) Commentary to Art 27 [1] explains, 'it may be that the effect of the facts which disclose a circumstance precluding wrongfulness may also give rise to the termination of the obligation'.

[40] ARSIWA (n 1) Commentary to Art 27.

[41] See ibid, Art 27(a).

[42] Note that the Commentary to Art 27 allows for a partial resumption of compliance as the situation triggering the defence recedes. This might suggest that the State could be partially exonerated when this occurs. Leaving aside the difficult theoretical questions that partial justifications can raise, the Commentary to Article 12 ARSIWA states that 'partial compliance' is nevertheless a breach of international law.

The reasoning of the Tribunal – that compensation is due because of the inherent character of the plea – confuses, or fuses, resumption of compliance with compensation. In short, it confuses, or fuses, the provisions in ARSIWA Article 27(a) and Article 27(b). Resumption of compliance with the underlying obligation at the end of the situation of necessity and compensation for material loss during the period of necessity relate to two different obligations. The former, resumption of compliance, is just a consequence of the underlying obligation no longer being in abeyance. The latter is a different – new – obligation of the State invoking necessity. This is an obligation that arises *as a result* of the loss caused by the act of necessity: in our example above, the loss caused by the failure to deliver the rice. To say that the invoking State must resume compliance with the underlying obligation – which is the consequence of the defence's temporary character – has no bearing on whether the invoking State is now burdened by a new obligation to pay compensation for losses caused during the defence.

This conclusion does not change by saying that payment of compensation can only occur after the necessity has ended. We still need to find a basis in positive law for this obligation to pay compensation. The former is a question of the performance of the duty (when it falls due), the latter one of its existence. The underlying obligation cannot – itself – sustain this duty. In the example above, the obligation is to deliver rice: it is not 'to deliver rice *or pay compensation*'. It is also not a duty derived from responsibility – namely, one of forms of reparation – because there has been no wrongful act: the failure to deliver rice, in our example, was justified by necessity. What is, then, the positive law source of this obligation to pay compensation? After all, loss occasioned by a permitted or lawful act is not typically one that requires compensation. In other words, liability for the injurious consequences of lawful acts is *not the norm*. Such liability is exceptional, and needs to be grounded on a positive law rule.[43]

No positive law source – customary or otherwise – was identified by either the Tribunal or the Annulment Committee to ground the duty of compensation. The Tribunal noted and set aside the question of the customary character of the defence of necessity, arguing that the parties

---

[43] The obligation to pay compensation in these circumstances is substantive, in that it guides State conduct, but when attached to justified conduct, determining whether it is owed will require the use of the law of State responsibility. To argue over the primary or secondary character of such an obligation distracts from the main point: in either case, such an obligation requires a basis in positive law.

agreed on the application of ARSIWA Article 25.[44] Notably, the Tribunal does not mention whether the parties agreed on the application of Article 27(b) and, more importantly, whether they agreed on the question of compensation. The Committee, in turn, only referred to the correspondence in the *Caroline* incident which, indeed, supports the proposition that necessity is only temporary but, as will be seen, does not support a duty to pay compensation for material loss caused by an act adopted in circumstances of necessity.

2.3 Denials

Other tribunals have denied the existence of a duty of compensation in cases of necessity. This is clearly the case of the *LG&E* Tribunal. In its Liability decision, the Tribunal noted that Article 27(b) was a without prejudice clause, and that it did not 'not specifically refer to the compensation for one or all the losses incurred by an investor as a result of the measures adopted by a State during a state of necessity.'[45] Whether compensation was due, said the Tribunal, depended on the interpretation of the defence in question. The Tribunal focused on Article XI of the BIT and found that no compensation was due since this provision 'establishes the state of necessity as a ground for exclusion from wrongfulness of an act of the State, and therefore, the State is exempted from liability.'[46] The Tribunal's decision is grounded on Article XI of the BIT, but to the extent that the Tribunal equated Article XI to the customary plea of necessity its conclusion can be extended to the latter as well. In line with this reasoning, the *LG&E* Tribunal – the only one to have accepted Argentina's plea – eventually excluded compensation for the period covered by the necessity defence.[47] The reasoning is circular: the circumstance precluding wrongfulness of necessity does not attract a duty of compensation *because* it is a circumstance precluding wrongfulness. But the whole point is whether compensation should be due *even if* something is a circumstance precluding wrongfulness. In short, the Tribunal chose where to allocate the loss (the investor) but failed to provide a reasoned argument or any evidence of a source in positive law for this conclusion.

---

[44] *EDF* (Award) [1167–8].
[45] *LG&E Energy Corp, LG&E Capital Corp, LG&E International Inc v Argentine Republic* (Decision on Liability of 3 October 2006) ICSID Case ARB/02/1 [260].
[46] ibid [261].
[47] *LG&E v Argentina* (Award of 25 July 2007) ICSID Case No ARB/02/1 [106–8].

The award in *Urbaser* could be read as a denial of the duty of compensation, but it is a more equivocal precedent. The Tribunal found that Argentina's necessity plea was satisfied,[48] but it denied the payment of damages to the claimants. However, the *ratio* of this decision seems to have rested on the fact that the failure of the investment was primarily attributable to claimants themselves,[49] and not on the non-existence of a duty of compensation in cases of necessity. Indeed, the Tribunal made no comments on the existence of this, despite the fact that the parties presented arguments in this regard.[50]

2.4 Agnosticism

Finally, other tribunals have taken a more agnostic stance. The Annulment Committee in *CMS* simply noted that Article 27(b) is a without prejudice clause and not a stipulation, and that it did not attempt to 'specify in which circumstances compensation could be due, notwithstanding the state of necessity.'[51] The Annulment Committee in *Sempra*, in addressing the difference between state of necessity and the BIT's non-precluded-measures clause, noted that no compensation was due in the latter case but that the question of compensation 'was not precluded' in the former. The Tribunal thus acknowledges the possibility that compensation could be due, without taking sides in the debate.[52]

3 Doing the Homework: What Evidence for a Customary Duty of Compensation?

Tribunals' divided opinions on this point are not unique. Far from it. Scholars are equally divided on the existence of a duty of compensation in cases of necessity. Thus, some scholars have argued that international law recognises an obligation to provide compensation in these cases,[53]

---

[48] *Urbaser v Argentina* (Award of 8 December 2016) ICSID Case No ARB/07/26 [709 ff].
[49] ibid [847]
[50] ibid [697] (claimants), [708] (respondent).
[51] *CMS* (Annulment) [146–7].
[52] *Sempra Energy v Argentina* (Annulment of 29 June 2010) ICSID Case No ARB/02/16 [118].
[53] Eg, A Reinisch & C Binder, 'Debts and State of Necessity' in JP Bohoslavsky & JL Černič (eds), *Making Sovereign Financing and Human Rights Work* (Hart 2014) 125–6; G Bücheler, *Proportionality in Investor-State Arbitration* (OUP 2015) 243, 290–6; C Binder & P Janig, 'Investment Agreements and Financial Crises' in M Krajewski & RT Hoffmann (eds), *Research Handbook on Foreign Direct Investment* (Edward Elgar 2019) 677–8.

whereas others have expressed doubts as to the existence of this duty.[54] Many of these scholars, however, regardless of their views on the existence, in positive law, of this duty, agree that compensation would be fair in such circumstances.[55]

In the case law and the literature on this topic, arguments as to the existence of a customary duty of compensation usually rely, as evidence, on the ILC's drafting of, and Commentary to, Article 27(b), and the case law.[56] As will be seen in the next two sections, however, the evidence in support of this duty is far from clear. Regardless of how one interprets the ILC's work on, and the Commentary to, Article 27(b), only a handful of States commenting on the draft expressly supported a duty of compensation generally, or in cases of necessity specifically. Indeed, the evidence of practice and *opinio juris* in favour of this duty is scant and vague (Section 3.1), and the precedents relied upon by tribunals and scholars alike to evidence the existence of the duty of compensation are equivocal at best (Section 3.2).

3.1 Missing Practice

According to Article 38(1)(b) of the ICJ Statute, customary international law is evidenced by the existence of a 'general practice accepted as law'.[57] The practice must be general in the sense that it is 'sufficiently widespread and representative, as well as consistent.'[58] It is not necessary for all States in the international community to engage in the practice, nor is it needed for the practice to be absolutely uniform. The threshold required for the identification of any given rule of customary law may vary by reference to the context.[59] Thus, it is arguable that in the case of very exceptional circumstances, like those that trigger the plea of necessity, the threshold is lower as there

---

[54] See Franke (n 12) 156–7; A Kent & A Harrington, 'The Plea of Necessity Under Customary International Law: A Critical Review in Light of the Argentine Cases' in C Brown & K Miles (eds), *Evolution in Investment Treaty Arbitration* (CUP 2011) 261–3; M Paparinskis, 'Investment Treaty Arbitration and the (New) Law of State Responsibility' (2013) 24 EJIL 617, 633; R Díaz Inverso, 'El estado de necesidad como circunstancia que excluye la ilicitud en la responsabilidad internacional de los Estados' (2015) 47 Revista de Derecho Público 49, 54.

[55] S Ripinsky, 'State of Necessity: Effect on Compensation' (2007) 4(6) TDM 1; JE Viñuales, *Foreign Investment and the Environment in International Law* (CUP 2012) 390.

[56] Reinisch & Binder (n 53) 125–6; Bücheler (n 53) 243, 290–6; Binder & Janig (n 53) 677–8.

[57] Statute of the International Court of Justice (adopted 26 June 1945, entered into force 24 October 1945) 33 UNTS 993; see also *North Sea Continental Shelf Cases (Federal Republic of Germany/Netherlands; Federal Republic of Germany/Denmark)* (Judgment) [1969] ICJ Rep 3 [44].

[58] ILC (n 14) Conclusion 8(1), and references cited in the Commentary.

[59] ibid, Commentary to Conclusion 8 [2].

will be fewer opportunities for States to engage in the relevant practice. This practice must be accompanied by *opinio juris*, namely, evidence that States engage in the relevant practice out of a sense of legal obligation (or legal entitlement).[60] As will be seen, there is almost no support in the practice and *opinio juris* of States for the duty of compensation in cases of necessity.

It seems fair to read the ILC's work on Article 27(b) as generally supportive of a duty of compensation in cases of necessity.[61] Special Rapporteurs Ago and Crawford supported it, as well as several members of the Commission. None of them wished to take too exacting a position on this matter, however, because of the scarcity of practice and of the variety of cases in which this duty might arise.[62] In this regard, the ILC's work mirrors that of scholars – a strong sense that it would be fair for compensation to be due.

Nevertheless, States' views on this duty have been much more mixed and, often, negative. Only three of the States commenting on the ILC's drafts, Germany,[63] Russia[64] and the UK,[65] explicitly accepted the possibility of the duty arising in situations of necessity. Other States like Denmark (speaking on behalf of the Nordic countries),[66] the Netherlands[67] and

---

[60] ibid, Conclusion 9(1), and references cited in the Commentary.
[61] See, in particular, supportive remarks during the debates on this provision: ILC, 'Summary Record of the 1614th Meeting' (18 June 1980) UN Doc A/CN.4/SR.1614, Comments of Riphagen [6] & Comments of Schwebel [18 & 20]; ILC, 'Summary Record of the 1616th Meeting' (20 June 1980) UN Doc A/CN.4/SR.1616, Comments of Schwebel [11] & Comments of Calle y Calle [17]; ILC, 'Summary Record of the 1617th Meeting' (23 June 1980) UN Doc A/CN.4/SR.1617, Comments of Tsuruoka [36]. There were no specific endorsements of a duty of compensation in cases of necessity on second reading; on this occasion, the debate centred on the expansion of the duty of compensation to all cases in which defences were invoked, so no specific comments were made of the individual defences or circumstances in which the duty was owed.
[62] See, in particular, Crawford's comments in ILC, 'Second Report on State Responsibility, by Mr James Crawford, Special Rapporteur' (17 March, 1 and 30 April, 19 July 1999) UN Doc A/CN.4/498 and Add.1–4, 84 [348].
[63] ILC, 'State Responsibility: Comments and Observations Received by Governments' (25 March, 30 April, 4 May, 20 July 1998) UN Doc A/CN.4/488 and Add.1–3, 136.
[64] UNGA, 'Report of the International Law Commission on the Work of its 52nd Session (Continued)' (4 December 2000) UN Doc A/C.6/55/SR.18, 10 [53] (indicating that this assumed the plea of necessity operated to 'exempt responsibility' and not to 'preclude wrongfulness').
[65] ILC, 'State Responsibility: Comments and Observations Received From Governments' (25 March 1998) UN Doc A/CN.4/488, 136.
[66] ILC, 'Report of the International Law Commission on the Work of its 51st Session (Continued)' (20 December 1999) UN Doc A/C.6/54/SR.22, 2 [3].
[67] ILC, 'Report of the International Law Commission on the Work of its 51st Session (Continued)' (13 January 2000) UN Doc A/C.6/54/SR.21, 7–8 [52]; ILC, 'Comments and Observations Received From Governments' (19 March, 3 April, 1 May and 28 June 2001) UN Doc A/CN.4/515 and Add.1–3, 57 (adding that it should be limited to *force majeure*, state of necessity and distress).

Poland[68] generally endorsed Article 27 (or its predecessor). Their statements, however, fall short of endorsing the actual existence of a duty of compensation following invocations of necessity.[69] Austria did not outrightly reject the possibility that a duty of compensation may arise in situations of necessity, but it warned that the provision required a more specific formulation since 'it would otherwise lead to the danger of possibly undercutting the effect of circumstances precluding wrongfulness.'[70] Other States were more negative. France rejected altogether the idea that compensation may arise in the event of a successful invocation of a defence,[71] and Chile rejected it in respect of a state of necessity in particular.[72]

Furthermore, in the context of judicial or arbitral proceedings, Hungary[73] and Slovakia[74] have acknowledged the existence of the duty, while Argentina[75] and Zimbabwe[76] have rejected it. Bolivia also addressed this duty in arbitral proceedings against a foreign investor, though its position is not entirely clear. It offered compensation to the investor for the taking of property, which it justified under the plea of necessity and argued that in this way it respected the 'hypothetical interests' of the United Kingdom (the other party to the BIT) and of the international community as a whole.[77] However, the case involved an expropriation and the primary rules on expropriation themselves require compensation.

Overall, as this review shows, just over a dozen States (out of nearly 200) have expressed views on the existence of a duty of compensation in cases of necessity. As Fernando Bordin has noted, few (if any) customary rules 'even those long viewed as established, can survive the brutal scrutiny of

---

[68] ILC, '51st Session' (n 67) 8 [57].

[69] These States endorsed, in a general manner, ARSIWA (n 1) Art 27 (or its predecessor Art 35). However, given the wording of Art 27 (and its predecessor) the most that can be inferred from this general support is that these States do not deny the possibility that compensation may arise even if a defence is successfully invoked.

[70] ILC (n 65) A/CN.4/488, 135.

[71] ibid.

[72] UNGA, 'Record of Meeting Held on 12 Nov 1980' (12 November 1980) UN Doc A/C.6/35/SR.47 [8–9].

[73] See, *Gabčíkovo-Nagymaros Project (Hungary/Slovakia)* (Oral Proceedings) [1997] CR 97/3 (translation), 87, CR 97/4, 24–5 [36], CR 97/5, 64 & CR 97/6 (translation), 60, 66.

[74] ibid, CR 97/11, 56–7.

[75] See *CMS v Argentina* (Award) [389]; *CMS v Argentina* (Annulment) [139]; *Enron v Argentina* [344–5]; *Sempra Energy v Argentina* [393–4]; *BG Group* [398].

[76] *Pezold* [615].

[77] *South American Silver* [535].

the magnifying glass'.[78] The two-element approach to the identification of customary law, endorsed by the ILC Conclusions, must be applied with flexibility.[79] Even with this caveat in mind, however, it seems clear that the practice available at present is insufficient and is, moreover, is inconsistent as the broad range of views shows. This makes it difficult to draw any conclusions as to the existence of a customary duty of compensation. While there seems to be a trend towards favouring the recognition of this duty in the case law and scholarship, to date, such trend has not been followed by States in their practice: the evidence available at present falls far short of the requirement of generality necessary to identify a rule of customary law.

3.2 Equivocal Precedents

Whether international tribunals can make or develop international law, in addition to just applying the law to specific facts, is a persistent and thorny question in international law.[80] It is also a question which eschews simple answers.[81] One thing, however, is clear: as a matter of the formal sources of international law, judicial decisions are, as stated in Article 38(1)(d) of the ICJ Statute, subsidiary means for the determination of rules of law. International courts and tribunals do not *make law*, as recently reaffirmed by the ILC work on the Identification of Customary Law.[82] But this is not to say that courts and tribunals cannot act as agents of legal development.[83] As observed by Rosalyn Higgins, former President

---

[78] F Bordin, 'A Glass Half Full? The Character, Function and Value of the Two-Element Approach to Identifying Customary International Law' (2019) 21 ICLR 283, 297.
[79] ibid.
[80] CJ Tams & A Tzanakopoulos, '*Barcelona Traction* at 40: The ICJ as an Agent of Legal Development' (2010) 23 LJIL 781, 782.
[81] One of the most important texts on this question is H Lauterpacht, *The Development of International Law by the International Court* (Stevens & Sons 1958). For more recent works considering this question, see the collection of essays edited by CJ Tams & J Sloan (eds), *The Development of International Law by the International Court of Justice* (OUP 2013); and 2015 Gaetano Morelli Lectures, published in E Cannizzaro & ors (eds), *Decisions of the ICJ as Sources of International Law?* (International and European Papers Publishing 2018). Other reference works will be referred to throughout this chapter, as they become relevant.
[82] ILC, 'Draft Conclusions' (n 14), Conclusion 13, Commentary.
[83] See, eg, RY Jennings, 'The Judiciary, International and National, and the Development of International Law' (1996) 45 *ICLQ* 1, 3; A Pellet, 'Article 38' in A Zimmerman & ors (eds), *The Statute of the International Court of Justice: A Commentary* (OUP 2006) 789; J Crawford, *Brownlie's Principles of Public International Law* (OUP 2012) 39–40.

of the ICJ, 'the very determination of specific disputes, and the provision of specific advice, does develop international law'.[84] To be sure, there are 'decisions and decisions', to paraphrase Jan Paulsson.[85] Some decisions will exert an influence in legal development and, again in Paulsson's words, 'become ever brighter beacons', while others 'flicker and die near-instant deaths'.[86] Judicial development of international law relies on the interactions with the decisions by other actors in this process: whether the decision is endorsed by States in their practice,[87] or it is followed by other tribunals. In turn, these interactions depend on a variety of factors such as whether the field is receptive to judicial development;[88] and whether the decision showcases certain attributes (including the authority of the tribunal, the composition of the tribunal, the context of the decisions, the size of the majority, and the quality of the reasoning).[89]

It thus seems worth examining the case law relied upon by the investment awards discussed earlier. As will be seen, the precedents invoked are, at best, equivocal on this point. In most of these cases, the existence of compensation can be explained on other, more plausible, legal bases. As such, they cannot be relied upon as evidence of the existence of a duty of compensation. It is not surprising, then, that none of these cases has become a 'bright beacon' on this point, as evidenced by how few States have endorsed the existence of the duty of compensation. The list below is not intended to be exhaustive, but merely to assess those cases that are usually cited by investment tribunals and by scholars in their analyses of the duty of compensation.

3.2.1 The Neptune (1797)

During the Napoleonic wars, *The Neptune*,[90] an American vessel on voyage from Charleston to Bordeaux, carrying rice among other things, was stopped and seized by the British navy in April 1795.[91] The Admiralty

---

[84] R Higgins, *Problems and Process: International Law and How We Use It* (OUP 1995) 302.
[85] J Paulsson, 'International Arbitration and the Generation of Legal Norms: Treaty Arbitration and International Law' (2006) 3(5) TDM 11.
[86] ibid.
[87] A Boyle & C Chinkin, *The Making of International Law* (OUP 2007) 301; Tams, 'Development by ICJ' (n 15) 97–8.
[88] Tams, 'Development by ICJ' (n 15) 95.
[89] ILC, 'Report of the International Law Commission on the Work of its 68th Session' (2 May–10 June and 4 July–12 August 2016) UN Doc A/71/10, Ch 5, Commentary to Conclusion 13, 109 [3]; see also Schreuer (n 15) 738–9; Boyle & Chinkin (n 87) 300–10.
[90] *The Neptune* (1797) 4 Moore Arbitrations 3843.
[91] For a historical-legal background to this dispute, see SC Neff, *The Rights and Duties of Neutrals* (Manchester University Press 2000) 63 ff.

Court of London ordered the sale of the *Neptune*'s cargo to the British Government at the invoice price plus 10% profit. The owner claimed that it was owed the commercial price at which the articles would have sold in Bordeaux.[92] Before the Commission established under the Jay Treaty,[93] the British rejected the claim arguing that the seizure was lawful as the merchandise constituted contraband and, in the alternative, the seizure was a lawful preemptive purchase to provide for a threatened famine.[94] On this latter claim, agents for the British Crown asserted that the 'capture was made under such circumstances of distress as rendered the act lawful against the neutral'.[95]

The British claim of pre-emptive purchase was understood by the Commissioners as a plea of necessity.[96] Deciding by majority, the Commissioners rejected the British argument[97] as the conditions of the plea were not met in fact.[98] Nevertheless, in his consideration of this plea, Commissioner Pinkney endorsed a duty of compensation in the following cases: 'Great Britain might be able to say to neutrals "You shall sell to us", but it does not follow that she could also say "You shall sell to us upon worse terms than you would have procured elsewhere in the lawful prosecution of your commerce"'.[99]

While the *Neptune* is often cited as evidence of the existence of a duty of compensation,[100] three important factors detract from the weight and precedential value of this case. First, the applicable law by the Commission included 'justice, equity and the law of nations',[101] such that very little can be inferred from this case as to the positive law between

---

[92] *Neptune* 3844.
[93] Treaty of Amity, Commerce and Navigation between his Britannic Majesty and the United States of America (Jay Treaty) (Great Britain & US) (adopted 19 November 1794, entered into force 29 February 1796) 52 CTS 249.
[94] *Neptune* 3844.
[95] As quoted by Commissioner Gore, ibid, Opinion of Mr Gore, 3846.
[96] *Neptune* 3873.
[97] ibid, Opinion of Mr Gore, 3853; ibid, Opinion of Mr Pinkney, 3874–5; ibid, Opinion of Mr Trumbull, 3885. Only these three (out of five) Commissioners in the majority issued written opinions.
[98] ibid, Opinion of Mr Gore, 3853; ibid, Opinion of Mr Pinkney, 3874–5.
[99] ibid 3875.
[100] See, eg, Bücheler (n 53) 290; R Manton, 'Necessity in International Law' (PhD thesis, University of Oxford, 2016) 211–12 <https://ora.ox.ac.uk/objects/uuid:0ee2dd8e-6eac-4364-b538-21ae5eb932a2/download_file?file_format=pdf&safe_filename=Ryan%2BManton%252C%2BNecessity%2Bin%2BInternational%2BLaw.pdf&type_of_work=Thesis> accessed 10 May 2022.
[101] Jay Treaty, art VII.

States at the time.¹⁰² Second, only one of the five Commissioners upheld the existence of this duty. Lastly, the Commission rejected the plea of necessity so Pinkney's statement was only *obiter*.

3.2.2 The Caroline Incident (1837)

In 1837, Canadian rebels were attempting to declare, and establish, an independent Republic of Canada in the British colony of Upper Canada (now Ontario). The US steamer the *Caroline* supplied Canadian rebels and their US recruits on Navy island, within Ontario, from the US shore of the Niagara river. On 29 December 1837, British forces entered US territory and apprehended and destroyed the *Caroline*, which was moored off Fort Schlosser in the American bank of the river.¹⁰³ The incident led to a protracted diplomatic correspondence between the two States, in which the notions of self-preservation, self-defence, and necessity were invoked. And it is indeed in relation to self-defence that the incident is renowned: the so-called 'Webster formula' of self-defence, still invoked today,¹⁰⁴ was articulated by the US Secretary of State, Daniel Webster, in a letter to his British counterpart.¹⁰⁵

The US demanded redress for Britain's wrong, including compensation for the value of the destroyed property, which it estimated at $5000 US dollars.¹⁰⁶ Britain disputed the illegality of its actions claiming to have acted in self-preservation and self-defence,¹⁰⁷ thus rejecting the claim for

---

[102] See S Heathcote, 'State of Necessity and International Law' (PhD Thesis No 772, Graduate Institute of International and Development Studies, 2005) 137.

[103] For a detailed exposition of the facts see H Jones, 'The *Caroline* Affair' (1976) 28 Historian 485.

[104] For example, see M Wood, 'The Caroline Incident – 1837' in T Ruys, O Corten & A Hofer (eds), *The Use of Force in International Law: A Case-Based Approach* (OUP 2018) 10–4.

[105] D Webster, 'Letter from Daniel Webster, US Secretary of State, to Henry Fox, British Minister in Washington, Dated 24 April 1841' in WR Manning (ed), *Diplomatic Correspondence of the United States: Canadian Relations*, Vol 3 (Carnegie Endowment 1943) 145.

[106] A Stevenson, 'Letter from Andrew Stevenson, United States Minister to Great Britain, to Lord Palmerston, British Foreign Secretary, Dated 22 May 1838' in WR Manning (ed), *Diplomatic Correspondence of the United States: Canadian Relations*, Vol 3 (Carnegie Endowment 1943) 449, doc 1445 & 451. The value of the destroyed property was estimated at US $5000.

[107] See, eg, H Fox, 'Letter from Henry Fox to John Forsyth, US Secretary of State, dated 6 February 1838' in WR Manning (ed), *Diplomatic Correspondence of the United States: Canadian Relations*, Vol 3 (Carnegie Endowment 1943) 422; L Palmerston, 'Letter from Lord Palmerston, British Foreign Secretary, to Andrew Stevenson, American Minister in London, Dated 27 August 1841' in WR Manning (ed), *Diplomatic Correspondence of the United States: Canadian Relations*, Vol 3 (Carnegie Endowment 1943) 644–5.

reparation. The parties eventually settled the dispute with a (feeble) apology from the UK, which nevertheless insisted on the permissibility of its actions. The issue of compensation did not ultimately play a role in the settlement of the dispute. But there is here an interesting twist. The letter sent by Lord Ashburton, on behalf of the UK, to Webster included the following paragraph:

> If the Boat which was destroyed could by any fair construction of the case have been considered as the private property of a citizen bona fide and innocently employed by him as a passage vessel, compensation for its loss might perhaps have been admitted, but it is notorious that it was part and parcel of the armament of the insurgent force, and I have reason to know, that the property in part, if not wholly, was in British subjects. Under such circumstances no question of compensation could be entertained or expected.[108]

A copy of this letter, with these words crossed over but still legible, was kept in the Public Record Office, at the Foreign Office in London.[109] This original letter was subsequently withdrawn at the request of Lord Ashburton and replaced with another letter, amended by agreement of the parties. This second letter did not include the paragraph just quoted on compensation. As Lord Ashburton explained to Lord Aberdeen in this connection, on subsequent consideration he had thought it 'expedient to suppress' this paragraph from his original note.[110]

The *Caroline* incident was referred to by the Annulment Committee in *EDF*, in considering the duty of compensation. But it is doubtful that this case actually supports a duty of compensation. First, Britain did not accept the principle that compensation was payable to the owner of *The Caroline*: even if the latter had been innocent, Ashburton only says that compensation 'might perhaps have been admitted'. Second, such a statement was

---

[108] WR Manning (ed), *Diplomatic Correspondence of the United States: Canadian Relations*, Vol 3 (Carnegie Endowment 1943) 770, note 1.

[109] ibid.

[110] As quoted in Ld Ashburton, 'Lord Ashburton's letter to Lord Aberdeen, Dated 13 August 1842' (*Avalon Project*, Yale University, 2021) <https://avalon.law.yale.edu/19th_century/br-1842d.asp#ash1> accessed 10 May 2022, which stated that: 'By my despatch No 14 of the 28th ult, I had the honour of sending your Lordship copy of my note to Mr Webster on the subject of the Caroline. It was on consideration thought expedient to suppress a paragraph of that note, which related to the question of compensation to the owner of the vessel. I have therefore to ask your Lordship's permission to substitute the accompanying corrected copy of that note, and to request that the former may be cancelled. There is no other difference between these copies but the omission of the paragraph above referred to'.

not communicated to the US and compensation was not actually paid to the owner of the steamer. Third, the legal principle at issue in this dispute remains contested: while some argue that the parties relied on the plea of necessity,[111] others have argued that the legal principle at issue was that of self-defence.[112]

3.2.3 Orr and Laubenheimer (1900)

Orr and Laubenheimer, two US citizens, were engaged in the banana trade, importing bananas to the United States from the Nicaraguan port of Bluefields, on the mouth of the Rama River.[113] Bananas grew in plantations along the banks of the river and its tributaries, and were transported to the port by tugboats. In 1894, in the course of suppressing an insurrection in Bluefield, a Nicaraguan general seized two of Orr and Laubenheimer's tugboats to transport troops down the Rama river to Bluefields. Orr and Laubenheimer subsequently claimed indemnity for damages sustained as a result of Nicaragua's alleged seizure and detention of the tugboats, and the matter was submitted to arbitration by agreement of the governments of the US and Nicaragua. In its decision, the Arbitrator stated that the 'rights incident to a state of war ... justify the use by any Government, in an emergency, of any private property found available.'[114] It went on: 'Full compensation, however, for all damage suffered by private parties must afterwards be made. But the obligation rests upon every party damaged to do all in his power to reduce his losses to a minimum. That is the law the world over...'[115]

This award was referred to by the Tribunal in *CMS* in support of the proposition that acts of necessity generate a duty of compensation for material loss. But that is reading too much into this short decision, for three reasons. First, as per the parties' agreement, Nicaragua 'waive[d] its denial of liability ... and agree[d] that said arbitrator may award such sum as he believe[d] said Orr and Laubenheimer ... to be justly entitled to'.[116]

---

[111] *The Caroline* is, for example, included in ARSIWA (n 1) Commentary to Art 25 [5]. It was also relied upon by the Annulment Committee in *EDF v Argentina*, when discussing the latter's plea of necessity, as discussed in Section 3.2.
[112] See Paddeu (n 16) 351–7, and references cited therein.
[113] *Orr and Laubenheimer*.
[114] ibid 40.
[115] ibid 40.
[116] Protocol of an Agreement Between the United States and Nicaragua for the Arbitration of the Amount of Damages to be Awarded Orr and Laubenheimer and the Post-Glover Electric Company (Nicaragua & US) (adopted 22 March 1900, entered into force 22 March 1900, terminated 16 June 1900) 15 RIAA 35, Art III.

Second, as a result of the waiver on the question of liability, the arbitrator did not need to, and did not, apply international law to the dispute: its task was to decide the amount of *just* compensation due. Finally, if there is a legal basis for Nicaragua's obligation to compensate, this is the right of angary. Pursuant to this right, as explained by Oppenheim, States engaged in hostilities are entitled to use the property of neutrals 'provided the articles concerned are serviceable to military ends and wants', and so long as, in every case, 'the neutral owner [is] fully indemnified.'[117]

3.2.4 Company General of the Orinoco (1905)

The case involved the rescission of concession contracts between Venezuela and a French Company, signed in the late 1880s. The contract was for the exploitation of vegetable and mineral resources on territory that Venezuela believed to be under its sovereignty.[118] Following protests by Colombia,[119] Venezuela rescinded the contract with the French company. Venezuela subsequently found that most of the territory in the concession was under the sovereignty of Colombia.[120] The company claimed compensation from Venezuela, and the matter came before the Franco-Venezuelan Mixed Commission. Umpire Plumley upheld the rescission but ordered the payment of compensation to the company. In his reasoning, he framed the question as one of necessity.[121] In his view:

> As the Government of Venezuela, whose duty of self-preservation rose superior to any question of contract, it had the power to abrogate the contract in whole or in part. It exercised that power and canceled [sic] the provision of unrestricted assignment. It considered the peril superior to the obligation and substituted therefor [sic] the duty of compensation.[122]

The peril, as the Umpire explained, came from multiple sources. It came from the Colombian government, which claimed sovereignty over much of the area under concession, and which threatened force to recover the territory, but also from the local population and businessmen who were

---

[117] L Oppenheim, *International Law – Vol 2: War and Neutrality* (Longmans 1906) 395 [365].
[118] *Company General of the Orinoco* 260.
[119] ibid 257–8.
[120] ibid 269.
[121] More specifically, the Umpire framed the question as one about 'self-preservation'. On the relation between a discrete (and general) rule of necessity and the right of self-preservation and why claims of self-preservation need not (and should not) be equated with invocations of such a discrete rule of necessity, see Paddeu (n 16) 346–63.
[122] *Company General of the Orinoco* 280.

dissatisfied by the monopoly granted to the company and who, with the support of the local government, revolted sometimes violently.[123]

As with the *Neptune*, there are a number of factors which may diminish the weight and precedential value of this decision in respect of the duty of compensation.[124] First, there is uncertainty as to the law actually applied by the Umpire to decide the case.[125] The Umpire was competent to take into account, in reaching his decision as to the need for compensation, 'the ethical precepts of international law, equity and good conscience'.[126] On the specifics of the case, the Umpire held that 'if there were aught of wrong towards the Company General of the Orinoco done or permitted by the respondent Government', then he may award 'damages if justice and equity so permit and so require.'[127] Ultimately, in his view, there was 'no inequity' in apportioning some of the loss caused to the company by the rescission on the Government.[128] The decision was thus apparently based on equitable considerations.

Second, even if by application of international law, the award of compensation can be explained on other legal bases. It could be explained as a case of compensation for wrongful conduct: the compensation paid was not for the damage caused by the rescission of the contract itself, but rather for the breach of the contract before its termination.[129] Or it can be explained as involving the application 'of the rule that compensation must be paid when foreign-owned property is expropriated in the public interest.'[130] This explanation is more convincing than the former, as it can account for the necessity-like reasoning of the Umpire.[131] Being able to account for this reasoning of the Umpire is particularly important for two reasons: first, because it is this aspect of the reasoning that scholars seize upon to provide support for the existence of a duty of

---

[123] ibid 281–2.
[124] eg Bücheler (n 53) 290–1.
[125] On which see Heathcote (n 102) 226–8.
[126] *Company General of the Orinoco* 277. As established by the terms of the Protocol Relating to the Settlement of Indemnities Between France and Venezuela (France & Venezuela) (adopted 19 February 1902) published in J Ralston & WT Sherman Doyle (eds), *Report of French-Venezuelan Mixed Claims Commission of 1902* (US GPO 1906) 1.
[127] *Company General of the Orinoco* 278.
[128] ibid 284.
[129] M Forteau, 'Reparation in the Event of a Circumstance Precluding Wrongfulness' in J Crawford, A Pellet & S Olleson (eds), *The Law of International Responsibility* (OUP 2010) 889.
[130] M Akehurst, 'International Liability for Injurious Consequences Arising Out of Acts Not Prohibited by International Law' (1985) 16 NYIL 3, 12, fn 45.
[131] Bücheler (n 53) 290.

compensation; and, second, because there are considerable doubts as to the recognition of a defence of necessity in the positive law of the time.[132] As Sarah Heathcote explains, there exist in international law primary rules 'in the image of necessity': these are substantive rules of international law that cater to a specific (factual) situation of necessity. A State's right to expropriate property is precisely one of these rules, as it can only be exercised in situations of public necessity. As the Umpire noted in the award, a situation of public necessity existed in Venezuela at the time, as a result of the external (from Colombia) and internal (local population) threats that the country was facing.[133] In such circumstances, the rescission of the concession was an expropriation of foreign-owned property due to necessity. The payment of compensation in this case was, therefore, a matter of the primary rule in question (expropriation) rather than one of the applications of the plea of necessity under the law of State responsibility.

3.2.5 Properties of Bulgarian Minorities in Greece (1926)

Following the exchange of minorities provisions in the post-World War I settlements, foreign refugees of Greek origin were transferred from Turkey to Greece. In order to house them, the Greek Government forced Bulgarian minorities to move out of their homes in Greece. The matter was considered by a League of Nations' Commission of Enquiry.[134] By the time the Commission issued its report, the Bulgarian minorities had left Greece and the Greek refugees were already settled in the homes. The Commission allowed that the take-over of Bulgarian property by Greece had been the result of a situation of what it termed 'force majeure'. Indeed, according to the report, to remove the Greek refugees to allow the return of the owners would have been impossible in these circumstances, as well as undesirable.[135] Nevertheless, the Commission argued that it could not be expected that the Bulgarian minorities would simply renounce their right to the homes, so it was just that they receive compensation for the value of their property.[136]

---

[132] See IV Hull, *A Scrap of Paper: Breaking and Making International Law During the Great War* (Cornell University Press 2014) 44–5; Paddeu (n 16) 382–6.
[133] Heathcote (n 102) 228–9.
[134] League of Nations, 'Report of the Commission of Enquiry on the Incidents on the Frontier between Bulgaria and Greece, Doc No C.727.M.270.1925.VII (Annex 815)' (1926) 7 LNOJ 196, 209.
[135] ibid 209.
[136] ibid.

The argument for a duty of compensation is more plausible in this instance, but it is not clear cut. The situation certainly seems to be one that could fit within the plea of necessity (as currently formulated): in order to protect one interest (housing Greek refugees), Greece infringed the rights of others (Bulgarian minorities). But here too there are a number of factors which may weaken this argument. To begin with, the Commission spoke of *force majeure* and not of necessity. Much of contemporary doctrine has tended to assume that *force majeure* and 'necessity' were used interchangeably at the time, but this view requires some nuance. The concepts are (and were) indeed different, and I have argued elsewhere that reference was made to *'force majeure'* during this period to address situations of necessity because international law did not recognise a rule of necessity at the time.[137] At any rate, even if this had been a case decided on a plea of necessity (at least in substance, if not expressly), it does not seem that the requirements of the plea were met. As Heathcote has argued, this was not a case of protecting a superior interest as against an inferior one: in this case, the interests were equal for 'why should Bulgarian minorities, who ... had only been in Greece for a decade or so ... be moved out of their homes to house refugees of Greek origins – the Smirna "Greeks" [who] had been in Turkey for centuries?'[138]

Once more, the Commission's decision is better explained on other legal bases: either as a situation of reparation for wrongful conduct or, as in the *Orinoco Company* case, as a case of expropriation for public necessity.[139] In any event, there are doubts as to whether the basis of the Commission's recommendation was premised on law at all. While its mandate was to 'establish the facts enabling the responsibility to be fixed, and supply the necessary material for the determination of any indemnities or reparation which may be considered appropriate', the Council did not specify the basis (legal or otherwise) upon which such 'responsibility' and 'indemnities' ought to be decided. Perhaps for this reason, Michael Akehurst has interpreted the Commission's finding as a political compromise.[140]

3.2.6 Gabčíkovo-Nagymaros (1997)

The dispute between Slovakia and Hungary concerned the unilateral termination of the Treaty of 1977, which envisaged a joint project between

---

[137] Paddeu (n 16) 382–6.
[138] Heathcote (n 102) 224.
[139] ibid 223–4.
[140] Akehurst (n 130) 12, fn 45.

the two States for the construction of a system of locks in the Danube, by Hungary. Among other things, Hungary invoked the plea of necessity to justify its unilateral termination of the Treaty. At the time of unilateral termination, both parties had commenced the works already. Slovakia had completed a section of works in one of the sectors, so the question as to whether any compensation was due to Slovakia as a result of the unilateral termination emerged. The ICJ rejected Hungary's plea of necessity, but it noted that 'Hungary [had] pointed out' that a duty to compensate Slovakia for the works undertaken existed.[141] The Court's statement was *obiter* and is not a direct endorsement by the Court of the duty: it is merely a description of Hungary's position. As such, not much weight can be given to the judgment itself.

More pertinent are, at any rate, the statements made by Hungary during the proceedings. Hungary raised the point multiple times during the oral phase of the proceedings.[142] In very clear terms, Hungary stated that

> Hungary recognizes that in modern international law the plea of necessity can only be admitted on a limited and strictly defined basis. 'Necessity' allows the sovereign State to commit what would otherwise be an unlawful act while avoiding international responsibility – though not the requirement to make appropriate compensation.

Slovakia's own views on the matter were less assertive. It recognised that the duty of compensation was required as a matter of fairness[143] and common sense, but it warned of the risk of States 'buying' their 'way out of [their] breaches of its international obligations'.[144]

4 Assessment

Investment tribunals have tackled the question of compensation in cases of necessity in numerous cases. Their conclusions on the point (almost always in *obiter*) are as varied as the reasoning behind them. A common thread among them is that they have, for the most part, failed to assess the positive law basis for the existence (or non-existence) of the duty of compensation. Only a handful of decisions name-check some precedents and cases, but none of them in any way refer to State practice or *opinio juris*.

---

[141] *Gabčíkovo-Nagymaros* (Oral Proceedings) [48].
[142] See, eg, ibid [48].
[143] This is the English translation of the statement found in the *Gabčíkovo-Nagymaros* (Oral Proceedings): CR 97/11, 54. Note that the original French version uses the term 'equité'.
[144] ibid 55.

To be sure, the question of compensation in cases of necessity is a philosophically and theoretically difficult one, having troubled legal scholars and theorists for many centuries.[145] It is a question that elicits intuitive and often strongly held opinions: it would be unfair for the affected party to bear the burden of the protection of others' interests. In short, it would be unfair to let the loss lie where it falls. And yet, the action that causes the loss is a permitted one, it is lawful behaviour, and under normal circumstances, we would not expect those acting lawfully to compensate losses caused by their actions. In the absence of a wrong, losses do lie where they fall: herein lies the dilemma at the heart of the duty of compensation. And yet, necessitated acts seem different from other lawful acts that cause loss. Indeed, necessitated acts have a baggage that other lawful acts do not: they evoke moral hazard and, in the history of international law, they evoke abusive behaviour by powerful States.

This baggage explains the intuitive perceptions of unfairness at the allocation of loss onto the affected party, and the support for a re-distribution of the loss onto the agent. It may also explain, at least partly, why investment tribunals have been sympathetic to the idea that States invoking necessity owe a duty of compensation to the affected parties. But this is no justification for these tribunals' omission to engage with the methods of law ascertainment: aside from the fairness and justness of the duty of compensation, is there evidence that this is required by positive law; is there evidence, in particular, of practice and *opinio juris* about the existence of this duty? As shown, there is not only limited practice and *opinio juris* on this duty, but the few precedents cited in investment decisions do not support, nor do they provide evidence of, the existence of a duty of compensation. The nobility of the sentiment is no substitute for the absence of positive law on the existence of this duty. Indeed, in asserting or deducing the duty of compensation in this manner, investment tribunals are closer to deciding the matter *ex aequo et bono*, for which they would need specific consent by the parties, than by application of the rules of international law, as they are mandated to do.

---

[145] For an overview of scholars' approach to this question, both historical and contemporary, see J Salter, 'Hugo Grotius: Property and Consent' (2001) 29 Political Theory 537; J Salter, 'Grotius and Pufendorf on the Right of Necessity' (2005) 26 HPT 285; SD Sugarman, 'The "Necessity" Defense and the Failure of Tort Theory: The Case Against Strict Liability for Damages Caused While Exercising Self-Help in an Emergency' (2005) 5(2) Issues in Legal Scholarship 1.

8

A Riddle Wrapped in a Mystery Inside an Enigma

Equitable Considerations in the Assessment
of Damages by Investment Tribunals

EMMANUEL GIAKOUMAKIS[*]

1 Introduction

It is perhaps trite to say that the principle of 'full reparation', enunciated by the Permanent Court of International Justice (PCIJ) in the *Chorzów Factory* case, has been widely recognised as the customary rule governing the reparation of internationally wrongful acts.[1] According to that judgment, where restitution is unavailable or insufficient, customary law requires the payment of compensation in the form of 'a sum corresponding to the value which a restitution in kind would bear [and] the award, if need be, of damages for loss sustained which would not be covered by restitution in kind or payment in place of it'.[2] Whilst the rights of private

---

[*] The views expressed in this chapter are personal and do not necessarily reflect those of the International Court of Justice or the United Nations. The author is grateful to Konstantina Georgaki, Andreas Kulick, Panos Merkouris, Nikiforos Panagis, Nikolaos Pavlopoulos and Maciej Żenkiewicz and for their invaluable comments on earlier drafts of this chapter. All errors and conclusions remain mine.

[1] *Certain Activities Carried Out by Nicaragua in the Border Area (Costa Rica v Nicaragua)* (Judgment) [2018] ICJ Rep 15 [29–32]; *Ahmadou Sadio Diallo (Guinea v DRC)* (Compensation) [2012] ICJ Rep 324 [13]; *Application of the Convention on the Prevention and Punishment of the Crime of Genocide (Bosnia and Herzegovina v Serbia and Montenegro)* (Judgment) [2007] ICJ Rep 43 [460]; *Legal Consequences of the Construction of a Wall in the Occupied Palestinian Territory* (Advisory Opinion) [2004] ICJ Rep 136 [152]; *Gabčíkovo-Nagymaros Project (Hungary/Slovakia)* [1997] ICJ Rep 7, 80 [149–50]; *The M/V Saiga (No 2) (Saint Vincent and Grenadines v Guinea)* (Judgment) [1999] 120 ITLOS Rep 10 [170–1]; *Papamichalopoulos and Others v Greece* (1995) Series A No 330-B [34–6]; *Velásquez-Rodríguez & ors v Honduras* (Reparations and Costs, Judgment of 21 July 1989) IACHR Series C No 7 [26]; *Eritrea's Damages Claims* (Final Award of 17 August 2009) (Eritrea-Ethiopia Claims Commission) XXVI RIAA 505, 524 [24 ff].

[2] *Case Concerning the Factory at Chorzów (Germany v Poland)* (Merits) [1928] PCIJ Rep Series A No 17, 27, 47.

entities are 'on a different plane' to those belonging to States, the damage suffered by an individual affords 'a convenient scale for the calculation of the reparation due to the State',[3] so the extent of the individual injury affords the metric for the calculation of damages at the inter-State level.

The International Law Commission (ILC) took *Chorzów Factory* as the basis for the elaboration of the rules governing the consequences of wrongful acts in the 2001 Articles on Responsibility of States for Internationally Wrongful Acts (ARSIWA).[4] In the Commentary to Article 31, the ILC explained that '[t]he responsible State's obligation to make full reparation relates to the "injury caused by the internationally wrongful act"'.[5] If restitution is unavailable or insufficient, '[t]he role of compensation is to fill in any gaps so as to ensure full reparation for damage suffered.'[6] Article 36 ARSIWA then states that '[t]he State responsible for an internationally wrongful act is under an obligation to compensate for the damage caused thereby, insofar as such damage is not made good by restitution', damage being understood as 'any financially assessable damage including loss of profits'.[7] Given that most Bilateral Investment Treaties (BITs) are silent as to the remedies applicable in case of their violation, investment tribunals have referred to Article 36 ARSIWA as reflecting the applicable standard of compensation,[8] and have recognised *Chorzów Factory* as an 'authoritative description' of customary law on the subject.[9]

In line with the *Chorzów Factory* standard, the determination of compensation seems to operate within three governing parameters.[10] First, the identification of the extent of the damage (material or moral) as a question of fact.[11] Second, the establishment of a sufficiently direct and

---

[3] ibid 28.
[4] ILC, 'Draft Articles on Responsibility of States for Internationally Wrongful Acts with Commentaries' (23 April–1 June and 2 July–10 August 2001) UN Doc A/56/10, reproduced in [2001/II – Part Two] YBILC 31, Commentary to Art 31 [2–3] (ARSIWA).
[5] ibid 91, Commentary to Art 31 [5].
[6] ibid 99, Commentary to Art 36 [3].
[7] ibid.
[8] *Vivendi (I) v Argentina* (Final Award of 20 August 2007) ICSID Case No ARB/97/3 [8.2.6–7]; *Ron Fuchs v Georgia* (Award of 3 March 2010) ICSID Case No ARB/07/15 [504, 532–4].
[9] *Crystallex International Corporation v Venezuela* (Award of 4 April 2016) ICSID Case No ARB(AF)/11/2 [847–8]; *ConocoPhillips v Venezuela* (Award of 8 March 2019) ICSID Case No ARB/07/30 [207–10].
[10] *Ahmadou Sadio Diallo* [14].
[11] *Opinion in the Lusitania Cases* (1923) VII RIAA 32, 39 ('[t]he fundamental concept of "damages" is (...) reparation for a *loss* suffered; a judicially ascertained *compensation* for wrong. The remedy should be commensurate with the loss, so that the injured party may be made whole'); see also *Wall Advisory Opinion* [152–3]; *Diplomatic and Consular*

certain causal nexus between the damage and the internationally wrongful act.[12] Third, the quantification, in monetary terms, of any 'financially assessable' damage through the application of an appropriate valuation methodology.[13] The final amount of compensation will vary depending on permutations of these factors. Conversely, factual or legal considerations beyond these parameters are generally deemed irrelevant to quantum.[14]

Within this conceptual framework, strongly influenced by private-law analogies from municipal tort law,[15] compensation has acquired a strong, 'damage-centric' focus, in the sense that it depends primarily – if not exclusively – on the demonstration of a financially assessable damage and a 'sufficiently direct and certain causal nexus' between the damage and the wrongful act.[16] Thus, at the final stages of its codification efforts the ILC decided to omit from the text of ARSIWA any provision allowing for extraneous factors to be taken into account in the determination of compensation beyond damage and causality, such as aggravating or mitigating circumstances, the gravity of the act, or limitations relating to proportionality.[17]

Staff in Tehran (USA v Iran) (Judgment) [1980] ICJ Rep 3 [90]; *Military and Paramilitary Activities in and against Nicaragua (Nicaragua v USA)* (Merits) [1986] ICJ Rep 16 [284]; *Gabčíkovo-Nagymaros Project* [152]; J Crawford, *Brownlie's Principles of Public International Law* (9th edn, OUP 2019) 553; H Grotius, *The Rights of War and Peace* (first published 1625, Richard Tuck ed, Liberty Fund 2005) Book II, ch XVII, sects I and II.

[12] ILC (n 4) 92, Commentary to Art 31 [9]; *Application of the Convention on the Prevention and Punishment of the Crime of Genocide* [460–2].

[13] ILC (n 4) 102–5, Commentary to Art 36 [7–32].

[14] An exception here is made by the ILC concerning the failure to mitigate damages: ILC (n 4) 93, Commentary to Art 31 [11]. The ILC does not, however, attempt to proffer a cognisable legal basis for this consideration.

[15] B Sabahi, *Compensation and Restitution in Investor-State Arbitration: Principles and Practice* (OUP 2011) 13–17 ('[n]owhere, perhaps, is this link (or the debt of international law to Roman law) more clearly demonstrated than in the (…) landmark *Chorzów Factory* case'). On the influence of rules governing tort liability under municipal legal systems and Roman law upon the standard of compensation under international law: ILC (n 4) 10 [27]; ILA Study Group on Use of Domestic Law Principles in the Development of International Law, 'Report' (Sydney Conference, 2018) [126–7, 157, 165]; H Lauterpacht, *Private Law Sources and Analogies of International Law* (Longmans 1927) 149.

[16] *Ahmadou Sadio Diallo* [14]; *Certain Activities* (n 1) [32]; ILC (n 4) 99, Commentary to Art 36 [4].

[17] ILC, 'Summary Records of the Meetings of the 31st Session' (14 May–3 August 1979) UN Doc A/CN.4/SER.A/1979, 26 [23, 30], 205 [22], 207 [14]; ILC, 'Report of the International Law Commission on the Work of its 31st Session' (14 May–3 August 1979) UN Doc A/34/10, Commentary to Draft Chapter V, 109 [11]; ILC, 'Summary Records of the Meetings of the 32nd Session' (5–25 July 1980) UN Doc A/CN.4/SER.A/1980, 80 [33], 96 [47]; ILC, 'Preliminary Report on the Content, Forms and Degrees of International Responsibility

A perusal of international jurisprudence, however, paints quite a different picture. In fact, early arbitral commissions,[18] the International Court of Justice (ICJ),[19] the Iran-US Claims Tribunal,[20] *ad hoc* inter-State tribunals,[21] as well as regional human rights courts,[22] have referred to equity (or, interchangeably, 'equitable considerations'[23]) as a normative proposition capable of affecting the determination of damages in ways not expressly contemplated in *Chorzów Factory*. Investment tribunals have followed a similar path, invoking equitable considerations for the determination of compensation due for violations of BIT provisions.[24] What this means in practice is unclear: despite the frequent invocation of equity for the purposes of determining compensation, international courts and tribunals have made little effort to explain the legal basis of these considerations or their underlying methodology.

(Part II of the Draft articles on State Responsibility), by Mr William Riphagen, Special Rapporteur' (1 April 1980) UN Doc A/CN.4/330 reproduced in [1980/II] YBILC 107, 112–13 [27, 34] & 128 [95]; ILC, 'Third Report on State Responsibility, by Mr James Crawford, Special Rapporteur' (15 March, 15 June, 10 and 18 July and 4 August 2000) UN Doc A/CN.4/507, 51 [161, 164], 49 [156(b)], 51 [162–3].

[18] VD Degan, *L'Equité et le Droit International* (Martinus Nijhoff 1970) 158–91.

[19] *Certain Activities Carried Out by Nicaragua in the Border Area* [35]; *Ahmadou Sadio Diallo* [24, 33–6]; *Judgments of the Administrative Tribunal of ILO Upon Complaint Made Against UNESCO* (Advisory Opinion) [1956] ICJ Rep 77, 100; *Armed Activities on the Territory of the Congo (Congo v Uganda)* (Reparations) [2022] ICJ Rep 1 [106, 164, 166, 181, 193, 206, 225, 258, 365].

[20] *Islamic Republic of Iran v USA* (Award of 2 July 2014) IUSCT Case Nos A15(IV) and A24 [230–1] ('investment jurisprudence has recognized the authority of international arbitral tribunals to determine equitably (ie, in equity *intra legem*) the amount of damages'); *Starrett Housing Corporation v Iran* (Final Award of 14 August 1987) IUSCT Case No 24 [339]; G Aldrich, *The Jurisprudence of the Iran-United States Claims Tribunal* (Clarendon 1996) 241.

[21] *Loan Agreement Between Italy and Costa Rica* (1998) XXV RIAA 21 [69–70].

[22] *Varnava & ors v Turkey* (2009) ECHR 1313 [224]; *Velásquez-Rodríguez* [25–7].

[23] According to A Gourgourinis, 'Equity in International Law Revisited (with Special Reference to the Fragmentation of International Law)' (2009) 103 ASIL Proc 79, 80, the words 'equity', 'equitable principles' and 'equitable considerations' are different facets of the same concept: equity denotes the 'normative process' whereas equitable principles or considerations denote the normative means. According to P Weil, 'L'Equité Dans La Jurisprudence de la Cour Internationale de Justice: Un Mystère en Voie de Dissipation?' in V Lowe & M Fitzmaurice (eds), *Fifty Years of the International Court of Justice* (CUP 1996) 123, the terminological confusion between equitable 'principles', 'processes', 'solutions' and 'results' evidences a reluctance to define the normative aspects of equity, but what matters is the result.

[24] *American Manufacturing & Trading, Inc v Zaire* (Award of 21 February 1997) ICSID Case No ARB/93/1 [7.02 & 7.16] (*AMT*); *Gold Reserve Inc v Venezuela* (Award of 22 September 2014) ICSID Case No ARB(AF)/09/1 [686]; *Técnicas Medioambientales Tecmed, SA v Mexico* (Award of 29 May 2003) ICSID Case No ARB (AF)/00/2 [190]. Tribunals have also

Arguably, the integration of equitable considerations in quantum analysis presents some significant advantages. From a procedural point of view, it allows for some flexibility in the fact-gathering process and enables the tribunal to award compensation even when objective circumstances preclude the injured party from producing sufficient evidence to substantiate its loss. The ICJ, for example, has invoked equitable considerations for the determination of compensation where the evidence was insufficient to enable a precise quantification, for 'it would be a perversion of fundamental principles of justice to deny all relief to the injured person, and thereby relieve the wrongdoer from making any amend for his acts.'[25] From a substantive point of view, the rigid or mechanical application of customary rules governing compensation might also lead to a juridical outcome that places too strong an emphasis on the extent of the injury caused by the wrongful act, in a manner disconnected from the context in which the injury arose, the nature of the unlawful act, or the respective interests and conduct of the parties. Thus, the application of equity to compensation enables the tribunal to 'infuse' elements of reasonableness and 'individualized justice' in its reasoning,[26] and arrive at a balanced outcome that accommodates the interests of both parties.

Be that as it may, equitable considerations may also give rise to complications in practice. In fact, an unprincipled application of equity to compensation may have serious repercussions for the legitimacy of the dispute settlement procedure. It might also affect the procedural rights of the parties and, ultimately, undermine the integrity of the decision itself. This complexity is exemplified in the International Centre for Settlement of Investment Disputes (ICSID) framework where *ad hoc* annulment committees have stated that if a tribunal misapplies the legal rules in favour of a settlement based on 'general equity', the award might be subject to annulment for manifest excess of power or a failure to state adequate reasons, within the meaning of Article 52(1)(b) and (e) of the Washington Convention.[27]

Outside the ICSID framework, the application of equitable considerations may also give rise to challenges to recognition and enforcement of arbitral

---

referred to equitable considerations in the context of compensation due for lawful nationalisation: *Kuwait v American Independent Oil Company* (Award of 24 March 1982) *Ad Hoc* Arbitration, 66 ILR 518 [77–8] (*Aminoil*).

[25] *Certain Activities Carried Out by Nicaragua in the Border Area* [35].
[26] F Francioni, 'Equity in International Law' [2013] MPEPIL 1399 [7].
[27] *MTD Equity Sdn Bhd v Chile* (Decision on Annulment of 21 March 2007) ICSID Case No ARB/01/7 [48 & 77]; *Amco Asia Corporation & ors v Indonesia* (Decision on Annulment of 16 May 1986) ICSID Case No ARB/81/1 [26–8].

awards. For instance, States have challenged the validity of arbitral awards relying upon equitable considerations before domestic courts, portraying them as attempts at awarding punitive damages in a manner contrary to international law.[28] Conversely, some municipal courts have attempted at re-opening certain arbitral awards, especially with regard to questions of compensation, invoking 'equity', 'fairness' or 'proportionality' as the legal basis for their judicial review.[29] This development may have serious implications for the finality of arbitral awards: a broadly-construed conception of 'equity' for quantum purposes may in fact be used as the trojan horse to re-open arbitral proceedings and substitute a tribunal's decision for the views of domestic courts, especially where large monetary awards are at stake.

In light of these challenges and the risk of protracted proceedings, it is imperative to develop an analytical framework for the operation of equity in the determination of compensation by investment tribunals. Against this background, this chapter argues that while investment arbitral tribunals are entitled to apply equitable considerations when determining compensation as a general principle of international law, this possibility is restrained by certain limitations beyond which the award might result in a legal error or an excess of powers. To that end, Section 2 will distinguish between the different forms that equity may take and examine the interpretative function of equity in the framework of compensation. Section 3 will examine the interpretative function of equity in the framework of customary norms of State responsibility, whereas Section 4 will argue that recourse to equity is subject to intrinsic and extrinsic limitations, emanating either from the nature of equity as an interpretative canon or from the procedural framework in which tribunals are bound to operate, respectively.

A few words are in order on the scope of this chapter. For analytical purposes, the term 'compensation' should be understood as a pecuniary remedy for the reparation of injury caused by an internationally wrongful act within the meaning of Articles 31 and 36 of ARSIWA. The relationship between equity and other forms of remedies, such as restitution or satisfaction, fall outside the scope of the analysis. In the same vein, equity may also have a bearing on the determination of 'compensation' that is due upon liability for injurious, yet *lawful* acts. Indeed, there are numerous treaty provisions that require the payment of 'fair', 'equitable' or 'just' compensation for

---

[28] *Gold Reserve Inc v Venezuela* (Venezuela's Motion to Dismiss Petition and to Deny Recognition of Arbitral Award, or in the Alternative, to Stay Enforcement of 12 June 2015) ICSID Case No ARB(AF)/09/1, 31, 36–7.

[29] *Al-Kharafi & Sons Co v Libya and Others* (Judgment of the Cairo Court of Appeal of 3 June 2020) *Ad Hoc* Arbitration [3–4 & 8–12].

acts that are not prohibited by international law, such as the expropriation of foreign investments[30] or the civil liability of economic operators for the harm caused to persons or the environment by hazardous or ultrahazardous activities.[31] Nevertheless, the interpretation of these treaty-specific provisions is a question of primary, not secondary, norms, which are subject to distinct rationales and present structural legal differences when compared to State responsibility. Thus, the meaning of equity within these treaty-specific regimes falls to be determined by reference to their distinctive teleologies and contextual specificities. Finally, even though equitable considerations are frequently integrated in computational models proposed by valuation experts[32] and the methodology employed by tribunals,[33] this chapter will only address the legal function of equity, as opposed to the use of equity in the process of valuation methodologies.

2 The Legal Basis for the Application of Equity to Compensation

Doctrinal analysis of the concept of equity typically begins with some preliminary questions regarding the normative character of equity and its functions in general international law. It is not, however, the purpose of this chapter to revisit the doctrinal debate surrounding the normativity of equity.[34] Suffice to say that, throughout the twentieth century, the development of international law has transformed equity from a non-legal

---

[30] *Compañia del Desarrollo de Santa Elena SA v Costa Rica* (Award of 17 February 2000) ICSID Case No ARB/96/1 [91–2 & 95]; U Kriebaum, 'Regulatory Takings: Balancing the Interests of the Investor and the State' (2007) 8(5) JWIT 717, 717 ff; *contra* E Lauterpacht, 'Issues of Compensation and Nationality in the Taking of Energy Investments' (1990) 8(1) JERL 241, 247–50 ('Attractive though the concept of equity may be in many situations, and perhaps as much beyond criticism as is mother love, we must recognise that it is not a concept that can be sprinkled like salt on every part of the law (…) it is not permissible to use equitable considerations to qualify the role of the various individual factors in a DCF calculation of value').

[31] For a detailed analysis, A Boyle & C Redgwell (eds), *Birnie, Boyle, and Redgwell's International Law and the Environment* (4th edn, OUP 2021) 226–33; A Boyle, 'Globalising Environmental Liability: The Interplay of National and International Law' (2005) 17(1) JEL 3, 5, 12, 19.

[32] WH Knull, ST Jones, TJ Tyler & ors, 'Accounting for Uncertainty in Discounted Cash Flow Valuation of Upstream Oil and Gas Investments' (2007) 25 JERL 268, 290, 298–300.

[33] *AMT v Zaire* [7.02]; *American International Group, Inc v Iran* (Award of 7 December 1983) IUSCT Case No 2, 4 IUSCTR 96, 109; *Amoco International Finance Corp v Iran* (Partial Award of 14 July 1987) IUSCT Case No 56, 83 ILR 500, 542–3, 570, 574–6, 587 [224–5, 252–5 & 258].

[34] See generally A Gourgourinis, 'Delineating the Normativity of Equity in International Law' (2009) 11(3) ICLR 327, 327 ff; *Maritime Delimitation in the Area Between Greenland*

concept[35] to a general principle of law within the meaning of Article 38(1)(c) of the PCIJ and later ICJ Statute.[36] As early as 1920, the Advisory Committee of Jurists, tasked with the preparation of the draft Statute for the PCIJ, understood equity as an integral part of international law to be applied by the World Court,[37] a point subsequently endorsed by the overwhelming majority of scholars and jurisprudence.[38]

Nevertheless, investment tribunals have not clearly articulated the legal basis for the application of equitable considerations to the assessment of damages. In *LIAMCO*, for example, the tribunal confusingly referred to equity as a 'general principle of law' under Article 38(2) of the ICJ Statute, instead of Article 38(1)(c).[39] In the same vein, the *Aminoil* Tribunal stated that 'redress will be ensured *ex aequo et bono*' without 'depart[ing] from principles of law', in plain contradiction to the terms of Article 38(2) of the ICJ Statute.[40]

It is, however, clear, that the application of equity as a general principle of law should not be confused with a decision *ex aequo et bono*. In the *North Sea Continental Shelf* cases, the ICJ drew a distinction between the power of the Court to settle disputes *ex aequo et bono* and equity as an integral part of international law (equity *intra legem*).[41] In *Tunisia/Libya*, the Court explained that 'the legal concept of equity is a general principle

---

and Jan Mayen (Judgment) [1993] ICJ Rep 38, Separate Opinion of Judge Weeramantry, 211 [52–102]; Weil (n 23) 121, 124 ff.

[35] G Ripert, 'Les Règles du Droit Civil Applicables aux Rapports Internationaux (Contribution à l'étude des principes généraux du droit visés au Statut de la Cour permanente de Justice internationale)' (1933) 44 RdC 565, 575–6; Degan (n 18) 15–17; *North Sea Continental Shelf Cases (Federal Republic of Germany/Netherlands; Federal Republic of Germany/Denmark)* (Judgment) [1969] ICJ Rep 3, Dissenting Opinion of Vice-President Koretsky, 154, 166.

[36] M Habicht, *Post-War Treaties for the Pacific Settlement of International Disputes* (HUP 1931) 1052; G Berlia, *Essai sur la Portée de la Clause de Jugement en Équité en Droit des Gens* (Université de Paris 1937) 74; T Gihl, 'Lacunes du droit international' (1932) 3 NordJIntlL 37, 54; H Lauterpacht, 'Règles Générales du Droit de La Paix' (1937) 62 RdC 96, 183–4; MO Hudson, *The Permanent Court of International Justice, 1920–1942, A Treatise* (Macmillan 1943) 617–18.

[37] Francioni (n 26) [6].

[38] W Friedmann, *The Changing Structure of International Law* (Stevens & Sons 1964) 197; C de Visscher, 'Contribution à l'etude des sources du droit international' (1933) 60 RDILC 395, 414 ff; S Rosenne, 'The Position of the International Court of Justice on the Foundations of the Principle of Equity in International Law' in A Bloed & P van Dijk (eds), *Forty Years International Court of Justice: Jurisdiction, Equity and Equality* (Europa Instituut 1988) 85, 108.

[39] *Libyan American Oil Company v Libya* (Award of 12 April 1977) *Ad Hoc* Tribunal, 62 ILR 140, 209 (*LIAMCO*).

[40] *Aminoil* [78].

[41] *North Sea Continental Shelf Cases* [88].

directly applicable as law.'[42] The Court, 'whose task is by definition to administer justice is bound to apply it.'[43] By contrast, dispute-settlement *ex aequo et bono* entails that a tribunal may act as an *amiable compositeur* for the 'adjustment of the respective interests' of the parties.[44] While the latter function requires express agreement by the parties (Article 42(3) of ICSID),[45] the former is not simply 'a matter of abstract justice', but a rule of law capable of generating legal obligations between States.[46]

Within the framework of *intra legem* equity, the ICJ has drawn a further distinction between equity *praeter* and *infra legem*.[47] Equity *praeter legem* acquires an autonomous normative function in case of *lacunae*, 'in order to remedy the insufficiencies of international law and fill in its *logical* lacunae.'[48] Conversely, *infra legem* equity consists in 'a method of interpretation of the law in force, and is one of its attributes.'[49] Leaving aside doctrinal objections against the traditional typology of equity,[50] this analysis will not focus on the *praeter legem* of equity: to the extent that the *Chorzów Factory* standard has received wide-spread acceptance in State practice and jurisprudence as reflecting customary law, it seems untenable to speak of a general 'gap' in State responsibility to which *praeter legem* equity could apply,[51] although it may always be possible to identify smaller gaps to which *praeter legem* equity may be of relevance.

Rather, it is the interpretative function of equity that is most pertinent to the customary rules governing the determination of compensation.[52] Thus, in *Amco v Indonesia* the ICSID annulment committee dismissed the idea that any mention of 'equitable considerations' in the award would

---

[42] *Continental Shelf (Tunisia/Libya)* (Merits) [1982] ICJ Rep 18 [71].
[43] ibid.
[44] *Frontier Dispute (Burkina Faso/Republic of Mali)* [1986] ICJ Rep 554 [28]; C Schreuer, 'Decisions Ex Aequo et Bono under the ICSID Convention' (1996) 11 ICSID Rev – FILJ 37.
[45] Eg, see *SARL Benvenuti & Bonfant v Congo* (Award of 15 August 1980) ICSID Case No ARB/77/2 [4.90–8]; *Atlantic Triton Company Limited v Guinea* (Award of 21 April 1986) ICSID Case No ARB/84/1.
[46] *Continental Shelf* [71]; *North Sea Continental Shelf Cases* [71].
[47] *Frontier Dispute* [28].
[48] *Barcelona Traction, Light and Power Company, Ltd (Belgium v Spain)* (Judgment) [1970] ICJ Rep 3, Separate Opinion of Judge Ammoun, 286 [42] (emphasis in the original); O Schachter, 'International Law in Theory and Practice' (1982) 178 RdC 15, 85.
[49] *Frontier Dispute* [28]; see also, M Akehurst, 'Equity and General Principles of Law' (1976) 25(4) ICLQ 801, 801–2.
[50] V Lowe, 'The Role of Equity in International Law' (1988) 4 Aust YBIL 54, 56, 59 ff; Gourgourinis (n 34) 330.
[51] I Marboe, *Calculation of Compensation and Damages in International Investment Law* (2nd edn, OUP 2017) [3.347].
[52] *Iran v USA* [230].

necessarily amount to a decision *ex aequo et bono*, and accepted that equitable considerations may 'form part of the law to be applied by the Tribunal' for the purposes of compensation.[53] In *Dogan v Turkmenistan* the annulment committee also stated that equitable considerations were 'inherent (…) in the interpretation of the law applied by the Tribunal.'[54] The committee in *MTD v Chile* developed this point further, stating that a tribunal is entitled to 'tak[e] into account considerations of fairness in applying the law', given that 'individual rules of law will often require fairness or a balancing of interests to be taken to account.'[55]

These propositions align with the general understanding of the hermeneutical function of equity as intimately linked with the requirements of good faith and reasonableness. Following a long tradition of jurists,[56] Schwarzenberger postulates that equity demands 'reasonableness and good faith in the interpretation and application of treaties'.[57] For '[e]ven in a relatively static environment, the need arises sooner or later to soften the harshness of *jus strictum* by the infusion of elements of equity and elasticity.'[58] In the same vein, certain authors have argued that equity may 'soften' or 'temper' the strict application of positive rules, by 'infusing elements of reasonableness and 'individualised' justice in their interpretation, whenever the applicable law leaves a margin of discretion',[59] or as a 'a normative flexifier [*sic*] mitigating the rigidity of application of positive international law'.[60]

---

[53] *Amco v Indonesia* (n 27) [26]–[28].

[54] *Adem Dogan v Turkmenistan* (Decision on Annulment of 15 January 2016) ICSID Case No ARB/09/9 [100].

[55] *MTD v Chile* [48 & 77].

[56] R Kolb, *La bonne foi en droit international public: Contribution à l' étude des principes généraux de droit* (Graduate Institute Publications 2000) 264, fn 545–7; R Phillimore, *Commentaries Upon International Law*, Vol II (T&JW Johnson 1855) 70 ('[a]ll international treaties are covenants *bonae fidei,* and are, therefore, to be equitably and not technically construed'); Baron É Descamps, 'L'Influence de la Condamnation de la Guerre sur l'Evolution Juridique Internationale' (1930) 31 RdC 394, 554 ('Quand le droit des gens universel affirme que les traités sont des conventions de bonne foi, il érige en règle l'obligation de les interpréter et de les appliquer avec toutes les suites que l'équité, notamment, leur donne suivant leur nature'); E Kaufman, 'Règles Générales du Droit de la Paix' (1935) 54 RdC 511 ('le principe de la bonne foi (…) [est] destiné à faire prévaloir les exigences de l'équité contre les pures formalités').

[57] G Schwarzenberger, 'Equity in International Law' (1972) YBWA 346, 357.

[58] G Schwarzenberger, 'The Fundamental Principles of International Law' (1955) 87 RdC 192, 379 & 301 ('[o]bservance of good faith, then, becomes equivalent to the infusion of considerations of equity in the moral sense into the treaty superstructure of international law').

[59] Francioni (n 26) [7]; M Fitzmaurice, 'International Protection of the Environment' (2001) 293 RdC 16.

[60] Gourgourinis (n 34) 327.

Insofar as *infra legem* equity has been mostly theorised at the level of treaty interpretation, the question arises whether its interpretative function extends to customary rules. In this regard, academic authors have raised a series of doctrinal objections against the possibility of interpreting customary norms *as such*, pointing towards the absence of a *written text* that could be analysed through the ordinary means of interpretation.[61] Without further delving into this wider doctrinal debate, it is sufficient to note that the applicability of *infra legem* equity to compensation has been relatively uncontested in practice: thus, in the *Armed Activities* case the ICJ made several references to equitable considerations at the reparations stage, and several judges acknowledged that recourse to equitable considerations in determining compensation 'is an application of equity *infra legem*'.[62] In *Total v Argentina*, the tribunal also noted that '[e]quitable considerations in the application of the law, including in performing calculation of damages, pertain to *aequitas infra legem* (…) and not *aequitas praeter legem* to use a Latin expression (equity within what the law admits)'.[63] Indeed, if *infra legem* equity can affect the interpretation of treaty-based rules, it stands to reason that it can also affect the interpretation of customary norms, which are framed at such level of generality that a further deductive process is required to particularise their content and meaning to the circumstances of each case.[64] The question, therefore, is not about whether equitable considerations may apply to the interpretation of customary law *in abstracto*, but rather about how that process comes to bear.

3 Lost and Found: Equitable Considerations in the Law of State Responsibility

Heretofore, academic authors have approached the principle of equity through the lens of primary rules governing inter-State relations, ranging

---

[61] Eg. T Treves, 'Customary International Law' [2006] MPEPIL 1393 [2]; VD Degan, *L'interprétation des accords en droit international* (Nijhoff 1963) 162. For a response to these arguments, P Merkouris, *Interpretation of Customary International Law: of Methods and Limits* (Brill 2023) (on file with the author).
[62] *Armed Activities on the Territory of the Congo*, Separate Opinion of Judge Iwasawa [5–15], Separate Opinion of Judge Yusuf [24] ('equitable considerations are of an essentially legal character (equity *infra legem*)').
[63] *Total SA v Argentina* (Award of 27 November 2013) ICSID Case No ARB/04/1, fn 39.
[64] P Merkouris, 'Interpreting the Customary Rules of Interpretation' (2017) 19 ICLR 126, 136–42.

from maritime boundary delimitation[65] to the exploitation and management of natural resources,[66] the 'fair and equitable treatment' standard in BITs,[67] or the law of the WTO.[68] By contrast, much less attention has been paid to the question whether – and if so, how – equity may affect the interpretation of secondary norms governing the consequences of wrongful acts,[69] even less so compensation.[70] As noted by Milano, the function of equity in the identification of remedies for wrongful acts

> is an aspect of the general principle of equity which has been under-investigated in the literature and one where the relationship between equity itself and the application of the ordinary rules of State responsibility, presumably of a customary nature, becomes crucial.[71]

However, recourse to equitable considerations for compensation purposes is not new.[72] States have instructed arbitral tribunals and mixed claims commissions to apply 'equity' to the assessment of damages arising from foreign claims as early as the 1794 Jay Treaty, where the US and Great Britain mandated the umpire to settle their claims to compensation on the basis of 'justice, equity and the law of nations'. But even where equity was not expressly mentioned in the arbitral agreement, this did not prevent arbitrators from invoking equity *proprio motu* for the determination of compensation.[73] Even though some of these early decisions were rendered *ex aequo et bono*,[74] some other tribunals invoked equity within

---

[65] D Nelson, 'The Roles of Equity in the Delimitation of Maritime Boundaries' (1990) 84(4) AJIL 837, 837 ff.

[66] T Franck, *Fairness in International Law and Institutions* (OUP 2012) 56 ff; United Nations Convention on the Law of the Sea (adopted 10 December 1982, entered into force 1 November 1994) 1833 UNTS 397, Arts 74, 83, 140, 155(2).

[67] Francioni (n 26) [22]–[28].

[68] A Gourgourinis, *Equity and Equitable Principles in the World Trade Organization* (Routledge 2016) 42–134.

[69] Gourgourinis (n 23) 81. On this distinction, see HLA Hart, *The Concept of Law* (Clarendon Press 1984) 77 ff.

[70] E Milano, 'General Principles *Infra, Praeter, Contra Legem*? The Role of Equity in Determining Reparation' in M Andenas & ors (eds), *General Principles and the Coherence of International Law*, vol 37 (Brill Nijhoff 2019) 67.

[71] ibid.

[72] For early writings on this question, see A Heffter, *Le Droit International Public de l'Europe* (first published 1844, Jules Bergson tr, 3rd edn, Cotillon Libraires 1873) [101–200]; C de Visscher, *De l'équité dans le règlement arbitral ou judiciaire des litiges de droit international public* (Pedone 1972) 57–66.

[73] Degan (n 18) 158–91.

[74] *Orinoco Steamship Company Case* (1910) XI RIAA 16, 240; *Attaque de la caravane du maharao de Cutch* (1927) II RIAA 821, 826; *Campbell* (1931) II RIAA 1145, 1157–8; *The Masonic* (1885) published in H La Fontaine, *Pasicrisie internationale* (Stämpfli 1902) 281–2.

the framework of legal reasoning, either as the normative basis for allowing a claim (*praeter legem*),[75] or as a legal principle capable of influencing the interpretation of customary law (*infra legem*).[76]

Eventually, the concept of equity found its way into the codification efforts of the ILC on the law of State responsibility. Originally, the 1930 Preparatory Committee of the Hague Conference stated in its 'Basis for Discussion No. 29' that '[r]esponsibility involves (…) an obligation to make good the damage suffered in so far as it results from failure to comply with the international obligation.'[77] This standard echoes the conventional understanding of the *Chorzów Factory* judgment that had been rendered by the PCIJ just the previous year. As early as 1956, however, Special Rapporteur Garcia-Amador recognised that, apart from the remedial function of compensation, there may also be some 'attenuating', 'extenuating' or 'aggravating' circumstances that can affect the extent to which a State is bound to compensate for injury caused to aliens in its territory.[78] This position, which signalled a departure from *Chorzów Factory*, became clearer in his subsequent reports, where he noted that, while

> the basic and at the same time general criterion, is that the reparation should be commensurate with the nature or extent of the actual injury (…) the reparation is not always strictly in keeping with the true nature or extent of the injury. Other factors generally come into play, such as the circumstances in which the injury occurred, the gravity, in special situations, of the act or omission imputable to the respondent State and, on occasion, factors justifying a reduction in the amount of the reparation.[79]

---

[75] *John Gill* (1931) V RIAA 157, 162; *Spillane* (1931) RIAA 290; *Règlement des prestations effectuées dans la Ruhr* (1927) II RIAA 797, 818; *Biens britanniques au Maroc espagnol: Réclamation No 51* (1925) II RIAA 615, 726; *Heny* (1903) IX RIAA 125, 134; *Compagnie de la Baie d'Hudson* (1869) published in in N Politis & AG de Lapradelle (eds), *Recueil Des Arbitrages Internationaux (1856–1872)* (Pedone 1923) 503, 512; *Harington et autres* (1862) published in N Politis & AG de Lapradelle (eds), *Recueil Des Arbitrages Internationaux (1856–1872)* (Pedone 1923) 155, 157–8.

[76] For an overview of pre-1960 arbitral jurisprudence, see Degan (n 18) 164 ff.

[77] League of Nations, 'Bases of Discussion Drawn up by the Preparatory Committee of the Hague Codification Conference' (1929) LoN Doc C.75.M.69.1929.V, 151.

[78] ILC, 'International Responsibility: Report by FV Garcia Amador, Special Rapporteur' (20 January 1956) UN Doc A/CN.4/96 reproduced in [1956/II] YBILC 173, 208–9 [183–91]; ILC, 'Summary Record of the 370th Meeting' (1956) UN Doc A/CN.4/SR.370, 230 [33].

[79] ILC, 'International Responsibility: Sixth report by FV Garcia Amador, Special Rapporteur' (26 January 1961) UN Doc A/CN.4/134 reproduced in [1961/II] YBILC 1, 30 [117]; see also, ILC, 'Report of the International Law Commission on the Work of its 27th Session' (5 May–25 July 1975) UN Doc A/10010/Rev. 1 reproduced in [1975/II] YBILC 47, 56 [42] & 59 [51] (referring to 'various circumstances whose existence (…) might preclude, attenuate or aggravate any wrongfulness of the conduct attributed to the State').

Special Rapporteur Ago did not submit a report on the consequences of internationally wrongful acts before his election to the ICJ. However, when discussing his eighth report on the circumstances precluding wrongfulness, several ILC members observed that, while certain circumstances may not preclude the wrongfulness of an act *qua*, they may nonetheless operate as mitigating factors for the purposes of reparation.[80] Special Rapporteur Ago acknowledged this point[81] and the commentary to draft Chapter V stated that circumstances precluding wrongfulness 'must not be confused with other circumstances which might have the effect not of precluding the wrongfulness of the act of the State but of attenuating or aggravating the responsibility entailed by that act', with regard to the content, form and degree of responsibility.[82] Even though neither Rapporteur expressly referred to 'equity' as the legal basis, they both acknowledged that it was possible for compensation to take into account not only the extent of the injury caused by the wrongful act, but additional factors as well.

The following year, Special Rapporteur Riphagen argued in favour of a 'qualitative' and 'quantitative' degree of proportionality between the characteristics of the unlawful conduct and the consequences in response thereto, including the level and amount of compensation.[83] Notably, since the *North Sea Continental Shelf* cases the ICJ has drawn a connection between the application of equitable principles and a 'reasonable degree of proportionality' to be observed by the respective decision-maker.[84] In the course of the debate on Riphagen's report, the principle of proportionality was expressly endorsed by some ILC members[85] (notably in the context of compensation[86]) but met with scepticism from others.[87]

Equitable considerations resurfaced with greater force at the last stages of the codification process. In his first report to the ILC, Special Rapporteur

---

[80] ILC, 'Summary 31st Session' (n 17) 26 [23, 30] & 205 [22].
[81] ibid 207 [14] ('there might be situations in which wrongfulness would not be precluded but in which account should be taken of the circumstances involved as attenuating circumstances in regard to fixing the amount and form of reparation for damage').
[82] ILC, 'Report 31st Session' (n 17), Commentary to Draft Chapter V, 109 [11].
[83] ILC, 'Preliminary Report International Responsibility' (n 17) 112–13 [27, 34], 128 [95]; ILC, 'Summary 32nd Session' (n 17) 80 [33], 96 [47].
[84] *North Sea Continental Shelf Cases* [93–4, 98 & 101.D.(3)].
[85] ILC, 'Summary 32nd Session' (n 17) 83 [15–17], 87–8 [11, 17, 21], 95 [36].
[86] ibid 88 [17], 91 [7] ('[a]nother aspect was that proportionality could act as a mitigating circumstance in the determination by the forum court or States concerned of the amount of reparation to be paid'); 95 [40] ('proportionality was the linchpin of Part II of the draft, and it applied equally to reparation').
[87] ibid, 82–4 [9, 25].

Arangio-Ruiz described the *Chorzów Factory* principle as too vague or sweeping a proposition, which does not settle all of potential legal issues involved, such as the 'relevance of the injured State's conduct', of the 'gravity of the wrongful act' or the 'degree of fault of the offending State'.[88] The following year, however, he explained that '[h]e had omitted express references to equity from the report because, as experience showed, such references were apt to be unhelpful. Needless to say, however, equity was implied in all legal rules and formed an essential and integral part of law.'[89] In his opinion, equity was intimately linked to the relevance of fault, wilful intent or negligence for the purposes of compensation.[90] In the same vein, other ILC members raised the question of the onerousness of the financial obligation upon the obligor State as an equitable consideration that could justify a proportional reduction of damages in some cases.[91] The Special Rapporteur expressly acknowledged the role of equity in the assessment of damages, but noted that 'it might be dangerous to refer expressly to [equity], since it was part and parcel of law and of any legal decision'.[92] Still, the original Commentary to Article 6*bis* stated that:

> There may be other equitable considerations *that militate against full reparation*, particularly in cases involving an author State with limited financial resources, but only to the extent that such considerations can be reconciled with the principle of the equality of all States before the law and the corresponding equality of the legal obligations of all States.[93]

It was, therefore, understood that the customary standard of full reparation could be balanced against equitable considerations, which could reduce the extent of reparation, including the amount of compensation. In his third report to the ILC, Special Rapporteur Crawford observed that international jurisprudence reflected

---

[88] ILC, 'Second Report on State Responsibility, by Mr Gaetano Arangio-Ruiz, Special Rapporteur' (9 and 22 June 1989) UN Doc A/CN.4/425 and Add.L reproduced in [1989/II] YBILC 1, 8 [21–2].
[89] ILC, 'Summary Records of the Meeting of the 42nd Session' (1 May–20 July 1990) UN Doc A/CN.4/SER.A/1990, 173 [41].
[90] ibid 173 [41].
[91] ibid 165 [57], 168 [7], 177 [6], 189 [31–2], 190 [39].
[92] ibid 198 [31].
[93] ILC, 'Draft Report of the ILC on the Work of its 45th Session, Addendum' (9 July 1993) UN Doc A/CN.4/L.484/Add.3, 5–6 [6 *bis*] (emphasis added). The text of the commentary was amended in ILC, 'Report of the International Law Commission on the Work of its 45th Session' (3 May–13 July 1993) UN Doc A/48/10, 60 [8] to read: ('There may be other equitable considerations that *might be taken into account* in providing full reparation') (emphasis added).

the wide variety of factual situations, the influence of particular primary obligations, evaluations of the respective behaviour of the parties (both in terms of the gravity of the breach and their subsequent conduct), and, more generally, a concern to reach an equitable and acceptable outcome.[94]

When international judges are making a complex judgment such as one regarding the amount of compensation, he observed, 'equitable considerations will inevitably be taken into account, whether acknowledged or not.'[95] He warned, however, that, 'while illustrations can be given of the operation of equitable considerations and of proportionality in international law, the attempt to specify them in detail is likely to fail.'[96] Given that the ILC was anxious to conclude its codification work before 2001, the Special Rapporteur made no effort to define 'equitable considerations' in detail. But the general proposition made it to the final commentary to Article 36 of ARSIWA (albeit with diluted wording), stating that:

> As to (…) the principles of assessment to be applied in quantification, these will vary, depending upon the content of particular primary obligations, an evaluation of the respective behaviour of the parties and, more generally, a concern to reach an equitable and acceptable outcome.[97]

It follows that the ILC understood that the customary standard of 'full reparation' would not always provide satisfactory solutions and that international tribunals could have recourse to equity, as a general principle of law, for the adjustment of compensation in such a way as to reflect additional factors, such as the parties' conduct and situation, the content of the primary norm breached, or an evaluation of their respective interests. While most Special Rapporteurs acknowledged the relevance of equity for compensation (including under the rubric of proportionality),

---

[94] ILC, 'Third report on State Responsibility, by Mr James Crawford, Special Rapporteur' (15 March, 15 June, 10 and 18 July and 4 August 2000) UN Doc A/CN.4/507, 51 [159] (internal references omitted).

[95] ibid.

[96] ibid.

[97] ILC (n 4) 100 [7], referring to Aldrich (n 18) 242; B Graefrath, 'Responsibility and Damages Caused: Relationship between Responsibility and Damages' (1984) 185 RdC 14, 101 (discussing the non-permissibility of punitive damages); L Reitzer, *La réparation comme conséquence de l'acte illicite en droit international* (Sirey 1938) 175 (suggesting that the principle of full reparation may at times be unsatisfactory and unhelpful); C Gray, *Judicial Remedies in International Law* (Clarendon 1987) 11 (discussing references to 'equity' in early arbitral awards) & 33–4 (discussing different types of injury); J Personnaz, *La Réparation du Préjudice en Droit International Public* (Sirey 1939) 98–109 (discussing the relevance of the source of the obligation to provide reparation, of the conduct of the parties and of their general situation on the determination of reparation).

it was agreed not to insert an express qualification to the text of the draft articles. However, far from discounting the relevance of equity in favour of a mechanical approach to quantum, the ILC suggested that *infra legem* equity forms part-and-parcel of the secondary rules of State responsibility and may have a bearing on the level of compensation. This proposition, reflected in the final commentary of ARSIWA after more than 50 years of discussions and buttressed by the contemporaneous and subsequent practice of courts and tribunals, is of key import for the interpretation of the rules governing compensation.[98]

4 Equitable Considerations in Investment Arbitration: Is There a Limit?

In line with the preceding analysis, investment tribunals have, expressly or impliedly, applied equitable considerations to the determination of compensation payable in case of unlawful acts. As early as 1982, for example, the *Aminoil* Tribunal observed that 'any estimate in money terms of amounts intended to express the value of an asset, of an undertaking, of a contract, or of services rendered, must take equitable principles into account'.[99] In *Amco v Indonesia*, the committee further stated that 'a tribunal applying international law may take account of equitable considerations in non-maritime boundaries cases', such as compensation.[100]

While this proposition is generally accepted in the literature,[101] there seems to be no consensus as to what these 'equitable considerations' might be. Commentators, practitioners and tribunals alike have proffered

---

[98] D Azaria, 'Codification by Interpretation: The International Law Commission as an Interpreter of International Law' (2020) 31(1) EJIL 171, 198.
[99] *Aminoil* [78].
[100] *Amco v Indonesia* [27].
[101] B Sabahi, K Duggal & N Birch, 'Principles Limiting the Amount of Compensation' in C Beharry (ed), *Contemporary and Emerging Issues on the Law of Damages and Valuation in International Investment Arbitration* (Brill Nijhoff 2018); Marboe (n 51) 155–7 [3.343-59]; SN Elrifai, 'Equity-Based Discretion and the Anatomy of Damages Assessment in Investment Treaty Law' (2017) 34(5) JInt'l Arb 835, 835–88; C Schreuer & ors, *The ICSID Convention – A Commentary* (CUP 2009) 636–7 [269–70]; M Kantor, *Valuation for Arbitration: Compensation Standards, Valuation Methods and Expert Evidence* (Kluwer 2008) 116 ('[t]he use of equitable considerations in the computation of compensation amounts is not uncommon, even if it is not always admitted (…) It also lies just beneath the surface of many judicial and arbitral decisions'); T Wälde & B Sabahi, 'Compensation, Damages, and Valuation in International Investment Law' in P Muchlinski, F Ortino & C Schreuer (eds), *Oxford Handbook of International Investment law* (OUP 2008) 1049, 1103–5.

a wide range of factors capable of influencing quantum (well beyond the *Chorzów* formula), albeit not always invoking equity as the relevant legal basis. On the one hand, it has been suggested that equitable considerations may justify an aggravated amount of compensation, in order to reflect the 'seriousness' or 'gravity' of the unlawful act,[102] or the subjective intent (or fault) of the wrongdoer State.[103] Similar considerations, however, evoked serious objections within the ILC during the codification process that led to the ARSIWA: despite the original proposals to enable damages reflecting the gravity of the breach,[104] the ILC eventually rejected the idea that compensation be used as a vehicle for the introduction of punitive damages.[105] The ICJ has also rejected the availability of punitive or exemplary damages, even in those cases involving the most serious violations of international human rights and humanitarian law.[106]

On the other hand, it has been suggested that equitable considerations may warrant an adjustment (or proportionate reduction) of compensation in order to accommodate additional, countervailing considerations, that relate either to the injured party or the wrongdoer State. As regards to the first category, some tribunals have sought to limit the amount of recoverable compensation by reference to the injured party's conduct that either precedes or follows the wrongful act. For example, in *Himpurna v PLN* the Tribunal applied the doctrine of abuse of right in favour of the respondent, in order to prevent the claimant's contractual rights from being extended 'beyond tolerable norms', also taking into account PLN's status 'as an arm of governmental policy acting in pursuit of the public welfare'. On that basis, it lowered the amount of compensation due referring to 'equitable principles'.[107]

---

[102] In *Gold Reserve v Venezuela* [615 & 668], the Tribunal awarded over $700 million in damages stating that, given the 'number, variety and seriousness of the breaches' by Venezuela of the FET standard, '[t]he compensation due to Claimant for such breaches should reflect the seriousness of the violation'.

[103] ILC, 'Special Rapporteur Arangio-Ruiz' (n 88) 173 [41].

[104] ILC, 'Report of the International Law Commission on the Work of its 48th Session' (6 May–26 July 1996) UN Doc A/51/10, 63 (Art 45, providing for 'damages reflecting the gravity of the infringement' in cases of gross infringement of the rights of the injured State).

[105] ILC (n 4) 99, commentary to Art 36 [(4)] ('Compensation corresponds to the financially assessable damage suffered by the injured State or its nationals. It is not concerned to punish the responsible State, nor does compensation have an expressive or exemplary character').

[106] *Armed Activities on the Territory of the Congo* [102]; see also *Ahmadou Sadio Diallo* [57]; *Certain Activities Carried Out by Nicaragua in the Border Area* [31].

[107] *Himpurna California Energy Ltd (Bermuda) v PT (Persero) Perusahaan Listruik Negara (Indonesia)* (Final Award of 4 May 1999) XXV YBCA 14, 71–3 [237–8] & 92–3 [325–31]. In

Conversely, international tribunals have endorsed the proposition that the amount of compensation must be reduced when the claimant has failed to take 'reasonable steps' to mitigate the injury caused.[108] Failure to mitigate damages has been understood as a matter that is notionally distinct from the contributory fault/negligence of the injured party in the occurrence of the wrongful conduct and the emergence of the harm, which is a matter related to the existence of causal nexus.[109] Insofar as tribunals have based the existence of a 'duty to mitigate damages' upon considerations of fairness,[110] this proposition may be interpreted as a specific form of equitable considerations that comes into play after the occurrence of the harm. In the same vein, the Arbitral Tribunal in the *Loan Agreement* case emphasised the 'equitable character' of the customary norms of compensation, which led the Tribunal to consider not only the 'technical' provisions of the treaty and loan agreements, but also the 'overall circumstances of the case, including the causes of delay, the misunderstandings (...) and generally the specific situation and conduct *of both Parties*, as well as the totality of the relations of amity and co-operation.'[111]

With respect to equitable considerations relating to the wrongdoer State, it is important to note that recent scholars have argued for the reconceptualisation of investment arbitration from a private-law-type arbitration into a form of 'public-law adjudication', which takes into consideration the public functions of the host State *vis-à-vis* its population in furtherance of the public interest and allows for some flexibility to the host State concerned. The public-law paradigm has found expression in

its 'Basis of discussion No 19', the Preparatory Committee of the 1930 Hague Conference also identified the 'provocative attitude' of the injured person as a factor capable of affecting the extent of a State's responsibility: ILC (n 4) 71–2 [(5)].

[108] See, for example, *AIG Capital Partners, Inc and CJSC Tema Real Estate Company Ltd v Kazakhstan* (Award of 7 October 2003) ICSID Case No ARB/01/6 [10.6.4]. In *MTD Equity Sdn Bhd v Chile* (Award of 25 May 2004) ICSID Case No ARB/01/7 [217 & 242–3], the Tribunal decided to reduce damages by 50% to reflect the fact that claimants had taken decisions that increased their risks and amplified their losses. See further *Gabčíkovo-Nagymaros Project* [80]; *Well Blowout Control Claim* (Report and Recommendations of UNCC of 15 November 1996) 109 ILR 479 [54].

[109] *Hulley Enterprises Limited v Russia* (Final Award of 18 July 2014) PCA Case No 2005–03/AA226 [1603].

[110] In *EDF v Argentina* (Award of 11 June 2012) ICSID Case No ARB/03/23 [1301] the Tribunal observed that it would be 'patently unfair to allow Claimants to recover damages for loss that could have been avoided by taking reasonable steps'. In *Middle East Cement Shipping and Handling Co SA v Egypt* (Award of 12 April 2002) ICSID Case No ARB/99/6 [167], the Tribunal held that '[t]he duty to mitigate (...) can be considered to be part of the General Principles of Law'.

[111] *Loan Agreement Between Italy and Costa Rica* [70–1 & 77].

investment arbitration in several ways, such as the principle of proportionality, legitimate expectations and the applicable standard of review.[112] Similar considerations have found their way into the assessment of damages.[113] For instance, it has been suggested that investment tribunals should either weigh the level of compensation against legitimate 'public interest' considerations motivating the unlawful conduct of the host State[114] or consider the circumstances surrounding the wrongful act, such as the occurrence of an armed conflict in the host State's territory.[115]

Within that context, the potentially 'crippling' effect that large sums of compensation may have for a host State's financial subsistence has been suggested as a potential equitable consideration that is relevant to quantum. In his separate opinion in the quantum phase of *CME v Czech Republic*, Sir Ian opined that the principles of compensation must be read within the framework of the BIT and noted that '[i]t would be strange indeed, if the outcome of a [BIT] took the form of liabilities "likely to entail catastrophic repercussions for the livelihood and economic well-being of the population"'.[116] Along similar lines, Paparinskis has argued in favour of an exception to the principle of full compensation, with a view to ensuring that '[r]emedies serve social as well as individual needs': to the extent that the bilateralist precepts of corrective justice that underlain *Chorzów Factory* have gradually evolved in a more communitarian direction, Paparinskis posits that the standard of compensation 'can be changed in line with the broader structural shifts in modern international law'.[117] Indeed, in the *Armed Activities* case the ICJ took note of Uganda's plea that a large amount of compensation would exceed its capacity to pay and seems implicitly to have endorsed the relevance of this legal ground by reference to the award by the Eritrea-Ethiopia Claims

---

[112] D Peat, *Comparative Reasoning in International Courts and Tribunals* (CUP 2019) 107–39.
[113] cf A Kulick, 'Sneaking Through the Backdoor – Reflections on Public Interest in International Investment Arbitration' (2013) 29(3) Arb Intl 435, 435–7.
[114] While Kulick (n 113) 438, 448 ff does not expressly refer to equity as the basis for 'public interest' considerations, he considers Brownlie's argument in *CME* (n 116) that 'considerations of fairness (…) must find reflection in the eventual calculation of compensation and damages' to be 'quite forceful'.
[115] *AMT v Zaire* [7.16–9]; *Chemin de fer de Sopron-Köszeg contre Autriche et Hongrie* (1929) II RIAA 961, 968; *Junghans (Germany v Romania) (Part Two)* (1940) III RIAA 1883, 1890; *France (Feuillebois) v Mexico* (1929) V RIAA 542, 543.
[116] *CME Czech Republic BV v Czech Republic* (Separate Opinion on the Issues at the Quantum Phase by Ian Brownlie of 14 March 2003) UNCITRAL [33 & 73–7]; see also *Spadafora (Colombia, Italy)* (1904) XI RIAA 1, 9–10.
[117] M Paparinskis, 'A Case Against Crippling Compensation in International Law of State Responsibility' (2020) MLR 1, 6–8.

Commission (EECC).[118] Ultimately, however, the Court was 'satisfied that the total sum awarded (…) remain[ed] within the capacity of Uganda to pay', although it ordered the payment of the sum in annual instalments, presumably in order to Uganda's ability to meet its people's basic needs.[119]

The foregoing remarks serve to show that equitable considerations are not a monolithic concept but are used as an umbrella term to denote a wide variety of factors and circumstances which have an influence upon quantum. To be sure, a detailed analysis of each these considerations would exceed the limited purpose of this chapter, but a key point stands out: whatever these 'equitable considerations' may be, it is suggested that investment tribunals do not have a *carte blanche* to subvert the customary principle of full reparation on the basis of 'abstract equity'.[120] Indeed, it is well settled that an investment tribunal 'must base its decision on objective and rational considerations which must be stated.'[121] The US' strong objections to the application of equitable considerations in the determination of compensation arising from the *Norwegian Shipowners* case aptly illustrates how an unprincipled application of equity to damages may have serious repercussions on the validity of the arbitral award and the integrity of the process.[122] As Judge Yusuf stated in the *Armed Activities* case,

> Equitable considerations (…) should be understood within the legal framework governing the judicial function of the Court. They cannot serve as the basis to dispense with the applicable rules altogether, or not to provide reasons for their applicability. The Court should have made an attempt at explaining how it intends to apply equity within the general framework of State responsibility and the procedural framework governing the fact-finding procedure before it'.[123]

---

[118] *Armed Activities on the Territory of the Congo* [109, 407].
[119] ibid [407–8].
[120] *Armed Activities on the Territory of the Congo*, Separate Opinion of Judge Yusuf [28] ('recourse to equitable principles is not unfettered [and] it should not be used to make good the shortcomings in a claimant's case by being substituted for evidence which could have been produced if it actually existed. Nor can equitable considerations be used as an excuse to depart from the Court's judicial function').
[121] Schreuer & ors (n 101) 637 [272]; A Broches 'The Convention on the Settlement of Investment Disputes between States and Nationals of Other States' (1973) 136 RdC 333, 394.
[122] *Norwegian Shipowners' Claims (Norway v USA)* (Award of 13 October 1922) I RIAA 307, 331, 339–40; Letter of Secretary of State to the Norwegian Minister at Washington: *Norwegian Shipowners' Claims* 344–6; CP Anderson, 'Letter of the Honorable Chandler P Anderson, American Arbitrator, to the Secretary General of the Permanent Court of Arbitration' reproduced in (1923) 17(2) AJIL 362, 399.
[123] *Armed Activities on the Territory of the Congo*, Separate Opinion of Judge Yusuf [24].

On that basis, it is submitted that, whilst *infra legem* equity may have a bearing on the interpretation of customary norms governing compensation, it is by its nature subject to certain limitations that may either be intrinsic to the 'general framework of State responsibility' or extrinsic to it, appertaining to the 'procedural framework governing the fact-finding procedure' before the respective court or tribunal. We shall examine these two kinds of limitations in turn.

4.1   Intrinsic Limitations *to* infra legem *Equity*

Intrinsic limitations emanate from the nature of equity as a canon of interpretation. As the *Institut de Droit International* noted in 1937, an international judge may be called upon to consider equitable considerations in the interpretation of norms, 'to the extent consistent with respect for the applicable law.'[124] If equity is supposed to operate within the limits of the law, its hermeneutical function must be understood by reference to the limitations applicable to *any* rule of interpretation. As a cognitive exercise, the process of interpretation is ordinarily restrained by the rule to which it relates and its possible meanings.[125] Essentially, any method of interpretation involves the selection of a meaning amongst a spectrum of possible meanings within a conceptual radius defined by the widest possible meaning.[126]

Within that hermeneutical process, *infra legem* equity assists the interpreter in both identifying the outer limits of the norm in question, and in selecting 'among several possible interpretations of the law the one which appears, in the light of the circumstances of the case, to be closest to the requirements of justice.'[127] While these analytical choices will not always be clear-cut, it is suggested that a tribunal cannot exceed the conceptual radius of a norm and select a meaning beyond its range on the basis of equitable considerations – for this would result in extending or altering the norm's content into something else.[128] Consequently, in the

---

[124] IDI, 'Resolution: On the Jurisdiction of the International Judge in Equity' (1937) 40 AIDI 140.
[125] As Hart has observed, every norm contains a 'core of settled meaning' surrounded by a 'penumbra of debatable cases', see HLA Hart, 'Positivism and the Separation of Law and Morals' (1958) 71(4) HLR 607.
[126] EP Hexner, 'Teleological Interpretation of Basic Instruments of Public International Organizations' in S Engel & R Metall (eds), *Law, State and International Legal Order– Essays in Honor of Hans Kelsen* (Tennessee University 1964) 119, 123; H Kelsen, *The Law of the United Nations* (Stevens & Sons 1950) xiv–xv.
[127] *Continental Shelf* [71]; Weil (n 23) 125.
[128] *Interpretation of Peace Treaties with Bulgaria, Hungary and Romania (Second Phase)* (Advisory Opinion) [1950] ICJ Rep 221, 229–30. For a detailed discussion of the inherent

South West Africa cases the ICJ rejected the applicants' contention that 'humanitarian considerations [we]re sufficient in themselves to generate legal rights and obligations' from the applicable treaties.[129] To do so would exceed the process of interpretation and result in rectification or revision of the treaty, whereas a court of law 'can take account of moral principles only in so far as these are given a sufficient expression in legal form.'[130]

The interpretative function of equity becomes much more complex in the realm of customary law, precisely because there is no authoritative text to be interpreted.[131] Depending on the availability and specificity of State practice and *opinio juris*, customary rules tend to be much more vague and flexible, leaving some scope for debate regarding the precise limits and content of the rule.[132,133] As Merkouris points out, customary rules exist at such level of abstraction that a further deductive process is required to particularise their meaning to the facts of each case.[134] Thus, customary law affords the decision-maker a wide margin of discretion in interpreting and applying abstract rules to the circumstances of each case. In the absence of textual limitations, it is here that *infra legem* equity has a key role to play by defining the contours of customary law or providing the basis from which to infer potential qualifications.

This does not mean that the output of the interpretative process will vary along with the proverbial foot of the Chancellor.[135] Nor should the application of equitable considerations to customary rules be understood as being 'freed from the moorings of international law (…) drifting towards elusive subjectivism with little room left for the necessary guarantee of the objectivity and predictability of the law.'[136] While *infra legem* equity to some

---

difficulties in distinguishing the interpretation of customary rules and its possible amendment/modification, Merkouris (n 61) Section VI (on file with the author).

[129] *South West Africa Cases (Second Phase) (Ethiopia v South Africa; Liberia v South Africa)* (Judgment) [1966] ICJ Rep 6 [49].

[130] ibid [91].

[131] C Grauer, 'The Role of Equity in the Jurisprudence of the World Court' (1979) 37 RDUT 101, 116; Akehurst (n 49) 807 fn 36 ('[a] conflict between equity and custom is less likely to arise, because the scope of a customary rule is usually less precise than the scope of a treaty provision').

[132] R Lapidoth, 'Equity in International Law' (1987) 81 ASIL Proc 138, 139.

[133] ibid 139.

[134] Merkouris (n 64) 136–42.

[135] F Orrego Vicuña, 'Le pied du chancelier continue de s'allonger: les principes généraux et l'équité en droit international' in M Kohen, R Kolb & DL Tehindrazanarivelo (eds), *Perspectives of International Law in the 21st Century: Liber Amicorum Professor Christian Dominicè in Honour of his 80th birthday* (Martinus Nijhoff 2012) 69.

[136] Francioni (n 26) [14].

extent involves the exercise of discretion,[137] it forms part of the applicable law and must, therefore, display a minimum degree of consistency. As Jennings observes, no reasonable litigant expects the decision of a court to be predictable; but the range of considerations used for a decision and the procedures or their application should certainly be predictable.[138]

In determining these potential limitations, useful lessons can be drawn from the practice of equitable considerations in other areas of international law. In the *North Sea Continental Shelf* cases, the ICJ explained that the interpretative function of equity was limited by the object and purpose of the customary principles governing the continental shelf and could not result in the *de novo* apportionment of maritime areas on the basis of distributive justice.[139] To hold otherwise would contravene the 'most fundamental of all the rules of law relating to the continental shelf'.[140] In *Libya/ Malta*, the Court further stressed the need for consistency and identified potential limitations to the application of equity to maritime delimitation:

> Th[e] justice of which equity is an emanation, is not abstract justice but justice according to the rule of law; which is to say that its application should display consistency and a degree of predictability; even though it looks with particularity to the peculiar circumstances of an instant case, it also looks beyond it to principles of more general application. This is precisely why the courts have, from the beginning, elaborated equitable principles as being, at the same time, means to an equitable result in a particular case, yet also having a more general validity and hence expressible in general terms.[141]

On that basis, the Court distinguished between those equitable considerations which are 'pertinent to the institution of the continental shelf as it has developed within the law' and may, therefore, qualify for inclusion in the rule (ie, circumstances of a geographical nature), and those 'which are strange to its nature' and cannot be used 'fundamentally' to alter its character.[142] Thus, the Court seems to have recognised certain limitations to the interpretative function of equity as a canon by reference to the content of the rule and its teleology.

The ICJ affirmed this proposition in *Barcelona Traction*, where it rejected Belgium's contention that the customary rule of diplomatic protection should have been extended to a company's shareholders on the

---

[137] A Pellet, 'Sources of International Law' [1992] *Thesaurus Acroasium*, vol 19, 291.
[138] RY Jennings, 'Equity and Equitable Principles' (1986) XLII Annuaire Suisse 27, 38.
[139] *North Sea Continental Shelf Cases* [18–20].
[140] ibid [19–20, 39].
[141] *Continental Shelf (Libya/Malta)* (Merits) [1985] ICJ Rep 13 [45].
[142] ibid [48].

basis of 'equitable considerations'.[143] In so doing, the ICJ emphasised the nature of the customary right to exercise diplomatic protection and explained that any different interpretation would render inoperable the 'original' right of the State and severely undermine 'the stability which it is the object of international law to establish in international relations.'[144] Thus, the Court implicitly confirmed that equitable considerations cannot be used to justify *any* possible exception within the interpretation of a customary norm in the framework of State responsibility and it is subject to certain limitations stemming from the rule's object and purpose.

Extending this logic to compensation for internationally wrongful acts, it is suggested that equitable considerations cannot contradict the object and purpose of the rule, which is to 'wipe out', as far as possible, 'all the consequences of the illegal act and re-establish the situation which would, in all probability, have existed if that act had not been committed'.[145] The implications of this point are two-fold. On the one hand, equity cannot circumvent the inherently remedial function of compensation: thus, the invocation of the 'seriousness' of the breach, the 'magnitude' of the damage, or the 'wilful intent' of the host State cannot serve as bases for awarding damages beyond and above the amount of injury suffered by the claimant. Such damages, essentially of an afflictive, punitive or exemplary character are foreclosed under modern international law[146] and an award to that effect might be *contra legem*.[147] At the same time, however, equitable considerations cannot obviate claims for damages altogether: as the PCIJ explained in *Chorzów Factory*, compensation constitutes an 'essential principle contained in the actual notion of an illegal act'. Even if compensation may be adjusted to accommodate a balancing exercise between competing interests at stake, this cannot detract from the core principle that 'the breach of an engagement involves an obligation to make reparation in an adequate form.'[148] A different understanding would essentially transform equity into a circumstance precluding wrongfulness, without a clear legal basis.

Within these two extremes, it is quite difficult to pinpoint the extent to which equity may affect quantum in the abstract. Each factor requires

---

[143] *Barcelona Traction (Second Phase)* 3 [92]–[101].
[144] ibid [97].
[145] *Chorzów Factory* 47.
[146] *Certain Activities Carried Out by Nicaragua in the Border Area* [31].
[147] cf Venezuela's application to set aside the award in *Gold Reserve* on the basis of having awarded 'punitive damages' under the veil of equitable considerations.
[148] *Case Concerning the Factory at Chorzów (Germany v Poland)* (Jurisdiction) [1927] PCIJ Rep Series A No 9, 21.

an independent legal analysis and a careful application of the customary principle to the facts of each case. But this does not mean that equity is a matter of chance.[149] Whilst Radi emphasises the 'casuistic normativity' of equity for the proposition that it is impossible to define *infra legem* equity in general legal terms,[150] international tribunals are required to state the reasons for their decisions, including on their interpretation and application of equity. As the committee stated in *Rumeli v Kazakhstan*,

> It is highly desirable that tribunals should minimise to the greatest extent possible the element of estimation in their quantification of damages and maximise the specifics of the ratiocination explaining how the ultimate figure was arrived at.[151]

Within that wider normative process of trial and error, equity may perform its essential role by introducing elements of flexibility and reasonableness into the law, without departing from the object and purpose of the rule being interpreted. As tribunals continue to expand and rationalise the ways in which equity affects their interpretation of the customary standard of compensation, these judicial pronouncements (and the attitude of States to these interpretations) will tend to harden into rules and legal principles, to the effect that 'the freedom to frame arguments and frame the reasoning leading to decisions in the court will be correspondingly reduced.'[152]

4.2 Extrinsic Limitations to Equitable Considerations: Between Alchemy and Science

The duty to state reasons brings us to the next point, which is the extrinsic limitations to the interpretative function of equity. Contrary to intrinsic limitations, extrinsic limitations do not relate from the *content* of the rule being interpreted but rather emanate from the tribunal's adjudicative authority and the procedural framework in which it is bound to operate. When a tribunal resorts to equity, it can neither exceed the scope of its jurisdiction nor can it disregard certain fundamental rules of procedure

---

[149] Remarks of Mr Roucounas in ILC (n 89) 185 [81].
[150] Y Radi, 'Promenade avec Aristote Dans les Jardins du Droit International: Réflexions sur L'équité et le Raisonnement Juridique des Juges et Arbitres Internationaux' in D Alland, V Chetail, O de Frouville & ors (eds), *Unity and Diversity of International Law* (Brill Nijhoff 2014) 358, 361–2.
[151] *Rumeli Telekom AS & or v Kazakhstan* (Decision of ad hoc Committee of 25 March 2010) ICSID Case No ARB/05/16 [178].
[152] Lowe (n 50) 74–5.

upon which its function is conditioned (cf. Article 52(1)(d) ICSID) – at least not without the validity of its decision being impinged. As a result, in *Klöckner v Cameroon*, the ICSID annulment committee annulled an arbitral tribunal's award for manifest excess of power *inter alia* on the basis that the tribunal had reached an 'equitable estimate' of damages, using 'approximate equivalents', and had, therefore, failed to state reasons as required by Articles 52(1)(e) and 48(3) of the ICSID Convention.[153]

The obligation to state reasons is of key import in the framework of compensation, where equity is typically associated with the lack of sufficient evidence to ascertain the precise extent of the injury.[154] The valuation of injury caused to long-term investments and commercial undertakings is a complex task, that often involves conflicting methodologies and inadequate evidence.[155] While it may be feasible to gauge the amount of *lucrum cessans* on the basis of business records from ongoing concerns, investment disputes frequently arise from still-born projects or failed contracts, where the value of profits can hardly be determined at all. As noted in *Santa Elena v Costa Rica*, investment tribunals enjoy a wide measure of discretion in making an approximation, 'taking into account all relevant circumstances (…) including equitable considerations'.[156]

Nevertheless, equitable considerations in the interpretation of the law must not be confused with the ordinary exercise of arbitral discretion in the appreciation of the facts.[157] As noted in *ADM v Mexico*, 'the assessment of damages for lost profits is not a precise science.'[158] Thus, the discretion of an arbitral tribunal in the calculation of damages arises from the uncertainty of the inquiry into lost profits, involving an inquiry with a counterfactual premise, namely, the consideration of the profits that would have been made if an illegal act – which did in fact occur – had not occurred.[159]

---

[153] *Klöckner Industrie-Anlagen GmbH & ors v Cameroon & Société Camerounaise des Engrais* (Ad hoc Committee Decision on Annulment of 3 May 1985) ICSID Case No ARB/81/2 [173–6].
[154] Marboe (n 51) 153 [3.343 ff].
[155] *Rumeli Telekom AS v Kazakhstan* [142]; M Whiteman, *Damages in International Law*, vol III (US GPO 1943) 1872.
[156] *Phillips Petroleum v Iran* (Award of 29 June 1989 (Award No 425-39-2)) IUSCT Case No 39, 21 IUSCT 79 [112 & 157]; *Starrett Housing Corporation v Iran* [339]; *Gold Reserve v Venezuela* [686].
[157] In this direction, T Marzal, 'Quantum (In)Justice: Rethinking the Calculation of Compensation and Damages in ISDS' (2021) 22 JWIT 249, 269–70.
[158] *ADM v Mexico* (Decision on Request for Correction, Supplementary Decision, and Interpretation of 10 July 2008) ICSID Case No ARB(AF) 04/05 [36].
[159] ibid.

In order to make these complex factual determinations, the tribunal will have to consider documentary evidence, witness testimony, admissions against interest, as well as expert reports and shall be the judge of the admissibility of any evidence adduced and of its probative value.[160] Inevitably, the assessment of the facts lies within the arbitrator's free evaluation of evidence (also known as the *conviction intime du juge*).[161] While this should be guided by a spirit of fairness, it is difficult to lay down precise legal rules of international law, upon which *infra legem* equity may come to bear as an interpretative canon.

By contrast, equitable considerations might affect the interpretation of the procedural rules governing the fact-finding process,[162] especially since investment tribunals consider themselves not to be bound to adhere to strict judicial rules of evidence.[163] In line with international case-law,[164] tribunals have relied upon equity to suggest that the fact that damages cannot be settled with certainty is no reason not to award damages when a loss has incurred.[165]

In this regard, tribunals have drawn a distinction between the allocation of the burden of proof and the standard of proof. It is well established that the claimant bears the onus to establish the conditions required by substantive law to corroborate a claim for damages.[166] The claimant must not only bring evidence in support of its allegations but must also convince the tribunal of their truth, lest they be disregarded for want, or insufficiency, of proof.[167] However, as the ICJ pointed out in *Diallo*, this rule may be applied flexibly in certain cases, especially where the respondent may be in a better position to establish certain facts.[168] Given that tribunals

---

[160] ICSID Rules of Procedure for Arbitration Proceedings (Arbitration Rules) (adopted 25 September 1967, entered into force 1 January 1968) Rule 34.
[161] *AAPL v Sri Lanka* (Final Award of 27 June 1990) ICSID Case No ARB/87/3 [56] rules (K-L).
[162] Weeramantry (n 34) [25].
[163] *AAPL v Sri Lanka* [56] rule (K).
[164] *Certain Activities Carried Out by Nicaragua in the Border Area* [35]; *Ahmadou Sadio Diallo* [33]; *Trail Smelter (United States, Canada)* (1941) III RIAA 1920.
[165] *Southern Pacific Properties (Middle East) Limited v Egypt* (Award of 20 May 1992) ICSID Case No ARB/84/3 [215]; *Swisslion DOO Skopje v FYROM* (Award of 6 July 2012) ICSID Case No ARB/09/16 [345]; *Vivendi v Argentina* [8.3.16] ('approximations are inevitable; the settling of damages is not an exact science'); *ADM v Mexico* [38].
[166] B Cheng, *General Principles of Law as Applied by International Courts and Tribunals* (reprinted, CUP 1987) 327; *Certain Activities Carried Out by Nicaragua in the Border Area* [33].
[167] *AAPL v Sri Lanka* [56] rules (I)-(J); *Middle East Cement* [89].
[168] *Ahmadou Sadio Diallo* [15].

have a relative freedom as to the allocation of the burden of proof,[169] equitable considerations may therefore warrant a shifting of the burden of proof, where the establishment of certain facts lies within the power of the respondent,[170] or where a party has impeded access to material evidence.

The *Archer Daniels* Tribunal took this reasoning a step further, noting that 'failure of a claimant to prove its damages with certainty, or to establish its right to the full damages claimed, does not relieve the tribunal of its *duty* to assess damages as best it can on the evidence available' (emphasis added).[171] This 'duty', endorsed by subsequent investment tribunals in compensation proceedings,[172] implies a gradual departure from the adversarial model of arbitration into a more inquisitorial system, a proposition that may have far-reaching implications for investor-State dispute settlement.[173] As Lord Neuberger has observed, 'an increase in arbitral powers must be accompanied by an increased responsibility'.[174] As mega-awards intimating claims over USD one billion plus continue to emerge, it seems likely investment tribunals will assert more control over the assessment of claims that may have serious impact on tax-payers' resources.[175] The progressive recognition of investment arbitration as a

---

[169] *Metal-Tech Ltd v Uzbekistan* (Award of 4 October 2013) ICSID Case No ARB/10/3 [238–9].

[170] For example, in the *Armed Activities on the Territory of the Congo*, the ICJ reversed the burden of proof with respect to Ituri, where the respondent was an occupying Power, expecting Uganda 'to establish (…) that a particular injury alleged by the DRC in Ituri was not caused by Uganda's failure to meet its obligations as an occupying Power.' In his Separate Opinion [6–21], Judge Yusuf criticised this 'radical reversal of the burden of proof' as unprecedented, imbalanced and inconsistent with the nature of the duty of vigilance incumbent upon the occupying Power as an obligation of due diligence, rather than an obligation of result.

[171] *Archer Daniels* [38].

[172] *Swisslion* [345].

[173] On the non-inquisitorial nature of investment arbitration, see A Mourre, 'Arbitration and Criminal Law: Jurisdiction, Arbitrability and Duties of the Arbitral Tribunal' in L Mistelis & S Brekoulakis (eds), *Arbitrability: International and Comparative Perspectives* (Kluwer 2009) 207, 229; T Giovannini, 'Ex Officio Powers to Investigate: When Do Arbitrators Cross the Line?' in D Baizeau & B Ehle (eds), *Stories from the Hearing Room: Experience form Arbitral Practice (Essays in Honour of Michael E Schneider)* (Kluwer 2015) 59, 68; A Redfern & M Hunter, *Law and Practice of International Commercial Arbitration* (Sweet & Maxwell 2004) [3–28].

[174] Ld Neuberger, 'Arbitration and Rule of Law' (Address Before the Chartered Institute of Arbitrators Centenary Celebration, Hong Kong, 20 March 2015) <www.supremecourt.uk/docs/speech-150320.pdf> accessed 1 June 2022.

[175] cf *World Duty Free Company v Republic of Kenya* (Award of 4 October 2006) ICSID Case No Arb/00/7 [181] ('as regards public policy (…) the law protects not the litigating parties but the public; or in this case, the mass of tax-payers and other citizens making up one of the poorest countries in the world').

form of public law adjudication might require tribunals to take a more active role in quantum, inquiring into possible mitigating circumstances for the assessment of compensation. Thus, when faced with a (relatively modest) claim of about USD 22 million against war-torn Zaire, the *AMT* Tribunal took the formal step of appointing a former World Bank official as an independent expert to evaluate damages suffered by the claimant, invoking 'its discretionary and sovereign power to determine the quantum of compensation'.[176] Such recourse to external expertise may provide as a legitimate alternative when the evidence on the record is not sufficient to justify a precise amount of compensation, as shown in the *Armed Activities* case, where the ICJ relied upon the analyses of two Court-appointed for the purposes of determining compensation for the loss of life and natural resource. However, it may also give rise to objections as unfairly interfering with the allocation of the burden of proof and tilting the balance in favour of one Party to the detriment of the other, contrary to the principles of a fair hearing and equality of arms and outsourcing the tribunal's function to the experts.[177]

On the other hand, investment tribunals have lowered the standard of proof invoking equitable considerations as the basic justification. In *Crystallex v Venezuela*, for example, the Tribunal distinguished between the *existence* of damage as a fact that must be proven 'with certainty' and the precise *quantification* of that damage which is not subject to the same degree of certainty, 'because any future damage is inherently difficult to prove.'[178] Similarly, the Tribunal in *Lemire v Ukraine* observed that 'less certainty is required in proof of the actual amount of damages; for this latter determination claimant only needs to provide a basis upon which the tribunal can, with reasonable confidence, estimate the extent of the loss.'[179] In *Impregilo*, the Tribunal also held that it would be unreasonable to require precise proof of the extent of the damage caused. Instead, reasonable probabilities and estimates would suffice as a basis for compensation.[180] The same principle was expressed by the EECC, which applied a differentiated standard of proof between the merits and the reparation phase:

---

[176] The expert evaluated *damnus emergens* at USD 4,452,500, but the Tribunal awarded approximately 9 USD million.
[177] *Armed Activities on the Territory of the Congo (Congo v Uganda)* (Order of 8 September 2020) [2020] ICJ Rep 264, Separate Opinion of Judge Sebutinde, 289–91.
[178] *Crystallex v Venezuela* [867–8]; *Tecmed SA v Mexico* [190].
[179] *Lemire v Ukraine* (Award of 28 March 2011) ICSID Case No ARB/06/18 [246].
[180] *Impregilo v Argentina* (Award of 21 June 2011) ICSID Case No ARB/07/17 [371].

The Commission has required clear and convincing evidence to establish that damage occurred, within the liability parameters of the Partial Awards. However, for purposes of quantification, it has required less rigorous proof. The considerations dictating the 'clear and convincing standard' are much less compelling for the less politically and emotively charged matters involved in assessing the monetary extent of injury.[181]

Again, however, a balance must be struck between competing interests. The function of procedural equity is limited by the requirements of due process from which a tribunal may not detract. As the Iran-US Claims Tribunal recalled in *Amoco*, '[o]ne of the best settled rules of the law on international responsibility of States is that no reparation for speculative or uncertain damage can be awarded.'[182] In the Tribunal's view, international law does not permit the use of a method which yields uncertain figures for the valuation of damages, even if the existence of damages is certain.[183] Thus, investment tribunals have generally rejected possible but contingent and indeterminate damages in the absence of evidence.[184] In *Diallo*, the ICJ also affirmed that, whilst an award of compensation relating to loss of future earnings inevitably involves some uncertainty, 'such a claim cannot be purely speculative'.[185] Nevertheless, as the Tribunal held in *Achmea I*, the requirement of proof must not be impossible to discharge. Nor must the requirement for reasonable precision in the assessment of the quantum be carried so far that the search for exactness in the quantification of losses becomes disproportionately onerous when compared with the margin of error.[186] Indeed, compensation matters are not capable of precise quantification because they depend on the exercise of judgmental factors that are better expressed in approximations or ranges.[187] That is particularly so where the absence of evidence is a result of the behaviour of the author of the damage[188] or results from a failure of the claimant to present its case. These are equitable considerations that require a further analysis, depending on the procedural framework governing the arbitral process.

---

[181] *Eritrea's Damages Claims* [36].
[182] *Amoco International Finance Corp v Iran* [238].
[183] ibid.
[184] *Southern Pacific Properties (Middle East) Limited v Egypt* [189].
[185] *Ahmadou Sadio Diallo* [49].
[186] *Achmea (I) v Slovakia* (Award of 7 December 2012) UNCITRAL, PCA Case No 2008-13 [323].
[187] *Starrett Housing Corporation v Iran* [338-9]; see also *Gold Reserve* [686].
[188] *Rumeli Telekom AS v Kazakhstan* [144-5]; *Sapphire International Petroleums Ltd v NIOC* (Award of 15 March 1963) 35 ILR 136, 187-8.

5 Conclusion

In 1939, Winston Churchill described Russia's foreign policy during World War II as 'a riddle wrapped in a mystery inside an enigma'.[189] There might be no better phrase to describe the use of equitable considerations by investment arbitral tribunals in the process of determining damages for violations of international law. This chapter may have been unable fully to unravel that mystery, but some useful lessons can be drawn. By now, the *Chorzów Factory* standard has been widely recognised as reflecting the customary standard governing reparation, but customary rules do not operate in a legal vacuum. International courts and tribunals have progressively acknowledged the general principle of equity as normative proposition capable of affecting the interpretation of customary norms, including secondary rules governing State responsibility. Even though the ILC avoided to articulate an express rule to that effect, it was well understood that equitable considerations had a role in the determination of compensation either as 'aggravating' or 'mitigating' circumstances.

Yet, *infra legem* equity is not unbound: it is subject to certain limitations that may either be intrinsic to its nature as an interpretative canon, or stemming from the procedural framework governing the function of the tribunal. Within these parameters, equity is not a magic spell that elides rational conceptualisation; to hold otherwise could have serious implications to the interpretative process and undermine the integrity of the procedure itself. And while it may be true that the assessment of damages is not always a precise science,[190] the opposite also holds true: '[e]quitable principles should not be used to make good the shortcomings in a claimant's case by being substituted for evidence which could have been produced if it actually existed: equity is not alchemy.'[191]

---

[189] D Carlton, *Churchill and the Soviet Union* (MUP 2000) 1.
[190] *ADC Affiliate Limited v Hungary* (Award of 2 October 2006) ICSID Case No ARB/03/16 [521].
[191] *Ahmadou Sadio Diallo*, Declaration of Judge Greenwood [5].

9

Conflict of Treaty Norms and Subsequent Agreements in Relation to the Interpretation of Treaties in International Investment Law

ŁUKASZ KUŁAGA

1 Introduction

There are several provisions in the Vienna Convention of the Law of Treaties (VCLT), reflecting customary law. Already in 1969, the VCLT was considered to be a partial codification of customary international law (CIL). Other rules of the VCLT constituted then developed into customary law.[1] Indeed, according to the commentaries to the VCLT the large majority of its provisions currently reflects custom.[2] As international investment law is a branch of international law based primarily on treaties[3] it is not surprising that the provisions of the VCLT and corresponding customary rules have been often interpreted and applied by investment

---

[1] DB Hollis, 'Introduction' in DB Hollis (ed), *The Oxford Guide to Treaties* (2nd edn, OUP 2020) 2; In general this phenomenon was identified by ICJ in North Sea Continental Shelf cases by stating that treaties 'may have an important role to play in recording and defining rules deriving from custom, or indeed in developing them', *North Sea Continental Shelf Cases (Federal Republic of Germany/Netherlands; Federal Republic of Germany/Denmark)* (Judgment) [1969] ICJ Rep 3, 27, 29–30; see also, Conclusion 11 of ILC, 'Draft Conclusions on Identification of Customary International Law, with Commentaries' (30 April–1 June and 2 July–10 August 2018) UN Doc A/73/10, reproduced in [2018/II – Part Two] YBILC 122.

[2] According to the authors of the commentary prepared under edition of Oliver Dörr and Kirsten Schmalenbach at least following provision of the VCLT can be considered as of customary character: Art. 11–18, certain elements of Articles 19–34, certain elements 35, 38, certain elements of Arts 39–41, 43, 46–8, 51–2, 56–63, O Dörr & K Schmalenbach (eds), *Vienna Convention on the Law of Treaties A Commentary* (2nd edn, Springer 2018); a similar position is presented by Mark Villiger: 'Since 1969, States, courts and authors have increasingly relied on the Convention, even before its entry into force, as an authoritative guide to the customary law of treaties. All in all, there is a certain probability that the Convention rules are declaratory', ME Villiger, *Commentary on the 1969 Vienna Convention on the Law of Treaties* (Brill 2009) 27; a similar position can be found in O Corten & P Klein (eds), *The Vienna Conventions on the Law of Treaties: A Commentary* (OUP 2011).

[3] According to UNCTAD there are 2558 international investment agreements in force – UNCTAD, 'World Investment Report 2022' (9 June 2022) UN Doc UNCTAD/WIR/2022, 65;

tribunals. Considering that the total number of investor-State dispute settlement (ISDS) cases had reached 1,190 by the end of 2021,[4] investment arbitration[5] has the potential to significantly influence the interpretation of the law of treaties, both in the rules contained in the VCLT as well as those confirmed by CIL.

The situation of parallel existence between treaty and customary rules demonstrates that it is not only a treaty's rules, but also the customary ones, that in practice can be, and in fact are, interpreted.[6] Furthermore, this scenario in particular proves that the content determination of customary rules can be, and is, accomplished through a different approach than the ascertainment of two classical elements of custom, that is, State practice and *opinio juris*.[7]

This chapter will focus on two issues discussed broadly by investment tribunals: rules on conflicts of treaty norms (Article 30 of the VCLT and corresponding CIL) and rules relating to subsequent agreements in relation to the interpretation of treaties (Article 31(3)(a) of the VCLT and corresponding CIL). Emphasis on these two examples of the interpretation of customary law in investment arbitration seems to be particularly pertinent as, in these two areas, tribunal's decisions seem to diverge from the approach, as reflected in the works of the International Law Commission (ILC), traditionally taken in general international law. Why do investment tribunals deviate from agreed understanding of rules on conflicts of norms? How they define the scope of these rules? And with respect to subsequent agreements, can they influence the CIL concerning the interpretation of treaties which envisage rights for individuals? These issues certainly call for a study on the matter.

The aim of this chapter is not to provide an extensive and exhaustive list of all such cases where the interpretation of the customary rules codified in Articles 30 and 31(3)(a) of the VCLT has occurred but rather to

---

nevertheless, custom remains an important source of international investment law – P Dumberry, *The Formation and Identification of Rules of Customary International Law in International Investment Law* (CUP 2016) 351–68.

[4] UNCTAD (n 3) 73.

[5] By investment arbitration this contribution understands arbitration to be governed under international investment agreements, that is, bilateral investment treaties, investment chapters in Free Trade Areas treaties and other agreement regulating rights both substantive and procedural rights of investors.

[6] P Merkouris, *Article 31(3)(c) VCLT and the Principle of Systemic Integration – Normative Shadows in Plato's Cave* (Brill 2015) 246.

[7] P Merkouris, *Interpretation of Customary International Law: of Methods and Limits* (Brill 2023).

highlight some most interesting examples which demonstrate the general approach of investment tribunals to these norms.

2 Interpreting Rules on Conflicts of Treaty Norms in Investment Arbitration

The issue of resolving conflicts of norms originating from different legal acts is central to every legal order.[8] In international law it is regulated in Article 30 of the VCLT and corresponding CIL. From the perspective of international investment law, the main issue that has arisen in the interpretation of this legal norm relates to the material scope of the entirety of Article 30, ie the reference in the title and paragraph 1 of this provision to treaties 'relating to the same subject matter'.[9]

The jurisprudence of investment arbitral tribunals has mainly referred to Article 30 VCLT in cases concerning the relationship between intra-EU investment treaties, or the intra-EU application of the Energy Charter Treaty[10] in relation to the Treaty on the Functioning of the European Union[11] (TFEU, or its predecessor – the Treaty Establishing the European Community[12]). In the former case, Article 30 of the VCLT was invoked by

---

[8] 'Conflict must be equated with breach. Hence, there is conflict of norms in case one norm breaches, has led or may lead to breach of another norm', J Pauwelyn, *Conflict of Norms in Public International Law: How WTO Law Relates to Other Rules of International Law* (CUP 2003) 489; similarly, see W Jenks, 'Conflict of Law-Making Treaties' (1953) 30 BYBIL 401; It is to be noted that in its report concerning fragmentation ILC proposed also broader definition of this term – ILC, 'Report on Fragmentation of International Law: Difficulties Arising from the Diversification and Expansion of International Law, finalised by Martti Koskenniemi' (13 April 2006) UN Doc A/CN.4/L.682, 24.

[9] Vienna Convention on the Law of Treaties (adopted 23 May 1969, entered into force 27 January 1980) 1155 UNTS 331, Art 30(1).

[10] The Energy Charter Treaty (adopted 17 December 1994, entered into force 16 April 1998) 2080 UNTS 95; this case law, due to the volume limitations of this contribution, will not be analysed here. However, it does not lead to different conclusions from the case law on intra-EU investment treaties. It is worth noting the key decisions in this area *Electrabel v Hungary* (Decision on Jurisdiction and Liability of 30 November 2012) ICSID Case No ARB/07/19 [4.176.]; *Sevilla Beheer & ors v Spain* (Decision on Jurisdiction, Liability and the Principles of Quantum of 11 Feb 2022) ICSID Case No ARB/16/27 [647]; *Masdar Solar v Spain* (Award of 16 May 2018) ICSID Case No ARB/14/1; *Vattenfall AB & ors v Germany* (Decision on the Achmea Issue of 31 August 2018) ICSID Case No ARB/12/12 [194], *Landesbank Baden-Württemberg & ors v Spain* (Decision on the Intra-EU Jurisdictional Objection of 25 February 2019) ICSID Case No ARB/15/45 [178].

[11] Treaty on the Functioning of the European Union (adopted 13 December 2007, entered into force 1 December 2009) [2016] OJ C202/1.

[12] Treaty Establishing the European Community (adopted 25 March 1957, entry into force 1 January 1958) [1997] OJ C340/173.

the respondent, most often a Central-Eastern European State, as an argument emphasising the priority of the EU Treaties – subsequent treaties, over investment treaties – earlier treaties, ie dating back to the 1990s. At times, arbitral tribunals have also commented on the concept of the 'same subject matter' against the background of the applicability of Article 59 VCLT, which is also considered to reflect a customary rule, and then referred their conclusions to the applicability of Article 30 of the VCLT, even if they noticed differences between the purposes of these provisions.[13]

As the ILC indicated in its report on fragmentation, adopting a narrow interpretation of this formulation could result in a number of potential treaty conflicts not being covered at all by this provision.[14] The Commission emphasised that:

> If conflict were to exist only between rules that deal with the "same" subject-matter, then the way a treaty is applied would become crucially dependent on how it would classify under some (presumably) pre-existing classification scheme of different subjects. But there are no such classification schemes.[15]

The ILC, therefore, opted for a flexible approach to the formulation of 'same subject matter'. Support for this position can be found in the Commission's commentary to the 1966 Draft Articles on the Law of Treaties,[16] where the view was expressed that this formulation was intended to broadly cover cases of incompatibility between treaty norms. This issue has rarely been a subject of consideration by international courts and tribunals. Similar reasoning to the position of the ILC can be found in GATT/WTO decisions. In *EC – Imposition of Anti-Dumping Duties on Imports of Cotton Yarn from Brazil* the panel stated that on the basis of analysis of a single of provision of the Multifibre Arrangement (MFA), the Anti-Dumping Agreement and the MFA were treaties 'relating to the same subject-matter'.[17] In the

---

[13] 'While Article 30 is, therefore, focused on particular provisions, the question under Article 59 is whether the entire treaty should be terminated by reason of the adoption of a later treaty relating to the same subject-matter. The very fact that these situations are treated separately in the VCLT points to the need under Article 59 for a broader overlap between the earlier and later treaties than would be needed to trigger the application of Article 30', *Achmea (I) v Slovakia* (Award on Jurisdiction, Arbitrability and Suspension of 26 October 2010) PCA Case No 2008-13 [240].

[14] ILC (n 8) [253].

[15] ibid [22].

[16] ILC, 'Draft Articles on the Law of Treaties with Commentaries' (4 May–19 July 1966) UN Doc A/CN.4/191, reproduced in [1966/II] YBILC 187, 214.

[17] WTO, *European Communities – Imposition of Anti-Dumping Duties on Imports of Cotton Yarn from Brazil – Report of the Panel* (4 July 1995) ADP/137 [540].

China – Measures Related to the Exportation of Rare Earths, Tungsten, and Molybdenum the Appellate Body acknowledged that all multilateral trade agreements annexed to the Marrakesh Agreement relate to the same subject matter without detailed examination.[18]

Arbitration decisions, however, have adopted a narrower understanding of Article 30 VCLT and, consequently, of the customary norm that this provision codifies. As was stated by the *Eastern Sugar* Tribunal, '[w]hile it is true that European Union law deals with intra-EU cross border investment, say between the Netherlands and the Czech Republic, as does the BIT, the two regulations do not cover the same precise subject-matter'.[19] The Tribunal underlined *inter alia* the existence of fair and equitable standard,[20] as well as the possibility for an investor to sue the host-State directly, as grounds to reject the 'equivalence argument'.[21] This approach has been upheld in many subsequent arbitration awards relating to intra-EU bilateral investment treaties (BITs).[22] In *EURAM*, the Tribunal rejected the interpretation that the 'same subject matter' can be

---

[18] WTO, *China – Measures Related to the Exportation of Rare Earths, Tungsten, and Molybdenum*, AB-2014-3, AB-2014-5, AB-2014-6 – Reports of the Appellate Body (7 August 2014) WT/DS431/AB/R, WT/DS432/AB/R, WT/DS433/AB/R [5.53].

[19] *Eastern Sugar BV (Netherlands) v Czech Republic* (Partial Award of 27 March 2007) SCC Case No 88/2004 [160].

[20] ibid [164].

[21] ibid [180]; this argumentation related to lack of 'access to an international and neutral dispute resolution forum in the form of international arbitration' was emphasised, ie by tribunals in *JSW Solar & Wirtgen v Czech Republic* (Final Award of 11 October 2017) PCA Case No 2014-03 [253]; *Anglia v Czech Republic* (Final Award of 10 March 2017) SCC Case No 2014/181 [116]; *Busta v Czech Republic* (Final Award of 10 March 2017) SCC Case No 2015/01 [116]; *Strabag & ors v Poland* (Partial Award on Jurisdiction 4 March 2020) ICSID Case No ADHOC/15/1 [8.138].

[22] *Binder v Czech Republic* (Award on Jurisdiction of 6 June 2007) UNCITRAL [63-5]; *Oostergetel v Slovakia* (Decision on Jurisdiction 30 April 2010) UNCITRAL [72-9, 86-7, 104]; *Achmea (I)* [239-42, 245-63, 273-7]; *European American Investment Bank AG (Austria) v Slovakia* (Award on Jurisdiction of 22 October 2012) UNCITRAL, PCA Case No 2010-17 [155-85, 213-34, 268-78]; *A11Y v Czech Republic* (Decision on Jurisdiction 9 February 2017) ICSID Case No UNCT/15/1 [177]; *Anglia v Czech Republic* [113-16 & 126]; *Busta v Czech Republic* [113-16 & 126]; *JSW Solar & Wirtgen* [241, 259-61]; *GPF GP Sàrl v Poland* (Award on Jurisdiction (Not Public) of 15 February 2017) SCC Case No V 2014/168 – see P Treder & W Sadowski, 'Poland', in C Nagy (ed), *Investment Arbitration In Central And Eastern Europe* (Elgar 2019) 283-367; *Marfin v Cyprus* (Award of 26 July 2018) ICSID Case No ARB/13/27 [584-91]; *United Utilities (Tallinn) v Estonia* (Award of 21 June 2019) ICSID Case No ARB/14/24 [545-59]; *Juvel & Bithell v Poland* (Partial Final Award 26 February 2019) ICC Case No 19459/MHM [368-89]; *Magyar Farming v Hungary* (Award of 13 November 2019) ICSID Case No ARB/17/27; *Strabag* [8.129-139]; *Muszynianka v Slovakia* (Award 7 of October 2020) PCA Case No 2017-08 [231-8].

equated to being applicable to 'the same facts', or having 'the same goal'.[23] The decision then subsequently elaborated that '[t]he subject matter of a treaty, in the Tribunal's understanding, therefore differs both from the concrete situations in which it will be applicable and from its goal'.[24] For this Tribunal, the crucial argument was that prior to the Lisbon Treaty the EU had no competence in relation to direct investment.[25] A narrow interpretation was also presented by the *Strabag* Tribunal which 'under[stood] the precondition of "same subject matter" as requiring the subject matters of the two treaties in question to be "identical"'.[26] Again, a similar position was expressed by the *Juvel* Tribunal: '[t]wo different treaties may apply simultaneously to the same set of facts without them having the same subject-matter. Further, if two treaties have the same goal but approach the achievement of that goal from two different perspectives, the treaties do not have the same subject-matter'.[27] The negative position of these tribunals, towards the applicability of the conflict of norms provisions, was primarily related to the far-reaching consequences that States could derive from the arguments in this regard, ie lack of jurisdiction of those tribunals to examine the case.[28]

It is significant that in most of the aforementioned decisions, the arbitral tribunals did *de facto* interpret CIL, as the VCLT was inapplicable. In the overwhelming majority of these cases, tribunals seemed to be unaware of this legal situation, as evidenced by the awards, which clearly indicate that they were applying the VCLT. This issue typically did not explicitly appear in the proceedings, as usually both the respondents and claimants seemed to also presume that the VCLT did apply after all.[29] This was the

---

[23] *European American Investment Bank AG (Austria)* [168].
[24] ibid [171].
[25] ibid [183]. A similar position was presented by Austria in an amicus curiae: 'the EU treaties and the BIT "have different objectives and a different content" with the former aiming at establishing a monetary and economic union in the wider context of a political union, while the latter is a specific treaty aiming solely at the promotion and protection of investments' [125].
[26] *Strabag* [8.135].
[27] *Juvel* [380].
[28] 'More importantly, it is difficult to see how Article 30 could deprive the Tribunal of jurisdiction based upon the Parties' consent derived from Article 8 of the BIT (whether operating the first stage, second stage or both), even if there may be circumstances in which a true incompatibility between the BIT and EU law arises. Any such incompatibility would be a question of the effect of EU law as part of the applicable law and, as such, a matter for the merits and not jurisdiction', *Achmea (I)* [272].
[29] 'Respondent has been a State Party to the VCLT since 28 May 1993; and the Netherlands since 9 April 1985. While the VCLT does not apply retrospectively, it is widely regarded as

case in disputes against Slovakia or the Czech Republic brought on the basis of 1990 BIT with the UK[30] (*A11Y, Anglia, Busta*), the 1990 BIT with Germany[31] (*Binder, JSW Solar*), or the 1992 BIT with the Netherlands[32] (*Eastern Sugar, Oostergetel, Achmea*), as the Czech and Slovak Republics were only bound by the VCLT in 1993. The same issue related to the disputes against Poland (which acceded to the VCLT in 1990) on the basis of the 1988 BIT with Austria[33] (*Strabag*) and 1987 BIT with Belgium and Luxembourg[34] (*GPF*[35]).

Conversely, the only cognizant approach in this respect in the cases involving intra-EU BITs was applied by the tribunal in *EURAM* on the basis of the 1990 Czechoslovakia-Austria BIT.[36] Considering the argument of Slovakia that the VCLT was not applicable and that only the corresponding CIL, with respect to Articles 30 and 59 VCLT (but not Article 65), being applicable, the Tribunal referred to the exchange of diplomatic notes between the States concerned confirming the succession of the BIT in 1994. This assertion allowed it to recognise that the BIT was concluded in 1994.[37] It is to be noted that the approach formulated by the tribunals on the same subject matter issue, where they decide incognizantly on the

---

reflecting customary international law. Respondent has argued on the basis of the provisions of the VCLT, and neither Party has suggested that the rules set out in the provisions which it discusses are not applicable to the BIT', *Achmea (I)* [231].

[30] Agreement between the Government of the United Kingdom of Great Britain and Northern Ireland and the Government of the Czech and Slovak Federal Republic for the Promotion and Protection of Investments (UK & Czech Republic) (adopted 10 July 1990, entered into force 26 October 1992).

[31] Treaty between the Federal Republic of Germany and the Czech and Slovak Federal Republic Concerning the Promotion and Reciprocal Protection of Investments (Germany & Czech Republic) (adopted 2 October 1990, entered into force 2 August 1992).

[32] Agreement on Encouragement and Reciprocal Protection of Investments between the Kingdom of the Netherlands and the Czech and Slovak Federal Republic (Netherlands & Czech Republic) (adopted 29 April 1991, entered into force 1 October 1992).

[33] Agreement between the Polish People's Republic and Republic of Austria on Promotion and Protection of Investments (Austria & Poland) (adopted 24 November 1988, entered into force 1 November 1989, terminated 16 October 2019).

[34] Agreement between the Government of the United Kingdom of Great Britain and Northern Ireland and the Government of the Polish People's Republic for the Promotion and Reciprocal Protection of Investments (UK & Poland) (adopted 8 December 1987, entered into force 14 April 1988).

[35] *GPF GP Sàrl v Poland* (Final Award of 29 April 2020) SCC Case No 2014/168.

[36] Agreement between the Republic of Austria and the Czech and Slovak Federal Republic on the Promotion and Protection of Investments (Austria & Czech Republic) (adopted 15 October 1990, entered into force 1 October 1991).

[37] *European American Investment Bank AG (Austria)* [77–81]. The Tribunal also confirmed the customary character of the VCLT's provisions [316].

basis of CIL (such as *Eastern Sugar, Oostergetel, Binder,* or *Achmea (I)*), has been recognised and followed by arbitral tribunals directly adjudicating under the VCLT.[38]

When reaching the conclusion that the conflict of norms provisions do not apply as prerequisite of 'the same subject matter' is not fulfilled – arbitral tribunals most often did not offer any suggestions on how to solve the problem of a conflict of such norms. Initially, this approach was a consequence of not perceiving existence of such a conflict at all. Tribunals have also continued to maintain such a position after the judgment of the Court of Justice of the European Union (CJEU) in the *Achmea* case, despite the fact that the CJEU unequivocally confirmed the existence of such a conflict.[39] Regardless, it is noticeable that since this judgment, arguments concerning the different material scope of the treaties has been increasingly and more clearly evoked by tribunals.[40] Significantly, arbitral tribunals have pointed to the lack of ISDS in the EU Treaties as the main argument for the difference, while the CJEU explicitly stated that ISDS is contrary to the EU Treaties. A culmination of this legal reasoning was the 2019 ruling in *Magyar Farming Company v Hungary* in which the Tribunal, while noting that Article 30 VCLT was inapplicable due to the treaties' differing subject matter,[41] determined:

> [The] [t]ribunal is not aware of the existence of, provisions in the VCLT or of norms of customary international law that would govern the resolution of possible conflicts between successive treaties that do not share the same subject matter.[42]

In conclusion, the case law of arbitral tribunals makes it necessary to analyse Article 30 VCLT's 'same subject matter' formulae in more detail. As it turns out, an element of this provision, overlooked even in the commentaries to the Convention,[43] may be a key argument for rejecting application of this rule. This position, if comprehensively applied, could prevent

---

[38] See, for example, *Muszynianka v Slovakia*.
[39] Case C-284/16, Slowakische Republik *v* Achmea BV, Judgment of the Court (Grand Chamber) of 6 March 2018, EU:C:2018:158.
[40] *Marfin v Cyprus* [587–8, 595]; *United Utilities (Tallinn) v Estonia* [545–59]; *Strabag* [8.139].
[41] In this respect the approach was taken that Article 30 of the VCLT could be applied with respect to relation between BIT concerned and the treaty which would cover all provision of the BIT in similar fashion, see the logic presented in *Magyar Farming v Hungary* [232].
[42] *Magyar Farming v Hungary* [237]. Similarly, in *Muszynianka v Slovakia* [237]: 'The Parties have not invoked any principle or customary norm of international law that would govern a possible conflict between treaties that do not share the same subject matter'.
[43] Villiger (n 2).

any practical application of Article 30 VCLT and its corresponding CIL. Thus, from a systemic perspective, this line of interpretation should not be upheld,[44] as it is difficult to assert that this potential interpretation of CIL presented by the arbitral tribunal would be followed by States or other international court and tribunals. The fact that approach of investment arbitration was clearly linked with the defense of its own jurisdiction by the tribunals has created circular or, perhaps, opportunistic lines of argumentation. This position, however, has been poorly embedded in general international law, which leads to a conclusion that its significance outside the framework of international investment law is limited. An alternative position would be recognising that this line of interpretation has led to significant gaps in conflict of rules under general international law.[45]

3 Subsequent Agreements in Relation to the Interpretation of Treaties

The second point under scrutiny concerns the subsequent agreements in relation to the interpretation of treaties regulated by Articles 31 (3)(a) VCLT. This issue was recently elaborated by the ILC in its 2018 Draft Conclusions on Subsequent Agreements and Subsequent Practice in Relation to the Interpretation of Treaties.[46] Articles 31(3)(a) VCLT provide:

> 3 There shall be taken into account, together with the context:
> (a) any subsequent agreement between the parties regarding the interpretation of the treaty or the application of its provisions.[47]

---

[44] EW Vierdag, 'The Time of the 'Conclusion' of a Multilateral Treaty: Article 30 of the Vienna Convention on the Law of Treaties and Related Provisions' (1988) 59 BYBIL 100; AA Ghouri, *Conflict of Treaties in Investment Arbitration* (Kluwer 2015) 166; ILC (n 8) 23, see also 117 & 254.

[45] Compare with '[i]t is doubtful, however, whether a narrow construction of the scope of article 30 is all that plausible to begin with. Such a conception finds no support in the drafting history of article 30 and, moreover, makes fairly little sense in any case. Surely, the drafters could not have intended to leave the important category of overlapping commitments in treaties relating to different subject matters completely out of the scope of the Vienna Convention, and merely to satisfy themselves with an article that would not even aspire to help resolve conflicts between overlapping commitments', J Klabbers, *Treaty Conflict and the European Union* (CUP 2010) 93.

[46] ILC, 'Draft Conclusions on Subsequent Agreements and Subsequent Practice in Relation to the Interpretation of Treaties, with Commentaries' (30 April–1 June and 2 July–10 August 2018) UN Doc A/73/10.

[47] See ibid, Conclusion 4, which defines subsequent agreement and subsequent practice: '1. A subsequent agreement as an authentic means of interpretation under article 31, paragraph 3 (a), is an agreement between the parties, reached after the conclusion of a treaty, regarding the interpretation of the treaty or the application of its provisions'.

As has been stated by the ILC,[48] and previously by international courts,[49] tribunals,[50] and investment tribunals,[51] the abovementioned rules also apply under customary law. Thus, these norms regarding interpretation could also be the object of interpretation as customary rules.[52] Such an approach has been applied by the WTO, where Article 31(3)(c) VCLT was considered to be custom in the *Measures Affecting the Production and Sale of Clove Cigarettes* case.[53] Concerning the most-favoured nation (MFN) clause, the whole of Article 31 VLCT as a customary rule has also been scrutinised in investment arbitration jurisprudence.[54]

Already in 1966, the ILC had confirmed that the joint intention of parties, which underpins the conclusion of a treaty, has a particular authority when identifying the meaning of that treaty, even after its conclusion.[55] This was in line with the ICJ's jurisprudence.[56] Regarding the legal effects

---

[48] ILC (n 46) Conclusion 2.

[49] See, for example, *Pulp Mills on the River Uruguay (Argentina v Uruguay)* (Judgment) [2010] ICJ Rep 14 [65]; *Dispute Regarding Navigational and Related Rights (Costa Rica v Nicaragua)* (Judgment) [2009] ICJ Rep 213 [47]; *Application of the Convention on the Prevention and Punishment of the Crime of Genocide (Bosnia and Herzegovina v Serbia and Montenegro)* (Judgment) [2007] ICJ Rep 43 [160].

[50] *Responsibilities and Obligations of States Sponsoring Persons and Entities with Respect to Activities in the Area* (Advisory Opinion of 1 February 2011) 2011 ITLOS Rep 10 [57]; *Award in Arbitration Regarding the Iron Rhine Railway Between the Kingdom of Belgium and the Kingdom of the Netherlands* (Decision of 24 May 2005) XXVII UNRIAA 35, 45.

[51] *National Grid plc v Argentina* (Decision on Jurisdiction of 20 June 2006) UNCITRAL [51]; *Canfor Corporation v USA* and *Tembec et al v USA* and *Terminal Forest Products Ltd v USA* (Order of the Consolidation Tribunal of 7 September 2005) UNCITRAL [59]; *Renco (I) v Peru* (Partial Award on Jurisdiction of 15 July 2016) ICSID Case No UNCT/13/1 [69]; *Venezuela US v Venezuela* (Interim Award on Jurisdiction of 26 July 2016) PCA Case No 2013-34 [49]; *Saluka Investments BV v Czech Republic* (Partial Award of 17 March 2006) UNCITRAL [296].

[52] P Merkouris, 'Interpreting the Customary Rules on Interpretation' (2017) 19 ICLR 154-5.

[53] WTO, *United States – Measures Affecting the Production and Sale of Clove Cigarettes – Report of the Appellate Body* (4 April 2012) WT/DS406/AB/R [267]; similar approach with respect to Art 31(3)(c) was applied in WTO, *European Communities – Measures Affecting the Approval and Marketing of Biotech Products – Report of the Panel* (21 November 2006) WT/DS291R, WT/DS292R & WT/DS293R [7.68-7.72].

[54] N Piracha, *Toward Uniformly Accepted Principles for Interpreting MFN Clauses: Striking a Balance Between Sovereignty and the Protection of Investors* (Kluwer 2021) 183-255.

[55] ILC (n 16) 221-2; a similar position was taken by the ILC in its work on reservations: 'The interpretation resulting from an interpretative declaration made in respect of a bilateral treaty by a State or an international organization party to the treaty and accepted by the other party constitutes an authentic interpretation of that treaty', ILC, 'Guide to Practice on Reservations to Treaties' (26 April-3 June and 4 July-12 August 2011) UN Doc A/66/10, reproduced in [2011/II] YBILC 26 [1.6.3].

[56] *Ambatielos (Greece v UK)* (Preliminary Objection) [1952] ICJ Rep 28 [43 & 75].

of subsequent agreements, it is worth noting, first of all, Conclusion 7(1) adopted by the ILC, which states that

> Subsequent agreements and subsequent practice under article 31, paragraph 3, contribute, in their interaction with other means of interpretation, to the clarification of the meaning of a treaty. This may result in narrowing, widening, or otherwise determining the range of possible interpretations, including any scope for the exercise of discretion which the treaty accords to the parties.[57]

In the commentary to this provision, the Commission recognised, *inter alia*, the possibility for the parties to depart, by a subsequent agreement, from the ordinary meaning of the words of a treaty and to give them special meaning within the context of Article 31(4) VCLT. A departure from the ordinary meaning of words may be particularly justified if it is considered that the parties, in concluding the treaty, intentionally wished to give them an evolving meaning or content, by using general expressions, to take account of developments in international law.[58]

The ILC's interpretation of Article 31(3)(a)-(b) VCLT can be compared to the position of arbitral tribunals on declarations or joint interpretations formulated by the parties to the treaty. One of the most famous examples of a subsequent agreement in international investment law is the interpretative note by the North American Free Trade Agreement (NAFTA) Commission,[59] which narrowed the scope of Article 1105 NAFTA. In particular, the arbitral tribunal in *Pope & Talbot* v *Canada* stated that 'were the Tribunal required to make a determination whether the Commission's action is an interpretation or an amendment, it would choose the latter'.[60] However, the tribunal found that this issue was not relevant as, regardless of the legal qualification of the note, its previous decision was consistent with it.[61] In the *Methanex* case, by contrast, the arbitral tribunal cited Oppenheim's position according to which

---

[57] ILC (n 46) Conclusion 7(1).
[58] *Dispute regarding Navigational and Related Rights* [64].
[59] NAFTA Free Trade Commission, 'Notes of Interpretation of Certain Chapter 11 Provisions' (*NAFTA FTC*, 31 July 2001) <https://2009-2017.state.gov/documents/organization/38790.pdf> accessed 30 July 2022.
[60] *Pope & Talbot Inc v Canada* (Award in Respect of Damages of 31 May 2002) UNCITRAL [47].
[61] ibid [56–64]. Other tribunals considered to be bound by the interpretative note: *ADF Group Inc v USA* (Award 9 January 2003) ICSID Case No ARB(AF)/00/1 [177]; *Waste Management v Mexico (Number 2)* (Award of 30 April 2004) ICSID Case No ARB(AF)/00/3 [91–3]; *Glamis Gold, Ltd v USA* (Award 8 June 2009) UNCITRAL [559].

authentic interpretation of the parties to the treaty 'overrides the ordinary principles of interpretation'.[62]

Besides the NAFTA Tribunal's approach, which was based on an explicit clause in NAFTA, the issue of joint interpretation as a subsequent agreement has featured significantly in disputes concerning intra-EU BITs and intra-EU applications of the ECT.[63] What is striking in the practice of tribunals in intra-EU disputes is that the readiness to accept any significance of such an interpretation is very limited, which differs from the position of the NAFTA tribunals. In the fundamental *Eskosol decision*, the Tribunal evaluated whether the *Declaration of the Governments of the Member States on the Legal Consequences of the Judgment of the Court of Justice in Achmea and on Investment Protection in the European Union of 22 EU-Member States* (EU Declaration)[64] was a subsequent agreement under Article 31(3)(a) VCLT.[65]

The Tribunal criticised the lack of detailed justification in the EU Declaration, although it did not explain its source for such a requirement.[66] It referred to the ILC's works, although, surprisingly, not to those related to subsequent agreements, but instead its work related to reservations.[67] Consequently, the Tribunal decided that the EU Declaration cannot be considered as a subsequent agreement as it does not refer to any particular provision of the ECT.[68] Following the judgment of Singapore

---

[62] *Methanex v USA* (Final Award of the Tribunal on Jurisdiction and Merits of 3 August 2005) UNCITRAL [23], citing R Jennings & A Watts (eds), *Oppenheim's International Law*, Vol 1 (9th edn, OUP 2008) 630.

[63] However, there were also other cases related to this issue – see, for example, *Canadian Cattlemen v USA* (Award on Jurisdiction of 28 January 2008) UNCITRAL [186–9]; *El Paso Energy International Company v Argentina* (Award of 31 October 2011) ICSID Case No ARB/03/15 [601–2]; *Telefónica SA v Argentina* (Decision of the Tribunal on Objections to Jurisdiction of 25 May 2006) ICSID Case No ARB/03/20 [111]; see also jurisprudence cited by K Magraw, 'Investor-State Disputes and the Rise of Recourse to State Party Pleadings As Subsequent Agreements or Subsequent Practice under the Vienna Convention on the Law of Treaties' (2015) 30 ICSID Rev 142, 161–6.

[64] EU Member States, 'Declaration of the Governments of the Member States on the Legal Consequences of the Judgment of the Court of Justice in Achmea and on Investment Protection in the European Union of 22 EU-Member States' (*European Commission*, 15 January 2019) <https://ec.europa.eu/info/publications/190117-bilateral-investment-treaties_en> accessed 30 July 2022; Ł Kułaga, 'Implementing Achmea: The Quest for Fundamental Change in International Investment Law' (2019) 39 Polish YBInt'l Law 227, 227–50.

[65] *Eskosol v Italy* (Decision on Termination Request and Intra-EU Objection of 7 May 2019) ICSID Case No ARB/15/50.

[66] ibid [215–6].

[67] ibid [220 & 224].

[68] ibid [222].

Court of Appeal in the *Sanum* case,[69] the *Eskosol* Tribunal cited an excerpt from the 1966 Commentary of the Draft Articles on the Law of Treaties to assert that subsequent agreements are only intended to clarify the findings of the treaty negotiations.[70] This element requires closer inspection as it has been repeated on several occasions by arbitral tribunals interpreting Article 31(3)(a) VCLT.[71]

As a matter of fact, a broader citation of the ILC's commentary in this respect does not in any way prejudge the accuracy of this position but rather (contrary to the conclusions drawn by the arbitral tribunals) emphasises in particular the significant nature of the subsequent agreements.[72] Furthermore, it is worth noting another extract from this decision: 'VCLT Article 31(3)(a) is not, however, a trump card to allow States to offer new interpretations of old treaty language, simply to override unpopular treaty interpretations based on the plain meaning of the terms actually used'.[73] This interpretation was subsequently cited by arbitral tribunals as rationale of their position in this respect, even when evaluating different legal situations.[74] Thus, in the view of the Tribunal in *Eskosol*, a subsequent agreement 'may "corroborate" or "support an interpretation that has already been determined by other methods," such as "the objective elements listed in articles 31 and 32 of the Vienna Convention,"

---

[69] *Sanum Investments (I) v Laos* (Judgment of the Court of Appeal of Singapore of 29 September 2016) PCA Case No. 2013-13, [2016] SGCA 57 [77].

[70] 'As the ILC's 1966 Commentaries on the Draft VCLT Articles discuss regarding this provision, "[a] question of fact may sometimes arise as to whether an understanding reached during the negotiations concerning the meaning of a provision was or was not intended to constitute an agreed basis for its interpretation"', *Eskosol v Italy* [222].

[71] Similarly, *Muszynianka v Slovakia* [203]; *Addiko Bank v Croatia* (Decision on Croatia's Jurisdictional Objection Related to the Alleged Incompatibility of the BIT with the EU Acquis of 12 June 2020) ICSID Case No ARB/17/37 [289]; *GPF GP Sàrl v Poland* (Final Award) [352].

[72] 'A question of fact may sometimes arise as to whether an understanding reached during the negotiations concerning the meaning of a provision was or was not intended to constitute an agreed basis for its interpretation [134] But it is well settled that when an agreement as to the interpretation of a provision is established as having been reached before or at the time of the conclusion of the treaty, it is to be regarded as forming part of the treaty. Thus, in the Ambatielos case the Court said: "…the provisions of the Declaration are in the nature of an interpretation clause; and, as such, should be regarded as an integral part of the Treaty…". Similarly, an agreement as to the interpretation of a provision reached after the conclusion of the treaty represents an authentic interpretation by the parties which must be read into the treaty for purposes of its interpretation' ILC (n 16) 221.

[73] *Eskosol v Italy* [223].

[74] *Muszynianka v Slovakia* [223].

but it cannot override the application of those elements'.[75] Finally, when the rights of individuals are impacted purportedly on the basis of general principles of law or CIL, the *Eskosol* decision supports the need for limitations upon the interpretative influence of subsequent agreements.[76] This position had already been presented by the *Enron* tribunal; according to which, no new interpretation of an International Investment Agreement (IIA) can 'affect rights acquired under the Treaty by investors or other beneficiaries'.[77]

Following the *Eskosol* decision, this restrained approach to subsequent agreements concerning the EU question (or so-called intra-EU objection) has been presented by other tribunals. According to the *Addiko Bank* Tribunal, EU member States do not have the right to interpret the TFEU, as this competence has been entrusted exclusively to the Court of Justice of the EU.[78] The *Strabag* Tribunal stated that '[f]rom the text of Article 31(3) VCLT, it is evident that such "extrinsic" elements, while informative to the context of a treaty, cannot be used to rewrite the ordinary meaning of the text of the treaty under interpretation'.[79]

In *Muszynianka*, subsequent agreements relating to interpretation, although recognised as CIL,[80] were considered as 'merely one element' that '[is] not an exclusive and dispositive method of treaty interpretation'.[81] Thus, the influence of subsequent agreements upon interpretation could be ruled out when, in the opinion of tribunal, it explicitly flows from the ordinary meaning.[82] The *Muszynianka* decision is extraordinary in this context as it totally ignored the bilateral declaration of the BIT's State Parties, which the Tribunal justified by the fact the declaration was linked to the EU Declaration. Analysis of the latter was sufficient according to the tribunal.[83]

---

[75] *Eskosol v Italy* [224]; similarly, *GPF GP Sàrl v Poland* [354].
[76] '[I]t would be inconsistent with general notions of acquired rights under international law to permit States effectively to non-suit an investor part-way through a pending case, simply by issuing a joint document purporting to interpret longstanding treaty text so as to undermine the tribunal's jurisdiction to proceed', *Eskosol v Italy* [226]; similarly, *Addiko Bank v Croatia* [290].
[77] *Enron v Argentina* (Award of 22 May 2007) ICSID Case No ARB/01/3 [33]; similarly, *Sempra Energy v Argentina* (Award of 28 September 2007) ICSID Case No ARB/02/16 [385–6]. See also, Opinion 1/17 *Accord ECG UE-Canada* [2019] ECLI:EU:C:2019:341 [236]; *Sanum (I) v Laos* [116].
[78] *Addiko Bank v Croatia* [286].
[79] *Strabag* [8.125].
[80] *Muszynianka v Slovakia* [225].
[81] ibid [222].
[82] ibid [223].
[83] *Muszynianka v Slovakia* [225].

With regard to the relationship between the rights of individuals and interpretation on the basis of Articles 31 (3)(a) VCLT, the Tribunal in *Green Power* noted that the competence of States in this respect can induce inequality between parties of an arbitral proceeding, as one of them could change – with retroactive effect – the text of the ECT. Nevertheless, in this monumental decision, the Tribunal acknowledged that no such situation arises with respect to the EU Declaration in the context of the relationship between ECT and the EU law.[84] Thus, what was crucial for the *Green Power* Tribunal was the interpretations made by the respondent and the investor's home-State, and not that this interpretation was not confirmed by all the parties of both applicable multilateral treaties.[85] Furthermore, the Tribunal, on one hand, seemed to support the position that subsequent agreements could not be applied retroactively if they related to the rights of individuals, but, on the other hand, stated that 'Spain's offer to arbitrate under the ECT is not applicable in intra-EU relations' without indicating any concrete moment in time when this offer's non-applicability took effect.[86]

As in the case of Article 30 VCLT – investment arbitration, in several cases, has interpreted Articles 31 (3)(a) VCLT and its customary counterpart. At least in one case (*Strabag*), only CIL was the subject of interpretation, as the VCLT was not applicable in the case. In this context it is to be noted that investment arbitration informs possible interpretations of Articles 31 (3)(a) in at least two areas – retroactive application and, connected with it, the impact on the rights of individuals.[87] Thus, although

---

[84] *Green Power Partners & SCE Solar v Spain* (Award of 16 June 2022) SCC Case No V2016/13 [380].

[85] 'Yet, being non-binding instruments and not reflecting a consensus of all EU Member States – let alone, and more importantly, all ECT Contracting Parties – the EU Member States Declarations cannot change the clear terms of the ECT or guide the Tribunal in seeking a harmonious interpretation', *RENERGY v Spain* (Award of 6 May 2022) ICSID Case No ARB/14/18 [371]; similarly, *Sevilla Beheer & ors v Spain* [670].

[86] *Green Power Partners & SCE Solar v Spain* [445 & 461] – compare '[w]ith a view to the arguments of amendment, suspension, or regarding the alleged effects of the EU Member States Declarations, the Tribunal further adds and recalls that even if suspension or amendment was the argued effect of either the EU Member States Declarations or the Achmea and Komstroy Judgments, any such effect would come too late in this case to affect or invalidate the consent perfected by the Parties at the relevant time, ie the date of the Request', *RENERGY v Spain* [348].

[87] G Zarra, 'Uses and Abuses of Authentic Interpretations of International Investment Agreements: Reflections on the Role of Arbitral Tribunals as Masters of the Judicial Function' (*EJIL:Talk!*, 28 August 2020) <www.ejiltalk.org/uses-and-abuses-of-authentic-interpretations-of-international-investment-agreements-reflections-on-the-role-of-arbitral-tribunals-as-masters-of-the-judicial-function/> accessed 4 July 2022.

'the parties to a treaty own the treaty and can interpret it',[88] their freedom in respect to international investment law is met with significant scrutiny and reticence from the arbitral tribunals. In fact: '[t]he only situations in which tribunals have been bound to follow the interpretive directions of the state parties are where the relevant treaty goes beyond the general VCLT rules and specifically provides for joint interpretations to be binding'.[89]

Such an approach tends to look at IIAs not only as a transaction between the parties,[90] which have full discretion as to how to apply the mutually agreed upon provisions, but as an agreement which relates also to other beneficiaries. As Anthea Roberts puts it:

> Instead of privileging the rights and powers of states and state-to-state tribunals (as in the first era) or investors and investor-state tribunals (as in the second era), we should move into a third era based on the ideas that investment treaty rights are granted to investors and home states on an interdependent basis.[91]

The problem with this line of reasoning is twofold. First, under international law, the State parties have the principal competence in the interpretation of treaties. This is not in any way changed by the fact that the interpretation can have a positive influence on their position in a dispute. It is still 'their' treaty.[92] Second, certainly, there is an accepted domestic practice of retroactive change in the interpretation of statutes[93]

---

[88] J Crawford, 'A Consensualist Interpretation of Article 31(3) of the Vienna Convention on the Law of Treaties' in G Nolte (ed), *Treaties and Subsequent Practice* (OUP 2013) 31; A Kulick (ed), *Reassertion of Control over the Investment Treaty Regime* (CUP 2017) 15 & 18–20.

[89] KN Gore & E Shirlow (eds), *The Vienna Convention on the Law of Treaties in Investor-State Disputes: History, Evolution, and Future* (Kluwer 2022) 26; see also, L Marotti, 'The Proliferation of Joint Interpretation Clauses in New International Investment Agreements: A Mixed Blessing?' (2020) 35 ICSID Rev 63, 63–81; Ł Kułaga, 'Interpretative Declarations as an Instrument of Transformation of International Investment Law: Measures for Restraining Judicial Activism' (author's translation) (2019) 81(3) Ruch Prawniczy, Ekonomiczny I Socjologiczny 53, 53–69.

[90] For such an approach see Opinion 1/17, Opinion of Advocate General Bot delivered on 29 January 2019 [107].

[91] A Roberts, 'State-to-State Investment Treaty Arbitration: A Hybrid Theory of Interdependent Rights and Shared Interpretive Authority' (2014) 55(1) HarvILJ 69.

[92] 'If the Contracting Parties interpret their BITs in one manner or another, this interpretation applies to the investors of both Parties', *Adamakopoulos & ors v Cyprus* (Statement of Dissent of Professor Marcelo Kohen of 3 February 2020) ICSID Case No ARB/15/49 [59].

[93] A van Aaken, 'Control Mechanisms in International Investment Law', in Z Douglas, J Pauwelyn & JE Viñuales (eds), *The Foundations of International Investment Law – Bringing Theory into Practice* (OUP 2014) 435.

or retroactive application of new precedents. The latter point has been evaluated by domestic constitutional and international courts and was, in principle, not found as violating the rule of law.[94] Thus, domestic law does not have to justify its departure from the VCLT or customary law rules on interpretation. The powers of State parties to interpret 'their' treaties is well-represented in the China–Australia Free Trade Agreement (ChAFTA)[95] which allows parties, in certain situations, to agree on whether the case pending before arbitral tribunal can be adjudicated due to the treaty constraints in this respect.[96] As a result, there is an evident tension between the right of State parties regarding treaty interpretation under general international law and the emerging tendency for this competence to be limited with respect to rights of investors.

4 Conclusions

The two mentioned rules, on the conflict of norms and the influence of subsequent agreements regarding the interpretation of treaties, exemplify that investment arbitration can not only impact the interpretation of

---

[94] 'Prospective overruling is not yet a principle known in English law', *Hindcastle Ltd v Barbara Attenborough Associates Ltd* [1996] UKHL 19; Case C-292/04 *Wienand Meilicke, Heidi Christa Weyde, Marina Stöffler v Finanzamt Bonn-Innenstadt* [2007] ECLI:EU:C:2007:132.

[95] China–Australia Free Trade Agreement (ChAFTA) (China & Australia) (adopted 24 October 2003, entered into force 20 December 2015).

[96] A Roberts & R Braddock, 'Protecting Public Welfare Regulation Through Joint Treaty Party Control: A ChAFTA Innovation' (*EJIL:Talk!*, 21 June 2016) <www.ejiltalk.org/protecting-public-welfare-regulation-through-joint-treaty-party-control-a-chafta-innovation/> accessed 30 July 2022; a similar solution, although not decisive for the tribunal, can be found in the Agreement Establishing the ASEAN–Australia–New Zealand Free Trade Area (adopted 27 February 2009, entered into force 10 January 2010) 2672 UNTS 3, ch 11, Art 25(6), which provides: 'Where an investor claims that the disputing Party has breached Article 9 (Expropriation and Compensation) by the adoption or enforcement of a taxation measure, the disputing Party and the non-disputing Party shall, upon request from the disputing Party, hold consultations with a view to determining whether the taxation measure in question has an effect equivalent to expropriation or nationalisation. Any tribunal that may be established pursuant to this Section shall accord serious consideration to the decision of both Parties under this Paragraph'; and the Free Trade Agreement between the Government of the Republic of Korea and the Government of the Socialist Republic of Viet Nam (Korea & Vietnam) (adopted 5 May 2015, entered into force 20 December 2015) Art 9.24, which provides that an interpretation issued by the treaty's Joint Committee 'shall be binding on a Tribunal … and an award … shall be consistent with that interpretation'; and ASEAN–Australia–New Zealand FTA Ch 11, Art 27(2): 'The tribunal shall, on its own account or at the request of a disputing party, request a joint interpretation of any provision of this Agreement that is in issue in a dispute'.

general international law concerning the responsibility of States, but they also have the potential to influence the law of treaties.

With respect to the first issue, it is to be noted that there exists a coherent line of tribunals decisions concerning relations between international investment agreements and EU treaties, which narrowly interpret the issue of 'the same subject matter' for possible conflicting treaty norms. Such an approach is particularly remarkable as it differs from the position taken by the ILC both in its work on the law of the treaties as well as in its study on the fragmentation of international law. Such a position differs also from the interpretations contained in two GATT/WTO decisions. Nevertheless, as this issue has not generally been the subject of scrutiny in international courts and tribunals in inter-State cases, investment awards cannot be disregarded as they represent the most extensive jurisprudence in this area. Still, from a systemic perspective, investment tribunals' line of argumentation leads clearly to fragmentation as they approach investment treaties as almost self-contained regimes, which are resilient to a conflict of rules analysis unless the two applicable treaties are almost identical. It is remarkable that even a year after publication of the ILCs report on fragmentation, whose main message was 'that the emergence of special treaty-regimes (which should not be called "self-contained") has not seriously undermined legal security, predictability or the equality of legal subjects',[97] investment tribunals, at least with respect to the application of conflict of norms rules, have initiated a process leading towards the opposite direction. In this respect, in my view, investment awards which interpret not only rules of the VCLT, but also their corresponding CIL rules, seem to have *pro futuro* limited value and should rather be considered to have incidental significance for general international law.[98] It seems that this approach taken by investment tribunals has been largely dictated by the need to defend their jurisdiction. What is striking is the number of cases in which tribunals were convinced that they could apply the VCLT when, in fact, only CIL was applicable in the respective case. This approach can also prove that at least with respect to rules with double force (treaty – customary) under international law, the method of interpretation can be similar to a large extent.

---

[97] ILC (n 8) 24, 248–9.
[98] This criticism was reflected by Hai Yen Trinh: 'arbitral tribunals have disregarded all or the basic interpretive tools required under international law, overrelied on supplementary means of interpretation, judicial decisions and scholarly writings, and liberally found a solely pro-investor object and purpose', TH Yen, *The Interpretation of Investment Treaties* (Martinus Nijhoff 2014) 4.

Regarding the VCLT and CIL rules on subsequent agreements several observations can be made. First, the ease with which arbitral tribunals reject interpretations formulated by States through subsequent agreements is striking. The analysis of these agreements is often rudimentary, absent, or the tribunal simply refers to other rulings – indicating that it considers these interpretations as their own – without sometimes paying attention to the difference in legal situations between the cases whose jurisprudence it cites. Second, tribunals have set out detailed requirements for the formulation of a declaration, without explaining the source for these requirements. Third, there is a considerable difference between tribunals referring to joint interpretations of State Parties, as envisaged by the treaty as binding (such as with NAFTA), and the tribunal assessing such interpretations through the lens of the VCLT or corresponding customary rules. With respect to the latter, tribunals tend to diminish the role of subsequent agreements by underlining the 'taken into account' formulae of Article 31(3) VCLT. Due to the laconic nature of the provisions of most of the investment agreements[99] (in particular so called 'old-generation' treaties),[100] this approach enables investment tribunals, through the interpretation of the 'ordinary meaning' of terms and the 'object and purpose' of a treaty, to maintain its far-reaching interpretative power.

What follows from these observations is, to my mind, the necessity of bringing consistency between the case law of international investment arbitration tribunals and general international law, both as regards conflict of norms as well as of the role subsequent agreement and subsequent practices. Thus, there is a continuous need for more grounding of investment jurisprudence in the realm of general international law.[101]

Still, investment arbitration can inform general international law in at least in two areas, which were not explicitly articulated by the ILC in its 2018 Conclusions, the retroactive application of interpretations and, connected with it, the impact on the rights of individuals. Certainly, in this respect, investment arbitration leans towards interpretations which

---

[99] '[A]s judge-made law and deeply imbued with the functional logic pervading the investment protection regime', A von Bogdandy & I Venzke, 'In Whose Name? An Investigation of International Courts' Public Authority and Its Democratic Justification' (2012) 23(1) EJIL 7, 9.

[100] 'Old treaties abound: more than 2,500 IIAs in force today (95 per cent of all treaties in force) were concluded before 2010' UNCTAD, 'Phase 2 of IIA Reform: Modernizing the Existing Stock of Old-Generation Treaties' (2017) (2) IIA Issues Note 1, 1.

[101] Such as with the Most Favoured Nation clause, see ILC, 'Final Report of the Study Group on the Most-Favoured-Nation Clause' (29 May 2015) UN Doc A/CN.4/L.852 [153 & 157].

restrain the rights of State parties as the 'masters' of treaties.[102] However, the line between rights of State parties and rights of the individual beneficiaries of the treaties (ie investors) has not yet crystallised. Thus, this trend coming from investment arbitration should be juxtaposed with the approach of other international tribunals and domestic constitutional courts' jurisprudence.

---

[102] E Methymaki & A Tzanakopoulos, 'Masters of Puppets? Reassertion of Control through Joint Investment Treaty Interpretation' in A Kulick (ed), *Reassertion of Control Over the Investment Treaty Regime* (CUP 2017) 173.

PART III

Interpreting Customary International Rules
Current Challenges

10

Police Powers in a Pandemic

Investment Treaty Interpretation and the Customary Presumption of Reasonable Regulation

OLIVER HAILES*

1 Introduction

In 1634, amid waves of bubonic plague, the governor of Ancona suspected that the Venetian consul had spread information detrimental to local commerce. The governor seized the consul's possessions and banished him 'under pretence that, contrary to public prohibition, he had caused goods to be unloaded in a time of contagion'.[1] An imbroglio of infectious disease and economic insecurity thus occasioned the arbitrary treatment of a foreign national and his property. In the realm of diplomatic protection, Emer de Vattel advised that the 'surest way' to settle such matters was by 'commercial treaty'; otherwise, 'custom is to be the rule'.[2] Four centuries later, thousands of treaties provide substantive standards and consent to arbitration in the cognate realm of investment protection. But these treaties have not supplanted the customary rule that there is no State responsibility for reasonable regulation of foreign investment. Effectively a presumption derived from territorial sovereignty, this rule has manifested in investment jurisprudence through the police powers doctrine, the right to regulate, and a margin of appreciation. Foregrounding the presumption of reasonable regulation helps to situate these arbitral trends from a generalist perspective and provides the baseline for interpretation

---

* Many thanks to Professor Jorge E Viñuales and the editors for helpful comments. The usual caveat applies. Thanks also to the Robert Stout Law Library of the University of Otago for providing me with access to its collection during my unplanned return to New Zealand.
[1] E de Vattel, *The Law of Nations; or, Principles of the Law of Nature, applied to the Conduct and Affairs of Nations and Sovereigns* (first published 1758, Joseph Chitty ed, 6th edn, Johnson 1844) book II, ch II, [34].
[2] ibid.

of investment treaties in another time of contagion: the COVID-19 pandemic and its economic aftermath.[3]

Section 2 reviews the demand for governments to impose a moratorium on investment treaty arbitration amid the COVID-19 pandemic. Modern treaty practice, however, already recognises the right to regulate as an affirmation of the customary position that each State may reasonably regulate foreign investment without violating international obligations. Section 3 recalls how this regulatory dimension of territorial sovereignty endured throughout the mid-century debate over the standard of compensation for nationalisation and the rise of investment treaty arbitration. The police powers doctrine is singled out as a formulation through which tribunals impose the burden on claimants to prove that a regulatory measure was unreasonable before it may be addressed as an alleged expropriation. By recognising the link between police powers and territorial sovereignty, we may realise the potential scope of the customary presumption of reasonable regulation. Section 4 identifies how this presumption may be integrated in the interpretation of investment treaties, addressing whether modern treaties may operate as *leges specialis*. Reasonable regulation is nevertheless presumed under the standard of fair and equitable treatment (FET) by determining legitimate expectations in light of the State's right to regulate or by applying a margin of appreciation. Section 5 reviews classical practice on the treatment of alien property in times of infectious disease and its contemporary lessons for investment treaty arbitration alongside the international health regulations of the World Health Organization (WHO), concluding that it should be very difficult to establish that an investment obligation has been violated by regulatory measures designed to mitigate the chronic character of today's entwined crises.

2   Treaty and Custom in the COVID-19 Pandemic

From the outset of the COVID-19 pandemic, public health measures threatened to undermine the ordinary conditions for private enterprise; the Spanish government, for example, empowered the Minister of Health

---

[3] COVID-19 describes the disease caused by a coronavirus, provisionally named 2019-nCoV and renamed SARS-CoV-2, which emerged in December 2019. On 11 March 2020, the Director-General of the World Health Organization described the outbreak as a pandemic: WHO, 'WHO Director-General's opening remarks at the media briefing on COVID-19' (*World Health Organization*, 11 March 2020) <www.who.int/dg/speeches/detail/who-director-general-s-opening-remarks-at-the-media-briefing-on-covid-19---11-march-2020> accessed 10 May 2021.

to requisition industrial property.[4] Rapidly, it became apparent that markets could not 'self-regulate in relation to all conceivable social and economic shocks', leading to 'interventions on a scale last seen in World War II'.[5] Scholars and practitioners published bulletins on whether such measures might trigger obligations to compensate foreign investors.[6] In light of the mounting crises, however, NGOs called on States to address proactively their exposure to costly claims. The Columbia Center on Sustainable Investment (CCSI), for instance, recommended an immediate moratorium on investment treaty arbitration and a permanent restriction on claims related to 'measures targeting health, economic, and social dimensions of the pandemic and its effects'.[7] The proposed moratorium would last until governments had agreed on principles to safeguard 'good faith recovery efforts'.[8]

CCSI's proposal was consistent with past demands for States to protect their right to regulate in the public interest.[9] Yet, the concerns of civil society, like much of the scholarly literature, have concentrated on perceived pitfalls of investment treaties and arbitral institutions rather than the customary foundations for investment regulation.[10] The intergovernmental reform agenda, moreover, has focused on procedural and institutional aspects of investment treaty arbitration.[11] In other words, efforts to suspend or recalibrate the practice of investment treaty arbitration have oddly illustrated the normative resilience of substantive investment law,[12] while overlooking sources of applicable law that reinforce the international lawfulness of health, social, and economic measures. A more

---

[4] Real Decreto 463/2020, de 14 de marzo, por el que se declara el estado de alarma para la gestión de la situación de crisis sanitaria ocasionada por el COVID-19, Art 13.
[5] A Tooze, *Shutdown: How Covid Shook the World's Economy* (Allen Lane 2021) 13.
[6] See, eg F Paddeu & K Parlett, 'COVID-19 and Investment Treaty Claims' (*Kluwer Arbitration Blog*, 30 March 2020) <http://arbitrationblog.kluwerarbitration.com/2020/03/30/covid-19-and-investment-treaty-claims> accessed 10 May 2021.
[7] P Bloomer & ors, 'Call for ISDS Moratorium During COVID-19 Crisis and Response' (*Columbia Center on Sustainable Investment*, 6 May 2020) <http://ccsi.columbia.edu/2020/05/05/isds-moratorium-during-covid-19> accessed 10 May 2021.
[8] ibid.
[9] See, eg G Van Harten & ors, 'Public Statement on the International Investment Regime' (*Osgoode Hall Law School*, 31 August 2010) <www.osgoode.yorku.ca/public-statement-international-investment-regime-31-august-2010> accessed 10 May 2021.
[10] cf JE Viñuales, 'Customary Law in Investment Regulation' (2014) 23(1) IYIL 23.
[11] UNCITRAL, 'Working Group III: Investor-State Dispute Settlement Reform' (*UNCITRAL*, 2021) <https://uncitral.un.org/en/working_groups/3/investor-state> accessed 10 May 2021.
[12] J Kurtz, JE Viñuales & M Waibel, 'Principles Governing the Global Economy' in JE Viñuales (ed), *The UN Friendly Relations Declaration at 50: An Assessment of the Fundamental Principles of International Law* (CUP 2020) 359–60.

constructive intervention than CCSI's proposed moratorium, therefore, would be to equip vulnerable polities with defence arguments derived from customary international law that might accommodate the dynamic character of regulatory measures amid chronic crises.[13]

While acknowledging that regulatory powers originate in custom, Catharine Titi argues that the right to regulate should be understood narrowly as an express treaty provision permitting a State to regulate in derogation of its commitments.[14] But one should resist the reflex to rely on treaty exceptions, which reproduces the popular perception that investment obligations normally forbid ambitious regulation.[15] In reality, the basic aim of CCSI's moratorium has long formed part of customary international law; by virtue of the police powers doctrine, governments may indeed adopt regulatory measures in good faith without compensating investors.[16] In modern treaties, moreover, parties have secured the presumptive lawfulness of their regulatory measures not by fashioning an exceptional right under treaty law, but by 'reaffirm[ing] their right to regulate within their territories to achieve legitimate policy objectives'.[17] As governments struggle to confront the pandemic and its aftermath, it is timely to review the enduring relevance of custom as the wellspring of investment regulation.

3   Investment Regulation under Customary International Law

To unearth the customary roots of regulatory power, it helps to survey some historical foundations of investment treaty arbitration. Modern standards of treatment, enforceable originally through diplomatic protection, emerged out of transitions from formal empire towards post-colonial

---

[13] This chapter does not consider exceptions reserved for acute emergency, such as jurisdictional carve-outs for measures protecting essential security interests or the customary plea of necessity as a circumstance precluding wrongfulness. On these modalities, see JE Viñuales, 'Defence Arguments in Investment Arbitration' (2020) 18 ICSID Rep 9. See also Chapter 7 of this volume.

[14] A Titi, *The Right to Regulate in International Investment Law* (Nomos 2014) 32–3. Cf LW Mouyal, *International Investment Law and the Right to Regulate: A Human Rights Perspective* (Routledge 2016) 8.

[15] J Arato, K Claussen & JB Heath, 'The Perils of Pandemic Exceptionalism' (2020) 114 AJIL 627, 631.

[16] See, eg, J Lee, 'Note on COVID-19 and the Police Powers Doctrine: Assessing the Allowable Scope of Regulatory Measures During a Pandemic' (2020) 13 CAAJ 229. Cf Section 5 below.

[17] Comprehensive Economic and Trade Agreement (CETA) between Canada, of the One Part, and the European Union and its Member States, of the Other Part (adopted 30 October 2016, provisionally entered into force 21 September 2017) [2017] OJ L11/23 Art 8.9.1.

independence and from coercive intervention towards peaceful means of dispute settlement.[18] Digging through juridical strata, three layers underpin the importance of custom in the regulation of foreign investment. First, the mid-century debate over the standard of compensation for nationalisation situates investment treaty arbitration as a relatively recent exception to the customary principle of permanent sovereignty over natural resources (PSNR). Secondly, before and during that debate, the regulatory dimension of territorial sovereignty was reaffirmed through instruments acknowledging the State's right to regulate and judicial dicta that investors bear the risk of regulatory change. Finally, the police powers doctrine is identified as an expression of territorial sovereignty by which investment tribunals may distinguish non-compensable regulation from compensable expropriation. By recognising the imbrication of police powers and territorial sovereignty, we may appreciate the general application of the customary presumption that reasonable regulation does not engage State responsibility to compensate foreign investors.

3.1 *Exceptional Character of Investment Treaty Arbitration*

A debate over compensation for nationalisation flared up in the era of decolonisation, framed by newly independent States as a manifestation of their PSNR.[19] Now a recognised principle of customary international law,[20] PSNR was a 'linchpin' of the movement for a New International Economic Order.[21] Through the 1974 Charter of Economic Rights and Duties of States (CERDS), the movement sought to fortify the economic content of self-determination by embedding a standard of 'appropriate compensation' in domestic jurisdiction.[22] But an earlier formulation of PSNR in the widely supported General Assembly resolution 1803 included

---

[18] OT Johnson & J Gimblett, 'From Gunboats to BITs: The Evolution of Modern International Investment Law' in KP Sauvant (ed), *Yearbook on International Investment Law & Policy 2010–2011* (OUP 2012).
[19] FV García-Amador, 'The Proposed New International Economic Order: A New Approach to the Law Governing Nationalization and Compensation' (1980) 12 LawAmer 1, 20 ff.
[20] *Armed Activities on the Territory of the Congo (Democratic Republic of the Congo v Uganda)* (Judgment) [2015] ICJ Rep 168 [244].
[21] U Özsu, 'Neoliberalism and the New International Economic Order: A History of "Contemporary Legal Thought"' in J Desautels-Stein & C Tomlins (eds), *Searching for Contemporary Legal Thought* (CUP 2017) 339–40.
[22] UNGA, 'Charter of Economic Rights and Duties of States' (12 December 1974) UN Doc A/RES/3281(XXIX), Art 2(2)(c) (CERDS).

the requirement of compensation 'in accordance with international law',[23] often decoded as 'prompt, adequate and effective payment'.[24] Capital-exporting States defended this standard during the drafting of CERDS, opposing its ultimate adoption.[25] Subsequent awards reaffirmed that nationalisation remained subject to an international standard of compensation and the fundamental principle of *pacta sunt servanda*.[26] Indeed, resolution 1803 provided that '[f]oreign investment agreements freely entered into by or between sovereign States shall be observed in good faith';[27] and that disputes over compensation should be settled 'through arbitration or international adjudication'.[28] Consistent with their right of entering into international agreements,[29] States consented to prospective arbitration of investment disputes under contract, statute, or treaty.[30] By the 1990s, investment treaty arbitration had emerged as an overgrown exception to the principle of PSNR.[31] Yet, it must not be overlooked that the nationalisation debate generated a variegated grammar of sovereign rights.[32] While the right to expropriate is one dimension of sovereignty, its bounds often blur with the State's right to regulate.[33]

3.2 Regulatory Dimension of Territorial Sovereignty

Regulatory authority over foreign investment is an extension of the State's plenary competence under customary international law to determine its internal priorities, often formulated as an expression of PSNR or the sovereign right freely to choose and develop an economic system.[34]

---

[23] UNGA, 'Permanent Sovereignty Over Natural Resources' (14 December 1962) UN Doc A/5217 [4] (PSNR).
[24] cf AJIL, 'Mexico – United States: Expropriation by Mexico of Agrarian Properties Owned by American Citizens' (1938) 32 AJIL Supp 181, 193.
[25] CN Brower & JB Tepe, 'The Charter of Economic Rights and Duties of States: A Reflection or Rejection of International Law?' (1975) 9(2) Intl Law 295, 304–9.
[26] See, eg *Texaco Overseas Petroleum et al v Libya* (Award on the Merits) (1977) 53 ILR 422 [58–91].
[27] PSNR (n 23) [8].
[28] ibid [4].
[29] SS 'Wimbledon' (UK & ors v Germany) (Judgment) [1923] PCIJ Series A No 1, 25.
[30] See J Paulsson, 'Arbitration Without Privity' (1995) 10 ICSID Rev 232.
[31] Kurtz & ors (n 12) 351–5.
[32] N Schrijver, *Sovereignty over Natural Resources: Balancing Rights and Duties* (CUP 1997) ch 9.
[33] J Crawford, *Brownlie's Principles of Public International Law* (9th edn, OUP 2019) 604.
[34] See PSNR (n 23) [2–3]; UNGA, 'Declaration on Principles of International Law Concerning Friendly Relations and Cooperation Among States in Accordance with the Charter of the United Nations' (24 October 1970) UN Doc A/RES/2625(XXV) Annex, The principle

Manifestations of regulation, as activities performed *à titre de souverain*, are often decisive in territorial disputes.[35] Indeed, the exclusive right to regulate, opined Max Huber in the *Island of Palmas case*, entails a corollary duty to regulate 'in a manner corresponding to circumstances'.[36] This notion of correspondence implies that measures must be reasonable, reflected in contextual gradations of deference.[37] In *Spanish Zone of Morocco Claims*, given the State's duty to maintain social order, responsibility for injury to foreign nationals was engaged only if local authorities acted in manifest abuse of their discretion; that is, beyond a margin of appreciation.[38] In the *North Atlantic Coast Fisheries Case*, moreover, Great Britain had a 'duty of preserving and protecting the fisheries' in its territorial waters, even though the United States had secured liberties for its nationals to exploit that resource.[39] British authorities enjoyed 'the right to make reasonable regulations' and the burden fell on the United States to prove that its liberties were violated by such measures.[40] These days, a State's duty to regulate may be triggered by treaties and customary principles requiring the protection of human rights and the prevention of environmental harm, even beyond its territory.[41] The basic right and manifold duties to adopt reasonable regulations in the circumstances, however, derive fundamentally from territorial sovereignty over internal affairs, which vastly predates the articulation of PSNR.[42]

In the *Oscar Chinn Case*, the Permanent Court of Justice held that '[f]avourable business conditions and goodwill are transient circumstances, subject to inevitable changes,' including 'the general trade depression and the measures taken to combat it'.[43] Throughout the

---

of sovereign equality of States [e]; CERDS (n 22) Art 2(2)(a); *Military and Paramilitary Activities in and Against Nicaragua (Nicaragua v USA)* (Merits) [1986] ICJ Rep 14 [263–4]; G Abi-Saab, 'Permanent Sovereignty over Natural Resources and Economic Activities' in M Bedjaoui (ed), *International Law: Achievements and Prospects* (UNESCO 1991) 597–615.

[35] *Territorial and Maritime Dispute (Nicaragua v Colombia)* (Judgment) [2012] ICJ Rep 624 [80–4].
[36] *Island of Palmas case (Netherlands v USA)* (1928) 2 RIAA 829, 839.
[37] cf E Shirlow, 'Deference and Indirect Expropriation Analysis in International Investment Law: Observations on Current Approaches and Frameworks for Future Analysis' (2014) 29 ICSID Rev 595.
[38] *Biens britanniques au Maroc espagnol* (Spain v GB) (1925) 2 RIAA 615, 645.
[39] *North Atlantic Coast Fisheries Case (GB v USA)* (1910) 11 RIAA 167, 187.
[40] ibid 180, 188.
[41] See *The Environment and Human Rights* (Advisory Opinion OC-23/17 of 15 November 2017) IACHR Series A 23 [141] ff.
[42] P Juillard, 'L'Évolution des Sources du Droit des Investissements' (1994) 250 RdC 9 [52–3].
[43] *Oscar Chinn Case (Britain v Belgium)* (Judgment) PCIJ Series A/B No 63, 88.

nationalisation debate, moreover, Third World initiatives to establish an international regulatory regime for multinational corporations were resisted by capital-exporting States, which insisted that regulation was strictly for domestic jurisdiction.[44] The range of compensable expropriations, therefore, never encompassed any deprivation of property or economic disadvantage resulting merely from taxation, monetary reform, or regulatory measures.[45] Commentary to the 1967 Organisation for Economic Cooperation and Development (OECD) Draft Convention on the Protection of Foreign Property, for instance, acknowledged 'the sovereign right of a State, under international law, to deprive owners, including aliens, of property which is within its territory in the pursuit of its political, social or economic ends' and that to 'deny such a right would be to ... interfere with its powers to regulate'.[46] The power to regulate may include placing limits on activities, including their wholesale prohibition for legitimate purposes such as environmental protection.[47] The financial risk of such measures is accordingly borne by foreign nationals.[48] The customary position that any loss arising from reasonable regulation does not violate international law remains salient in contemporary investment jurisprudence, including through the police powers doctrine.

3.3 Development of the Police Powers Doctrine

While some depict the police powers doctrine as a recent innovation,[49] others have traced its deeper genealogy.[50] Derived from the Greek *politeia*, the notion of police as prudent regulation originated in administrative manuals of France and Germany, later adopted by William Blackstone

---

[44] S Pahuja & A Saunders, 'Rival Worlds and the Place of the Corporation in International Law' in J von Bernstorff & P Dann (eds), *The Battle for International Law: South-North Perspectives on the Decolonization Era* (OUP 2019) 156.

[45] LB Sohn & RR Baxter, 'Responsibility of States for Injuries to the Economic Interests of Aliens' (1961) 55 AJIL 545, 551–3. See also *Kügele v Polish State* (1932) 6 ILR 69 (on taxation); *Furst Claim* (1960) 42 ILR 153 (on monetary reform).

[46] OECD, 'Draft Convention on the Protection of Foreign Property' (1967) 7 ILM 117, 125. cf CERDS (n 22) Art 2(2)(a).

[47] *Dispute regarding Navigational and Related Rights (Costa Rica v Nicaragua)* (Judgment) [2009] ICJ Rep 213 [126–8].

[48] See, eg, *Deutsche Amerikanische Petroleum Gesellschaft Oil Tankers* (1926) 2 RIAA 777, 794; *USA (Dickson Car Wheel Company) v Mexico* (1931) 4 RIAA 669, 681–82.

[49] See eg A Pellet, 'Police Powers or the State's Right to Regulate: *Chemtura v Canada*' in M Kinnear & ors (eds), *Building International Investment Law: The First 50 Years of the ICSID Convention* (Kluwer 2015).

[50] See eg S Legarre, 'The Historical Background of the Police Power' (2007) 9 UPaJConstL 745.

and Adam Smith.[51] By the influence of Vattel,[52] police power as the conceptual basis for public regulation of private property evolved through the United States constitutional law and migrated to Argentina.[53] On the international stage, the concept featured in significant developments towards property protection: the jurisprudence of mixed claims commissions;[54] the 1930 Hague Conference;[55] the 1961 Harvard Draft;[56] scholarly debates;[57] the Restatements of Foreign Relations Law;[58] and the jurisprudence of the Iran-United States Claims Tribunal.[59] The police powers doctrine then entered investment treaty arbitration to shield measures from claims of indirect expropriation,[60] including health,[61] licensing,[62] environmental,[63] bankruptcy,[64] and financial regulation.[65]

For two decades, investment tribunals have recognised the police powers doctrine as custom.[66] States reiterate that customary status in their submissions as respondents and non-disputing parties.[67] The resulting

---

[51] ibid 748–61.
[52] ibid 753.
[53] See respectively JL Sax, 'Takings and the Police Power' (1964) 74 YLJ 36; S Berensztein & H Spector, 'Business, Government, and Law' in G della Paolera & AM Taylor (eds), *A New Economic History of Argentina* (CUP 2003) 339–41.
[54] See, eg *Poggioli Case* (1903) 10 RIAA 669, 691.
[55] S Rosenne (ed), *League of Nations Conference for the Codification of International Law (1930)*, Vol 2 (Oceana 1975) 684–5.
[56] Sohn & Baxter (n 45) 551–3.
[57] See eg JF Williams, 'International Law and the Property of Aliens' (1928) 9 BYBIL 1, 23–8; AP Fachiri, 'International Law and the Property of Aliens' (1929) 10 BYBIL 32, 51–4.
[58] American Law Institute, *Restatement (Second) of Foreign Relations Law* (American Law Institute 1965) [197]; American Law Institute, *Restatement (Third) of Foreign Relations Law* (American Law Institute 1987) [712].
[59] *Sedco, Inc v National Iranian Oil Company and Islamic Republic of Iran* (Award of 17 September 1985) IUSCT Case Nos 128 and 129 [90]; *Too v Greater Modesto Insurance Associates and United States of America* (Award of 29 December 1989) IUSCT Case No 880 [26–9].
[60] For the first known reference, see *SD Myers, Inc v Canada* (Statement of Defence of 18 June 1999) UNCITRAL [55].
[61] Eg *Methanex Corporation v USA* (Final Award of the Tribunal on Jurisdiction and Merits of 3 August 2005) pt IV, ch D [15].
[62] Eg *UAB E energija (Lithuania) v Republic of Latvia* (Award of 22 December 2017) ICSID Case No ARB/12/33 [1067–101].
[63] Eg *Chemtura Corporation (formerly Crompton Corporation) v Canada* (Award of 2 August 2010) UNCITRAL [266].
[64] Eg *AMF Aircraftleasing Meier & Fischer GmbH & Co KG, Hamburg (Germany) v Czech Republic* (Final Award of 11 May 2020) PCA Case No 2017-15 [624].
[65] Eg *Marfin v Cyprus* (Award of 26 July 2018) ICSID Case No ARB/13/27 [825–30].
[66] Eg *Feldman v Mexico* (Award of 16 December 2002) ICSID Case No ARB(AF)/99/1 [103–6].
[67] Eg *Lone Pine Resources Inc v Canada* (Gouvernement du Canada Contre-Mémoire of 24 July 2015) ICSID Case No UNCT/15/2 [491–528].

decisions, as 'subsidiary means for the determination of rules of law',[68] have further developed the 'scope, content and conditions' of police powers.[69] The doctrine effectively is a screening mechanism between the right to expropriate with compensation and the right to regulate without compensation.[70] While few treaties refer explicitly to police powers,[71] many now reflect the content of custom in interpretative annexes.[72] The Tribunal in *Philip Morris v Uruguay* rendered a typical formulation in its finding that branding restrictions and health warnings on cigarette packaging did not constitute indirect expropriation of intellectual property: 'the State's reasonable *bona fide* exercise of police powers in such matters as the maintenance of public order, health or morality, excludes compensation even when it causes economic damage to an investor'.[73]

As Jorge Viñuales explained, 'the lack of public purpose, discrimination, arbitrariness, due process, effects and/or prior specific assurances' should be understood as 'considerations of good faith', which serve not as 'cumulative requirements' of the police powers doctrine but rather as 'indicia guiding a broader assessment of regulatory reasonableness' by reference to circumstances of the case and the applicable treaty standard.[74] While the standard of reasonableness gives leeway to arbitral discretion,[75] tribunals have applied that standard in a broadly deferential manner by

---

[68] Statute of the International Court of Justice (adopted 26 June 1945, entered into force 24 October 1945) 1 UNTS 993, Art 38(1)(d).

[69] *Philip Morris Brand Sàrl (Switzerland), Philip Morris Products SA (Switzerland) and Abal Hermanos SA (Uruguay) v Uruguay* (Award of 8 July 2016) ICSID Case No ARB/10/7 [295] (*Philip Morris v Uruguay*).

[70] *Suez & Interagua v Argentina* (Decision on Liability of 30 July 2010) ICSID Case No ARB/03/17 [128] (*Suez v Argentina*).

[71] cf Investment Agreement for the COMESA Common Investment Area (adopted 23 May 2007, not yet in force) Art 20(8) <https://investmentpolicy.unctad.org/international-investment-agreements/treaty-files/3092/download> accessed 10 May 2021.

[72] Eg, Comprehensive and Progressive Agreement for Trans-Pacific Partnership (adopted 9 March 2018, entered into force 30 December 2018) [2018] ATS 23, annex 9-B. cf Section 4.2 below. Notably, an interpretative protocol to the very first bilateral investment treaty provided that 'measures taken for reasons of public security and order, public health or morality shall not be deemed as discrimination': Treaty between the Federal Republic of Germany and Pakistan for the Promotion and Protection of Investments (Germany & Pakistan) (adopted 25 November 1959, entered into force 28 April 1962) 457 UNTS 24, protocol [2].

[73] *Philip Morris v Uruguay* [295].

[74] Viñuales (n 13) [93].

[75] C Henckels, *Proportionality and Deference in Investor-State Arbitration: Balancing Investment Protection and Regulatory Autonomy* (CUP 2015) 119.

requiring the absence of arbitrariness through some link between a rational policy and the adopted measure.[76]

Not to be conflated with its domestic expression,[77] the police powers doctrine under customary international law is an operative formulation of the regulatory dimension of territorial sovereignty.[78] This nexus is evident in the *Iron Rhine Arbitration*, wherein the Netherlands 'forfeited no more sovereignty than that which is necessary' for Belgium to exercise it treaty rights and, thus, 'retain[ed] the police power throughout that area,' including the power to establish health, safety and environmental standards.[79] The Tribunal effectively presumed no derogation from territorial sovereignty, albeit conditioned by good faith and reasonableness.[80] While such presumptions have eroded in some contexts,[81] reaffirmation of regulatory powers in recent treaties has reinforced a general presumption that 'investment treaties were never intended to do away with their signatories' right to regulate'.[82]

3.4 Customary Presumption of Reasonable Regulation

The principled starting point under customary international law, reflected in the police powers doctrine, is to presume that regulation is a reasonable manifestation of territorial sovereignty. 'Presumptively', recalled James Crawford, 'the ordering of persons and assets is an aspect of the domestic jurisdiction of a state and an incident of its territorial sovereignty'.[83] In the *Brewer, Moller and Co Case*, moreover, the German-Venezuelan Commission endorsed the 'uniform presumption of the regularity and validity of all acts of public officials'.[84] Rosalyn Higgins further referred to a 'weighty presumption' when measures are introduced by 'normal

---

[76] See, eg *AES Summit Generation Limited and AES-Tisza Erömü Kft v Hungary* (Award of 23 September 2010) ICSID Case No ARB/07/22 [10.3.9].
[77] *Suez v Argentina* [150].
[78] JE Viñuales, 'Sovereignty in Foreign Investment Law' in Z Douglas, J Pauwelyn & JE Viñuales (eds), *The Foundations of International Investment Law: Bringing Theory into Practice* (OUP 2014) 329–36.
[79] *Award in the Arbitration regarding the Iron Rhine ("Ijzeren Rijn") Railway between the Kingdom of Belgium and the Kingdom of the Netherlands* (Decision of 24 May 2005) 27 RIAA 35 [87].
[80] ibid [163].
[81] *Dispute regarding Navigational and Related Rights* (n 47) [48].
[82] *Invesmart, BV v Czech Republic* (Award of 26 June 2009) UNCITRAL [498].
[83] Crawford (n 33) 596.
[84] *Brewer, Moller & Co Case (Germany v Venezuela)* (1903) 10 RIAA 423, 423.

legislative processes of a democratic parliament'.[85] This presumption's contemporary relevance was reaffirmed by the partially dissenting arbitrator in *Philip Morris v Uruguay*, Gary Born, who endorsed: 'the presumptive lawfulness of governmental authority under customary international law, as well as respect for a state's sovereignty, particularly with regard to legislative and regulatory judgments regarding its domestic matters'.[86]

Plainly, this presumption would be rebutted if a claimant proved that an impugned regulation was adopted in bad faith.[87] Several tribunals have also found that a State's failure to comply with requirements of domestic law prevented its reliance on the police powers doctrine.[88] But the presumptive character of the police powers doctrine has significant implications for the burden of proof, given the party who asserts must prove.[89] If the doctrine was pleaded as an exception, tribunals might wrongly require the State to justify its regulatory measures.[90] In *Servier v Poland*, however, the Tribunal dismissed the claimant's submission that the police powers doctrine was an 'affirmative defence' for which the respondent had to 'prove the negative' by demonstrating 'an absence of bad faith and discrimination, or the lack of disproportionateness in the measures taken'.[91] The respondent had shown the domestic legal basis for its decisions not to renew marketing authorisations for pharmaceutical products.[92] The claimant thus had to prove that those decisions were inconsistent with a legitimate exercise of police powers.[93] While this burden allocation is surely correct, its basis is not merely evidential but rather reflects the customary presumption that each State is entitled to regulate in the reasonable pursuit of its priorities and may indeed be

---

[85] R Higgins, 'International Law and the Reasonable Need of Governments to Govern' in R Higgins (ed), *Themes and Theories: Selected Essays, Speeches and Writings in International Law* (OUP 2009) 791.

[86] *Philip Morris v Uruguay* (Concurring and Dissenting Opinion of Gary Born of 8 July 2016) ICSID Case No ARB/10/7 [141] (hereinafter *Philip Morris* Dissent).

[87] Eg, *Deutsche Bank AG v Sri Lanka* (Award of 31 October 2012) ICSID Case No ARB/09/02 [483–4, 522–4].

[88] Eg, *Quiborax v Bolivia* (Award of 16 September 2015) ICSID Case No ARB/06/2 [201–27].

[89] *Karkey Karadeniz Elektrik Uretim AS v Islamic Republic of Pakistan* (Award of 22 August 2017) ICSID Case No ARB/13/1 [497].

[90] Eg, *Bahgat v Arab Republic of Egypt* (Final Award of 23 December 2019) PCA Case No 2012–07 [230].

[91] *Les Laboratoires Servier, SAS, Biofarma, SAS and Arts et Techniques du Progres SAS v Republic of Poland* (Final Award of 14 February 2012) UNCITRAL [579, 583].

[92] ibid [582].

[93] ibid [584].

required to regulate in the circumstances, such as a duty to adopt legislation for the 'protection of health and life of humans'.[94]

Beyond the context of expropriation, the presumption of reasonable regulation is apparent in other customary rules, foremost the minimum standard of treatment.[95] The well-known *Neer* standard provides that 'an unsatisfactory use of power included in national sovereignty' amounts to 'an international delinquency' when conduct amounts 'to an outrage, to bad faith, to wilful neglect of duty' or 'to an insufficiency so far short of international standards that every reasonable and impartial man would readily recognise its insufficiency'.[96] This formulation is often adopted to determine the content of the customary minimum standard or the related treaty standard of FET.[97] In *Al Tamimi v Oman*, moreover, the Tribunal observed that the 'high threshold' for breach of the minimum standard requires a claimant to 'confront' the State's 'margin of discretion in exercising its police powers to enforce its existing laws'.[98] Weaving together these strands, we may say there is a general presumption that a State is not responsible for loss suffered by a foreign investor as a result of reasonable regulation.

4 Integrating Custom through Investment Treaty Interpretation

This chapter has thus far bracketed the matter of how custom forms a part of applicable law in investment treaty arbitration. Most investment treaties require disputes to be determined in accordance with the treaty simpliciter or alongside rules of international law.[99] No treaty is a 'self-contained closed legal system'; however, each must be 'envisaged within a wider juridical context' through the integration of 'rules from other sources'.[100] This section explores how the police powers doctrine has been incorporated in arbitral reasoning through the principle of systemic integration, which permits the customary presumption of reasonable

---

[94] ibid [39].
[95] For property protection as an element of the minimum standard involving an inquiry of 'deferential reasonableness', see M Paparinskis, *The International Minimum Standard and Fair and Equitable Treatment* (OUP 2013) 218–28. See further Section 5.1 below.
[96] *USA (LFH Neer) v Mexico* (1926) 4 RIAA 60 [4].
[97] See, eg *Glamis Gold, Ltd v United States* (Award of 8 June 2009) UNCITRAL [598–626].
[98] *Al Tamimi v Oman* (Award of 3 November 2015) ICSID Case No ARB/11/33 [443–7].
[99] Y Banifatemi, 'The Law Applicable in Investment Treaty Arbitration' in K Yannaca-Small (ed), *Arbitration under International Investment Agreements* (2nd edn, OUP 2018) [19.10].
[100] *Asian Agricultural Products Ltd v Republic of Sri Lanka* (Final Award of 27 June 1990) ICSID Case No ARB/87/3 [21].

regulation to be taken into account generally in treaty interpretation. Modern treaties include bespoke protection of the State's regulatory powers, which could operate as *leges specialis*. Arbitral recognition of the State's right to regulate and a margin of appreciation, however, hints at the tacit integration of the customary presumption within the FET standard.

4.1 Systemic Integration of the Customary Presumption

One way of bringing custom into the interpretative process is by referencing a customary concept as the 'ordinary meaning' under Art 31(1) or as a 'special meaning ... the parties so intended' under Art 31(4) of the Vienna Convention on the Law of Treaties (VCLT).[101] But, consider the obligation not to 'take any measures depriving, directly or indirectly, investors ... of their investments'.[102] The ordinary meaning of 'measures' is 'wide enough to cover any act' and 'imposes no particular limit on their material content or on the aim pursued thereby'.[103] In *Saluka v Czech Republic*, however, the Tribunal considered that 'the concept of deprivation' allowed for integration of the 'customary international law notion that a deprivation can be justified if it results from the exercise of regulatory actions aimed at the maintenance of public order'.[104] The Tribunal in *El Paso v Argentina* similarly interpreted an expropriation standard in light of custom, requiring the claimant to show that 'general regulations are unreasonable, that is, arbitrary, discriminatory, disproportionate or otherwise unfair' before determining whether they neutralised property rights to constitute indirect expropriation.[105] Rather than direct reference to custom, these tribunals interpreted the obligation in light of the distinction between compensable expropriation and non-compensable regulation embodied in the police powers doctrine,

---

[101] Vienna Convention on the Law of Treaties (adopted 23 May 1969, entered into force 27 January 1980) 1155 UNTS 331.
[102] Agreement on Encouragement and Reciprocal Protection of Investments Between the Kingdom of The Netherlands and the Czech and Slovak Federal Republic (Netherlands & Czech Republic) (adopted 29 April 1991, entered into force 1 October 1992) 2242 UNTS 205, Art 5.
[103] *Fisheries Jurisdiction (Spain v Canada) (Jurisdiction)* (Judgment) [1998] ICJ Rep 432 [66].
[104] *Saluka Investments BV v Czech Republic* (Partial Award of 17 March 2006) UNCITRAL [254].
[105] *El Paso Energy International Company v Argentina* (Award of 31 October 2011) ICSID Case No ARB/03/15 [240–1] (*El Paso v Argentina*). Many tribunals improperly invert this inquiry: see, eg *Windstream Energy LLC v Canada* (Award of 27 September 2016) PCA Case No 2013–22 [284].

which served as an organising principle around which to structure the applicable standard and burden of proof.

The principle of systemic integration applied in *Saluka* and *El Paso* is the chief means by which the customary presumption of reasonable regulation may be incorporated in arbitral practice.[106] Under Art 31(3)(c) of the VCLT, an interpreter must take into account, together with context, 'any relevant rules of international law applicable in the relations between the parties', including customary rules.[107] But tribunals seldom formulate precisely the rule, its relevance, or its applicability between the parties.[108] For clarity, therefore, the presumption of reasonable regulation may be formulated as the rule that there is *no State responsibility to compensate for reasonable regulation of foreign investment*. The elastic element of reasonableness might provoke the complaint that norms of investment law are too nebulous to qualify as custom.[109] But the 'inchoate character' of a rule is 'by no means fatal to its legal character' so long as it generates 'an adequate apparatus of precise principles'.[110] Investment treaty arbitration may well serve as that apparatus, transforming the customary criterion of reasonableness into determinate standards of review.[111] Tribunals need not address the elements of *opinio juris* and concordant practice, in any event, when investment disputes tend to concern the evolving content of custom rather than its formation.[112] Moreover, the presumption of reasonable regulation is a well-established expression of territorial sovereignty, for which general practice accepted as law is axiomatic. As a customary rule, therefore, it is applicable in relations among all States and would doubtless be relevant to any investment treaty standard.[113]

---

[106] See generally, C McLachlan, 'Investment Treaties and General International Law' (2008) 57 ICLQ 361, 369–74.
[107] *Oil Platforms (Iran v USA)* (Judgment) [2003] ICJ Rep 161 [40–2].
[108] P Ranjan, 'Police Powers, Indirect Expropriation in International Investment Law, and Article 31(3)(c) of the VCLT: A Critique of *Philip Morris v Uruguay*' (2019) 9 AsianJIL 98, 107–20.
[109] cf J d'Aspremont, 'International Customary Investment Law: Story of a Paradox' in T Gazzini & E de Brabandere (eds), *International Investment Law: The Sources of Rights and Obligations* (Martinus Nijhoff 2012).
[110] I Brownlie, 'Legal Status of Natural Resources in International Law (Some Aspects)' (1979) 162 RdC 245, 270–1.
[111] cf O Corten, 'The Notion of "Reasonable" in International Law: Legal Discourse, Reason and Contradictions' (1999) 48 ICLQ 613, 620–4.
[112] *Mondev International Ltd v USA* (Award of 11 October 2002) ICSID Case No ARB(AF)/99/2 [113].
[113] Ranjan (n 108) 117–18.

4.2 Investment Treaties as Leges Specialis

The chapeau of Art 31(3) of the VCLT provides that an interpreter must take into account any relevant rules 'together with the context'. Some argue that the sparse context of investment obligations supports the operation of investment treaties as *leges specialis* in respect of the police powers doctrine.[114] This view might support the 'sole effect' approach to indirect expropriation, which focuses on the deprivation caused by a measure regardless of regulatory intent.[115] But 'the persistence of the regulatory powers of the host State is not the accidental result of the failure of investment treaties to eliminate them', observed Vaughan Lowe; such powers remain 'an essential element of the permanent sovereignty of each State over its economy'.[116]

Given the reaffirmation of the right to regulate in modern treaties, the context of investment treaty standards should generally permit systemic integration of the customary rule that there is no State responsibility for reasonable regulation.[117] In *Bear Creek v Peru*, however, the Tribunal held that an express provision for general exceptions – modelled on Art XX of the General Agreement on Tariffs and Trade (GATT) – was 'an exclusive list' precluding the application of 'other exceptions from general international law', including 'the police powers exception [sic]'.[118] The provision stated that 'nothing in this Agreement shall be construed to prevent a Party from adopting or enforcing measures necessary ... to protect human, animal or plant life or health'.[119] While these terms arguably imply a presumption in favour of such measures, the Tribunal imposed the burden of proving their necessity on the respondent.[120] That treaty exception, therefore, should not have precluded the presumptive operation of the police powers doctrine, given a *lex generalis* and a *lex specialis* should have the same character as either a device limiting the scope of a treaty obligation (by distinguishing a regulatory

---

[114] ibid 121–4.
[115] R Dolzer, 'Indirect Expropriations: New Developments?' (2002) 11 NYU Envtl LJ 64, 79 ff.
[116] V Lowe, 'Regulation or Expropriation?' (2002) 55(1) CLP 447, 450.
[117] cf *Philip Morris v Uruguay* [300–1].
[118] *Bear Creek Mining Corporation v Perú* (Award of 30 November 2017) ICSID Case No ARB/14/21 [472–3] (*Bear Creek v Peru*).
[119] Free Trade Agreement between Canada and the Republic of Peru (Canada & Peru) (adopted 29 May 2008, entered into force 1 August 2009) Can TS 2009 No 15, Art 2201.1(3)(a) (Canada–Peru FTA).
[120] *Bear Creek v Peru* [477].

measure from an alleged expropriation) or an affirmative defence (for which a State bears the burden).[121]

Another ground on which the *Bear Creek* Tribunal excluded the police powers doctrine was the 'very detailed provisions' on expropriation.[122] An interpretative annex materially provided:

> Except in rare circumstances, such as when a measure or series of measures is so severe in the light of its purpose that it cannot be reasonably viewed as having been adopted and applied in good faith, non-discriminatory measures of a Party that are designed and applied to protect legitimate public welfare objectives, such as health, safety and the environment, do not constitute indirect expropriation.[123]

Yet, these terms reflect custom, incorporating typical indicia of police powers and imposing upon claimants the burden of proving such measures are disproportionate.[124] Indeed, in *Eco Oro v Colombia*, the Tribunal held that an identical annex did not exclude but rather 'reflect[ed] the more general doctrine of police powers in customary international law', such that 'awards on the police powers doctrine … may provide some guidance (by analogy)' in 'interpreting and applying the provisions'.[125] By entering investment treaties, States may well agree to transform the customary presumption into a more determinate test by specifying factors that arbitrators must address in their assessment of a measure's proportionality in light of its purpose.[126] While an interpretative annex could thus operate as *lex specialis* in regard to indirect expropriation, the customary presumption would remain relevant in the interpretation of other standards, including full protection and security[127] and protection against

---

[121] C Henckels, 'Scope Limitation or Affirmative Defence? The Purpose and Role of Investment Treaty Exception Clauses' in L Bartels & F Paddeu (eds), *Exceptions in International Law* (OUP 2020) 367.

[122] *Bear Creek v Peru* [473].

[123] Canada–Peru FTA (n 119) annex 812.1(3).

[124] C Titi, 'Police Powers Doctrine and International Investment Law' in A Gattini, A Tanzi & F Fontanelli (eds), *General Principles of Law and International Investment Arbitration* (Brill 2018) 338–9.

[125] *Eco Oro Minerals Corp v Colombia* (Decision on Jurisdiction, Liability and Directions on Quantum of 9 September 2021) ICSID Case No ARB/16/41 [626].

[126] cf *Military and Paramilitary Activities in and Against Nicaragua* [178] (treaties may establish 'mechanisms to ensure implementation' of customary rules); *Legality of the Threat or Use of Nuclear Weapons* (Advisory Opinion) [1996] ICJ Rep 226 [25] ('[t]he test … falls to be determined by the applicable *lex specialis*').

[127] This standard of due diligence requires governments 'to take reasonable acts within their power to prevent the injury … when states are, or should be, aware of a risk of injury': N Junngam, 'The Full Protection and Security Standard in International Investment Law: What

unreasonable and discriminatory measures.[128] Let us now consider the most frequently violated of all investment obligations.[129]

4.3 Tacit Integration Through Fair and Equitable Treatment

The FET standard has long been criticised for arbitral expansion beyond textual warrant.[130] Tribunals adopted the framework of legitimate expectations, for instance, to determine whether a State acted unfairly.[131] Modern treaties have since narrowed the notion of FET to the customary minimum standard and thus the circumstances in which interference with expectations may violate investment obligations.[132] It is through the framework of legitimate expectations, however, that we witness further expression of the customary presumption of reasonable regulation as alpha and omega of the FET standard in the respective guises of the right to regulate and a margin of appreciation.

To establish that an expectation has been defeated, tribunals typically require a claimant to prove three interlocking elements: an unfulfilled commitment; reliance when the investment was made; and reasonableness of that reliance, allied to the first element where the commitment was implicit.[133] In *El Paso*, the Tribunal held that there can be 'no legitimate expectation for anyone that the legal framework will remain unchanged in the face of an extremely severe economic crisis'.[134] Seldom do tribunals spell out the customary roots of such reasoning, treating the State's regulatory authority as a matter of fact rather than a legal presumption. In *Suez v Argentina*, however, the Tribunal recognised that the police powers doctrine and the State's right to regulate under the FET standard were in

---

and Who is Investment Fully[?] Protected and Secured From?' (2018) 7 AUBLR 1, 54. Notably, the classical practice points to a 'presumption against responsibility' of a State for injuries to foreign investors caused by non-State actors: FV García-Amador, LB Sohn & RR Baxter, *Recent Codification of the Law of State Responsibility for Injuries to Aliens* (Oceana 1974) 27.

[128] This non-impairment standard largely overlaps with FET: A Reinisch & C Schreuer, *International Protection of Investments: The Substantive Standards* (CUP 2020) 846–51.

[129] J Bonnitcha, LN Skovgaard Poulsen & M Waibel, *The Political Economy of the Investment Treaty Regime* (OUP 2017) 94.

[130] M Sornarajah, *Resistance and Change in the International Law on Foreign Investment* (CUP 2015) ch 5.

[131] M Potestà, 'Legitimate Expectations in Investment Treaty Law: Understanding the Roots and Limits of a Controversial Concept' (2013) 28 ICSID Rev 88.

[132] See, eg CETA (n 17) Art 8.9.2.

[133] C McLachlan, L Shore & M Weiniger, *International Investment Arbitration: Substantive Principles* (2nd edn, OUP 2017) [7.184].

[134] *El Paso v Argentina* [373–4].

fact 'duplicative' inquiries.[135] In other words, each inquiry is a reformulation of the customary presumption tailored to a different standard.[136] Acknowledging the common source of the police powers doctrine and the right to regulate helps us better to understand the customary drivers of arbitral convergence on contextual inquiries into the reasonableness of government conduct, regardless of the applicable treaty standard.[137]

An emerging consensus that the FET standard preserves the State's right to regulate was complicated by disputes regarding fiscally prudent adjustments to renewable energy incentives.[138] The jurisprudence divided into 'two schools of thought' as to whether legislative regimes constituted specific commitments that guaranteed tariffs would not change.[139] Arguments based on the State's right to regulate 'miss the point', quipped the majority in *Greentech v Italy*, when there were 'repeated and precise assurances to specific investors' that tariffs would remain fixed for two years.[140] In *RREEF v Spain*, however, the majority recalled that the absence of an express reference to the State's right to regulate under the Energy Charter Treaty did not mean it was excluded from applicable law.[141] As a matter of principle, 'an international obligation imposing on the State to waive or decline to exercise its regulatory power cannot be presumed' absent an 'unequivocal' commitment; 'more so when it faces a serious crisis'.[142] In the majority's view, 'there can be no doubt that States enjoy a margin of appreciation in public international law'.[143]

The margin of appreciation is an established principle of the European Court of Human Rights (ECtHR) that has been adopted by several tribunals applying the FET standard.[144] The majority in *Philip Morris v Uruguay* held

---

[135] *Suez v Argentina* [148].
[136] cf JE Alvarez, 'The Public International Law Regime Governing International Investment' (2011) 344 RdC 193, 423.
[137] F Ortino, *The Origin and Evolution of Investment Treaty Standards: Stability, Value, and Reasonableness* (OUP 2020) ch 3.
[138] YS Selivanova, 'Changes in Renewables Support Policy and Investment Protection under the Energy Charter Treaty: Analysis of Jurisprudence and Outlook for the Current Arbitration Cases' (2018) 33 ICSID Rev 433.
[139] *Masdar Solar v Spain* (Award of 16 May 2018) ICSID Case No ARB/14/1 [490].
[140] *Greentech Energy Systems A/S, NovEnergia II Energy & Environment (SCA) SICAR, and NovEnergia II Italian Portfolio SA v Italy* (Final Award of 23 December 2018) SCC Case No V 2015/095 [450].
[141] *RREEF v Spain* (Decision on Responsibility and on the Principles of Quantum of 30 November 2018) ICSID Case No ARB/13/30 [241] (*RREEF v Spain*).
[142] ibid [244].
[143] ibid [242].
[144] Viñuales (n 13) [94–8].

that such a margin required 'great deference to governmental judgments of national needs in matters such as the protection of public health'.[145] Due to the complexity of scientific and policy assessments, the 'sole inquiry' was whether the measures were adopted with 'manifest lack of reasons' or 'in bad faith'.[146] Partially dissenting arbitrator Born believed such a margin was 'neither mandated nor permitted' under international law, finding instead that treaty and custom required a 'minimum level of rationality and proportionality'.[147] Yet, the concept may be viewed as another iteration of the customary presumption that Born himself endorsed.[148] A margin of appreciation serves as the final layer of deference in determining the reasonableness or proportionality of regulatory measures,[149] reflecting the epistemic advantage of local authorities and their relative proximity to mechanisms of accountability.[150] These practical and normative factors assumed real significance in the COVID-19 pandemic, which transpired as 'a collection of national epidemics' shaped by interwoven social and biological factors.[151]

5   Reasonable Regulation in a Pandemic

Since the outbreak of COVID-19, the *Bischoff Case* has become a salient authority.[152] In 1898, Caracas police detained the carriage of a foreign national, which they supposed to have transported persons infected with smallpox. The police had acted on false information and eventually offered to return the carriage. Reflecting the customary presumption of reasonable regulation, the German-Venezuelan Commission held: 'Certainly during an epidemic of an infectious disease there can be no liability for the reasonable exercise of police power, even though a mistake is made.'[153] This final section fleshes out that prescient dictum by reviewing the classical practice on diplomatic protection in times of contagion and its contemporary lessons for investment treaty arbitration, highlighting how tribunals may interpret treaty standards in light of another codification

---

[145] *Philip Morris v Uruguay* [399].
[146] ibid [399–401].
[147] *Philip Morris* Dissent (n 86) [87], [139]. See also, G Born, D Morris & S Forrest, '"A Margin of Appreciation": Appreciating Its Irrelevance in International Law' (2020) 61 HarvILJ 65.
[148] See fn 86.
[149] See, eg *RREEF v Spain* [468].
[150] cf *Jahn and others v Germany* ECHR 2005-/VI 55 [91].
[151] F Paddeu & M Waibel, 'The Final Act: Exploring the End of Pandemics' (2020) 114 AJIL 698, 700.
[152] *Bischoff Case* (1903) 10 RIAA 420.
[153] ibid 420.

of reasonable regulation – the proportionality inquiry under Art 43 of the International Health Regulations (IHR).[154] The inherent limits of the IHR, however, mean that many claims arising from the COVID-19 pandemic and its economic aftermath should be resolved by integrating the customary presumption of reasonable regulation through the police powers doctrine, the right to regulate, or a margin of appreciation.

5.1   Classical Practice

The eminent digests contain a cluster of cases in which the British Foreign Office and the United States Department of State held that injury to property during an epidemic did not entitle a foreign national to compensation. In 1875, the destruction of property by Turkish authorities to combat plague entitled British nationals to compensation only if local subjects were compensated.[155] Similarly, in 1894, Brazilian authorities destroyed the watermelon crop of the US nationals to prevent the spread of cholera.[156] The State Department found such measures were 'justified under the circumstances' and accepted the Brazilian view that any claims must go before local courts.[157] The apparent standard of national treatment reflected the ubiquity of epidemics and the reciprocal need to maintain discretion without hypocrisy.[158] There was nevertheless a reasonableness requirement. In the 1893 case of *Lavarello*, Italy was awarded partial indemnity of a trader's travelling expenses and spoilage of his merchandise because Cape Verdean sanitary authorities had exceeded their powers and arbitrarily withdrew an initial order permitting him to unload.[159] In *Bischoff*, moreover, the State was 'liable for damages for the detention of the property for an unreasonable length of time and injuries to the same during that period'.[160] The unlawful conduct of injured foreigners was also a relevant factor in the reasonableness inquiry.[161]

---

[154] International Health Regulations (adopted 23 May 2005, entered into force 15 June 2007) 2509 UNTS 79 (IHR).
[155] C Parry (ed), *A British Digest of International Law*, Vol 6 (Stevens & Sons 1965) 350.
[156] JB Moore, *A Digest of International Law*, Vol 6 (US GPO 1906) 751–2.
[157] ibid 751.
[158] In 1892, the State Department refused to request the relaxation of Colombia's quarantine because the United States had also imposed rigid measures: JB Moore, *A Digest of International Law*, Vol 2 (US GPO 1906) 146.
[159] MM Whiteman, *Damages in International Law*, Vol 2 (US GPO 1937) 879–82.
[160] *Bischoff Case* 420.
[161] In 1885, the Foreign Office refused to entertain the claims of injured companies that had flouted sanitary regulations: Moore (n 156) 144.

The limits of reasonable regulation in the time of cholera were well articulated in the 1861 case of the *Azorian*, a British vessel that was ordered by local authorities in Tenerife to perform quarantine despite its clean bill of health upon departure. The Queen's Advocate complained:

> The fact of the 'Azorian' (alone) being treated in this unjust manner without any *bonâ fide* reason, and whilst free communication was taking place between London and all Parts of Spain, by land and sea, is so unreasonable, and *primâ facie* indefensible, that the mere assertion of the technical legal power of the Board of Health to do as it did will not satisfy the British Government.[162]

There had been no 'symptom of disease on board during the voyage'; Spain did not even pretend that the 'arbitrary and unjustifiable' quarantine measure was 'necessary to prevent infection, or that it was done in every (or any) other case'.[163] In a neglected passage of his leading monograph, Martins Paparinskis addressed the *Azorian* as an exemplary case of the distinction between compensable and non-compensable measures in State practice of the nineteenth century.[164] He accordingly adopted the *Azorian* case as a yardstick of classical customary law in his assessment of the modern jurisprudence on property rights in the ECtHR[165] and the Inter-American Court of Human Rights,[166] which he further linked to the formulation of arbitrariness by the International Court of Justice in the *ELSI* case[167] and arbitral interpretation of the FET standard in *Saluka*.[168] Following the grain of the *Azorian* case, Paparinskis believed these authorities point towards a consistent method of examining regulatory measures that are alleged to have breached international law: deference to 'the legitimacy of the purpose and means chosen to pursue it as such (unless they are entirely indefensible)' coupled with 'formal and procedural safeguards against abuse in their

---

[162] Parry (n 155) 292.
[163] ibid.
[164] Paparinskis (n 95) 224.
[165] Eg *Sporrong and Lönnroth v Sweden* IHRL 36 (ECHR 1982) [66–74].
[166] Eg *Chaparro Álvarez and Lapo Íñiguez v Ecuador* (Preliminary Objections, Merits, Reparations, and Costs, Judgment of 21 November 2007) IACHR Series C No 170 [183–218].
[167] *Elettronica Sicula SpA (ELSI) (USA v Italy)* (Judgment) [1989] ICJ Rep 15 [128] ('a wilful disregard of due process of law, an act which shocks, or at least surprises, a sense of juridical propriety').
[168] See ELSI [128] ('a wilful disregard of due process of law, an act which shocks, or at least surprises, a sense of juridical propriety'); *Saluka v Czech Republic* [307] (requiring conduct 'reasonably justifiable by public policies' which 'does not manifestly violate the requirements of consistency, transparency, even-handedness and nondiscrimination').

implementation (the absence of which permits a more critical engagement with the ends and means)'.[169]

Tracing the classical practice concerning past pandemics through to modern customary law, therefore, strengthens the presumption of reasonable regulation; rebutted when a claimant proves that government conduct was unreasonable because, for instance, requirements of domestic law were arbitrarily applied, discriminatory, or knowingly violated.[170] A mid-century study observed that State responsibility would be engaged only 'if health or quarantine regulations are imposed not *bona fide* to protect public health, but with the real, though unavowed, purpose of ruining a foreign trader'.[171] As Born would later put it, each State 'possesses broad and unquestioned sovereign powers to protect the health of its population'.[172] As a further corollary of territorial sovereignty, however, Hersch Lauterpacht (in his work for the United Nations Secretariat) underscored each State's 'obligation to take measures both of a preventive nature and of active co-operation with other States against the spread of disease and epidemics'.[173] The pioneering instance of such cooperation was the 1851 International Sanitary Conference of a dozen European States on the 'standardization of quarantine regulations',[174] followed by six conferences before the first binding convention on infectious disease.[175] The World Health Assembly, composed of WHO Members, is the contemporary forum for intergovernmental cooperation, authorised to adopt regulations 'designed to prevent the international spread of disease'.[176] Given that there are 196 parties to the IHR, it is highly likely that a tribunal would take into account any relevant rules in investment treaty claims arising from the COVID-19 pandemic, notably the restriction on additional health measures.

---

[169] Paparinskis (n 95) 242.
[170] cf measures adopted in a 'rapidly developing public health emergency' may be *ultra vires* but 'nevertheless reasonable, necessary and proportionate': *Borrowdale v Director-General of Health* [2020] NZHC 2090 [290].
[171] BA Wortley, *Expropriation in Public International Law* (CUP 1959) 110.
[172] *Philip Morris* Dissent (n 86) [90].
[173] ILC, 'Survey of International Law in Relation to the Work of Codification of the International Law Commission' (10 February 1949) UN Doc A/CN.4/1/Rev.1 [58] citing *Trail Smelter (United States, Canada)* (1941) 3 RIAA 1905.
[174] N Howard-Jones, *The Scientific Background of the International Sanitary Conferences 1851–1938* (WHO 1975) 12.
[175] International Sanitary Convention (adopted 30 January 1892, entered into force 1 November 1893). See further S Murase, 'Epidemics and International Law' (2021) 81 Annuaire de l'Institut de Droit International 37, 45–7.
[176] Constitution of the World Health Organization (adopted 22 July 1946, entered into force 7 April 1948) 14 UNTS 185, Art 21(a).

5.2 Current Prognosis

Two broad categories of regulatory response to the COVID-19 pandemic might give rise to an investment treaty claim: overreach and underreach.[177] Given the fear of regulatory chill animating CCSI's proposed moratorium,[178] responsibility for alleged overreach has been our focus in this chapter.[179] It is nevertheless worth observing how the IHR sets both a floor and a ceiling for internationally lawful health measures. Parties are required to share information with WHO so the Director-General may determine whether an extraordinary event constitutes a 'public health emergency of international concern' (PHEIC),[180] posing 'a public health risk to other States through the international spread of disease' and 'potentially requir[ing] a coordinated international response'.[181] Subject to procedural requirements,[182] the Director-General issues 'temporary recommendations', which may include 'health measures' to be implemented by a party experiencing the PHEIC or by other parties 'without delay' and 'in a transparent and non-discriminatory manner'.[183] The obligation to implement recommended health measures thus serves as the regulatory floor.[184] Reflecting 'the principles of international law', however, the IHR reaffirms 'the sovereign right to legislate and to implement legislation in pursuance of their health policies' while 'uphold[ing] the purpose' of the IHR.[185] That purpose is, in a word, proportionality: the IHR were designed not merely 'to prevent, protect against, control and provide a public health response to the international spread of disease' but to do so in ways that are 'commensurate with and restricted to public health risks' and 'avoid unnecessary interference with international traffic and trade'.[186]

---

[177] cf DE Pozen & KL Scheppele, 'Executive Underreach, in Pandemics and Otherwise' (2020) 114 AJIL 608.
[178] See Section 2 above.
[179] Whether underreach could breach the standard of full protection and security falls beyond this chapter. See fn 127.
[180] IHR (n 154) Arts 5–12.
[181] ibid Art 1.
[182] ibid Art 49.
[183] ibid Arts 15(2) & 42.
[184] See, eg WHO, 'Statement on the Fourth Meeting of the International Health Regulations (2005) Emergency Committee Regarding the Outbreak of Coronavirus Disease (COVID-19)' (*WHO*, 1 August 2020) <www.who.int/news/item/01-08-2020-statement-on-the-fourth-meeting-of-the-international-health-regulations-(2005)-emergency-committee-regarding-the-outbreak-of-coronavirus-disease-(covid-19)> accessed 27 April 2021.
[185] IHR (n 154) Art 3(4).
[186] ibid Art 2.

Elaborating upon the ceiling of proportionality, Art 43(1) provides that the IHR 'shall not preclude' parties from implementing 'additional health measures' in accordance with their domestic law and international obligations in order to achieve a 'greater level of health protection than WHO recommendations'. Additional health measures, however, 'shall not be more restrictive of international traffic and not more invasive or intrusive to persons than reasonably available alternatives that would achieve the appropriate level of health protection'. In determining whether to implement additional health measures, parties are required by Art 43(2) to base their determinations upon scientific principles; available scientific evidence of a risk to human health, or where such evidence is insufficient, the available information including from WHO and other relevant intergovernmental organisations and international bodies; and any available specific guidance or advice from the WHO. The IHR also must be implemented 'with full respect for the dignity, human rights and fundamental freedoms of persons'.[187]

Article 43 of the IHR bears a striking resemblance to Art 5.6 of the SPS Agreement,[188] under which a complaining member of the World Trade Organization (WTO) must establish that there is a reasonably available measure that achieves the responding member's appropriate level of sanitary or phytosanitary protection and is significantly less restrictive to trade.[189] Without digressing into how WTO law should inform its interpretation,[190] it suffices to note that Art 43 of the IHR could be considered more relevant than custom in the interpretation of investment treaty standards.[191] Like the interpretative annex on indirect expropriation in *Bear Creek* and *Eco Oro*, the proportionality inquiry under Art 43 of the IHR is

---

[187] ibid Art 3(1). cf International Covenant on Economic, Social and Cultural Rights (adopted 16 December 1966, entered into force 3 January 1976) 993 UNTS 3, Art 12(2)(c) (on 'prevention, treatment and control of epidemic' as 'steps to be taken ... to achieve the full realization' of 'the right of everyone to the enjoyment of the highest attainable standard of physical and mental health').

[188] Agreement on the Application of Sanitary and Phytosanitary Measures (adopted 15 April 1994, entered into force 1 January 1995) 1867 UNTS 493. See DP Fidler, 'From International Sanitary Conventions to Global Health Security: The New International Health Regulations' (2005) 4 Chin J Int Law 325, 382–3.

[189] WTO, *India – Measures Concerning the Importation of Certain Agricultural Products – Report of the Appellate Body* (4 June 2015) WT/DS430/AB/R [5.203].

[190] cf R Habibi & ors, 'The Stellenbosch Consensus on Legal National Responses to Public Health Risks: Clarifying Article 43 of the International Health Regulations' (2022) 19 IOLR 90, 45–51.

[191] See eg *Continental Casualty v Argentina* (Award of 5 September 2008) ICSID Case No ARB/03/9 [192].

the applicable *lex specialis* for the regulation of infectious disease, setting a floor of recommendations and a ceiling of proportionality.[192] If WHO were to advance this position in an *amicus* brief,[193] a tribunal may be persuaded that the IHR determine the parameters of reasonable regulation during a PHEIC.[194]

Yet there are limits to the relevance of the IHR. As defined under Art 1.1, 'health measure' means 'procedures applied to prevent the spread of disease or contamination', but excludes 'law enforcement or security measures'. Restrictions on additional health measures are determined by reference to temporary recommendations during a PHEIC, which expire automatically after three months unless extended.[195] The proportionality inquiry under Art 43, moreover, balances additional health measures against restrictions on 'international traffic', defined under Art 1.1 as 'the movement of persons, baggage, cargo, containers, conveyances, goods or postal parcels across an international border, including international trade'. This definition notably excludes cross-border flows of capital and financial instruments, let alone assets owned by foreign investors within a State's territory; the IHR does even not cover the same subject matter as investment treaty arbitration.[196] Given these temporal and material limitations, the proportionality inquiry under Art 43 has minimal relevance for claims arising from the full gamut of regulatory responses to the social and economic disruptions caused by the COVID-19 pandemic.

In addition to the inbuilt limits of the IHR, it is important to recall that the principle of systemic integration is directed to the interpretation of investment treaties, not to the application of conflicting rules.[197] While the IHR may take general priority over custom in the regulation of infectious disease, an investment treaty is the product of (usually) bilateral negotiation in respect of investment promotion and protection, which may be considered a *lex specialis* in respect of the multilateral IHR.[198]

---

[192] See fn 123–6.
[193] cf *Philip Morris v Uruguay* (n 69) [37–9].
[194] On the potential significance of WHO's scientific evidence and legal submissions, see CE Foster, 'Respecting Regulatory Measures: Arbitral Method and Reasoning in the *Philip Morris v Uruguay* Tobacco Plain Packaging Case' (2017) 26(3) RECIEL 287.
[195] IHR (n 154) Art 15.3.
[196] See M Waibel, 'Subject Matter Jurisdiction: The Notion of Investment' (2021) 19 ICSID Rep 25.
[197] R Yotova, 'Systemic Integration: An Instrument for Reasserting the State's Control in Investment Arbitration?' in A Kulick (ed), *Reassertion of Control over the Investment Treaty Regime* (CUP 2016) 185.
[198] cf *Continental Casualty v Argentine Republic* [244–5].

Modern investment treaties increasingly make express provision for health measures and future treaties could actively seek to harness private capital towards public health goals through specialised mechanisms for settling health-related investment disputes.[199] In general, however, the proportionality inquiry under Art 43 of the IHR may be considered in certain claims arising from health measures during a PHEIC, but it does not supplant the customary presumption of reasonable regulation defended throughout this chapter and its manifestations in investment jurisprudence: the police powers doctrine, the right to regulate, and a margin of appreciation.

From its microscopic origin, the COVID-19 pandemic has spawned planetary crises of a social, economic, and fiscal character. Yet the State remains the locus of regulatory power in an international legal system founded on the rights and duties of territorial sovereignty. While all States are equal in their sovereignty, the asymmetric impact of the pandemic has exposed unequal institutional capacities. Past tribunals have accommodated local circumstances in determining the reasonableness of government conduct; 'the heritage of the past as well as the overwhelming necessities of the present and future'.[200] In *Philip Morris v Uruguay*, the majority was satisfied that the FET standard did not 'preclude governments from enacting novel rules', even if these were 'in advance of international practice', provided they had 'some rational basis' and were 'not discriminatory'.[201] Conversely, the Tribunal in *Genin v Estonia* found that procedures adopted by a central bank that fell short of 'generally accepted banking and regulatory practice' did not violate the FET standard in light of Estonia's transition status and 'the emergence of state institutions responsible for overseeing and regulating areas of activity perhaps previously unknown'.[202] Such factors must likewise inform how a diligent investor would reasonably expect governments to address the economic recession and social dislocation caused by the COVID-19 pandemic.[203] It should be very difficult for claimants to rebut the customary presumption of reasonable regulation without

---

[199] F Baetens, 'Protecting Foreign Investment and Public Health Through Arbitral Balancing and Treaty Design' (2022) 71 ICLQ 139.
[200] *Mamidoil Jetoil Greek Petroleum Products Societe Anonyme SA v Albania* (Award of 30 March 2015) ICSID Case No ARB/11/24 [629].
[201] *Philip Morris v Uruguay* [430].
[202] *Genin, Eastern Credit Limited, Inc and AS Baltoil v Estonia* (Award of 25 June 2001) ICSID Case No ARB/99/2 [348, 364].
[203] Eg, *Teinver v Argentina* (Award of 21 July 2017) ICSID Case No ARB/09/1 [668–78].

clear evidence of bad faith or discriminatory treatment, more so when threats to human rights convert the State's right to regulate into a duty to regulate.[204]

6 Conclusion

At the time of writing, the annulment committee in *Tethyan Copper Company v Pakistan* found that enforcement of an award of USD 5.9 billion would not compromise the 'capacity to respond promptly and effectively to a pandemic' despite Pakistan's reliance on loans from the International Monetary Fund 'to address the economic impact of the COVID-19 shock'.[205] If the committee's insouciance were reflected in an award on the merits, that would surely provoke more calls for a moratorium or broader exceptions to investment treaty arbitration. The police powers doctrine, the right to regulate, and a margin of appreciation, however, are all examples of an ostensibly 'new jurisprudence' focused on finding 'space for flexibility within the primary rules themselves'.[206] The customary presumption of reasonable regulation, as a longstanding expression of territorial sovereignty, is the underlying driver of these doctrines. While Art 43 of the IHR may have some relevance in determining the proportionality of health measures during a PHEIC, the economic aftermath of the pandemic presents a broader opportunity for governments, counsel and arbitrators to revive the general rule that there is no State responsibility for reasonable regulation of foreign investment. Investment treaty arbitration, rather than acting as an unmitigated constraint on regulatory powers, may both guard against arbitrary treatment by governments and transform the ambitious measures of successful respondents into lasting legal principle in the face of overbearing investors.

---

[204] cf *Urbaser v Argentina* (Award of 8 December 2016) ICSID Case No ARB/07/26 [1205–10]. See fn 187.
[205] *Tethyan Copper v Pakistan* (Decision on Stay of Enforcement of the Award of 17 September 2020) ICSID Case No ARB/12/1 [155–7].
[206] Arato, Claussen & Heath (n 15) 635.

11

Bilateral Investment Treaties, Investor Obligations and Customary International Environmental Law

MADHAV MALLYA

1 Introduction

In 2016, Nigeria and Morocco signed a Bilateral Investment Treaty (BIT), which mandated that the foreign investor conduct an Environmental Impact Assessment (EIA) in accordance with domestic law and that both the foreign investor and the host State apply the precautionary principle to the investment.[1] The BIT also required that foreign investors comply with the international environmental obligations of the host State while operating the investment.[2] This treaty follows upon the heels of several other regional model international investment frameworks which require similar obligations.[3] BITs rarely impose obligations of conduct on foreign investors, given that they are not considered a means of economic regulation,[4] and their primary objective is the promotion and protection of

---

[1] Reciprocal Investment Promotion and Protection Agreement Between the Government of the Kingdom of Morocco and The Government of the Federal Republic of Nigeria (Morocco & Nigeria) (adopted 3 December 2016, not yet in force) Art 14 (Hereinafter Nigeria–Morocco BIT).

[2] Nigeria–Morocco BIT (n 1) Art 18(3).

[3] The language of the precautionary principle clause in the Nigeria–Morocco BIT is identical to the language in the South African Development Committee (SADC) Model BIT and the ECOWAS Common Investment Code. The SADC Model BIT also states that the application of the precautionary principle by investor and investments shall be described in the environmental impact assessment. The ECOWAS Common Investment Code further highlights various aspects of EIA and mandates that environmental and social impact assessment be made available to the general public and local affected communities. In addition, the investor is required to perform restoration, using appropriate technologies for any damage caused to the natural environment and provide necessary environmental information to the competent national environmental authorities, together with measures and costs necessary to avoid and mitigate against potentially harmful effects.

[4] See P Muchlinski, 'Negotiating International Investment Agreements: New Sustainable Development Oriented Initiatives' in S Hindelang, M Krajewski & ors (eds), *Shifting Paradigms in International Investment Law: More Balanced, Less Isolated and Increasingly Diversified* (OUP 2016) 41.

investments. However, these treaties represent a new paradigm in investment treaty drafting. They try to hold foreign investors accountable for potential violations of domestic and international environmental norms. Further, both the precautionary principle and EIA are rules of customary international law.[5] Their inclusion in BITs gives rise to two pertinent issues.

First, though the precautionary principle and EIA are recognised as rules of Customary International Law (CIL), their status as CIL has been highly debated because they are, in essence, rules of procedure, and their form and content vary from jurisdiction to jurisdiction.[6] Therefore, for these rules to create binding obligations upon foreign investors, the host State must have first recognised these rules as CIL. This recognition may happen through domestic law or the ratification of an international treaty or even any other action of the host State which demonstrates acceptance of the rule.

Second, are foreign investors, most of whom are private multinational corporations, directly bound by these rules because of their inclusion in a BIT? Multinational Corporations as non-state actors are not considered to be subjects of international law[7] and, while Investor-State Dispute Settlement (ISDS) tribunals have recognised that they need to operate the investment and act in accordance with the domestic and international environmental obligations of the host State, they have been reluctant to recognise that foreign investors may have any direct environmental obligations with the host State.[8]

To discuss these issues, this chapter will be divided into three parts. The first part will briefly document how the international investment law regime has evolved from an isolated regime, focusing only on investment promotion and protection, to a regime which is trying to take investor responsibility into account. The second part of this chapter will discuss the incorporation of the precautionary principle and EIA as investor

---

[5] P Marie-Dupuy & JE Viñuales, *International Environmental Law* (CUP 2015) 61, 68.

[6] OW Pederson, 'From Abundance to Indeterminacy: The Precautionary Principle and its Two Camps of Custom' (2014) 3(2) TEL 323, 327.

[7] The Tribunals in *Urbaser v Argentina* and *David Aven v Costa Rica* were confronted with the question of whether multinational corporations had the same international human rights and environmental obligations as state actors. Both Tribunals concluded that there was a certain degree of responsibility on multinational corporations to ensure that they operated within the host state's legal obligations. However, those obligations were not identical to those of nation states and in both cases, the relevant investment frameworks did not impose any direct obligation. See *Urbaser v Argentina* (Award of 8 December 2016) ICSID Case No ARB/07/26 [1207–10]; and *David Aven v Costa Rica* (Final Award of 18 September 2018) ICSID Case No UNCT/15/3 [743].

[8] *Urbaser v Argentina* [1210]; *David Aven v Costa Rica* [743].

obligations into BITs, with reference to their status as CIL. It will correspondingly examine how these rules may bind the foreign investor if the host State has recognised them as CIL.

While the BITs analysed in this chapter seek to impose obligations on foreign investors, they also require the host State to apply some of these rules in conjunction with the foreign investors. Therefore, the third part of this chapter will be divided into two sections. It will first discuss how the inclusion of these rules of customary international environmental law in investment treaties will affect host States and whether host States can be held accountable by foreign investors for not implementing the precautionary principle or following EIA procedures.

The second part will discuss the decisions of investor-State arbitral tribunals towards the international environmental obligations of foreign investors as non-State actors. It will argue that while the inclusion of environmental rules in investment treaties is a welcome step towards ensuring investor responsibility, tribunals are not yet ready to acknowledge that foreign investors have responsibility towards the host State unless such obligations are a part of general international law or incorporated in domestic law.[9] It will also situate these decisions within the systemic reluctance of public international law frameworks to impose international environmental obligations on non-State actors such as multinational corporations. Most international efforts to regulate the environmental obligations of multinational corporations place the onus on State parties to create obligations of compliance, rather than create any direct obligation.[10]

2 A Brief History of Environmental Regulation in Investment Treaties

The first BITs focused solely on investment promotion and protection, following a capital exporting model, which sought to protect investments in new nations and former colonies from nationalisation.[11] Initially, only a

---

[9] ibid [1210].
[10] See J Wouters & AL Chane, 'Multinational Corporations in International Law' in M Noorman, A Reinisch & C Ryngaert (eds), *Non-State Actors in International Law* (Bloomsbury 2017) 239.
[11] K Miles, *The Origins of International Investment Law: Empire, Environment and the Safeguarding of Capital* (CUP 2013) 19–20. Miles argues that the content and form of foreign investment protection cannot be separated from its socio-political context and the rules on foreign investment protection evolved throughout the 'colonial encounter' as a tool to protect the interests of capital exporting States and their nationals. She further

handful of BITs were signed between developed and developing nations, in part because of resistance from the New International Economic Order (NIEO) movement and the Permanent Sovereignty over Natural Resources (PSNR) resolution.[12] It was only in the early 1990s that certain States began signing investment treaties, following the collapse of the Soviet Union and the realisation that foreign capital was needed for economic development.[13]

By the early 2000s, States had begun challenging the legitimacy of BITs, arguing that they were a restraint on the sovereign regulatory power of the host State, especially since the threat of investment arbitration could prove costly to developing host States – the concept of 'regulatory chill'.[14] The signing of the North American Free Trade Agreement (NAFTA) in 1994, led to developed economies like the US and Canada finding themselves as respondents in investment treaty arbitration, because domestic environmental regulation was often challenged by foreign investors.[15] Many erstwhile capital importing States became exporters of capital and several BITs were signed between developing countries.[16] These reasons contributed to States' rethinking of the regulatory scope of BITs, beginning with the model US and Canada BITs of 2004 and 2006 respectively.[17]

---

argues that colonial capital exporting States portrayed the European form and content of international law, along with its particular conceptions of property, private wealth, economy and regulation as being the basis for the evolution of international investment law as a mechanism which protected only the investor.

[12] KJ Vandevelde, 'A Brief History of International Investment Agreements' (2005) 12 UCDavis JInt'l L& Pol'y 57.

[13] ibid 174. Terming it the *Global Era*, Vandevelde observes that the victory of market ideology following the collapse of the Soviet Union and loss of alternatives to foreign investment as a source of capital acted as a catalyst for the growth of international investment agreements.

[14] K Tienhaara, 'Regulatory Chill and the Threat of Arbitration' in C Brown & K Miles (eds), *Evolution in Investment Treaty Law and Arbitration* (CUP 2011).

[15] Two early cases where the United States found itself as a respondent were *Methanex v USA* (Final Award of the Tribunal on Jurisdiction and Merits of 3 August 2005) UNCITRAL and *Glamis Gold, Ltd v USA* (Award of 8 June 2009) UNCITRAL. In the former, the Canadian investor producing Methanol challenged the California ban of the additive MTBE of which Methanol was a component. In the latter, the Canadian investor sough compensation from California for a regulation that required the restoration and backfilling of Native American sites. In both cases, the Tribunal held that expropriation had not occurred.

[16] An analysis of the Database of BITs on the International Centre for Settlement of Investment Disputes website shows that more BITs were signed between 1978 and 1995 and onwards, rather than before 1978. Moreover, several BITs signed in the 1980s and 1990s were between developing nations. See ICSID, 'Database of Bilateral Investment Treaties' (*ICSID*, 2022) <https://icsid.worldbank.org/resources/databases/bilateral-investment-treaties> accessed 1 June 2022.

[17] The 2012 US Model BIT, Art 12(5) specifically states that nothing shall prevent the State parties from taking measures or undertaking regulations to protect the environment. Likewise, Annex B of the Treaty excludes non-discriminatory regulatory objectives to protect the environment from the scope of expropriation. Of course, these provisions are also present in the

These BITs contained Exception Clauses and Non-Precluded Measures to regulate the investment, a common component of most BITs today.[18]

> Since then, BITs have continued the trend of allowing the host State to regulate the investment. However, it is rare to see BITs impose obligations of environmental conduct on investors and host States. Countries use IIAs to attract foreign investment and as observed recently, it does not appear likely that express investor obligations of conduct will be included in investment treaties in the immediate future, since they may serve as deterrent to the signing of investment treaties and investors may shy away from making investments.[19]

Admittedly, the BIT models being discussed in this chapter are a unique exception to BIT drafting practices, envisaging that both investors and host States will play a role in the environmental management of the investment. While the treaty drafting language does not have precedent, the objective of this chapter is to give an overview of the investor obligations enshrined in these treaties so that their implications from both the perspective of investors and host States can be understood.

2004 US model BIT. The increased scope of regulation in the US Model BIT is a reflection of the North American Free Trade Agreement (NAFTA) (adopted 17 December 1992, entered into force 1 January 1994) 32 ILM 289; Canada, '2004 Model Agreement for the Promotion and Protection of Investments' (*Canadian Government*, 2004) <https://investmentpolicy.unctad.org/international-investment-agreements/treaty-files/2820/download> accessed 1 June 2022; USTR, '2012 U.S. Model Bilateral Investment Treaty' (USTR, 2012) <https://ustr.gov/sites/default/files/BIT%20text%20for%20ACIEP%20Meeting.pdf> accessed 1 June 2022; USTR, '2004 Model Bilateral Investment Treaty' (USTR, 2004) <https://ustr.gov/sites/default/files/U.S.%20model%20BIT.pdf> accessed 1 June 2022.

[18] A way in which states attempt to promote sustainable development and green economy objectives is the use of exceptions and reservations in IIAs. By exceptions, States ensure that their ability to regulate certain fields will not be restricted by investment treaties. Exceptions can be in several forms, ie, sector-specific treaty reservations, general exceptions such as measures relating to the protection of 'human, animal or plant life or health' or Non-Precluded Measures which are intended to exempt certain subject areas such public health, public security and morality from the scope of the treaty or specific treaty obligations.' These are standardised clauses found in almost all treaties. See MW Gehring & A Kent 'International Investment Agreements and the Emerging Green Economy: Rising to the Challenge' in F Baetens (ed), *Investment Law Within International Law* (CUP 2013) 187, 204. A clause which allows cause for exceptions to a country's liability in an international investment agreement regarding matters such as public health, public order, environmental matters, essential security interests, etc. Non precluded measures preclude the wrongfulness of a nation's regulatory liability in such areas. They are a form of exception clauses.

[19] See M Krajewski, 'A Nightmare or a Noble Dream? Establishing Investor Obligations Through Treaty-Making and Treaty-Application' (2020) 5(1) BHRJ 105, 128. Krajewski observes that recent treaty-making practice in international law does not seem to move towards including clear and precise binding human rights obligations for investors. Consequently, it seems unlikely that investor obligations to respect human rights will emerge in the foreseeable future in international treaty making or treaty-application. The Nigeria–Morocco BIT appears to be an exception to the rule.

3 Integrating Customary International Environmental Law in Investment Treaties

3.1 Treaty Drafting Practices

Over the past decade or so, several regional model investment treaties have tried to integrate the EIA and the precautionary principles as investor obligations. The clauses in the Nigeria–Morocco BIT are based on similar clauses from other model treaties as well the International Institute for Sustainable Development Model BIT.[20] In addition, the African Union in 2016 produced the Draft Pan African Investment Code, a comprehensive document which seeks to protect the environment through investor obligations and promote investment protection in the African continent.[21] However, are these obligations couched in terms which make them directly binding on foreign investors or is their enforceability dependent on domestic law or the host State's international environmental obligations?

Article 14(1) of the Nigeria–Morocco BIT mandates 'that investors or the investment shall comply with environmental assessment screening and assessment processes applicable to their proposed investments prior to their establishment as required by the laws of the host state or home state, whichever is more rigorous'.[22] Article 14(3) states that

> investors, their investments, and host state authorities shall apply the precautionary principle to their environmental impact assessment and to decisions taken in relation to a proposed investment, including any necessary mitigation [sic] or alternative approaches of the precautionary principle by investors and investments shall be described in the environmental impact assessment they undertake.[23]

Article 18(3) states that '[i]nvestors and investments shall not manage or operate the investments in a manner that circumvents international environmental, labour and human rights obligations to which the host state and/or home state are parties'.[24]

---

[20] See H Mann, K Van Moltke, LE Peterson & ors, 'International Institute for Sustainable Development Model International Agreement on Investment for Sustainable Development, Negotiators Handbook' (*IISD*, Aril 2006) <www.iisd.org/system/files/publications/investment_model_int_handbook.pdf> accessed 1 June 2022 (hereinafter IISD Model BIT).

[21] See African Union Commission, 'Draft Pan African Investment Code' (December 2016) <https://au.int/sites/default/files/documents/32844-doc-draft_pan-african_investment_code_december_2016_en.pdf> accessed 1 June 2022 (hereinafter Draft PAIC).

[22] Nigeria–Morocco BIT (n 1) Art 14(1).

[23] ibid, Art 14(3).

[24] ibid, Art 18(3).

These clauses are almost identical to the corresponding clauses of the International Institute of Sustainable Development (IISD) Model Investment Agreement. Article 12(a) of the IISD Model Agreement provides for investors to comply with the EIA processes of the home State or the host State, whichever is more rigorous.[25] The only addition is that Article 12(a) calls for the parties to adopt a minimum standard of EIA at their first meeting and comply with these standards on all occasions. Likewise, Article 12(d) requires investors to apply the precautionary principle to their investments.[26] Article 14(d) is identical to Article 18(3) of the Nigeria–Morocco BIT.[27]

While the South African Development Community (SADC) Model BIT also adopts identical language to the Nigeria–Morocco BIT and SADC Model BIT, it goes a step ahead and prescribes the International Finance Corporation's (IFC) performance standards on environmental and social impact assessments as an alternative to home State and host State laws.[28] Likewise, the Economic Committee of West African States (ECOWAS) Common Investment Code also adopts the precautionary principle and EIA as investor obligations but only mandates the investor to undertake an EIA and social impact assessment of proposed business activities and investments with respect to natural environment and the local population in the relevant jurisdiction. It also only mandates the investor to apply the precautionary principle to the EIA or social impact assessment, including any mitigating approaches.[29]

Finally, the Pan African Investment Code (PAIC) does not mention the precautionary principle but simply mandates the investor to conduct an EIA.[30] However, the Nigeria–Morocco BIT, IISD Model Investment Agreement, ECOWAS Common Investment Code and the PAIC incorporate these obligations to try and hold the investor accountable for the violation of environmental norms; they do not, however, prescribe any standard to be followed for the implementation of the precautionary principle and EIA. In the absence of a domestic law incorporating EIA or

---

[25] IISD Model BIT (n 20) Art 12(a).
[26] ibid, Art 12(d).
[27] Nigeria–Morocco BIT (n 1) Art 18(3); ibid 14(d).
[28] SADC, 'SADC Model Bilateral Investment Treaty Template: With Commentary' (*SADC*, July 2012) Art 13.1 <www.iisd.org/itn/wp-content/uploads/2012/10/sadc-model-bit-template-final.pdf> accessed 1 June 2022.
[29] ECOWAS, 'ECOWAS Common Investment Code (ECOWIC)' (July 2018) arts 27(1)(b-d) <https://wacomp.projects.ecowas.int/wp-content/uploads/2020/03/ECOWAS-COMMON-INVESTMENT-CODEENGLISH.pdf> accessed 1 March 2022.
[30] Draft PAIC (n 20) Art 37(4).

the precautionary principle, these investor obligations may be rendered nugatory. Moreover, even if the investor must act in accordance with the host State's international obligations, which may include the host State's recognised rules of CIL, it will be difficult for the investor to implement these rules in the absence of domestic law. It is only the SADC Model BIT which expressly prescribes the IFC standards in absence of rigorous domestic standards.[31] However, the adoption of these standards is subject to an agreement between the investor and host State. Therefore, does the inclusion of these CIL obligations in BITs have any real significance for investor obligations, or are they just window dressing without any real effect? The next subsection, which discusses the customary nature of the precautionary principle and EIA, will try to answer this question.

3.2 Customary International Law Status of the Precautionary Principle and Environmental Impact Assessment and Their Relevance as Investor Obligations

3.2.1 The Precautionary Principle

The Precautionary Principle was first incorporated into international environmental agreements in the 1980s, though precautionary thinking had been present in domestic environmental policy.[32] The basic underlying idea behind this concept is that the lack of scientific certainty about the actual or potential effects of an activity must not prevent States from taking appropriate measures.[33] The most accepted formulation of the precautionary principle is in the Rio Declaration. Principle 15 states that:

> In order to protect the environment, the precautionary approach shall be widely applied by states according to their capabilities. Where there are threats of serious or irreversible damage, lack of full scientific certainty shall not be used as a reason for postponing cost-effective measures to prevent environmental degradation.[34]

---

[31] Supra SADC (n 28).
[32] P Sands, J Peel, A Fabra & ors, *Principles of International Environmental Law* (CUP 2012) 34–5.
[33] Marie-Dupuy & Viñuales (n 5) 61. The main thesis of the precautionary principle is that in the face of serious risk to or grounds (as appropriately qualified) for concern about the environment, scientific uncertainty or the absence of complete proof should not stand in the way of positive action to minimise risks or take actions of a conservatory, preventative or curative nature; see also *Southern Bluefin Tuna Cases (NZ v Japan; Australia v Japan)* (Provisional Measures, Order of 27 August 1999) 1999 ITLOS Rep 280, Separate Opinion of Judge Laing [14].
[34] UNGA, 'Report of the United Nations Conference on Environment and Development' (16 March 1992) UN Doc A/RES/47/190 (Rio Declaration) principle 15.

The precautionary principle is not so much a *principle,* as it is a *rule* or a *standard.*[35] This dichotomy marks a controversy regarding its actual status as a rule of customary international law. Though it has been included in several transboundary environmental treaties, all of which reflect the approach echoed in the Rio Declaration, its status as a CIL rule has been debated.[36] The debate surrounding its normative content also has a spillover effect in its application, as is it a rule that obligates a State to act irrespective of scientific uncertainty. Does such a spillover, therefore, shift the burden of proof to the proponent of a project (ie, the investor), or is it simply a standard which States may include in its domestic laws and policies, with varying environmental standards and thresholds?[37]

There is one school of thought which argues that it is CIL, simply, based on the frequency of its inclusion in multilateral treaties and declarations, while another school of thought argues that it is not customary international law since actual State practice is difficult to prove empirically.[38]

---

[35] Pederson (n 6) 329.

[36] For a detailed list of treaties containing the precautionary principle or incorporating a precautionary approach, See J Peel, *The Precautionary Principle in Practice* (Federation Press 2005). For example, some treaties define the precautionary principle and then apply it. The Convention to Ban the Importation into Forum Island Countries of Hazardous and Radioactive Wastes and to Control the Transboundary Movement and Management of Hazardous Wastes within the South Pacific Region (adopted 16 September 1995, entered into force 21 October 2001) 2161 UNTS 91, Art 1: '"Precautionary principle" means the principle that in order to protect the environment, the precautionary approach shall be widely applied by Parties according to their capabilities. Where there are threats of serious or irreversible damage, lack of full scientific certainty shall not be used as a reason for postponing cost effective measures to prevent environmental degradation', Art 13(3) of the same convention; likewise, the preamble of the Cartagena Protocol on Biosafety to the Convention on Biological Diversity (adopted 29 January 2000, entered into force 11 September 2003) 39 ILM 1027, reaffirms the precautionary approach contained in Principle 15 of the Rio Declaration on Environment and Development. Article 1 states that 'In accordance with the precautionary approach contained in Principle 15 of the Rio Declaration on Environment and Development, the objective of this Protocol is to contribute to ensuring an adequate level of protection in the field of the safe transfer, handling and use of living modified organisms resulting from modern biotechnology that may have adverse effects on the conservation and sustainable use of biological diversity, taking also into account risks to human health, and specifically focusing on transboundary movements'.

[37] Sands & ors (n 32) 61: 'Even if the existence of a customary precautionary principle could be admitted, its content would still have to be defined. Is it an obligation to take action despite the lack of sufficient evidence about the danger that an activity poses to the environment? Or is it, rather, a simple authorisation to take such measures?'.

[38] According to the non-custom camp, since the principle is ill defined, it is difficult to prove empirically, see Pederson (n 6) 329.

This is the classic *rule vs standard* dialectic.[39] CIL is often difficult to prove and depends upon whether widespread State practice (and corresponding *opinio juris*) can be established.[40] This grey area has not been resolved by the decisions of several international courts and tribunals, which have adopted what may be called a *precautionary approach*, where they have been reluctant to recognise the principle as CIL. This reluctance stems from the fact that while international treaties may enshrine the rule, its application, form and content differs across jurisdictions, which poses a challenge in establishing definitive State practice.

In the *Southern Bluefin Tuna* case, New Zealand and Australia filed for provisional measures restraining Japan from unilaterally designing and undertaking an experimental fishing programme.[41] Both New Zealand and Australia requested that the parties act consistently in accordance with the precautionary principle.[42] In their decision, the Tribunal did not expressly mention the precautionary principle, but stated that even though they could not conclusively assess the scientific evidence presented by the parties, further measures must be taken to preserve the rights of the parties and to avert further deterioration of Bluefin Tuna and that the parties must act with prudence and caution to ensure that effective conservation measures are taken.[43]

Though the Tribunal did not expressly mention the precautionary principle, several separate opinions clarified the approach of the Tribunal, lending clarity to the application of the precautionary principle. Judge

---

[39] ibid 334. According to Pederson, this dialectic plays out where controversy arises concerning the enactment of a legal directive or norm. Preference may be given to rules over principles, depending on which virtues and vices or vice versa. The non-custom camp prefers the conception of rules over broader principles.

[40] The custom camp primarily relies on widespread State practice to bolster its stand that the precautionary principle is CIL. Since *opinio juris* is a state of mind, there is difficulty in attributing it to a State, and therefore, it has to be deduced from a State's actions and pronouncements. A rule is often considered to be CIL by being codified in multilateral conventions – in fact, so much so, that a judge no longer has to ascertain from the practice what the alleged rule requires, see H Thirlway, *The Sources of International Law* (OUP 2005) 80. The ICJ, in *Military and Paramilitary Activities in and against Nicaragua (Nicaragua v USA)* (Merits) [1986] ICJ Rep 16, 98 [186], explained that for a rule to be considered customary it dd not consider that the corresponding practice must be in absolute conformity with the rule. Rather, it is sufficient that the conduct of States should, in general, be consistent with such rules.

[41] *Southern Bluefin Tuna Cases (NZ v Japan; Australia v Japan)* (Provisional Measures, Order of 27 August 1999) 1999 ITLOS Rep 280 [28–9].

[42] ibid [34].

[43] ibid [77].

Laing stated that adopting an *approach* (sic), rather than a principle, appropriately imports a certain degree of flexibility and tends, though not dispositively, to underscore reticence about making pronouncements about desirable normative structures.[44] Judge Treves, while regretting that the precautionary principle was not expressly stated in the order of the Tribunal, underscored the importance of the Tribunal adopting a precautionary approach even though it was reluctant in taking a position whether it was a binding position of international law. Observing that the measures prescribed by the Tribunal aimed at stopping the deterioration of the Southern Bluefin tuna stock, it was essential that the Tribunal adopt a precautionary approach since there was scientific uncertainty whether the situation of the stock had improved.[45] In fact, he equated the notion of precaution with 'caution', an aspect inherent in the very notion of precautionary measures.[46]

Reinforcing this approach, in the *EC Asbestos* dispute, the WTO Appellate body adopted a precautionary approach, stating that member States have the undisputed right to determine the level of health protection they deem appropriate and that Canada, the proponent of the exports, would have to prove that their 'controlled use' alternative would achieve the same level of protection.[47] In the *Nuclear Tests* case, the separate dissenting opinions of Judges Weeramantry and Palmer supported the idea of the Precautionary Principle being a rule of customary international law relating to the environment.[48] In the *EC-Hormones* dispute, the

---

[44] ibid, Separate Opinion of Judge Laing [19].
[45] ibid, Separate Opinion of Judge Treves [8].
[46] ibid.
[47] WTO, *European Communities – Measures Affecting Asbestos and Asbestos-Containing Products – Report of the Appellate Body* (12 March 2001) WT/DS135/AB/R [53].
[48] In the *Nuclear Tests* case, Judge Palmer (dissenting) observed that the norm involved in the precautionary principle has developed rapidly and may now be a principle of customary international law. Judge Weeramantry (dissenting) observed that reversing the burden of proof was an essential element to guarantee an effective protection of the environment and give full force to the legal obligations tending to ensure this protection. New Zealand argued that France should prove the absolute innocuity of nuclear tests in the South Pacific. See *Request for an Examination of the Situation in Accordance with Paragraph 63 of the Court's Judgment of 20th December 1974 in the Nuclear Tests (New Zealand v France)* [1995] ICJ Rep 288, Dissenting opinion by Judge ad hoc Sir Geoffrey Palmer [91] & Dissenting opinion by Judge Weeramantry 343. The reluctance to directly refer to the precautionary principle as custom is reflective of the lack of uniform conception of the principle. In the *Pulp Mills* decision, the ICJ observed that the precautionary principle may be relevant in the interpretation and application of the provisions of the disputed treaty. Within the context of the Nigeria–Morocco BIT, the inclusion of the precautionary principle may provide clear guidance as to the environmental management procedures to be followed by the

WTO Appellate Body, while noting that the Precautionary Principle did not override the treaty obligation of Article 5.7 of the WTO Agreement on Sanitary and Phytosanitary Standards to base measures on a risk assessment, noted that it would be unnecessary to take a position on whether the precautionary principle had been authoritatively formulated as a general principle of customary international law, since 'responsible, representative governments commonly act from perspectives of prudence and caution where risks are irreversible...'.[49]

3.2.2 Environmental Impact Assessment

Like the Precautionary Principle, the status of EIA as customary international law is not established. While it may be argued that it is custom in a transboundary context, given the number of treaties and tribunal decisions which stress its importance,[50] it is not referred to in a transnational context to the treaties discussed in this chapter. Rather, the reference to EIA will be within the domestic context. Still, it has been observed that human rights law has greatly expanded through the adoption of wide-ranging international conventions, even with the typical difficulty in establishing a practice based customary law.[51] Since many of these conventions have been ratified by almost all States, it is argued that the norms embodied in those conventions are binding on non-parties, leading to a customary law of human rights.[52] It might be argued that even though an EIA has been recognised as customary in a transboundary context, it has developed as a customary norm of international environmental law, where the rule of conducting an *impact assessment* is customary rather than the context in which it is undertaken.

---

investors; see *Pulp Mills on the River Uruguay (Argentina v Uruguay)* (Merits) [2010] ICJ Rep 14 [164].

[49] WTO, *European Communities – Measures Concerning Meat and Meat Products (Hormones) – Report of the Appellate Body* (13 February 1998) WT/DS26/AB/R, WT/DS48/AB/R [124].

[50] Convention on Environmental Impact Assessment in a Transboundary Context (adopted 25 February 1991, entered into force 10 September 1997) 1989 UNTS 309. In the *Case Concerning Pulp Mills* [204] the ICJ observed, 'that a practice has developed which in recent years has gained so much acceptance among states that it may now be considered a requirement under general international law to undertake an environmental impact assessment where there is a risk that the proposed industrial activity may have a significant adverse impact in a transboundary context, in particular, on a shared resource'.

[51] Thirlway (n 40) 72.

[52] ibid 73.

It is evident that while the customary status of the precautionary principle as rule *per se* is debated, courts and tribunals appear to treat the precautionary approach as customary. What is the significance of this approach for BITs? It could be argued that by placing the onus of applying the precautionary principle in the context of an EIA on the investor and the host State, a BIT is trying to adopt a precautionary approach, giving credence to what may be termed a *customary approach* instead of customary rule. The significance of this inclusion cannot be underestimated. BITs, which have traditionally only obligated host States to protect the investment, could now require environmental cooperation between the investor and host State. The inclusion of these CIL rules in BITs also promotes the host State's right to regulate the investment, though of course, domestic frameworks or standards would have to be adopted to give effect to these rules creating investor obligations.[53]

While these treaties try to ensure that the host State regulates the investment in accordance with its international legal obligations and places affirmative obligations of conduct on the investor, it remains to be seen whether and how investor-State dispute settlement tribunals may interpret these clauses and agree with the objectives of such inclusion. This question is discussed in the following section.

4 The Interpretation of Environmental Obligations by Investor-State Arbitration Tribunals

While the precautionary principle and EIA clauses in the treaties discussed above have not yet been interpreted by any investor-State arbitration tribunal, they have implications for investors and host States alike. This section examines the jurisprudence of investor-State arbitration tribunals, which discuss the host State's environmental obligations towards foreign investors – both substantive and procedural. Subsequently, it will discuss the approach of tribunals towards the environmental obligations of foreign investors.

---

[53] India has recently diluted its environmental screening procedures to attract greater investment. It allows certain projects of strategic importance to be cleared without screening and has reduced the timeline for public participation. Therefore, even if a BIT were to include the application of a precautionary approach, it would depend on whether domestic law provides for that approach. See Indian Government, 'Ministry Of Environment, Forest And Climate Change: Notification' (*Gazette of India*, 23 March 2020) Extraordinary, pt II, sect 3, subsect (ii) <http://environmentclearance.nic.in/writereaddata/Draft_EIA_2020.pdf> accessed 1 June 2022.

4.1 Procedural Implications for Host States

Foreign investors have often challenged the procedures used by the host State to apply the precautionary principle to the investment or to challenge the EIA methodology employed by the host State to assess the investment.[54] Consequently, tribunals have adjudicated on the legitimacy of application of these procedural rules. Investors have also argued that host State's neglect of the environment has led to a diminishment of value of the investment. These decisions are discussed below.

The *Bilcon*[55] decision concerned the denial of a permit to conduct mining activities in Nova Scotia following the recommendation of an environmental joint review panel (JRP). On the grounds of procedural fairness, the majority of the tribunal concluded that the review panel had acted in breach of Canadian environmental law, which amounted to a breach of the international minimum standard of treatment. The Tribunal held that it was a serious breach of the law on procedural fairness that Bilcon was denied reasonable notice of the 'community core values' standard of the environmental JRP as well as a chance to seek clarification and respond to it.[56] The Tribunal emphasised that while legislatures could adopt rigorous and comprehensive environmental regulations, including assessments, those regulations had to be actually implemented and carried out.[57]

The *Bilcon* award highlights the importance of an effective and transparent impact assessment procedure prior to the establishment of the investment and could work as a call to host States to incorporate such clauses into BITs, in order to ensure stability and transparency of investment projects.[58] Such impact assessment mechanisms, along with adopting a precautionary approach, could include public participation in the form of information sharing and consultation which would increase the likelihood of potential impacts, the disclosure of all alternatives and the reasons for rejection of certain alternatives based on a measure of accountability.[59]

---

[54] H Davies, 'Investor-State Dispute Settlement and the Future of the Precautionary Principle' (2016) 5(2) Br J A Leg Studies 449, 454.

[55] *Bilcon v Canada* (Award of 17 March 2015) PCA Case No 2009-04.

[56] ibid [534].

[57] ibid [597-8].

[58] MW Gehring, 'Impact Assessments of Investment Treaties' in MC Cordonier Segger, MW Gehring & AP Newcombe (eds) *Sustainable Development in World Investment Law* (Kluwer Law 2011) 149-50.

[59] ibid.

In *Allard v Barbados*, the claimant claimed that the host State failed to take the necessary environmental protection measures and contributed to the contamination of the claimant's eco-tourism site.[60] These actions violated the FET and expropriation standards of the investment.[61] While the Tribunal noted that the host State was not responsible for the contamination of the eco-tourism site, and therefore, the terms of the BIT were not violated,[62] it did note that the claimant bought the land for economic development even before submitting an environmental management plan or conducting an EIA, against the warnings of State officials.[63]

The decisions in these awards may be relevant to scenarios where both the investor and the host State have the responsibility of ensuring the environmental viability of a project. The Nigeria–Morocco BIT and the African model treaties, which create such a scenario, do not explain what they mean by these clauses. Nonetheless, some educated guesses can be made as to potential interpretative implications that may arise with respect to these clauses.

First, procedurally speaking, the host State will be bound to be transparent with the investor about environmental screening procedures. Moreover, if a host State alleges that an investor is responsible for environmental degradation, the host State cannot evade responsibility if proper procedures have not been followed or if a project has been approved even without environmental sanction. Therefore, the host State may share liability with a foreign investor for environmental degradation.

Second, an investor cannot argue that environmental procedures were not informed or that the host State did not follow due procedures and that action of the host State led to a diminishment in the economic value of the investment. A joint reading of the obligations in the Nigeria–Morocco BIT, the ECOWAS treaty, and the SADC Model and to some extent, the PAIC, emphasise that the obligation to conduct an EIA employing the precautionary approach is on the investor, in conjunction with the host State and that there is a certain duty of responsibility.[64]

---

[60] *PA Allard v Barbados* (Award of 27 June 2016) PCA Case No 2012–06 [3].
[61] ibid.
[62] ibid [226].
[63] ibid [224].
[64] There may also be a certain benefit in the investor co-operating with the host State in conducting an environmental screening of the investment. *Bear Creek Mining Corporation v Peru* (Award of 30 November 2017) ICSID Case No ARB/14/21 [39]. In *Bear Creek Mining Corporation v Peru* (Partial Dissenting Opinion of Professor Philippe Sands of 30 November 2017) ICSID Case No ARB/14/21, Sands argued in his dissenting opinion

4.2 Investor-State Arbitration and Investor Obligations

BITs do not expressly impose environmental obligations of conduct on foreign investors, whether in accordance with domestic law or international law. Consequently, tribunals have rarely had a chance to expound upon investor obligations from a general international law perspective. The limited jurisprudence on investor obligations usually involves counterclaims. However, even these instances have been marked by a reluctance on the part of tribunals to expressly recognise investor obligations unless they are treaty obligations or a general principle of international law.[65] In general, tribunals have also been reluctant to recognise human rights defences raised by host states.[66]

Both the Nigeria–Morocco BIT and the SADC Model Treaty recognise the domestic and international environmental obligations of foreign investors. However, international environmental treaties do not impose any obligations on non-State actors and, while domestic law may place a precautionary burden of proof on a private actor, the onus to apply the principle and decide is on a State party.[67] Therefore, to what extent would clauses that mandate that foreign investor conduct an EIA and apply the precautionary principle, in accordance with the international legal obligations of the host State, have credence before an investor-State arbitration tribunal? Further, would such tribunals be willing to hold foreign investors liable in accordance with international law? The following analysis discusses the jurisprudence on investor obligations to answer this question.

In *Aven v Costa Rica*, the respondent claimed that the suspension of the claimant's real estate project was in pursuit of legitimate environmental interests protected under the Central America-Dominican Republic Free Trade Agreement (DR-CAFTA)[68] and in accordance with Costa Rica's domestic and international environmental obligations.[69] The respondent

---

that investors are obliged to adhere to human rights in particular, to minimise any potential damages which investors could suffer. See also, T Ishikawa, *The Role of International Environmental Principles in Investment Treaty Arbitration: Precautionary and Polluter Pays Principles and Partial Compensation* (Brill 2016) 245.

[65] *Urbaser v Argentina* [1207].

[66] JH Fahner & M Happold, 'The Human Rights Defence in International Investment Arbitration: Exploring the Limits of Systemic Integration' (2019) 68(3) ICLQ 741, 758.

[67] See, Peel (n 36), where most environmental treaties place the onus of applying the precautionary principle on State parties.

[68] For the full text of the DR-CAFTA, see Free Trade Agreement between Central America, the Dominican Republic and the United States of America (DR-CAFTA) (adopted 5 August 2004, entered into force 1 January 2009).

[69] *David Aven v Costa Rica* [385].

also argued that sound and efficient measures to protect the environment is key to the implementation of the treaty.[70] Chapter 17 of the DR-CAFTA expressly reserved space for environmental issues.[71] While making these arguments, the respondent maintained that neither the treaty nor the customary international law exonerates the claimants from complying with Costa Rica's framework for the protection of the environment.[72] However, the respondent did not emphasise which rule of customary international law applied to the claimants.[73]

One of the respondent's key contentions was that the burden of proof was reversed on the party allegedly causing the risk of harm, that is, the claimant had the burden of disclosing to the host State, the existence of protected wetlands and forests on the construction site.[74] The respondent tied this obligation to the precautionary principle, recognised in its domestic biodiversity law which provided that 'the burden of proof … shall correspond to whom requests the approval, the permit, or the access to biodiversity, or who is accused of having caused environmental harm'.[75] The respondent linked these obligations in its domestic law to its international obligations under the Ramsar and Biodiversity Conventions.[76]

The Tribunal sided with the respondent and found that the claimant had a duty to advise the environmental authorities in matters that affect any impact to the environment, and to evidence that no adverse impact was to occur as a result of the development, and that this duty arose under domestic law.[77] Therefore, the burden of proof was with the claimant when applying for a permit to demonstrate the absence of non-permitted pollution, degradation or affectation.[78] A pertinent question arises from this ruling, relevant to our central analysis.

First, the Tribunal did not hold the claimant responsible in accordance with international law or the precautionary principle, *per se*, but rather

---

[70] ibid.
[71] ibid. Article 17.2 of the DR-CAFTA recognises a Party's right to enforce its environmental laws. Article 17.12 further recognises that the implementation of multilateral environmental agreements is critical to achieving the objectives of those agreements. Article 10.11 allows a State Party to adopt, maintain or enforce any measure, consistent with its investment obligations, to ensure that investment activity in its territory is undertaken in a manner sensitive to environmental concerns.
[72] ibid.
[73] ibid [394].
[74] ibid [444].
[75] ibid.
[76] ibid [417–18].
[77] ibid [552].
[78] ibid [553].

in accordance with domestic law which incorporated the precautionary approach. The claimant had a duty under the domestic biodiversity law to advise the competent authority in matters that affect any impact to the environment and to evidence that no adverse impact was to occur as a result of the development.[79]

Therefore, even if a BIT does say that a foreign investor must apply the precautionary principle and conduct an EIA, the tribunal will be bound to decide in accordance with the domestic law of that State, rather than an absolute rule, even if that rule is embodied in the treaty. This approach again gives rise to the *rule vs standard* dialectic. Even if the BIT states that the investor must operate the investment in accordance with the host State's international obligations and apply the precautionary principle, the application of such rule will happen in accordance with domestic law, even if the host state has ratified environmental treaties which imbibe the precautionary approach.[80] It is, therefore, difficult to gauge the efficacy of the investor obligations in the Nigeria–Morocco BIT and draft PAIC from a purely international law perspective, even more so since these BITs are not in force.

Tribunals have also been reluctant to import investor obligations into investment treaties unless the treaty expressly mentions obligations.[81] In the *Aven* dispute, the host State also filed a counterclaim alleging that the claimant was responsible for environmental damage. Though the Tribunal recognised that the claimant was bound by the environmental measures taken by the host State under the DR-CAFTA, it observed that the treaty did not place any direct affirmative obligation on foreign investors.[82] Of course, an arbitral tribunal's ruling may differ regarding a treaty which expressly places obligations on the investor. In such cases, as the model treaties discussed in this chapter suggest, in the absence of a domestic legal framework the question of being held liable in accordance with international law would arise.[83]

The *Urbaser v Argentina* dispute is more relevant in the context of discussing the relationship between human rights treaties and the international investment law regime. However, the reasoning employed by the Tribunal

---

[79] ibid [552–3].
[80] *Urbaser v Argentina* [1210]. The Tribunal observed that the investor was only bound by the BIT and domestic law – ensuring the human right to water was the responsibility of the host State.
[81] ibid [1207].
[82] *David Aven v Costa Rica* [743].
[83] Please see Section 2.1 of this chapter.

is of some significance to understanding how the rules of international environmental law within investment treaties may apply to foreign investors.

In their counterclaim, Argentina argued that they suffered damage since the claimant failed to make the necessary level of investment, which would have guaranteed the human right to water and sanitation.[84] Their position was that under the concession contract and applicable regulatory framework, the claimants assumed investment obligations, which gave rise to bonafide expectations that the investment would be made and guarantee the human rights to water and sanitation. By failing to make these investments, the claimants violated the principles of good faith and *pacta sunt servanda* recognised by both Argentina and international law.[85] The claimant, on the other hand, argued that it was Argentina's regulatory actions which prevented them from making the investment and that the Argentine Republic should be the true guarantor of human rights, and not a private party.[86] The investor also argued that the treaty did not place any express obligations on the investor and, therefore, the counterclaim of the host State faced the insurmountable challenge of being presented in the context of a BIT which did not create obligations for the investor or subject the investor to the rules of Argentine or international law.[87] While Argentina agreed that the responsibility of the investor originated under international law *per se*, through the concession framework, it argued that the Universal Declaration on Human Rights placed obligations on private parties and had achieved the status of customary international law.[88]

In making its decision whether the investor had any positive obligation to guarantee human rights, the Tribunal referred to the dispute resolution clause of the Spain–Argentina BIT, which stated that disputes had to be decided in accordance with the general principles of international law. Using this clause as a steppingstone to further its arguments, the Tribunal ruled that a BIT cannot be an isolated, asymmetric set of rules, which only focuses on investment protection.[89] However, this is where the Tribunal showed a reluctance to read and express human rights obligation upon the investor within the treaty. The guarantee of human rights should be borne solely by the State, and the investor had a duty to ensure that its operations did not obstruct the host State from fulfilling its human rights

---

[84] *Urbaser v Argentina* [1156].
[85] ibid.
[86] ibid.
[87] ibid [1167].
[88] ibid [1158].
[89] ibid [1201].

obligations.[90] For such an obligation to exist, it should be part of another treaty or represent a principle of general international law.[91]

The precautionary principle and EIA are not substantive rights. Rather within the international and transnational context, they are procedurally binding on State parties in terms of application and implementation. If the reasoning of the *Urbaser* Tribunal were to be followed, there is no international treaty obligation, or any general principal of international law independent of the investment treaty, which obligates private investors to implement these obligations. Therefore, it seems unlikely that tribunals would budge from their narrow stance on the international law-based obligations of investors. This reluctance stems not only from the ambiguity surrounding the international environmental obligations of non-State actors but also whether arbitrators will accept the validity of a treaty which directly imposes international obligations on investors. Irrespective of their status in general international law, most treaties only mandate that investors act in accordance with domestic law and even these obligations rarely extent to obligations of conduct.[92]

The question of whether international obligations can be imposed on non-State actors or not remains unanswered. The next section explores this question from the wider perspective of those frameworks which try to impose environmental and human rights obligations on multinational corporations. It situates this discussion within the unique conception of international investment law, a regime which gives international rights to foreign investors but does not impose liabilities upon them.

5   The Environmental Liability of Foreign Investors as Non-State Actors – An International Law Perspective

The tribunals in the *Urbaser* and *Aven* counterclaims made similar observations that 'it can no longer be admitted that companies operating internationally are immune from becoming subjects of international

---

[90] ibid [1210].
[91] ibid [1207].
[92] See R Yotova, 'Compliance with Domestic Law: An Implied Condition in Treaties Conferring Rights and Protections on Foreign Nationals and Their Property?' in J Klingler, Y Parkhomenko & C Salonidis (eds), *Between the Lines of the Vienna Convention? Canons and Other Principles of Interpretation in Public International Law* (Kluwer 2018) 307. She observes that compliance with domestic law rarely extends to obligations of conduct – most requirements of compliance are in regard to admission of investments, the definition of investment or limit the application of the treaty to investments made in accordance with the laws of the host State. However, this does not mean that investors are necessarily bound by the environmental obligations of the host State.

law'.⁹³ This observation was because several international instruments encouraged non-State actors to observe human rights and environmental obligations and investment treaties themselves expected investors to abide by host State measures to protect the environment. However, this is where the buck stopped, and the tribunals were unable to express themselves any further on the issue of the environmental liability of foreign investors. This limitation arose because general principles of international law do not recognise the international environmental liabilities of non-State actors. Indeed, while there are several soft law efforts to draft human rights codes for transnational multinational corporations like the 'UN Draft Norms on the Responsibilities of Transnational Corporations and Other Business Enterprises with Regard to Human Rights', the 'Guiding Principles on Business and Human Rights' and the 'Third Draft of the Open Ended Intergovernmental Working Group (OEIGWG)', these instruments place the onus of regulation and enforcement on State parties and do not consider, in-depth, environmental obligations.⁹⁴

There are historic and economic factors which have given investors, as private non-State actors, certain rights in international law to have their investments protected and file claims against States for a decrease in the value of the investment,⁹⁵ but they have not been imposed with reciprocal obligations. While a discussion on this dichotomy remains beyond the scope of this chapter, it is important to try and understand what the nature of environmental obligations imposed on foreign investors by the Nigeria–Morocco BIT and the PAIC are.

To that extent, do these BITs try to equate foreign investors and State parties with the same obligations? Or is there a greater burden on State parties to ensure the compliance of these norms along with cooperation and participation of the investor? The answer is, perhaps, the latter. The

---

⁹³ *Urbaser v Argentina* [1195].
⁹⁴ See Wouters & Chane (n 9) 239. See UN Sub-Commission on the Promotion and Protection of Human Rights, 'Economic, Social and Cultural Rights: Norms on the Responsibilities of Transnational Corporations and Other Business Enterprises with Regard to Human Rights' (26 August 2003) UN Doc E/CN.4/Sub.2/2003/12/Rev2 (Draft Norms); UNHRC, 'Report of the Special Representative of the Secretary-General on the Issue of Human Rights and Transnational Corporations and Other Business Enterprises, John Ruggie' (21 March 2011) UN Doc A/HRC/17/31 [13]; and UNHRC, Text of the third revised draft legally binding instrument with the concrete textual proposals submitted by States during the seventh session, UNHRC, 'Text of the Third Revised Draft Legally Binding Instrument with the Textual Proposals Submitted by States During the Seventh Session of the Open-Ended Intergovernmental Working Group on Transnational Corporations and Other Business Enterprises With Respect to Human Rights' (28 February 2022) UN Doc A/HRC/49/65/Add.1.
⁹⁵ Miles (n 10).

obligation to conduct an EIA applying the precautionary principle, and to follow the international environmental obligations of the host State, would be in conjunction with the independent obligation of the host State to ensure that its investment is in accordance with its domestic and international legal obligations. It is difficult to imagine a scenario where these obligations could be construed as being imposed solely on investors.

It will be useful to take inspiration from Alvarez' idea that international lawyers should spend their time addressing which rules may apply to corporations, rather than thinking about whether corporations are subjects of international law or not.[96] While acknowledging that corporations do have international responsibilities, he cautions that these responsibilities cannot be the same as those of State parties simply because corporations are not the equivalent of States or natural persons.[97] Therefore, a tribunal will not agree that an investor has the responsibility of ensuring the human right to water, but can agree that the investor has the responsibility of ensuring that the precautionary approach is followed while conducting an EIA, provided there are binding legal frameworks which provide for such obligations. International law does not directly hold multinational corporations responsible for human rights violations and, therefore, the drafters of investment treaties must align the obligations of conduct they place on foreign investors with their domestic legal frameworks, ensuring that their international legal obligations have been assimilated into those domestic legislations applicable to foreign investors.

6   Conclusion

Many of the treaties discussed in this chapter have not yet come into force and, in fact, the PAIC has been relegated to the status of a policy document.[98] However, the unique aspect of these treaties is that they adopt

---

[96] JE Alvarez, 'Are Corporations "Subjects" of International Law' (2011) 9(1) Santa Clara Journal of International Law 1, 31. Alvarez suggests that multinational corporations cannot have the same obligations as State parties – rather, they have obligations to protect and respect the human rights obligations of the host State through the conception of due diligence. To arrive at this reasoning, he borrows from the *UN Draft Norms on the Responsibilities of Transnational Corporations and Other Business Enterprises with Regard to Human Rights*, which requires multinational corporations to respect human rights and to avoid causing adverse human rights impacts. See, UNHRC 'Report of the Special Representative of the Secretary General on the Issue off Human Rights and Transnational Corporations and Other Business Enterprises, John Ruggie' (7 April 2008) UN Doc A/HRC/8/5 [3].
[97] ibid 34.
[98] Krajewski (n 19).

a precautionary approach and mandate both investor and host State to assess the environmental impact of an investment with caution. In fact, the customary status of the precautionary approach is further legitimised with its integration in investment treaties. Though these environment CIL rules may bind only State parties, their inclusion in non-environmental treaties could be a step towards ensuring that State parties clearly delineate procedures for their implementation.

The reader may possibly think that this chapter started on an optimistic note, with its highlighting of the integration of customary international environmental law in investment treaties and its exploration of the possibilities of crafting investor obligations. However, it ends on a slightly pessimistic note, concluding that the efficacy of these obligations would primarily depend on domestic law mechanisms and by simply including these obligations in a treaty, even if they are CIL, is not enough. However, it is hoped that these treaties, and this chapter, mark the beginning of trying to find a solution to a problem that has plagued the study of international investment law for the past few years.

12

The Role of Customary International Law in International Investment Law Remedies

The Curious Case of Natural Resources

FILIP BALCERZAK[*]

1 Introduction

The growing number of investor-State arbitrations shed a light on the role of customary international law in the context of remedies. In virtually every arbitral award based on international investment treaties, when tribunals find that respondent States have violated their obligations, stemming from the underlying treaties, they make explicit reference to the *Chorzów Factory* judgment. They find that the principle that an award should 'wipe out all the consequences of the illegal act and re-establish the situation which would, in all probability, have existed if that act had not been committed' reflects customary international law. Sometimes, additional reference is made to the Draft Articles on Responsibility of States for Internationally Wrongful Acts (ILC Articles) to confirm that the calculations which follow are rooted in customary international law. This is commonly repeated, but often no detailed analysis follows. Instead, tribunals simply proceed to calculate compensation guided by the principle that a methodology should be applied which does not result in a 'speculative' outcome.

This chapter analyses some of the issues which arise in this context. First, what is the real meaning of references to the *Chorzów Factory* judgment in virtually every investment arbitral award? Is customary international law helpful in determining remedies, or is it merely a shortcut which allows the tribunals to proceed to compensation calculations? Second, why are references to remedies other than compensation, which are available under customary international law, so rare in investor-State

---

[*] The article is part of the research project number 2018/28/C/HS5/00087 financed by the National Science Centre Poland.

arbitrations?[1] Is there a place for restitution or declaratory awards in international investment law? Third, what are the differences between the consequences of lawful expropriation and the consequences of treaty breaches in the light of customary international law?

The issues discussed in this chapter are particularly visible in disputes concerning renewable energy and early-stage mining projects, both of which fall within a broad definition of the natural resources sector. Therefore, the final part of this chapter concerns the methodologies available for calculations of compensation for treaty breaches, explained by way of examples of disputes concerning the flagged industries.

2 The *Chorzów Factory* Judgment as the Textualisation of Customary International Law

In its judgment, issued on 13 September 1928, the Permanent Court of International Justice (PCIJ) observed as follows:

> The essential principle contained in the actual notion of an illegal act – a principle which seems to be established by international practice and in particular by the decisions of arbitral tribunals – is that reparation must, as far as possible, wipe out all the consequences of the illegal act and reestablish the situation which would, in all probability, have existed if that act had not been committed. Restitution in kind, or, if this is not possible, payment of a sum corresponding to the value which a restitution in kind would bear; the award, if need be, of damages for loss sustained which would not be covered by restitution in kind or payment in place of it – such are the principles which should serve to determine the amount of compensation due for an act contrary to international law.[2]

Even back in 1928, this principle was 'established by international practice'.[3] Thus, the first pre-requisite (*usus*) for considering it as customary international law has been met. In 1987, the US–Iran Claims Tribunal

---

[1] Traditionally, the term 'compensation' was used in connection with the consequences of a legal act, whereas the term 'damages' in connection with the consequences of an illegal act. At present, that distinction is often blurred in practice. See S Ripinsky & K Williams, *Damages in International Investment Law* (BIICL Law 2008) 4; TW Wälde & B Sabahi, 'Compensation, Damages and Valuation' in P Muchlinski, F Ortino & C Schreuer (eds), *The Oxford Handbook of International Investment Law* (OUP 2008) 1052–3. For the purposes of this chapter, the author decided to avoid the semantic dispute on the use of terminology and uses the term 'compensation' with respect to the consequences of both legal and illegal acts, following the wording of the ILC Articles.
[2] *Case Concerning the Factory at Chorzów (Germany v Poland)* (Merits) [1928] PCIJ Series A No 17, 47.
[3] ibid.

noted that 'in spite of the fact that it is nearly sixty years old, this judgment is widely regarded as the most authoritative exposition of the principles applicable in this field, and is still valid today'.[4] It has been confirmed on uncountable occasions since then.[5] Thus, the second condition, *opinio juris sive necessitatis*, has also been met.[6] In the context of investor-State disputes, States not only commonly adopt this position but also enforce and recognise arbitral awards rendered on this basis as final and binding.

The *Chorzów Factory* principle is reflected in the ILC Articles.[7] Even though the ILC Articles 'seek to formulate, by way of codification and progressive development, the basic rules of international law concerning the responsibility of States for their internationally wrongful acts', their respective provisions codify, not progressively develop, the principle reflected in the *Chorzów Factory* judgment.[8]

---

[4] *Amoco v Iran* (Partial Award (Award No 310-56-3) of 14 July 1987) IUSCT Case No 56, 15 IUSCT 189 [191].

[5] For example: *Case Concerning the Gabčíkovo-Nagymaros Project (Hungary/Slovakia)* (Judgment) [1997] ICJ Rep 7 [149]; Arrest *Warrant of 11 April 2000 (Congo v Belgium)* (Judgment) [2002] ICJ Rep 3 [76]; *Avena and Other Mexican Nationals (Mexico v USA)* (Judgment) [2004] ICJ Rep 12 [119]; *Legal Consequences of the Construction of a Wall in the Occupied Palestinian Territories* (Advisory Opinion) [2004] ICJ Rep 136 [152]. In investor-State arbitrations, see, for example: *Unglaube v Costa Rica* (Award of 16 May 2012) ICSID Case No ARB/08/1 & ARB/09/20 [306]; *ADC Affiliate Limited v Hungary* (Award of 2 October 2006) ICSID Case No ARB/03/16 [484–5]. In other fora, see also, for example: *The M/V 'Saiga' (No 2) (Saint Vincent and the Grenadines v Guinea)* (Judgment) [1999] ITLOS Rep 10 [170]; *Papamichalopoulos and Others v Greece (Article 50)* (1995) Series A No 330-B [36].

[6] See, for example, MW Reisman & RD Sloane, 'Indirect Expropriation and its Valuation in the BIT Convention' (2004) 74 BYBIL 115, 133, who describe the *Chorzów Factory* principle as a 'lodestar' for the general principles of international law on compensation. For the two elements of custom see, for example: J Crawford, *Brownlie's Principles of Public International Law* (9th edn, OUP 2019) 22–5.

[7] E De Brabandere, *Investment Treaty Arbitration as Public International Law* (CUP 2014) 177.

[8] J Crawford, 'State Responsibility' [2020] MPEPIL 1093 [31]; N Rubins, V Sinha & B Roberts, 'Approaches to Valuation in Investment Treaty Arbitration' in CL Beharry (ed), *Contemporary and Emerging Issues on the Law of Damages and Valuation in International Investment Arbitration* (Brill Nijhoff 2018) 172; De Brabandere (n 7) 178; Ripinsky & Williams (n 1) 32; *Nykomb v Latvia* (Arbitral Award of 16 December 2003) SCC Case No 118/2001, 38; *LG&E v Argentina* (Award of 25 July 2007) ICSID Case No ARB/02/1 [31]; *Siemens AG v Argentina* (Award of 17 January 2007) ICSID Case No ARB/02/8 [350]; *Biwater Gauff v Tanzania* (Award of 24 July 2008) ICSID Case No ARB/05/22 [773]; *Tza Yap Shum v Peru* (Award of 7 July 2011) ICSID Case No ARB/07/6 [253–4]. The Tribunal in *OperaFund v Spain* summarised: 'the relevant principles of customary international law are derived from the PCIJ Judgment in the Chorzów Factory Case and are recorded in Articles 31–38 of the ILC Draft Articles' (*OperaFund v Spain* (Award of 6 September 2019) ICSID Case No ARB/15/36 [609]).

The ILC Articles precisely define that Part Two thereof (which includes remedies) 'does not apply to obligations of reparation to the extent that these arise towards or are invoked by a person or entity other than a State'.[9] This 'is without prejudice to any right, arising from the international responsibility of a State, which may accrue directly to any person or entity other than a State'.[10] Despite that, they have been continuously referred to in investor-State arbitrations.[11] Depending on how one assesses the nature of investors' rights under investment treaties, they are applicable either directly or *mutatis mutandis*. One possible theoretical approach is that investment treaties create investors' own substantive and procedural rights (being States' obligations towards investors, which would allow for Part Two of the ILC Articles being applied only *mutatis mutandis*).[12] Another possible approach is that investment treaties create procedural rights which can be applied to trigger arbitral proceedings related to alleged breaches of obligations owed to the State of the investor's nationality (being obligations owed to the other contracting State, and not to the investors themselves, which would allow for Part Two of the ILC Articles being applied directly).[13]

The *Chorzów Factory* judgment is frequently referred to by arbitral tribunals in cases based on investment treaties.[14] The tribunals consider the *Chorzów Factory* judgment as reflecting customary international law and, therefore, playing a pivotal role in determining remedies available in investor-State arbitrations. Even though the starting point for determining the remedies available in each case is always the text of the applicable

---

[9] ILC, 'Draft Articles on Responsibility of States for Internationally Wrongful Acts with Commentaries' (23 April–1 June and 2 July–10 August 2001) UN Doc A/56/10, reproduced in [2001/II – Part Two] YBILC 31, 87–8, commentary to Art 28 [3] ('ILC Articles'); in similar vein: ILC Articles, 95, commentary to Art 33 [4].

[10] ILC Articles (n 9) Art 33(2)

[11] PM Protopsaltis, 'Shareholders' Injury and Compensation in Investor-State Arbitration' in P Pazartzis & Panos Merkouris (eds), *Permutations of Responsibility in International Law* (Brill Nijhoff 2019) 188–9. See, for example, *SD Myers v Canada* (Partial Award of 13 November 2000) UNCITRAL [312–15]; *CME Czech Republic BV v Czech Republic* (Partial Award of 13 September 2001) UNCITRAL [583]; *Arif v Moldova* (Award of 8 April 2013) ICSID Case No ARB/11/23 [559]; cases mentioned in (n 8). Only occasionally the tribunals recognise that the ILC Articles do not apply – for example: *Wintershall v Argentina* (Award of 8 December 2008) ICSID Case No ARB/04/14 [113].

[12] De Brabandere explains that 'the rules and principles relating to the forms of reparation are, however, similar when it is a nonstate entity that is entitled to invoke the responsibility of a state' – De Brabandere (n 7) 178, fn 12.

[13] For broader considerations see: F Balcerzak, *Investor–State Arbitration and Human Rights* (Brill Nijhoff 2017) 236–8.

[14] Examples of cases referred to in (n 8) and (n 11).

investment treaty,[15] most treaties remain silent on the issue of remedies for their breach, although a few exceptions exist.[16] Thus, customary international law becomes relevant, as it governs issues that are not regulated in an applicable international treaty.[17]

The *Chorzów Factory* principle 'is precise, strict, and unchangeable as a principle, but flexible and useful in a myriad of different scenarios'.[18] Its biggest advantage sometimes turns out to be its disadvantage – tribunals have frequently failed to sufficiently analyse the application of this customary international law rule. Instead, they often tend to take a 'shortcut' and proceed to calculation of compensation, simply observing that this is 'consistent with the principles set forth' in the *Chorzów Factory* judgment.[19]

3 Restitution as the Primary Remedy

Under the *Chorzów Factory* principle, restitution is the default remedy for violations of a State's international obligations.[20] Only when restitution 'is not possible' should the 'payment of a sum corresponding to the value

---

[15] ILC Articles (n 9) Art 55.
[16] By way of an example, see 'The Energy Charter Treaty' (adopted 17 December 1994, entered into force 16 April 1998) 2080 UNTS 95, Art 26(8) ('ECT'); 'Agreement Between the United States of America, the United Mexican States, and Canada ('USMCA')' (adopted 10 December 2019, entered into force 1 July 2020) Art 14.D.13(1)(b), which replaced the North American Free Trade Agreement ('NAFTA') (adopted 17 December 1992, entered into force 1 January 1994) 32 ILM 289, Art 1135, which has a similar wording; see also, 'Convention on the Settlement of Investment Disputes Between States and Nationals of Other States' (adopted 18 March 1965, entered into force 14 October 1966) 575 UNTS 159, Art 54(1), which refers solely to enforcing 'the pecuniary obligations' imposed by arbitral awards.
[17] For example, the final sentence of the preamble to the Vienna Convention on the Law of Treaties (adopted 23 May 1969, entered into force 27 January 1980) 1155 UNTS 331 (VCLT), states: 'Affirming that the rules of customary international law will continue to govern questions not regulated by the provisions of the present Convention'.
[18] I Marboe, 'Assessing Compensation and Damages in Expropriation Versus Non-Expropriation Cases' in CL Beharry (ed), *Contemporary and Emerging Issues on the Law of Damages and Valuation in International Investment Arbitration* (Brill Nijhoff 2018) 134–5. It is 'a double-edged sword in the sense that it not only enables flexibility when responding to the variety of factual situations but also introduces subjectivity and discretion in the application of the legal principles' – Ripinsky & Williams (n 1) 21.
[19] *Metalclad v Mexico* (Award of 30 August 2000) ICSID Case No ARB(AF)/97/1 [122]. *Foresight v Spain* can serve as another example, where the Tribunal decided that 'the Claimants are in principle entitled to full compensation for Spain's violation of Article 10(1) ECT. The Tribunal shall now turn to the Parties' respective submissions on quantum' – *Foresight v Spain* (Final Award of 14 November 2018) SCC Case No 2015/150 [438].
[20] There is a 'primacy of restitution' – ILC Articles (n 9) 96, commentary to Art 35 [3]; it is a 'first-ranked' remedy – Wälde & Sabahi (n 1) 1057.

which a restitution in kind would bear' be awarded.[21] This is re-affirmed in Article 36(1) of the ILC Articles, according to which a State responsible for an internationally wrongful act 'is under an obligation to compensate for the damage caused thereby, insofar as such damage is not made good by restitution'.

Therefore, under customary international law, the broad concept of 'reparation' is divided into three subcategories: restitution, compensation and satisfaction, each being a different type of remedy. Restitution is a default remedy and a primary obligation of a State which violates an investment treaty.[22] However, sometimes full reparation may only be achieved by combining different forms of reparation.[23]

From a theoretical perspective, the possibility of arbitral tribunals awarding restitution in investor-State disputes has been recognised for many years.[24] This theoretical possibility has been confirmed as available in investor-State arbitrations.[25] In light of the above, it may be surprising that investor-State arbitral awards almost always comprise a compensation payment.[26] Only sometimes does this result from a particular substantive law being applicable to the dispute.[27] Typically, investment treaties do not address remedies at all, so they also do not preclude the possibility of restitution.

---

[21] *Factory at Chorzów*, 47. This should happen together with 'damages for loss sustained which would not be covered by restitution in kind or payment in place of it', which opens the floor for a discussion of moral damages. However, that issue falls outside the scope of this chapter.

[22] Rubins et al (n 8) 172.

[23] ILC Articles (n 9) 95, commentary to Art 34 [2] 95.

[24] For example: C Schreuer, 'Non-Pecuniary Remedies in ICSID Arbitration' (2004) 20(4) Arbitration International 325, 331–2.

[25] *Pezold v Zimbabwe* (Award of 28 July 2015) ICSID Case No ARB/10/15 [700, 723], in [1020.1] which actually ordered restitution. In other cases, tribunals have confirmed that this is possible, but decided on facts of the case not to order restitution – for example: Enron v Argentina (Decision on Jurisdiction of 14 January 2004) ICSID Case No ARB/01/3 [79, 81]; Micula (I) v Romania (Final Award of 11 December 2013) ICSID Case No ARB/05/20 [1309–11]; Micula (I) v Romania (Decision on Jurisdiction and Admissibility of 24 September 2008) ICSID Case No. ARB/05/20 [166–8]; Al-Bahloul v Tajikistan (Final Award of 8 June 2010) SCC Case No V (064/2008) [63]; cases mentioned in (n 32).

[26] C Malinvaud, 'Non-pecuniary Remedies in Investment Treaty and Commercial Arbitration' in AJ van den Berg (ed), *50 Years of the New York Convention: ICCA International Arbitration Conference* (Kluwer Law International 2009) 210. Compensation is 'perhaps the most commonly sought in international practice' in general, not merely in investor-State arbitration. See ILC Articles (n 9) 99, commentary to Art 36 [2].

[27] See examples in (n 16). Even though ECT, NAFTA and USMCA formally allow restitution, they require restitution orders to permit the alternative of paying compensation.

Most probably, the main reason for tribunals paying insufficient attention to restitution is the way in which claims are framed. Claimants have the right to choose which form of remedies they seek.[28] The way in which claims are framed binds the tribunals, which cannot go beyond the remedies sought by the claimants.[29] It is rare in practice for investors to seek remedies other than compensation.[30] It was rightly commented that 'the ultimate goal of the claimant in an investment treaty arbitration is almost always the payment of compensation for the harm it believes it has suffered at a host State's hands'.[31]

Recent awards rendered against Spain suggest that this approach may be revisited in practice. In *Eiser v Spain*, *Masdar v Spain*, *Antin v Spain*, *RREEF v Spain*, *RWE v Spain*, *PV Investors v Spain* and *Watkins v Spain*, the claimants primarily sought restitution and only asked for compensation if restitution was not awarded.[32] None of the tribunals in these cases declined the theoretical possibility of awarding restitution.[33] However, each tribunal arrived at the conclusion that restitution was inappropriate on the facts of the particular case.

Such an approach seems to be justified in the Spanish saga cases, which concern alleged violations of investment treaties arising due to changes in the general regulatory framework. Restitution can be replaced by

---

[28] ILC Articles (n 9) 120, commentary to Art 43 [6].

[29] Wälde & Sabahi (n 1) 1059. This principle is expressed in the Latin maxim *non ultra petita*.

[30] Malinvaud (n 26) 221; Schreuer (n 24) 329; Balcerzak (n 13) 221–2. Sometimes, after initially presenting the claim for restitution, it was abandoned in the course of the proceedings – for example: *South American Silver v Bolivia* (Award of 22 November 2018) PCA Case No 2013-15 [797].

[31] Rubins et al (n 8) 171.

[32] *Eiser v Spain* (Final Award of 4 May 2017) ICSID Case No ARB/13/36 [155, 425]; *Masdar Solar v Spain* (Award of 16 May 2018) ICSID Case No ARB/14/1 [554–5]; *Antin v Spain* (Award of 15 June 2018) ICSID Case No ARB/13/31 [631]; *RREEF v Spain* (Decision on Responsibility and on the Principles of Quantum of 30 November 2018) ICSID Case No ARB/13/30 [11, 473]; *RWE v Spain* (Decision on Jurisdiction, Liability and Certain Issues of Quantum of 30 December 2019) ICSID Case No ARB/14/34 [681–3]; *PV Investors v Spain* (Final Award of 28 February 2020) PCA Case No 2012-14 [665] (although the claim for restitution 'was abandoned' in the course of the proceedings); *Watkins Holdings v Spain* (Award of 21 January 2020) ICSID Case No ARB/15/44 [632–4]. Notably, the claimants in all of these cases were represented by the same law firm.

[33] Although the Tribunal in *Cube v Spain* observed that ordering restitution is 'beyond the proper scope of the powers of the Tribunal and is moreover plainly materially impossible and disproportionately burdensome'. The claimant did not request restitution, so this observation was made by the tribunal without having heard the parties' submissions on that issue. See *Cube v Spain* (Decision on Jurisdiction, Liability and Partial Decision on Quantum of 19 February 2019) ICSID Case No ARB/15/20 [460].

compensation not only where restitution is 'not possible' (as expressly stated in the *Chorzów Factory* judgment and recognised in Art 35 of the ILC Articles), but also if restitution is 'unavailable' or 'inadequate'.[34]

It would be either impossible, or at least extremely difficult, to comply with an award which ordered the restitution of previously applicable laws and regulations.[35] Moreover, the Tribunals in *Eiser v Spain, Antin v Spain* and *Watkins v Spain* observed that ordering restitution could give rise to doubts as to the permissibility of limiting State sovereignty.[36] The Tribunal in *Masdar v Spain* concluded that it could 'unduly burden' the respondent's 'legislative and regulatory autonomy'.[37] The Tribunal in *RWE v Spain* observed that the case was 'plainly not an appropriate case for restitution', as it involved regulations 'generally applicable across a very important sector in Spain' and restitution 'would obviously involve a burden to the Respondent out of all proportion'.[38]

The 'sovereignty concern' is well founded in the context of treaty violations caused by changes to generally applicable regulatory frameworks, as happened in the Spanish saga cases. It is less justified in cases concerning treaty breaches targeting a specific, individual investor. In such cases, the approach adopted by Energy Charter Treaty (ECT), North American Free Trade Agreement (NAFTA) and the United States Mexico Canada Agreement (USMCA) provide useful guidance on how to mitigate the sovereignty concern related to restitution by ordering that the respondent 'may pay monetary damages and any applicable interest in lieu of restitution'.[39] This solution is not a deviation from the *Chorzów Factory* principle.[40] Arbitral tribunals have the possibility to adopt a similar approach in investment disputes based on investment treaties other than ECT, NAFTA or USMCA. This is certainly so if the claimant presents an explicit request for such relief. However, even if a claimant's request is framed in

---

[34] ILC Articles (n 9) 99, commentary to Art 36 [3].
[35] *Masdar v Spain* [563].
[36] *Eiser v Spain* [425]; *Antin v Spain* [636-7] ('disproportional to its interference with the sovereignty of the State compared to monetary compensation'); *Watkins v Spain* [674] (restitution 'is an inappropriate remedy because the Respondent has a sovereign right to take appropriate legislative and regulatory measures to meet public interests').
[37] *Masdar v Spain* [559]. In similar vein *RREEF v Spain* [473].
[38] *RWE v Spain* [685], adding that breaches of the ECT were found only with respect to part of the claimant's plants.
[39] NAFTA, Art 1135(1)(b). The same wording was repeated in USMCA, Art 14.D.13(1)(b), which replaced NAFTA. Similarly, ECT, Art 26(8), provided that the respondent 'may pay monetary damages in lieu of any other remedy granted'.
[40] Marboe (n 18) 117.

a traditional manner – ie, it requests restitution and, only if restitution is impossible, compensation as an alternative – this opens the door for the tribunal to order restitution with the possibility to pay compensation *in lieu* of restitution.

Alternatively, tribunals can award restitution, stipulate a time limit within which it must materialise and proceed to ordering compensation only if the respondent fails to perform the specific obligation imposed upon it. Although no publicly available arbitral award reveals that this theoretical possibility has already been applied in practice, an analogy can be made from some tribunals' approach of deferring a decision on compensation to await both parties' initiative to provide a joint experts' report, whilst at the same time securing an alternative scenario if the parties cannot or do not wish to reach an agreement.[41]

Restitution may occur alongside compensation, not merely as an alternative.[42] With respect to an income-generating business, a return of the asset alone would not fully compensate the investor, as it would not compensate the income lost by that business in the intervening period.[43] In such a case, restitution should take place 'in combination' with compensation, as explicitly stated in Article 34 of the ILC Articles.[44] Only then is the principle of full reparation met.[45] Similarly, restitution should take place 'in combination' with compensation if an expropriated asset has lost its value since it was taken away. Otherwise, the claimant would be in a worse position if the asset were returned to him than if he received compensation.[46]

4   No Place for Declaratory-Only Awards

Satisfaction is a third type of remedy available for the violation of treaty obligations. This remedy comes into play insofar as the injury 'cannot be made good by restitution or compensation'.[47] In this sense, an award itself, which declares the wrongfulness of State actions, can constitute satisfaction – a form of reparation.[48]

---

[41] For example: *RREEF v Spain* [597]; *Cube v Spain* [532].
[42] *Bernhard von Pezold v Zimbabwe* [925, 1020.2].
[43] Rubins et al (n 8) 172–3.
[44] Marboe (n 18) 117.
[45] ILC Articles (n 9) 95, commentary to Art 34 [2].
[46] Rubins et al (n 8) 172–3.
[47] ILC Articles (n 9) Art 37(1).
[48] ILC Articles (n 9) 106–7, commentary to Art 37 [6]; the Tribunal in *Europe Cement v Turkey* expressly recognised 'the reasoning and conclusions set out in this Award' as 'a

This remedy has little, if any, relevance in investor-State disputes. First, no investor would ever decide to commence costly arbitral proceedings solely to achieve this purpose. Therefore, a declaratory-only award by itself would be considered a 'paper victory' and a *de facto* loss, rather than one which results in meaningful reparation being granted.

Second, the award must be made public if the claimant is to receive satisfaction within the above meaning. Many arbitral awards remain unpublished, notwithstanding a certain tendency towards transparency.[49] The fact that an award will remain confidential would require an arbitral tribunal to order the State to issue 'an acknowledgement of the breach, an expression of regret, a formal apology or another appropriate modality', rather than simply issuing an award which declares that certain treaty provisions were infringed.[50]

Although theoretically possible, there is nothing in the public domain to suggest that a claim has ever been framed in that manner, ie requesting exclusively declaratory relief.[51] Claimants invariably request declaratory relief in conjunction with compensation (and sometimes restitution).[52]

5 Compensation for Lawful Expropriation

When looking at compensation, it is important to differentiate between lawful expropriation and violations of investment treaties, including unlawful expropriation.[53]

Expropriation as such is not prohibited under general international law.[54] On the contrary, States have a right to expropriate alien property.[55]

---

form of "satisfaction" for the Respondent' (*Europe Cement v Turkey* (Award of 13 August 2009) ICSID Case No ARB(AF)/07/2 [181]).

[49] For example: United Nations Convention on Transparency in Treaty-based Investor-State Arbitration (Mauritius Convention on Transparency) (adopted 10 December 2014, entered into force 18 October 2017) No 54749.
[50] ILC Articles (n 9) Art 37(2).
[51] Which binds tribunals (n 29).
[52] For example: *Enkev v Poland* (First Partial Award of 29 April 2014) PCA Case No 2013-01 [121]; *RREEF v Spain* [11].
[53] Or, to word it differently, between 'treaty violative' and 'treaty compliant' expropriations. See S Ratner, 'Compensation for Expropriations in a World of Investment Treaties: Beyond the Lawful/Unlawful Distinction' (2017) 111(1) AJIL 7, 16.
[54] MN Shaw, *International Law* (8th edn, CUP 2017) 627.
[55] R Dolzer & C Schreuer, *Principles of International Investment Law* (2nd edn, OUP 2012) 136; *Siag v Egypt* (Award of 1 June 2009) ICSID Case No ARB/05/15 [428]. On the division between compensable (expropriatory) and non-compensable (non-expropriatory)

Investment treaties do not alter this situation. In fact, most explicitly reaffirm States' right to expropriate. They do, however, define the conditions which must be met by expropriatory action before it will comply with States' international obligations. The standard conditions of lawful expropriation include the existence of a public purpose, non-discrimination, due process and 'prompt, adequate and effective compensation'[56] (or similar wording having the same meaning).[57] The last condition is typically accompanied by a determination of the valuation date and applicable interest rate.[58]

The most essential element in defining compensation – adequate – is linked with the objective value of the expropriated investment, which is equated with its 'fair market value'.[59] The fair market value is understood as reflecting 'the price at which a willing buyer would buy, and a willing seller would sell, no party being under any type of duress and both parties having good information about all relevant circumstances involved in the purchase'.[60] 'Effective' means that compensation must be 'fully realizable', whilst 'prompt' means 'paid without delay'.[61]

The above is not, however, a remedy for an internationally wrongful act.[62] The applicable legal principles differ between compensation, as one

---

States' actions see, for example: M Żenkiewicz, 'Compensable vs. Non-Compensable States' Measures: Blurred Picture Under Investment Law' (2020) 17(3) MJIEL 362.

[56] For example: art VI of the Agreement Between the Government of Canada and the Government of the Republic of Poland for the Promotion and Reciprocal Protection of Investments (Canada & Poland) (adopted 6 April 1990, entered into force 22 November 1990) ('BIT Poland - Canada (1990)'). This reflects the Hull formula – Wälde, Sabahi (n 1) 1068.

[57] For example, 'genuine' having the same meaning as 'adequate', ie 'fair market value'. See *Rusoro Mining v Venezuela* (Award of 22 August 2016) ICSID Case No ARB(AF)/12/5 [646–7].

[58] For example, the Agreement Between the Government of Canada and the Government of the Republic of Poland for the Promotion and Reciprocal Protection of Investments (Canada & Poland) (adopted 6 April 1990, entered into force 22 November 1990) ('BIT Poland - Canada (1990)') Art VI ('Such compensation shall be based on the real value of the investment at the time of the expropriation, shall be made within two months of the date of expropriation, after which interest at the rate agreed between the investor and the Contracting Party concerned and in no case less than the London Inter Sank Offered Rate (LISOR) shall accrue until the date of payment [...]').

[59] Marboe (n 18) 123; Guideline IV(3) of the World Bank, 'Legal Framework for the Treatment of Foreign Investment, Vol 2: Report to the Development Committee and Guidelines on the Treatment of Foreign Direct Investment' (*World Bank Report*, 25 September 1992) reproduced in (1992) 31 ILM 1363, Guideline IV(3); see also, Poland Business and Economic Relations Treaty (USA & Poland) (adopted 21 March 1990, entered into force 6 August 1994) Art VII(1): 'Compensation shall be equivalent to the fair market value of the expropriated investment [...]'.

[60] *Rusoro Mining v Venezuela* [751]; see also, *Khan Resources v Mongolia* (Award on the Merits of 2 March 2015) UNCITRAL [378].

[61] Marboe (n 18) 122.

[62] De Brabandere (n 7) 179; *ADC v Hungary* [481].

of the conditions of lawful expropriation, and compensation, as a remedy for unlawful expropriation.[63]

In this context, a question arises whether a failure to fulfil this condition of lawful expropriation (ie the condition of paying 'prompt, adequate and effective compensation') by itself means that the expropriation becomes unlawful. Many tribunals have ruled in favour of this approach.[64] Others have decided that non-fulfilment of the compensation prerequisite does not, by itself, render the expropriation unlawful.[65] However, the latter cases concerned situations where the respondent States accepted their obligation to pay compensation, but the parties were unable to agree on the amounts due. The Tribunal in *Tidewater v Venezuela* found that this was 'not a case where the State took assets without any offer of compensation. The record does not demonstrate a refusal on the part of the State to pay compensation. Rather, it discloses that the Parties were unable to agree on the basis or the process by which such compensation would be calculated and paid'.[66] Similarly, in *Venezuela Holdings v Venezuela* the negotiations on compensation took place and the respondent State 'made proposals during those negotiations'.[67] This allows the conclusion that expropriation should be considered as legal if all other conditions have been met (aside from the payment of compensation) and the respondent State has made 'a good faith effort to comply with the compensation requirement' (even if unsuccessfully).[68] If, on the other hand, the respondent State declines to pay any compensation at all, the failure to fulfil this condition suffices to consider the expropriation unlawful. In line with the above, any indirect expropriation would always amount to unlawful

---

[63] Ripinsky & Williams (n 1) 65–6; Marboe (n 18) 132–3; *ADC v Hungary* [499]; *Siemens v Argentina* [352]; *Tza Yap Shum v Peru* [253]; *Quiborax v Bolivia* (Award of 16 September 2015) ICSID Case No ARB/06/2 [326]; *Tidewater v Venezuela* (Award 13 March 2015) ICSID Case No ARB/10/5 [142]; *ConocoPhillips v Venezuela* (Decision on Jurisdiction and Merits of 3 September 2013) ICSID Case No ARB/07/30 [342–3].

[64] For example, *Pezold v Zimbabwe* [497–8]; *Unglaube v Costa Rica* [305]; *Crystallex v Venezuela* (Award of 4 April 2016) ICSID Case No ARB(AF)/11/2 [716].

[65] For example: *Tidewater v Venezuela* [140]; *Venezuela Holdings v Venezuela* (Award of 9 October 2014) ICSID Case No ARB/07/27 [301] (this award was annulled, but not in the part referred to – *Venezuela Holdings v Venezuela* (Decision on Annulment of 9 March 2017) ICSID Case No ARB/07/27 [196(4)]).

[66] *Tidewater v Venezuela* [145].

[67] *Venezuela Holdings v Venezuela* (Award) [306]. Similarly, *ConocoPhillips v Venezuela* [362].

[68] MW Friedman & F Lavaud, 'Damages Principles in Investment Arbitration' in JA Trenor (ed), *The Guide to Damages in International Arbitration* (3rd edn, Global Arbitration Review 2018) 104.

expropriation, as it is not compensated and involves no attempt to negotiate the amount of compensation payable.

6 Remedies Available for Treaty Breaches

As noted above, compensation for lawful expropriation is linked with the 'fair market value' of the expropriated object, typically with the valuation date set immediately prior to expropriation and increased by the applicable interest rate. If an expropriation does not meet the conditions of being lawful, it should not have taken place at all. In such a situation, reparation should 'wipe out' all of its consequences. The principle of full reparation rooted in customary international law does not provide any guidelines on how to determine the financial situation of the victim of a treaty breach.[69]

The aim is to put the claimant in the same situation as it would have been 'but for' the breach. In the first place, this may justify restitution in kind, as noted above. In the context of compensation, there are two vital differences between the compensation calculated as a condition for lawful expropriation and the compensation calculated as a remedy for unlawful expropriation. These relate to: (i) the date of valuation and (ii) the possibility to use *ex post* information during the calculation.[70]

As noted earlier, compensation for lawful expropriation is typically calculated on the basis of the fair market value shortly prior to the time at which the asset was taken. Calculating compensation for unlawful expropriation offers more flexibility. It allows the same date to be chosen as would apply in the case of lawful expropriation (ie immediately prior to the taking), but it offers an alternative – ie the date of the award.[71] This is in line with the principle of putting the claimants in the situation they would have been in 'but for' the breach. The PCIJ itself noted in the *Chorzów Factory* judgment that compensation

> is not necessarily limited to the value of the undertaking at the moment of dispossession, plus interest to the day of payment. This limitation would only be admissible if the Polish Government had had the right to

---

[69] Marboe (n 18) 126.
[70] In addition, compensation for unlawful expropriation can cover additional harm, beyond the loss of the property. See Ratner (n 53) 21.
[71] For example: *ADC v Hungary* [497, 499]; *Pezold v Zimbabwe* [813]; *Quiborax v Bolivia* [370, 377]; *Siemens v Argentina* [352]; *Kardassopoulos v Georgia* (Award of 3 March 2010) ICSID Case No ARB/05/18 [514]; *El Paso Energy International Company v Argentina* (Award of 31 October 2011) ICSID Case No ARB/03/15 [704, 706].

expropriate, and if its wrongful act consisted merely in not having paid to the two Companies the just price of what was expropriated.[72]

In the words of the US–Iran Claims Tribunal in *Phillips Petroleum v Iran*, the difference is – apart from restitution – 'whether compensation can be awarded for any increase in the value of the property between the date of the taking and the date of the judicial or arbitral decision awarding compensation'.[73]

Another difference is the possibility to make use of *ex post* information – ie information which became available only after the expropriation took place. In the case of lawful expropriations, calculations are based on data available at the moment just prior to the taking, which reflects 'the price at which a willing buyer would buy, and a willing seller would sell' with the knowledge they would have actually had on the valuation date.[74] Customary international law allows a different approach – ie relying on any available information, including *ex post* knowledge.[75] The 'only subsequent known factors relevant to value which are not to be relied on are those attributable to the illegality itself'.[76]

These differences can result in higher amounts of compensation when compared to compensation for lawful expropriation. As was summarised by the Tribunal in *Quiborax v Bolivia*: 'This is easily explained by a reference to restitution: damages stand in lieu of restitution which would take place just following the award or judgment. It is also easy to understand if one keeps in mind that what must be repaired is the actual harm done, as opposed to the value of the asset when taken.'[77] This may become relevant in practice. For example, with respect to unlawfully taking a mining concession, it would not be surprising if, at the moment of taking, the deposit estimations suggest that a specific amount of mineral resource exists, but subsequently the deposit turns out to be larger, thereby increasing the amount of due compensation.

At the same time, these differences should not result in a lower compensation for unlawful expropriation than for lawful expropriation. It is possible for an expropriated investment to lose its value between the expropriation date and the date of the award. If this occurs, compensation for

---

[72] *Factory at Chorzów* 47.
[73] *Phillips Petroleum v Iran* (Award of 29 June 1989 (Award No 425-39-2)) Case No 39, 21 IUSCT 79 [110].
[74] See (n 60).
[75] Ripinsky & Williams (n 1) 256; *El Paso Energy v Argentina* [704]; *Quiborax v Bolivia* [370, 379].
[76] *Amco v Indonesia* (Award of 31 May 1990) ICSID Case No ARB/81/8 [186].
[77] *Quiborax v Bolivia* [377].

lawful and unlawful expropriation should be calculated on the same basis, ie based on the value of the asset at the time of expropriation, plus interest.[78] This is in line with customary international law, which provides that restitution – if possible – should be awarded together with compensation for any loss which is not covered by restitution. If compensation is the only remedy available, the claimant is entitled to compensation 'in the amount of the asset's higher value' between the expropriation date and the date of the award. This is because the State which violated international law bears 'the risk of unanticipated events decreasing the value of an expropriated asset over that time period', not the individual who suffered the loss.[79]

An important differentiation in this context arises with respect to a division between unlawful expropriation and other treaty breaches. It goes without saying that the *Chorzów Factory* principle finds application to all violations of investment treaties' provisions, not solely unlawful expropriation.[80]

In this context, restitution could play a more important role in the future.[81] In terms of compensation, if violations of multiple standards are found, typically, tribunals consider it sufficient to calculate compensation for unlawful expropriation as covering the whole loss suffered.[82] This is in line with the *Chorzów Factory* principle, which requires that no

---

[78] Marboe (n 18) 132–3.

[79] *Hulley Enterprises v Russia* (Final Award of 18 July 2014) PCA Case No AA 226 [1768]; *Yukos Universal Ltd v Russia* (Final Award of 18 July 2014) PCA Case No AA227 [1768]; *Veteran Petroleum v Russia* (Final Award 18 July 2014) PCA Case No AA 228 [1768]. Another scenario is that the value of the expropriated investment initially increased after the expropriation but decreased later. To allow the claimant to choose the most favorable moment between the expropriation date and the date of the award, the claimant would need to satisfy the burden of proof that it would have disposed of the property at the 'peak' of its value, which would rarely be capable of being established.

[80] For example: *Unión Fenosa v Egypt* (Award of 31 August 2018) ICSID Case No ARB/14/4 [10.96]; *Murphy v Ecuador* (Award of 6 May 2016) PCA Case No AA434 [423]; *Lemire v Ukraine* (Award of 28 March 2011) ICSID Case No ARB/06/18 [149]; *White Industries v India* (Final Award of 30 November 2011) UNCITRAL [14.3.3]; *Novenergia II v Spain* (Final Award of 15 February 2018) SCC Case No 2015/063 [807].

[81] The use of non-financial remedies for non-expropriatory treaty violations include examples such as an order to refrain from discriminatory treatment, to re-issue an administrative or judicial decision in full compliance with due process, or to seek other administrative remedies that provide full satisfaction – Wälde & Sabahi (n 1) 1115–16.

[82] For example: *Vivendi (I) v Argentina* (Final Award of 20 August 2007) ICSID Case No ARB/97/3 [8.2.8]; in *BG Group v Argentina* the Tribunal observed that while it was 'disinclined to automatically import' standard of fair market value envisaged for lawful expropriation, 'this standard of compensation is nonetheless available by reference to customary international law' and applied it to breach of the fair and equitable treatment and prohibition of unreasonable measures – *BG Group v Argentina* (Final Award of 24 December

overcompensation takes place.[83] It results from a pragmatic approach: typically, other breaches would result in a compensation award of equal or less value than the compensation due in the case of unlawful expropriation.[84]

7 Methodologies of Calculating Compensation in the Light of the *Chorzów Factory* Principle

Within the legal framework discussed above, when calculating compensation tribunals must decide which methodology to apply. In each case, the choice of methodology is fact dependent. In the words of the Tribunal in *Antin v Spain*: 'there are no right or wrong valuation methods, but different methods that are appropriate depending on the specific circumstances of the case'.[85] Whichever methodology is applied, typically, compensation 'cannot be determined with mechanical precision'.[86] What matters is that the arbitrators are comfortable that the methodology applied is not 'speculative'.[87] Reluctance towards a speculative outcome is one of the key factors which influences arbitrators when choosing the methodology for calculating compensation.

Keeping in mind the above, it is possible to make a few general comments on the methodologies typically available in investor-State arbitrations. From a theoretical perspective, they can be divided into two classifications: (i) backward-looking and (ii) forward-looking.[88]

2007) UNCITRAL [422]. The standard of compensation for expropriation is 'relatively well established' when compared to compensation for breaches of other standards commonly found in investment treaties. See Wälde & Sabahi (n 1) 1082.

[83] ILC Articles (n 9) 105, commentary to Art 36 [33].

[84] Although, for example, in *Novenergia v Spain*, the value of the claim for expropriation was lower than the claim for violation of other ECT standards – *Novenergia v Spain* [811].

[85] *Antin v Spain* [688].

[86] *Eiser v Spain* [473]. Tribunal in *Masdar v Spain* rejected test of 'confidence approaching absolute certainty' – *Masdar v Spain* [576]. Tribunal in *Infrared v Spain* observed: 'no model or methodology for assessing damages can determine with absolute precision the loss visited on an investor by a regulatory change, given the many uncertainties and variables inherent in projecting revenues, costs and risk over time. The method used must rather be reasonable in the light of all the circumstances' – *Infrared v Spain* (Award of 2 August 2019) ICSID Case No ARB/14/12 [533].

[87] *Novenergia v Spain* [820].

[88] Rubins et al (n 8) 185; Ripinsky & Williams (n 1) 193, 214. It remains unclear how to categorise asset-based methodologies, which value investments by summing up their individual assets (Ripinsky & Williams (n 1) 218). This group consists of book value, replacement value and liquidation value methodologies. Whilst book value is clearly a backward-looking methodology (Rubins et al (n 8) 198), classification of the remaining two into this category is more debatable.

Probably the most common backward-looking methodology considers the amounts actually invested ('sunk costs') and seeks to return this amount to the investor. The advantage of this methodology is that the outcome is based on actual figures, which avoids any speculation.[89] The disadvantage is that it does not compensate for lost profits.[90] As such, it does not place the claimant in a situation in which it would have been 'but for' the treaty breach, as required by customary international law. No reasonable investor decides to undertake an investment with the sole purpose of receiving back the amount it originally invested after a period of time.

This shortcoming is partially cured by ordering pre-award interest.[91] This is envisaged by Art. 38 of the ILC Articles, which states that interest may be 'necessary in order to ensure full reparation'.[92] Pre-award interest 'should compensate a claimant for the deprivation of money owed to it between the date of the harm suffered and the award'.[93] The economic rationale behind interest is to reflect the 'cost of money that a lender is willing to be paid to part with his money for a given period of time'.[94] Pre-award interest, therefore, brings 'past losses […] to present value' and compensates for loss stemming from the fact that the investors were not 'in possession of the funds' to which they were entitled and they had 'either to borrow funds at a cost or were deprived of the opportunity of investing these funds at a profit'.[95] As such, it reflects the time value of

---

[89] Wälde & Sabahi (n 1) 1072–3.

[90] ibid 1066, in the context of the backward-looking methodologies and the traditional division between *damnum emergens* and *lucrum cessans*. Similarly, on ibid 1073, when they provide an example of investment in petroleum, where most exploration wells are unsuccessful (dry), but they 'get compensated by the few successful results of a drilling campaign. This means that the value of the successful exploration is – often by a multiple – much more than the expenditures incurred. In essence, expenses have either to be multiplied by the exploration risk (historic method) or in this situation (and other comparable situations where a particular high risk is overcome) one needs to look at comparable transactions and forecasts of future income. A combination of historic cost (adjusted by exploration risk), future income, and market-value-based valuations is here called for'.

[91] Their object is considered to 'ensure full reparation in accordance with the Chorzów principle' – I Uchkunova & O Temnikov, 'A Procrustean Bed: Pre- and Post-award Interest in ICSID Arbitration' (2014) 29(3) ICSID Rev 648, 651; for example: *Occidental v Ecuador* (Award of 5 October 2012) ICSID Case No ARB/06/11 [834]; *Vivendi (I) v Argentina* [9.2.6].

[92] ILC Articles (n 9) 108, commentary to Art 38, [7], *a contrario* 105, commentary to Art 36 [33].

[93] CL Beharry, 'Prejudgment Interest Rates in International Investment Arbitration' (2016) 8(1) JIDS 56, 56–7. Gotanda defines interest as compensation 'for the temporary withholding of money' or 'for the loss of the use of money'. See JY Gotanda, 'Compound Interest in International Disputes' (2003) 34(2) Law & PolIntBus 393, 395–6.

[94] Beharry (n 93) 61.

[95] *Quiborax v Bolivia* [513].

money and the decreasing purchasing power of money over time. It does not compensate investors for the fact that they did not obtain a profit from the investment.[96]

For the above reason, 'sunk costs' can be used as a 'reality check' of the outcome reached by applying other methodologies.[97] They can serve as the primary methodology only if forward-looking ones are unavailable in a particular case. The two most common forward-looking methodologies are: (i) income based and (ii) market based.[98]

Income-based methodology, also known as the Discounted Cash Flow (DCF) method, calculates the present value of an investment's anticipated future cash-flows during its useful life.[99] As such, it provides for a fair market value of a 'going concern'.[100] It aims at compensating lost profits which the investment was supposed to generate, but was unable to because of the treaty breach.[101] Application of this method requires the ability to forecast future earnings.

Market-based methodology determines the value of an investment by comparing it to similar investments traded on the open market. Whilst DCF 'computes the present value of the business's future earnings' directly, the market-based approach does so indirectly 'because it incorporates market values of comparable businesses'.[102] Application of this method requires the existence of comparable transactions (concerning similar projects or companies, if an investment is implemented through a special purpose vehicle having one asset).[103]

---

[96] This is possible when using forward-looking methodologies. For example, the Tribunal in *Quiborax v Bolivia* included interest accrued on past cash flows in the total value of past cash flows calculated using the Discounted Cash Flow method. See *Quiborax v Bolivia* [515].

[97] For example: *Eiser v Spain* [474].

[98] However, some authors classify the market-based approach as a backward-looking methodology – Wälde & Sabahi (n 1) 1070–1, 1074.

[99] Ripinsky & Williams (n 1) 195; see also G Rush, K Sequeira & M Shopp, 'Valuation Techniques for Early-Stage Businesses in Investor-State Arbitration' in CL Beharry (ed), *Contemporary and Emerging Issues on the Law of Damages and Valuation in International Investment Arbitration* (Brill Nijhoff 2018) 273.

[100] This is understood as meaning that a business is in operation and has a track record of cash flows – *Antin v Spain* [689]. This is the prevailing approach in the case law, but from the financial perspective it is not necessarily a pre-condition for applying the DCF method – KF Schumacher & H Klönne, 'Discounted Cash Flow Method' in CL Beharry (ed), *Contemporary and Emerging Issues on the Law of Damages and Valuation in International Investment Arbitration* (Brill Nijhoff 2018) 212.

[101] Ripinsky & Williams (n 1) 279, 289.

[102] ibid 212.

[103] 'Market capitalization', calculated based on a price of shares on the stock market would also fall within the category of market-based methodology – Rubins et al (n 8) 190.

Forward-looking methods are commonly applied in business reality, outside the context of litigation.[104] For example, they are recognised in industry standards for valuating mineral properties.[105] They are based on market indicators. Thus, even though they represent a degree of subjectivity and uncertainty, this in itself should not preclude their application.[106]

8   The Curious Case of the Natural Resources Sector

Investor-State arbitration case law reveals the reluctance of arbitral tribunals to apply forward-looking valuation methods to early-stage projects, particularly those which have not yet started to generate any income. With respect to such projects tribunals tend to consider the DCF method as 'too speculative and uncertain',[107] 'unattractive and speculative',[108] requiring 'too many unsubstantiated assumptions' and being 'overly speculative',[109] requiring an investment to be 'a going concern with a proven record of profitability'.[110] The tendency with respect to comparable transactions is to consider them as 'not sufficiently comparable'[111] or to find that they do not 'support a clear conclusion' regarding comparability.[112] Instead, tribunals prefer to look at the amounts actually invested ('sunk costs')[113] or other backward-looking methods, such as offers actually received in the past to acquire the relevant investment.[114]

In cases where tribunals have decided not to apply the DCF method to early-stage mining projects, they did not preclude the use of the method

---

[104]   Rush et al (n 99) 262, 288; Schumacher & Klönne (n 100) 207.
[105]   For example, CIMVAL Standards and Guidelines 2003 provide that an income-based approach may be a suitable method of valuation for any type of mineral property save for an exploration property (CIMVAL, 'Standards and Guidelines for Valuation of Mineral Properties: Special Committee of the Canadian Institute of Mining, Metallurgy and Petroleum on Valuation of Mineral Properties' (*CIMVAL*, 2003) 22 <https://mrmr.cim.org/media/1020/cimval-standards-guidelines.pdf> accessed 1 June 2022). This was confirmed in CIMVAL Code 2019 (CIMVAL, 'The CIMVAL Code for the Valuation of Mineral Properties' (*CIMVAL*, 2019) 16 <https://mrmr.cim.org/media/1135/cimval-code-november2019.pdf> accessed 1 June 2022).
[106]   Rubins et al (n 8) 200.
[107]   *Bear Creek Mining Corporation v Peru* (Award of 30 November 2017) ICSID Case No ARB/14/21 [604].
[108]   *Khan Resources v Mongolia* [392].
[109]   *Al-Bahloul v Tajikistan* [96].
[110]   *Caratube v Kazakhstan* (Award of 27 September 2017) ICSID Case No ARB/13/13 [1094].
[111]   *Khan Resources v Mongolia* [398].
[112]   *South American Silver v Bolivia* [838]; similarly, *Caratube v Kazakhstan* [1133].
[113]   *Bear Creek v Peru* [604]; *South American Silver v Bolivia* [866]; *Caratube v Kazakhstan* [1164].
[114]   *Khan Resources v Mongolia* [410–1].

per se, but merely decided that it was not applicable to the facts of the given case.[115] Rightly so, as the methodology itself is in line with the *Chorzów Factory* principle.

There are examples to show that the DCF method can also be applied in disputes concerning early-stage mining projects. In *Tethyan v Pakistan* case, the Tribunal awarded compensation based on a 'modern DCF'. It observed that, among other matters,

> the question whether a DCF method (or a similar income-based valuation methodology) can be applied to value a project which has not yet become operational depends strongly on the circumstances of the individual case. The first key question is whether, based on the evidence before it, the Tribunal is convinced that in the absence of Respondent's breaches, the project would have become operational and would also have become profitable. The second key question is whether the Tribunal is convinced that it can, with reasonable confidence, determine the amount of these profits based on the inputs provided by the Parties' experts for this calculation [...].[116]

Both prerequisites were met in the case. The Tribunal in *Crystallex v Venezuela* observed, in the context of a gold mine project which had not commenced production, that:

> the Claimant has established the fact of future profitability, as it had completed the exploration phase, the size of the deposits had been established, the value can be determined based on market prices, and the costs are well known in the industry and can be estimated with a sufficient degree of certainty. [...] In this case only forward-looking methodologies aimed at calculating lost profits are appropriate in order to determine the fair market value of Crystallex's investment.[117]

This is in line with standard industry practices such as CIMVal Standards and Guidelines 2003. Also, the Tribunal in *Gold Reserve v Venezuela*,

---

[115] For example, the Tribunal *in Khan Resources v Mongolia* [392] observed: 'in this particular case, there are a number of additional factors and uncertainties which, in the Tribunal's view, make the use of the DCF method unattractive and speculative'. The Tribunal in *Al-Bahloul v Tajikistan* [74–6] observed that 'under exceptional circumstances DCF-analysis might be appropriate where the investment project at issue had not started operation', which 'might be justified, inter alia, where the exploration of hydrocarbons is at issue. The determination of the future cash flows from the exploitation of hydrocarbon reserves need not depend on a past record of profitability. There are numerous hydrocarbons reserves around the world and sufficient data allowing for future cash flows projections should be available to allow a DCF-calculation'. The Tribunal did not apply DCF because 'no hydrocarbons have yet been found' in the disputed concessions.
[116] *Tethyan Copper v Pakistan* (Award of 12 July 2019) ICSID Case No ARB/12/1 [330, 335].
[117] *Crystallex v Venezuela* [878, 880, 882–3], relied on estimations of proven and probable reserves and measured and indicated resources in accordance with international standards.

where the experts for both parties used the DCF method, applied it to non-production property.[118]

This case law reveals that the DCF method can indeed be applied to early-stage mining projects.[119] Relevant factors in the fact-assessment include whether a sufficient degree of certainty has been achieved regarding projections of future profitability (such as knowledge of the size of the mineral deposit,[120] predictability of price fluctuations strengthened by resource type[121] and reliable mining cashflow analysis prepared prior to the dispute having arisen),[122] combined with the claimant's standing (such as a historical record of financial performance,[123] whether it has a demonstrated commitment and capacity – both financial and organisational – to progress to the production stage).[124]

These observations find support in the Spanish saga case law, concerning investments in the renewable energy sector (which is considered to fall within the field of natural resources).[125] In most of these cases, when tribunals found that the underlying investment treaty had been infringed, they decided to apply the DCF method.[126] The tribunals did not consider it too speculative. The lifetime of the investments (power plants) was foreseeable. This can be compared to the expected lifetime of a mine and the production period of a particular deposit. The commodity price (electricity)

---

[118] *Gold Reserve Inc v Venezuela* (Award of 22 September 2014) ICSID Case No ARB(AF)/09/1 [830]: 'Although the Brisas Project was never a functioning mine and therefore did not have a history of cashflow which would lend itself to the DCF model, the Tribunal accepts the explanation of both Dr Burrows (CRA) and Mr Kaczmarek (Navigant) that a DCF method can be reliably used in the instant case because of the commodity nature of the product and detailed mining cashflow analysis previously performed'.

[119] From a financial perspective, the limitations identified by tribunals 'are not impediments per se to applying the DCF method', but rather factors to be included in the DCF models – Schumacher & Klönne (n 100) 211–12.

[120] *Crystallex v Venezuela* [880]; *Khan Resources v Mongolia* [391].

[121] *Crystallex v Venezuela* [879].

[122] *Rusoro Mining v Venezuela* [759].

[123] ibid.

[124] *Khan Resources v Mongolia* [392].

[125] R Caldwell, D Chodorow & F Dorobantu, 'Valuing Natural Resources Investments' in CL Beharry (ed), *Contemporary and Emerging Issues on the Law of Damages and Valuation in International Investment Arbitration* (Brill Nijhoff 2018) 293.

[126] *Eiser v Spain* [465]; *Novenergia v Spain* [818, 820]; *Masdar v Spain* [575, 581]; *Antin v Spain* [688–91]; *Foresight v Spain* [474, 530]; *Cube v Spain* [478]; *Infrared v Spain* [521]; *OperaFund v Spain* [621]; *Watkins v Spain* [689]; *PV Investors v Spain* [691, 697]; *SolEs v Spain* (Award of 31 July 2019) ICSID Case No ARB/15/38 [488]; *9REN v Spain* (Award of 31 May 2019) ICSID Case No ARB/15/15 [407]. The ECT was the applicable investment treaty in these cases.

was foreseeable. This can be compared to the commodity price of natural resources such as gold, copper or gas.[127] Developing projects in both fields requires large, upfront investments.[128]

In the renewable energy sector, an important element allowing for DCF calculations was the highly regulated nature of the industry, minimising the expected fluctuations of future cash flows. In the words of the Tribunal in *Novenergia v Spain*, the DCF method 'is considered particularly suitable for valuating income-streams that are regulated (as opposed to unregulated business that is more exposed to market fluctuations)'.[129] Thus, the DCF method was applied not only to 'going concerns', but also to investments which began generating income shortly prior to the respondent's regulatory changes, which violated the investment treaty.[130] This is a major difference between mining and renewable energy disputes. Whereas mining disputes also concern a highly-regulated industry, this factor is not related to State subsidies and, therefore, has limited impact on future cash flows.

9 Conclusions

The *Chorzów Factory* principle reflects customary international law governing remedies for treaty breaches. As such, it applies to violations of international investment treaties. It entitles claimants in investor-State arbitrations to seek restitution prior to compensation or satisfaction.

Claimants have a right to choose the remedy they wish to seek. If claimants seek restitution, tribunals have the power to award it, unless this is explicitly precluded by the underlying treaty or is impossible (or at least inadequate) due to the facts of a particular case. Restitution was considered as inadequate in the Spanish saga cases, which concerned

---

[127] Caldwell et al (n 125) 302–3.
[128] ibid 294. The difference is that although the development of a renewable energy power plant is a long process which takes several years, it is still shorter than an investment in developing a mine, which is preceded by exploration activities.
[129] *Novenergia v Spain* [820]. See also *Cube v Spain* [478]; *Infrared v Spain* [535].
[130] In *Eiser v Spain* [121] the plants began operation in 2012; in *Masdar v Spain* [98–9] – at the end of 2011; in *Infrared v Spain* [57–8] in 2012; in *RREEF v Spain* [169, 173] one of the power plants became operational in 2013, although the other one was operational already in 2008. Contested violations of the ECT concerned a series of measures taken between 2012 and 2014, whereas the respondent 'crossed the line' in June 2014; for example: *Eiser v Spain* 458; see also: Caldwell et al (n 125) 300–1; in *NextEra v Spain*, however, an operational history of less than 1 year was the basis for refusing to apply the DCF method – *NextEra v Spain* (Award of 12 March 2019) ICSID Case No ARB/14/11 [643, 647].

treaty violations resulting from the adoption of new laws and regulations. Ordering restitution in this context was considered as potentially limiting State sovereignty. Tribunals can award restitution with the possibility to pay compensation *in lieu* of restitution, to overcome similar concerns in cases concerning individually applied measures.

A declaratory-only award is considered as a 'paper victory' and the *de facto* loss of the case, rather than as having obtained satisfaction, a meaningful form of reparation. Such an award is disproportionate when compared to the costs of arbitral proceedings and its significance is undermined by the confidentiality of the bulk of investor-State arbitral awards.

In practice, claimants rarely consider any remedy other than compensation. The *Chorzów Factory* principle seems to be used by claimants as a shortcut to proceed to calculating compensation. There is nothing reproachable in this, and the precise manner in which claims are framed is binding on tribunals, which cannot go beyond the remedies sought by the claimants. This explains, however, the reasons why remedies other than compensation – restitution and satisfaction, available under customary international law – are only occasionally considered in investor-State arbitrations.

With respect to compensation, differences exist between compensation for lawful expropriation (compensation is a prerequisite of any lawful expropriation) and compensation as a remedy for unlawful expropriation. The latter can be higher, as it can be calculated as of the date of the award and it can make use of *ex post* information. This understanding of the customary international law governing compensation appears to be already settled in investor-State arbitral case law.

There is no infallible approach to choosing the methodology for calculating compensation for treaty breaches. However, the choice of forward-looking (income-based) methods is generally available in cases concerning all sectors of the economy, including in disputes concerning early-stage mining projects and renewable energy power plants. There are identifiable patterns in the case law, showing that (i) in principle, arbitral tribunals are reluctant to apply forward-looking valuation methods to early-stage projects, particularly those which have not begun to generate any income, but (ii) if a number of factual elements exist, this initial reluctance can be overturned. This U-turn is easier in renewable energy disputes than in mining disputes, because the highly-regulated nature of the renewable energy industry is closely related to State subsidies, which allow the expected fluctuations of future cash flows to be minimised.

13

A TWAIL Engagement with Customary International Investment Law

Some Strategies for Interpretation

NINA MILEVA[*]

1 Introduction

The intellectual movement of Third World Approaches to International Law (TWAIL) is now a well-established strand of critical thought within the international legal discourse. At its core, TWAIL unveils the hierarchical nature of the international legal system and undertakes critical investigations which unearth power relationships within the international community.[1] While nowadays some may argue that the term TWAIL or the reference to third world States is anachronistic, it is important to understand that TWAIL is not a reference to a particular geographical constellation in international law. This is all the more so if we consider that States traditionally grouped under the 'third world' heading have since changed the political, economic or social traits that originally earned them this categorisation.[2] Rather, TWAIL represents a perspective which is 'critical of the universalizing mission and occidental authority of Eurocentric international legal scholarship and practice',[3] and is not

---

[*] Nina Mileva is a PhD candidate and lecturer at the University of Groningen. This contribution is based on research conducted in the context of the project 'The Rules of Interpretation of Customary International Law' ('TRICI-Law'). This project has received funding from the European Research Council (ERC) under the European Union's Horizon 2020 Research and Innovation Programme (Grant Agreement No 759728).

[1] JT Gathii, 'The Promise of International Law: A Third World View' (2021) 36(3) American University International Law Review 377; JT Gathii, 'The Agenda of Third World Approaches in International Law' in J Dunoff & M Pollack (eds), *International Legal Theory: Foundations and Frontiers* (CUP 2022) ch 7.

[2] A Bianchi, *International Law Theories: An Inquiry into Different Ways of Thinking* (OUP 2016) 203–4.

[3] Gathii 2022 (n 1). For an additional commentary on the geographical counterparts of these categories, see JC Okubuiro, 'Application of Hegemony to Customary International Law: An African Perspective' (2018) 7 Global Journal of Comparative Law 232.

necessarily tied to a geographical Statist space. This reflects first the non-homogeneous ideological make-up of States traditionally considered as belonging to the third world, as well as the fact that nowadays one may often find the wretched and the dispossessed among societies traditionally considered to be part of the Global North. Thus, members of the TWAIL intellectual movement may not always share a geographical space and yet be united in 'a sensibility and a political orientation'.[4]

Historically, there have been different ways that TWAIL scholars have chosen to engage with international law, varying from complete denunciations of the system to more constructive attempts to deploy existing legal structures with a view to enacting change.[5] In this chapter, I will sketch out a discussion of customary international law (CIL) interpretation as an example of constructive engagement with international investment law (IIL) from a TWAIL perspective. I will build on the existing TWAIL scholarship, which has engaged in criticism of IIL as a regime and of the theory of CIL as a source of international law (Section 2). Having outlined the existing critique, I will turn to a discussion of CIL interpretation as a potential tool for reconciling some of the harsh, but merited, criticism coming from the TWAIL perspective with a continued engagement with and reliance on international (investment) law.

First, relying on the example of the minimum standard of treatment of aliens (MST) – one of the oldest customary rules of the international investment regime – I will argue that interpretation plays a crucial role in the construction of customary rules and is central to their evolution and continued existence (Section 3). Having established this, I will move to my final argument as to how this awareness of the function of interpretation in CIL can help us constructively engage with IIL from a TWAIL perspective (Section 4). Here, I will outline strategies for interpretation which may be deployed from the TWAIL perspective in order to address the perceived problems in the regime of IIL. Put differently, I will argue that the awareness of what interpretation is and how it functions in CIL opens up new avenues for addressing problems within both particular customary rules and, more generally, international (investment) law. It is at the stage

---

[4] L Eslava & S Pahuja, 'Between Resistance and Reform: TWAIL and the Universality of International Law' (2011) 3 Trade, Law and Development 103, 104; See also K Mickelson, 'Rhetoric and Rage: Third World Voices in International Legal Discourse' (1998) 16(2) Wisconsin International Law Journal 353.

[5] Bianchi calls this TWAIL's 'ambivalent posture towards international law', variously regarding international law as either the problem or the solution to the world's injustices. Bianchi (n 2) 207–8.

of interpretation of customary rules that particular criticism can be raised and potentially resolved. In this sense, interpretation is a tool that may be utilised to address and potentially improve upon problematic rationales underlying the rule or the larger system in which it operates. While this presents great emancipatory potential with regard to argumentative strategies that may be developed, it also has its limitations. An evaluation of the limitations of the argument as well as some summary observations are thus addressed in the conclusion (Section 5).

2 The Criticism of Customary International Investment Law from the TWAIL Perspective

It is not surprising to observe that TWAIL scholarship is very critical of the regime of IIL. The TWAIL intellectual tradition in international law originates from decolonisation. It is a school of thought which perceives the international legal system as one built on power disparity, exploitation, and unequal relations. On this understanding, international law as a system reflects the interests of powerful States, and these interests are deployed through various legal doctrines including the doctrine of CIL. Here CIL is considered problematic both generally as a category in the sources doctrine,[6] and more specifically on the level of individual customary rules.[7] These problems of CIL are set in the wider historical context which links the development of international law to the colonial encounter between European States and the violently colonised non-European world.[8] It is thus not surprising to find particularly strong criticism among TWAIL scholars aimed at the system of IIL, and the (customary) rules contained therein.[9]

Historically, one of the strongest concerted TWAIL efforts at both criticising and reforming the international economic legal order was the

---

[6] BS Chimni, 'Customary International Law: A Third World Perspective' (2018) 112(1) AJIL 1, 4–12; GRB Gallindo & C Yip, 'Customary International Law and the Third World: Do Not Step on the Grass' (2017) 16(2) Chin J Int Law 251; JP Kelly, 'Customary International Law in Historical Context: The Exercise of Power without General Acceptance' in BD Lepard (ed), *Reexamining Customary International Law* (CUP 2017) 47; see also KJ Heller, 'Specially Affected States and the Formation of Custom' (2018) 112(2) AJIL 191.

[7] Kelly (n 6) 59–73 particularly focusing on the origins of the customary MST; A Anghie, *Imperialism, Sovereignty and the Making of International Law* (CUP 2007) 214.

[8] Anghie (n 7).

[9] M Sornarajah, 'Mutations of Neo-Liberalism in International Investment Law' (2011) 3 Trade Law and Development 203; M Sornarajah, *The International Law on Foreign Investment* (3rd edn, CUP 2010).

New International Economic Order (NIEO).[10] This was an initiative of Third World States aided by TWAIL scholars aimed at reforming regimes such as the IIL via a concentrated legislative effort at the United Nations General Assembly. The initiative concerned a reformation of key areas such as foreign direct investment, the rules of nationalisation and expropriation, the criteria applied to compensation, and the fora for dispute settlement in this area.[11] While highly ambitious, this initiative was met with little success. Pushback from Western States as well as various complex forms of financial domination deployed in the international system undermined the reformative effort, and the battle for a NIEO was largely lost.[12] The limited success of the NIEO has spurred what some have called a second generation[13] of TWAIL scholars, more disenchanted with international law, and focused on uncovering its continuously hegemonic traits. It is among this scholarship that much of the criticism of the contemporary IIL system can be found.

A central trait of this criticism revolves around the underlying rationale of IIL. The assumption upon which IIL is constructed is that foreign investment is so essential to economic development that its operation must be facilitated by near absolute protection of the foreign investment/investor.[14] This assumption, however, remains contested among critical scholars, as case studies demonstrate that foreign investment can be hugely exploitative and damaging to host economies.[15] This has led Sornarajah to observe that while the potential of foreign investment to aid development must be recognised, the absolute protection of investment in international law enables 'the instrumentalism of free market fundamentalism' to fragment international law 'without paying heed to prescriptions of law relating to the environment, human rights or labour standards'.[16] Similarly, Odumosu has demonstrated that in the context of

---

[10] UNGA, 'Charter of Economic Rights and Duties of States' (12 December 1974) UN Doc A/RES/3281(XXIX); See also, M Bedjaoui, *Towards a New International Economic Order* (Holmes & Meier 1979).

[11] Bianchi (n 2) 213.

[12] See, however, Bianchi who argues that the NIEO effort yielded changes in the international law-making process by introducing the notion of soft-law, and introducing a relative vision of normativity in this respect. Bianchi (n 2) 214.

[13] A Anghie & BS Chimni, 'Third World Approaches to International Law and Individual Responsibility in Internal Conflicts' (2003) 2 Chin J Int Law 78.

[14] Sornarajah 2011 (n 9) 204.

[15] J Linarelli, ME Salomon & M Sornarajah, *The Misery of International Law: Confrontations with Injustice in the Global Economy* (OUP 2018) 145–74.

[16] Sornarajah 2011 (n 9) 205.

investment dispute settlement, this overwhelming focus on investment protection has all but erased legitimate grievances of local populations affected by investments, and also significantly restricted the extent to which host States might balance the protection of foreign investment with the protection of other local interests.[17]

The criticism of the underlying rationale of IIL often goes hand in hand with a critique of its historical origin, as well that of specific customary rules operating in the system. For instance, Kelly traces the customary MST to early natural law doctrines on the freedom of commerce and the rights to hospitality and sociability of Vittoria and Grotius, developed to legitimise the extension of the European colonial empires and the exploitation of peoples and resources encountered in the process.[18] Similarly, Anghie unpacks the relationship between State responsibility and the customary MST to demonstrate that Western States re-established colonial relationships of power with former colonies through what was ostensibly neutral international law.[19] Thus, while the formal process of decolonisation got rid of colonial empires, legal doctrines formed in the colonial period survive today and perpetuate problematic logics in the contemporary context of international law. On this point, Pahuja persuasively demonstrates that in moments when the Third World attempted to dispute existing structures in international law (such as with the NIEO), this was met with a response by the First World, which claimed the universality of values so as to discredit attempted alternatives.[20]

A related criticism here is the structure of dispute settlement inIIL. Scholars have pointed out the asymmetry inherent in the fact that while foreign investors may bring suit against host States, the opposite is not true.[21] Moreover, the rationale inherent in many BITs, trade agreements, and customary rules automatically puts host States on the defensive should there be an attempt to limit foreign investment in favour of the protection of local environment or peoples.[22] The obvious counter-argument here is that States willingly admit foreign investment by signing BITs or trade agreements,

---

[17] IT Odumosu, 'The Law and Politics of Engaging Resistance in Dispute Settlement' (2007) 26 Penn State Int Law Rev 251.
[18] Kelly (n 6) 51–74.
[19] Anghie (n 7) 210–15.
[20] S Pahuja, *Decolonising International Law: Development, Economic Growth and the Politics of Universality* (CUP 2011) 102–71.
[21] Linarelli, Salomon & Sornarajah (n 15) 147; G Abi-Saab, 'The Third World Intellectual in Praxis: Confrontation, Participation, or Operation behind Enemy Lines' (2016) 37(11) Third World Quarterly 1957, 1969.
[22] See, for example, the reasoning of the Tribunal in *Técnicas Medioambientales Tecmed, SA v Mexico* (Award of 29 May 2003) ICSID No ARB(AF)/00/2 [119–32].

thereby subjecting themselves also to potential dispute settlement and the application of (customary) investment law. However, this argument potentially neglects the larger socio-economic context in which this 'willingness' takes place. Moreover, often political elites in States which conclude foreign investment agreements do not, in fact, represent or purport to protect the rights of some local populations, and thus, the asymmetry grows. Investment dispute settlement treats the State as a unitary entity, and as such, the interests of different local communities which might be differently affected by a particular foreign investment project are all subsumed under it.[23]

Having briefly outlined the lines of criticism levelled at customary IIL from the TWAIL perspective, I now turn to a discussion of CIL interpretation as the next step in the argument.

3 The Interpretation of Customary International Investment Law

This section first outlines more generally the nature and role of interpretation in the context of customary international law, before turning to the more concrete example of the customary MST as an illustration of these more general observations.

3.1 What Constitutes Interpretation of Customary International Law

Legal interpretation is the process of determining the scope and content of legal rules. It can be distinguished from rule-identification, which is the act of establishing whether a legal rule exists. Thus, interpretation is the process of discerning or clarifying the meaning of an existing legal rule, and takes place when a general rule is applied to particular facts.

CIL interpretation is the process that takes place after a customary rule has been identified. Once a rule of CIL is identified for the first time through an assessment of State practice and *opinio juris*, its existence is not restricted to the moment where it was identified for the first time; rather it is a continuous one. When the same rule is invoked in subsequent cases before the same or a different judicial body, the judicial body does not usually go into the exercise of re-establishing that the rule in question is a customary one by reassessing State practice and *opinio juris*.[24] Instead, the rule is *interpreted*

---

[23] Odumosu (n 17) 265–99.
[24] See, for instance, *North Sea Continental Shelf Cases (Federal Republic of Germany/Netherlands; Federal Republic of Germany/Denmark)* (Judgment) [1969] ICJ Rep 3, Dissenting Opinion of

within the given legal and factual context of the new case at hand. Moreover, outside of the dispute-settlement context, a customary rule does not only exist in the isolated moments when it is identified for the purposes of a particular case. Rather, its existence in the complex of international legal relations is also a continuous one. In this sense, interpretation allows us to account for the continued existence and operation of a customary rule. Within the timeline of existence of a CIL rule, interpretation takes place after the periods of formation and identification of the rule.[25] Identification yields a general rule of CIL, based on an inductive analysis of State practice and *opinio juris*.[26] It is important to note that a form of interpretive reasoning may also take place at this stage, in the sense of assessment of the relevant practice and *opinio juris*. The identification exercise includes choices in the selection of certain custom-formative practices over others in order to infer the general rule, as well as the choices in how we describe these practices which lead to the identification of the rule.[27] The reasoning employed in these choices and descriptions is by necessity interpretative. However, this is not an interpretation of a customary rule because this rule has not been confirmed to exist yet. Rather, what happens at the stage of identification is an evaluation of the evidence of State practice and *opinio juris* in order to assess whether they qualify for the purposes of establishing a customary rule and whether they in fact point to the existence of a customary rule.[28] Some scholars do employ the term 'interpretation' to also refer to the reasoning that takes place at the stage of identification.[29] However, a distinction must be maintained between what might be labeled as interpretation

---

Judge Tanaka, 183; *Arrest Warrant of 11 April 2000* (Congo v Belgium) (Judgment) [2002] ICJ Rep 3 [52–4]; *Pulp Mills on the River Uruguay (Argentina v Uruguay)* (Judgment) [2010] ICJ Rep 14 [101–2, 204]; *Mondev International Ltd v USA* (Award of 11 October 2002) ICSID Case No ARB(AF)/99/2 [113]; See also, P Merkouris, *Article 31(3)(c) VCLT and the Principle of Systemic Integration: Normative Shadows in Plato's Cave* (Brill 2015) 241.

[25] For an earlier discussion of this concept of a CIL timeline, see N Mileva, 'The Role of Domestic Courts in the Interpretation of Customary International Law: How Can We Learn from Domestic Interpretive Practices?' in P Merkouris, J Kammerhofer & N Arajärvi (eds), *The Theory, Practice, and Interpretation of Customary International Law* (CUP 2022) 453, 458–61, <www.cambridge.org/core/services/aop-cambridge-core/content/view/630 E681903F80296865C48617CCA5C14/9781316516898c21_453-480.pdf/role_of_domestic_courts_in_the_interpretation_of_customary_international_law.pdf>.

[26] Merkouris (n 24) 134–5.

[27] O Chasapis Tassinis, 'Customary International Law: Interpretation from Beginning to End' (2020) 31(1) EJIL 235, 240–4.

[28] On this point, see for more details, ILC, 'Draft Conclusions on Identification of Customary International Law, with Commentaries' (30 April–1 June and 2 July–10 August 2018) UN Doc A/73/10, reproduced in [2018/II – Part Two] YBILC 122, Conclusion 6, Conclusion 10.

[29] See, for instance, A Roberts, 'Traditional and Modern Approaches to Customary International Law: A Reconciliation' (2001) 95(4) AJIL 757; N Banteka, 'A Theory of

at the stage of identification and what is interpretation in the strict sense of an existing CIL rule. This is because these two operations are substantively different with respect to both their content and their outcome. The reasoning employed at identification is concerned with questions about the relevance and weight to be given to evidence of State practice and *opinio juris*, and the outcome of this reasoning is a binary one – a CIL rule is either determined to exist or it is not. The reasoning employed in interpretation is concerned with the determination of the content of the CIL rule and how this rule applies to the case at hand, and this reasoning may have a variety of outcomes depending on the rule being interpreted and the legal and factual circumstances it is being interpreted in. It is only by distinguishing these two operations that we may adequately capture the fact that the interpretation manifests differently in the context of CIL, that it is subject to a different methodology than that of identification, and it performs specific functions.

A related consideration in this context is who interprets. Formally, international law does not allocate interpretive authority with a single entity. Depending on the circumstances, interpretive authority may lie with a court, a State, or even a non-governmental entity.[30] All these actors together form the epistemic community of international law, and as such contribute broadly to the way legal rules are interpreted.[31] Nevertheless, judicial interpretation holds a prominent role in international law.[32] In

---

Constructive Interpretation for Customary International Law Identification' (2018) 39(3) MichJInt'l Law 301; DB Hollis, 'The Existential Function of Interpretation in International Law' in A Bianchi, D Peat & M Windsor (eds), *Interpretation in International Law* (OUP 2015) 78.

[30] M Waibel, 'Interpretive Communities in International Law' in A Bianchi, D Peat & M Windsor (eds), *Interpretation in International Law* (OUP 2015) 147, 155–8; see also, Azaria who speaks of the interpretive authority of the ILC, D Azaria, 'Codification by Interpretation: The International Law Commission as an Interpreter of International Law' (2020) 31(1) EJIL 171.

[31] See A Bianchi, 'Epistemic Communities' in J d'Aspremont & S Singh (eds), *Concepts for International Law: Contributions to Disciplinary Thought* (Edward Elgar 2019) 251; Waibel (n 30) 147; I Johnstone, 'Treaty Interpretation: The Authority of Interpretive Communities' (1991) 12(2) MJInt'l Law 371. See also, Linderfalk who discusses various interpreters through the distinction between operative interpretation (performed by national courts, civil servants, military officials, diplomatic personnel, international courts and arbitration tribunals, international organisations, and other authorities empowered to decide on issues concerning the application of international agreements) and doctrinal interpretation (performed by scholars). U Linderfalk, *On the Interpretation of Treaties: The Modern International Law as Expressed in the 1969 Vienna Convention on the Law of Treaties* (Springer 2007) 12.

[32] See R Mackenzie, C Romano & Y Shany (eds), *The Manual on International Courts and Tribunals* (2nd edn, OUP 2010); G Hernandez, 'Interpretative Authority and the International Judiciary' in A Bianchi, D Peat & M Windsor (eds), *Interpretation in International Law* (OUP 2015) 166.

the subsequent discussion I focus on judicial interpretation for two reasons. First, because in the practice of international law, questions of interpretation tend to arise in the context of disputes and be formulated with a judge or arbitrator in mind.[33] Put differently, the bulk of the judicial role in international law consists of interpretation.[34] In this regard, and without prejudice to the interpretation of CIL by other actors, examples of CIL interpretation are most likely to be found in the jurisprudence of courts and tribunals. Second, because in international law judicial decisions possess what has aptly been described as a 'centrifugal normative force' – other international legal actors tend to follow judicial reasoning, and judicial decisions can be 'substantively constitutive' of international law.[35] 'That normative effect is exacerbated when dealing with *unwritten* sources of law, in particular customary international law [...]: there is no balancing between the text, its authors, and the interpreter in such situations, and the certainty of judicial reasoning holds and intrinsic appeal'.[36]

An examination of jurisprudence dealing with the interpretation of CIL indicates that interpretation performs two important functions in the continued existence of customary rules – a constructive/concretising function and an evolutive function.[37] The constructive/concretising function refers to the fact that interpretation is the process through which the content of general customary rules is fleshed out and specified. Customary rules are often formulated in broad terms, and require precisely the act of interpretation to arrive at more concrete findings of their content.[38] In this sense, it is through interpretation that we arrive at more specific sub-elements of a general customary rule, or more specific sub-obligations

---

[33] A Bianchi, 'The Game of Interpretation in International Law: The Players, the Cards, and Why the Game is Worth the Candle' in A Bianchi, D Peat & Windsor (eds), *Interpretation in International Law* (OUP 2015) 34, 41.

[34] Hernandez (n 32) 167.

[35] ibid, 166; See also, A Zidar, 'Interpretation and the International Legal Profession: Between Duty and Aspiration in A Bianchi, D Peat & M Windsor (eds), *Interpretation in International Law* (OUP 2015) 133, 134; H Kelsen, *Pure Theory of Law* (UC Press 1967) 354–5.

[36] Hernandez (n 32) 166 [emphasis added]. See also, Waibel who discusses the centrality of judicial interpretation in international law with a particular focus on national courts as interpreters of international law. Waibel (n 25) 155–8.

[37] For an earlier discussion of these two functions, see P Merkouris & N Mileva, 'ESIIIL Reflection: Introduction to the Series "Customary Law Interpretation as a Tool"' (2022) 11(1) ESIL Reflections 1 <https://esil-sedi.eu/wp-content/uploads/2022/08/ESIL-Reflection-Merkouris-Mileva.pdf> accessed 24 June 2023.

[38] S Sur, 'La créativité du droit international' (2013) 363 RdC 21, 295; A Orakhelashvili, *The Interpretation of Acts and Rules in Public International Law* (OUP 2008) 496.

that flow from it. Merkouris also refers to this as the *collapsing* function of interpretation.[39] The evolutive function of interpretation refers to the fact that interpretation is crucial in the continued existence of CIL rules, and their adaptation to new developments of fact or law. Contrary to some views, customary rules are not static legal rules which have no place in modern legal systems.[40] Rather, customary rules are by their nature dynamic because they move together with the community from whose conduct they emerge. As such, they require interpretation in order to be able to respond to emerging new circumstances.[41] For an illustration of these two functions relevant to our present discussion, let us briefly consider the example of the customary MST.

3.2 The Interpretation of the Customary MST and the Functions of CIL Interpretation

The customary status of MST is uncontested, and support for this may be found widely among States, tribunals, and scholarly writings. What is, however, in question is its precise content.[42] As argued above, customary rules necessarily come in a general format, and the MST is one among many examples which confirms this. This is certainly both a virtue and a vice of custom. The generality of customary rules makes them particularly fit to answer to a variety of circumstances, and thus regulate a variety of situations that may arise in international law. In a scenario where multiple legal regimes might interact or bind different actors differently, general customary rules present a least common denominator of legal obligation. In the context of the MST, its customary status means that obligations flowing from it apply to all States, including those that may not have

---

[39] ibid.
[40] For a discussion on this, see CA Bradley, 'Customary International Law Adjudication as Common Law Adjudication' in CA Bradley (ed), *Custom's Future: International Law in a Changing World* (CUP 2016) 34; BD Lepard, 'Customary International Law as a Dynamic Process' in CA Bradley (ed), *Custom's Future: International Law in a Changing World* (CUP 2016) 62; O Sender & M Wood, 'Custom's Bright Future: The Continuing Importance of Customary International Law' in CA Bradley (ed), *Custom's Future: International Law in a Changing World* (CUP 2016) 360; J Tasioulas, 'Customary International Law and the Quest for Global Justice' in A Perreau-Saussine & JB Murphy (eds), *The Nature of Customary International Law: Legal, Historical and Philosophical Perspectives* (CUP 2007) 307.
[41] On this point, see N Mileva & M Fortuna, 'Environmental Protection as an Object of and Tool for Evolutionary Interpretation' in G Abi-Saab et al (eds), *Evolutionary Interpretation and International Law* (Hart 2019) 152.
[42] P Dumberry, *The Formation and Identification of Rules of Customary International Law in International Investment Law* (CUP 2016) 97.

entered into any bilateral investment treaties (BITs), and may also be invoked by any foreign investor irrespective of whether or not their State of origin has entered into a BIT with the State where they've made an investment.[43] Moreover, in new legal situations not covered by conventional rules, customary law may prove a source of regulation that can be extended by analogy.[44] This is arguably what indeed happened with the customary MST, which had originally broadly applied to the treatment of aliens and was later also extended to the property of aliens as well as their investments. At the same time, the generality of customary rules also leads to vagueness, and this is a challenge to the legal certainty and predictability that actors might desire in particular legal scenarios or in international law more generally. The customary MST has indeed been criticised for its vagueness, its inability to provide clear standards for behaviour, and even its 'normative weakness'.[45]

Historically, the formulation of the MST is traced back to a 1910 address by the American Secretary of State, Elihu Root, who expressed the view that an international standard is necessary in order to guarantee appropriate treatment by host countries to the nationals of another country.[46] Root's formulation, however, was quite vague, and did not in fact provide for a more concrete content of the standard beyond a claim that such a standard existed and was recognised by civilised countries.[47] A more concrete expression of the content of the MST is ascribed to the US–Mexico Claims Commission in its *Neer* award.[48] Much like the formulation

---

[43] ibid, 96.
[44] See on this the reasoning of Germany with respect to customary rules applying to cyber operations. German Government, 'On the Application of International Law in Cyberspace – Position Paper' (*Auswärtiges Amt*, March 2021) <www.auswaertiges-amt.de/blob/2446304/32e7b2498e10b74fb17204c54665bdf0/on-the-application-of-international-law-in-cyberspace-data.pdf> accessed 26 July 2022.
[45] J d'Aspremont, 'International Customary Investment Law: Story of a Paradox' in Gazzini, T & de Brabandere, E (eds), *International Investment Law: The Sources of Rights and Obligation* (Brill 2012) 5, 34.
[46] E Root, 'The Basis of Protection to Citizens Residing Abroad' (1910) 4 ASIL Proc 16, 21. 'There is a standard of justice, very simple, very fundamental, and of such general acceptance by all civilized countries as to form a part of the international law of the world'.
[47] See on this the detailed analysis in M Paparinskis, *The International Minimum Standard and Fair and Equitable Treatment* (OUP 2013) 39–63.
[48] *USA (LFH Neer) v Mexico* (Award of 15 October 1926) 4 RIAA 60 [4]. See Patrick Dumberry also flags other contemporaneous cases as relevant to the emergence of the minimum standard. Dumberry (n 42) 65, referencing *USA (Harry Roberts) v Mexico* (Award of 2 November 1926) 4 RIAA 77; *France (Affaire Chevreau) v UK* (Award of 9 June 1931) 2 RIAA 1113; and *USA (Hopkins) v Mexico* (1926) 4 RIAA 41.

expressed by Secretary Root, however, the *Neer* award did not express the MST with the protection of foreign investments or property in view. Rather, it was concerned with the more specific scenario of alleged failure to investigate the murder of an alien, and the more general standard of denial of justice in the context of treatment of aliens.[49] Thus, while *Neer* is considered the classical starting point of MST, both States and tribunals have recognised that MST is not frozen in time to this formulation.[50] The shift from a more general standard of denial of justice to the more specific rationale of protection of foreign investment and property is not insignificant. As Paparinskis aptly demonstrates in his genealogy of the standard, in post-World War 2 discussions of the MST there is a marked 'shift of the paradigm that the standard was meant to regulate', including now a focus on property and the personality of the foreign investor.[51] This focus on the protection of property rights and protection of foreign investment is the primary area of application of the MST today.[52]

TWAIL scholarship has offered its own take on why this shift occurred.[53] What we are more concerned with for the purposes of this section is how these changes in perspective were operationalised in the standard by means of interpretation. As the upcoming discussion will demonstrate, while the customary MST was initially expressed in general terms, its content in the context of investment law has been made more concrete and specific through interpretation by various investment tribunals. Moreover, it is also through interpretation that the MST has evolved over time.

Early mentions of the MST as a customary rule relevant in the context of investment protection can be found in the reasoning of the ICJ in the *ELSI* case. Here, the court acknowledged that the relevant treaty standard of treatment 'must conform to the minimum international standard',[54] and found that this minimum standard includes the element of 'denial of

---

[49] Paparinskis (n 47) 48–54.
[50] See, for instance, the positions of both USA and Canada as expressed during the proceedings of *ADF Group Inc v USA*. *ADF Group Inc v USA* (Canada's Second Article 1128 Submission of 19 July 2002) ICSID Case No ARB(AF)/00/1 [8–10]; *ADF Group Inc v USA* (Transcript of Hearing: Day 2 of 16 April 2002) ICSID Case No ARB(AF)/00/1, 492–3.
[51] Paparinskis (n 47) 64, 65–7. See also the discussion in the ILC on State responsibility, discussing also an international standard in relation to the protection of property of aliens. ILC, 'Summary Records of the 8th Session' (23 April–4 July 1956) [1956/1] YBILC 1, 233–8.
[52] H Dickerson, 'Minimum Standards' [2013] MPEPIL 845 [12–13].
[53] See discussion in Section 2 above.
[54] *Case concerning Elettronica Sicula SpA (ELSI) (USA v Italy)* (Judgment) [1989] ICJ Rep 15 [111]. This makes sense in light of the fact that the relevant treaty provision provided for 'the full protection and security required by international law'.

procedural justice'.⁵⁵ The reasoning of the ICJ with regard to the denial of procedural justice as an element of the customary MST has been referenced by various investment tribunals similarly faced with the need to specify the content of the general customary standard. For instance, in its award in respect of damages, the *Pope and Talbot* Tribunal relied on the reasoning in *ELSI* when seeking to define the arbitrariness requisite for a finding of denial of justice as part of the MST.⁵⁶ In *Mondev International Ltd*, this reference was part of a broader interpretation of the customary MST. Here, the Tribunal began by decoupling the customary MST in the context of investment protection from the minimum standard broadly outlined in *Neer*.⁵⁷ It then proceeded to interpret the customary MST evolutively so as to account for changes of law that have taken place in the broader legal environment in which the rule operates.⁵⁸ While this may, at first glance, seem expansive, it is interesting to note that the Tribunal also acknowledged the limitations of its interpretive power, and professed to remain within the limits posed by the customary MST.⁵⁹ After examining the relevant legal developments in the period since *Neer*, the *Mondev* Tribunal came to the conclusion that under the customary MST investments are entitled to fair and equitable treatment and full protection and security.⁶⁰ Having outlined the content of the customary MST in this way, the Tribunal went on to examine the applicable standard of denial of justice which would render treatment unfair or inequitable. Here it relied, among other, on the reasoning of the ICJ with respect to the nature of arbitrariness as a denial of justice, and accepted the ICJ definition of arbitrary conduct 'as that which displays a willful disregard of due process of law, … which shocks, or at least surprises, a sense of judicial propriety'.⁶¹ In addition to the ICJ's reasoning in *ELSI*, the *Mondev* Tribunal also relied

---

⁵⁵ ibid. In the particular circumstances, however, the court found that the temporal delay in proceedings complained by the applicant did not amount to such a denial. ibid [112].
⁵⁶ *Pope & Talbot Inc v Canada* (Award in Respect of Damages of 31 May 2002) UNCITRAL [63].
⁵⁷ *Mondev International Ltd v USA* (Award of 11 October 2002) ICSID Case No ARB(AF)/99/2 [113–15].
⁵⁸ ibid [116]. '[…] In the light of these developments it is unconvincing to confine the meaning of "fair and equitable treatment" and "full protection and security" of foreign investments to what those terms – had they been current at the time – might have meant in the 1920s when applied to the physical security of an alien. To the modern eye, what is unfair or inequitable need not equate with the outrageous or the egregious'.
⁵⁹ ibid [119–20].
⁶⁰ ibid [121–5].
⁶¹ ibid, referring to *Elettronica Sicula SpA (ELSI)* [128].

on the *Azinian* Tribunal for an even more detailed interpretation of denial of justice, thus also accepting into its definition elements such as refusal to entertain a suit, undue delay, inadequate administration of justice and malicious misapplication of the law.[62]

I flag this cross-reference to the reasoning of other tribunals because it is illustrative of the role of judicial interpretation in the construction of both customary rules more generally and the customary MST more specifically. In light of the general nature of CIL, it is not at all surprising that courts will borrow from each other when interpreting rules in *pari materia*. What is noteworthy in this cross-referencing is that the interpretive reasoning does not remain limited to the particular case, but carries over to subsequent cases as well. It is attached to the rule beyond the context of the specific case in that it has specified the content which is now considered to be an expression of the rule. In this sense, interpretation affects the content of the customary rule more generally as it exists continuously in international law. We may similarly observe this in the reasoning of the *Loewen Group Inc* Tribunal, which relied on the reasoning in *Pope & Talbot*, *ELSI* and *Mondev* to elucidate what would constitute arbitrariness amounting to a denial of justice in breach of the customary MST.[63] The constructive role of interpretation is illustrated perhaps most strongly by the reasoning of the Tribunal in *Waste Management*. Here, having surveyed the previous jurisprudence of a number of investment tribunals, the *Waste Management* Tribunal arrived at the following finding:

> Taken together, the *S.D. Myers*, *Mondev*, *ADF* and *Loewen* cases suggest that the minimum standard of treatment of fair and equitable treatment is infringed by conduct attributable to the State and harmful to the claimant if the conduct is arbitrary, grossly unfair, unjust or idiosyncratic, is discriminatory and exposes the claimant to sectional or racial prejudice, or involves a lack of due process leading to an outcome which offends judicial propriety—as might be the case with a manifest failure of natural justice in judicial proceedings or a complete lack of transparency and candour in an administrative process. In applying this standard it is relevant that the treatment is in breach of representations made by the host State which were reasonably relied on by the claimant.[64]

---

[62] *Azinian v Mexico* (Award of 1 November 1999) ICSID Case No ARB(AF)/97/2 [99–103].
[63] *Loewen Group, Inc and Raymond L Loewen v USA* (Award of 26 June 2003) ICSID Case No ARB(AF)/98/3 [131–3].
[64] *Waste Management, Inc v Mexico* ("Number 2") (Award of 30 April 2004) ICSID Case No ARB(AF)/00/3 [98].

The Tribunal here comes up with a very specific definition of the customary MST as a set of concrete elements and obligations. I would argue that this kind of construction of the customary MST, as a general rule made up of various specific legal sub-obligations, is a product of interpretation. This is certainly not an entirely novel observation, as several authors have made similar claims as to the 'umbrella-like' character of MST.[65] Building on their observations, I would merely argue more specifically that it is through interpretation particularly that the content of the general customary MST was developed and concretised. Why this is important is because this act of concretisation through interpretation does not remain restricted to the case at hand, but carries over to reasoning in subsequent cases both before the same tribunal and others that might follow it. Thus, we may envisage a general customary rule in case A whose content gets concretised through interpretation to contain element A1, where that element is carried over to the subsequent case B. Should further concretisation through interpretation take place in case B, whereby the customary rule is found to also contain element B1, elements A1 and B1 would now carry over to subsequent case C, and so on. In this way, interpretation affects the content of general customary rules not only for purposes of one specific case but also throughout the continuous existence of that customary rule overall and generally in international law. That this transcends adjudication becomes evident when we consider that often States rely on earlier judicial reasoning to argue the content of customary rules in subsequent cases. Thus, this constructive function of interpretation finds its way into State practice as well, thereby penetrating the very process of custom-creation by States.[66]

While this brief analysis of case law demonstrates how the customary MST has evolved and been constructed through judicial interpretation, this trend has not gone without criticism. For one, scholars have noted that this form of development of the standard through a case-by-case

---

[65] P Dumberry, 'Fair and Equitable Treatment: Its Interaction with the Minimum Standard and its Customary Status' (2017) 1(2) Brill Research Perspectives in International Investment Law and Arbitration 1, 17–18; See also, A Newcombe & L Paradell, *Law and Practice of Investment Treaties: Standards of Treatment* (Kluwer 2009); Paparinskis (n 47).

[66] Giannakopoulos and Monga refer to this as a 'feedback loop'. C Giannakopoulos & M Monga, 'History as Interpretative Context in the Evolutionary Interpretation of FET in International Investment Law' in G Abi-Saab et al (eds), *Evolutionary Interpretation and International Law* (Hart 2019) 297, 308.

application is not coherent and may lead to discrepancies in the way the standard is applied and enforced.[67] Furthermore, scholars have criticised this expansion through interpretation for developing investment protection obligations which arguably do not flow from the customary standard or the conduct of States.[68] For instance, several awards have read into the standard a requirement for a stable and predictable regulatory environment owed to investors,[69] which does not necessarily flow from the customary MST.[70] Similarly, and relying on the conviction that the customary MST should be interpreted evolutively,[71] the *Bilcon* Tribunal also found that the standard requires a 'fair opportunity for review' to be extended to the investor,[72] which once again is not obvious from the customary MST. On this critical note, it has also been observed that in the context of NAFTA proceedings there is a conflation of the customary MST with the treaty standard enshrined in Article 1105 NAFTA.[73] Thus, tribunals often make interpretive findings concerning the customary MST by relying on the treaty standard and relevant rules for treaty interpretation, which is problematic.[74] Nevertheless, it has been observed that the content of the standard is likely to continue being 'created through the dispute-settlement process',[75] and no universal international codification

---

[67] Dickerson (n 52) [23].

[68] JH Fahner, 'Maximising Investment Protection under the Minimum Standard – A Case Study of the Evolutive Interpretation and Application of Customary International Law in Investment Arbitration' (2023) 12(1) ESIL Reflections 1 <https://esil-sedi.eu/esil-reflection-maximising-investment-protection-under-the-minimum-standard-a-case-study-of-the-evolutive-interpretation-and-application-of-customary-international-law-in-investment-arbitration-2/> accessed 24 June 2023.

[69] See, for instance, *Windstream v Canada* (Award of 27 September 2016) PCA Case No 2013–22 [379]; *Eco Oro Minerals Corp v Colombia* (Decision on Jurisdiction, Liability and Directions on Quantum of 9 September 2021) ICSID Case No ARB/16/41 [805–21].

[70] Fahner (n 68).

[71] *Bilcon v Canada* (Award on Jurisdiction and Liability of 17 March 2015) PCA Case No. 2009–04 [433–6].

[72] ibid [603].

[73] The pertinent portion of the North American Free Trade Agreement (NAFTA) (adopted 17 December 1992, entered into force 1 January 1994) 32 ILM 289, Art 1105 is: 'Each Party shall accord to investments of investors of another Party treatment in accordance with international law, including fair and equitable treatment and full protection and security'. In an interpretative note issued in 2001, NAFTA parties clarified that Art. 1105 prescribes the customary MST as the relevant standard of treatment to be afforded to investments, that this standard includes fair and equitable treatment and full protection of security, and these latter two do not require treatment in addition to or beyond the customary MST.

[74] See on this point Fahner (n 68) criticising the reasoning in *Pope & Talbot* in these terms.

[75] Dickerson (n 52) [23].

or clarification effort seems imminent.[76] Bearing these observations in mind, let us now turn to a discussion of how these traits of interpretation in the context of CIL rules may be conducive to a TWAIL engagement with customary IIL.

4 A TWAIL Approach to the Interpretation of Customary International Investment Law

In outlining a potential TWAIL approach to the interpretation of customary international investment law, I join the chorus of critical scholars who have taken the proverbial good with the bad in attempting to devise critique without dismissing international law as a whole. This, I believe, reflects what Sundhya Pahuja has aptly named a 'critical faith' – maintaining faith in international law despite firmly comprehending its problematic complicity with power.[77] At the centre of such an engagement with international law lies the need to deconstruct international law's claim to universality in order to trace problematic elements and potentially resolve them. This entails recognising 'both the contingency of any value put forth as universal and the frame of reference supporting the universal claim'.[78] This I would argue is a task that can be achieved at the stage of interpretation. With this in mind, this section outlines three potential strategies which rely on the constructive and evolutive functions of interpretation in the context of CIL. These strategies represent modes of engagement with customary international investment law from the TWAIL perspective which rely on interpretation in order to draw out and address the problems inherent in the law, without dismissing the system as a whole. They represent what Georges Abi Saab has humorously dubbed 'operating behind enemy lines' – a mode of engagement with problematic aspects of international law premised on the understanding that it is better to attempt change from within than from outside.[79]

One might question the value of engaging with international investment law from a TWAIL perspective in this 'internal' way. The benefit of this kind of engagement lies in the opportunity to engage familiar professional

---

[76] However, see Dumberry discussing Article 8.10 of the EU-Canada Comprehensive Economic and Trade Agrement (CETA) as bypassing the uncertainty inherent in the customary MST by codifying particular obligations which ostensibly derive from the customary standard. Dumberry (n 65) 42–45.
[77] Pahuja (n 20) 1.
[78] ibid, 260.
[79] Abi-Saab (n 21) 1957.

language that is intelligible to the broader 'target audience' (courts, lawyers, States, scholars). Moreover, it also lies in the power to speak and be heard that comes from remaining within an arena of discussion rather than abandoning it.[80] This type of TWAIL engagement with international law capitalises on the existing structures in order to deploy what might be considered a subversive argument aimed at the amelioration of perceived biases. At the same time, it is important to acknowledge that professionals participating in international legal argumentation have a responsibility of maintaining what has been dubbed a 'methodological honesty' in their development of arguments concerning the content and purpose of international legal rules. The persuasiveness of any legal argument depends upon maintaining the idea of international law as a formal system according to which answers to legal questions can be derived from sources and principles whose validity depends on the internal logic of the system.[81] In this sense, the interpretive strategies suggested below are not attempts to argue in bad faith or misrepresent existing legal rules. Rather, the objective is to explore avenues of argumentation that promote the interpretation of customary rules in a way that accounts for their historically problematic origin and promotes their re-construction in a manner consistent with contemporary developments and values in the broader system.

The interpretive strategies suggested below are informed, amongst others, by the regime bias approach (alternatively also called the regime bias *critique*) developed by TWAIL scholars engaged with the various legal regimes of international economic governance.[82] The regime bias approach is aimed at uncovering how rules of the legal regimes making up the international economic order are constructed in a way that disempowers particular members of the system, inconsistently with the 'liberal promise of even-handedness'.[83] This approach looks particularly at the way rules of international trade, commerce, and investment are

---

[80] See, for instance, BS Chimni, 'Third World Approaches to International Law: A Manifesto' in A Anghie et al (eds), *The Third World and International Order: Law, Politics and Globalization* (Brill 2003) 47.

[81] R Collins & A Bohm, 'International Law as Professional Practice: Crafting the Autonomy of International Law' in J d'Aspremont et al (eds), *International Law as a Profession* (CUP 2017) 67.

[82] JT Gathii, 'Third World Approaches to International Economic Governance' in R Falk, B Rajagopal & J Stevens (eds), *International Law and the Third World* (Routledge 2008) 255; G Van Harten, 'TWAIL and the Dabhol Arbitration' (2011) 3(1) Trade, Law and Development 131; AR Hippolyte, 'Correcting TWAIL's Bind Spots: A Plea for a Pragmatic Approach to International Economic Governance' (2016) 18 ICLR 34.

[83] Gathii (n 82) 255-6.

construed, and identifies a differential manner in which the rules are interpreted and applied when the interests of the Third World are at stake.[84] Some of the main insights of the regime bias approach include the observation that international law is not a neutral and objective set of rules but rather an instrument employed in the context of power relations, and the finding that international institutions may interpret and apply international law in ways that are systemically biased against Third World interests.[85] For instance, using the example of the Dabhol investment arbitration before the International Chamber of Commerce (ICC), Van Harten argues that the ICC construed its role broadly to include not only arbitration on the basis of the pertinent investment contract but also what was in effect a review of domestic regulatory choices and a disciplining of constituencies in the Third World.[86] While the main contribution of the regime bias approach is critical, scholars have also used its rationale to propose reform within the international investment regime. For example, Hippolyte advocates for Third World countries to develop their own BIT models, which would focus on modes of investment attuned to their particular concerns, or to establish alternative regional investment arbitration centres.[87] Similarly, Odumosu flags mechanisms within investment arbitration proceedings such as the *amicus curiae* brief or public interest arguments, which may be a way for subaltern voices to be heard and considered in the otherwise insular investment proceedings.[88]

The regime bias approach is instructive because it demonstrates the inherent plasticity of legal rules, which becomes apparent at the stage of interpretation. It counters the image of a stable and neutral international investment law regime and reveals some of the biases which are woven into rules during the act of interpretation. Thus, the regime bias approach does not only shed light on certain problematic rationales operating in the investment law regime but also flags interpretation as a viable 'entry point' for TWAIL counter-arguments and resistance. Bearing in mind that throughout the analysis in this chapter I have focused on judicial interpretation and the function of interpretation in the dispute settlement context, the strategies sketched below are focused primarily on interpretation in dispute settlement and operate differently depending on one's

---

[84] Van Harten (n 82) 147–60.
[85] ibid, 137.
[86] ibid, 148–60.
[87] Hippolyte (n 82) 50–2.
[88] Odumosu (n 17) 271–87.

positionality in the process.[89] In this sense, they are also differentially suitable for different actors who might want to engage with international law from the TWAIL perspective.

The first possible strategy in the context of CIL interpretation is advancing evolutive interpretative claims which push for a reconsideration of the rule's content in light of factual or legal changes in the broader normative environment in which the rule operates. Depending on the rule in question, this would entail different argumentative strategies. For instance, when advancing an evolutive interpretative claim for the customary MST, this type of engagement consists of answering two connected questions: (i) can an argument be made that there is a need to interpret the rule dynamically in order to capture a change in the legal environment in which the rule operates? and (ii) are there competing rationales that may be taken in consideration and affect the interpretation of the rule accordingly? In relation to the first question, in the context of the customary MST, it has been argued persuasively that given the generality of the rule the elements which form part of its content are inherently dynamic and as such require evolutive interpretation.[90] Claims for evolutive interpretation may thus persuasively be made any time it can be shown that there is a need to interpret the rule dynamically in order to capture a change in the relevant standards or normative environment in which the rule operates. Answering question two entails, as a first step, recognising and stating plainly the rationale that the customary MST is driven by. This rule is largely focused on the protection of foreign investment, premised in turn on the ideology of economic development. Recognising this enables us to situate the historical development of the rule and understand how it has come to be what it is today. Having done that, we are able to evaluate how the rule plays out in the modern context, and which claims regarding its evolution are likely to work. Are there competing rationales – such as, for instance, the protection of the environment or human rights – that may be taken into consideration and that affect the interpretation of the rule accordingly? These may be found in other regimes as relevant treaty rules

---

[89] See on this point Georges Abi-Saab: 'The interpretative operation yields a final product, also referred to as "interpretation", consisting of a rendering of the meaning of the interpreted text. In evaluating the "authority" of this final product, ie, the weight it carries in the eyes of the community, particularly the legal community, one has to keep in mind the interpreter's status and position: interpretation by whom and for what purpose?'. G Abi-Saab, 'Introduction: A Meta-Question' in G Abi-Saab et al (eds), *Evolutionary Interpretation and International Law* (Hart 2019) 7, 10.

[90] Giannakopoulos & Monga (n 66) 303–4.

applicable between the parties, or in competing customary rules which have developed later than the customary MST and afford protection to, for instance, the environment or indigenous peoples. Interpretation entails, amongst other things, a balancing exercise,[91] and as such, it is capable of striking a balance between the rationale of economic development and these competing interests and competing rationales.

In the context of this strategy of engagement, interpretation functions as a sort of controlled 'arguing space' wherein competing argumentative strategies are deployed. This strategy is suited to TWAIL advocates and practitioners participating in relevant litigation. The limits here are of course the forum in which one attempts to advance evolutive interpretative claims, as well as the instructions of the party one is representing. For example, with respect to the limitation posed by the forum, it has been observed that certain formats of investment arbitration, such as ICSID arbitration, are inherently tilted in favour of the protection of foreign investors.[92] Thus, attempting to argue for evolutive interpretation, which balances the protection of investors with the protection of say the environment or indigenous groups, may not always be successful. With respect to the limitation posed by the party one is representing, it has been observed that the arguments deployed by, for instance, counsel representing States are limited in scope and content by the previous consultations and instructions of their client.[93] In this regard, any TWAIL arguments advanced by counsel on behalf of a State would be limited accordingly. Another relevant consideration here is that sometimes strategic engagement with litigation in this way may lead to adverse effects if the proposed interpretation is not accepted by courts.[94] Thus, for instance, an

---

[91] J Paine, 'The Judicial Dimension of Regime Interaction beyond Systemic Integration' in S Trevisanut, N Giannopoulos & R Roland Holst (eds), *Regime Interaction in Ocean Governance: Problems, Theories and Methods* (Brill 2020) 184.

[92] Abi-Saab argues that 'In contrast to the WTO […] when it comes to ICSID arbitrations, the enemy is clearly there. Not only is the procedure tilted in favor of foreign investors (for example, they can initiate arbitration against the host State, but the reverse is not possible), but so are also a good majority of the players in the system, who do not hesitate grossly to misinterpret the rules of international law to suit their private purposes.' Abi-Saab (n 19) 1969.

[93] J Batura, J Hettihewa & P Kulish, '"I resigned because Russia had become an absolutely indefensible client": an Interview with Alain Pellet' (*Völkerrechtsblog*, 4 July 2022) <https://voelkerrechtsblog.org/de/i-resigned-because-russia-had-become-an-absolutely-indefensible-client/> accessed 25 July 2022.

[94] See on this point T Sparks, N Nedeski & G Hernández, 'Judging Climate Change Obligations: Can the World Court Rise to the Occasion? Part II: What Role for International Adjudication?' (*Völkerrechtsblog*, 30 April 2020) <https://voelkerrechtsblog.org/judging-climate-change-obligations-can-the-world-court-raise-the-occasion-2/> accessed 25 July 2022.

unsuccessful argument for evolutive interpretation may lead to a consolidation of the undesirable content of the rule.

An alternative to this strategy would be the strategy of arguing for a restrictive interpretation of a CIL rule. In the context of the customary MST, this would entail arguing for a stringent customary standard of treatment which has a high threshold of breach. This may involve similar argumentative strategies to the ones described above, only deployed in the 'opposite direction'. More specifically, it may involve argumentative strategies which hark back to the older *Neer* standard and early investment arbitration which maintained it, arguing for a limitation of the customary standard to the high threshold described therein. These argumentative strategies may rely on exo-legal findings which show that expanding investment protection in the past has been to the detriment of local communities, and has potentially violated standards of environmental protection, or human and labour rights.[95] In this context, they may argue that a stringent customary standard, coupled with a balancing exercise, which considers rationales such as public policy or the protection of the local environment or communities, yields a narrow interpretation of the customary MST and the rights and protections extended to the investor. Alternatively, they may rely on a doctrinal positivist argument arguing that the expansion of the customary MST through interpretation is illegitimate and inconsistent with State practice. In this regard, it has been argued, for instance, that arguments which attempt to draw a uniform standard from widespread investment treaties as a form of State practice are unsubstantiated because while these treaties are many in number, their content as to the treatment of investors is varied and fails the uniformity requirement for CIL.[96] This strategy may be particularly fit for TWAIL advocates or governmental advisors who are representing or advising States.

A final strategy in the context of CIL interpretation is what I would call 'interpreting against the grain'. This strategy consists of devising innovative arguments as to the (re)interpretation of general customary rules, with a view to forwarding a new rationality previously unexplored in the rule.[97]

---

[95] See as an example of this strategy the argument developed by Sornarajah (n 9) 208.
[96] ibid, 225–6.
[97] See, for example, Sparks, Nedeski and Hernández who argue that '[i]n the context of catastrophic climate change legal analysis must understand State responsibility collectively: as *shared responsibility*', and thus, argue for an interpretation of the no-harm rule which imposes more demanding obligations on states for their share in global emissions. T Sparks, N Nedeski & G Hernández, 'Judging Climate Change Obligations: Can the World Court Rise to the Occasion? Part I: Primary Obligations to Combat Climate Change' (*Völkerrechtsblog*, 30 April 2020) <https://voelkerrechtsblog.org/judging-climate-change-obligations-can-the-world-court-raise-the-occasion/> accessed 25 July 2022.

In this context, one can rely on existing CIL doctrine more generally and the customary MST more specifically and utilise some of its inherent plasticity[98] to argue for a possible remoulding of the content. Interpretation here opens a sort of 'reasoning space' in which the problematic origin of a rule can be scrutinised and interpretive arguments deployed to resolve it. Can certain past practices and rationalities withstand modern scrutiny when placed against contemporary values espoused in the system? This is one of the central questions that may be asked when an older general customary rule such as the MST is being interpreted in the modern context. The resulting answer is a normative argument which might claim that the protection of investment to the detriment of the environment or human wellbeing is incompatible with contemporary values. A similarly plausible argument in this vein would be that the unitary notion of Statehood inherent in the construction of the investor-State relationship is incompatible with the heterogeneous make-up of States, which often comprise of different communities with varying interests.[99] This strategy would best fit a TWAIL scholar who develops their argument from the position of scholarship.[100] On this point, an important caveat is that 'the authority of scholars is not an institutional, procedural, or social one, but purely an epistemic one'.[101] The authority of interpretative arguments developed by scholars is limited accordingly.

This strategy may also be suited to an NGO or grassroot movement which has been granted the right to appear as *amicus curiae* in the context of an investment arbitration. For instance, in the context of ICSID proceedings, pursuant to Rule 37(2) of the Rules of Procedure for Arbitration Proceedings, a non-disputing party may be granted a right to intervene in the proceedings. This kind of intervention is meant to 'assist the Tribunal in the determination of factual or legal issue related to the proceeding by bringing a perspective, particular knowledge or insight that is different from that of the disputing parties'.[102] Similar provision for non-disputing

---

[98] The 'inherent plasticity' of CIL is a term borrowed from the work of Chasapis Tassinis, and refers to the ability of custom to be molded into different shapes and lead to rules of different scope, without the need to add new state practice and *opinio juris* to the pool of evidence each time. Chasapis Tassinis (n 27) 248–55.

[99] Odumosu (n 17) 269.

[100] See, for example, the call of BS Chimni for a 'postmodern approach' to custom. Chimni (n 6).

[101] A Peters, 'Realizing Utopia as a Scholarly Endeavour' (2013) 24(2) EJIL 533.

[102] ICSID Rules of Procedure for Arbitration Proceedings (Arbitration Rules) (adopted 25 September 1967, entered into force 1 January 1968) Rule 37(2)

party intervention is made in the context of NAFTA proceedings.[103] This represents the opportunity to inject subaltern voices into the proceedings when their interests are otherwise not represented by the State. Using the tool of a non-disputing party intervention, actors may put forward interpretive arguments which highlight the asymmetry inherent in the investor-State relationship, and the adverse effects this has to the rights and interests of local communities. This strategy is of course limited by the tribunal's willingness to grant standing to non-disputing parties, as well as the scope of such participation.[104] For instance, the *Glamis Gold* Tribunal allowed the Quechan Indian Nation to submit their views as a non-disputing party because it felt that the submission would not cause an undue burden or delay.[105] On the other hand, the *Pezold* Tribunal rejected indigenous participation on the reasoning that the rights of indigenous communities fell outside of the scope of the dispute and that allowing for such participation may unfairly prejudice the claimant (investor).[106] Moreover, it has been argued that even if such participation is granted, the extent to which an investment tribunal would seriously consider the interests of subaltern communities is limited.[107]

A tangential opportunity to the one described here is in the training and education activities undertaken by a TWAIL scholar. For instance, in response to TWAIL scholarship, which has called for a conceptual change in the CIL doctrine, d'Aspremont has argued that a more fruitful avenue to pursue this change would be in the early stages of legal education, by targeting the production of ideas and beliefs about customary international law. The objective here would be to use the malleability of the CIL doctrine to empower scholars and practitioners of the periphery to develop persuasive subversive arguments.[108]

---

[103] FTC, 'Statement of the Free Trade Commission on Non-Disputing Party Participation' (*FTC*, 7 October 2003) <www.sice.oas.org/tpd/nafta/commission/nondispute_e.pdf> accessed 25 July 2022.

[104] For instance, Rule 37(2) of the ICSID Rules of Procedure for Arbitration Proceedings indicates that 'After consulting both parties, the Tribunal *may* allow a person or entity [...] to file a written submission' and that such a submission may not 'disrupt the proceeding or unduly burden or unfairly prejudice either party'. ICSID Rules of Procedure for Arbitration Proceedings (n 102) Rule 37(2).

[105] *Glamis Gold, Ltd v United States* (Decision on Application and Submission by Quechan Indian Nation of 16 September 2005) UNCITRAL [11–13].

[106] *Pezold v Zimbabwe* (Procedural Order No 2 of 26 June 2012) ICSID Case No ARB/10/15 [48–63].

[107] Odumosu (n 17) 256–7.

[108] J d'Aspremont, *The Discourse on Customary International Law* (OUP 2020) 84–7. In particular, d'Aspremont argues that '[i]nstead of striving to reinvent the doctrine of

5 Concluding Observations

This chapter has presented an idea for a constructive TWAIL approach to the interpretation of customary international investment law. This idea reflects the view that while there is a lot of relevant and legitimate criticism against the existing system of international investment law, desired change cannot be achieved if one completely dismisses the existing system. Thus, I have sketched out the so-called interpretative strategies which rely on existing structures in international law in order to affect systemic change. The argument developed here is an attempt to reconcile some of the harsh but merited TWAIL criticism with a continued engagement with the existing system of international law.

This argument also has its limitations. First, the conclusions reached in Section 3 with respect to the constructive function of interpretation in the context of the customary MST are preliminary, insofar as they were reached on the basis of a small exploratory sample of investment arbitration cases. In this sense, the conclusions can and should be tested on a broader sample of cases, as well as through examples of other customary rules.[109] Second, as the discussion in Section 4 illustrates, the strategies for interpretation as potentially deployed from the TWAIL perspective are limited by the role and position of the actor who is trying to deploy them. Finally, the strategies proposed here cannot address all the criticism levelled from the TWAIL perspective. The proposals made in Section 4 are limited to issues which arise, may be argued, and potentially resolved at the stage of interpretation.

---

customary international law, we must invest in strategies that draw on the malleability and fluidity of the current doctrine of customary law and facilitate the types of argumentation that "de-centre" the First World'.

[109] See, however, an analysis with similar conclusions about the constructive role of interpretation with respect to the customary rule of prevention. N Mileva, 'The Role of Customary International Law Interpretation in the Balancing of Interests at Sea: The Example of Prevention' (*TRICI-Law Research Paper Series 010/2020*, 2020) <https://tricilawofficial.files.wordpress.com/2021/06/mileva_rps-010-2020.pdf> accessed 25 July 2022.

PART IV

Concluding Thoughts

Custom and Its Interpretation in International Investment Law

14

Custom and Its Interpretation in International Investment Law

Final Musings

PANOS MERKOURIS, ANDREAS KULICK,
JOSÉ MANUEL ÁLVAREZ-ZARATE AND
MACIEJ ŻENKIEWICZ*

1 The Continued Relevance of Custom in International Investment Law

At first glance, one may think of international investment law (IIL) as a response to custom (or lack thereof), instead of a field of its application. Indeed, modern IIL and arbitration arguably have developed in order to fill the void provoked by the challenges to the Hull formula and other custom regarding the treatment of aliens, especially post-1945 and, most notably, through the New International Economic Order (NIEO). Hence, one may be inclined to wonder whether an inquiry into the relationship of custom and IIL, as this edited volume intends, represents a rather skewed or anachronistic choice of topic.

However, in fact, the opposite is the case. Looking at the practice of international investment tribunals as well as the central discussions in international legal scholarship, general international law and most of all customary international law (CIL) is pervasive, if not to say ubiquitous. The interpretation and application of customary rules and principles is the bread and butter of IIL and arbitration. Interpretation, termination or provisional application of treaties, attribution of conduct, circumstances precluding wrongfulness or reparation and other remedies are but a few examples of how CIL permeates the IIL and arbitration. Custom is of pivotal importance in nearly every single investment dispute. Even beyond

---

* This contribution is based on research conducted in the context of the project 'The Rules of Interpretation of Customary International Law' ('TRICI-Law'). This project received funding from the European Research Council ('ERC') under the European Union's Horizon 2020 Research and Innovation Programme (Grant Agreement No 759728).

customary treaty law and the rules of State responsibility, the recourse to and discussion of standards and principles such as the international minimum standard of treatment (MST), inter alia, is a frequent sight in investment arbitration practice. In the following few pages, we offer some final musings on key themes that permeate and connect not only the contributions in this volume but the general engagement both in academia and in practice with international investment law and CIL.

2   Musings on Custom and International Investment Law

Despite the preponderance of academic and jurisprudential focus on the identification of CIL through the classical two-element approach, ie State practice and *opinio juris*, with all the associated problems that this approach and its misapplication entails,[1] there is also the oft-neglected aspect of the *interpretation* of customary rules. Even the International Law Commission (ILC) itself, in its 2018 Draft Conclusions on Identification of Customary International Law, accepted the reality of the distinction between the existence of a customary rule and its content determination,[2] although it decided to leave this and the concept of change and evolution of customary rules from the scope of its work.[3] In other topics being considered by the ILC at the same time, as, for instance, on *jus cogens* and on immunities of State officials from foreign criminal jurisdiction, the inevitability and utility of CIL interpretation has also found its way more explicitly in the reports of Special Rapporteurs, the Draft Conclusions and the corresponding commentaries.[4]

It is not just in the expert works of the ILC that interpretation of customary rules can be spotted. Quite the contrary. International and

---

[1] See contributions by Dumberry (Chapter 1), El Boudouhi (Chapter 2), Mejía-Lemos (Chapter 3) and Álvarez-Zarate (Chapter 4) in this volume.

[2] ILC, 'Report of the International Law Commission on the Work of its 70th Session' (30 April–1 June and 2 July–10 August 2018) UN Doc A/73/10, 124 [4]. The Netherlands made this distinction more forcefully in its comments to the Draft Conclusions; The Netherlands, 'ILC Draft Conclusions on Identification of Customary International Law – Comments and Observations by the Kingdom of the Netherlands' (2018) 1, [5] <https://legal.un.org/ilc/sessions/70/pdfs/english/icil_netherlands.pdf> accessed 1 August 2022.

[3] ILC (n 2) 122–4.

[4] ILC, 'Fifth Report on Immunity of State Officials from Foreign Criminal Jurisdiction, by Concepción Escobar Hernández, Special Rapporteur' (14 June 2016) UN Doc A/CN.4/701 [136 & 150]; ILC, 'Peremptory Norms of General International Law (*jus cogens*): Text of the Draft Conclusions and Draft Annex Provisionally Adopted by the Drafting Committee on First Reading' (29 May 2019) UN Doc A/CN.4/L.936, Draft Conclusion 20 [10(3) & 17(2)].

domestic jurisprudence is replete with such examples.[5] CIL interpretation by international courts and tribunals is ubiquitous across all regimes of international law. Such interpretation contributes not only to the refinement, clarification of the content of the customary rule (the 'collapsing function' of CIL interpretation), but also, on occasion and depending on the circumstances, to its evolution (the 'evolutive function' of CIL interpretation).[6]

IIL could not possibly be an exception to this pattern. As the various contributions of this edited volume[7] aptly and amply demonstrate several sub-sets of rules on State responsibility and the law of treaties raise intriguing points as to the manner in which, and the variety of methods employed by investment arbitration tribunals when they interpret and apply these customary rules. Irrespective of whether this variation can be unequivocally distilled in certain patterns, or is sometimes the unfortunate result of incorrect and uninformed interpretations and applications of CIL, what is indisputable is that the identification scheme of focusing solely on State practice and *opinio juris* is woefully incapable of making sense of the multifariousness of tools and methods employed by these courts and tribunals. Contrarily, if one views these through the prism of interpretation, one can clearly see familiar patterns.

The same holds true for the 'evolutive function' of the interpretation of CIL as evinced by the contributions in Part III of this volume.[8] Evolutive interpretation allows rules to breathe and grow like a 'living tree' that reacts to changes in fact and in law, and adapts to new challenges and new factual situations. The same flexibility, which ensures the continued relevance of the rule, can also be seen in the case of CIL. To add to this, this 'evolutive function' combined with the 'collapsing function' of interpretation may allow the use of interpretation as a tool that can help if not course-correct, or at least address and partially mitigate some of the

---

[5] For detailed examples and the particular methods of interpretation used, see P Merkouris, *Interpretation of Customary International Law: of Methods and Limits* (Brill 2023).
[6] That is, of course, not to say that these two functions of CIL interpretation are completely separate and distinct from each other, but as in treaty interpretation they overlap. In more detail, see: P Merkouris & N Mileva, 'ESIL Reflection – Introduction to the Series "Customary Law Interpretation as a Tool"' (2022) 11(1) ESIL Reflections 1 <https://esil-sedi.eu/wp-content/uploads/2022/08/ESIL-Reflection-Merkouris-Mileva.pdf> last accessed 24 June 2023.
[7] See, in particular, Lekkas (Chapter 5), Ventouratou (Chapter 6), Paddeu (Chapter 7), Giakoumakis (Chapter 8) and Kulaga (Chapter 9) in this volume.
[8] Hailes (Chapter 10), Mallya (Chapter 11) and Balcerzak (Chapter 12) in this volume.

warranted criticisms that have been levelled, among others by the Third World Approaches to International Law (TWAIL) movement, against the formation of CIL.[9]

That is not to say, of course, that interpretation is a panacea or a *deus ex machina* that can solve everything that has been and is wrong with IIL, and international law in general. If anything, it is less of a *deus* and more of a ghost in the machine or in the shell,[10] which can contribute to the rule being more attune to the current pulse of the society.

In this context and as already mentioned, any discourse on IIL cannot but engage with critical theories on international law, and most notably, the perspective and insight offered by the intellectual movement of TWAIL. This is a point that deserves further attention. Colonialism and imperialism have been central in the discussion among scholars and States for their opposing interests in political, cultural and legal matters[11] with former colonies and their former rulers. Legal and subaltern studies from the UK, India, the United States and Latin America,[12] have coincided in questioning Western universalism versus particularism. This refers to whether colonialism and its civilising mission still has effects on an inclusion-exclusion discourse.[13] Yet, in the construction of a modern global society, where the world system rests, it has been claimed that 'Third World' voices have not been heard, or have been ignored or relegated.[14] In the case of CIL in Investment Law, it is crucial to clarify, bolster

---

[9] Mileva (Chapter 13) in this volume.

[10] For 'ghost in the machine', see A Koestler, *Ghost in the Machine* (Macmillan 1967), and even earlier, G Ryle, *The Concept of Mind* (Hutcheson 1949); for 'ghost in the shell', see M Oshii, 'Ghost in the Shell' (Shochiku 1995).

[11] M Koskenniemi, *The Gentle Civilizer: The Rise and Fall of International Law 1870–1960* (CUP 2001); A Anghie, *Imperialism, Sovereignty and the Making of International Law* (CUP 2004)

[12] See, eg E Said, *Orientalism* (Random House Inc 1978); R Guha & G Spivak, *Selected Subaltern Studies* (OUP 1988). See also authors such as: H Bhabha (from the US) and W Mignolo, E Dussel and E Quijano (from Latin America).

[13] Koskenniemi (n 11) 130 ('exclusion in terms of a cultural argument about the otherness of the non-European that made it impossible to extend European rights to the native'); Anghie (n 11) 3–4 ('"Third World" sovereignty appeared quite distinctive as compared with the defining Western sovereignty ... [where] the civilizing mission, the grand project that has justified colonialism as a means of redeeming the backward, aberrant, violent, oppressed, underdeveloped people of the non-European world by incorporating them into the universal civilization of Europe').

[14] E Said, *Orientalism* (25th anniversary edn, Penguin 2003) Preface; ('In the process the uncountable sediments of history, a dizzying variety of peoples, languages, experiences, and cultures, are swept aside or ignored, relegated to the sandheap along with the treasures ground into meaningless fragments that were taken out of Baghdad').

and/or create means to compel the system to listen to the said voices and not to repeat the mistakes of the past. This would result in more legitimate outcomes in the identification and interpretation of the CIL rule.

TWAIL might be placed and understood as part of a wider set of scholarly writings that has adopted some of its concepts from the discussions on post-colonial critical theory. It is characterised by a pattern of continuity in the use of power in the construction of international law and investment law. However, over time, one might see different reactions to imperialism from former colonies and regions. On the one hand, since the revolutionary wars of independence, former Latin-American colonies endorsed the posture on international law. For instance, in 1832, Andrés Bello claimed that local law applied to foreigners who should be protected or judged in local courts and given national treatment in such courts.[15] This was resurrected by Carlos Calvo, in 1863, who laid it on the international discussion table with the US and European States. Later, in 1902, Luis M Drago opposed the use of force by western powers to claim foreign debts.[16] On the other hand, in the mid-twentieth century, newly decolonised States from Africa and Asia made other claims to the international community, including that of a NIEO, and confirming/establishing permanent sovereignty over their natural resources to promote development.[17] Mohammed Bedjaoui stands out as one of its prominent pioneers.[18] Together with Latin American countries, which supported these positions as 'Third World', their interests in reversing colonialism were placed on the international agenda and even were recognised in international instruments.[19] This despite opposition by the Global North that promoted a swift treatification of investment protection.

Thus, the confrontation between the Global North and the Third World has not been successful in including the aforementioned interests in formal treaties. If TWAIL's claims are to be integrated into the formal system of international law, a constructive discussion of the interpretation of customary international investment law is required. Accordingly, Mileva's[20]

---

[15] A Bello, *Principios de Derecho de Gentes* (2nd edn, Printing Press Bruneau 1840) 63, 67, 70–1, 76 & 89.
[16] See Mileva (Chapter 13) in this volume.
[17] Angie (n 11) 211.
[18] M Bedjaoui, *Towards a New International Economic Order* (Holmes & Meier 1979).
[19] The NIEO was addressed in the UN through the Declaration on the Establishment of a New International Economic Order (UNGA Res 3201/1974) and with the Charter of Economic Rights and Duties of States (UNGA Res 3281/1974).
[20] Mileva (Chapter 13) in this volume.

proposal of including TWAIL's legal arguments in such discussions, within the existing system might be one option. This may help in avoiding throwing the baby out with the bathwater, ie achieving legitimate change without dismissing the formal structures of international law. In other words, based on the constructive/'collapsing' and evolutive functions of interpretation of CIL[21] new developments of both fact and law would be taken into account in the interpretation of existing customary norms, and thus, 'Third World' States' interests would be more fairly represented in the content determination of these norms.[22]

An additional point of entry of TWAIL considerations in IIL could be through the inclusion of clauses in investment treaties that would provide clarity on the policy space recognised by States regarding, for example, the protection of the environment. This should set a different context for arbitrators to decide differently from the norm on the content of the MST if the said policy space clause was not included in the treaty. The MST clause has been considered a CIL rule that was included in bilateral investment treaties, in the midst of the twentieth century.[23] At the time, environmental or development provisions did not manifest in such treaties. Environmental clauses have been included in second generation treaties and BIT models.[24] Tribunals' decisions based on such second-generation treaties should take into account the new legal developments when interpreting the customary MST provision. After all, they have the responsibility to maintain 'a "methodological honesty" in their development of arguments concerning the content and purpose of'[25] these rules.

However, one can still find examples in investment arbitration that surprisingly both from a methodological and an outcome perspective, seem to lean in a different direction, as in the case of *Eco Oro Minerals Corp v Colombia*[26] where the interpretation of the MST did not consider the

---

[21] Merkouris & Mileva (n 6).
[22] An example of this would be, for instance, taking into account the Third World States' interests on sustainable development.
[23] See on that subject: M Paparinskis, *The International Minimum Standard and Fair and Equitable Treatment* (OUP 2013); P Dumberry, *The Fair and Equitable Treatment Standard: A Guide to NAFTA Case Law on Article 1105* (Kluwer 2013) 13–46; JM Álvarez-Zarate & DM Beltran Vargas, 'El derecho consuetudinario en el derecho internacional de inversiones' in JM Álvarez-Zarate & M Żenkiewicz (eds) *El derecho internacional de las inversiones* (Universidad Externado de Colombia 2021) 63–4.
[24] Eg Canada-Colombia Free Trade Agreement (Canada & Colombia) (adopted 21 November 2008, entered into force 15 August 2011).
[25] Mileva (Chapter 13) in this volume.
[26] *Eco Oro Minerals Corp v Colombia* (Decision on Jurisdiction, Liability and Directions on Quantum of 9 September 2021) ICSID Case No ARB/16/41.

environmental exception of Article 2201(3).[27] This led to the State being found responsible for breaching the treaty. The investor claimed that Colombia had breached Article 805 'relating to the customary international law minimum standard of treatment of aliens, including fair and equitable treatment'.[28] The Tribunal said that under CIL the MST had evolved 'as indeed international customary law itself evolves'.[29] However, it disregarded that environmental protection would take precedence, as investment protection and environmental protection 'must co-exist in a mutually beneficial manner'.[30]

Eco Oro Minerals Corp v Colombia demonstrates that arbitral tribunals may, on occasion, resist an evolutive interpretation when this would favour the State. This, in the case of investment law, may be further accentuated by the fact that arbitral tribunals more frequently base their decisions on previous cases where the BIT did not have environmental or human rights provisions.[31] That is not to say that an evolutive interpretation should always be opted for. Far from it. However, arbitral tribunals such as in the case of *Eco Oro Minerals Corp v Colombia* should be cognisant and vigilant of the relevant standards and the way the normative context in which the rule operates may have changed, and adapt accordingly. Disregarding such changes might need the development of an education strategy to avoid costly outcomes that are also at dissonance with the contemporary international legal system and society in general.

A need for an improvement in the methodology and reasoning employed by investment tribunals can also be felt in the context of 'secondary rules'. While the terminology is not fully consistently applied in

---

[27] Article 2201(3) of the Treaty provides as follows: '(3) For the purposes of Chapter Eight (Investment), subject to the requirement that such measures are not applied in a manner that constitute arbitrary or unjustifiable discrimination between investment or between investors, or a disguised restriction on international trade or investment, nothing in this Agreement shall be construed to prevent a Party from adopting or enforcing measures necessary:
  (a) To protect human, animal or plant life or health, which the Parties understand to include environmental measures necessary to protect human, animal or plant life and health;
  (b) To ensure compliance with laws and regulations that are not inconsistent with this Agreement; or
  (c) For the conservation of living or non-living exhaustible natural resources.'
[28] *Eco Oro Minerals Corp v Colombia* [383].
[29] ibid [744].
[30] ibid [744, 748 & 828].
[31] W Alschner, *Investment Arbitration and State-Driven Reform, New Treaties, Old Outcomes* (OUP 2022) 6–8.

international legal scholarship, 'secondary rules' usually are considered to constitute those rules that are 'rules about rules':[32] the 'common grammar'[33] of international law that determines how primary rules, ie international rights and obligations, are to be established, interpreted, applied or what are the conditions and consequences of breaches of international obligations.[34] The law on the international responsibility of States constitutes an integral part of those secondary rules of international law. It is of a customary nature only, not enshrined in an international treaty, and features prominently in IIL and arbitration, as the contributions in Part II of this volume attest.

In a recent study, undertaken at the event of the Articles on the Responsibility of States for Internationally Wrongful Acts' (ARSIWA) 20th anniversary and published as part of a symposium in a special double issue in Vol 37 of the ICSID Review, Esmé Shirlow and Kabir Duggal count no less than 136 arbitral awards and decisions that refer to the ARSIWA for the period of 2011–2020 alone, with 219 overall in the 20-year span from 2001–2020.[35] As the late James Crawford noted in his 10th anniversary review in the same journal in 2011, the ARSIWA are 'considered by courts and commentators to be in whole or in large part an accurate codification of the customary international law of state responsibility'.[36] In a similar vein, according to Hobér, 'there is general consensus that the ILC Articles accurately reflect customary international law on state responsibility'.[37] Investment arbitration tribunals also routinely stress that the ARSIWA are 'widely regarded as a codification of customary international law'[38] and that they have been applied as 'declaratory of customary international law'.[39] However, not all of the ARSIWA have accrued to

---

[32] cf HLA Hart, *The Concept of Law* (3rd edn, OUP 2012) 94.

[33] PM Dupuy, 'A Doctrinal Debate in the Globalisation Era: On the "Fragmentation" of International Law' (2007) 1 EJLS 1, 4.

[34] cf J Pauwelyn, *Conflict of Norms in Public International Law – How WTO Law Relates to Other Rules of International Law* (CUP 2003) 159 (they 'regulate other norms, that is they may address the creation, application, interplay, suspension, termination, breach of enforcement of other norms of international law').

[35] E Shirlow & K Duggal, 'Special Issue on 20th Anniversary of ARSIWA: The ILC Articles on State Responsibility in Investment Treaty Arbitration' (2022) 37 ICSID Rev 378, 380, Figure 1.

[36] J Crawford, *State Responsibility: The General Part* (1st edn, CUP 2013) 43.

[37] K Hobér, 'State Responsibility and Attribution' in P Muchlinski, F Ortino & C Schreuer (eds), *The Oxford Handbook of International Investment Law* (OUP 2008) 549, 553.

[38] *Noble Ventures Inc v Romania* (Award of 12 October 2005) ICSID Case No ARB/01/11 [69].

[39] *EDF (Services) Ltd v Romania* (Award of 8 October 2009) ICSID Case No ARB/05/13 [187].

custom. Their customary nature needs to be established individually and carefully in each instance – a task in which investment tribunals have only partly succeeded.[40]

Among the plethora of issues arising from the interaction of the customary rules on State responsibility with IIL in general and addressed in or inspired by the contributions in this volume in particular, two stand out in particular. First, as the contributions in this volume acknowledge,[41] identification of custom is one thing, the interpretation of a customary norm quite another.[42] In the case of State responsibility, the peculiarity exists that most other customary rules, whether of a primary or secondary nature, do not feature in a written document. Custom is an unwritten source of international law. Sometimes, it might find expression in a written text, which at the same time usually constitutes a primary source of international law in its own right, ie a treaty – with most of the Vienna Convention on the Law of Treaties (VCLT) arguably the most prominent case in point. Alas, the ARSIWA are a written text, but not a treaty. However, the draft articles the ILC submitted to the UN General Assembly, which unanimously accepted them, very much have the looks of a treaty text. This may be one of the reasons why, as several of the contributions confirm,[43] many investment tribunals appear to treat the ARSIWA very similarly to a treaty, seemingly also applying interpretation rules similar to Articles 31 and 32 VCLT to the ARSIWA. A bit like Andri, the protagonist in Max Frisch's play *Andorra*,[44] the ILC Articles, by repeatedly being attributed a different identity, somewhat assume such new identity. Arguably, such attribution to one thing of something else until it becomes this other thing is the very essence of custom: this is at least how a new rule of custom emerges – if the breach of a rule is repeated long enough and 'accepted as law', such breach becomes the new customary rule. However, a lacklustre treatment as quasi-treaty is hardly conducive to apt application of interpretive rules to something that is manifestly not a treaty.

---

[40] Positive example: *Cargill, Inc v Mexico* (Award of 18 September 2009) ICSID Case No ARB(AF)/05/2 (NAFTA) [381]; negative example: *MCI Power Group LC & New Turbine, Inc v Republic of Ecuador* (Award of 31 July 2007) ICSID Case No ARB/03/6 [42].
[41] Eg Lekkas (Chapter 5) in this volume.
[42] On the specifics of the distinction and its implications and consequences, see P Merkouris, 'Interpreting the Customary Rules on Interpretation' (2017) 19 ICLR 126.
[43] cf, eg Lekkas (Chapter 5), Paddeu (Chapter 7) and Giakoumakis (Chapter 8) in this volume.
[44] M Frisch, *Andorra* (P Hutchison tr, Routledge 1994).

Second, as evinced by several of the pieces in this volume,[45] the reasoning of arbitration tribunals on both identification and interpretation of the customary rules of State responsibility has room for improvement. As, for example, Federica I Paddeu illustrates in her contribution on compensation in cases of necessity, tribunals have often merely asserted the existence of a customary rule, without undertaking much effort to support such assertion with reasoning and evidence, while others tend to make doubtful deductions.[46] As mentioned before, these defects are not an outlier. No doubt, investment tribunals are not alone in their oftentimes rather questionable approach to custom identification or interpretation, as Talmon so aptly demonstrated vis-à-vis the determination of customary rules by the International Court of Justice (ICJ).[47] However, even given their, sometimes, limited interest in coherence and consistency of method, possibly due to their nature as *ad hoc* tribunals and the limited grounds of annulment under Article 52 of the ICSID Convention, investment tribunals' practice also could do better in this regard.

3   Concluding Thoughts

Despite the undeniable 'treatification' of IIL,[48] that should not lead one to the erroneous assumption that, as a direct consequence of this, other sources of law and custom, in particular, become gradually and increasingly more irrelevant in this particular filed of international law. Contrarily, customary rules remain of fundamental importance in what has been called 'the age of treatification of international investment law'.[49] This holds true on more than one levels: (i) with respect to both the customary primary rules specific to IIL and the customary secondary rules; and (ii) with respect to the stage of its identification as it does also to the stage of its interpretation. Furthermore, custom, both in its primary rule and secondary rule incarnation, potentially will even grow further in its importance to IIL and arbitration, considering the seemingly increasing

---

[45] cf Lekkas (Chapter 5), Ventouratou (Chapter 6), Paddeu (Chapter 7) and Giakoumakis (Chapter 8) in this volume.

[46] cf Paddeu (Chapter 7) in this volume.

[47] cf S Talmon, 'Determining Customary International Law: The ICJ's Methodology between Induction, Deduction and Assertion' (2015) 26 EJIL 417, 434 et seq.

[48] JW Salacuse, 'The Treatification of International Investment Law' (2007) 13(1) Law & Bus Rev Am 155.

[49] P Dumberry, 'A Few Observations on the Remaining Fundamental Importance of Customary Rules in the Age of Treatification of International Investment Law' (2016) 34(1) ASA Bulletin 41.

trend of what may be dubbed if not a 'de-treatification' then at least a decrease in the number of treaties (or treaty ratifications) relating to IIL.[50]

Even with the justified criticisms about false narratives and the creation of custom being a reflection of prior and current power structures, the study of custom and its function across all stages of its life-cycle has a lot to yield. Both these criticisms and the general academic inquiries into the lacunae of custom (at the identification as well as the interpretation/content-determination stages) contribute to the gradual refinement of our understanding of how custom works, how it is used, what gaps it has and how it can adapt to modern challenges and new circumstances.

The contributions to the present edited volume have hopefully given the reader a peek into the inner workings and continued relevance of custom and its interpretation in IIL, highlighted that the study of custom has still a lot of mysteries to yield and demonstrated that custom and international investment law go hand in hand, entangled in a never-ending dance. And since these are 'final musings', as the etymology of the name of the Muse of dancing, Terpsichore, reveals there is 'delight [to be found] in [such] dancing'!

---

[50] Eg the termination of bilateral investment treaties, in intra-EU constellations and beyond, of the ICSID Convention.

BIBLIOGRAPHY

Books

Aldrich G, *The Jurisprudence of the Iran-United States Claims Tribunal* (Clarendon 1996)

Alschner W, *Investment Arbitration and State-Driven Reform, New Treaties, Old Outcomes* (OUP 2022)

Amerasinghe CF, *Evidence in International Litigation* (Martinus Nijhoff 2005)

American Law Institute, *Restatement (Second) of Foreign Relations Law* (American Law Institute 1965)

American Law Institute, *Restatement (Third) of Foreign Relations Law* (American Law Institute 1987)

Anghie A, *Imperialism, Sovereignty and the Making of International Law* (CUP 2004)

d'Aspremont J, *The Discourse on Customary International Law* (OUP 2020)

Balcerzak F, *Investor–State Arbitration and Human Rights* (Brill Nijhoff 2017)

Bedjaoui M, *Towards a New International Economic Order* (Holmes & Meier 1979)

Bello A, *Principios de Derecho de Gentes* (2nd edn, Printing Press Bruneau 1840)

Berlia G, *Essai sur la Portée de la Clause de Jugement en Équité en Droit des Gens* (Université de Paris 1937)

Bianchi A, *International Law Theories: An Inquiry into Different Ways of Thinking* (OUP 2016)

Blackaby N, Partasides C, Redfern A & ors, *Redfern and Hunter on International Arbitration* (OUP 2009)

Bonnitcha J, Skovgaard Poulsen LN & Waibel M, *The Political Economy of the Investment Treaty Regime* (OUP 2017)

Bos M, *A Methodology of International Law* (Asser 1984)

Boyle A & Chinkin C, *The Making of International Law* (OUP 2007)

Boyle A & Redgwell C (eds), *Birnie, Boyle, and Redgwell's International Law and the Environment* (4th edn, OUP 2021)

Bücheler G, *Proportionality in Investor-State Arbitration* (OUP 2015)

Byers M, *Custom, Power and the Power of Rules: International Relations and Customary International Law* (CUP 1999)

Carlton D, *Churchill and the Soviet Union* (MUP 2000)

Caron D & Caplan L, *The UNCITRAL Arbitration Rules: A Commentary* (2nd edn, OUP 2013)
Carreau D & Juillard P, *Droit international économique* (LGDJ 1998)
Cheng B, *General Principles of Law: As Applied by International Courts and Tribunals* (Stevens 1953)
Cheng B, *General Principles of Law as Applied by International Courts and Tribunals* (reprinted, CUP 1987)
Corten O & Klein P (eds), *The Vienna Conventions on the Law of Treaties: A Commentary* (OUP 2011)
Crawford J, *The International Law Commission's Articles on State Responsibility: Introduction, Text and Commentaries* (CUP 2002)
Crawford J, *Brownlie's Principles of Public International Law* (OUP 2012)
Crawford J, *State Responsibility – The General Part* (1st edn, CUP 2013)
Crawford J, *Brownlie's Principles of Public International Law* (9th edn, OUP 2019)
De Brabandere E, *Investment Treaty Arbitration as Public International Law* (CUP 2014)
Degan VD, *L'interprétation des accords en droit international* (Martinus Nijhoff 1963)
Degan VD, *L'Equité et le Droit International* (Martinus Nijhoff 1970)
Diehl A, *The Core Standard of International Investment Protection: Fair and Equitable Treatment* (Kluwer 2012)
Dolzer R & Schreuer C, *Principles of International Investment Law* (2nd edn, OUP 2012)
Dolzer R & Stevens M, *Bilateral Investment Treaties* (Martinus Nijhoff 1995)
Dörr O & Schmalenbach K (eds), *Vienna Convention on the Law of Treaties: A Commentary* (2nd edn, Springer 2018)
Đorđeska M, *General Principles of Law Recognized by Civilized Nations (1922–2018): The Evolution of the Third Source of International Law through the Jurisprudence of the Permanent Court of International Justice and the International Court of Justice* (Brill 2020)
Dumberry P, *The Fair and Equitable Treatment Standard: A Guide to NAFTA Case Law on Article 1105* (Kluwer 2013)
Dumberry P, *The Formation and Identification of Rules of Customary International Law in International Investment Law* (CUP 2016)
El Boudouhi S, *L'élément factual dans le contentieux international* (Bruylant 2013)
Franck T, *Fairness in International Law and Institutions* (OUP 2012)
Friedmann W, *The Changing Structure of International Law* (Stevens & Sons 1964)
Frisch M, *Andorra* (P Hutchison tr, Routledge 1994)
García-Amador FV, Sohn LB & Baxter RR, *Recent Codification of the Law of State Responsibility for Injuries to Aliens* (Oceana 1974)
Gardiner R, *Treaty Interpretation* (2nd edn, OUP 2015)
General Claims Commission (US & Mexico), *Opinions of Commissioners Under the Convention Concluded on 8 September 1923 Between the United States and Mexico*, Vol 1 (US GPO 1927)

Ghouri AA, *Conflict of Treaties in Investment Arbitration* (Kluwer 2015)
Gore KN & Shirlow E (eds), *The Vienna Convention on the Law of Treaties in Investor-State Disputes: History, Evolution, and Future* (Kluwer 2022)
Gourgourinis A, *Equity and Equitable Principles in the World Trade Organization* (Routledge 2016)
Grotius H, *The Rights of War and Peace* (first published 1625, Richard Tuck ed, Liberty Fund 2005)
Guha R & Spivak G, *Selected Subaltern Studies* (OUP 1988)
Habicht M, *Post-War Treaties for the Pacific Settlement of International Disputes* (HUP 1931)
Habicht M, *Analysis of the Treaties in Post-War Treaties for the Pacific Settlement of International Disputes*, Part II (HUP 1931)
Hart HLA, *The Concept of Law* (Clarendon Press 1984)
Hart HLA, *The Concept of Law* (3rd edn, OUP 2012)
Heffter A, *Le Droit International Public de l'Europe* (first published 1844, Bergson J tr, 3rd edn, Cotillon Libraires 1873)
Henckels C, *Proportionality and Deference in Investor-State Arbitration: Balancing Investment Protection and Regulatory Autonomy* (CUP 2015)
Hepburn J, *Domestic Law in International Investment Arbitration* (OUP 2017)
Higgins H, *Problems and Process: International Law and How We Use It* (OUP 1995)
Howard-Jones N, *The Scientific Background of the International Sanitary Conferences 1851–1938* (WHO 1975)
Hudson MO, *The Permanent Court of International Justice, 1920–1942: A Treatise* (Macmillan 1943)
Hull IV, *A Scrap of Paper: Breaking and Making International Law During the Great War* (Cornell University Press 2014)
Ishikawa T, *The Role of International Environmental Principles in Investment Treaty Arbitration: Precautionary and Polluter Pays Principles and Partial Compensation* (Brill 2016)
Jennings J & Watts A (eds), *Oppenheim's International Law*, Vol 1 (9th edn, OUP 2008)
Kantor M, *Valuation for Arbitration: Compensation Standards, Valuation Methods and Expert Evidence* (Kluwer 2008)
Kelsen H, *The Law of the United Nations* (Stevens & Sons 1950)
Kelsen H, *Pure Theory of Law* (UC Press 1967)
Kinnear M, Biorklund A & Hannaford JFG, *Investment Disputes Under NAFTA: An Annotated Guide to NAFTA Chapter 11* (Kluwer Law 2006)
Klabbers J, *Treaty Conflict and the European Union* (CUP 2010)
Koestler A, *Ghost in the Machine* (Macmillan 1967)
Kokott J, *The Burden of Proof in Comparative and Human Rights Law: Civil and Common Law Approaches with Special Reference to the American and German Legal Systems* (Kluwer Law International 1998)

Kolb R, *La bonne foi en droit international public: Contribution à l'étude des principes généraux de droit* (Graduate Institute Publications 2000)

Koskenniemi M, *The Gentle Civilizer: The Rise and Fall of International Law 1870–1960* (CUP 2001)

Kotuby CT & Sobota LA, *General Principles of Law and International Due Process: Principles and Norms Applicable in Transnational Disputes* (OUP 2017)

Kulick A (ed), *Reassertion of Control over the Investment Treaty Regime* (CUP 2017)

Kurkela M & Turunen S, *Due Process in International Commercial Arbitration* (OUP 2010)

Lauterpacht H, *Private Law Sources and Analogies of International Law* (Longmans 1927)

Lauterpacht H, *The Development of International Law by the International Court* (Stevens & Sons 1958)

Laviec JP, *Protection et promotion des investissements, étude de droit international économique* (PUF 1985)

Linarelli J, Salomon ME & Sornarajah M, *The Misery of International Law: Confrontations with Injustice in the Global Economy* (OUP 2018)

Linderfalk U, *On the Interpretation of Treaties: The Modern International Law as Expressed in the 1969 Vienna Convention on the Law of Treaties* (Springer 2007)

López Cárdenas CM, *La desaparición forzada de personas en perspectiva histórico jurídica: su origen y evolución en el ámbito internacional* (Editorial Universidad del Rosario 2017)

Mackenzie R, Romano C & Shany Y (eds), *The Manual on International Courts and Tribunals* (2nd edn, OUP 2010)

Manning WR (ed), *Diplomatic Correspondence of the United States: Canadian Relations*, Vol 3 (Carnegie Endowment 1943)

Marboe I, *Calculation of Compensation and Damages in International Investment Law* (2nd edn, OUP 2017)

Marie-Dupuy P & Viñuales JE, *International Environmental Law* (CUP 2015)

McLachlan C, Shore L & Weiniger M, *International Investment Arbitration: Substantive Principles* (OUP 2007)

McLachlan C, Shore L & Weiniger M, *International Investment Arbitration: Substantive Principles* (2nd edn, OUP 2017)

Merkouris P, *Article 31(3)(c) VCLT and the Principle of Systemic Integration: Normative Shadows in Plato's Cave* (Brill 2015)

Merkouris P, *Interpretation of Customary International Law: Of Methods and Limits* (Brill 2023)

Miles K, *The Origins of International Investment Law: Empire, Environment and the Safeguarding of Capital* (CUP 2013)

Montt S, *State Liability in Investment Treaty Arbitration* (Hart 2009)

Moore JB, *A Digest of International Law*, Vol 2 (US GPO 1906)

Moore JB, *A Digest of International Law*, Vol 6 (US GPO 1906)

Mouyal LW, *International Investment Law and the Right to Regulate: A Human Rights Perspective* (Routledge 2016)
Muchlinski P, *Multinational Enterprises and the Law* (2nd edn, OUP 2007)
Neff SC, *The Rights and Duties of Neutrals* (MUP 2000)
Newcombe A & Paradell L, *Law and Practice of Investment Treaties: Standards of Treatment* (Kluwer 2009)
OECD, *International Investment Law: A Changing Landscape: A Companion Volume to International Investment Perspectives* (OECD Publishing 2005)
Oppenheim L, *International Law – Vol 2: War and Neutrality* (Longmans 1906)
Orakhelashvili A, *The Interpretation of Acts and Rules in Public International Law* (OUP 2008)
Ortino F, *The Origin and Evolution of Investment Treaty Standards: Stability, Value, and Reasonableness* (OUP 2020)
Paddeu F, *Justification and Excuse in International Law: Concept and Theory of General Defences* (CUP 2018)
Pahuja S, *Decolonising International Law: Development, Economic Growth and the Politics of Universality* (CUP 2011)
Paparinskis M, *The International Minimum Standard and Fair and Equitable Treatment* (OUP 2013)
Parry C (ed), *A British Digest of International Law*, Vol 6 (Stevens & Sons 1965)
Pauwelyn J, *Conflict of Norms in Public International Law: How WTO Law Relates to Other Rules of International Law* (CUP 2003)
Peat D, *Comparative Reasoning in International Courts and Tribunals* (CUP 2019)
Peel J, *The Precautionary Principle in Practice* (Federation Press 2005)
Phillimore R, *Commentaries Upon International Law*, Vol II (T&JW Johnson 1855)
Piracha N, *Toward Uniformly Accepted Principles for Interpreting MFN Clauses: Striking a Balance Between Sovereignty and the Protection of Investors* (Kluwer 2021)
Redfern A & Hunter M, *Law and Practice of International Commercial Arbitration* (Sweet & Maxwell 2004)
Reinisch A & Schreuer C, *International Protection of Investments: The Substantive Standards* (CUP 2020)
Reitzer L, *La réparation comme conséquence de l'acte illicite en droit international* (Sirey 1938)
Ripinsky S & Williams K, *Damages in International Investment Law* (BIICL 2008)
Rosenne S (ed), *League of Nations Conference for the Codification of International Law (1930)*, Vol 2 (Oceana 1975)
Ryle G, *The Concept of Mind* (Hutcheson 1949)
Sabahi B, *Compensation and Restitution in Investor-State Arbitration: Principles and Practice* (OUP 2011)
Said E, *Orientalism* (Random House Inc 1978)
Said E, *Orientalism* (25th anniversary edn, Penguin 2003)
Salacuse JW, *The Law of Investment Treaties* (OUP 2010)

Salacuse JW, *The Three Laws of International Investment National, Contractual, and International Frameworks for Foreign Capital* (OUP 2013)
Sandifer D, *Evidence before International Tribunals* (UVA Press 1975)
Sands P, Peel J, Fabra A & ors, *Principles of International Environmental Law* (CUP 2012)
Schill S, *The Multilateralization of International Investment Law* (CUP 2009)
Schreuer C & Dolzer R, *Principles of International Investment Law* (OUP 2008)
Schreuer C & ors, *The ICSID Convention: A Commentary* (2nd edn, CUP 2009)
Schwarzenberger G, *International Law*, Vol 1 (3rd edn, Stevens and Sons 1957)
Shaw MN, *International Law* (6th edn, CUP 2006)
Shaw MN, *International Law* (8th edn, CUP 2017)
Schrijver N, *Sovereignty over Natural Resources: Balancing Rights and Duties* (CUP 1997)
Sornarajah M, *The International Law on Foreign Investment* (2nd edn, CUP 2004)
Sornarajah M, *The International Law on Foreign Investment* (3rd edn, CUP 2010)
Sornarajah M, *Resistance and Change in the International Law on Foreign Investment* (CUP 2015)
Spanish Treaty Claims Commission, *Rules and Regulations of Practice and Procedure: Adopted and Amended from Time to Time by the Commission, Together with a Copy of the Organic Act and Other Papers* (US GPO 1902)
Tams CJ & Sloan J (eds), *The Development of International Law by the International Court of Justice* (OUP 2013)
Thirlway H, *The Sources of International Law* (OUP 2005)
Titi A, *The Right to Regulate in International Investment Law* (Nomos 2014)
Tooze A, *Shutdown: How Covid Shook the World's Economy* (Allen Lane 2021)
Tudor I, *The Fair and Equitable Treatment Standard in International Foreign Investment Law* (OUP 2008)
Vandevelde K, *United States International Investment Agreements* (Kluwer 2002)
de Vattel E, *The Law of Nations; Or, Principles of the Law of Nature, Applied to the Conduct and Affairs of Nations and Sovereigns* (first published 1758, Chitty J ed, 6th edn, Johnson 1844)
Villiger ME, *Commentary on the 1969 Vienna Convention on the Law of Treaties* (Brill 2009)
Viñuales JE, *Foreign Investment and the Environment in International Law* (CUP 2012)
de Visscher C, *De l'equité dans le règlement arbitral ou judiciaire des litiges de droit international public* (Pedone 1972)
Weiler T, *The Interpretation of International Investment Law: Equality, Discrimination and Minimum Standards of Treatment in Historical Context* (Martinus Nijhoff 2013)
Whiteman MM, *Damages in International Law*, Vol 2 (US GPO 1937)
Whiteman MM, *Damages in International Law*, Vol 3 (US GPO 1943)

Wilson RR, *The International Law Standard in Treaties of the United States* (HUP 1953)
Wortley BA, *Expropriation in Public International Law* (CUP 1959)
Yen TH, *The Interpretation of Investment Treaties* (Martinus Nijhoff 2014)

Chapters in an Edited Volume

van Aaken A, 'Control Mechanisms in International Investment Law' in Douglas Z, Pauwelyn J & Viñuales JE (eds), *The Foundations of International Investment Law – Bringing Theory into Practice* (OUP 2014)

Abi-Saab G, 'Permanent Sovereignty over Natural Resources and Economic Activities' in Bedjaoui M (ed), *International Law: Achievements and Prospects* (UNESCO 1991)

Abi-Saab G, 'La Commission du Droit International, la codification et le processus de la formation de droit international' in *Making Better International Law: The International Law Commission at 50* (UN 1998)

Abi-Saab G, 'Introduction: A Meta-Question' in Abi-Saab G et al (eds), *Evolutionary Interpretation and International Law* (Hart 2019)

Álvarez-Zárate JM & Beltrán Vargas DM, 'Desafíos del arbitraje de inversión en los sectores minero-energético en América Latina' in Castillo LFM & Villanueva C (eds), *Anuario iberoamericano en Derecho de la Energía, Vol II, Regulación de la transición Energética* (Universidad Externado de Colombia 2019)

Álvarez-Zarate JM & Beltrán Vargas DM, 'El derecho consuetudinario en el derecho internacional de inversiones' in Álvarez-Zarate JM & Żenkiewicz M (eds), *El derecho internacional de las inversiones* (Universidad Externado de Colombia 2021)

d'Aspremont J, 'International Customary Investment Law: Story of a Paradox' in Gazzini T & de Brabandere E (eds), *International Investment Law: The Sources of Rights and Obligations* (Martinus Nijhoff 2012)

d'Aspremont J, 'The Custom-Making Moment in Customary International Law' in Merkouris P, Kammerhofer J & Arajärvi N (eds), *The Theory, Practice, and Interpretation of Customary International Law* (CUP 2022)

Baetens F, 'Keeping the Status Quo or Embarking on a New Course? Setting Aside, Refusal of Enforcement, Annulment and Appeal' in Kulick A (ed), *Reassertion of Control over the Investment Treaty Regime* (CUP 2017)

Banifatemi Y, 'The Law Applicable in Investment Treaty Arbitration' in Yannaca-Small K (ed), *Arbitration under International Investment Agreements* (2nd edn, OUP 2018)

Berger B, 'The Use of Experts in International Arbitration: Specific Issues Relating to Legal Experts' in Besson S & Frey H (eds), *Expert Evidence: Conflicting Assumptions and How to Handle them in Arbitration* (Juris Publishing 2021)

Bianchi A, 'The Game of Interpretation in International Law: The Players, the Cards, and Why the Game Is Worth the Candle' in Bianchi A, Peat D & Windsor M (eds), *Interpretation in International Law* (OUP 2015)

Bianchi A, 'Epistemic Communities' in d'Aspremont J & Singh S (eds), *Concepts for International Law: Contributions to Disciplinary Thought* (Edward Elgar 2019)

Binder C & Janig P, 'Investment Agreements and Financial Crises' in Krajewski M & Hoffmann RT (eds), *Research Handbook on Foreign Direct Investment* (Edward Elgar 2019)

Berensztein S & Spector H, 'Business, Government, and Law' in della Paolera G & Taylor AM (eds), *A New Economic History of Argentina* (CUP 2003)

Bradley CA, 'Customary International Law Adjudication as Common Law Adjudication' in Bradley CA (ed), *Custom's Future: International Law in a Changing World* (CUP 2016)

Caldwell R, Chodorow D & Dorobantu F, 'Valuing Natural Resources Investments' in Beharry CL (ed), *Contemporary and Emerging Issues on the Law of Damages and Valuation in International Investment Arbitration* (Brill Nijhoff 2018)

Cheng B, 'Some Remarks on the Constituent Element(s) of General (or So-Called Customary) International Law' in Anghie A & Sturgess G (eds), *Legal Visions of the 21st Century: Essays in Honour of Judge Christopher Weeramantry* (Kluwer 1998)

Chimni BS, 'Third World Approaches to International Law: A Manifesto' in Anghie A et al (eds), *The Third World and International Order: Law, Politics and Globalization* (Brill 2003)

Collins R & Bohm A, 'International Law as Professional Practice: Crafting the Autonomy of International Law' in d'Aspremont J et al (eds), *International Law as a Profession* (CUP 2017)

Cordero Moss G, 'Tribunal's Power v Party Autonomy' in Muchlinski P, Ortino F & Schreuer C (eds), *Oxford Handbook of International Investment Law* (OUP 2008)

Crawford J, 'A Consensualist Interpretation of Article 31(3) of the Vienna Convention on the Law of Treaties' in Nolte G (ed), *Treaties and Subsequent Practice* (OUP 2013)

Crawford J, 'The International Court of Justice and the Law of State Responsibility' in Tams CJ & Sloan J (eds), *The Development of International Law by the International Court of Justice* (OUP 2013)

Daillier P, 'The Development of the Law of Responsibility through the Case Law' in Crawford J, Pellet A & Olleson S (eds), *The Law of International Responsibility* (OUP 2010)

Dolzer R & von Walter A, 'Fair and Equitable Treatment – Lines of Jurisprudence on Customary Law' in Ortino F, Liberti L, Sheppard A & ors (eds), *Investment Treaty Law: Current Issues* II (BIICL 2007)

Donovan DF, 'Re-examining the Legal Expert in International Arbitration' in HKIAC (ed), *International Arbitration: Issues, Perspectives and Practice: Liber Amicorum Neil Kaplan* (Wolters Kluwer 2019)

Dumberry P, 'Fair and Equitable Treatment' in Schacherer S & Mbengue MM(eds), *Foreign Investment Under the Comprehensive Economic and Trade Agreement (CETA)* (Springer 2018)

Dumberry P, 'Fair and Equitable Treatment' in Bungenberg M & Reinisch A (eds), *Canada-European Union Comprehensive Economic and Trade Agreement (CETA): Article-by-Article Commentary* (Nomos/Hart 2021)

Forteau M, 'Reparation in the Event of a Circumstance Precluding Wrongfulness' in Crawford J, Pellet A & Olleson S (eds), *The Law of International Responsibility* (OUP 2010)

Fox H, 'Letter from Henry Fox to John Forsyth, US Secretary of State, dated 6 February 1838' in Manning WR (ed), *Diplomatic Correspondence of the United States: Canadian Relations*, Vol 3 (Carnegie Endowment 1943)

Friedman MW & Lavaud F, 'Damages Principles in Investment Arbitration' in Trenor JA (ed), *The Guide to Damages in International Arbitration* (3rd edn, Global Arbitration Review 2018)

Franke F, 'The Custom of Necessity in Investor-State Arbitrations' in R Hofmann & CJ Tams (eds), *International Investment Law and General International Law* (Nomos 2011)

Gathii JT, 'Third World Approaches to International Economic Governance' in Falk R, Rajagopal B & Stevens J (eds), *International Law and the Third World* (Routledge 2008)

Gathii JT, 'The Agenda of Third World Approaches in International Law' in Dunoff J & Pollack M (eds), *International Legal Theory: Foundations and Frontiers* (CUP 2022)

Gehring MW, 'Impact Assessments of Investment Treaties' in Cordonier Segger MC, Gehring MW & Newcombe AP (eds), *Sustainable Development in World Investment Law* (Kluwer Law 2011)

Gehring MW & Kent A, 'International Investment Agreements and the Emerging Green Economy: Rising to the Challenge' in Baetens F (ed), *Investment Law Within International Law* (CUP 2013)

Giannakopoulos C & Monga M, 'History as Interpretative Context in the Evolutionary Interpretation of FET in International Investment Law' in Abi-Saab G et al (eds), *Evolutionary Interpretation and International Law* (Hart 2019)

Giovannini T, 'Ex Officio Powers to Investigate: When Do Arbitrators Cross the Line?' in Baizeau D & Ehle B (eds), *Stories from the Hearing Room: Experience from Arbitral Practice (Essays in Honour of Michael E Schneider)* (Kluwer 2015)

Henckels C, 'Scope Limitation or Affirmative Defence? The Purpose and Role of Investment Treaty Exception Clauses' in Bartels L & Paddeu F (eds), *Exceptions in International Law* (OUP 2020)

Hernandez G, 'Interpretative Authority and the International Judiciary' in Bianchi A, Peat D & Windsor M (eds), *Interpretation in International Law* (OUP 2015)

Hexner EP, 'Teleological Interpretation of Basic Instruments of Public International Organizations' in Engel S & Metall R (eds), *Law, State and International Legal Order–Essays in Honor of Hans Kelsen* (Tennessee University 1964)

Higgins R, 'International Law and the Reasonable Need of Governments to Govern' in Higgins R (ed), *Themes and Theories: Selected Essays, Speeches and Writings in International Law* (OUP 2009)

Hobér K, 'State Responsibility and Attribution' in Muchlinski P, Ortino F & Schreuer C (eds), *The Oxford Handbook of International Investment Law* (OUP 2008)

Hollis DB, 'The Existential Function of Interpretation in International Law' in Bianchi A, Peat D & Windsor M (eds), *Interpretation in International Law* (OUP 2015)

Hollis DB, 'Introduction' in Hollis DB (ed), *The Oxford Guide to Treaties* (2nd edn, OUP 2020)

Jarrosson C, 'L'expertise juridique' in Reymond C (ed), *Liber amicorum Claude Reymond: Autour de l'arbitrage* (Litec Paris 2004)

Johnson OT & Gimblett J, 'From Gunboats to BITs: The Evolution of Modern International Investment Law' in Sauvant KP (ed), *Yearbook on International Investment Law & Policy 2010–2011* (OUP 2012)

Kelly JP, 'Customary International Law in Historical Context: The Exercise of Power without General Acceptance' in Lepard BD (ed), *Reexamining Customary International Law* (CUP 2017)

Kent A & Harrington A, 'The Plea of Necessity Under Customary International Law: A Critical Review in Light of the Argentine Cases' in Brown C & Miles K (eds), *Evolution in Investment Treaty Arbitration* (CUP 2011)

Kurtz J, Viñuales JE & Waibel M, 'Principles Governing the Global Economy' in Viñuales JE (ed), *The UN Friendly Relations Declaration at 50: An Assessment of the Fundamental Principles of International Law* (CUP 2020)

Langford M, Behn D & Lie R, 'The Revolving Door in International Investment Arbitration' in Føllesdal A & Ulfstein G (eds), *Judicialization of International Law: A Mixed Blessing?* (OUP 2018)

Leben C, 'L'évolution du droit international des investissements' in SFDI & IHEI (eds), *Un accord multilatéral sur l'investissement: d'un forum de négociation à l'autre?* (Pedone 1999)

Lepard BD, 'Customary International Law as a Dynamic Process' in Bradley CA (ed), *Custom's Future: International Law in a Changing World* (CUP 2016)

Lévesque C & Newcombe A, 'Commentary on the Canadian Model Foreign Promotion and Protection Agreement' in Brown C (ed), *Commentaries on Selected Model Investment Treaties* (OUP 2013)

Losari JJ & Ewing-Chow M, 'Legitimate Countermeasures in International Trade Law and Their Illegality in International Investment Law' in Pazartzis P & Gavouneli M (eds), *Reconceptualising the Rule of Law in Global Governance, Resources, Investment and Trade* (Bloomsbury 2016)

Malinvaud C, 'Non-pecuniary Remedies in Investment Treaty and Commercial Arbitration' in van den Berg AJ (ed), *50 Years of the New York Convention: ICCA International Arbitration Conference* (Kluwer Law International 2009)

Marboe I, 'Assessing Compensation and Damages in Expropriation Versus Non-Expropriation Cases' in Beharry CL (ed), *Contemporary and Emerging Issues on the Law of Damages and Valuation in International Investment Arbitration* (Brill Nijhoff 2018)

Mazeaud D, 'L'expertise de droit à travers l'*amicus curiae*' in Frison-Roche MA & Mazeaud D (eds), *L'expertise* (Dalloz 1995)

Mejía-Lemos D, 'General International Law and International Investment Law: A Systematic Analysis of Interactions in Arbitral Practice' in Chaisse J et al (eds), *Handbook of International Investment Law and Policy* (Springer Singapore 2020)

Methymaki E & Tzanakopoulos A, 'Masters of Puppets? Reassertion of Control through Joint Investment Treaty Interpretation' in Kulick A (ed), *Reassertion of Control Over the Investment Treaty Regime* (CUP 2017)

Milano E, 'General Principles *Infra, Praeter, Contra Legem*? The Role of Equity in Determining Reparation' in Andenas M & ors (eds), *General Principles and the Coherence of International Law*, Vol 37 (Brill Nijhoff 2019)

Mileva N & Fortuna M, 'Environmental Protection as an Object of and Tool for Evolutionary Interpretation' in Abi-Saab G et al (eds), *Evolutionary Interpretation and International Law* (Hart 2019)

Mileva N, 'The Role of Domestic Courts in the Interpretation of Customary International Law: How Can We Learn from Domestic Interpretive Practices?' in Merkouris P, Kammerhofer J & Arajärvi N (eds), *The Theory, Practice, and Interpretation of Customary International Law* (CUP 2022)

Mourre A, 'Arbitration and Criminal Law: Jurisdiction, Arbitrability and Duties of the Arbitral Tribunal' in Mistelis L & Brekoulakis S (eds), *Arbitrability: International and Comparative Perspectives* (Kluwer 2009)

Muchlinski P, 'Negotiating International Investment Agreements: New Sustainable Development Oriented Initiatives' in Hindelang S, Krajewski M & ors (eds), *Shifting Paradigms in International Investment Law: More Balanced, Less isolated and Increasingly Diversified* (OUP 2016)

Orrego Vicuña F, 'Le pied du chancelier continue de s'allonger: les principes généraux et l'équité en droit international' in Kohen M, Kolb R & Tehindrazanarivelo DL (eds), *Perspectives of International Law in the 21st Century: Liber Amicorum Professor Christian Dominicè in Honour of his 80th birthday* (Martinus Nijhoff 2012)

Owada H, 'The International Law Commission and the Process of Law-Formation' in UN(ed), *Making Better International Law: The International Law Commission at 50* (UN 1998)

Özsu U, 'Neoliberalism and the New International Economic Order: A History of "Contemporary Legal Thought"' in Desautels-Stein J & Tomlins C (eds), *Searching for Contemporary Legal Thought* (CUP 2017)

Paddeu F, 'The Impact of Investment Arbitration in the Development of State Responsibility Defences' in Tams CJ, Schill SW & Hofmann R (eds), *International Investment Law and General International Law* (Edward Elgar 2023)

Pahuja S & Saunders A, 'Rival Worlds and the Place of the Corporation in International Law' in von Bernstorff J & Dann P (eds), *The Battle for International Law: South-North Perspectives on the Decolonization Era* (OUP 2019)

Paine J, 'The Judicial Dimension of Regime Interaction beyond Systemic Integration' in Trevisanut S, Giannopoulos N & Roland Holst R (eds), *Regime Interaction in Ocean Governance: Problems, Theories and Methods* (Brill 2020)

Palmerston L, 'Letter from Lord Palmerston, British Foreign Secretary, to Andrew Stevenson, American Minister in London, Dated 27 August 1841' in Manning WR (ed), *Diplomatic Correspondence of the United States: Canadian Relations*, Vol 3 (Carnegie Endowment 1943)

Pellet A, 'Article 38' in Zimmerman A & ors (eds), *The Statute of the International Court of Justice: A Commentary* (OUP 2006)

Pellet A, 'The ILC's Articles on State Responsibility for Internationally Wrongful Acts and Related Texts' in Crawford J, Pellet A & Olleson S (eds), *The Law of International Responsibility* (OUP 2010)

Pellet A, 'Police Powers or the State's Right to Regulate: *Chemtura v Canada*' in Kinnear M & ors (eds), *Building International Investment Law: The First 50 Years of the ICSID Convention* (Kluwer 2015)

Protopsaltis PM, 'Shareholders' Injury and Compensation in Investor-State Arbitration' in Pazartzis P & Merkouris P (eds), *Permutations of Responsibility in International Law* (Brill Nijhoff 2019)

Radi Y, 'Promenade avec Aristote Dans les Jardins du Droit International: Réflexions sur L'équité et le Raisonnement Juridique des Juges et Arbitres Internationaux' in Alland D, Chetail V, de Frouville O & ors (eds), *Unity and Diversity of International Law* (Brill Nijhoff 2014)

Reinisch A & Binder C, 'Debts and State of Necessity' in Bohoslavsky JP & Černič CL (eds), *Making Sovereign Financing and Human Rights Work* (Hart 2014)

Reghizzi ZC, 'General Rules and Principles on State Responsibility and Damages in Investment Arbitration: Some Critical Issues' in Gattini A, Tanzi A & Fontanelli F (eds), *General Principles of Law and International Investment Arbitration* (Brill 2018)

Rosenne S, 'The Position of the International Court of Justice on the Foundations of the Principle of Equity in International Law' in Bloed A & van Dijk P (eds), *Forty*

Years International Court of Justice: Jurisdiction, Equity and Equality (Europa Instituut 1988)

Rubins N, Sinha V & Roberts B, 'Approaches to Valuation in Investment Treaty Arbitration' in Beharry CL (ed), *Contemporary and Emerging Issues on the Law of Damages and Valuation in International Investment Arbitration* (Brill Nijhoff 2018)

Rush G, Sequeira K & Shopp M, 'Valuation Techniques for Early-Stage Businesses in Investor-State Arbitration' in Beharry CL (ed), *Contemporary and Emerging Issues on the Law of Damages and Valuation in International Investment Arbitration* (Brill Nijhoff 2018)

Sabahi B, Duggal K & Birch N, 'Principles Limiting the Amount of Compensation' in Beharry C (ed), *Contemporary and Emerging Issues on the Law of Damages and Valuation in International Investment Arbitration* (Brill Nijhoff 2018)

Sender O & Wood M, 'Custom's Bright Future: The Continuing Importance of Customary International Law' in Bradley CA (ed), *Custom's Future: International Law in a Changing World* (CUP 2016)

Shany Y, 'Jurisdiction and Admissibility' in Romano C, Alter K & Shany Y (eds), *The Oxford Handbook of International Adjudication* (OUP 2013)

Solomou A, 'Exceptions to a Rule Must be Narrowly Construed' in Klinger J, Parkhomenko Y & Salonidis C (eds), *Between the Lines of the Vienna Convention?* (Kluwer 2019)

Spielmann O 'Applicable Law' in Muchlinski P, Ortino F & Schreuer C (eds), *The Oxford Handbook of International Investment Law* (OUP 2008)

Stevenson A, 'Letter from Andrew Stevenson, United States Minister to Great Britain, to Lord Palmerston, British Foreign Secretary, Dated 22 May 1838' in Manning WR (ed), *Diplomatic Correspondence of the United States: Canadian Relations*, Vol 3 (Carnegie Endowment 1943)

Tams CJ, 'The Development of International Law by the International Court of Justice' in Cannizzaro E & ors (eds), *Decisions of the ICJ as Sources of International Law?* (International and European Papers Publishing 2018)

Tasioulas J, 'Customary International Law and the Quest for Global Justice' in Perreau-Saussine A & Murphy JB (eds), *The Nature of Customary International Law: Legal, Historical and Philosophical Perspectives* (CUP 2007)

Tienhaara K, 'Regulatory Chill and the Threat of Arbitration' in Brown C & Miles K (eds), *Evolution in Investment Treaty Law and Arbitration* (CUP 2011)

Titi C, 'Police Powers Doctrine and International Investment Law' in Gattini A, Tanzi A & Fontanelli F (eds), *General Principles of Law and International Investment Arbitration* (Brill 2018)

Treder P & Sadowski W, 'Poland' in Nagy C (ed), *Investment Arbitration in Central and Eastern Europe* (Elgar 2019)

Tzanakopoulos A, 'We Who Are Not as Others: Sanctions and (Global) Security Governance' in Geiß R & Melzer N (eds), *The Oxford Handbook of the International Law of Global Security* (OUP 2021)

Ünüvar G, 'The Vague Meaning of Fair and Equitable Treatment Principle in Investment Arbitration and New Generation Clarifications' in Kjær AL & Lam J (eds), *Language and Legal Interpretation in International Law* (OUP 2022)

Viñuales JE, 'Sovereignty in Foreign Investment Law' in Douglas Z, Pauwelyn J & Viñuales JE (eds), *The Foundations of International Investment Law: Bringing Theory into Practice* (OUP 2014)

Waibel M, 'Interpretive Communities in International Law' in Bianchi A, Peat D & Windsor M (eds), *Interpretation in International Law* (OUP 2015)

Wälde TW & Sabahi B, 'Compensation, Damages and Valuation' in Muchlinski P, Ortino F & Schreuer C (eds), *The Oxford Handbook of International Investment Law* (OUP 2008)

Webster D, 'Letter from Daniel Webster, US Secretary of State, to Henry Fox, British Minister in Washington, Dated 24 April 1841' in Manning WR (ed), *Diplomatic Correspondence of the United States: Canadian Relations*, Vol 3 (Carnegie Endowment 1943)

Weil P, 'L'Equité Dans La Jurisprudence de la Cour Internationale de Justice: Un Mystère en Voie de Dissipation?' in Lowe V & Fitzmaurice M (eds), *Fifty Years of the International Court of Justice* (CUP 1996)

Wood M, 'The Caroline Incident – 1837' in Ruys T, Corten O & Hofer A (eds), *The Use of Force in International Law: A Case-Based Approach* (OUP 2018)

Wouters J & Chane AL, 'Multinational Corporations in International Law' in Noorman, M, Reinisch A & Ryngaert C (eds), *Non-State Actors in International Law* (Bloomsbury 2017)

Yamashita T, 'Investors in the Formation of Customary International Law' in Droubi S & d'Aspremont J (eds), *International Organisations, Non-State Actors, and the Formation of Customary International Law* (MUP 2020)

Yotova R, 'Systemic Integration: An Instrument for Reasserting the State's Control in Investment Arbitration?' in Kulick A (ed), *Reassertion of Control over the Investment Treaty Regime* (CUP 2016)

Yotova R, 'Compliance with Domestic Law: An Implied Condition in Treaties Conferring Rights and Protections on Foreign Nationals and Their Property?' in Klingler J, Parkhomenko Y & Salonidis C (eds), *Between the Lines of the Vienna Convention? Canons and Other Principles of Interpretation in Public International Law* (Kluwer 2018)

Zidar A, 'Interpretation and the International Legal Profession: Between Duty and Aspiration' in Bianchi A, Peat D & Windsor M (eds), *Interpretation in International Law* (OUP 2015)

Articles

Abi-Saab G, 'The Newly Independent States and the Rules of International Law: An Outline' (1962) 8 *How LJ* 100

Abi-Saab G, 'The Third World Intellectual in Praxis: Confrontation, Participation, or Operation behind Enemy Lines' (2016) 37(11) *Third World Quarterly* 1957

Aguilar Alvarez G & Park WW, 'The New Face of Investment Arbitration: NAFTA Chapter 11' (2003) 28 *YJIL* 365

AJIL, 'Article 27. Violation of Treaty Obligations' (1935) 29 *AJIL Supp* 1077

AJIL, 'Mexico – United States: Expropriation by Mexico of Agrarian Properties Owned by American Citizens' (1938) 32 *AJIL Supp* 181

Akehurst M, 'Equity and General Principles of Law' (1976) 25(4) *ICLQ* 801

Akehurst M, 'International Liability for Injurious Consequences Arising Out of Acts Not Prohibited by International Law' (1985) 16 *NYIL* 3

Akinsanya A, 'International Protection of Direct Foreign Investments in the Third World' (1987) 36 *ICLQ* 58

Al Faruque A, 'Creating Customary International Law Through Bilateral Investment Treaties: A Critical Appraisal' (2004) 44 *IJIL* 312

Alvarez JE, 'Bit on Custom' (2009) 42 *NYU J Intl L & Pol* 17

Alvarez JE, 'The Public International Law Regime Governing International Investment' (2009) 344 *RdC* 292

Alvarez JE, 'Are Corporations "Subjects" of International Law' (2011) 9(1) *Santa Clara Journal of International Law* 1

Alvarez JE, 'The Return of the State' (2011) 20(2) *Minn JIntlL* 223

Álvarez-Zárate JM, 'Legitimacy Concerns of the Proposed Multilateral Investment Court: Is Democracy Possible?' (2018) 59(8) *BCLRev* 2765

Anderson CP, 'Letter of the Honorable Chandler P Anderson, American Arbitrator, to the Secretary General of the Permanent Court of Arbitration' reproduced in (1923) 17(2) *AJIL* 362

Angie A & Chimni BS, 'Third World Approaches to International Law and Individual Responsibility in Internal Conflicts' (2003) 2 *Chin J Int Law* 78

Arato, J, Claussen K & Heath JB, 'The Perils of Pandemic Exceptionalism' (2020) 114 *AJIL* 627

d'Aspremont J, 'The Idea of 'Rules' in the Sources of International Law' (2014) 84 *BYBIL* 103

d'Aspremont J, 'Three International Lawyers in a Hall of Mirrors' (2019) 32 *LJIL* 367

Azaria D, 'Codification by Interpretation: The International Law Commission as an Interpreter of International Law' (2020) 31(1) *EJIL* 171

Baade HW, 'Proving Foreign and International Law in Domestic Tribunals' (1978) 18(4) *VaJInt'l L* 619

Baetens F, 'Protecting Foreign Investment and Public Health: From Arbitral Balancing via Treaty Reform to Synergy by Design?' (2022) 71 *ICLQ* 139

Baker TE, 'The Impropriety of Expert Witness Testimony on the Law' (1992) 40 *UKanLRev* 325

Banteka N, 'A Theory of Constructive Interpretation for Customary International Law Identification' (2018) 39(3) *MichJInt'l Law* 301

Barrera B, 'The Case for Removing the Fair and Equitable Treatment Standard from NAFTA' (2017) 128 *CIGI Papers* 10

Bedjaoui M, 'Expediency in the Decisions of the International Court of Justice' (2000) 71 *BYBIL* 1

Beharry CL, 'Prejudgment Interest Rates in International Investment Arbitration' (2016) 8(1) *JIDS* 56

Berman F, 'Treaty "Interpretation" in a Judicial Context' (2004) 29 *YaleJIntlL* 291

Blandford AC, 'The History of Fair and Equitable Treatment Before the Second World War' (2017) 32(2) *ICSID Rev* 294

von Bogdandy A & Venzke I, 'In Whose Name? An Investigation of International Courts' Public Authority and Its Democratic Justification' (2012) 23(1) *EJIL* 7

Bordin FL, 'A Glass Half Full? The Character, Function and Value of the Two-Element Approach to Identifying Customary International Law' (2019) 21 *ICLR* 283

Born G, Morris D & Forrest S, '"A Margin of Appreciation": Appreciating Its Irrelevance in International Law' (2020) 61 *HarvILJ* 65

Boyle A, 'Globalising Environmental Liability: The Interplay of National and International Law' (2005) 17(1) *JEL* 3

Broches A, 'The Convention on the Settlement of Investment Disputes between States and Nationals of Other States' (1973) 136 *RdC* 333

Brower C & Tepe J, 'The Charter of Economic Rights and Duties of States: A Reflection or Rejection of International Law?' (1975) 9(2) *Intl Law* 295

Brower C, 'Evidence Before International Tribunals: The Need for Some Standard Rules' (1994) 28(1) *Int'l L* 47

Brownlie I, 'Legal Status of Natural Resources in International Law (Some Aspects)' (1979) 162 *RdC* 245

Caron D, 'The ILC Articles on State Responsibility: The Paradoxical Relationship between Form and Authority' (2002) 96 *AJIL* 857

Charney J, 'Universal International Law' (1993) 87(4) *AJIL* 529

Chasapis Tassinis O, 'Customary International Law: Interpretation from Beginning to End' (2020) 31(1) *EJIL* 235

Chimni BS, 'Customary International Law: A Third World Perspective' (2018) 112(1) *AJIL* 1

Choudhury B, 'Evolution or Devolution? Defining Fair and Equitable Treatment in International Investment Law' (2005) 6(2) *JWIT* 297

Christol CQ, 'International Liability for Damage Caused by Space' (1980) 74(2) *AJIL* 346

Cohen D & Goldman Z, 'Like It or Not, Unilateral Sanctions Are Here to Stay' (2019) 113 *AJIL Unbound* 146

Corten O, 'The Notion of "Reasonable" in International Law: Legal Discourse, Reason and Contradictions' (1999) 48 *ICLQ* 613

Cox Alomar R, 'Investment Treaty Arbitration in Cuba' (2017) 48(3) *U Miami Inter-Am L Rev* 1

Crawford J, 'The ILC's Articles on Responsibility of States for Internationally Wrongful Acts: A Retrospect' (2002) 96 *AJIL* 874

Crawford J, 'Investment Arbitration and the ILC Articles on State Responsibility' (2010) 25 *ICSID Rev* 127

Crawford J, 'State Responsibility' [2020] *MPEPIL* 1093

Crook JR, 'Applicable Law in International Commercial Arbitration: The Iran-U.S. Claims Tribunal Experience' (1989) 83(2) *AJIL* 278

Davies H, 'Investor-State Dispute Settlement and the Future of the Precautionary Principle' (2016) 5(2) *Br J A Leg Studies* 449

Descamps É, Baron, 'L'Influence de la Condamnation de la Guerre sur l'Evolution Juridique Internationale' (1930) 31 *RdC* 394

Desierto DA, 'The Outer Limits of Adequate Reparations for Breaches of Non-Expropriation Investment Treaty Provisions: Choice and Proportionality in Chorzòw' (2017) 55(2) *ColumJ Transnat'l L* 395

Díaz Inverso R, 'El estado de necesidad como circunstancia que excluye la ilicitud en la responsabilidad internacional de los Estados' (2015) 47 *Revista de Derecho Público* 49

Dickerson H, 'Minimum Standards' [2013] *MPEPIL* 845

Dolzer R, 'New Foundations of the Law of Expropriation of Alien Property' (1981) 75(3) *AJIL* 553

Dolzer R, 'Indirect Expropriations: New Developments?' (2002) 11 *NYU Envtl LJ* 64

Dolzer R, 'Fair and Equitable Treatment: A Key Standard in Investment Treaties' (2005) 39(1) *IntI Law* 87

Dumberry P, 'Are BITs Representing the 'New' Customary International Law in International Investment Law' (2010) 28 *Penn State Int Law Rev* 675

Dumberry P, '"Cross Treaty Interpretation" en Bloc or How CAFTA Tribunals Are Systematically Interpreting the FET Standard Based NAFTA Case Law' *The Law and Practice of International Courts and Tribunals* (forthcoming 2023)

Dumberry P, 'Moving the Goal Post! How Some NAFTA Tribunals Have Challenged the FTC Note of Interpretation on the Fair and Equitable Treatment Standard Under NAFTA Article 1105' (2014) 8(2) *WAMR* 251

Dumberry P, 'A Few Observations on the Remaining Fundamental Importance of Customary Rules in the Age of Treatification of International Investment Law' (2016) 34(1) *ASA Bulletin* 41

Dumberry P, 'Has the Fair and Equitable Treatment Standard become a Rule of Customary International Law?' (2016) 8(1) *JIDS* 155

Dumberry P, 'The Importation of the Fair and Equitable Treatment Standard Through MFN Clauses: An Empirical Study of BITs' (2016) 17 *ICSID Rev* 229

Dumberry P, 'Fair and Equitable Treatment: Its Interaction with the Minimum Standard and its Customary Status' (2017) 1(2) *Brill Research Perspectives in International Investment Law and Arbitration* 1

Dupuy PM, 'A Doctrinal Debate in the Globalisation Era: On the "Fragmentation" of International Law' (2007) 1 *EJLS* 1

Eagleton C, 'Measure of Damages in International Law' (1929) 39(1) *YLJ* 52

Elrifai SN, 'Equity-Based Discretion and the Anatomy of Damages Assessment in Investment Treaty Law' (2017) 34(5) *JInt'l Arb* 835

Encinas de Munagorri R, 'L'ouverture de la Cour de cassation aux *amici curiae*' [2005] *RTD civ* 88

van Ert G, 'The Admissibility of International Legal Evidence' (2005) 84 *CanBar Rev* 31

Eslava L & Pahuja S, 'Between Resistance and Reform: TWAIL and the Universality of International Law' (2011) 3 *Trade, Law and Development* 103

Fachiri AP, 'International Law and the Property of Aliens' (1929) 10 *BYBIL* 32

Fahner JH & Happold M, 'The Human Rights Defence in International Investment Arbitration: Exploring the Limits of Systemic Integration' (2019) 68(3) *ICLQ* 741

Fahner JH, 'Maximising Investment Protection under the Minimum Standard – A Case Study of the Evolutive Interpretation and Application of Customary International Law in Investment Arbitration' (2023) 12(1) *ESIL Reflections* 1 <https://esil-sedi.eu/esil-reflection-maximising-investment-protection-under-the-minimum-standard-a-case-study-of-the-evolutive-interpretation-and-application-of-customary-international-law-in-investment-arbitration-2/>

Fauchald OK, 'The Legal Reasoning of ICSID Tribunals – An Empirical Analysis' (2008) 19(2) *EJIL* 301

Fidler DP, 'From International Sanitary Conventions to Global Health Security: The New International Health Regulations' (2005) 4 *Chin J Int Law* 325

Fitzmaurice G, 'The Law and Procedure of the International Court of Justice: International Organizations and Tribunals' (1952) 29 *BYBIL* 1

Fitzmaurice M, 'International Protection of the Environment' (2001) 293 *RdC* 16

Foster CE, 'Respecting Regulatory Measures: Arbitral Method and Reasoning in the *Philip Morris v Uruguay* Tobacco Plain Packaging Case' (2017) 26(3) *RECIEL* 287

Francioni F, 'Equity in International Law' [2013] *MPEPIL* 1399

Gaja G, 'Interpreting Articles Adopted by the International Law Commission' (2015) 85 *BYBIL* 10

Gallindo GRB & Yip C, 'Customary International Law and the Third World: Do Not Step on the Grass' (2017) 16(2) *Chin J Int Law* 251

Gantz DA, 'The Evolution of FTA Investment Provisions: From NAFTA to the United States – Chile Free Trade Agreement' (2003) 19(4) *AmUIntl LRev* 679

García-Amador FV, 'The Proposed New International Economic Order: A New Approach to the Law Governing Nationalization and Compensation' (1980) 12 *LawAmer* 1

Gathii JT, 'The Promise of International Law: A Third World View' (2021) 36(3) *American University International Law Review* 377

Gihl T, 'Lacunes du droit international' (1932) 3 *NordJIntlL* 37

Gotanda JY, 'Compound Interest in International Disputes' (2003) 34(2) *Law & PolIntBus* 393

Gourgourinis A, 'Delineating the Normativity of Equity in International Law' (2009) 11(3) *ICLR* 327

Gourgourinis A, 'Equity in International Law Revisited (with Special Reference to the Fragmentation of International Law)' (2009) 103 *ASIL Proc* 79

Gourgourinis A, 'The Distinction between Interpretation and Application of Norms in International Adjudication' (2011) 2 *JIDS* 31

Gourgourinis A, 'General/Particular International Law and Primary/Secondary Rules: Unitary Terminology of a Fragmented System' (2011) 22 *EJIL* 993

Graefrath B, 'Responsibility and Damages Caused: Relationship between Responsibility and Damages' (1984) 185 *RdC* 14

Grauer C, 'The Role of Equity in the Jurisprudence of the World Court' (1979) 37 *RDUT* 101

Grotto A, 'Monetary Gold Arbitration and Case' [2008] *MPEPIL* 175

Guha-Roy SN, 'Is the Law of Responsibility of States for Injuries to Aliens A Part of Universal International Law?' (1961) 55 *AJIL* 866

Guzman AT, 'Why LDCs Sign Treaties That Hurt Them: Explaining the Popularity of Bilateral Investment Treaties' (1998) 38(4) *VaJIntlL* 64

Habibi R & ors, 'The Stellenbosch Consensus on Legal National Responses to Public Health Risks: Clarifying Article 43 of the International Health Regulations' (2022) 19 *IOLR* 90

Haeri H, 'A Tale of Two Standards: 'Fair and Equitable Treatment' and the Minimum Standard in International Law' (2011) 27 *Arb Intl* 34

Haight GW, 'International Organizations OECD Resolution on the Protection of Foreign Property' (1968) 2(2) *Int'l L* 326

Handl G, 'The Environment: International Rights and Responsibilities' (1980) 74 *ASIL Proc* 222

Hart HLA, 'Positivism and the Separation of Law and Morals' (1958) 71(4) *HLR* 607

Heller KJ, 'Specially Affected States and the Formation of Custom' (2018) 112(2) *AJIL* 191

Henckels C, 'Protecting Regulatory Autonomy through Greater Precision in Investment Treaties: The TPP, CETA and TTIP' (2016) 19(1) *J Intl Econ Law* 27

Herrero Rubio A, 'Curso De 1955 De La Universidad De Valladolid en Vitoria' (1956) 9(1/2) *REDI* 281

Herz JH, 'Expropriation of Foreign Property' (1941) 35(2) *AJIL* 243

Hippolyte AR, 'Correcting TWAIL's Bind Spots: A Plea for a Pragmatic Approach to International Economic Governance' (2016) 18 *ICLR* 34

Hudson MO, 'The Seventh Year of the Permanent Court of International Justice' (1929) 3(1) *AJIL* 1

IDI, 'Resolution: On the Jurisdiction of the International Judge in Equity' (1937) 40 *AIDI* 140
International Organization, 'International Court of Justice' (1959) 13(3) *Int'l Org* 446
Jadeau F & Gélinas F, 'CETA's Definition of the Fair and Equitable Treatment Standard: Toward a Guided and Constrained Interpretation' (2016) 13(1) *TDM* 1
Jenks W, 'Conflict of Law-Making Treaties' (1953) 30 *BYBIL* 40
Jennings RY, 'The Progressive Development of International Law and its Codification' (1947) 24 *BYBIL* 301
Jennings RY, 'Equity and Equitable Principles' (1986) XLII *Annuaire Suisse* 27
Jennings RY 'The Judiciary, International and National, and the Development of International Law' (1996) 45 *ICLQ* 1
Jiménez De Aréchaga E, 'International Law in the Past Third of a Century' (1978) 159 *RdC* 1
Johnstone I, 'Treaty Interpretation: The Authority of Interpretive Communities' (1991) 12(2) *MJInt'l Law* 371
Jones H, 'The Caroline Affair' (1976) 28 *Historian* 485
Juillard P, 'L'évolution des sources du droit des investissements' (1994) 250 *RdC* 76
Junngam N, 'The Full Protection and Security Standard in International Investment Law: What and Who is Investment Fully[?] Protected and Secured From?' (2018) 7 *AUBLR* 1
Kaufman E, 'Règles Générales du Droit de la Paix' (1935) 54 *RdC* 511
Kaufman Hevener N & Mosher SA, 'General Principles of Law and the UN Covenant on Civil and Political Rights' (1978) 27(3) *ICLQ* 596
Kessedjian C, 'Le tiers impartial et indépendant en droit international: Juge, arbitre, médiateur, conciliateur – Cours général de droit international' (2019) 403 *RdC* 56
Kill T, 'Don't Cross the Streams: Past and Present Overstatement of Customary International Law in Connection with Conventional Fair and Equitable Treatment Obligations' (2008) 106 *MichLRev* 853
Klein Bronfman M, 'Fair and Equitable Treatment: An Evolving Standard' (2006) 10 *Max Planck YrbkUNL* 615
Knull WH, Jones ST, Tyler TJ & ors, 'Accounting for Uncertainty in Discounted Cash Flow Valuation of Upstream Oil and Gas Investments' (2007) 25 *JENRL* 268
Krajewski M, 'A Nightmare or a Noble Dream? Establishing Investor Obligations Through Treaty-Making and Treaty-Application' (2020) 5(1) *BHRJ* 105
Kriebaum U, 'Regulatory Takings: Balancing the Interests of the Investor and the State' (2007) 8(5) *JWIT* 717
Kułaga Ł, 'Implementing Achmea: The Quest for Fundamental Change in International Investment Law' (2019) 39 *Polish YBInt'l Law* 227
Kułaga Ł, 'Interpretative Declarations as an Instrument of Transformation of International Investment Law: Measures for Restraining Judicial Activism' (author's translation) (2019) 81(3) *Ruch Prawniczy, Ekonomiczny I Socjologiczny* 53
Kulick A, 'Sneaking Through the Backdoor – Reflections on Public Interest in International Investment Arbitration' (2013) 29(3) *Arb Intl* 435

Lachs M, 'Teachings and Teaching of International Law' (1976) 151 *RdC* 164
Lapidoth R, 'Equity in International Law' (1987) 81 *ASIL Proc* 138
Lauterpacht E, 'Issues of Compensation and Nationality in the Taking of Energy Investments' (1990) 8(1) *JERL* 241
Lauterpacht H, 'Règles Générales du Droit de La Paix' (1937) 62 *RdC* 96
Lee J, 'Note on COVID-19 and the Police Powers Doctrine: Assessing the Allowable Scope of Regulatory Measures During a Pandemic' (2020) 13 *CAAJ* 229
Legarre S, 'The Historical Background of the Police Power' (2007) 9 *UPaJConstL* 745
Lévesque C, 'Influences on the Canadian Model FIPA and US Model BIT: NAFTA Chapter 11 and Beyond' (2006) 44 *CanYBIL* 255
Lowe V, 'The Role of Equity in International Law' (1988) 4 *Aust YBIL* 54
Lowe V, 'Regulation or Expropriation?' (2002) 55(1) *CLP* 447
Lowenfeld AF, 'Investment Agreements and International Law' (2003) 42 *ColumJ Transnat'l L* 123
Magraw K, 'Investor-State Disputes and the Rise of Recourse to State Party Pleadings as Subsequent Agreements or Subsequent Practice under the Vienna Convention on the Law of Treaties' (2015) 30 *ICSID Rev* 142
Maier HJ, 'The Role of Experts in Proving International Human Rights Law in Domestic Courts: A Commentary' (1996) 25 *GaJInt'l& CompL* 205
Mann FA, 'British Treaties for the Promotion and Protection of Investments' (1981) 52 *BYBIL* 241
Marks S, 'Expropriation: Compensation and Asset Valuation' (1989) 48(2) *CLJ* 170
Marotti L, 'The Proliferation of Joint Interpretation Clauses in New International Investment Agreements: A Mixed Blessing?' (2020) 35 *ICSID Rev* 63
Marzal T, 'Quantum (In)Justice: Rethinking the Calculation of Compensation and Damages in ISDS' (2021) 22 *JWIT* 249
Mayeda G, 'Playing Fair: The Meaning of Fair and Equitable Treatment in Bilateral Investment Treaties' (2007) 41(2) *JWT* 273
McLachlan C, 'Investment Treaties and General International Law' (2008) 57 *ICLQ* 361
Mendelson MH, 'Compensation for Expropriation: The Case Law' (1985) 79(2) *AJIL* 414
Merkouris P, 'Interpreting the Customary Rules on Interpretation' (2017) 19 *ICLR* 126
Merkouris P & Mileva N, 'ESIL Reflection: Introduction to the Series "Customary Law Interpretation as a Tool"' (2022) 11(1) *ESIL Reflections* 1 <https://esil-sedi.eu/wp-content/uploads/2022/08/ESIL-Reflection-Merkouris-Mileva.pdf>
Metzger SD, 'Property in International Law' (1964) 50(4) *VaLRev* 594
Mickelson K, 'Rhetoric and Rage: Third World Voices in International Legal Discourse' (1998) 16(2) *Wisconsin International Law Journal* 353
Moremen PM, 'National Court Decisions as State Practice: A Transnational Judicial Dialogue?' (2006) 32 *NCJInt'l L& ComReg* 259
Muir Watt H & Creach M, 'Expertise sur la teneur du droit étranger' [2016] *Répertoire de droit international* (Dalloz 2016)

Muir Watt H & Creach M, 'Notion d'expertise' [2016] *Répertoire de droit international* (Dalloz 2016)

Murase S, 'Epidemics and International Law' (2021) 81 *Annuaire de l'Institut de Droit International* 37

Nelson D, 'The Roles of Equity in the Delimitation of Maritime Boundaries' (1990) 84(4) *AJIL* 837

Nollkaemper A, 'Constitutionalization and the Unity of the Law of International Responsibility' (2009) 16 *IJGLS* 535

Odumosu IT, 'The Law and Politics of Engaging Resistance in Dispute Settlement' (2007) 26 *Penn State Int Law Rev* 251

OECD, 'Draft Convention on the Protection of Foreign Property' (1967) 7 *ILM* 117

Okubuiro JC, 'Application of Hegemony to Customary International Law: An African Perspective' (2018) 7 *Global Journal of Comparative Law* 232

Olleson S, 'Attribution in Investment Treaty Arbitration' (2016) 31 *ICSID Rev* 457

Orellana MA, 'International Law on Investment: The Minimum Standard of Treatment (MST)' (2004) 3 *TDM* 1

Paddeu F & Waibel M, 'The Final Act: Exploring the End of Pandemics' (2020) 114 *AJIL* 698

Paparinskis M, 'Investment Arbitration and the Law of Countermeasures' (2009) 79 *BYBIL* 264

Paparinskis M, 'Investment Treaty Arbitration and the (New) Law of State Responsibility' (2013) 24 *EJIL* 617

Paparinskis M, 'A Case Against Crippling Compensation in International Law of State Responsibility' (2020) 83(6) *MLR* 1 *MLR* 1

Paparinskis M, 'The Once and Future Law of State Responsibility' (2020) 114 *AJIL* 618

Paulsson J, 'Arbitration Without Privity' (1995) 10 *ICSID Rev* 232

Paulsson J, 'International Arbitration and the Generation of Legal Norms: Treaty Arbitration and International Law' (2006) 3(5) *TDM* 11

Paulsson J & Petrochilos G, 'Neer-ly Misled?' (2007) 22(2) *ICSID Rev* 242

Pauwelyn J, 'Editorial Comment: Adding Sweeteners to Softwood Lumber: The WTO–NAFTA "Spaghetti Bowl" Is Cooking' (2006) 9 *JIEL* 197

Pauwelyn J, 'The Use of Experts in WTO Dispute Settlement' (2008) 51(2) *ICLQ* 325

Pederson OW, 'From Abundance to Indeterminacy: The Precautionary Principle and its Two Camps of Custom' (2014) 3(2) *TEL* 32

Pellet A, 'Sources of International Law' [1992] *Thesaurus Acroasium*, Vol 19

Pellet A, 'L'adaptation du droit international aux besoins changeants de la société internationale' (2007) 329 *RdC* 9

Peters A, 'Realizing Utopia as a Scholarly Endeavour' (2013) 24(2) *EJIL* 533

Picherack JR, 'The Expanding Scope of the Fair and Equitable Treatment Standard: Have Recent Tribunals Gone Too Far?' (2008) 9(4) *JWIT* 264

Potestà M, 'Legitimate Expectations in Investment Treaty Law: Understanding the Roots and Limits of a Controversial Concept' (2013) 28 *ICSID Rev* 88

Pozen DE & Scheppele KL, 'Executive Underreach, in Pandemics and Otherwise' (2020) 114 *AJIL* 608

Preiswerk R, 'New Developments in Bilateral Investment Protection – With Special Reference to Belgian Practice' (1967) 3 *RBDI* 173

Ranjan P, 'Police Powers, Indirect Expropriation in International Investment Law, and Article 31(3)(c) of the VCLT: A Critique of *Philip Morris v Uruguay*' (2019) 9 *AsianJIL* 98

Ratner SR, 'Compensation for Expropriations in a Word of Investment Treaties: Beyond the Lawful/Unlawful Distinction' (2017) 111(1) *AJIL* 7

Reisman MW & Sloane RD, 'Indirect Expropriation and its Valuation in the BIT Convention' (2004) 74 *BYBIL* 115

Ripert G, 'Les Règles du Droit Civil Applicables aux Rapports Internationaux (Contribution à l'étude des principes généraux du droit visés au Statut de la Cour permanente de Justice internationale)' (1933) 44 *RdC* 565

Ripinsky S, 'State of Necessity: Effect on Compensation' (2007) 4(6) *TDM* 1

Roberts A, 'Traditional and Modern Approaches to Customary International Law: A Reconciliation' (2001) 95(4) *AJIL* 757

Roberts A, 'State-to-State Investment Treaty Arbitration: A Hybrid Theory of Interdependent Rights and Shared Interpretive Authority' (2014) 55(1) *HarvILJ* 69

Root E, 'The Basis of Protection to Citizens Residing Abroad' (1910) 4 *AJIL* 521

Romero Jiménez M, 'Considerations of NAFTA Chapter 11' (2001) 2 *CJIL* 243

Root E, 'The Basis of Protection to Citizens Residing Abroad' (1910) 4 *ASIL Proc* 16

Ryan MC, 'Glamis Gold, Ltd v The United States and the Fair and Equitable Treatment Standard' (2011) 56(4) *McGill LJ* 919

Ryngaert C & Hora Siccama D, 'Ascertaining Customary International Law: An Inquiry into the Methods Used by Domestic Courts' (2018) 65 *NILR* 1

Salacuse JW, 'The Treatification of International Investment Law' (2007) 13(1)1 *Law & Bus Rev Am* 155

Salter J, 'Hugo Grotius: Property and Consent' (2001) 29 *Political Theory* 537

Salter J, 'Grotius and Pufendorf on the Right of Necessity' (2005) 26 *HPT* 285

Sax JL, 'Takings and the Police Power' (1964) 74 *YLJ* 36

Schacherer S, 'TPP, CETA and TTIP Between Innovation and Consolidation – Resolving Investor-State Disputes Under Mega-Regionals' (2016) 7(3) *JIDS* 631

Schachter O, 'International Law in Theory and Practice' (1982) 178 *RdC* 15

Schreuer C, 'Decisions *Ex Aequo et Bono* under the ICSID Convention' (1996) 11 *ICSID Rev – FILJ* 37

Schreuer C, 'Fair and Equitable Standard (FET): Interaction with Other Standards' (2007) 4(5) *TDM* 68

Schreuer C, 'Investment Disputes' [2013] *MPEPIL* 517

Schreuer C, 'The Development of International Law by ICSID Tribunals' (2016) 31(3) *ICSID Rev* 728

Schwarzenberger G, 'The Fundamental Principles of International Law' (1955) 87 *RdC* 192

Schwarzenberger G, 'Equity in International Law' (1972) 26 *YBWA* 346
Schwebel SM, 'Investor-State Disputes and the Development of International Law: The Influence of Bilateral Investment Treaties on Customary International Law' (2004) 98 *ASIL Proc* 27
Schwebel SM, 'Is Neer far from Fair and Equitable?' (2011) 27(4) *Arb Intl* 555
Selby JM, 'State Responsibility and the Iran-United States Claims Tribunal' (1989) 83 *ASIL Proc* 240
Selivanova YS, 'Changes in Renewables Support Policy and Investment Protection under the Energy Charter Treaty: Analysis of Jurisprudence and Outlook for the Current Arbitration Cases' (2018) 33 *ICSID Rev* 433
Shirlow E, 'Deference and Indirect Expropriation Analysis in International Investment Law: Observations on Current Approaches and Frameworks for Future Analysis' (2014) 29 *ICSID Rev* 595
Shirlow E & Duggal K, 'Special Issue on 20th Anniversary of ARSIWA: The ILC Articles on State Responsibility in Investment Treaty Arbitration' (2022) 37 *ICSID Rev* 378
Sloane R, 'On the Use and Abuse of Necessity in the Law of State Responsibility' (2012) 106 *AJIL* 447
Sohn LB & Baxter RR, 'Responsibility of States for Injuries to the Economic Interests of Aliens' (1961) 55 *AJIL* 545
Sommerich OC & Busch B, 'The Expert Witness and the Proof of Foreign Law' (1953) 38 *Cornell L Rev* 125
Sornarajah M, 'Mutations of Neo-Liberalism in International Investment Law' (2011) 3 *Trade Law and Development* 203
Sugarman SD, 'The "Necessity" Defense and the Failure of Tort Theory: The Case Against Strict Liability for Damages Caused While Exercising Self-Help in an Emergency' (2005) 5(2) *Issues in Legal Scholarship* 1
Sur S, 'La créativité du droit international' (2013) 363 *RdC* 21
Talmon S, 'Determining Customary International Law: The ICJ's Methodology between Induction, Deduction and Assertion' (2015) 26 *EJIL* 417
Tams CJ & Tzanakopoulos A, 'Barcelona Traction at 40: The ICJ as an Agent of Legal Development' (2010) 23 *LJIL* 781
Thomas JC, 'Reflections on Article 1105 of NAFTA: History, State Practice and the Influence of Commentators' (2002) 17(1) *ICSID Rev* 26
Torres F, 'Revisiting the Chorzów Factory Standard of Reparation – Its Relevance in Contemporary International Law and Practice' (2021) 90(2) *Nord J Intl L* 190
Treves T, 'Customary International Law' [2006] *MPEPIL* 1393
Tzeng P, 'Investments on Disputed Territory: Indispensable Parties and Indispensable Issues' (2017) 14 *Braz J Int Law* 121
Uchkunova I & Temnikov O, 'A Procrustean Bed: Pre- and Post-award Interest in ICSID Arbitration' (2014) 29(3) *ICSID Rev* 648
UNCTAD, 'Phase 2 of IIA Reform: Modernizing the Existing Stock of Old-Generation Treaties' (2017) (2) *IIA Issues Note* 1

Vandevelde K, 'A Comparison of the 2004 and 1994 US Model BITs' (2008–2009) 1 *YB Intl Invest L&Pol* 291

Van Harten G, 'TWAIL and the Dabhol Arbitration' (2011) 3(1) *Trade, Law and Development* 131

Vasciannie S, 'The Fair and Equitable Treatment Standard in International Investment Law and Practice' (1999) 70(1) *BYBIL* 99

Vierdag EW, 'The Time of the 'Conclusion' of a Multilateral Treaty: Article 30 of the Vienna Convention on the Law of Treaties and Related Provisions' (1988) 59 *BYBIL* 100

Viñuales JE, 'Customary Law in Investment Regulation' (2014) 23(1) *IYIL* 23

Viñuales JE, 'Defence Arguments in Investment Arbitration' (2020) 18 *ICSID Rep* 9

de Visscher C, 'Contribution à l'etude des sources du droit international' (1933) 60 *RDILC* 395

Vitta E, 'Responsabilidad De Los Estados' (1959) 12(1/2) *REDI* 11

Waibel M, 'Subject Matter Jurisdiction: The Notion of Investment' (2021) 19 *ICSID Rep* 25

Wilde Jr PS, 'El Derecho Internacional y el Petróleo Mexicano' (1940) 7(26(2)) *Trimestre Económico* 271

Williams JF, 'International Law and the Property of Aliens' (1928) 9 *BYBIL* 1

Wilson MJ, 'Demystifying the Determination of Foreign Law in US Courts: Opening the Door to a Greater Global Understanding' (2011) 46(5) *Wake Forest LRev* 887

Woolsey LH, 'The Expropriation of Oil Properties by Mexico' (1938) 32(3) *AJIL* 519

Yntema HE, 'The Treaties with Germany and Compensation for War Damage. IV: The Measure of Damages in International Law' (1924) 24(2) *ColumLRev* 134

Żenkiewicz M, 'Compensable vs. Non-Compensable States' Measures: Blurred Picture Under Investment Law' (2020) 17(3) *MJIEL* 362

Unpublished/Thesis/Online/Working Paper Series

Heathcote H, 'State of Necessity and International Law' (PhD Thesis No 772, Graduate Institute of International and Development Studies, 2005)

Manton R, 'Necessity in International Law' (PhD thesis, University of Oxford, 2016) <https://ora.ox.ac.uk/objects/uuid:0ee2dd8e-6eac-4364-b538-21ae5eb932a2/download_file?file_format=pdf&safe_filename=Ryan%2BManton%252C%2BNecessity%2Bin%2BInternational%2BLaw.pdf&type_of_work=Thesis>

OECD, '"Indirect Expropriation" and the "Right to Regulate" in International Investment Law' (OECD Working Papers on International Investment 2004/04, 2004)

Pinchis-Paulsen M, 'The Life and Death (and Re-Birth) of "Fair and" "Equitable Treatment:" A Historical Examination of Twentieth Century International Trade and Investment Law Treaty-Making and Political Decision-Making' (PhD Thesis, King's College London, 2017)

Websites

ALI & UNIDROIT, 'ALI/UNIDROIT Principles of Transnational Civil Procedure' (*UNIDROIT*, 2006) <www.unidroit.org/instruments/civil-procedure/ali-unidroit-principles/>

Ashburton Ld, 'Lord Ashburton's letter to Lord Aberdeen, Dated 13 August 1842' (*Avalon Project, Yale University*, 2021) <https://avalon.law.yale.edu/19th_century/br-1842d.asp#ash1>

Batura J, Hettihewa J & Kulish P, '"I resigned because Russia had become an absolutely indefensible client": An Interview with Alain Pellet' (*Völkerrechtsblog*, 4 July 2022) <https://voelkerrechtsblog.org/de/i-resigned-because-russia-had-become-an-absolutely-indefensible-client/>

Bloomer P & ors, 'Call for ISDS Moratorium During COVID-19 Crisis and Response' (*Columbia Center on Sustainable Investment*, 6 May 2020) <http://ccsi.columbia.edu/2020/05/05/isds-moratorium-during-covid-19>

CEPEJ, 'European Judicial Systems – Edition 2014 (2012 data): Efficiency and Quality of Justice' (*EEEI*, 9 October 2014) <https://experts-institute.eu/wp-content/uploads/2018/03/extract-rapport-2014-en.pdf>

CIMVAL, 'Standards and Guidelines for Valuation of Mineral Properties: Special Committee of the Canadian Institute of Mining, Metallurgy and Petroleum on Valuation of Mineral Properties' (*CIMVAL*, 2003) <https://mrmr.cim.org/media/1020/cimval-standards-guidelines.pdf>

CIMVAL, 'The CIMVAL Code for the Valuation of Mineral Properties' (*CIMVAL*, 2019) <https://mrmr.cim.org/media/1135/cimval-code-november2019.pdf>

van Ert G, 'The Reception of International Law in Canada: Three Ways we Might Go Wrong' (*Canada in International Law at 150 and Beyond Paper No 2*, 2018) <www.cigionline.org/sites/default/files/documents/Reflections%20Series%20Paper%20no.2web.pdf>

EU Member States, 'Declaration of the Governments of the Member States on the Legal Consequences of the Judgment of the Court of Justice in Achmea and on Investment Protection in the European Union of 22 EU-Member States' (*European Commission*, 15 January 2019) <https://ec.europa.eu/info/publications/190117-bilateral-investment-treaties_en>

FTC, 'Statement of the Free Trade Commission on Non-Disputing Party Participation' (*FTC*, 7 October 2003) <www.sice.oas.org/tpd/nafta/commission/nondispute_e.pdf>

German Government, 'On the Application of International Law in Cyberspace – Position Paper' (*Auswärtiges Amt*, March 2021) <www.auswaertiges-amt.de/blob/2446304/32e7b2498e10b74fb17204c54665bdf0/on-the-application-of-international-law-in-cyberspace-data.pdf>

ICJ, 'Speech by HE Mr Abdulqawi A Yusuf, President of the International Court of Justice, on the occasion of the Seventy-Third Session of the United Nations General Assembly' (*Statements by the President*, 25 October 2018) <www.icj-cij.org/public/files/press-releases/0/000-20181025-PRE-02-00-EN.pdf>

ICSID, 'Database of Bilateral Investment Treaties' (*ICSID*, 2022) <https://icsid.worldbank.org/resources/databases/bilateral-investment-treaties>

Indian Government, 'Ministry of Environment, Forest And Climate Change: Notification' (*Gazette of India*, 23 March 2020) <http://environmentclearance.nic.in/writereaddata/Draft_EIA_2020.pdf>

Italaw, 'Expert (Legal Opinion)' (*Italaw*, 2022) <www.italaw.com/browse/expert-legal-opinions>

Lew JDM, 'Iura Novit Curia and Due Process' (*Queen Mary Law Research Paper Series No 72/2010*, 1 January 2011) <http://dx.doi.org/10.2139/ssrn.1733531>

Mann H, Van Moltke K, Peterson LE & ors, 'International Institute for Sustainable Development Model International Agreement on Investment for Sustainable Development, Negotiators Handbook' (*IISD*, April 2006) <www.iisd.org/system/files/publications/investment_model_int_handbook.pdf>

Mileva N, The Role of Customary International Law Interpretation in the Balancing of Interests at Sea: The Example of Prevention' (*TRICI-Law Research Paper Series 010/2020*, 2020) <https://tricilawofficial.files.wordpress.com/2021/06/mileva_rps-010-2020.pdf>

NAFTA Free Trade Commission, 'Notes of Interpretation of Certain Chapter 11 Provisions' (*NAFTA FTC*, 31 July 2001) <https://2009-2017.state.gov/documents/organization/38790.pdf>

Neill J, 'Chorzów Factory and Beyond: Case Law Update' (*Landmark Chambers*, August 2018) <www.landmarkchambers.co.uk/wp-content/uploads/2018/08/Presentation-JN-Chorzow-Factory.pdf>

Neuberger Ld, 'Arbitration and Rule of Law' (Address Before the Chartered Institute of Arbitrators Centenary Celebration, Hong Kong, 20 March 2015) <www.supremecourt.uk/docs/speech-150320.pdf>.

Newcombe A, 'The Strange Case of Expert Legal Opinions in Investment Treaty Arbitrations' (*Kluwer Arbitration Blog*, 18 March 2010) <http://arbitrationblog.kluwerarbitration.com/2010/03/18/the-strange-case-of-expert-legal-opinions-in-investment-treaty-arbitrations/>

Paddeu F & Parlett K, 'COVID-19 and Investment Treaty Claims' (*Kluwer Arbitration Blog*, 30 March 2020) <http://arbitrationblog.kluwerarbitration.com/2020/03/30/covid-19-and-investment-treaty-claims>

SCC, '2017 Arbitration Rules' (*SCC*, 1 January 2020) <https://sccinstitute.com/media/1407444/arbitrationrules_eng_2020.pdf>

Sender O & Wood M, 'The International Court of Justice and Customary International Law: A Reply to Stefan Talmon' (*EJIL:Talk!*, 30 November 2015) <www.ejiltalk.org/the-international-court-of-justice-and-customary-international-law-a-reply-to-stefan-talmon/>

Sparks T, Nedeski N & Hernández G, 'Judging Climate Change Obligations: Can the World Court Rise to the Occasion? Part I: Primary Obligations to Combat Climate Change' (*Völkerrechtsblog*, 30 April 2020) <https://voelkerrechtsblog

.org/judging-climate-change-obligations-can-the-world-court-raise-the-occasion/>

Sparks T, Nedeski N & Hernández G, 'Judging Climate Change Obligations: Can the World Court Rise to the Occasion? Part II: What Role for International Adjudication?' (*Völkerrechtsblog*, 30 April 2020) <https://voelkerrechtsblog.org/judging-climate-change-obligations-can-the-world-court-raise-the-occasion-2/>

Tzeng P, 'The Doctrine of Indispensable Issues: Mauritius v United Kingdom, Philippines v China, Ukraine v Russia, and Beyond' (*EJIL:Talk!*, 14 October 2016) <www.ejiltalk.org/the-doctrine-of-indispensable-issues-mauritius-v-united-kingdom-philippines-v-china-ukraine-v-russia-and-beyond/>

UNCITRAL, 'Working Group III: Investor-State Dispute Settlement Reform' (*UNCITRAL*, 2021) <https://uncitral.un.org/en/working_groups/3/investor-state>

VanDuzer JA, 'Investor-State Dispute Settlement in CETA: Is It the Gold Standard?' (*CD Howe Institute Commentary No 459*, 4 October 2016) <www.cdhowe.org/sites/default/files/attachments/research_papers/mixed/Commentary%20459.pdf>

Van Harten G, 'ISDS in the Revised CETA: Positive Steps, But Is It a "Gold Standard"?' (*CIGI Investor-State Arbitration Commentary Series*, 20 May 2016) <www.cigionline.org/publications/isds-revised-ceta-positive-steps-it-gold-standard>

Van Harten G & ors, 'Public Statement on the International Investment Regime' (*Osgoode Hall Law School*, 31 August 2010) <www.osgoode.yorku.ca/public-statement-international-investment-regime-31-august-2010>

WHO, 'WHO Director-General's opening remarks at the media briefing on COVID-19' (*World Health Organization*, 11 March 2020) <www.who.int/dg/speeches/detail/who-director-general-s-opening-remarks-at-the-media-briefing-on-covid-19---11-march-2020>

WHO, 'Statement on the Fourth Meeting of the International Health Regulations (2005) Emergency Committee Regarding the Outbreak of Coronavirus Disease (COVID-19)' (*WHO*, 1 August 2020) <www.who.int/news/item/01-08-2020-statement-on-the-fourth-meeting-of-the-international-health-regulations-(2005)-emergency-committee-regarding-the-outbreak-of-coronavirus-disease-(covid-19)>

Zarra G, 'Uses and Abuses of Authentic Interpretations of International Investment Agreements: Reflections on the Role of Arbitral Tribunals as Masters of the Judicial Function' (*EJIL:Talk!*, 28 August 2020) <www.ejiltalk.org/uses-and-abuses-of-authentic-interpretations-of-international-investment-agreements-reflections-on-the-role-of-arbitral-tribunals-as-masters-of-the-judicial-function/>

Other

Oshii M, 'Ghost in the Shell' (Shochiku 1995)

INDEX

Abi-Saab, G., 8, 323
actual draft, 13, 15
admissibility of evidence, 25, 27
ALI/UNIDROIT principles, 29
ambivalent arbitral practice, 126–8
Anti-Dumping Agreement, 214
applicable rules of law, 95, 99, 103
Argentina, 39, 54, 56, 60, 61, 65, 66, 279
Articles on State Responsibility for Internationally Wrongful Acts (ARSIWA)
  compensation for material loss, 151
  content of applicable rules
    means of interpretation, 110–13
    textual approach, 105–10
  formal status of, 95–100
  interpretation, patterns of, 105–10
  justification, patterns of, 100–5
  law on State responsibility
    interpretation of, 113–16
    unity of, 116–20
  proportionality, requirement of, 135
  standard of compensation, 180
Austria, 166
award, 54

backward-looking methodology, 300
bankruptcy, 241
Belgium, 66, 67, 202, 217, 243
Berman, F., 138
bilateral investment treaties (BITs), 3
  actual drafting, 13
  fair and equitable treatment standard in, 190
  FET obligation, 11
  foreign investors, 261
  legitimacy of, 264
  remedies, 180
Bordin, F.L., 166
Born, G., 255
Bulgarian minorities, property of, 175–6
burden of education, 42
burden of proof, 34, 206–8, 244, 247, 269, 276, 277
Burkina Faso/Singapore BIT, 68

Canada, 16, 17, 19, 21, 55, 57, 58
Canada–United States–Mexico Agreement (CUSMA), 18
the *Caroline* incident, 170–2
case-by-case approach, 117, 118
Cerro Negro Project, 59
Charter of Economic Rights and Duties of States (CERDS), 9, 237
Charter of the United Nations, 65, 67
Cheng, Bin, 81
Chicago Convention, 145, 146
China/Mexico BIT, 68
China–Australia Free Trade Agreement (ChAFTA), 227
Chorzów Factory case, 73, 81, 84, 179, 285–8
  calculating compensation, 299–302
  damages
    after, 81–3
    before, 77–81
    present, 84–6
  restitution, 288–92
Churchill, W., 210
Columbia Center on Sustainable Investment (CCSI), 235

commercial arbitration, influence of, 29–32
Company General of the Orinoco, 173–5
compensation. *See also* duty of compensation
  Chorzów Factory case, 299–302
  equity. *See* equitable consideration
  lawful expropriation, 293–6
  material loss, 151
Comprehensive Economic and Trade Agreement between the European Union and Canada (CETA), 4
  FET clause, 19–20
conflict of treaty norms, 213–19
copper, 305
counterclaims, 148–9
countermeasures
  ambivalent arbitral practice, 126–8
  application of, 125
  vs. counterclaims, 148–9
  customary requirements of, 134–7
  investors' rights, 130–4
  lex specialis principle, 128–30
  as prior internationally wrongful act, 144–5
  US–Mexico sugar war, 126–8
COVID-19 pandemic, 252, 253, 258, 259
  classical practice, 253–5
  current prognosis, 256–60
  treaty and custom in, 234–6
Crawford, J., 243
customary international law (CIL), 336–44
  constitutive elements of, 33–7
  functions of, 316–23
  identification, 46, 47, 54–60
  interpretation of, 312–16
  relevance of, 335–6
  State practice in, 54–60
  TWAIL approach, 323–30
customary presumption
  reasonable regulation of, 243–5
  systemic integration of, 246–7
Czech Republic, 215, 217

damages
  Chorzów decision
    after, 81–3
    before, 77–81
    present, 84–6
de Vattel, E., 233
decision-making process, 40, 99
declaratory-only award, 292–3, 306
denial of justice principle, 6, 44, 318–20
Denmark, 165
Discounted Cash Flow (DCF) method, 83, 301, 302, 304
Dolzer, R., 10
domestic courts
  influence of, 29–32
  State practice in, 47–53
Dominican Republic-Central America Free Trade Agreement (CAFTA-DR), 57, 277, 278
due process, 6, 20, 24
  principle of, 18
  procedural equity, function of, 209
duty of compensation
  agnosticism, 163
  assertions, 156–8
  assessment, 177–8
  Bulgarian minorities, property of, 175–6
  the *Caroline* incident, 170–2
  Company General of the Orinoco, 173–5
  deductions, 158–62
  denials, 162–3
  equivocal precedents, 167–8
  Gabčíkovo-Nagymaros, 176–7
  lost and found, 189–95
  material loss, 151–4
  missing practice, 164–7
  the *Neptune*, 168–70
  Orr and Laubenheimer, 172–3

Eagleton, Clyde, 77
'effective control' test, 107, 117
electricity, 304
Energy Charter Treaty (ECT), 251
Environmental Impact Assessment (EIA), 272–3
environmental liability, foreign investors, 280–2
environmental protection, 139, 240, 275, 328, 341

environmental regulation, history of, 263–5
equitable consideration
  application of, 183
  compensation, 185–9
  extrinsic limitations to, 204–10
  limitations, 195–200
Eritrea-Ethiopia Claims Commission (EECC), 199
EU-Canada CETA, 41
European Court of Human Rights (ECtHR), 251, 254
expansive approach, 145–8
expert witnesses, in investment arbitration, 23
expropriation
  lawful, 293–6
  unlawful, 293–6

fair and equitable treatment (FET), 3
  actual drafting of, 15
  CETA, 19–20
  emergence of, 10–14
  interpretations of, 16
  tacit integration, 250–2
fair market value, 294, 296, 301
financial regulation, 241
foreign investments
  expropriation of, 185
  importance of, 149
  legal protections, 10
  regulation of, 233, 237
  regulatory authority, 238
  settlement of, 46
foreign investors
  assets owned by, 258
  environmental liability of, 280–2
  investment protection for, 3
  legal protection, 3, 10
  minimum standard of protection to, 8
  obligations of, 261–3
  rights of, 149
foreign-owned property, 174, 175
formalist analysis, 33–7
forward-looking methodology, 301, 302
France, 166, 240
Free Trade Commission ('FTC'), 16

gas, 305
Geneva Convention, 80, 86, 89
German-Venezuelan Commission, 243, 252
Germany, 165, 217, 240
gold, 305
gunboat diplomacy, 6

Hague Conference (1930), 241
Harvard Draft (1961), 241
health, 241
Heathcote, S., 175
Herz, J.H., 80
Higgins, R., 243
host States
  power of, 141–4
  procedural implications for, 274–5
Hudson, M.O., 80
human rights protection, 139, 239

ILC Draft Conclusions, 35
illegal expropriations, 74, 76, 84, 88
income-based methodology, 301
India, 111, 338
Indian Model BIT, 22
infra legem equity, 187, 189, 195, 200
  intrinsic limitations to, 200–4
International Court of Justice (ICJ), 27, 34
  expansive approach, 145–8
  judges of, 42
International Finance Corporation (IFC), 267
International Institute of Sustainable Development (IISD), 267
International Investment Agreements (IIAs), 54, 71
International Law Commission (ILC), 33, 180
  duty of compensation, 165
international law experts, 26
investment arbitration, 29
investment protection treaties
  countermeasures, interaction of, 137–41
  investors' rights, 130–4

investment regulation, 236–7
investment treaty arbitration, 155, 234–6
  exceptional character of, 237–8
investor obligations, 276–80
investors' rights
  host States, power of, 141–4
  nature of, 130–4
investor-State arbitration, 21, 119, 127, 143, 276–80
investor-State dispute settlement proceedings (ISDS), 54, 212
  challenge of, 60
  State practice in, 54–60
Iran-U.S. Claims Tribunal (IUSCT), 82
Iran-United States Claims Tribunal, 241
iura novit arbiter principle, 42

Jay Treaty (1974), 169, 190
Jennings, J., 202
joint review panel (JRP), 274

Latin America, 6, 338
law on State responsibility
  equitable considerations in, 189–95
  interpretation of, 113–16
  unity of, 116–20
lawful expropriation. *See* expropriation
legal experts
  admissibility, 32
  appointment of, 27
  battle of, 26
  scarcity of, 28
  testimonies, 35
  use of, 30
  witnesses, 34, 37, 43
legal experts, types of, 26
legal opinions, in investment arbitration, 25–9
leges specialis, 19–20
legitimacy, struggle for, 40–4
lex specialis principle, 128–30
  countermeasures, interaction of, 137–41
licensing, 241
Lisbon Treaty, 216
Lowe, V., 248
Luxembourg, 217

market-based methodology, 301
material loss, compensation for, 151–4
Merkouris, P., 159, 201, 316
Mexico, 17, 58, 127, 131, 135, 136, 141, 144
Mexico/Singapore BIT, 68
minimum standard of treatment (MST)
  concept of, 3–4
  customary status of, 316–23
  historical foundation of, 5–7
  Newly Independent States, challenges, 8–10
  return of, 14–18
Multifibre Arrangement (MFA), 214

national law experts, 26
natural resources sector, case of, 302–5
the Neptune, 168–70
Netherlands, 21, 165, 215, 217, 243
Neuberger, L., 207
New International Economic Order (NIEO), 264, 310, 339
Newly Independent States, 8–10
Nigeria–Morocco BIT, 266, 267, 275, 276, 281
North American Free Trade Agreement (NAFTA), 7, 15, 264
  arbitration proceedings, 16
  claims of breaches, 129
  Commission, 221
  interpretation of, 55
  Parties, 16
  US breaches of, 140

OECD Draft Convention (1967), 11, 240
Organisation for Economic Cooperation and Development (OECD), 5, 11, 12, 45
Orr and Laubenheimer, 172–3

Paddeu, F., 344
Pan African Investment Code (PAIC), 267
Paparinskis, M., 141, 198
party-appointed expert witnesses, 24, 25

Paulsson, J., 43
Permanent Sovereignty over Natural Resources (PSNR), 237, 264
Poland, 166, 217
police powers doctrine, 233, 236, 237, 249, 250, 253, 259, 260
  development of, 240–3
post-award proceedings, 46, 47, 54
  State practice in, 60–9
power plants, 304
pre-award interest, 300
precautionary principle, 268–72
principle of proportionality, 192, 198
prior internationally wrongful act, 144–5
public health emergency of international concern (PHEIC), 256

quantum/industry experts, 26

racial discrimination, 34
Ramsar and Biodiversity Conventions, 277
reasonable regulation, presumption of, 243–5
renewable energy power plants, 306
renewable energy sector, 305
restitution, 288–92
Return of the State, 21
rights of foreigners, 6
rights of investors. *See* investors' rights
Rio Declaration, 268
Roberts, A., 226
Root, Elihu, 7
Russia, 165, 210

SADC Model Treaty, 276
satisfaction, 289, 292
Schreuer, C., 10
Second World War, 7, 9
Singapore/Colombia BIT, 68
Slovak Republics, 217
South African Development Community (SADC) Model BIT, 267
Spanish Treaty Claims Commission of 1901, 78
standard of compensation, 84
State practice

CIL identification, 54–60
ISDS, 54–60
nature of, 47–53
in post-award proceedings, 60–9
significance of, 47–53
subsequent agreements, 219–27
sunk costs, 301
systemic integration, principle of, 246–7

Talmon, S., 156
territorial sovereignty, 233, 237, 243
  regulatory dimension of, 238–40
textual approach, 105–10
Third World Approaches to International Law (TWAIL), 309–12
  customary international investment law, 323–30
Titi, C., 236
Transpacific Partnership agreement, 18
treaty drafting practices, 266–8
Treves, T., 271
Trojan horse of legal expertise, 37–40
two-element approach, 46, 54, 55, 57, 62, 67–9, 167, 336. *See also* customary international law (CIL)

UK, 165, 171, 338
UK–Argentina BIT, 153
UNCITRAL Arbitration Rules (2013), 28
UN General Assembly (UNGA), 64, 72, 93, 343
United Nations Conference on Trade and Development (UNCTAD), 6
United Nations General Assembly, 8
United States, 16–18, 30, 32, 49, 60, 338
Universal Declaration on Human Rights, 279
unlawful expropriation. *See* expropriation
US–Mexico sugar war, 126–8
US Model BIT, 16, 18

Vienna Convention on the Law of Treaties (VCLT), 211, 212, 246, 343
Viñuales, J., 242

Washington Convention, 183
Webster formula, 170
Weiler, T., 12
Wood, M., 52, 53
Woolsey, L.H., 81

World Bank, 208
World Trade Organization (WTO), 28, 144–5, 257
   dispute settlement system, 126